Narrative Art and Poetry
in the Books of Samuel

volume III

THRONE AND CITY

STUDIA SEMITICA NEERLANDICA

edited by

For publications in the series see page 441

J. P. Fokkelman

NARRATIVE ART AND POETRY IN THE BOOKS OF SAMUEL

a full interpretation based on stylistic and structural analyses

volume III

THRONE AND CITY
(II Sam. 2-8 & 21-24)

VAN GORCUM 1990
Assen/Maastricht, The Netherlands

The publication of this book was made possible through a grant from the Netherlands Organisation for the Advancement of Research (N.W.O.).

CIP-DATA KONINKLIJKE BIBLIOTHEEK, DEN HAAG

Fokkelman, J.P.

Narrative Art and Poetry in the Books of Samuel: a full interpretation based on stylistic and structural analyses / J.P. Fokkelman. – Assen (etc.): Van Gorcum
Vol.III: Throne and City (II Sam.2-8 & 21-24). – Ill. –
SISO 226.4 UDC 22.015 NUGI 639
Subject heading: Samuel (Bible); text analysis.
ISBN 90 232 2546 5

Translation: Mrs. L. Waaning-Wardle
Jacket design, light module on cover and illustrations: Joost van Santen in co-operation with the author.
Cover photograph: Caspar van Santen.
Layout: Van Gorcum, Assen, The Netherlands.
Printed by Van Gorcum, Assen, The Netherlands.

Contents

ACT FIFTEEN: II SAM.21-24

Chapter I

Introduction

§ 1. *What a single verse can do*

Just as the previous volume ended with the analysis of a poem, the dirge of David marking the end of the large section "The Crossing Fates", so towards the close of this my third volume of studies on Samuel, I shall again devote my attention to poetry. The great hymn of David, a poem of not less than 53 verses in II Sam.22, is to be discussed, together with a short poem at the beginning of ch.23 entitled "The Last Words of David". Before applying myself to this task I would like to give a finger exercise in stylistics to brush up our awareness of the power and compactness of Hebrew lyrics.

To this end I would like to concentrate on a poem consisting of a single verse only. We came across it in our reading of I Sam.15[1] where I was principally concerned with the shrewd and surprising manipulation employed by the speaker Samuel to allow the butt of his remarks, the Amalekite king Agag, to discover for himself the fact of his own imminent execution. There is, however, so much more to be said about this verse which goes, if we remember, like this:

> *ka'ăšęr šikk^{e}lā nāšīm ḥarbękā*
> *ken tiškal minnāšīm 'immękā*

The parallelism governing the two verse halves is constituted from the very outset by the first pair of words. The words "as...// so..." both introduce a

[1] See NAPS II, p.109.

clause and provide the semantic basis for a comparison. The style of the verse is taut: one sentence of two four-word clauses formed by eight paired words, according to the scheme abcd//a'b'c'd'. The parallelism becomes conspicuous by the unmodified repetition of "women" in the third position and the return of the root *š-k-l* in the predicate. Both cola begin with *k*- and end with a rhyme on the same consonant, i.e. -*kā*.

These forms of similarity are interwoven with forms of dissimilarity which also contribute to the parallelism.[2] Of central importance are the various tenses of the verb (past versus imminent future) and the different forms its root takes (pi'el: qal = factitive : intransitive), together with the many/one contrast of the women, and especially the combination of the two words "sword ... mother" which resist being harnessed together as a word pair, but whose agreement in position (d-d') and rhyme on the possessive pronoun already give us food for thought. They form the semantic centre of gravity for the whole because they are the point of its rhetorical manipulation. Both clauses are ascendant and the content of each can be understood only at the end since the last word is the subject. Moreover, the position of the subject is somewhat anomalous. Non-literary language would have placed both the subject of the first colon, and that of the second, immediately after the initially positioned predicate (*škl* in the feminine): scheme PSO,[3] but the subjects "your sword" and "your mother" have been deferred here.[4] Changing places with the word "women", which is now adjacent to the predicate, would have created an unpleasant identical rhyme, but would have done the most damage by interfering with the emergence of the point.[5]

The comparison is a source of friction since it places the unique situation of one mother next to a general, or iterative, situation (i.e. of women in the plural). This raises the question of the nature of the relationship between the particular and the general here. Does the unique situation of colon B come under the latter category as a matter of course? Perhaps an ordinary Israelite

[2] With reference to the extensive ring composition comprising the rebellion of Absalom, I stated (NAPS I, pp.282-3 and 312) that correspondence consists not only of similarity but also of difference, and often exists in hybrid forms of equivalence and dissimilarity. This has also been recognised by Adele Berlin in her book "The Dynamics of Biblical Parallelism", Bloomington 1985, in her discussion (pp.2-3, 11-12) of Jakobson's definition of literariness and the concept of equivalence it contains, which she applies in chs.II-V. Cf. *infra* ch.IV note 47.

[3] P = predicate, O = object, S = subject, C = complement. PSO would be the non-literary variant of colon A, whilst colon B would be PSC in "ordinary" linguistic usage.

[4] The actual poetic syntax with which we are dealing in I Sam.15:33 is, therefore, after the short word denoting comparison: POS//PCS.

[5] The reader can sense this by trying it out for himself: the clauses *šklh ḥrbk nšym // tškl 'mk mnšym* neither sound right nor function well.

soldier, whom I can picture as standing by listening, might indeed think that the prospective childlessness of Agag's mother is the normal state of affairs, an implementation of the harsh rules of war. But such an idea is sure to meet with resistance in the mind of the addressee himself. In his pride this Amalekite king had never thought of his mother as simply being one of "the women". And the reader is confronted by the fact that the speaker, the prophet Samuel, makes special mention of that one loss and employs poetic diction to do so. He also notices that this statement anticipates an event due to take place any minute now, and that it functions, therefore, as an announcement. It is now difficult for him to think that nothing is really wrong.

What could be the law which accounts for colon B being an application of the rule in colon A? Does the shift from pi'el to qal in the predicate shed any light on the matter? The factitive action of Agag (*škl* in the pi'el) has taken a heavy toll of victims; this verb form is, therefore, highly transitive and is indeed accompanied by an object in the plural. Its place is then taken by a qal form which is intransitive. Does the speaker wish to suggest by this, that the death just announced is a more or less autonomous or matter-of-course process, a natural event and not something which has been set in motion and completed by the hand of man? At the end of the cola which lead to the surprising words "sword" and "mother" – coerced into a tense combination by the rhyming suffix and an identical metrical accent[6] – the reader refuses to believe in a process of nature taking its course. His suspicions are aroused as he hears the precision lock click shut. Agag himself, the listener who enjoys ultimate precedence above all other listeners (both present and future) since this verse is about his own skin, does not believe that no weapon is involved in rendering his mother childless. The omission of the word "sword" in colon B bears an ironic relationship to, and is not at all in iconic agreement with, Samuel's treatment of Agag a few moments later: he hacks the king to pieces.

The ellipse of the sword in colon B breaks through the symmetry which had created, three times already, a pair of words. The "as" at the beginning was neatly answered by "so"; the perfect of *škl* had received an imperfect as correspondent whereby the feminine ending, as it were, rotated round the stem and the feminine afformative changed into a feminine preformative, and "women" was succeeded by "among women". These three implementations of parallelism build up a pattern in the reader's mind and he now expects symmetry in the d-d' position once more. All the greater the shock at the

[6] Thanks to the pausal forms at the end of the clauses the Masoretic Hebrew of our verse exhibits the rhythmic pattern (or if you prefer: the metrical foot as unit of an accentual metre) o ó o for the words in position d, which also probably covered the premasoretic forms.

occurrence of "your mother". She is, it is true, the grammatical subject, just as "sword" is in position d, but of suffering rather than action. The powerful agent *ḥrbk*, which does not know when to stop, is replaced by the *patiens* whose loss is unique. Samuel has calculated exactly – that is, poetically! – the cruelty of the impending execution.

I keep on searching for the nature of the similarity between colon A and colon B, for the symmetry is too great to be exhausted already. Samuel does not place the two situations of childless women in the syntactical framework of "your sword..., that is why your mother ... ". If he had done so we should have recognised immediately the language of an AJI, an announcement of judgement to an individual,[7] with its bipartite structure of crime and punishment, past and near future. But Samuel is a prophet, and the individual threatened by a prophet with an oracle of doom is often a king. The prose immediately following Samuel's verse expressly exhibits the sacral dimension of the execution carried out by Samuel.[8] This provides us with sufficient information to venture the proposition that the verse's broadly based synonymy discreetly suggests the symmetry of the *talio*. It is not difficult to indeed construe such a connection between the two halves of the verse. Their relationship is, however, causal rather than one which states reasons, and it could be paraphrased something like this: "because of the fact that you've always availed yourself of violence, you shall inevitably meet your end in the same way." This is, therefore, not so much a matter of a natural process as an intrinsic one. "The violence which you have regularly made use of has activated a process whereby you must die a violent death"; or: "the point of your death penalty is made obvious by your violence".

Whatever the precise formulation of this train of thought might be, the fact remains that the symmetry of the two halves of the verse stands for a necessary connection between the bloodshed of yesterday and the execution which is about to take place. In this the prophet's "sentence" (both as compound sentence and as judgement) is very close to several other AJI's. It is comparable with the oracle which Elijah had to utter against king Ahab after the latter had confiscated Naboth's vineyard: "Would you murder and take possession? In the very place where the dogs lapped up Naboth's blood, the dogs will lap up your blood too" (I Ki.21:19). Here too the symmetry imparts a compelling quality to the judgement, and this verse also allows the

[7] I use Cl. Westermann's term (in "Grundformen prophetischer Rede", 2nd ed., Munich 1964), viz., 'das Gerichtswort an den Einzelnen', translated by 'Announcement of Judgement to the Individual'.

[8] I 15:33d reads, straight after the line of poetry, "And Samuel hewed Agag in pieces *before the LORD* in Gilgal."

addressee to reach for himself the conclusion that his end is near, albeit it in a less spectacular form than I Sam. 15 does.

Let us put it like this then. The scheme "as...so..." masks the more legal scheme "because...therefore".[9] Perhaps this legal template has been concealed because Agag's behaviour towards his victims was without trial, let alone mercy. Now he too shall be summarily and relentlessly executed. The one authority to whom he could appeal, Samuel himself, is also omitted from the text. What is more, the power of this symmetry means that there must be no exceptions. Surely you do not think that the fate you have meted out to many women will pass your own mother by, Agag? In this sense we can indeed state that the rule deduced from colon A is applied by Samuel to Agag.

At this point I wonder if the preposition *min*, which has been added to the second half of the verse (as the only morpheme without a counterpart in the other half of the verse!) can be easily understood. Is it partitive, separative, or comparative? How would Agag classify his mother in respect of the women, inclusive or exclusive? Is she to become childless as a member of this group (in which case *min* would be partitive), or in a manner different from the women (separative), or in a way which would make her worse off than they (comparative)? The exclusive borders on the comparative: on the basis of the unique and close relationship with the first woman in his life, an ordinary mortal will hold his mother in greater esteem than other women. But I imagine that someone as high-born as this king will be continually faced with the temptation to accord his mother a place above and beyond the whole of womankind in general. Perhaps Agag's total lack of respect for other mothers was the other side of the coin of his love for his mother, which would explain why the uniqueness of the tie other mothers have with their children simply did not occur to him at all.

This is not historical description but gap-filling, on the part of the reader, about the king. It is, nevertheless, admissible because the Agag who emerges from colon A is a fearsome and ruthless warrior. And warriors do not have the time nor the psychological scope to envisage the tenderness of mother

[9] Compare also the fate of the Canaanite king Adoni-bezek in Judg.1:4-8. When the Israelites had defeated him "they cut off his thumbs and his big toes". When given the floor, in verse 7, he remarks, "Seventy kings, with thumbs and big toes cut off, used to pick up scraps under my table; *as* I have done, *so* God has requited me." This is the first time that the construction *k'šr//kn* occurs in Judges; what is more the symmetry here is made explicit by the character himself. And if this enemy king points to the factor of God in his own fate, how much more may we then expect the judgement of God in Samuel's verse! – See also Judg.15:11, the third occurrence of as/so in Judges.

and child. They have to adopt a macho attitude and, in order to survive, often repress, forget or ignore their own vulnerability. In any case Agag's sword has raged indiscriminately, and I suspect that not all his victims were combatants. His negation, or to put it more strongly, his repeated destruction of what is unique and vulnerable now breaks him down, and Samuel states, in the second half-verse, that the mother of the king too must be totally included in the ranks of inconsolable women (*min* inclusive). The coercive quality of the pair of words as/so fastens her in place, she will no longer be able to step outside these ranks.

In this way a simple syllable is seen to have a history and a dialectic of its own. 'My mother doesn't come under this category', says Agag. 'Does!' snaps Samuel. The prophet compels the ruler to return to his origins and forces him to face his own vulnerability, after the former has considered the vulnerability of so many in the first half-verse. And Agag has to admit to something which he would otherwise have continued to unequivocally deny with a sweep of his sword: he too was once a child, dependent, weak. For him the comparison as/so ultimately includes the insight that he has little cause to exalt himself above the people; he too came naked into the world. In the announcement of his imminent death, and through the grief of the mothers in mourning, this insight now dawns on Agag.

The reader, just like the writer, is in the privileged position of being able to examine the issue in a story, debate, or verse, first from one angle and then from another. Perhaps we can assign one more effect to the dynamics of the word *min*. By utilising the technique of inverted quotation in his dirge David has brought the Song of Deborah within close range; here too we encounter a verse with *minnāšīm*, viz. Judg.5:24. This line is also about a woman, but since it expresses praise – and also because of the woman's action – it is diametrically opposed to the colon which brings sorrow to Agag's mother. "Most blessed of women be Jael, wife of Heber the Kenite, most blessed of women in tents." Is it not true to say that the preposition in this *tᵉbōrak minnāšīm* is a synthesis of the inclusive and the exclusive? Jael belongs to the ranks of women, insofar as the women of Israel do not need to fall outside the effective scope of the poetess Deborah's blessing; Jael dominates the ranks of women through her unexpected deed, which is as bloody as it is liberating, and is pre-eminently worthy of praise – more than the others (*min* comparative) – for her act. This has the following consequences for the verse in I Sam.15. Because the sword of Agag finally turns against him, the queen mother can no longer enjoy the exclusive status of great lady. Once again I am reminded of Judg.5 where, after the stanza in which the praises are sung of the woman who hammered a tent pin into the ground, another stanza follows which actually shows the mother of Sisera in the upper part of the palace, surrounded by ladies-in-waiting; they are still bragging, filled with illusions as to the outcome of the battle, (but what on earth could be keeping the general?). The mother of Agag is to become just another ordinary woman insofar as she must join the group of women who have been rendered childless. But she is, at the same time, brought to the fore out of the group, by the special attention the poem pays to her.

What is actually uttered in a text should also be understood in relation to what is left unsaid. Our poem is an excellent example of this principle at work. It is characterised by a multiple ellipse and derives much of its power from what is omitted in relation to what is stated. I shall begin with colon A. What Samuel says here is much more arresting than "you have killed many people". The first ellipse is that of the victims, whose number and gender – not in the grammatical sense here! – remain indefinite. And this is exactly why I do not accept that those who have been killed are only soldiers. Agag would more likely have fought his enemies with the ban – until the moment that Saul ought to have eradicated him as part of the ban commanded by God (I 15:3). What does this omission of men, women and children mean? It seems to me that the ellipse is an image of the destructive power of the warrior Agag and his utter contempt for the victims. They did not enter his mind for a moment and now they are absent from the text as well. Samuel's words ignore those whom Agag has always literally ignored; the prophet finds the exact turn of phrase to express indiscriminate bloodthirstiness.

The second ellipse is a double literary device since it is realised by metonymy. The subject of eradication in colon A is not the person of Agag but "your sword". The speaker does not show us Agag at war, he sees only the inexorable sword of Agag as it rampages incessantly on the field of battle. This is the image used to depict the robot-like efficiency of the killer Agag, and it is heightened by the iterative nature of the action as well as by the factitive and the transitive aspects of the stem formation of *škl.*[10] Agag

[10] Notice how the effect of this kind of metonymy is dependent upon the context. At the end of *The Crossing Fates*, in the dirge of David, we encountered a whole series of weapons as metonyms for their bearers. "The shield of the heroes" in stanza 1 was a figure of speech for avoidance, for sorrow still repressed; when grief breaks out (especially for Jonathan) the final verse places "the weapons of war" in a pair of words with "the heroes", making the contiguity, upon which the convention of metonymy is based, graphic. In the central stanza the bow and the sword are dominated by the tribute paid to Saul and Jonathan as heroes; and they are personified in their actions, which produces a gripping point of contact with I 15:33.

In some of the oracles of the Later Prophets the metonym of the sword – elaborated upon to such an extent that it attains the status of an independent agent – represents the scale and irrevocability of the approaching catastrophe. See, for example, various verses in Ezek.21 and Is.34:6.

continues to be ignored in colon B and one might sense, perhaps, the indirectness of the approach via "your mother" (the counterpart, after all, in position d') as a fresh instance of metonymy. In any case, it is a stroke of literary genius to sentence someone to death without even mentioning him in the text.[11]

The action mentioned in the first half-verse is not carried out by Agag, but by an object. This too can be interpreted as a result of his reifying attitude (*Verdinglichung*) towards his enemies, if not more of his fellow-men. Smouldering within this vicarious instrument is the potential criticism that Agag is without empathy and, in repressing his own vulnerability, is incapable of responsibility for his own actions. And insofar as the sword substitutes the warrior I can detect traces of personification in the use of metonymy.[12] After all the repeated action of rendering women childless is attributed to his sword. But now Agag can conveniently blame his sword each time he wishes to avoid his responsibility and provide himself with an excuse in the form of "the sword always takes its toll" – the sort of rationalisation which reminds us of David as a criminal (II 11:25). It is ironic, therefore, that this substitution is met by a similar one in the main clause.

There are three additional ellipses in the second half-verse. We fail to find mention of the execution, the executioner, and his instrument. What Samuel says in colon B is far more gripping than "that's why I'm now going to kill you with my sword". I will be brief about the ellipse of the execution since I have explained previously the verse's direct rhetorical hit in making Agag deduce his own end, before he can meaningfully reconstruct the content of the main clause. The moment element d' falls into place in the abcd//a'b'c'd' sequence Agag hears the manacles click shut on his wrists. There is, however, yet another elliptical aspect, both at this point and in the first half-verse, adhering to the choice of *škl*, and that is that "rendering/becoming childless" as charge and sentence is also a kind of metonymy, since it is based on a shift of cause and effect. In both the first and second halves of the verse death is indirectly announced via the mothers and their grief. Initially this seems to be a kind of discretion exercised in view of the harshness of death. But upon

[11] There is only one slight restriction to this. Via the possessive suffix *-kā* Agag is, in fact, present, as addressee and virtual vocative: but what I mean by his absence from the text is that he is not provided with a complete lexeme, and may not, therefore, perform a syntactical function as subject, object or complement.

[12] This is supported by a reminder of the central stanza of David's dirge, where sword and bow carry out human actions. Compare this with the devouring of people by bushes and trees in II Sam.18, which, for the rest, comes under "metaphor".

reconsideration or reflection this discretion is seen to aid the manipulation of the one indicted, which makes the sentence an even more stinging blow.

Samuel has also omitted to mention his own person as executioner, ellipse number four. Once more I am reminded of the announcement of judgement to an individual. In this kind of situation the prophet sees himself only as a messenger, one who must faithfully pass on, unaltered, the judgement of another; his own person is of no importance. This is also what happens here. Samuel himself is irrelevant and is not involved in a personal vendetta. The deliberate silence surrounding his own contribution is designed to convey the disinterestedness of the penalty; and its irrevocability too, inasmuch as Samuel does not wish to be present in the text of the sentence as the proper authority for an appeal or a hoped-for reprieve.

The fifth ellipse consists of "your sword", in colon A, being the only element in the abcd sequence to receive no synonym in colon B. The executioner's instrument is, therefore, absent. No instrument can now divert our attention from the fate of that one mother. The absence of the Israelite sword cuts short the exaltation of the murder weapon with which Agag was so elated in the first half of the verse. So the repeated action of an object terminates in the unique passion of a woman.

Apart from this verse one might think that war was the concern of men rather than women. In several places not far from our verse, however, this view is refuted – as much by prose as by poetry – by Jael and the mother of Sisera, for example, or by the woman who threw a millstone down onto the head of the tyrant. But how fares the man-woman polarity in this poem against the Amalekite? Communication goes from man to man, it is true, and the killing in the verse returns to the man with whom it had so often originated. But there is one word which, by remaining unchanged, is absolutely identical in both halves of the verse and that is the word "women". Even more striking is the fact that everything which can possibly be inflected in the poem, six out of a total of eight words, is feminine! This is effected by the choice of the tandem "sword//mother" as subject[13] – after which the predicate.

The frequency of feminine forms in relation to male matters is, to put it mildly, remarkable. For the doomed man Agag this means, both from the outset and on second thoughts, that the message is ineluctable: he too is a

[13] The grammatical contingency of *ḥrb* being feminine in Hebrew is now exploited for stylistic ends. A datum which is linguistically and semantically neutral, is no longer so when it functions as a knot in a literary network. This probably also holds good in the case of the plural "women" which happens to have a masculine ending. This makes for an ironic effect, in our verse, at the point where *signifiants* and *signifiés* meet.

child of a mother, and the fact that he has ignored this dimension is going to spell disaster for his mother. Subsequently I accord the women their relevant place in regard to ellipses 2 and 4: over against and around the omission of the two men, who are all that matter here and now, is the suffering presence of many women.

The highly complex reality of the poem is full of friction, contrasts, displacements and elliptical hiatuses. Many of these *écarts* and differences signal the strain and inconsequence of king Agag's behaviour and attitude. Whilst these instances of tension are thus exposed by the power of literary language – through its cruel beauty – retribution, intending to gain the upper hand, becomes visible. The suffering of the one woman who enjoys special mention answers the suffering of the many, so that justice is done. All this is held together in a cast-iron mould: the scheme and the dominating syntax of comparison.

§ 2. *A primary survey of the subject matter*

This book closes the gap between *The Crossing Fates* and *King David* by dealing with II Sam.2-8 and 21-24. Its subject matter links the long account of Saul's doom and downfall in I 13-31 & II 1 with the section on David's moral and psychological decline, II 9-20 & I Kings 1-2. This obtains completely at any rate for chs.2-8, but can it also be said of 21-24, the group of passages which end the books of Samuel as they have been handed down to us? The answer is, yes and no.

The insertion of II Sam.21-24 is just as ambiguous as that of I Kings 1-2. The Act with which the book of Kings opens is the only passage which really treats the question of who is to succeed David as the central issue.[14] It can be regarded as the tailpiece of "King David" as well as being used for the beginning of I Kings. The latter is, however, justified only on condition that I Kings be treated as a part of (or at least within the province of) the Former Prophets. All kinds of details and motifs in I Kings 1-2, such as the poisonous rage of David against Joab and Shimei for example, can only be understood thanks to information provided by II Samuel. No wonder, since the analyses in *King David* have demonstrated just how much I Kings 1-2 forms an inextricable part of the composition of "King David" which is divided

[14] The polemic obverse of this sentence is – I would like to repeat it just once more, because I keep coming across the old and erroneous description in specialist literature – that the so-called Succession Story (or History) does not exist.

exactly into four Acts.[15]

Joining up I Kings 1-2 with II Sam.9-20 involves skipping II Sam.21-24. The decision to miss out II Sam.21-24 was a diachronic one which is presupposed by linking II Sam.9-20 and Kings 1-2. After taking this diachronic step I provided a synchronic reading of "King David" and my interpretation of this section has, in turn, borne out the appropriateness of the diachronic step by demonstrating, at different levels, that the Acts of this section have the order AB-B'A', on the grounds of (amongst other reasons) characters and thematics. These Acts, therefore, form a complete sequence.

The omission of II Sam.21-24 was, however, only temporary, and it is now time to do justice to this passage. It rounds off the books of Samuel in the form in which they have come down to us. The location of this subject matter has little to be said for it aesthetically because it interrupts the continuity of the "King David" section. But those who have become familiar with it will be able to confirm experientially that inserting it elsewhere would be much more disrupting. Considering a location after II Sam.1 would involve severing at least an equal number of links. The rate at which II 2 fits in with Saul's end, or, in other words, the speed with which David comes to power, would be removed. The hymn would then make too early an appearance as certainly would the poem "The Last Words". II 21 and 24 reveal a David who has established himself in Jerusalem as king over all Israel, and that is a piece of information which does not fit in until after II 5-6 (the conquest and religious esteem of Jerusalem).

We have now arrived at the subject of chronology in II Sam. 21-24. In this respect the block looks two ways like Janus. By definition the function of the "Last Words" is closure. The adjacent hymn, which also serves to round off the whole, befits a long-established king. Half of it is a song of thanksgiving, in which he looks back on the conquests God has granted him and which have made him into a powerful ruler. The location of the song in II 22 makes it into a mainstay which, together with the lyric poetry of II 1 (the dirge) and the Psalm of Hannah in I 2, supports the entire composition of I and II Samuel; the three poems ensure a programmatic beginning, middle and end to the Bible book.

These data mean that the block cannot function at a point after II Sam.8. But other particulars would not be out of place there chronologically.

[15] I would like to briefly reiterate the typographic convention adopted previously – whereby "The Crossing Fates" and "King David" refer to the titles which I have given to passages of Hebrew text (viz., I Sam.13-31 + II Sam.1 and II Sam.9-20 + I Ki.1-2), whilst *King David* and *The Crossing Fates* refer to (the titles of) my interpretations, i.e. NAPS I and II.

Somehow or other there is a connection between 21:7 and 9:1 (the cripple Mephibosheth is spared by David because of the latter's special bond with Jonathan). The liquidation of Saul's inheritance, in this case an instance of blood-guilt on the part of David's predecessor against a Canaanite enclave, can best be placed, on the time scale, at the beginning of David's reign. Thematically it would link up well with Act IX (= II Sam.2-5:5) where the throne of Israel is at stake in the confrontations between the Judean David and the Saulides. In addition there is the annalistic subject matter on David's heroes which is to be found in the second half of chs.21 and 23. The anecdotes in 21 and the list of names in 23 record certain deeds and the names of "the heroes of David" in order to honour them and they look back especially on the previous period, shortly before and shortly after Saul's death, when David was still primarily a military leader and had enough on his hands what with the shaking off of Philistine oppression. As it is this subject matter could be situated on the scale of narrated time sometime after II 1 or 5.

What we see, therefore, in II Sam.21-24 is a curious mixture of very early and very late material; lyric poetry providing closure. One begins to suspect that chronology is not so important here. Such an assumption is confirmed by the observation that neither are the surrounding stories, II 21 (first half) and 24, in the least accorded a precisely determined place on a chronological scale by the writer or redactor.[16] Time adjuncts are so conspicuous by their absence in the Gibeon affair and in the account of the plague and the threshing floor, that I have been led to the opinion that the shaping of time is amorphous throughout the entire Act, and that it differs radically in this respect from the other 14 Acts in Samuel.

I do not say that Act XV is amorphous in itself. On the contrary, the Act does have a definite structure but one which is not of a narrative kind. The last block of text in Samuel consists of six literary units belonging to three very different genres. These genres are arranged in pairs in a concentric scheme and the units also exhibit quantitative alternation,[17] in the sense that each genre is represented in a short and an extended form:

[16] Notice how vague the description "in the days of David" is at the beginning of II 21. The first word of II 24 forms a thematic link with ch.21 (for more information see ch.VIII below) rather than a chronological (consecutive) link with what has just taken place.

[17] The terms 'short' and 'long' are, in the scheme which follows, relative rather than absolute; i.e, they are mutually determined. The story in 21:1-14 is, measured against an absolute standard (the average length of all Hebrew stories, for example), probably of medium length, but in comparison with ch.24, short, etc. Apart from this the poems also turn out to be very long and short respectively if measured against the rest of Hebrew poetry.

A	story (short)	blood-guilt and execution	21:1-14
B	annals (short)	four heroes from Gath	vv.15-22
C	poetry (long)	hymn and song of thanksgiving	22:1-51
C'	poetry (short)	"Last Words"	23:1-7
B'	annals (long)	David's heroes: deeds and names	23:8-39
A'	story (long)	census, plague, compassion	24:1-25

When a scheme like this occurs I am in the habit of finding out straightaway how important the consequences are for the content, and then stating them. Arrangements like this increase richness of meaning and form the basis for a more precise interpretation. But this is not the case here if I am right. The concentric nature of the six units remains one of outward appearances and their ring composition gives an unalterable impression of artificiality, even though the passages in A-A' and B-B' take each other into account.[18] That is why I am of the opinion that this sequence is usually rightly called an appendix *vis-à-vis* the rest of Samuel and that it was the right decision to locate it at the end.

What I have managed to ascertain is that the sequential or syntagmatic axis, right from I Sam.13 up to and including II 20, is not to be burdened by the insertion of the block II 21 to 24, because the analyses put forward in NAPS I-III show that Acts IV through XIV have a structure of their own which is convincing, and that they form a series which is not to be interrupted. I have also pointed out the striking temporal indeterminacy which characterises II 21-24, and which underlines the isolation of the appendix. But none of this alters the fact that the given text of I and II Sam. ends with the block. It is, therefore, important, in the final part of this book, to listen carefully to what the passages constituting (Act, or rather) group XV have to say, and to arrive at a clear assessment as to their own particular meaning first of all. Perhaps, on this basis, it will then be possible to get beyond the mere label "appen-

[18] In "The Narrative Covenant", San Francisco 1987, David Damrosch refers to this block as one of the cases "where a unified oral tradition is certainly not present". Somewhat further down the same page, 237, he says: "here ... the technique [viz., of ring composition] survives as the natural organizational method even though literacy has replaced the need for aids to oral memory and even though no special dramatic movement is being created." Damrosch agrees with Meir Sternberg who, in "The Poetics of Biblical Narrative: Ideological Literature and the Drama of Reading", Bloomington 1985, p.40, supplies "the chiastic pattern that rounds off Samuel" and in whose opinion: "It is suggestive that the most conspicuous and large-scale instance of chiasm in Samuel applies to a hodgepodge that has the least pretensions to literariness and, even with the artificial design thrown in, hardly coheres as more than an appendix. Granted that form can produce or imply an artistic function, it still cannot enthrone one regardless of context, which includes the matter enformed and the rules governing their union."

dix" and to specify the contribution of II 21-24 to the whole. This contribution does not function very effectively on the syntagmatic axis and does not belong there in the first place, but there is a good chance of placing it on the paradigmatic axis.

In anticipation of the research to be conducted *infra* in chapters VII and VIII I look on the Bible book Samuel as a composition with a double ending. The reader can react to this by employing one of two possible reading strategies. The first option is to treat the composition as a self-contained unit and adhere strictly to the given text. This means that Act XV must be left where it is, viz. after the rebellion of Absalom, and viewed as the conclusion of the Bible book. This method involves sacrificing the completion and compelling continuity of the section "King David"; the decision on the succession (I Kings 1-2) now being reserved for the following Bible book. Such an approach will never get beyond level 12, since it restricts itself to the book as a relative unity.[19] The second strategy moves a level higher and sees Samuel as part of the Former Prophets or the so-called Deuteronomistic History. In this reading the limits of the book scarcely function as a dividing line any more. One is then free to read the "King David" section as a complete series, and to re-enact it in one's mind. At the same time the block II 21-24 is to be envisaged as a paradigmatic aside kept out of the narrative flow.

II Samuel 2-8 consists of two groups of stories. The first group, Act IX, occurs in 2:1-5:5 and is bounded by a double anointing. The members of David's own tribe are the ones to accept him as king first, followed by the rest of Israel seven years later. Strictly subjected to the criterion of space the Act is seen to be a unity. Everything which is of importance takes place in, proceeds from, makes for, or has close ties with, the ancient city of Hebron in Judah, where David is in residence as king of the South.[20] The fragments at the

[19] I call to mind that, in ch. 1 of the foregoing volume, I described the text as a hierarchy of 12 levels. Following the six levels of the texture there are the sequences and speeches (level 7), subscenes (8), the scene is 9, we meet groups of stories (Acts) at level 10, at level 11 the sections (the first is, for example, I Sam.1-12) and on level 12 the Bible book. Then, at level 13, there is the Deuteronomistic History and at 14, the mass of Genesis through Kings, whilst 15 is the Hebrew Bible.

[20] The name Hebron occurs 18 times in Act IX. Before this it occurs in I 30:31 only, where it actually anticipates II 2 (at the end of I 30 David does indeed do preliminary work on the territory of Judah!); after this the name appears in 5:13 where it actually refers back, and finally Hebron is the place where Absalom too wishes to declare his royal status (15:7,9,10).

beginning and end of the Act mention Hebron by name, and the three well-proportioned stories in between all end up with a grave in this city.[21]

As soon as David has ascended the throne of all Israel he moves on by conquering Jerusalem and choosing it as his royal capital.[22] So much attention is paid to this city of non-Israelite origins in the second group of passages (Act X = II Sam.5:6-8:18), that its significance cannot be covered by the criterion of space alone. The importance of this city goes a step further by reaching thematic proportions at various times here. The acquisition and expansion of Jerusalem is David's first goal, and it is at the same time the actantial object of 5:6-12. This ancient city subsequently receives sacral prestige when David enters with the ark in ch.6 – the building of the temple is the sequel, notices the reader of the Former Prophets – and we shall also see that the thematic attention paid to Jerusalem acquires a particular shape in chapters 7 and 8. In chapter 7 David receives, via an oracle given to the prophet Nathan, the promise of YHWH that his dynasty shall be a long-lasting one and that Zion shall be His chosen dwelling place. In chapter 8 the narrator sums up the conquests, on all sides, of the powerful monarch of a united Israel.

In both chapters concentration on the spatial aspect is coupled with a special treatment of time. In the long speech of 7:5-16 the speaker looks far and systematically into the future in a way no mortal man can do. Chapter 8 is not the normal way of looking at consecutive actions in the past. By being, in principle, exhaustive in his survey of victories, the narrator breaks out of the rule that the past ought to be reported as a chronological succession of events. The sequence itself might well be chronological, but in chapter 8 the narrator steps out of reported time to such an extent that, accompanied by us, he departs from the moment at which the story has arrived, i.e. somewhere at the beginning of David's reign in Jerusalem. He is highly anticipatory several times, and makes his omniscience felt in this way at the strategic moment when he wishes to bring an entire section to a close. From then on he has his hands full with David's internal conflicts and those of the court, II 9-20, and

[21] For the sake of clarity: there are three fragments, linked together in parallel form, in 2:1-11, and at the end, 5:1-3 (or 5). When I say "three stories", I mean 2:12-32, 3:6-39 and 4. Later I will divide the narrative mass of ch. 3 into two scenes, 3:6-21 and 22-39.

[22] At the beginning of this volume I would like to remark that such a report is not meant to be taken historically, but is aimed at a literary text and its narrative nature. We do not know how much time passed between the second anointing and the campaign which turned Jebus into Jerusalem.

that is why it suits his purpose to gather the military successes together into ch.8 and keep them away from the section on David's moral fall.[23]

The connection made between time and space in Act IX is unmistakable. The prominence of the city of Hebron is quickly coupled with a deliberate measurement of the length of David's rule over Judah. The eleventh verse of chapter two, a sentence which, via its length and wealth of information is designed to indicate the end of the first literary unit, states that David reigned for seven and a half years in Hebron. And his time of prosperity there is expressed in the form of a separate list of "sons which were born to David in Hebron", in 3:2-5. The Act ends with a new, twofold measurement of time in 5:4-5 which underlines the change of capital from Hebron to Jerusalem by an explicit mention of both names. This information is eye-catching, because the figure mentioned for David's Jerusalem period is an anticipation which once again springs out of the narrative flow, and because the note 5:4-5 is so located that it can be taken to be both the end of Act IX and the beginning of Act X. In any case it marks their mutual boundary.

This system of space and time co-ordinates, present in each story and usually worthy of note, also performs its customary task in II Sam.2-8 and efficiently discharges its duty to the subject matter. The subject matter – in careful contrast to the thematics which must be allowed to emerge by meticulous analysis – can be referred to very briefly: in Act IX the appointed leader of Judah ascends the throne of a united Israel via a phase of civil war and in Act X David's power is consolidated as he rules from Jerusalem. Obviously such matters, of political relevance and national scope, benefit from the exact pinpointing in time and space extended to us here.

Attainment of power plus consolidation: this division of subject matter, which is reflected in the title of this volume, *Throne and City*, is one of the factors which indeed make Acts IX and X into a duo. Their complementary nature is also made visible by other means. Both groups begin with the hero's change of capital and in both cases God's sanction is inserted in the opening scene: the oracle which guides David in 2:1 and the mention in ch.5 of God, who is solemnly referred to by His official title in verse 10b, and whose support is once again recognised in verse 12a. Then there is the parallelism which originates with the narrator's mention of numerical and geographic data from David's two periods of rule, in two different places; these interrup-

[23] The one time that the successful war in the Transjordan needs to be mentioned, since it forms the background to the David-Bathsheba-Uriah triangle, the narrator ensures, in ch.10, that the success is credited to the courageous Joab and Abishai and, at the end of 12, that David's seizure of the citadel of Rabbath-Ammon is arranged by Joab and that it is, moreover, a formality which did not cost David the slightest effort.

tions of the flow of events, by his formulaic survey, occur at the beginning of IX and X (in 2:11 and 5:4-5, as we have already seen).

There is yet another case of parallelism which abandons the chronology. It comprises 3:2-5 and 5:13-16 and consists of two lists of sons of David, one with those born in Hebron and the other with those born in Jerusalem. Both these summaries are, the time they are offered, largely proleptic *re* the place the births occupy on the narrative time scale. Most, if not all, of the children enumerated in ch.5 are yet to be born, viz. in the period to be related after ch.5. Both series come, in their Acts, after a first (and also) decisive military triumph of David.[24] David's progeny are not only a token of his fertility; by means of the strategic localisation of the two series these children symbolise their father's future and prosperity by supplying the prospects of a well-manned dynasty. Shortly afterwards, in ch.7, this dynasty proves to be long-lasting indeed, and one which is the point of the oracle of God, via the prophet.[25]

Parallelism can also be based on a case of opposites.[26] The fact that Acts IX and X are a pair is something which emerges from the contrast generals versus no generals. All the military operations in IX are performed by the commanders-in-chief of the competing kings Ishbosheth and David. We see Joab and Abner only, flanked by their armies and two rows of twelve champions, in the civil war in ch.2.[27] The political consequences of the war are set out in ch.3

[24] The term "decisive" means, in the case of 2:17-32, that the battle of Gibeon between the armies under the commands of Joab and Abner is exemplary; the record of this is, as it happens, the only passage in Act IX which makes the civil war visible. Chapter five vv.17-25, in Act X, is "decisive" insofar as David now has done with the Philistines altogether; that is, with the enemy which became increasingly powerful in I Sam. (for the purpose of, amongst other things, ensuring Saul's doom), and achieved, in I 31, a great victory against Saul and his followers, and which immediately appears with an army after David's conquest of the central enclave of Jebusites (which action finally betrays his intention to become a formidable opponent of the coastal cities alliance). Note that the narrator, in Act IX, is ever silent on the subject of the Philistines, an attitude which no contemporary historiographer can afford when describing the months and years subsequent to a great military clash. This is an interesting indication that this particular art of storytelling obeys different rules, and has other aims in view, than those which spring to mind if we label it historiography. I do not say that Samuel is not, in fact, historiography, but what I would like to point out is that the relationship story/history is a subtle one, being extremely difficult to disentangle.

[25] It almost goes without saying that both being blessed with children and the prospect of a dynasty assume an ironic aspect in the section "King David", being undermined in such a way as to endanger the succession.

[26] This phenomenon is perhaps, for the reader, the most well-known of all in Hebrew poetry and is one in which verse halves are able to exhibit so-called antithetic parallelism. The phenomenon of opposition can, therefore, be found there, in the texture, on level 6.

[27] Joab's two brothers, Asahel and Abishai, are also given a secondary role in chapter 2.

and are largely borne by the constructive activity of Abner (for David) and the destructive behaviour of Joab. David is chiefly present as receiver or addressee (*destinataire*). The same kind of situation is in force in ch.4 where all he does is receive and react: he receives the severed head of his rival and rewards the assassins with a death sentence. The David of Act X is, on the other hand, extremely active and all kinds of military campaigns are credited exclusively to him, whilst the name of Joab has disappeared.[28] David is the initiator and sole hero of the double raid on the Philistines in ch.5.[29] He is the one to lead the great procession in ch.6 and no one else deserves a mention besides this dancing priest-king. Finally ch. 8, in the annalistic style of the ancient Near East, joins a whole series of victories together which are linked exclusively with the name of the king; this is no place for generals.

The absence of the general(s) is in harmony with the sacral nature of Act X. This takes us on to another case of opposition. Whilst God is virtually absent in Act IX,[30] He is repeatedly and emphatically present in Act X. He is referred to several times by his full, solemn title, "the Lord of Hosts, the God of Israel",[31] and He intervenes personally and in an extraordinary way several times – which is exceptional for the books of Samuel. God answers twice when David consults the priestly oracle (ch.5) and in ch.7. He reveals himself via a "prophetic" oracle to David, after rejecting the king's fine idea to build a temple. It is the most extensive revelation of God in the books of Samuel and the content of it is of fundamental, indeed even of world-wide historical, importance. A short while earlier God had unexpectedly interrupted the entry of the ark with a fatal blow, and had made everyone tremble before His aspect as *numen tremendum*, 6:7.

A small but poignant instance of opposition is the princess Michal's return to the stage. She appears at the centre of both Acts.[32] In IX she is pointedly

[28] This is not altered by the fact that the general is, in fact, mentioned in the short list of top officials at the end of chapter 8.

[29] I restrict myself to mortals at this point. It will be up to chapter 5 to bring to light the fact that God has a special and decisive part to play according to/in the text of 5:17-25.

[30] He is mentioned as an agent only at the beginning, in 2:1, where he is important and sends David to Hebron via the priestly oracle. Afterwards He is represented only through what characters say: 2:5-6,27, 3:18,28,39, 4:9 and 5:2. They do not use the title "Lord of Hosts".

[31] Straightaway in 5:10 (David's prosperity sanctioned), then in 6:2c (the name of the ark), in 7:8b (the messenger formula, exordium of the divine promise) and in 7:26b (acknowledgement by David in his prayer of thanksgiving, cf 28ab). A striking example of polarity, in ch.8, is that of YHWH as subject (v.6c//14d, both clauses being in a pivotal position) and as indirect object (in v.11ab and, virtually, in 7b).

[32] In Act IX this occurs in the middle of the central story 3:6-21, and in Act X the clash between David and Michal is to be found at the end of ch.6, outside this chapter's plot which concerns the installation of the ark.

mentioned by David. He wants her to be extradited and returned to him, and it is painful to see how much the woman who genuinely loved David is treated as a mere pawn in the political game by this her first husband, 3:13-16. In X matters come to a head in the form of a conflict between David, who is returning home, and the isolated daughter of a king who (literally and metaphorically) looks down on her husband's ecstatic dance in the streets of Jerusalem, 6:20-22. As a result Saul's daughter is to remain childless. The twofold appearance of Michal can be summed up as the contrast between remarriage and barrenness, or, a little more abstract, between apparent attraction and permanent repudiation. Paltiel's disconsolate love (3:16) makes us experience even more keenly the coolness of the reception David has in store for her.

Chapter 8 is rounded off by a series of eight lines which mention David's top officials. But this small passage forms not only the conclusion to the list of victories (a function at level 9), but to that of the Act as well plus the section containing it. This strikes us as we notice that this paragraph of summary is repeated virtually in its entirety at the end of ch.20.[33] The only matter which the writer, or redactor, does not dare to duplicate is 8:15, especially the clause with the value judgement, i.e. 15b: "and David executed judgement and justice unto all his people". This ought to be omitted altogether what with the moral discomfiture of David. Apart from this the two passages, 20:23-26 and 8:16-18, are identical. They function at levels 10 and 11 and constitute a parallelism, which provides Acts X and XV, as well the section "Throne and City", with closure.[34]

At this point I would like to provide a survey of the stories, which, for the benefit of the reader, will be described very briefly. The original text which concerns us here has, we have already noticed, several short paragraphs of an annalistic nature; a short list of children here, a series of officials there. The conscious insertion of these brief passages reveals their structural importance. They are all so short, however, that I will refrain from giving them a special number in my count of the literary units. They do not constitute a story or scene and, whilst enumerating and delineating the units, I will now and again include them in the preceding unit.

[33] As I remarked in vol.II under the Corrigenda, I ought to have included 20:23-26 in the Hebrew colometric text of *King David*.

[34] I would like to add that the caesura between Acts IX and X is, on the other hand, a minor one. This is another indication of the close relationship between the two Acts. Act Nine ends with the formulas of David's government in 5:4-5, a slight closure I would say, after which X, without circumlocution or marking features, continues with David who, in v.6, advances up to the walls of Jebus for the siege.

There are six literary units in Act IX. They are framed by the two anointings of David, and the most obvious thing to do is see whether there is any more concentric order. But this attempt fails. Interestingly enough the events dealt with are, in fact, quite clearly of a concentric nature but their ring composition is only partially covered by the delineation of the textual units. The literary units are as follows:

1) 2:1-11: a small group consisting of three fragments, vv.1-4b/4c-7d/8-11, shows that the post-Gilboa vacuum of power was filled by a Saulide monarchy in the north and east, and by the monarchy of David in Judah.
2) 2:12-3:1: civil war. The armies of David and Ishbosheth confront each other at Gibeon. Preliminaries occur in 2:12-17: the generals Abner and Joab both appoint twelve champions but their combat ends indecisively. In the battle which follows the armies fight it out and Joab's side is victorious. During the pursuit Abner sees himself forced to kill a brother of Joab, Asahel by name, who refuses to turn aside (vv.18-23). When darkness falls Abner and Joab negotiate a cease-fire and the armies part, vv.24-31. In 3:2-5 a list of six children, whom David fathered in Hebron, is added on.
3) 3:6-21: a quarrel about a woman results in the outbreak of a conflict between Abner and Ishbosheth. Abner announces that he is about to go over to the other side. When he wants to bring Israel under David's rule the latter demands that Michal be extradited. Abner secures the political support of the tribes of Israel, appears in Hebron and settles the transference of power with David.
4) 3:22-39: whilst departing Abner is murdered by Joab, to the great embarrassment of David the politician. He pronounces a curse on his general, organises a solemn state funeral and honours Abner with a dirge and a grave in Hebron. The two halves of ch.3 are scenes which have their own plot and issue, but they belong together like the two halves of a diptych.
5) 4:1-12: the weak king Ishbosheth, robbed of Abner's support, is now murdered by two of his army sergeants during his siesta. They take his head to David, but he has them executed as murderers. An intermezzo reports how the son of Jonathan has become a cripple (v.4).
6) 5:1-3 consists of not more than one sequence in which the elders of Israel go to Hebron and anoint David king of Israel. The formulas of the periods of David's reign in Hebron draw the Act to a close, vv.4-5.

Now for the events as they function like links in the chain of the history (in the literary sense of the term: the successive events referred to in the story and underlying it) upon which this narrative of six instalments is based. We find, in 3:30, during a short interval in a day of hectic politics in Hebron, an aside, a moment of information provided for us by the omniscient narrator. Joab is supposed to have murdered Abner to pay him back for the killing of Asahel. In this way a correspondence between the two deaths, each as cruel and as colourful as the other, is brought about. This now helps to construct a ring composition after all:

A David anointed king of Judah
  B Abner makes Ishbosheth king in Mahanaim
    C civil war, battle of Gibeon; Abner kills Asahel
  B' Abner-Ishbosheth conflict, Abner goes over to David
    C' Joab kills Abner because of his brother
  B" Ishbosheth no longer has Abner's support and is liquidated
A' David anointed king of Israel

Actually there is only one point at which this scheme departs from the order of the literary units. It divides the part 2:1-11, which forms the beginning, into two points. The concentric structure of the decisive moments is so striking that it will guide and deepen our insight during interpretation. I will confine myself here to one quick look at the ring composition. In the first instance I have introduced a B-B'-B" series for the sake of the political weight of the general Abner, who makes and breaks a king. But upon further examination it becomes clear that 3:6-21 contains the turning point. Here Abner defects to the other side and as a symbol of this there is the extradition of Michal as well. The Act has its own macroplot from 2:1 through 5:3 and can readily be investigated in actantial terms. David is the hero from start to finish and his quest is to obtain the double crown. His strongest opponent is not the king but the general of the other side. The latter changes from opponent to helper in the actantial scheme in 3:8-10 and 12, after which the house of Saul collapses like a pack of cards. That is why I am now going to alter one label in the ring composition: B' will justifiably be referred to as X from now on, because it is the true axis; the seven events form the series ABCXCBA.

Finally I would like to survey the stories which Act X offers:
7) 5:6-12: David conquers Jerusalem and extends it; in an appendix another list of children follows, vv.13-16.
8) 5:17-25: the Philistines advance against Jerusalem, but David, supported by God's oracle, manages to defeat them in two battles.
9) 6:1-22: David transfers the ark, in a great and solemn procession, to Jerusalem after a numinous incident (vv.6-10); clash with Michal during homecoming.

10) 7:1-29: David's suggestion to build a temple meets with Nathan's approval but God's disapproval. God reveals Himself via Nathan (v.4sqq.) and promises David a long-lasting dynasty (vv.8-16). David responds with a long prayer of thanksgiving (vv.18-29).
11) 8:1-14 provides, in principle, a complete, and therefore anticipatory, list of David's military successes on all sides and vv.15-18 round off the section with a list of top officials.

INTERPRETATION OF ACT IX
(II SAM.2-5:5)

ומלכת בכל אשר תאוה נפשך

Chapter II

Who shall have dominion over Israel?

§ 1. *The exposition (II Sam.2:1-11)*

Assuming that the First Book of Samuel has been rounded off by the dirge of David we now find ourselves at the true beginning of II Samuel. The first literary unit consists of three paragraphs or sequences, which I call A, B and C here. They are kept together and segmented by a parallelism which links up their closing sentences and repeatedly mentions David as king of Judah. The main issue is now quite distinct therefore, notwithstanding Abner who wants something quite different. The closing sentences of A, B and C are as follows:

4b	*wayyimš^{e}ḥū šām*	*'et Dāwīd*	*l^{e}męlęk*	*'al bēt Y^{e}hūdā*
7d	*w^{e}gam 'ōtī*	*māš^{e}ḥū*	*bēt Y^{e}hūdā*	*l^{e}męlęk 'ălēhęm*
11	*(...) hāyā*	*Dāwīd*	*męlęk b^{e}ḥębrōn*	*'al bēt Y^{e}hūdā (..)*

In each first half of these sentences David and the predicate keep changing places as do the words "king" and "house of Judah" in the second half, so that the sentences are systematically traversed and integrated by four chiasmuses. One of the results of this is that the four elements from (the central relative clause of) v.11 are, after all that crisscrossing, in the same position and order again as in 4b. On the syntagmatic axis all three sentences have a pleasantly undulating rhythm formed by the regular alternation of proper names and an ordinary word from the pair anoint/king.[1] This far-reaching and continuing effect ensures that the lines form a series, and that the paragraphs in vv.1-4b, vv.4c-7d and 8-11 affect one another and obtain the same kind of closure.

Parallelism guides our reading of the tripartite unit. Each time we are led to David's kingship over Judah. In this way the passage states its theme and identifies the true hero for us. This is a welcome phenomenon because without the structural force emanating from the parallelism of the closing sentences, the paragraphs would become so detached as to endanger their unity (i.e. their belonging together). And it is also welcome because what emerges from the narrative is an unmistakable opponent, who installs a puppet king on a second throne somewhere else.

For the reader with a historical bent paragraph C seems to confirm the idea of balance between two kings and their small kingdoms. But the reader with an eye for literature feels that this view is undermined in different ways; one of these is the power of the book's beginning (vv.1-4b). In little more than a stroke of the pen – fifty-four words all told – David has moved and become king in Hebron. An element of breakneck speed is immediately introduced into the narrative, and this adds momentum to the new phase in David's career. How does paragraph A manage to achieve this?

The colometric exterior of vv.1-4b at once reveals that this short passage can be divided into two halves consisting of a dialogue and a report from the narrator. Nevertheless, the sum total of everything that is uttered is expressed in a mere eight words. The narrator has succeeded in apportioning this scant amount to two speakers who both speak twice. David and God neatly take it in turns in the twofold back and forth of question and answer. David needs two and four words respectively for his questions, God answers both times with one word only; a shorter dialogue is hard to imagine. David asks for an oracle and gets one straightaway. This time the narrator wishes to lose no more time by explaining procedure. He knows that we can fall back on previous passages in which David found himself in difficulties, i.e. at Keilah and Ziklag.[2] What counts now is the fact of consulting the oracle, and the content of God's answer.

[1] In v.7d the name David is replaced by the word "me" since David is the speaker; in v.11 the predicate "anoint" is replaced by *hāyā*. In v.11 the process of alternation moves somewhat faster because the name Hebron has been added. Removing the clause from the series with 4b and 7d, we prefer to visualise it in three waves of ordinary word + name: *hāyā Dāwīd / mẹlẹk bᵉḤẹbrōn / ʻal-bēt Yĕhūdā.*

[2] See I Sam.23:9-12 and 30:7-8, where David asks his priest Abiathar to approach with the ephod, the priestly oracle. Compare this also with Saul and the ark in I 14:18-19. We also meet

David asks: "Shall I go up to one of the cities of Judah?" A question which it is difficult to regard as open as he already knows where he is going. David heads for the provisional goal of his political existence without delay, and God just gives confirmation. The first question evinces a binary choice; it can be answered only in one of two ways, either by yes or no. The second question is different, viz. "where shall I go?" Now the benevolent deity tells him exactly which direction he is to take, mentioning the name of the largest and most central city in Judah. Hebron also occurred in the list of names at the end of I 30; even though still sojourning in the political wilderness, David was, at that time, assiduously working on his comeback and was plying his tribal homeland with the haul yielded by his campaigns as vassal.

The key word of the concise dialogue which the Masoretes, with a fine feeling for economy, included in its entirety in v.1, is the verb of movement "go up". The cluster of preterits forming the brief piece of narrator's text (vv.2-4) begins with it, *wayyaʿal*, v.2a, so that removal gets underway immediately after the speech. Verse 3a rounds off the removal, by complementing the one long sentence filling v.2 with a chiastic syntax,[3] and by allowing the series of four qal forms of *ʿlh* to culminate in a hiphʿil, which transfers the whole retinue to Judah in a single transitive action. David's leadership is not only apparent from the force of this causative form, of which he is the only subject, but also from the qal singular.[4] David is at the apex of a widening series: one man – two women – his men and their families.

The women receive special attention; 2b in particular attends to this, with its three names and two *nisbe* forms.[5] Which functions are being fulfilled here? In the first place the mention of the two women is a sequel to the

the question and answer form twice in 23:10-12; the questions of David contain thirty(!) and eight words respectively, God replies with two one-word answers each time. Chapter 30 verse 8 shows that this can be set about in a very different way: one question of five words, one answer of six words.

[3] The rhyme *nāšāw* with *ʾănāšāw* is surrounded by qal and hiphʿil forms of the verb. Or, in other words: the word order in 2a + 3a is chiastic syntax: predicate + persons (subject) versus persons (object) + predicate.

[4] Even though the word *gam* is not necessary for the creation of a singular at the beginning of v.2, its location distances "his two wives" somewhat. For a predicate in the singular in spite of a plural subject see, for example, I 23:5a, 25a, 26:7a, 28:8b. But not only there; the narrator is about to employ the same technique to highlight Abner's dominance in the northern kingdom: in 2:12 and 17.

[5] Since Abigail is expressly/still referred to as "the wife of Nabal" I find it better to retain the masculine form *hakkarmᵉlī*, via which it alludes to Nabal – than to make it into a feminine referring to Abigail.

outcome of I 25 where Ahinoam gets a place next to Abigail in v.43, and where the number two is also found. After this incident the number of wives is kept at two. One also suspects that the perilous episode between Maon and Carmel is being called to mind here. The fact that Abigail still gets the apposition "the wife of Nabal", years after the death of this gentleman-farmer,[6] argues for this. The use of this epithet after her name is embarrassing, almost contemptuous towards David. But at the same time it might also be a political hint. With this gifted and tactful woman at his side David is more easily enabled to rely on the support of the tribe of Caleb, in which she and her large farm enjoy prominence. Another good reason for calling I 25 to mind is that the central speech of Abigail is of exceptional importance in that chapter and that it emphatically drew David's attention to his future as king; this prolepsis – the hint of the broad apposition in 2:2b – is now fulfilled.

The second function of the extensive reference to the women is that a connection with, and a contrast to, I 30 thus arises. In this chapter the exile David had to experience a perilous separation from his wives, as also did his men. Here too the women were mentioned by name and origin one after the other, in v.5. This danger is now past and gone, and settling down has become the order of the day as against the wanderings prior to it. And just as the women and children of David's comrades are not forgotten in I 30, so II 2:3a mentions them and their menfolk in "every man *with his household*".

The women – I now arrive at the third and perhaps the most important function – also contribute to the man/woman polarity, which is just as important in this Act as it is in a number of others. Their presence precedes the list of children (3:2-5), which quickly establishes David's fertility as king of Judah and brings up the number of wives from two to six. The words which state their origins, "of Jezreel", and, "of Carmel", with their roots *zr'* and *krm* fit in well with the idea of fertility; in other words, their etymology is re-animated by their context.[7] At the end of I 25 the two women of Judah faced Michal who had been taken away from David by Saul. This difference is developed dramatically in Acts IX and X. Whilst the house of David flourishes, the Saulidic princess becomes isolated; even though she returns to David's side in ch.3, the last we hear of her in the text – at the end of

[6] Apart from which it is in complete agreement with I 30:5 where exactly the same thing took place: *wa'ăbīgayil 'ešęt Nābāl hakkarmᵉlī.*

[7] Jezreel (from *yizra'* + *'el*) itself means "God sows". Additional occurrences of literary finesse are that Carmel rhymes with Jezreel, and that the names of the ladies exhibit striking similarities: rhyming words of kinship ("my brother" // "my father", elements in many theophoric names followed by segholate forms (*no'am* and *gayil*).

ch. 6 – is her barrenness. No blessing rests upon a linking of the two dynasties, the much frustrated marriage of the daughter of Saul and the man of Judah is without issue.

The movement in vv.2-3a ends in the serenity of settling down – "they went to live in the city of Hebron". This *wayyešebū* contrasts with the same form in 31:7 which refers to the Philistine occupation of Israelite cities, after their victory at Gilboa. The construct state pair "cities *of* Hebron" looks less odd, as soon as one sees that this plural is the counterpart of "the cities of Judah",[8] and probably means 'the cities surrounding Hebron' or, 'the cities which come under Hebron'. I do not expect that Hebron alone could have absorbed the sudden arrival of thousands of people.

The large group of remigrants is given a special welcome. "And the men of Judah came, and they anointed David king over the house of Judah there." This is the great culmination of the journey, and, to be sure, of this sequence. But what stands out is that it is mentioned almost in passing, as something which is so selfevident – after everything which has gone before, on the grounds of what we already know about David's calling – that it takes up little room in any case. God's participation does not even extend to this event: the oracle restricts itself to sanctioning, and stipulating the destination of, the removal. David's residing in Hebron has already received divine authorisation, his throne there – in this passage at any rate – is not something awaiting sacral sanction. The anointing is an initiative of the men of Judah. It is a purely secular, political ratification of what has already been laid down sacrally much earlier, i.e. when the prophet found the young man in Bethlehem and "anointed him in the midst of his brothers" in I 16. And that is also why the anointing in Hebron is something which concerns "the house of Judah" only; at the moment there is no room for pretensions going beyond the military and political reach of Judah.

The five sentences of the narrator contain both the name "Hebron", which brings a pause, in the middle, i.e. 3b, and at their limits the reference "there" occurs next to the name of the hero. The preceding long verse 1 ended with the revelation of the name of the city, so that we can state that everything which happens in vv.2-4 is based on this. The final three clauses all end on geographical names: Hebron – Judah – Judah. David's going up there (*'ālā*) is completed by his dominion over (*'al*) the region.

[8] This correspondence especially meets the eye because the movements (go up to, settle in) are complementary, and are highly representative for the two halves of paragraph A, and because 1c and 3b are symmetrical in the sense that they are both situated at exactly the same distance from the beginning as from the end.

Paragraph B occurs in v.4c-7d and commences with a change of subject.[9] People (this is my interpretation of the plural) tell David that "it is the men of Jabesh in Gilead who buried Saul."[10] In this way a third passage on the relation between the first king and the city in Gilead has come about; located at this point it forcefully links the beginning of II Sam. with the previous two sections, in which the despairing city was unexpectedly relieved by a charismatic Saul in action (I 11) and where we were told, at the end of I 31, what happened to the body of Saul after it had been mutilated by the Philistines. Just as the death of the king on the battlefield, the subject matter of the narrator's lines in I 31:1-7, was reflected in the lines of a character in II 1 – which, as we saw, was a curious mixture of an authentic eyewitness account and two well thought-out lies – in the presence of David, so at this point also the narrator's lines on his funeral (31:11-13) are followed by a character's lines on Saul's last rites. The characters' passage is a message initially, and subsequently a long and carefully worded "letter" of David to the Jabeshites, which takes up practically the entire sequence. The importance attached by the sender to this message delivered by word of mouth, is apparent from the fact that he sends messengers in the plural. This group is, therefore, a true mission, originating from a powerful man and not from a private person. David's use of the plural signifies his homage to Saul, whom he refers to as the lord of Jabesh.

David's letter is well-wrought and many-sided. Its structure becomes clear as we trace the alternation of volitive and preterit verb forms, and observe the articulating function of *w^e^ʿattā* which occurs twice. The speech consists, therefore, of 3 + 3 + 4 clauses[11] and the structure can be shown as follows. There are three parts. Each part takes up one column and can be read vertically, therefore.

[9] At least this is what I assume; in view of the topic and their distance from the catastrophe it does not go without saying that the Judaeans, the subject in 4b, are still the subject in 4c. The change of subject is unmarked and that could be the reason why the Masoretes did not begin a new verse here. For evidence see Appendix I.

[10] What is being emphasised here is not whether or not Saul received a burial, but the question of who saw to it. That is why the men of Jabesh are brought to the fore in the sentence; likewise *'ăšęr* is to be understood as being between them and their predicate.

[11] I hesitate as to the proper colometry at the end of v.5. The words *wattiqb^e^rū 'ōtō* are themselves a clause, but these words which explain "you do out of *ḥęsęd*" in 5d are still dependent on *'ăšęr* syntactically. Is it not better to insert them at the end of 5d, therefore?

wish //	wishes //	wishes
5c	*w*^{e}*ʿattā* 6a	*w*^{e}*ʿattā* 7a
	gam 6b	7b
'ăšer +	*'ăšer* +	*kī* +
2 preterits:	preterit:	2 preterits:
motivation 5de	motivation 6c	motivation 7c
		gam 7d

David begins by blessing the Jabeshites, his motivation for which he explains in 5de. He then utters, in two clauses (6ab), a desire[12] for retribution based on the same motivation (6c). These two parts belong together closely and exhibit much parallelism. The third step is very different, and as a consequence of this the second *w*^{e}*ʿattā* is a weightier hinge than the first. David now extends double encouragement to the Jabeshites in 7ab, after which the link is no longer *'ăšęr* but the conjunction *kī*. He concludes with two more lines containing the antithesis of life and death and a change of atmosphere which marks the point of the whole letter.

The first two parts are highly parallel and belong together as good deed plus reward. The parallelism rests on various supports. The opening volitive clauses 5c and 6a both contain God's personal name, the kinds of motivation which follow begin identically with the series *'ăšęr ʿăśītęm ha ... hazzę̄*, 5d//6c. The relationship between the parts is a very close one due to the fact that, after the exordium "blessed ... ", four clauses follow in 5d-6e, which all use the verb "do" according to the pattern a-b-b-a: the perfect "you have done" occurs in 5d + 6c and encircles the forms of the imperfect in 6a and 6b, the short or jussive form (the strong desire "may *yhwh* ... do to you") and the full form ("I shall ... do to you") respectively.

I would like to take a close look at all this activity; who are the subjects, what is the tense, and what is the object? I will begin with the object, which repeatedly requires two words: its referent is exactly the same in all four clauses, even though the formulation varies and the way in which it does so is not without importance. Everything centres around "solidarity" each time. The first act of this *ḥęsęd* is "what you did for your lord", says David, and he explains what he means at once: you have buried him. All other details which at that time were added to it in the narrator's report are no longer what matters, of chief importance is that Saul's soul should find peace in a decent

12 Strictly speaking 6b is a promise and not a wish. But as this promise has a volitional element and line 6b runs notoriously parallel to 6a, I have called 6ab two wishes in the scheme.

grave; the men of Jabesh have seen to this – in the face of so much difficulty! But even this consideration is now left aside – which is what David now gratefully recognises. I notice that the narrator lets him begin with the value judgement "this deed of solidarity" in 5d, and only then lets him go on mentioning the fact itself in 5e. We become aware of the fact that practically the entire passage is of an evaluative nature.

David is not able to speak on behalf of God and he uses, therefore, the jussive of a strong wish in 6a to indicate the retribution of God. In this line for *yhwh* he intensifies the object "solidarity" – and this is a favourite of poets especially – into the splendid pair *ḥęsęd wę'ĕmęt*. The active form of 6a is a good complement of the passive construction with *lyhwh* in 5c. What David hopes for, from God for Jabesh, he can contribute towards himself, and now he uses in 6b the long form of *'śh* to make a promise himself: "for my part I will also do something good like this for you." The speaker has placed his activity on the same level as God's and in so doing has taken his place right next to God. Our speaker is not overly modest! In order not to crassly prolong this parallel David does not repeat the word *ḥęsęd* in his own line, 6b, but replaces it with *haṭṭōbā*.[13] The object makes its fourth appearance in 6c where, as final element, it is inconspicuous, so that the series ends with a simple: "this matter". The demonstrative pronoun of this, which also occurred in 5d and 6b, guarantees that the referent stays the same. It is David's desire and promise that the solidarity which the Jabeshites have shown might be rewarded and mirrored.

If David plans to do good to the people of Jabesh and if he also expects that God will reward their community for its loyalty, why does he then have to encourage them, in addition, to take heart in v.7? This is motivated by a *kī* clause in 7c which fills the entire verse with a kind of atmosphere other than the one which the two preceding ones had. A good understanding of the closing part is highly dependent on the question as to whether or not 7d is governed by the conjunction *kī*. In my opinion the proper relationship between 7ab, 7c and 7d only becomes visible, and their logic sufficiently clear, if one views 7d as a separate, independent addition to 7abc.[14] Whatever

[13] Neither does David dare to copy the designation *'immākęm* for the indirect object in 6a; he replaces it with *'itt^{e}kęm* in 6b. The words *ḥsd* and *ṭwb* are well-known as a word pair in poetry, see p.238 of Y. Avishur's "Stylistic Studies of Word-Pairs in Biblical and Ancient Semitic Literatures", Neukirchen-Vluyn, 1984 (AOAT 210).

[14] The opinion that 7d does in fact depend on *kī* we see, for example, in the English parataxis in the JPS rendering: "Now take courage and be brave men; for your lord Saul is dead and the House of Judah have already anointed me king over them." The KJ says approximately the same

the case might be, the high tone and style of vv.5-6 make way for the tense, in one sense perilous, present with which the whole of verse 7 is concerned. God has disappeared from the text and practical politics obtrudes itself. Jabesh is now vulnerable after the Philistine victory and can no longer rely on the protection of king Saul: "your master is dead." David implies this painful situation when he puts fresh heart into the city (with the three words of 7a), and it is now only natural that he doubles his encouragement with the three words of 7b which complete a synonymous parallelism. Because v.7 occupies itself with the threatening present, it is better to place the realisation of the blessing and the retribution desired by David somewhere else on the time scale, a few years into the future for example, when David will have succeeded in eliminating Philistine pressure and establishing the foundations for a strong Israel.

Against the negative fact of Saul's death David places the positive announcement of a new beginning; one that is defined in terms of his own coming to the throne. The introductory and emphatic *gam 'ōtī* is the counterpart of the already equally emphatic *gam 'ānōkī* with which he placed himself on the same plane as God in 6b.[15] Quasi self-effacing he now makes himself into the object of other people's activity; he does not want to create the impression that he himself was the initiator.[16] "However, as far as I am concerned [I

thing. I do not find this convincing because the content of 7c and 7d is so different as to ensure that the positive and negative statements cannot be bracketed together with 7ab in a clean logical order. In any case the loss in 7c renders the encouragement fitting, if not essential, whilst the anointing of David actually implies a promise for Jabesh, that in due course, perhaps speedily, it can expect assistance from Judah. Naturally 7d is also connected to 7ab but not with the same link *kī* which connects 7c with them. Another sin against logic is to be found in an initially attractive rendering in the LV: "be courageous men; since although your lord Saul is dead, the House of Judah has anointed me king over it." The concessive connection does not tally; this becomes apparent if we check it out by replacing death with life: "although your Lord Saul is alive they have anointed me king". This logic is sound, even though not applicable to II Samuel (remarkably enough it does apply to I Sam., after Ch.16!).

[15] This is all the more convincing since the first person does not occur in the rest of the speech. As far as the word *gam* is concerned, its translation here is a subtle business, as it so often is elsewhere. In 6b it is still chiefly additive and the redundant *'ānōkī* before the predicate itself already ensures emphasis on the first person. In 7d *gam* does more than fulfill its other and customary chief funcion of emphasis; it marks the turn to "now something completely different". My translation is, therefore, as follows: "Be courageous (*bis*), for your lord Saul is dead; as far as my own position is concerned, however, the house of Judah has anointed me king over it".

[16] David could have said, therefore: "and I have ascended the throne ... " etc., or *wā'ęmlok*, etc. Notice that "they have anointed me" is in line with v.4b; it is, after all, as a member of the series 4b-7d-11 also part of a larger entity.

would just like to get something off my chest here, and that is] I am the one who has been anointed king by Judah." This is the only sentence which contains something entirely new to the people of Jabesh. But are we able to evaluate this kind of communication? We simply cannot establish what this news, which, as a piece of information, differs entirely from the rest of the speech, actually wants to say when it comes down to it, and whether it is embarrassing or not. That David still includes the fact in his letter is something one might interpret as being very assertive, and also as a piece of clever politics. One might also find it embarrassing, or not very tactful, after so many splendid and pious clauses, to see how easily David places his promotion next to – I just manage to avoid saying: links it with – the death of Saul.[17] David has recognised Saul as "*your* lord" twice; this is obliging and to be valued as a form of loyalty, yet his loyalty does not go so far as to include himself by referring to Saul as "our lord". His own attitude to Saul he keeps behind the scenes here, and the possessive suffix which he does choose is a hardly noticeable sign of aloofness.

In any case the political reading is worthy of elaboration, since the speech is, and remains, a message of a leader to a community and there is nothing against assuming that David has considered the political implications of his message in depth. Moreover, the letter is a form of diplomatic correspondence. Verse 7d is, then, the point of the whole, which means that David meanwhile uses a sprat to catch a mackerel as he hopes to gain more territory than just Judah. It is not a promise of immediate military support and is unable to be this as yet, in phase 1 of David's rise to power. It is a reminder rather, one which capably makes a start by charming the audience for David: you were loyal to the previous ruler, and that earns my praise and respect; I won't forget you, and when the time comes I shall take your interests fully into consideration.[18]

We can track down the rhetorical achievement of David's message if we assess the incidence of conjunctions and disjunctions. Four parties are present in the letter: David and Saul, God and "you" (i.e. the inhabitants of Jabesh).[19] The relations which the speech of David introduces between these parties are almost all conjunctive. Out of a conceivable six, five are to be

[17] After all the stylistic embellishment in the preceding seven clauses 7c is hard and outspoken: Saul is dead, and 7d is businesslike and without the trimmings as well.

[18] Whilst on the subject of regarding and not forgetting: compare similar expressions of Abigail as she points out David's future to him in her central speech. Or Joseph in Gen.40:14.

[19] There is yet a fifth character, viz. Judah. Because this group only appears in the closing line I will not be subjecting it to consideration in this part of my argument; the Judah-David relationship is clearly conjunctive also.

found in the text.[20] They are, in short, as follows:
(1) the one with the umbrella function is that of David with Jabesh. He sends the community a positively worded letter in which he communicates a blessing and a promise, recognises loyalty, extends encouragement, and announces a new development.
– Jabesh-Saul is conjunction (2): seeing to the funeral is valued as an act of solidarity, the king is mentioned twice as "your lord";
(3) the speaker also, therefore, considers the conjunction Yhwh-Jabesh as blessing and retribution.
– the conjunctions (4) and (5) are surprising and have something precarious about them. The fourth, David-Yhwh, remains implicit and is created by David's placing himself on a level with God in the doing of good (6b is highly parallel with 6a); he who listens carefully, already notices the ideological legitimisation of a king. Chronologically all this activity of the ruler can only follow 7d, the anointing, so that the promise of 6b anticipates the information on David's royal status. Conjunction (5) is David-Saul: the new king refrains from any suggestion of a false note or criticism of his predecessor, he recognises him insofar as he himself, as successor, would like to see the loyalty shown to Saul praised and rewarded.

Disjunctions are absent. David is so discerning as to allow *one* conjunction to remain behind the scenes, and that is the Yhwh-Saul one. This is all too obvious, since Saul has so long been out of favour that such a conjunction cannot be asserted without hypocrisy. Most of the conjunctions are in the form of one-way communication, principally as a result of the fact that Saul is dead and the text is no longer to return to the fortunes of Jabesh. What keeps the conjunctions together the most, and with them the message itself, is plural symmetry or reflection which is fed by the idea of reciprocal loyalty and can easily be placed on a chronological axis: Jabesh has shown itself loyal to Saul; I, David, reflect this in my recognition, and God will reflect it in His blessing and reward. In this way all the parties are brought close together by means of a rhetorical strategy from which it is difficult to withdraw without being taken for a kind of wet blanket at the graveside.

In addition to this comprehensive letter what strikes us is that a sequel fails to emerge; the city responds neither with a message of appreciation, nor with a call for help, nor with the hint that, in due course, it will be willing to serve under David. We simply do not hear any more on Jabesh. This raises the

[20] Each of the four characters can be linked to the other three; 4 x 3 = 12. But these twelve links are reversible (David-Saul and Saul-David form one relation) making for six relationships, therefore.

interesting question as to why, in spite of this, the narrator has created this sequence at all, locating it here as he does without sequel or realisation. A possible answer to this would consist of different parts. One of these is that a long speech acts as like a window through which we can look at the character of the one who speaks; this letter contributes much to the characterisation of David as a swiftly acting politician and a courteous and level-headed diplomat who carefully formulates his words. I myself would be inclined to add a word of non-cynical appreciation here, viz. that David as God's elect, and, as yet, as a man of integrity, was sincerely moved by, and grateful for, the loyalty of the Jabeshites. After all, he has just shown greatness by honouring Saul personally in poetical form, in the dirge.

The inclusion of the message could also imply that the point of view of the narrator himself is being intimated. He himself at the end of I 31 had already indirectly paid tribute to the loyalty and courage of the Jabeshites by carefully unfolding their journey by night and their deep mourning. Now he decides, once again, to honour them, this time through his hero's holding a mirror to their virtue. On balance he found it structurally desirable to include the message of the funeral and the evaluation of David, in order to complete the two units (I 31 and II 1) which were devoted to Saul's death by the narrator and a character respectively. In continuation of this chapters 2-4 are all to end with a funeral.

Paragraph C, vv.8-11, is narrator's text throughout and its primary function is to supply information. This is apparent from the fact that its total of sixty-three words contains twenty names. Space and time are prominent here, in the specific application of reigns and the territories governed. The narrator commands a view of all of this and poses as chronicler for a short paragraph.

He begins with an inversion which introduces a new subject. It is Abner who finally receives a proper introduction as a character, from the section II Sam.2-8.[21] Two phrases in apposition announce his origins and his military profession. The two halves of the long sentence full of names are as rhythmic as waves; this effect is produced by their ending on the name which is, for the moment, still the point of orientation, Saul. Now we meet Abner for the first time, as a powerful gent.[22] The bare fact of the words chosen, "he took

[21] Both Abner and Job receive their real introduction as characters for the first time in Act IX even though they have made their appearance earlier. This is not such a bad decision for we are going to see that this duo actually does figure prominently here.

[22] Abner fulfilled a secondary role only in what has gone before, as a non-informed commandant of Saul at the end of I 17 and as a target of David's derision in I 26.

Ishbosheth", suggests that he has an authoritarian hold, and this impression is confirmed by two hiph'il forms which effectively express his power: "he took him to Mahanaim and made him king". Ishbosheth, the son of Saul, is not only the grammatical object, he is, both as a character and politically, the handiwork of the general. Abner's being mentioned first is iconic, he is the initiator and is an actantial subject with his own quest. The Saulide is only a puppet and Abner is the strong man, in a construction which makes a brief attempt to continue the kingdom of Saul. Another function fulfilled by the inversion is a temporal one. Verse eight is probably a flashback, "in the meantime Abner had installed the son of Saul", which indicates that the vacuum of power, after the elimination of Saul, was filled on both sides more or less at the same time. This accentuates the parallelism of the issue in paragraphs A and C, and heightens the idea of competition.

The territory assigned to Ishbosheth is covered by an enumeration, in verse 9, which begins with the eastern province, of which Mahanaim is the capital in this passage; next our attention is focused on this side of the Jordan and four areas are mentioned in a consistent north-south movement.[23] The series ends with the area which is farthest away from the new residence and borders on Judah, that of the tribe of the Saulides, Benjamin, and culminates in a summary, viz., "in short, the whole of Israel".[24] The set formula for age and length of reign, familiar from Kings, is now applied, in v.10b, to Ishbosheth. The text's insertion, close by, of how this contrasts with David,[25] makes me wonder whether the figures on Ishbosheth are principally of literary and ironic import rather; in which case Ishbosheth is a man who comes to power fairly late and survives, even though in the prime of life, only for a very short time.[26] David's Judah period alone is several times longer.[27]

[23] On the grounds of this pattern it seems probable to me that Asher – a name which we obtain by re-punctuating the impossible *'ăšurī* (see also Appendix I) – is a designation, understood *pars pro toto*, of Galilee.

[24] A *waw explicativum* occurs after the name Benjamin; notice the word order which follows it, with *kullō* after Israel, which might designate closure.

[25] In the neighbourhood: next to the figures of v.10 are those of David in v.11, and because 2:11 is a preamble to 5:4-5 which expressly repeats the Judaean figures, I include that passage.

[26] In NAPS II I expressed an opinion on the lacuna and the dubious number concerning Saul in I 13:1. Are the "two years" of rule which Saul receives there a model, or the copy, of the two years of Ishbosheth? There might be a literary connection. An additional (indeed speculative) step further: in view of II 2:10 might we regard the "forty years" as Saul's age in 13:1? Not only the age of Ishbosheth, but also that of Jonathan assume that Saul was at least sixty years of age when he died in I 31. In II 4:4 Jonathan has a little boy of five years when he himself dies, and in I 13-14 Jonathan is already adult (he has great military responsibility).

[27] If we insert 2:10 next to the complete formula of the age and reign of David, next to 5:4 (which

The appearance of the monarchical formula at this point is an indication, in principle, that the file on Ishbosheth is already closed. The only thing which we are still to hear about him is, indeed, his political demise (3:6sqq.), quickly followed by his physical one (II 4). The exposition itself keeps up appearances for the moment and presents the following balance between the two kings:

- Ishbosheth has much territory / but little time
- David has little territory / but a lot of time.

Verses 10a and 11 undermine the importance of the Saulide by taking the paragraph back to David, and verse 11, by the mere fact of its length alone, fifteen words in all, puts the Saulide in the shade. The line is well-proportioned, and constructed around a relative clause containing three names.[28] It has two functions especially here, i.e. providing contrast with the son of Saul (as a duplication of 5:5a)[29] and closure (as a member of the series 2:4b-7d-11). The narrator not only surveys David's reign in Hebron but creates a prolepsis by publicising its figures in advance; these are two unmistakable signs in the text of his omniscience and his perspective, at a place of closure.

A-B-C together. Now that we have the basic essentials on the Saulide, the main point in the literary unit 2:1-11 is complete and clear. Israel (in the broad sense) now has two kings and the question is whether or not the country is willing and able to bear this. The trio ABC forms the exposition of the whole Act and supplies the subject matter enabling the macroplot of Act IX to get underway. The exposition contains the seeds of conflict between a regime created by a high-handed general and a monarchy announced long ago by a prophet and currently recognised by a community. The power of the king of Judah, and that of the general, cannot be automatically added up to benefit the nation; on the contrary, they threaten to exhaust one another's resources. Next to David a phrase appears four times having a specific function in this unit viz., "the house of Judah".[30] This term is connected

is itemised in v.5) therefore, the shift of the literary or symbolic number forty is relevant perhaps: the hero David has already been reigning for as long as Ishbosheth lived before he ascended his ephemeral throne.

[28] The first three words rhyme with the final four and take care of the count; the relative clause which completes the 4b-7d-11 series occurs in between.

[29] The contrast is marked lexically by the particle *'ak* at the beginning of v.10c.

[30] The combination *bēt ye hūdā* occurs especially in the poetry of the Later Prophets (twenty-six times), and also once in Nehemiah and four times in Chronicles. Absent from the Torah, the term occurs in the Former Prophets exclusively in II Sam.2 (four times), I Ki.12:21 and 23, and II Ki.19:30 (a remnant of Judah shall remain: message of God to king Hezekiah, to be conveyed by Isaiah).

with 3:1, but especially takes us on to I Ki.12. This is, however, the chapter of the rift which takes place after the reign of Solomon! "The house of Judah" is found in v.21 where the arrogant Rehoboam wants to go to war to nullify the division, but also in v.23 where God himself forbids the struggle via an oracle and in so doing endorses the trauma of the split. This connection is a tip for us to read the beginning of II Samuel in the light of I Ki.12. One of the insights provided by such a reading is that Israel's partition into two is already prefigured here and that dissension is the birth trauma of the united country of David and Saul.

Now we are able to survey how the three paragraphs relate to one another. Great harmony between David, God and Judah is to be found in A, whilst the report of C takes a look at the other side and signifies a divided nation. The pseudo-dual of the name Mahanaim is animated by this piece of information: ascending the throne in the north-east results in "two camps".[31] Sequence B is in between and functions more or less like an intermediary. It is connected with C since it also looks at Gilead, but is also linked to A by its being a reaction of the newly crowned David. The location of his message is a delicate one. His evaluation of Jabesh's final tribute to Saul follows his own anointing, but precedes the installation of the other king. This means that the text of 2:5-7 can be the message of a king without simultaneously stirring up trouble in another man's territory. If David had brought his monarchy to the attention of the Jabeshites after the establishment of a Saulide ruler in Mahanaim, then his letter would have been an act of provocation towards the new regime, if not a *casus belli*, thus forming a questionable mixture of pious words and power politics. The writer has avoided putting things into this kind of a bad light by locating vv.5-7 in position B. David officially recognised the courage of the Jabeshites quicker than Saul's kinsfolk were able to reorganise themselves. Spatially speaking the Hebron-Jabesh line of communication in B nevertheless keeps on mediating between the entirely Judaean paragraph A and that of Abner in C, and David's information in 7d is the first sign of his possible expansion.

Another characteristic feature of the A-B-C series is the undulating movement of life-death-life, inasmuch as A and C announce the coming to power of a new generation, whilst B is a flashback to the death of Saul preconditional

[31] The place-name Mahanaim is not a proper dual, but might so function in a literary context. My reason for suggesting this here is that the place-name's first appearance in Genesis – Kings amply capitalises on the pseudo-dual, Gen.32 (as I have worked out in NAG *ad loc.*) and because duality in the violent form of warfare is depicted with precision straightaway in 2:12sqq. (whereby 2:9 does not neglect to mention the place-name Mahanaim once again.)

to David's coming to power. This succession of present-past-present goes for the most part together with the relationship of report and speech. A is for the most part report, but has a short dialogue, B consists almost exclusively of the spoken word, C consists entirely of report and information provided by the narrator. The preparatory nature of 2:1-11 is apparent from the frequency of proper names, primarily of characters and their territory. Seventeen names occur in A, there are 12 in B, and as many as 20 in C; 49 names altogether out of a total of 182 words.

The text is open enough to allow for an alternative reading. We might look at the events from the perspective of the heirs of the tribe of Saul. This does in fact involve radically turning the tables. David becomes the opportunistic parvenu who splits the nation by decking his regional power out with a crown. His official appearance on the stage of history is a dangerous attack on the Saulide continuity aimed at by Abner and forced, in the first instance, to make a new start in the Transjordan. Those sharing the Benjaminite point of view on the matter will, after all, be able to summon up little appreciation for the message of the newcomer David to a city which, *nota bene*, is not far from Mahanaim, also in the territory of the Transjordan, which feels closely committed to Saul, her one-time liberator. How dare David take it into his head to come between them with fine words!

§ 2. *An exemplary day of warfare,* 2:12-32

The fact of two kings in one country is quite explosive and quickly leads to strife. The text reserves room for warfare in 2:12-32, a complex unit of three tableaux. Two armies meet each other in the first and place two lines of champions opposite one another. A close-up of a young man who pursues the enemy leader is offered by the central tableau, whilst the third tableau announces a cease fire and the sides' going their separate ways. The second and the third part of the unit smoothly shade into one another via vv.24 and 25; they have key words in common and complement each other temporally by reporting what has taken place during the day and after sundown on the battlefield. The first tableau vv.12-16, through this but also through its own particular structure, is isolated and merits the appellation 'prelude'.

The relative independence of this opening is indicated by a boundary. In v.17 the overview and the organising activity of the narrator is very much present, and the two lines composing it form a parallelism with 3:1, which also has the perspective of the omniscient narrator. At this moment I will show only a half of the figure of speech:

17a wattᵉhī hammilḥāmā qāšā ʿad mᵉʾōd bayyōm hahū
3:1 wattᵉhī hammilḥāmā ʾărukkā bēn bēt šāʾūl ubēn bēt dāwīd
These lines commence with an unmistakable anaphora and together with their nominal predicate no longer take part in the chain of action. Their content is complementary, for whilst 17 only comments on this one day, 3:1 generalises about the war, summarises the whole course of events and reveals the result. The terms "house of Saul" and "house of David" suggest symmetry just once more, but to no avail; the balance finally tips in favour of Judah, 3:1bc.

A. The Prelude, 2:12-17
Armies advance from two different directions and meet each other at Gibeon. They take up symmetrical positions in v.13c. They allow themselves to be represented by a group of twelve champions, and their deployment exhibits a striking symmetry, v.15bc. This type of equality is characteristic of their combat and its horrifying result, v.16. The two times twelve meet their deaths at the same time, *yaḥdāw*. But what is now striking is that this word already occurred in v.13b, and that the meaning of this adverb is rather redundant – not to mention pleonastic – in the context of an encounter (*pgš* is the verb there).[32] This redundancy betrays the fact that the location of *yaḥdāw* in v.13 has to do with structure. The adverb is one of the indicators of a concentric symmetry which governs all the parts:

A 12+13a the parties: 2 kings, 2 generals, 2 armies
  B 13b encounter at Gibeon, *yḥdw*
    C 13c *yšb*: symmetrical encampment around the pool
      D 14abc Abner's proposal ...
      D' 14de ... accepted by Joab
    C' 15abc *qwm*: symmetrical deployment twelve/twelve
  B' 16abc combat, champions *yḥdw* dead (16d ... in Gibeon)
A' 17ab battle, one army defeats the other (1 general, 1 king)

To the outside are the two largest collectives, the armies of both sides, and the names of the princes. Because such large-scale warfare does not suit Abner, he puts forward his proposal that this should be carried out by two small

[32] If A and B meet each other then this must occur, by definition, "at the same time". That is why *yḥdw* is difficult to translate in v.13. The subject is that of 13a, "Joab and the servants of David", and my rendering of 13b would be as follows: "They met them [sc. Abner and his army] at the pool of Gibeon, [where both sides arrived] at the same time".

collectives. In C'B' the twelve plus twelve represent the armies under pressure in BC. Their encampment (indicated by *yšb*) is uneasy, and is replaced by the "rising up" of champions who must channel the increasing tension and drain it off by means of twelve duels. In the middle there are two individuals who speak to one another. Thus the concentric order makes room for characters on three levels and makes use of the difference between report and speech by filling the middle, D-D', with a dialogue which attempts to find a solution.

I would like to postpone determining the significance of the symmetrical structure and would first like to discuss the text in a cursory order of appearance. Verse twelve is long and contains many names as a result of its introductory function. Both Abner and Ishbosheth appear here along with their patronymics. Abner is mentioned first of all again, meriting once more the appellation of initiator. At the close of the verse the beginning and end of the campaign receive a tidy mention in "from Mahanaim to Gibeon". This army makes an appearance, therefore, in the southernmost part of his territory, in a Canaanite enclave of the tribe of Benjamin. The narrator, conceding nothing to our historical curiosity, withholds their objective; but we are aware of the fact that this expedition takes Abner close to the Judaean border and we doubt if the other side is pleased with this.

The army of David appears at the same time in Gibeon, and its leader, Joab, is also introduced to us by his patro-, no, by his matronymic in this case. This is indeed the passage in which the important actor is introduced by both the prefatory lines of v.13a and 18a.[33] The lines of v.12 and 13a are each other's complement, a fact which is made visible as an inclusio offering the military manoeuvre of marching out. At the beginning of v.12 and at the end of v.13 this verb forms part of a chiastic syntax, which itself once again surrounds the two place-names.[34] Our historical interest is once again frustrated, but my speculation is that Joab finds it a prudent defensive measure not to allow Abner to get too close but to confront him beyond the borders of David's territory. What is now striking is that neither side attacks. They are still controlling themselves apparently. What takes place is a tense setting up of camp on both sides of the pool; the words of 13c are identical for both sides. There is a temporary cessation of movement. The text is so restrained that a pinpointing of the significance of the water is not easy. The pool separates

[33] Prior to this Joab had no part to play in events. He was mentioned by name just once but only as reference point when his brother Abishai came into action alongside David, in I 26:6.

[34] The constructions *wayyeṣē* + personal names and personal names + *yāṣāʾū* surround that of "from Mahanaim to Gibeon".

and unites the sides who both need a lot of water. Motionless, available and centrally situated the pool reflects the great stir on all sides.

The centre-piece is a talk in which Abner takes the initiative once more. Without further ado he puts forward a proposal in two very brief clauses. The narrator omits all details. In (narrated) reality the gentlemen must have already engaged in a certain amount of negotiating, about the champions for example, whose exact number we are informed of for the first time in verse 15. This frugality means that only the core of the proposal is allowed to take up the centre position, which makes it easier for the narrator to introduce symmetry here as well, i.e. in the abridgement. Joab's minimum length reaction, the single word of 14e, is one of approval and mirrors the first word of Abner.[35]

How are we to evaluate Abner's proposal? The general proposes a combat between the representatives of both sides. I see this as one of three alternatives, two of which he does not want to, or which he cannot, carry out. The general is apparently not keen on a large-scale conflict which would require all the troops. This could be evidence of sense and moderation. But on the other hand Abner does not want, or cannot enter into, a conflict without weapons. That war is politics pursued by other means can, after all, be turned around. One can choose to speak through diplomats rather than weapons. Why is this something which Abner does not want? He does not put forward the suggestion that both armies should withdraw an hour's or a day's march away. What kind of duress is he under? Is he subject to the great stress of a very tense situation in which two armed forces lie in wait for each other and mutual distrust swiftly mounts? Would not failure to fight mean loss of face for a policy maker who is influenced, among other things, by the need to keep on being tough and other machismo considerations, and who now decides, therefore, that in any case "something must be done"?

What Abner proposes has the look of a tournament whose result is to be decisive for the two sides. After he has started to speak of "the young men" – the customary euphemism – in 14b, and has set their "rising up" against the impasse of their mutual sitting down (*yšb* of 13c), waiting, and lying in wait, the point arrives in 14c with an apt verb "they must make sport before us." In view of the way in which it is carried out I take the "making sport", in vv.15-16, to mean "hold a tournament", but in reality it is a serious

[35] The repetition of someone else's most significant word as a way of saying "yes" is a well-known feature in classical Hebrew. But included in a literary expression such echoing can be assigned more functions. We saw this clearly in NAPS I, for example, when II Sam. 20:17, or I Ki.2:13, was being discussed.

combat. Its bloody outcome reveals that "making sport" is a remarkable choice of words: probably the understatement of an old war-horse, part of military jargon from time immemorial, full of euphemisms which denote the most terrible things, but avoid adding more pain to the soft heart hidden behind the soldier's rough exterior.

Euphemisms attempt to reduce hard facts to manageable proportions. Abner suggests combat but its form and very limited scale are, and remain, an attempt to prevent mass bloodshed. As soon as Joab has uttered an echo of Abner's *yāqūmū*, the narrator follows on with his own report, *wayyāqūmū* in 15a. This word marks a quantitative balance in the text.[36] What precedes it in 12-14, a sketch of the situation plus dialogue, is preparatory, what follows it in 15-17 is real action, in duplicate.

The two small groups temporarily replace the two large ones, and they neatly line up opposite one another: 15a has the connotations of a well-drilled marching to battle stations and the pair 15bc exhibit great symmetry by the repetition of the number mentioned.[37] And what a number! Twelve for both sides – does this mean that both sides are laying claim to the twelve tribes of Israel in its entirety?[38] Something hair-raising clings to the use of the sacred number in an arena about to run red with blood. In 15b it is noticeable that the king is referred to in full by his patronymic; in this way the twelve men from the north have been accorded a formal and official designation, as if the narrator were a clerk of the court.

The real action in this part of the text is, at the same time, its dramatic climax, 16abc. The twelvefold duel is very succinctly rendered in the two lines 16ab, which form a parallelism thanks to the rhyme on *re'ehū*, "his companion = his opponent", and to the appearance of two parts of the body, head and side, both introduced by the same preposition. The sole verb appears at the beginning and shows us at a glance the plurality of the combatants. Immediately afterwards the idiomatic expression for reciprocity, *'īš ... re'ehū*, appears, which determines that six words follow in the

[36] The text (of the prelude, 2:12-17, therefore) employs forty-three words before and forty-three words after the *wayyaqūmū* of the narrator.

[37] The symmetry exhibits asymmetry in the names following the number. In 15c there is one name only in "the servants of David". In 15b there are two names. It is noticeable that the name of King Ishbosheth does not occur until the second position, in order to explain the name of the tribe (there is a waw explicativum after Benjamin). Ishbosheth's being made secondary is a continuing strategy, as we shall see.

[38] Further applicability to the tribes of Israel is not easy because each group of twelve comes from one tribe only; the first twelve soldiers consist largely of Benjaminites and the second twelve largely of Judaeans.

singular. It is employed in both lines and produces the semblance of individuality which can rescue no one from anonymity but nevertheless gives a vital and quasi-detailed picture of the twenty-four man to man combats. The twofold nature of the parallelism 16ab, which is iconic for each pair of soldiers standing face to face, is obliterated by that one short line of death, 16c, in which all come together; their unity is present lexically in the adverb *yaḥdāw* which ends the combat. The alternation of plural and quasi-singular can also be seen from the two words of 16c: the verb in the plural and the adverb of the root "one" exhibit a synchronous falling in battle. In this way a descending series of 4 + 3 + 2 words has come about which stands for intense exertion plus the crucial picture plus the dying together. In its entirety the series shows how quickly the twelvefold duel has ended.

What a gruesome tableau! And what a contrast between the significance of the clash and the craftsmanship of the narrator! The symmetries are at their most effective in vv.15-16 indeed, and culminate in the collective dying, two by two, twelve times. Does such terrible perfection actually exist? I can hardly imagine that killing could be so precise and so synchronous in reality. In my opinion what is happening in verse 16 is that the writer is no longer engaging in his customary realism, but transcends its limits and his equally concise and hermetic shaping of the perfect symmetry is a kind of surrealism. Looking at v.16b once again I find *wᵉḥarbō bᵉṣad reʿehū*. This must be the crucial line because it mentions the weapon and at this moment each champion receives the fatal thrust. But there is no verb in this verse of all things, and the description does not mention the fatal thrust which the loser receives but the fatal thrust which the winner deals! Syntactically speaking 16b is "only" a circumstantial clause next to 16a, but the chronological location[39] of 16b resists its playing a secondary role or merely providing additional information and suchlike. Both qua action and semantics 16b attempts to explode its syntactic bonds.

In spite of this 16b, the only line without a verb, cannot succeed in denying its nature. It is and remains a nominal clause without action.[40] The narrator has created a still life of death the moment all action dies, the instant the

[39] I would like to repeat it once more: *this is the moment* at which each champion receives the fatal thrust!

[40] In the colometric text I have accorded 15bc their own lines it is true, but their syntactic content is a double apposition with the *mspr* of 15a. What we can in fact say is that the symmetrical duplicate and the enumerative character (or the nominal mass) of 15bc slow down the tempo of narration – the narration time required by ten words, if we count the word 'Ishbosheth' as one word – which makes them anticipate the silence which falls in v.16 well.

twelve-fold duality is obliterated in the uniformity of death. Taken literally the 16ab pair (with a report in 16a and a description in 16b) just mentions the action of twenty-four young men, and 16c reports the sequel. But the expression of reciprocity makes the reader work and leads him to discover the *passio*, the suffering, of twenty-four young men.

We are now approaching the deepest reason as to why the narrator has arranged the prelude in the form of an ABCDD'C'B'A' series. In the still life various forms of duality come together and end in a uniformity as cold and perfect as death. The symmetries which put us on to the trail of the concentric structure signify a repeated mirroring or the unity of a duality. The two armies engage in the same marching out and setting up camp around the pool, after their arrival at the same time in Gibeon. Their leaders reach complete agreement in a brief talk and send two lines of champions, which are exactly the same, into the arena. Their combat and its result have a surrealistic kind of symmetry. But the background to all these mirrorings and symmetries is the nation's being torn apart, the rivalry of two small kingdoms. The different forms of unity and equality are expressions of duality. The text of vv.12-16 is itself the linguistic arena in which unity and duality pursue one another.

The narrator gives the reader breathing space. In 16d the text leaves the narrative flow and the momentariness of reported action. The omniscient narrator exhibits his grasp of, and his distance from, the subject matter through the introduction of an aetiological note on "that place" in Gibeon. The line is an aside supplying information. Such an enduring name immortalises the scene of the twenty-four champions' combat: "The Field of the Stone Knives". This name is a metonym for the combat or the bloodshed, which makes grief and bitterness manageable by avoiding their mention. But it is the metonym itself which has something lugubrious and horrifying about it. The specification added by a short relative clause ("which is in Gibeon") refers back to the beginning, particularly to the place-name in 13b. Perhaps we might be permitted to construe a contrast between the pool with its living water and the rocky[41] quality of the blood-soaked field turned cemetery. Once again, therefore, the shift from encounter to bloody clash is indicated by one or two details from the pair B-B'.

[41] I am now playing with the etymology of the stone knives, the *ṣurīm*, which are as hard as a rock, *ṣūr*, in contrast with the flowing movement of the water. This game can be justified lexicographically, see Josh.5:2sq., Ps.89:44 (two places in which *ṣur* occurs next to *ḥrb* and the words explain one another!) and Job 22:24, and HAL s.v. I *ṣur*, II *ṣur*, and I *ṣor* (pp.953ab, 954a and 985b). Though the conjectural reading which HAL puts forward for our verse (p.953b below: read *ḥęlqat haṣṣiddīm*) I reject as redundant.

The game of symmetry cannot go on for ever. The result of the combat is the sum of 12 + 12 = 0. It is a draw experienced by both camps as a deadlock and not as a fresh reason to negotiate. The general battle which now breaks out drastically terminates the series of equilibria which started in v.12 only to end in the indecisiveness of v.16c. The narrator expressly remains present in v.17 through a survey provided by various means. Even though the scale of the combat is suddenly a hundred times greater, he sums it up with "[the war =] the battle" and does not take the trouble to report it at length. The battle "was very hard on that day": no action but a nominal predicate through which the narrator supplies a judgement or at any rate a considered opinion and betrays his temporal distance. We hold our breaths for a moment. Is the impasse of an identical number of victims to continue in the escalation of the battle? No, now the balance tips radically. Further along it becomes apparent, from vv.30-31, that for every soldier of Joab's army killed in battle twenty soldiers of Abner perish; a formidable imbalance which tempts us to speculate as to the great difference in military experience and motivation between the Saulide camp and that of David.

The closing line does not use an active form to say that Joab wins but a passive one to say that Abner gets defeated. This is a better counter-balance for 12a and 14a where Abner's image was one of a strong man who takes the initiative.[42] It is noticeable that the parallelism of names in 12-13a, on two levels of leadership (general + king) gets a curious counterpart in v.17b. Two plus two names do not occur, neither do two names of identical rank, but the general of the losing side is combined with the king of the winning side. In this way Abner's power is dealt a heavy blow, but Joab stays in the background because the narrator does not wish to characterise him at this stage. The terminus is formed by the man who remains the most important even though he is absent from the scene. In addition the name of Ishbosheth is ousted by that of Israel, and this too, in comparison with 12 and 15b, is asymmetrical.

B. An incident on the battlefield, 2:18-23

Asahel's pursuit of Abner is an incident which took place whilst the battle was in progress, it is not the report of the battle. We can tell this, among other things, from the place which this B scene takes in reported time. Because the result of the day of war between the two armies has already been given in v.17, the last hour of Asahel is a flashback. The position of the camera

[42] Notice that the *wqtl*-form of 12 and 17b, in both cases, does not agree with the plural subject; something which underlines the dominance of Abner. See also note 4 above.

underlines this. If we call the view of the armies in vv.12-13 and 17 a long range shot, and the report of the two rows of champions a medium one, then it becomes clear that what we get in vv.18-23 is a close-up. In 19-23d we exclusively monitor two people and only in 23ef and 24 does our field of vision become broader to be able to include the regrouping of the armies around sunset. Because the text, via v.24, flows into the cease fire, we can include even 25-28 in the flashback. The precise point where the text catches up with narrated time already covered in 17b is the body count of vv.30-31. This taking stock lies within the focalisation of the collective character of the victors; the count taken by Joab's men covers the result of v.17b and is the complement of the focalisation of the narrator so clear in this line. The narrator has, therefore, not only postponed releasing the figures, but has left the process of arriving at them in the hands of a character as well. The return journey of the Benjaminite army and that of David's men in vv.29 and 32 respectively take place the same night and are the first thing that happens after the result of v.17b.

The facts of space and time work together in the service of the structure. It begins with the presence of three brothers on the battlefield in v.18, "and there were ... " Via a series of wyqtl forms we reach the double inversion of 24bc where the sun goes down on those engaged in combat. Complementary facts of space are to be found in 24c and 25c. Subsequently a new series of actions conveys us towards its terminus which is neatly marked by an indication of the time, the sunset of v.32d.

Verse 18a allows itself to be felt as an opening line by introducing a trio of actors. Two of them, Joab and Abishai, we know already because they undertook part of the action in I 26 and a short time ago in II 2:12sqq. The third, their brother Asahel, is brought out to the front for his own special introduction with a nominal clause. He is characterised by a quality, that of speed. And immediately the narrator sends him out in pursuit, by v.19a, so that he can give free rein to his excellence. This speed is given an extra accent thanks to the embellishment of a simile which makes us think of Jonathan for a minute; Asahel is as swift "as one of the gazelles in the field". But whilst the poet of 1:19 called his bosom friend a gazelle straightaway – but at the same time enigmatically – via a metaphor, Asahel is only one of a group. Is this a first subversive tarnishing of his specialty on the part of the narrator, who considers it his business to let us witness how Asahel perishes through underestimating his opponent and overestimating his own ability? Maybe Asahel is not so unique as he thought he was. My reading of v.21 will support this view presently. I would like to make one more connection with what has gone before. The poet referred to Saul and Jonathan as "swifter than eagles, stronger than lions". Asahel meets the demands of the first comparative and overtakes the general of the enemy, but will he turn out to be stronger than the lion Abner?

Whatever the case might be, this introduction of characters is rather unusual because three brothers are mentioned by name at the same time and are classified under their mother. The phrase "sons of Zeruiah" opens a series, the most difficult moments of which we have already seen[43]; David has his hands full with this tough family which quickly returns again as a group in 3:39. But why do all three brothers have to receive a mention if Asahel is the hero at the moment? The answer is that they are needed in the subtraction sum of which v.18a, 19a and 24a are the components:

18a Joab, Abishai and Asahel, the three sons of Zeruiah, were present there.

19a Asahel pursued Abner.

24a Joab and Abishai pursued Abner.

The subtraction sum goes like this, "three minus one is two", at Asahel's expense. The lines which form the boundaries of 19a and 24a define the route which Asahel's exit must follow. In between those two the word "pursue" does not occur any more, and this brings us to a paradox. The pursuit of Abner by Asahel further consists exclusively of Abner's attempt to get Asahel to end the pursuit for his own good, and its subsequent failure. And that is why the scene consists mainly of dialogue, vv.20-22, after which v.23 is reserved for the fatal thrust of the spear in Asahel's belly.

The last thing the absence of *rdf* wants to say is that Asahel is no longer engaged in pursuit. From v.19a on he is running, and Abner is running in front of him. There are various verbs of movement in the text and mostly they are connected with *the* key word for Asahel, "after, behind". It appears three times in close succession in 19ab+20a, and is finely illustrated[44] and replaced by "did not turn to go to the right or to the left" in 19b and 21b. The contrast between the two applications of *nṭh* is striking and includes the

[43] The series continues (via 3:39) with the pair 16:10 and 19:23, as part of the corresponding scenes which I have discussed in *King David*; and the singular "son of Zeruiah" accompanies one of the brothers in I 26:6, II 2:13,18, 8:16, 14:1, 16:9, 18:2, 19:22, 21:17, 23:18,37, and I Ki. 1:7, 2:5,22; cf finally II Sam.17:25.

[44] Notice that these first three occurrences of *'aḥărē* exhibit creative variations at once: in 19a we go straight forward with Asahel "after Abner", in 19b Asahel refuses to turn aside from going "after Abner", which is the opposite of his alternatives "to the right and to the left"; and in 20a the preposition occurs chiastically after Abner, who is so good as to turn round – in order to give the matter a twist.

difference between Abner and Asahel right away. In 19b the turning to go is equipped with the negative, the other key word for Asahel, and leads to "after Abner" which is combined with the separative *min*, Asahel does *not* want to turn aside (...) from behind Abner. The other combination, "turning to the right or to the left", does not come from the narrator but proceeds out of Abner's own mouth in 21b. Abner confronts Asahel with other options and urges him to choose them.[45] In this piece of positive advice, which is developed in 21cd, there is no room for the negative at all. The "turn aside" + separative "from ... after" (*bis*) is cleverly replaced by *(lā)sūr mē'aḥărē* (also *bis*: 21e//22b), "to turn aside from behind".

What is driving Asahel can be deduced from the parallelism which exists between 19a and 19b. The positive line on Asahel's pursuit must be duplicated and varied, finds the narrator at this point, by a negative line, 19b, about neither turning aside to go to the right nor to the left. This duplication is in itself already a hint at the young man's obsession. Apart from this 19a has a programmatic function; it consists of the title action of which the rest is a development. In v.20 Abner turns around towards Asahel and the narrator gives form to this by turning around the word order of the name Abner and the preposition. The first act of turning around warns us to prick up our ears attentively, the second ought to have been a warning to Asahel to be sure and take in what the general had to say to him, or merely to notice that this war-horse was not even ill-disposed towards him. The dialogue now begins in v.20, but it is not, in fact, a dialogue at all. With the exception of one short word – the revealing "I" – Asahel says nothing, and the narrator allows Abner to give three talks; a short one by way of introduction, v.20b, and two serious speeches in vv.21 and 22, that spell out the difference between life and death for the good listener (the reader who is up to the demands of this passage for example) and for the bad listener who is addressed, Asahel. The last thing which Abner's loquacity signifies is that he is a prattler. He shows himself to be an older and wiser man who does his utmost best to somehow get what he has to say into the obstinate young man's thick head, and is not ready by a long chalk to give up trying to talk him round after the first refusal. Only after Asahel's second refusal does Abner take action, and only then in a situation of *force majeure*, he has to finally defend himself.

[45] Even the marginal difference between *and* and *or* is revealing as regards the difference between Asahel and Abner. The pursuer Asahel refuses to turn to the right *and* to the left, 19b, and wants to go in one direction only, in order to be able to overcome Abner. The pursued general is insistent with Asahel: "turn aside, to the right *or* to the left and seize one of the soldiers" (this is, in fact, underlined twice by *l^ekā* with an eye to Asahel's own interest, i.e. saving his life). Abner offers more than just one option as an alternative.

Abner's two speeches are introduced by a moment of question-and-answer contact in v.20, to which an injustice would be done if we were to view it purely as an identification procedure. For one thing, when Abner asks "Are you Asahel?", his question already implies recognition and this is evidence that the speaker is a keen-eyed observer. What he does is to verify what he already thought he had seen. But he wants to be sure first; if it had turned out to be someone other than Asahel he could have used his spear at once. He asks Asahel himself for verification – a form of establishing the person to person kind of contact usually noticeable by its absence in a battlefield situation. This to-ing and fro-ing also aims at establishing contact. In the well-known model of Roman Jakobson this is called phatic communion.[46]

I can detect a certain amount of concern for Asahel in the general's attitude, and I think there are two sides to this. On the one hand the experienced fighter finds it somewhat embarrassing to have to make a mess of the swift hunter with his spear; when it comes down to it Asahel is no match for him. On the other hand Abner can see problems looming up over the horizon in connection with the fact that this young man is the brother of his adversary, Joab. He is about to put this into words. In any case the general's turning around means that he is no crazed fighter who kills and cuts down everything right and left indiscriminately. There is something he wants to discuss, and even though he finds himself in a difficult situation he puts himself out, making room for both parties to collect their wits.

Asahel answers yes, but his one-word answer means more than it says. What he gives voice to, in the Hebrew fashion, is "I" and this is characteristic of him. Although in a different way from the money-loving messenger of II 1 who was characterised by a threefold *'ānōkī*, and yet also similar,[47] Asahel

[46] His communication model with six components and six corresponding functions is to be found in his well-known paper of 1960 "Linguistics and Poetics", and is at present also to be found in the posthumous volume of Roman Jakobson, "Language in Literature" (Harvard University Press, 1987). I would like to call to mind two examples of phatic communion. Also in a context of war, the introduction to the negotiations which the wise woman wishes to conduct with Joab occurs in II 20:17; it is a double dialogue with two phatic moments coming from her. One might also remember the decisive moments that God calls "Abraham!" and he obediently replies *hinnenī*.

[47] Thinking through a possible parallel between the Amalekite and Asahel we quickly see interesting *tertia comparationis*. Being present on the field of battle is crucial to both, speed is of importance to each of them (we saw that the messenger had to personally attend to the scoop's arrival in Ziklag), both are out for the first prize (in the case of the messenger this is the regalia, proof of Saul's death which will yield him a messenger's rich reward) and both pay for their miscalculation and their being a prey to their own desires, with their deaths. Notice that within each *tertium comparationis* the variations between the messenger and Asahel are great.

too is possessed by a single idea, or more accurately by the ambitious desire to secure the first prize on the battlefield, viz., Abner's head. This kind of fixation, blind to all else, is an extreme example of the regimen of the ego. As far as the narrator is concerned he need say no more. Which is exactly what happens: in response to Abner's suggestions Asahel's negative answers, which perhaps took the form of the spoken word, are not given as the spoken word, as character's text, but as narrator's text: in v.21e and 23a the narrator replaces Asahel and it is he who reports that Asahel continually refuses.[48]

Abner's two speeches are related to one another as foreground to background, since the general begins with the here and now in v.21, and when that does not help he supplies background considerations in v.22 to motivate his counsel to turn aside. The first speech consists of three imperatives in the qal, through which Abner directly addresses Asahel. They are all followed by a *lᵉkā*, which – to put it in Latin – seems to be a *dativus ethicus* insofar as it can be done without in every line, but upon reflection has the force of a *dativus commodi* at least. Abner uses it to express his concern about the young man and draws his attention to a better understanding of his own interests. The suffix is heard twice more in 21b as a possessive pronoun. The general does not restrict himself to the advice of turning aside, the negative option of his remaining out of range, but takes the trouble to point out the positive options to the left and right of Asahel's route: surely you can seize some soldier or other and take his armour? Death is an ellipse here, Abner waives mentioning that the elimination of such an adversary is prerequisite to Asahel's cleaning him out. I notice, in addition, that the expression "turn aside to the right or the left" originates with the narrator in v.19b but is now uttered by the general. Is there a lot of difference between the two points of view?

"Some soldier or other" is what I just wrote. In Hebrew this is literally "one of the boys", and I note that a similar description was used for Asahel himself in the introduction. I see a connection between 18b and 21c which says: it is better for Asahel to keep away from the enemy top man because the latter is really unique. Let him, like one of the gazelles in the wilds, set his sights on "one of the soldiers" in the field; that is much more suitable for him.

Asahel does not let the three imperatives make an impression on him,

[48] Notice how the five words of 21e are abbreviated and varied in 23a. Asahel's name still occurs in 21e in order to commit him to his responsibility for himself, and the adversary is still present in the text in "from after him". And then there is the subtle difference between Asahel's "not wanting to" and his "refusing" [sc. to leave off his pursuit], which implies increasing obstinacy.

"and he was not willing to turn aside". The general reacts to this characteristic negation as follows: "And Abner said again to Asahel", etc. He decides to venture another attempt and the narrator underlines this by the pleonastic addition of the little word *'ōd* to the *wayyōsef* of v.22a. Now Abner becomes deadly serious. His first line, 22b, repeats the first line of the previous speech, 21b, with variation, and keeps on implying the advice of putting away another combatant of course, even though this is no longer included in the text. A subtlety which the narrator contributes to the exchange is that he puts into Abner's mouth exactly the same verb for "turn aside" which occurred in the narrator's text in 21e and which was subject there to Asahel's stubborn 'no'.

The main point is to be found in 22cd. Forgotten are the imperatives, what we are now listening to is language of a much more emotional kind in the form of rhetorical questions, and we see Abner himself appear in these two lines as a party, in the first person.[49] Self-interest is the criterion once again, but now that of Abner is central. For Abner the elimination of Asahel is so senseless; it would entail his subsequently facing a much more formidable adversary, says the word order of 22c + 22d. Behind the question of 22c the terrible prospect of 22d looms up, a confrontation with his equal Joab. Thinking about this opens up an abyss of dreadful uncertainty for the speaker and sounds ominous to the reader, in view of the outcome in ch.3. From the standpoint of composition v.22d is, of course, an anticipation of the Joab-Abner encounter of ch.3 and is, therefore, a line with integrating force.

After various forms of horizontal movement which attractively vary with one another, 22c suddenly introduces a vertical movement with a fatal force which is able to call a radical halt to all that horizontal effort. The verb there, "strike, kill", is so central that it too undergoes the shift from the one voice to the other: the narrator is to take it over from the speaker to indicate the death of Asahel, in 23b. It is sometimes a useful practice to give rhetorical questions the answer which they suggest. The answer to 22c ought to go something like this: no reason at all [to smite you], to 22d: there is no way [I could look your brother in the eye after killing you]. This reveals to us just how much Abner lands in a dilemma. I would now like to itemise how Abner is to suffer unacceptable harm should Asahel fail to take his advice and a clash results. The first option is: Abner does not defend himself and Asahel quickly

[49] The first morpheme for the first person even occurs already at the end of the first, imperative line, v.22b; a good preparation for the 'I' as subject in 22cd. The "from behind me" is the variant of, and much more direct than, the "your right or your left side" in v.21b.

kills him; this is unacceptable to the general, therefore. The second option is basically just as unpleasant: Abner defends himself and sees himself forced to eliminate Asahel; in which case Joab will probably revenge his brother and Abner will still die. But perhaps in this case there is a slight chance of escape. Which might sound something like this: Abner takes action in self-defence on the battlefield; if he manages to keep out of Joab's way until the end of the war, will Joab then abandon implementing a vendetta since he has no right to engage in it? For the reason that the civil right to carry out a vendetta is not applicable to someone who, in a situation of civil war, has killed a fellow-countryman? This is a subtle legal question concerning which he is not in a position to consult his lawyer at that moment, and he is even in less of a position to try to assess Joab's opinion.[50]

Just as was the case in the preceding speech, Abner also succeeds here in getting "you" once into each of his three lines. His concern has continued and is stressed by an internal rhyme of three words ending on *-ā*. Whilst the speech of v.21 shrank gradually, the final speech in v.22 actually grows:
21bcd = 7 + 4 + 4 words (with 15 + 12 + 9 syllables respectively)
22bcd = 3 + 3 + 6 words (with 7 + 7 + 12 syllables respectively).

The value of what Abner has said becomes even clearer if we consider the way in which he did not express himself: no snorting, no insulting or deprecating language, in spite of the fact that such language is available and that he knows he can add its force. He does not exhibit any kind of superior attitude. When he has to put the fatal blow into words he uses an *irrealis* and is in no way pleased with the idea, so that we cannot call v.22c a threat – it is at most a warning, and a telling one at that. Abner really makes a genuine attempt to deter the other person from his disastrous resolution. His realism is mature, humane and urgent. Should Asahel remain adamant, Abner is quite clearly and entirely vindicated as to what must take place.

Asahel is imperturbable in his obsession. The brevity of v.23a reflects an attitude which is abrupt and disdainful towards the other man, and "he refused" is even more blunt than "he was not willing" (21e) of which it is a variant. That Asahel does not utter a word in the text suggests that he does not consider the other worthy of being addressed. Whereupon the fatal action takes place, for the report of which the narrator takes over the decisive verb *nkh* (hiph.) from Abner himself. This line, 23b, and the next give two new and virtuoso twists to the word *'aḥărē* which characterised Asahel's fixation and turn the word against him physically and violently: he gets the butt of Abner's spear in the belly and with such an force that the weapon

[50] Naturally I will return to this question when the time comes, viz. in 3:27-30.

comes out of his back. With an unexpected reverse impact – Abner probably did not turn around while he was doing it, the surprise is complete – Asahel is given a lesson in 'do it or else!' The way in which he is killed is particularly ignominious to his pride as a hunter. Verse 23bcd are the visual and dramatic climax of the text, and the denouement of the simple plot.

The deadly weapon of the previous tableau was the sword, here it is the spear. We recognise this pair which formed a *leitmotiv* in the section "The Crossing Fates" and which was especially typical of Saul. It now works much mischief once again, bringing misery and grief. Of the two times twelve champions it was very briefly stated: they fell together. Verse 23d uses more words for Asahel: "he fell there and died *taḥtāw*." Up to now we read of the speed and all the horizontal movement of this young man who seems to personify precipitation. This showed how much his ego and his desire for the first prize stretched his centre of gravity to a point outside himself, so that he miscalculated his own potential on the one hand and underestimated the fighting experience of his opponent on the other and was no longer capable of taking his cautioning to heart. Now his great speed is brought to a halt and the spear indicates the exact spot where his point of gravity belongs: in his – I say it now in the Japanese way and in agreement with certain eastern martial arts – *hara*; the Hebrew equivalent, *haḥomeš*, is no chance occurrence in the text. Now Asahel is able to coincide with himself and the return of his point of gravity is indicated with a significant *taḥtāw*. This preposition – which together with *nfl* makes the vertical visible as well – not only means "on the spot" (i.e. where he was), but flows into the temporal signifying "immediately" just as the English or the Dutch "ter plekke" do.[51]

We have reached the end of the contact between Asahel and Abner and we are now able to get an idea of their interaction. There is a rhythm of regular alternation to be found in what they do:

Asahel pursues (*lō nāṭā* ...)	v.19
Abner turns around and speaks	vv.20-21d
Asahel keeps up his pursuit (*lō 'ābā* ...)	v.21e
Abner speaks and cautions with urgency	v.22
Asahel [keeps on pursuing because he] refuses *lāsūr*	v.23a
Abner (2x concretely *'aḥărē*)	v.23b-d

[51] In ch.3 we are given another example of this, also with *taḥat*; see, in addition, Appendix I on this occurrence, 3:12a.

The cessation of Asahel's movement broadens out into something else as the passing warriors see the bloodbath and stop. The entire line on Asahel's death is included in v.23a in a relative clause.[52] Not only is the narrative tempo slowed down at a suitable moment, but the way in which the death of Asahel comes into view for the passers-by is also presented in a like manner. In the meantime the camera has zoomed back to a medium shot in order to be able to take in the new character. There is an entire group of lookers-on who forget the pursuit and stand motionless around the victim, fallen and bleeding. His still life has points of contact with the previous bloody tableau.[53]

Every one who passed by stood shocked and silent. Every passer-by? There are two immediate exceptions to this; the two remaining sons of Zeruiah carry on what their brother Asahel had begun. The parallelism and complementary nature of 24a regarding 19a is so great that Joab and Abishai actually chase Abner themselves, and the probable reason for this is that they have either seen or been informed of their brother's death. There is but little time for an attempt at immediate revenge and they are the only ones who fail to pause at the body of Asahel. The two lines 23f and 24a almost clash because of this difference.

The passage consisting of vv.18-24a forms a seamless whole with the next passage, 25-32, via 24bc. The connection between the two chiefly lies in the movement of the pursuers (24a) being continued in v.24c, and that of those pursued being set forth in 25a. But there is also actually a connection between the two passages as regards the coming to a halt which is movement's opposite:

- 23f *wayya'amdū*: shocked passers-by around the body of Asahel pausing to grasp what has happened.
- 25c *wayya'amdū*: square of regrouping Benjaminites
- 28b *wayya'amdū*: Joab's army finally stop their pursuit.

This is a good example of variation in repetition. The same verb is used three times, but its meaning is different each time. Around sunset we hear three times how movement founders and this series takes us on to the last topic: the cease fire and separation of the troops. Abner and his men stand on the one hill at the edge of the desert, Joab and his men on the other (24c//25c). The third part of this war story begins in the same way the first did, therefore: two

[52] Moreover the "on the spot" of 23d which bore reference to Asahel is replaced by the verb "they stood still" 23f, which refers to the passers-by.

[53] Not only is *npl* to be found here and there but *māqōm* is too. The one place is immortalised by the name given to it, the other achieves longevity through the attention of so many and through the picture in v.23ef.

armies face one another in symmetrical positions. One day of warfare is over, however.

C. Cease Fire and Separation of Troops, vv.25-32

Buttressed by the fresh motivation of revenging their brother, Joab and Abishai want to carry on with the pursuit of Abner, but they are quickly frustrated in their attempt by the fall of darkness. The lines of 24bc together form a hinge which is striking through its double inversion of the same verb "come". Their syntactical scheme X + qtl indicates synchronicity.[54] The going down of the sun not only completes passage B and a day of warfare, but together with the sunrise of 32d forms a framework for the approaching night, so that passage C is clearly delineated.

The moment the sun goes down the pursuers reach the outskirts of the inhabited world; behind them, hours away, lies the city where it all began, Gibeon, and before them, in the east, lies the desert which Abner must cross whilst fleeing with his army. Three complements of place having a striking rhythm and a gimel in an alliterative key position supply us with this information in 24c.[55] The camera swings round and our attention is drawn towards the other side: v.25. Abner is finally surrounded by his own men, which produces a new variant of meaning for the nth occurrence of "behind" Abner. Heavy losses have been suffered, but the hopelessly scattered ranks now succeed to find each other in time to organise a good defensive formation. The regrouping leads to a square on the top of a hill; an identical rhyme underlines this process.[56]

At the moment the camera is unable to register anything more because it is completely dark, the narrator switches to aural means and has Abner call

[54] Comparable passages which employ this type of syntax in order to indicate synchronicity are I 9:5ab,11,14,27, II 13:30ab, 15:32 and 37, and Gen.15:12.

[55] Each complement consists of three words; the gimel, a consonant which is not frequent in Hebrew, is evenly distributed and displays the pair *gibʿat ... gibʿōn* around *gīᵃḥ*. Although we have no identification of the names Giach and Amma aṭ our disposal, the third complement (combined with the time factor of the pursuit) nevertheless gives an impression of where we now find ourselves on the map. The exact geographical location is, by the way, less important than the literary datum hill//hill of 24c//25c.

[56] The rhyme, or the epiphora, is made up of the numeral "one" upon which 25b and c end. I translate it at the end of 25c pregnant with "on top of *one and the same* hill". See also Appendix I. This "unity" is semantically connected with, since it is the realisation of, the "gather themselves together" of 25a.

from the one hill to the other.[57] In vv.26-27 a round of dialogue ensues. Once again Joab and Abner get the opportunity to speak, Abner is the initiator once more and obtains Joab's assent. This makes the dialogue into the counterpart of the one in v.14. The first talk between the generals initiated the use of weapons by proclaiming a tournament which had the effect of a lighted fuse in a keg of gunpowder; a second talk must now put an end to this.

The speeches of Abner and Joab both have three lines each which increase from short to long[58] and are geared to one another in a testy contrast: three rhetorical questions from a despairing Abner are answered by a highly irritated Joab, with the gravity and rhetorical emphasis of an oath formula in three lines:

Abner, v.26

b Must the sword devour forever?
c Don't you know how bitterly it's going to end?
d How long will you delay ordering your troops to stop the pursuit of their kinsmen?

Joab, v.27

b As God lives,
c *kī* if you hadn't spoken up,
d *kī* the troops would already have given up the pursuit of their kinsmen this morning!

Abner is not only the initiator, he is now the actual party making a request: he wants a cease fire from Joab. He speaks of the far distant, indeed apparently inaccessible, future because his questions speak of bloodshed which will never end until it ends bitterly. Each line has a temporal phrase to this end. The *lānęṣaḥ* of 26b and the *'ad-mātay* of 26d denote his – to a certain extent acted out, embroidered for the sake of drama – despair evoked by this receding horizon, and surround the word *'aḥărōnā* of 26c, which is the culmination and the temporal outcome of the *'aḥărē* series.[59] Continuing violence will only produce bitterness, says the middle part. The expressive "forever" takes the lead in 26b and "the sword" receives a verb which

[57] I recall how David shouted from the one hill to the other in I 26, after Saul had been symbolically emasculated. The text of 26:13 also has *wy'md* and *r'š* as here in 2:25c. One might also call that situation a situation of civil war and the contact there also took place in the dark. The butt of David's derision there was Saul's general ... Abner himself!

[58] Quantities: the speeches have just as many lines as Abner's two speeches in vv.21 and 22. The numbers of words here are as follows: 3 + 6 + 8 in v.26, 2 + 3 + 8 in v.27 (notice the epiphoric close of 26d//27d). The syllable count is: 8 + 15 + 18 in v.26, and 6 + 6 + 18 in v.27. Verse 26d and 27d are of the same length *re* syllables and words.

[59] The words *lānęṣaḥ* and *'ad mā(tay)* are to be found in the poetry, as a word pair: Ps.79:5 and 89:47, and compare 9:19.

functions in an absolute way; the total absence of an object signifies just how great its toll of casualties is on all sides.[60] The metaphor "eat", which has perhaps become small change itself, is somewhat activated by a word for taste, 'bitter', which is applicable to the survivors.

The questions 26b and c are launched by anaphora. Their temporal phrases are to be found at the beginning and end, after which those of 26d occur initially. In 26c the speaker is being manipulative: "don't you know" suggests great stupidity, which can still be redeemed as long as the addressee hurries up and gives Abner what he wants. In 26d Abner does not choose a simple sentence like "how long is your army going to pursue mine?" but the turn of phrase "until when will you not say (= will you not give the order) to the soldiery to turn back?" Abner suggests by this an attitude of refusal on the part of Joab which is reminiscent of that of Asahel who would not hear of turning aside. In addition he speaks of "turning back from following after their brothers" (= kinship). This too is manipulative. After a day of fighting at his own suggestion he now resorts to the emotional argument of kinship, placing all the responsibility for the war against brothers on the shoulders of the other side. The use of the word brother in the presence of Joab at this time is dangerous. In any case the latter is going to hark back to it at the close of his own speech.

These questions have a polarising effect on Joab. He reacts with their antipole and gives assurances with a double anaphoral *kī* forming an oath. The compound sentence 27cd is in impeccable Hebrew which is usually incorrectly rendered, so that Joab's point is lost.[61] What the text actually says is: "If you had not spoken, then truly the soldiery would have left this morning already, each one from following his brother!"[62] What Joab means is

[60] The metaphor "eat" occurs also in II 11:25d, where the tyrant uses another turn of phrase to convey the weapon's devouring left and right (*kī kāzō wᵉkāzę̄ tōkal hęḥāręb*), and there is the creative comparison in 18:18b.

[61] A serious methodological mistake is made here: because it is initially difficult to determine the lines along which the oath develops, what happens is that the most likely interpretation is chosen first and the Hebrew text is then adapted to it by changing *lūlē* to *lū* (its opposite!) or by taking *habboqęr* to mean "the following morning", which is untenable. The correct approach is the other way around: recognise that the Hebrew is utterly sound, translate the sentence without associations and mind-bending ideas, then and only then look for a plausible interpretation. See further Appendix I.

[62] We must, therefore, with Goslinga p.54sq., return to the classics of our 17th century, the KJ, and the SV, which kept to the MT. Keil is also correct. The fate of 27cd in the JPS is curious: initial conditional clause correct, main clause incorrect, and the other way around in the note offering an alternative!!

not very difficult to grasp for those who have learned to trust structure. The exchange of the generals is the counterpart of their first dialogue in v.14. The content of Joab's answer in v.27 confirms that structural connection; what he means is this: if you had not proposed a tournament this morning, then as far as I am concerned there would have been no need for a fight.

A stylistic element which confirms this reading is the fact that Joab ends with the expression for reciprocity – revolving around the now prevailing *'aḥărē*! – which was so characteristic for the prelude and its fan of symmetries. What he implies is that the reciprocity had already become a destructive and suffocating proximity as early as this. And he now behaves as if he has found it altogether unnecessary from the very beginning. Joab wants to outdo his competitor in this far reaching motion in the only area where he can still command strength, i.e. that of rhetoric. Joab's irritation is apparent from the sober quality of his "this morning", with which he answers and cuts short the puffed up temporality of Abner's questions.[63] Just like that of Abner his most central line has a perfect in the second person and a negative, his last four words are almost identical.[64] But Joab does not really answer the question as to a bitter end; he postpones it for an occasion which suits him better, one in which Abner is to experience it physically, 3:27.

The general who had advised Asahel *lāsūr me'aḥărē* has now had to entreat the latter's brother *lāšūb me'aḥărē*. Even though he wants to revenge his brother, Joab complies with this. He can wait and postpone his aim without relinquishing it. He thinks it is better to stop now, for military reasons I imagine. Just one more look at his use of language: formally speaking he does not reply to the question; he does not simply or forthrightly say: all right, I will cut short the battle. Taken literally his reaction is not an answer, only an *irrealis* which does not concern itself with the terms of the request.[65] This betrays resentment in this case. On the grounds of ch.3 we "know" what Joab is thinking: 'my time will come, I'll get you yet man!' At this stage we are able to compare the two sons of Zeruiah. Asahel cannot let go, but Joab

[63] In this interpretation of the text one can defend the view that the *habboqęr* (in which the article is still deictic, as in *hayyōm* = today) of 27d does double duty and is potentially operative as modifier of *dbrt*. In any case the three far-reaching temporal phrases of Abner are now paired with two practical ones of Joab: there is an *'āz* next to *mhbqr*.

[64] As a consequence of this one might ask oneself whether 26bcd and 27bcd which are indeed parallel, also exhibit the pattern ABC-ABC. I do not find the connection B-B for 26c-27c compelling. As far as 26b and 27b are concerned one might construe a death-life antithesis, and link *nṣḥ* with God, thanks to the fact that God has already been called the *Nṣḥ Yśr'l* in I 15.

[65] A good parallel of this complying and not complying with an urgent request is the oath with which David, in response to Abigail's plea, forswears the use of violence in I Sam.25; this is also put in the *irrealis*, uses a double *kī* and the conditional particle *lūlē*, see NAPS II p.515sqq.

can. Asahel does not let go even though it is necessary and it is pointed out to him. Joab does let go, for as long as it is necessary at any rate. Joab is able to keep track of the situation and weigh up the pros and cons, which means that he can afford a long postponement, but he does maintain the pursuit of Abner – even though it takes the form of a quest which remains invisible for a long time. After a while maybe Abner thought that he might get let off without injury, perhaps the Abner of ch.3 thought that as a brand new ally of David he could avoid a confrontation. The narrator is silent on this, leaving it to the imagination of the reader.

The part about the separation of the troops, which completes the unit in vv.28-32, is so constructed that the withdrawal of the two armies is split up and grouped around the death toll. Verse 28 consists of twice times two lines for Joab's side, and verse 29 contains twice times two lines for that of Abner. First we hear the ram's horn sounding through the darkness in verse 28a. Joab manages to stop at last; the final *wayya'amdū* occurs in 28b and halts the entire army, not (as in 23e) an arbitrary group. The halt is the long-awaited continuation of 24c in which the men of Judah had reached their position. Only after negotiations has a point been reached at which Joab finally wants to withdraw his men from the battle. This moment is underlined by the pair 28cd. This is a striking example of *parallelismus membrorum* which draws the series of lines on the pursuit to a close with its anaphoral "no more" and its "*rdf* after".

The coming to a halt of the one makes the movement of the other possible. Abner withdraws through the desert in the night and crosses the Jordan. The repetition of *hlk* helps us to arrange the lines in pairs and to accord an acceptable meaning to *bitrōn*. It cannot be other than an apposition in 29c, and because 29a links a specific time to the departure, what 29c can offer is a specific location. In this way the spatial co-ordinate, which indicates the end of the journey in the second pair of lines, complements the temporal co-ordinate of the first pair. The repetition of *kol* introduces balance in the pairs. Placed after the crossing of the Jordan, "the entire cleft" presumably means a wadi which runs parallel to the Jabbok and is now followed by the defeated army; as a datum in the narrative cluster it complements "the whole night" of 29a. The march, twice as wearisome after an exhausting day of war, takes the soldiers to Mahanaim. The narrator could have said that "each returned to his tent" as in II 20, where Joab also halted a campaign after negotiations by the blowing of the ram's horn. But he chooses to offer the pseudo-dual, close by "the cleft". The situation has indeed become one of two camps and a chasm between them. This too can be inferred from the rhyme *bitrōn-ḥębrōn*. Joab's pulling out with his army in 32cd is clearly both parallel and opposite to that of the Benjaminites.[66] Both sides receive a whole night for the return march from the narrator but only the winning side is greeted by a sunrise: "Day broke upon them in Hebron". The root in this name has a meaning which is opposite to the *btr* of the cleft.[67] So what is suggested to us via a play on words is that the winners come back to the city of fellowship and friendship whilst the losers cannot shake off the aspect of duality: this cleft takes them to "Mahanaim".[68] The partiality behind the allocation of the sunrise ensures that the rising and setting of the sun obtain a symbolic meaning. The rising stands for the increasing power of David's kingdom and for the career of Joab; the setting[69] brings rescue on a physical level, it is true, for Abner and his army, but on a symbolic level it signifies the decline of the Saulidic kingdom and that of the military career of Abner. (The political career and the physical existence of Abner end at the same time in 3:22sqq. and this too is to be marked by the going down of the sun.)

Verse 30ab seems redundant after v.24 and 28. But 30a establishes with exactitude the fact that Joab personally "returned from following after Abner". The narrator has taken over a character's verb once again; *šūb* belonged to the tired almost pleading Abner of 26d! His name in 30a is the ironic replacement of "their brothers" at the end of 26d. At the same time 30a formally concludes the movement of 24a. Verse 30b refers back too, the verb "to gather" is the complement of Abner's regrouping in 25a.

The death count is striking. For every Judean killed there are twenty bodies of the other side. There is a subtle difference in focalisation between 30c and 31a, even though these lines are adjacent to one another. The Judean figures lie within the scope and interest of Joab and his men, thanks to the

[66] Again there is the verb *hlk*, again "all that night", again the name of the general followed by "and his men" and again a place-name as finishing point.

[67] I acknowledge my indebtedness to Dr. A.S. Rodrigues Pereira (The Hague) who drew my attention to this play on words. See Appendix I for the root *btr*.

[68] Alonso Schökel also translates the name by *Los Castros* in NBE. Buber fails to translate the name at this point, but inserts *Doppellager* after the Hebrew name at the beginning of Gen.32.

[69] In the "historical" reality which lies behind the narrated world the sun rises and sets over everyone; but not in the narrated world, here the narrator has the unprecedented option of mentioning things or omitting them. The sunset of v.24 holds good for both armies it is true, but it has a link with 32 which grants the sunrise to Judah only. This piece of information is retroactive in its effect, to the detriment of Abner. He and his army no longer emerge from the darkness, Joab and his army do. Notice that the question of the light encroaches upon 29c in *habbitrōn*. The view that this is a spatial term supports – and is supported by – the one-sided apportioning of daybreak. This need not be used as an argument against the likelihood computed by Arnold, that Abner did not arrive in Mahanaim until around noon. The point is that the narrator does not allow this to become apparent in the text and that he has his reasons for doing so.

verb *wypqdw* which the narrator gives them, whilst the total Saulide losses are established by the omniscient narrator and are related to us in an informative tone. Once again he pushes the puppet king out of the text by regarding the Benjaminites as "the men of Abner", in approximately the same way as in v.17b, the line where this body count naturally belongs. Verse 31a thus ends with the general's personal name, a location which makes us shudder, because the preceding line ended with his victim Asahel. The choice of words of v.31 is remarkable for even more reasons. Instead of one passive line in the spirit of 17b there are two and they distinguish the killing in the transitive and active "strike" of David's soldiers (31) from the intransitive "die" of the Benjaminites. But these two verbs also marked the death of the young man in v.23. By being the only one mentioned by his own name in 30c, his importance matches that of the nineteen, and the remarkable complementary nature of 31 a and b wants to compensate his death.

Asahel is once more brought to the fore via his name and receives two more lines of attention (from the narrator and) from the Judaeans. He is now buried where he belongs, "in the grave of his father" which is to be found in the city where David comes from. This place is about half way along the route which Joab must travel. But we learn of this only after the caring moment when they "lifted up Asahel" etc. Verse 32cd ensures that we reconstruct the burial as a detainment during the return journey. But it is not the darkness of the grave which has the last word but the light which hails the survivors as victors.

Afterword: survey of a period, 3:1 and 2-5

The narrator surveys the period in its entirety in the three lines of 3:1 and informs us of its general trend, coming out in favour of David and being unfavourably disposed to the Saulides. These lines are nominal clauses which report duration in various ways. Insofar as they describe a process they are of general import, in contrast to the particular nature of what took place in 2:12-32. But they still belong here since they continue the game of symmetry and asymmetry. Let us begin with the instances of symmetry: the two sides are designated by "the house of x/y" in v.1a and because of this seem to keep each other neatly in balance for a moment.[70] Together with the designations in 2:15b,25a,31a they give the impression that the struggle was more of a family feud than a national battle between two armies. Then there is the equilibrium formed by 1b and 1c. They tidily run their parallel course and

[70] The terms *bēt* + proper noun of 3:1 partly explain why the narrator was using the rare term *bēt Yᵉhūdā* (*cf* note 30 above) in 2:1-11.

form a synonymous *parallelismus membrorum* for the time being, up until their final words "strong/weak" where their paths diverge into an antithetic parallelism. The balance finally tips in favour of David. Now it becomes noticeable that he, contrary to the closure of 1a, is mentioned in person in v.1b, whilst the other side remains "the house of Saul". The singular of v.1b is given the connotation of power, the plural in v.1c that of lack of leadership or unity. The brief but telling symmetry of the omission of Ishbosheth's name and its replacement by that of his dead father belongs here. In this way the contrast is made specific: David, the person who is chosen by God, faces a group which represents the old regime which is indeed the family of a reprobate. Subsequently verses 2-5 immediately go to work for David by laying the foundations of a dynasty. The duration which 3:1 stands for with its nominal predicate (*wattᵉhī hammilḥāmā 'ărukkā*) is, as we have already seen, the successor to and the complement of the pronounced intensity (*wattᵉhī hammilḥāmā qāšā*) in 2:17a, and the balance tips from the particular (2:17b) to the general (3:1bc). This is the envelope into which the battle of 2:18-32 is put.

The genealogical material of 3:2-5 consists of the enumeration of six children who receive one line each with a mention of a different mother each time. Surrounding this is the envelope of vv.2a and 5b, which are almost identical and connect the births with David's Hebron period. This brings us to the fact of the list's location being well-timed. The potency of David need not be noted immediately but must on no account appear too late. Its location here precludes the idea that David starts to bloom only after Abner has handed over the rest of Israel. This topic plus that of his coronation as king over all Israel can be completed without interruption after this list. In regard to what has gone before the location of 3:2-5 illustrates David's growth, which was established in the area of military politics in v.1.

The series of births is achronistic for the most part; it breaks through the chronological reporting of events which forms the context. The order of the births is laid down exactly by the ordinal numbers, but they are not anchored in the time scale in any way. They are the product of the narrator's overview and at the same time provide the reader with a certain degree of distance from what is actually happening alongside them (in the rest of the Act). We are given a brief interval from the violence of war. As a six-fold unit without relation to individual moments in time, its parts create the impression of covering the entire Hebron period.[71] Minor variations reduce the monotony

[71] In theory the children could have all been born in the same week; in practice this is extremely hard to believe and I assume they were spaced out to a certain extent.

of the very even list.[72] In comparison with the great variety of other genealogical material in the Hebrew Bible the equal attention each son receives is exceptional. The list is to receive a counterpart for the Jerusalem period in the following Act: in 5:13-16, after David has been invested in his new capital.

The first two sons have mothers which have already been presented to us a few times during the absence of Michal as the two wives of David. This forms a link with 2:2 and his entry into Hebron. The first-born, Amnon, later receives a leading role in ch.13 (in Act XII). Absalom and Adonijah, sons 3 and 4, we know as important pretenders to the throne in chs.15-20 and I Ki. 1-2 (i.e. Acts XIII and XIV). The mention of Absalom's mother's own royal descent agrees with ch.13 in which Absalom takes refuge with "Talmai, the king of Geshur". We are to hear nothing more of the sons which occur in the second, fifth and sixth positions.[73]

[72] The numbers one and two are given the special terms *bᵉkōr* and *mišnę̄*, with we which we hav already become acquainted in I 8:2 (sons of Samuel) and I 17:13 (the elder brothers of David): their mother is introduced with the preposition *lᵉ* and brings those characteristics with her which have already been discussed in connection with 2:2. Three sons follow being called "son of c/d/e"; the mother of Absalom gets extra details. The mother who is mentioned last has a characteristic of her own too, see note below.

[73] The rather redundant epithet "wife of David" of the sixth mother is perhaps a sign that the list is now complete and helps to contribute to the list's framework.

Chapter III

The generals keep their kings occupied

The stories which take up ch.3 occur in vv.6-21 and vv.22-39. They form two halves of a diptych which I could call, for short, 'Abner *agens*, Abner *patiens*' in view of the action. In the first half Abner goes over to the other side and takes "all Israel" with him; this transfer of power is the pivot of the Act as a whole. Abner is busy becoming king-maker for the second time. But later, in the second half, he is suddenly reduced to an actantial object: Joab murders him (vv.22-30), David mourns for him (vv.31-39).

§ 1. *The great about-turn: Abner goes over to the other side*, II Sam.3:6-21

In this story the two camps are unequally represented. All we see of the Judaean side is David whose solid position in Hebron begins to exert a magnetic force. On the other side there are, however, six characters: the reigning son of Saul, a daughter and a concubine, the citizen to whom Michal is married, and especially the strong man and the nation, which is sometimes referred to as "all Israel" and at others consists of "the elders of Israel" and Benjamin.[1]

This unit is a good example of subject matter and theme not being the same. Whilst the theme only gradually emerges from the details of a patient stylistic and structural analysis, the subject matter can be determined right away. Successively we see three changes take place which together make up the plot. They differ greatly according to nature and level, but flow from each other

[1] For the sake of completeness I would like to mention here the remaining characters who are collective: different groups of messengers who journey to and fro, and Abner's twenty man diplomatic mission to Hebron.

and order most of the relations between the characters. The first change is that Abner has taken a concubine of Saul, now Ishbosheth's by law, to bed with him. This leads to an enormous row between the king and the general, vv.7-11. Pouring out his wrath upon the trembling Ishbosheth, Abner announces change no.2, a veritable land-slide. He announces he is going to hand over Israel to David, and before Ishbosheth's very eyes opens relevant diplomatic relations with Hebron. David is prepared to conclude an agreement with Abner, but on condition that his wife is returned to him, and so it happens; Abner separates Michal, the princess who married David for love but who was taken away from him by Saul, from her present husband Paltiel and takes her to Hebron, vv.12-16. In vv.17-19 Abner is busy preparing the ground for the political landslide; in 20-21 he is the guest of honour in Hebron and makes a deal with David.

The three changes turn almost everything upside down. The conjunctions Rizpah-Ishbosheth, Abner-Ishbosheth, Michal-Paltiel and Israel-Ishbosheth, are broken up into the same number of disjunctions. The disjunctions David-Michal, David-Abner, and David-Israel are lifted and changed into conjunctions. In the first instance the number of changes suggests the following arrangement of the text:

– vv.6-11 Abner and Ishbosheth, breach
– vv.12-16 diplomatic relations: Michal is handed over
– vv.17-21 Abner working for David

This temporary division of the text into three is supported, and at the same time clearly expressed, in a figure which depicts the most relationships and shifts.[2] It forms a triangle which should be read anti-clockwise in order to follow the changes:

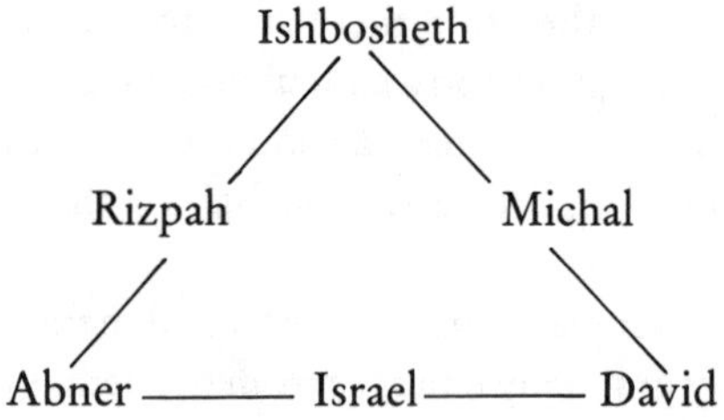

The rulers are situated at the points of the triangle, in between them along the sides are the objects of exchange (two ladies and a nation), and they undergo shift. Ishbosheth is the great loser. Yesterday the concubine Rizpah was

[2] My thanks are due to Dr. A.S. Rodrigues Pereira, who put me on to the idea of the triangle.

taken away from him, today he has to relinquish a sister, and tomorrow he is to lose his country and his position. Abner is the great initiator. He is the one who effects the first and the third shift, whilst he directs the one in the middle, the handing over of Michal demanded by David. David is the great receiver here. He gets back the princess and this symbolizes at once how he gets the whole nation under his protection. This story gives a unique form to the intimate combinations of sex, power and politics.

Space is effectively used for the game of conjunctions and disjunctions. Abner's political trajectory – which largely coincides with the narrative trajectory consisting of the links of the plot – becomes visible in terms of geography and contact. At the beginning we see the general in the Saulide residence, whilst at the end he is a guest of David in Hebron as an ally. These paragraphs face each other as breach and covenant, but both contain direct contact between general and king. They are separated from each other by a series of messages in the centre, which have a mediating function as indirect contacts. In vv.12-16 there is a coming and going of emissaries, who travel backwards and forwards between the strong man in Mahanaim and the strong man in Judah. They are go-betweens, instruments through which the great about-turn decided upon by Abner is to be prepared. There are two rounds of questions and answers. In its entirety the first is made up of direct speech in the form of a talk between Abner and David in vv.12-13; an offer of the general's meets with David's approval, but on one condition. This condition is the subject of the second exchange, vv.14-16. This contact is not by chance only half speech. David has his demand officially presented to the one who is formally his colleague (Ishbosheth!), who no longer has any choice. His consent means that the demand is put into operation, and has taken on the form of a narrator's report. In this way Michal is extradited. For Abner turning her over is a detail at the end of the decisive campaign through which he wins the political support of the tribes in vv.17-19 and which culminates in his visit to Hebron. Here is the survey of the sequential analysis which is based on space and contact:

sequence 1	*over there*	Abner versus Ishbosheth, breach	vv.7-11
sequence 2	*over there-here*	Abner to David: offer of covenant	v.12
	here-over there	David to Abner: right, bring Michal	v.13
sequence 3	*here-over there*	David to Ishbosheth: hand over Michal	v.14
	over there-here	Ishbosheth to David: sends Michal	vv.15-16
sequence 4	*over there-here*	Abner canvasses the tribes pro David	vv.17-19
sequence 5	*here*	Abner as David's guest, pact	vv.20-21

We now have at our disposal a division into three parts and one into five. Is the structure of the story able to cover one of them? I await the result of the stylistic analysis which now follows, before noting the structure.

The conflict between Abner and Ishbosheth, vv.6-11

Verse 6 is an introduction which does not report action but provides information on the situation. The temporal half, v.6a, reaches back over the list of 3:2-5 to pick up the thread again, resuming with seven out of its nine words the comparison v.1 made between "the house of Saul and the house of David". We now go down one level, from the conflict between states to the situation in the Saulide camp, and once again come across the word *ḥzq*, now in favour of Abner; but to whose detriment is not mentioned here. I hear two shades of meaning in the hithpa'el participle used. The first says that "Abner was the dominant personality in the house of Saul" which is late news, since we had already deduced this from the inversions and hiph'il forms. The other shade of meaning, obtained by an imitative rendering of the hithpa'el form, is interesting and attractive for a narrator to exploit: "Abner behaved as if he were the boss in Saul's house." Being the boss in the sense of having taken the initiative and being daring is all right so far, but if you behave like the boss whilst you are formally under the king then something is bound to go wrong.

This interpretation is immediately confirmed by the fact that Abner has not been able to keep away from the harem of his king and has been to bed with the concubine Rizpah. It is true this piece of information has been prepared by the narrator in v.7a, but the sexual offence is not something we hear about from the narrator's own mouth; he informs us indirectly through the offended Ishbosheth who lets fly at the general in 7c. Reaching for the harem means reaching for power and at least giving rise to the impression of being a pretender to the throne. It is going to cost someone like Adonijah his head, is what we read in the ambiguous affair of Abishag in I Ki.1-2.[3] Does reaching for Rizpah really mean, in Abner's case, that the general aspires to the throne? I would like to postpone my answer to this question for another five verses.

After the temporal construction of v.6a the first main clause itself exhibits an inversion, which causes the general to be brought to the fore again. This is the first hint of his receiving the leading role in the chapter. That he is not

[3] And someone like Absalom marked the total breach with his father the moment he marched into Jerusalem by enacting, on the roof of the palace, the sexual possession of the remaining part of David's harem; see *ad loc.* in NAPS I, Ch. VIII.

even compared to Ishbosheth in v.6b, something which we could have expected as the symmetrical continuation of vv.1 and 6a, is an ellipse of this king which does not bode him much good as far as his power is concerned. And then there are v.7a and c in addition. The one line does not couple the concubine to Ishbosheth, but to his father Saul. The other line is its echo; in his blaming the general, couched in the well-known form of a rhetorical question with "why?", Ishbosheth virtuously refers to Rizpah as "the concubine of my father", as if he is much too afraid to say "my concubine", as if he is not capable of taking on the responsibility of putting himself forward as lord of Rizpah therefore, or of having his own authority prevail. It looks as if Saul is the norm, both for the general who is the strong man "in the house of Saul" and for the present king. What is the state of affairs regarding Ishbosheth's sense of self-respect?

The end of v.7 ("the concubine of my father") points back to the beginning, "Saul had a concubine", so that the verse is framed by a chiasmus. This is a reason for my paying even more attention to it. In regard to the whole v.7 has the task of stating the problem which gets the plot going. The clash with Ishbosheth is the beginning of a long route which will finally take Abner to Hebron, to someone who ... is stronger than he is. Verse 7 is rather special. It ties in very closely with the introduction by commencing with the name on which v.6b ended, that of Saul. As regards time this introduction is a flashback. A young lady is dug up from the past whose name, position in society, and origins are given. All this is stated in two short nominal clauses, which we recognise as the technique for introducing a character to us. Therefore the line 7a creates the expectation that this women will be appearing in the developments which are about to take place. The narrator has put us on the wrong track in this, since she gets no role here.[4] Or does she? There are two remarkable facts. In the appendix II 20-24 Rizpah gets a leading role, not more than half a story long, but unforgettable.[5] And here in II 3 the change implemented with her is replaced and succeeded by another change which concerns an actual daughter of Saul. It too reaches back into the past and has even more to do with sex and power. Apart from that, what a contrast v.7 forms with the list of vv.2-5! Six women in their full dignity are mentioned in it, not concubines, but mothers who, as such, build up the strength of "the house of David", the powerful ruler of Judah; but here in v.7 there is

[4] They are only mentioned briefly by two other characters, in their speeches, by Ishbosheth in 7c and by Abner in 8f (notice how vaguely she is referred to, by the generic term *hā'iššā*).

[5] One of the good reasons for including the appendix, II Sam.21-24, in the section "Throne and City".

one concubine from the paternal past, as the object of a vulgar quarrel which splits those at the top in "the house of Saul."

The narrator has, in v.7, refused to determine on his own authority whether Abner is having an affair with Rizpah or, at any rate, has committed an indiscretion with the concubine. He has coupled Rizpah with Saul and not with Saul's son, and Ishbosheth follows his example in this as the speaker in v.7c. These two reductions of the might, indeed the person, of Ishbosheth are carried almost beyond endurance (might I say: *ad absurdum?*) in 7b, probably through the form in which the text has been handed down to us, since the name of the king is missing in the Masoretic text whilst qua information he cannot be done without as subject.[6] The surprising thing is, nevertheless, that the dropping of "Ishbosheth" resists being pure chance or a slip in the process of being handed down, insofar as it significantly links up with an Ishbosheth strategy which we can pinpoint a number of times and which consists of his person being forced out of the text. This treatment of Ishbosheth is iconic for his weakness. His being omitted or being suppressed, to which he contributes himself, iconically stands for the message that he is a nobody.

Abner becomes angry. On initial evaluation, whatever else may be said of him, he has a very strong personality, and in all probability is highly authoritarian and not used to being contradicted. But this is not the only thing which is the matter: he became "very angry" states the text. His rage is more severe than the business in question itself; the decision with its enormous consequences, announced in his long speech, is out of all proportion to the Rizpah affair. I deduce from this that the reproach he gets from Ishbosheth is merely the last straw which broke the camel's back. Abner explodes in the presence of Ishbosheth, after months of pent-up frustration. He has had enough of his own project. He probably set out with a genuine desire to continue Saulide rule, but right from the beginning he must have experienced serious disappointments with Ishbosheth, who turned out to be only a puppet, and with unfavourable military developments. Being on the receiving end of a moral reprimand from the puppet he now holds in contempt, is what really puts the cat among the pigeons.

[6] After noting 6ab + 7a the reader comes to a *wayyōmęr* without mention of a subject in 7b, and this means that what is actually required grammatically is the linking of that singular masculine form to the nearest masculine singular which preceded it in the text. But (after *šem* has been skipped) this is Saul, who has been dead for a long time. *Wayyōmęr* can only be understood with Ishbosheth as the subject (the correctness of which link can be proved only at the end of v.8a), but the absence of the name is still unbearable.

His speech occurs in vv.8c-10b and is the largest speech in the entire Act.[7] It is precision-made right down to the quantities involved. Around the 9a axis, which is the exordium of an oath, four clauses occur twice and consist of the same number of words; 25 in 8c-f and 25 in 9b-10b. The middle of the middle is the moment when Abner, by swearing an oath, takes maximum responsibility for what he spells out and commits himself irrevocably to it; he utters his own name there in a curse on himself.[8] The division of the speech into two parts is analogous to many two-part speeches without an oath which hinge on the word *w^e'attā*. There, and here, the part which precedes the hinge consists of a statement of information, or a description of the situation which the speaker wishes to bring up, whilst the second half is volitional and propels the action forward with a wish, a command or a recommendation, and suchlike.

In the first half Abner looks to the present. After a scornful opening (8c) a double *hayyōm* frames its three clauses with arguments about yesterday and today. The construction of the second half is much tauter and works with pairs right the way through. After the double *kō* clause of the oath a pair of clauses of the "as ... so" scheme follow, underlined by an anaphoral *kī*, and culminating in two infinitive clauses which begin anaphorally with a hiph'il form and are a pair qua content as well. The first half is about proven loyalty, the second about the opposite intention, defection.

Abner starts to imprecate. This is language of a very emotional kind which reveals that he has been deeply affected. The rhetorical question makes it seem as though Ishbosheth looks down on him as if he were a "dog's head from Judah". This seems to be an inversion and projection of Abner's own unuttered disdain for the other. Yet at the same time one might seriously ask just how scared Abner is of being treated with contempt himself, that he needs to engage in projection in this way. His sense of self-respect is shaky as soon as the mirror of morality is held up to him. We can be sure of this, the criticism of Ishbosheth in itself is totally justified.

Subsequently Abner points out his loyalty towards the dynasty. Here and in 10a he talks about "the house of Saul". This is the third time the phrase is used in duplicate, after the comparison of 3:1 and the introduction of v.6a. In all cases the name of Ishbosheth is avoided, so that we can count six dents in his prestige. Abner does not speak of his loyalty to the person of this king, the

[7] Abner's speech has 57 words; David's message to Jabesh had 51.

[8] The word *l^e'abner* is the centremost of (the seven words of) v.9a, in between the twins of *kō* + verb forms; and it is the twenty-ninth word out of a total of fifty-seven which make up the entire speech.

narrator does not wish to compare him with David. Both force Ishbosheth so far back into his family, that he is not even allowed to appear in their choice of words as a representative of the Saulides!

Just as Ishbosheth spoke of "the concubine of my father", so Abner adds the apposition "your father" to the name Saul. The norm of his loyalty was in no way the son but the father. He continues to go on about his loyalty with two appositions, "his kinsmen and his friends" whose suffixes serve only to strengthen the normative position of Saul. At last the first direct "you" occurs in 8e – but as an object of a verb, which both qua meaning and stem form (a hiph'il once again) is characteristic of Abner. "I have not delivered you into the hand of David", says the general, but such words have a paradoxical effect at this moment and send shivers down Ishbosheth's spine: Abner shows he is capable of such a deed and can take it into consideration; several lines later it has actually come to this and the political fate of Ishbosheth is sealed with a pair of verb forms which turn the force of the hiph'il against him, v.10ab. Abner contrasts his own loyalty up to the present moment (*hayyōm* up front in 8d) with what his boss is doing to him at the same moment (*hayyōm* as the end of 8f): in the eyes of the general Ishbosheth is inspecting or spying (*pqd*) which he can only see as a sickening nagging "about a *faux pas* with that woman". Between the lines Abner suggests that Ishbosheth is not worthy of his dedication, which provides the former with moral justification for breaking free from his narrow-minded lord.

The speech turns on the axis of v.9a exchanging loyalty for a total breach. In the middle of these opening words of an oath Abner places his own name at the place where he could have made do with a simple *lī*.[9] In its present form it sounds more solemn. Abner is now busy hammering out the dents in his own ego and brings a few more surprising devices to bear. The first is that his own oath bases itself on another oath, an oath of ... God himself. Abner legitimises his defection with a word of God Himself – with a dexterity we can observe time and time again in the history of the relations between church and state. Abner now poses as someone who decisively and willingly implements what God decides for the nation. The critical reader or journalist interrupting the general to ask why he had not allowed himself to be guided by such obedience from the very start would now, of course, be thrown into jail by the strong man for insulting behaviour against authority ....

[9] The double clause of self-cursing occurs nine times in Sam.-Ki., and once in Ruth. In five cases the form "me" follows God's "doing" (that is to say punishing), in three cases personal names follow (next to Abner still David in I 25:22, and Jonathan in I 20:13); in I 14:44 nil (but permlt. Mss, according to the BHS apparatus, have "me") and in I 3:17 in actual fact "you".

With suspect precision Abner "remembers" that God had sworn an oath to David, v.9b. And without the slightest trace of an attack of modesty, Abner is about to put this oath into operation, 9c. There is, however, a slight friction in 9bc to be detected by the careful listener, in the form of a change from the third to the first person. In the guise of a troublesome journalist we could throw another critical spanner in the works here, by posing, in the space between 9b and c, the question: is God unable to effectuate for Himself what He has sworn? Why do you suddenly consider yourself to be the indispensable doer of God's will? There is a striking parallel between Abner's quoting the oath according to the scheme "as ... so" and the word of power which is the centre and turning point of the lengthy unit on the Davidic succession, I Ki.1.[10] In the first place the parallel is based on the fact that the one oath is piled on top of the other, in the sense that a mortal is swearing something which, according to him, is merely a repetition of what God has sworn. Both passages are about David's throne and undivided power; in the one case it is put into David's hands, and in the other it passes out of his hands into those of his son. They frame David's career, therefore. But in both cases the antecedent cannot be found: the oath of God which Abner calls upon here, as does David at the end of his life, is not given! Judged severely it is the product of human imagination which is at work, in order to simulate ad hoc piety and to give one's own resolution the glitter (or the appearance) of divine legitimacy. A more charitable reading of the situation is, however, possible. It is a (textual) fact that David has been chosen by God as leader of this nation.[11] This is what is being recognised at this moment, and is being put into words by Abner in his own way, even though there is no formal oath of God which he can fall back on. To put it yet another way: Abner has finally reached the point of relinquishing his resistance to the career of David which enjoys God's blessing; a fact he had personally noticed several times when he was general under Saul.

The rhetorical device which Abner pulls out of the hat in v.9bc is his having God's sworn resolution and his own activity flow into one another. This is ingeniously ratified by God's oath being taken up into his and in reverse, his

[10] It concerns I Ki. 1:29-30, the decisive pronouncement of the aged David; see NAPS I *ad loc.* in ch.XIII, and p.367 which gives the concentric scheme of the composition.

[11] Election applies much less forcefully to Solomon; what is clear, however, at the end of II 12 (vv.24-25) is that the narrator already anticipates his succeeding David by paying special attention to Solomon's birth and his second name, which is etymologically related to that of his father (via the proximity of **ydd* and **dwd*).

own being taken up into God's. We can see the first by looking at the text: the oath of God (*šb'*) is quoted *in* the oath of Abner (which has the character of an *'ālā*, a curse on oneself: see v.9a), a previous utterance has been included in a current speech act of the general. But in terms of election and history Abner's oath has been taken up into that of God, Abner does nothing but repeat what has already been decided a long time ago by the one who is really in power, and reports for the duty of obediently taking part in the historical process already set in motion much earlier by God's word. Perhaps the scheme "as ... so" with its content "He has sworn// I put it into operation" has, in both texts, been inspired by, and wants to be an allusion to or a variant of, the formula of obedience which we regularly come across in the Torah: "and Noah (Moses, etc.) did as God had commanded", *ka'ᵃšęr* + verb *ṣwh* ... *ken* + verb *'śh*.

Up to now all this is in the inverted commas which a cynical reception wants to put round the speech of someone who, in reality, is engaged in the perpetration of power politics and is almost sadistically harassing his puppet with pious words. But the curious thing about this is that the thesis "Abner as willing instrument of God" seen on the level of a higher plan is still seriously legitimised in the scheme of the writer. In the long run Abner is a character who is allowed to come forward several times as an actor in a design which stretches far back, and of which David's career is merely a part. On a spiritual level the weakness of Ishbosheth and the strength of Abner provide the leverage used by God to realise David's ascendancy.

The fusion of God's original oath and its execution by Abner is given a sequel and a new face in v.10. Its language is first of all the vehicle of what, according to the speaker, God once swore. It revolves around two complementary matters: the removal of the monarchy from the Saulides and the placing of David on the throne of all Israel, 10a//10b. But how ambiguous is the content of the oath! This is something the reader notices in answering the question as to who is the actual subject of the action. Is it Abner himself – in which case the subject of 9c is unchanged, and remains in operation – or is it God, who was the subject in 9b, and who is recognised by the speaker as the real policy maker? Are they both subject, inseparable? The rhetoric of the general is so subtle that it is no longer possible for the listener to detect where divine initiative ends and human activity begins. With this brilliantly ambiguous move Abner has completed his strategy of religious self-legitimisation. The present lack of observable difference between God and Abner, does, however, turn against the speaker by lending itself to a psychological criticism of him: is it not true to say that Abner, through his fusing of divine authority and personal power politics, betrays his desire to be above both sides, exalted beyond all criticism? Is there any appreciable difference between this and self-glorification?

The words of v.10 themselves are worthy of our attention. Abner places a pair of infinitives up front, and once again we recognise the powerful transitiveness of hiph'il forms. They face the negative hiph'il of 8e ("I have not delivered you"). The two verbs which he has chosen are, moreover, an apt sequel to the two hiph'il narrative forms with which it all began. They reflect 2:8b and 9a where the general "transferred" the Saulide candidate to the Transjordan residence and "made him king" over Israel. The same actions now operate in reverse, the powerful arm now takes away what he once had given. Abner is able to make and break a king according to his own discretion – is this not suspiciously very much akin to divine power? After the infinitives the parallelism of lines 10a//b continues on the matters of monarchy and throne, which are, as abstract and concrete variables, complementary. They engage in opposite relationships with "the house of Saul" and David respectively, since they are taken away and offered; first the disjunction, then the conjunction. After the name of Saul emptiness follows in 10a, since there is nothing left to rule over. After the name of David a pack of four names follows in 10b being arranged in two merismuses. At last "Israel and Judah" stand side by side as brothers, and their being complementary is again intensified by a pair of city names. The well-known "from Dan to Beersheba", here forming a parallel with the names of the two countries, occurs as a merismus for the entire, indeed for the unified, state.[12]

The orator has undergone a *volte-face*. In his first line the name of Judah does duty as a term of abuse, in the last line it is used in a positive way and occurs harmoniously next to the name of his own territory. In the adjacent lines (8d and 10a) we see the contrast of Abner's loyalty to the Saulides (the preposition is *'im*) versus his departure (with preposition *min*).

Abner's speech has curious points of contact with the second longest speech of the Act, David's message to the Jabeshites. Both look across the

[12] Is the pair "from Dan to Beersheba" actually so well-known? I expect so. But when I check it, the famous pair appears to be used in seven places only. The distribution is interesting: five times in Samuel, and twice just across the boundary. The merismus occurs in I 3:20 (general acknowledgement of Samuel), twice in 24, vv.2 and 15, further in the bombastic rhetoric with which Hushai hoodwinks Absalom (17:11); and, finally, in Judg.20:1 (the nation shocked after an atrocity in Gibeah) and I Ki.5:5 (the ideal peace of the Solomonic empire). These two can be seen as a polarity around Sam., and the places in chs.3 and 24 can also be construed as a polarity. Another special circumstance is that "from Dan to Beersheba", in II 24:2-3 and in I Ki.5, accompanies the pair "Israel and Judah".

border in their first sentence, Abner to include Judah in a term of abuse, David in his wish that the city in the northern kingdom might be blessed. David praises the loyalty (*ḥęsęd*) of others towards their lord Saul, Abner praises his own loyalty towards the house of Saul.[13] Both set their own action alongside God's and end their speeches with the monarchy of David. After the closing line of David, by which he informs Jabesh of his anointing, we can understand the speaker's imagining this city as a Transjordanian bridgehead for his future expansion. And now, two stories later, the moment has arrived for presenting the northern kingdom to David on a silver platter. The decision behind this occurs in a speech which is given in another city in the Transjordan and saws the legs off the Saulide throne. "Be strong" were David's words of encouragement. Subsequently he showed himself stronger than the Benjaminite undertaking, and now the strong man of the northern kingdom (Abner *mitḥazzeq*) is to deploy his strength for the unification of Israel and Judah under this selfsame David. The duality which "Mahanaim" stood for has now almost run its course.

Hebrew narration is sparing in information on the thoughts and feelings of its characters. However, we see the notation of the interlocutors around the speeches here. The speechless fear of Ishbosheth corresponds to Abner's loquacious fury; he is quite petrified by this harangue. So much so that he fails to utter one single word more not only for the rest of this story but for the duration too. And as we notice that his name in v.11 has once again disappeared in an ellipse, we are forced to conclude that there is almost nothing left of this king. The only thing which remains for him to do is to presently obey a command (v.14). He extradites princess Michal (v.15) and that is the only action of his we know of. As a kind of figure of impotence and as a symbol for the *patiens* he is to make a final appearance, and how: asleep in bed where two murderers creep up on him and kill him for gain, ch.4.

The centre: emissaries come and go, vv.12-16

This speech is shocking: it is a public, infuriated and brazen desertion. And that is not all. Abner means what he says and takes measures to put his words into action immediately. I say "immediately": the text expresses this with the word *taḥtāw*, which means "on the spot" and shades into the temporal.[14]

[13] David made a parallel in 2:6a//b of God's activity (the volitional form *ya'aś*), and his own activity (imperf., full form, 1st. person). Abner also uses the volitional form for God's activity in v.9a (*ya'aśę̄*), and his own activity (imperfect, full form, 1st person, an assurance) coincides with and/or realises what God has sworn (sc. to do, v.9b).

[14] See Appendix I for an extensive justification of this interpretation of *tḥtw*.

"On the spot", that is to say whilst still face to face with his lord, Abner sends emissaries to David. Abner is, therefore, prepared to defy and make laughable the authority of Ishbosheth whilst the ruler himself is standing by. This is once again a demonstration of power, nobody can stop this man.

An interim phase of diplomatic negotiations now ensues in which the formal structure of two centres of power is dismantled and the centre of gravity moves in stages, at a brusque tempo however, to Hebron. The text contains a double exchange of messages. This might be expressed, woodenly, in a fourfold "he sent messengers" and four speeches. Our narrator avoids monotony, however, and introduces variation in the order of appearance, in the persons and in his means of inserting them, whether or not they speak:

- 12a "Abner immediately sent messengers to David" covenant offer
- 13a "and he [= David] said" agreement, on one condition
- 14a "David sent messengers to Ishbosheth" give me my wife Michal
- 15a "Ishbosheth sent [men] and took her away."

There is, therefore, no simple alternation Abner + David, Abner + David. Surprisingly the general is replaced once by his king. And if we include these two under the label S for their dynasty and refer to David by his own initial we can see the chiasmus in the communication: S + D and D + S. The two speeches of David are central, flanked by a word and a deed from Mahanaim. Thinking this centre through I notice that no change of subject takes place from v.13 to v.14 and I conclude that David's communiqués to the general and the king of the northern kingdom are synchronous, instead of belonging to different rounds of communication. I would like to correct the picture regarding the interchange, it is threefold rather than fourfold:

a) Abner takes the initiative and he sends a proposal to David only (one verse).

b) David replies with demands for both the general and the king (two verses);

c) both Abner and Ishbosheth contribute towards the execution of David's demand and extradite Michal (two verses).

In this way David's word of power occurs in duplicate in the middle of the literary unit and princess Michal is placed at the centre in duplicate as the issue of David's repeated demand. Is this broken marriage going to be healed?

Abner gets three lines from the narrator. He begins very briefly, almost in riddles with the question, v.12b, "who has a country?" Because Abner, v.12d, is fully aware of his own key position and this line assumes that Israel is in his hands, I take 12b to be a rhetorical question with the (understood) answer: 'I do' (in other words, 'Abner').[15] The question is, however, very short and entirely lacking in further modification; we do not know what it aims at. Which makes it ambiguous enough to allow for the opposite answer: you. In this case Abner admits that he is not able to check the flow of history. The narrator immediately adds an explanatory "that is to say" (the *lēmor* of 12b) and places it between Abner's words, so that the general explains himself with: "Just make your covenant with me!" The underlining of the imperative with the cohortative *-ā* rhymes with a strikingly added *-kā*. In my view this makes the request sound urgent, and I venture the reading that Abner is already giving David a lot of room to move and more or less says to him: you can now dictate the terms of the agreement. The sequel appears to confirm this. Abner has stretched out his hand and David grasps it whilst responding with the demand for Michal's extradition. This demand is not a minor one, since it concerns a loaded question between the previous king and his son-in-law, a serious conflict which by the mere fact of being mentioned at this point receives much political symbolism.

The last sentence of Abner's opening move is once again typical of him. He begins nominally with three words which might have proceeded, word for word, out of the mouth of God himself: "See, my hand is with you." Then Abner crystallises what his hand consists of, or is worth, with a characteristic hiph'il form *hāšeb*, which is the semantic successor and equal of the *ha'ᵃbīr* of 10a and denotes the same about-turn: I shall make "all Israel go over to you". In the meantime a series of objects has arisen through the connection 10a-10b-12d, and they are all to become David's possession: monarchy – throne – nation.

The narrator does not waste any time and effort by announcing, in v.13a, the sending of messengers. He makes do with a bare *wayyōmẹr* in order to introduce David's answer. The standing alone of "he said" suggests an immediate and resolute response from David. His speech shows that he knows exactly what he wants, now that an offer has been made. David begins by agreeing. His first clause is one syllable long and creates the impression that his affirmation involves no small print. Also the operation or validity of the predicative *ṭōb* is not restricted by surrounding modifications, and in this respect David's first clause accords with Abner's first clause. His second

[15] The passage is disputed, but I do not detect any flaws apart from the quick repetition of *l'mr* and the absence of the article in front of *'rṣ*; very poor reasons for taking recourse to an emendation. Nevertheless my explanation is put forward with hesitation. With "I, Abner" I follow Goslinga and CT, who take recourse to emendation as little as I do, and Hertzberg, who makes, however, a *tḥty 'rṣ* link and emendation (not a proper understanding of the meaning permitted by the preposition).

clause takes over all the words of Abner's second clause and betrays the fact that David has understood the projecting *-kā* well. The general had requested: "make *your* covenant with me" and the shifters "your" + "me" of that short clause have the persons of David + Abner as referents. David has picked up the two suffixes meticulously. He maintains the order of appearance of the persons involved, places a quasi-redundant "I" in front, through which the clause consists of four not three words and he turns the shifters around: "Right! *I* shall make a covenant with *you*. Only ... ". He has created a chiastic follow-up through these morphemes. This you-me // I-you reflection suggests to Abner prompt and willing compliance with his request. After which the telltale little word *'ak* follows to shatter the listener's illusions.

David's speech in v.13 is the axis of the whole unit, and the speech hinges on that one little syllable for "only ... ". The beginning of 13d still seems innocent for one moment: there is just one more detail to which I would like to draw your attention. The turn of phrase reminds us of how Bathsheba asked "just one small petition" of king Solomon, in Adonijah's favour.[16] But the parallel is, at the same time, a warning, since that "little question" had fatal consequences. The little word "only" is really a hinge, for the speaker turns around it to something quite different. The new issue is brought to the fore as object in 13d, whilst the pronouns of 13c, increasing by one syllable, remain the same and keep enclosing the predicate:

– 13c *'ănī 'ękrot 'ittᵉkā*		+ object: covenant
	hinge: *'ak*	
– 14c object: one thing		*'ānōkī šō'el mē'itᵉkā*

We see a chiasmus which fulfills two functions. As a figure of closure AB-BA firstly it makes clear that the one condition which David insists upon, Michal's return to him, essentially and indissolubly belongs to the agreement which is to be concluded. As a cruciform construction the trope makes the difference between the two halves visible, the change of tack from easy agreement to inexorable demand.

Abner's third clause concerned the transference of the nation. David's third clause concerns "one thing", which has to be a token of this trans-

[16] See I Ki.2:20b, with its strikingly similar word order and pronouns. The wife of another and the throne were the issue there as well. I also note that v.18bc, in the same passage, is remarkably similar to II Sam.3:13bc. For the passage in I Kings see NAPS I, p.392-397.

ference and provide evidence that Abner is as good as his word. In David's speech the topic of "transferring Israel" is exchanged, therefore, for something which seems much smaller but is not, the extradition of Michal. The exchange does not, however, signify replacement, since Michal's coming represents and symbolizes the coming of Israel.

In relation to what follows verse 13d functions as an introduction. David uses its final word, a *lēmor* once again, to say in turn[17] that he is now going to talk in practical terms. Then 13efg follow, an AXA construction, the middle line of which forms the point since it divulges the name of Michal. The coming of her person is that one thing which is announced by 13d. With a play on words, borrowed from the words of the text, we can sum up David's point as follows: I ask (*šō'el*) for the daughter of *šā'ūl*. The Act commenced with a questioning David; he asked God the way and received a throne. Now he demands, from the opposition, the return of his wife as a sign that the second throne is to be his. The text of 13f is, to a certain extent, irregular, but can be restored if we assess the proper value of the pattern of repetitions in 13efg.[18] The line with the name of the princess has exactly the same number of words as the line with "only one thing": 13d and 13f have seven words. Around and in between we find four words each time. After the exclamation "good!" there is, therefore, the regular alternation of 4 + 7 + 4 + 7 + 4 words.[19] The lines 13e and g are antithetical as not seeing versus seeing of "my person" (the rhyme *'ęt pānāy*) and surround Michal like an escort. I view them as a significant literary repetition: 'the difference, my good Abner, between getting to talk to me and not getting to talk to me, is Michal'. One could render the compound sentence as follows: "you will not come

[17] If the first *lēmor* (which has just been used in v.12b) is not uttered by the narrator but by Abner himself – which we cannot exclude – then we may regard the *lēmor* of David in 13d as a sly dig, an ironic echoing of the general.

[18] For more information see Appendix I *ad loc.*

[19] Just as is justified in Appendix I, the redundant *lpny* of 13f must first be dropped. A piece of additional information on quantity: Michal, as embodiment of the about-turn, makes me wonder whether or not her name in 13f is (or was) perhaps the centremost word. The unaltered version of the BHS (if, like the Masoretes, we write the name Ishbosheth as two words) contains 297 words; no. 149 is, then, the centremost word and is the "your coming" of 13g. In my version, which relocates the name Ishbosheth in v.7b but drops the *lpny* of 13f, there are 298 words and the middle of this even number lies between *bb'k* and *lr'wt*. Little changes if we insert an original Eshbaal (which always counts as one word) in (7b,) 8a, 14a, 15a. Deleting a *l'mr* in v.12 does not help either. I give up the exercise, satisfied with the fact that David's demand is the structural centre of the composition, and the person of Michal the stake.

into my presence unless you bring Michal daughter of Saul when you come before me."[20]

By choosing the form of a double negative (not ... unless), David makes his demand into a warning at the same time. We can clarify this if we provide, by way of contrast, alternative positive phraseology such as: "bring Michal with you, when (instead of the conditional 'if') you come before me," something which the narrator could have written also. In the crucial third clause of his speech Abner used "his" hiph'il to indicate the transference of power (not to mention: his arrogating the process). In a flash of telling irony David now answers with a well-chosen hiph'il in his crucial clause. He does not want to speak of the general's coming (*bw'* in the qal, 13g) before he has pointed out that Abner has to "bring" (*bw'* in the hiph'il) the woman. Abner must bring "Michal, the daughter of Saul" says David, which is not the same as "my wife, Michal", which expression David keeps for Ishbosheth in v.14. The businesslike nature of politics and the shift of power is what it is all about now, and once again the name of Saul is used as a gauge: what used to be Saulidic now becomes Davidic. The fact that David is supported by sound legal grounds is not what counts now in the negotiations between king and strong man; the aspect of marriage rights is reserved for v.14.

The omission of "sending messengers" in v.13a accentuates the action in, and the fullness of, v.14a: "David sent messengers to Ishbosheth, the son of Saul." Now there is no ellipse of Ishbosheth, and that is because David addresses him officially. The apposition "the son of Saul" ensures that Saul remains the gauge and directs our attention to the fact that David does not, in the first instance, address his colleague from Mahanaim, neither does he address the private person of Ishbosheth. No, he addresses the representative of the family of Saul who has the most legal liability regarding Michal. The apposition "the son of Saul" in 14a is parallel to, and related to, "the daughter of Saul", the apposition which the speaker David had added to the name of Michal in 13f. The one case of quasi-redundancy presupposes and answers to the other. David does not send a messenger but messengers, and this plural also is a token of the official nature of the message; only a genuine delegation will do in view of the gravity of the text.

The temporal aspect of v.14a is not marked, but interesting. This mission is just as much a reaction of David to the initiative of Abner as his prompt

[20] In this rendering I am mixing words from the NEB and the JPS. The JPS begins with: "Do not appear before me" and the NEB with "you do not come". I diverge from both by taking the *lō tir'ę̄* of v.13e to be neither prohibitive nor indicative, but something in between in the form of the threat: 'you will not succeed, unless ... '

answer (v.13) to Abner himself. This group must have been sent out at well-nigh the same time as the counter proposal to the general. The simultaneousness accentuates the differences between David's clauses on Michal. He gives Ishbosheth an order without beating about the bush, *t^e^nā*, and allows the name of the princess to be preceded by a word which is the decisive framework of reference for a good understanding of what precisely is being claimed. The word is "my wife" and receives many echoes: after the name Michal a relative clause occurs which rhymes twice on *'ištī* and consists of consonants all of which alliterate, so that the essential quality of Michal is included in a repeated form, in that *'ăšęr 'ēraśtī lī*. In this way an object of not less than ten words has arisen after the abrupt-sounding "give!" David quotes his own past in the subordinate clause for a special reason. "Michal, whom I have acquired for a hundred foreskins of the Philistines." The use of the *bet pretii* indicates that David mentions the bride's price which he has paid. He is not now saying that he has submitted twice as many, but uses the number 100 to indicate that this was Saul's condition and that he settled up accurately. David does not express grief for the loss of Michal, neither does he mention, in the presence of the Saulides, her significance as a pawn in the political game, but he speaks of justice. He lays claim to his property.[21] It was taken away from him and that was unjust.

By pleading the contract mentioned in I Sam.18, David cleverly includes other aspects: he was, at that time, the only real national hero who had an answer to the enemy, and without these triumphs he would not have become allied by marriage to Saul himself. The barbaric detail of the foreskins brings the same network of metonymic links into this passage as the ones I discussed in connection with I 18. Via the concrete entity of the foreskins we arrive at the topic of potency, and the subject of marriage touches upon this as well. David's might yields him a bond with the king's daughter, Saul's demand creates warfare which fails to turn against David but provides him instead with a new opportunity of demonstrating his strength, and the bond itself is a token of strength. One of the links has become a sound and connects the beginning of a long object concatenation with the end: *'ištī* returns and has to be released from *p^e^lištīm*. The *'ēraśtī* mediates through its sound and position, and states the context. The metonymic network which realises such powerful links between sex and power is, apart from this, prepared by the collision with which the story started. At that point Rizpah formed the intersection of sexual interest, justice and power.

[21] In the marriage and property laws of ancient Israel the wife was, after all, *b^e^'ūlat ba'al*, as Gen.20 expresses it in terms as splendid as they are efficient.

The Saulide gets his name again in v.15a, from the narrator this time, and he sends people out. After the *wayyišlaḥ* of v.12 and 14a we begin to think of more diplomacy. And we get it wrong. Ishbosheth takes measures for once, but he only does what he has just been required to do. His *wayyišlaḥ* flows immediately into a *wayyiqqaḥ* which puts the command of David into operation and quickly and summarily wrests Michal away from the man with whom she found love. Opposite the double *'ęt'išti 'ęt mīkal* of the first husband is the separation indicated twice by *me'im* "away from her husband, from Paltiel". In both cases the personal name follows the decisive "my wife / her husband". The polarity has already been announced by the pair give/take at the beginning of 14b/15b.

If some kind of mishap during the handing down of the text had caused v.16 to disappear, we would have noticed little or nothing of it. The rest of the passage keeps on being coherent and gripping enough. What can the function of v.16 be though, and what is the contribution of this miniature of three people on the road? We read its four lines attentively. The second husband now receives one full and expressive line for himself from the narrator, who by means of two effective absolute infinitives gives a poignant description of Paltiel's inability to part from his wife. He is, in the best sense of the word, "her husband", and the narrator allows room for its expression: he gives the verb in 16a the explicit subject *'īšāh*. Not only does he go "with her", whereby this *'ittāh* rhymes with "her husband"; but also, as soon as the movement has been depicted and shaded in emotionally with the beautiful pair *hālōk ubākō*, the narrator, on the brink of a pleonasm, joins Paltiel to his wife with a new preposition: "behind her". This husband turns the "cleaving" of the woman to the man, of which the last verse of Gen.2 speaks, upside down. But there is venom in the preposition *'aḥărē* which turns against him. The word causes him, in comparison with his *'ittāh* which shows him to be still at her side, to drop back as someone who cannot keep pace with developments; he becomes the loser who must remain *behind* in tears.

For Paltiel the place Bahurim is the frontier. From this Benjaminite location, the city of Jerusalem – viewed politically, the future creation of David – comes into view to the right of the small company travelling south. The name has in itself a positive ring to it, but its significance for Paltiel will always be a painful one. My reading of the name in this context is the abstract form "election" and I observe that it alliterates with his lamenting and his falling behind – ... *bākō 'aḥăręhā ... baḥūrīm*; daring to conclude that Paltiel's bitter loss is the inevitable corollary of Michal's place in David's history. David's being chosen is the brick wall Paltiel walks into.

The narrator has revealed his respect for the loser and wishes to accord space to it in the text with the careful brush strokes of his infinitives. But opposite the movement motivated by devotion (*wylk ... hlwk*) he now places a movement going in the opposite direction. This is imposed on Paltiel by somebody who can really snarl, Abner. Curtly this soldier – who has just abandoned his own loyalty of his own free will – barks out his command "go away, return" in two monosyllables. The first, *lek*, faces the *wayyelęk* of 16a, the second, *šūb*, is immediately put into operation, 16d. Just one more question: why does Abner snarl so? I suggest two answers to this. The sudden presence of Abner in this miniature suggests how embarrassing it is for the strong man to have to function as a lieutenant in an escort and to carry out a mission formally sent by the despised Ishbosheth. The enforced separation taking place before his very eyes is a very real and emotional consequence of his own decision and disloyalty. This is bound to produce a spectacle of confrontation. Abner is neither the first nor the last tough man to snarl in the presence of so much gentleness and tenderness.

Abner at work for David, vv.17-21

Now that we have suddenly seen Abner at Michal's side, we expect a report on the rest of his journey and how he escorts her to Hebron to bring her to her first and lawful husband. The latter had himself linked the arrival of the one with the arrival of the other in the central speech. Nothing doing, however! After v.16 we are confronted by an ellipse on the level of construing sequences. The narrator does not devote one word to the reception of Michal and we hear nothing more of her until, three chapters later, she has a nasty clash with king David when he comes home after the procession with the ark. I would like to postpone my evaluation of this hiatus for a while.

Abner does make an appearance in Hebron, in the text, but mention of the fact is postponed until v.20a. If we now read v.17, then what we see is another topic, the canvassing of the socio-political grass roots by the general, and we notice an inversion in v.17a. This piece of syntactical intervention not only indicates a change of subject after 16d, but also marks a break in chronological progress: "the word of Abner has been with the elders of Israel." That is a flashback. The question now is: what is the extent of this analepsis? In 19a, which pays special attention to the position of the tribe of Benjamin, Abner is still travelling about talking tribesmen round, and 19b reports a movement of completion: Abner is about to lay the results he has harvested before David. With "he went" v.20a joins up seamlessly[22] with "Abner came to David in

[22] When the announcement "he went" stands alone, it can also include the arrival. What we have here, however, is the pair *wayyelęk* + *wayyābō*, which articulates Abner's journey with the

Hebron." It is inserted, unnoticed, into the thread of recommenced chronological narrative to which our attention is made to revert. This is the way in which the contours of the analeptic sequence are given: verses 17-19 reach back.[23]

Abner can feel strong once more. The sequence of his political handiwork and his arrival in Hebron are characterised by the constant explicit mention of his name, up to six times and one after the other in the narrator's text, and he is almost always subject.[24] His power is also apparent from the choice of words in v.17a, with its nominal phrase *d^e^bar 'abner*, combined with *hyh*. We are used to this construction in the form "the word of *yhwh* came to X", see, for example 24:11. That it is now applied to Abner indicates that he acts with great authority; and, which is one step further, with some venom, that Abner imagines that he is equal to God in power. In the meantime the narrator includes groups as new characters, the elders of Israel and the tribe of Benjamin. Up to now the transfer of power was the subject of decision-making and talks. Now the great amount of work which is necessary to achieve this must be done. Abner must journey to the different tribes and he must ever apply himself to the task of ripening his audience for the far-reaching change. As a historian the reader estimates that such a process would have taken months at least. Our narrator manages to summarise the whole process of talking them round in a single speech consisting of four lines only, 17b-18c. And Abner's campaigning he sums up in a two-line report which he uses to form a frame around the speech: 17a and 19a report the *dbr* of Abner and are complementary as far as his audience is concerned. What is striking, in addition to this, is that Benjamin gets a separate line. This is understandable, since it is the tribe which provided the first king. The Benjaminites must now be brought to the point, not so much of rejoicing at the idea of David becoming king as being at least prepared to recognise the inevitability of the shift and to reconcile themselves to the loss of their dynasty. This is surely the hardest nut for Abner to crack on his long tour, and he keeps this task until last. There are two more reasons why this is appropriate, geography and

polarity of going away (including 'being underway' if necessary) and arriving. The poles now occur exactly on either side of the sequence boundary: 19b and 20a; the same duo of verbs of movement in 4:5ab and 7f + 8a (where *bw'* occurs in the hiph'il this time).

[23] The inversion was actually esteemed by Driver, LV, Buber. The analeptic sequence has rightly been given its own paragraph in the typography of the BJ and the JPS.

[24] Reading the context of the speech in vv.17b-18c I note the occurrence of the name of Abner in 17a-19a-20a-20b-21a, and still further, in 21e. The trio of 19ab20a is especially striking. Notice that the name is indispensable only in 17a, 19a, and 21a. The narrator could have omitted it in 19b and 20a, and replaced it by *lō* in 20b and by *'ōtō* in 21e.

Michal. The territory of Benjamin borders on Judah, so that Abner, immediately after canvassing the Saulide homeland can travel on to David with his final report. At the same time he can easily pick up Michal and take her to Hebron.

The speech which Abner makes, in sundry variations, during his campaign, once again turns on the hinge *w*^{e}*'attā*, so that we are led to expect two halves; in actual fact there are three parts. The first line, v.17b, begins with establishing the situation that has to serve the speaker as a platform in order to subsequently want, require, or promote something. This volitional part consists of one word only here! It is the imperative *'ăśū* which is not restricted by any object or complement, grows, because of this, in strength, and gains the nature of a sheer appeal. "Do it!" – and for those listeners who do not want to get going yet part three of the speech follows, a motivation in which the general, once again, allows God to put in an appearance. The personal name *yhwh* is expressly placed in front of the verb. Verse 18b is a variant of the quotation formula and introduces 18c, an embedded speech of God himself, which the speaker would actually like to insist is a genuine quotation.

Abner's opening sentence begins with a temporal phrase. Its two halves, "yesterday" and "the day before yesterday", are underlined with a rare double *gam*, so that their twofold nature emerges more.[25] This encourages me to accord them the interpretation that *t*^{e}*mōl* refers to the short period of time (one, at most two, years) after Saul's death and *šilšōm* refers to the period before, when David began to manifest himself as a power factor. The verb consists of the periphrastic combination *hyh* + part. which indicates duration in the past tense. What Abner now contends is remarkable and partly turns against him. All that time, he says to the representatives of the ten tribes, "you have been seeking David as king over you." If that had been absolutely untrue, Abner would have provoked protest and irritation in his audience, and the rhetorician is too clever for this. I assume, therefore, that what Abner says is to an important extent correct. But then it becomes clearly visible that Abner's own project, the truncated Saulide state, was a forced and high-handed construction which was really doomed to an inglorious collapse. Looked at another way the obverse of 17b is an admission of personal failure. In connection with this it is striking that Abner, throughout the

[25] Here and in 5:2, the sequel to Israel's choice of David, a double *gam* is intertwined with the two temporal terms. This double *gam* also occurs elsewhere, in Ex.4:10 and I Chr.11:2. Also compare the expression *gam t*^{e}*mōl gam hayyōm* which occurs in Ex.5:14 and I Sam.20:27. The double *gam* of II 3:17 cannot be viewed separately from the double *gam* of v.19.

course of his entire speech, does not this time use any form whatsoever of the first person. He speaks in the language of 'you all' as the Americans would say. After the broad sentence with the previous history Abner finds that he can be extremely brief in his recommendation. That which 'you all' have always wanted, you must now put into practice; the temporal aspect "now" of the hinge faces the "previously" of verse 17b as complement.

The motivation marked by the conjunction *kī* which follows is a shortened form of the doctrine of David's election. Because it now suits him Abner, the strong man, makes God dance to the tune of his power politics once more. The critical question as to why he did not place his resources at David's disposal before, he would have brushed away like an irritatingly buzzing gnat. The embedded speech of God also places a personal name at the beginning, in a complement which thereby receives emphasis: "it is my servant David, by whose hand I will save my people." My servant David and not someone else. The long sentence contains first two parties with whom God has an intimate relationship: my servant and my people; *'abdī* and *'ammī*, thanks to rhyme and alliteration, are welded into the unity of partners who are thrown into each other's arms and simultaneously enjoy God's favour. At the end of v.18c there are two more parties, first the name of one people, the Philistines, i.e. the group whose pressure yesterday and today is the source of the most concern, and then, generalising at the end with the inclusion of a climactic waw: "yes, all their enemies." Their power, metonymically present in a double *yad*, requires counterbalance; that's why "the hand of David" comes first. As far as his own hand is concerned, about which he had so pretentiously spoken to David in 12d, Abner is, this time, deferentially silent. One can base an entire actantial programme on this one sentence of 18c, which intimately keeps together its object, subject and predicate in the middle and separates the champion and his opponents, placing them at the edges.[26]

In v.9 Abner had been so free as to include an oath of God within his own oath and to point to David's election in the past. This speech had, as we have seen, a double layer, one of political opportunism on the general – king level

[26] I complete the actantial scheme here, because it is the valid background of so many stories in Joshua-Judges-Samuel; only the individual actors change, not the pattern of liberation.

According to II Sam.3:18c God is the subject, his quest is liberation (the actantial object) for the benefit of the *destinataire* (the addressee, receiver) Israel, whilst David is naturally the first helper, and the Philistines etc., the opponents. One could also shift God into the corner of the *destinateur* (sender, granter), making the hero, in this case David, the subject of the same quest. See NAPS II, pp.26, 143 and 171 on this.

of communication, and one of spiritual truth on the level of story – reader. Abner does the same thing here, in v.18, whilst he speaks to the grassroots support. He quotes the promise once made by God in order to endorse the election of David. And once again his political manoeuvering, which smacks of religious hypocrisy, is finally taken into the service of the divine goal which directs David's career. The spurious sounding piety of 18c utters a truth which is the extension of previous divine words about the election of David (I 17:46sq. and its echoes in I 19:5, 20:15 and 24:21), but also those about the first king, whose task was, likewise, to liberate the people from the Philistines on the field of battle (I 9:16, cf 8:20; and 7:8 on Samuel himself and his intervention).

The narrator completes the sequence with 19ab and also uses a double *gam* himself. That of Abner ordered the temporal, his is complementary and spatial.[27] The Benjaminite audience completes the national campaign of Abner, 19a, after which, as climax, David can also be visited, 19b. Four out of the five words of 19a reappear in 19b, but 19b surpasses its predecessor with an extra series of words. This contains four personal names, first the pair David and Hebron, then the pair Israel and Benjamin. The latter double repeats the addressees of 17a and 19a and gets a sustained appearance in Abner's account, 2x *kol*. The long sentence, with a record number of seventeen words, is, therefore, the recapitulation of the results of Abner's campaign and rounds off the paragraph with its fullness. Another nice detail is that Abner makes a report on the view of all and delivers it in Hebron; the double *b^{e}'oznē* is answered by the double *b^{e}'ēnē*, during the rounding off of the chore the visual and the auditive supplement each other. Apart from this, what is the view of all? What does the long object clause "all that was good in the eyes of Israel and Benjamin" consist of precisely? Are they in complete agreement with Abner's view on the political situation? Looked at in a down-to-earth way it does not occur in the text. In retrospect what is now striking is that an ellipse has followed v.18: Abner's listeners have received no speech from the narrator to disclose their position.

The closing sequence begins with the appearance of Abner. He has himself accompanied by a complete delegation. Isn't someone being hidden behind this group? I continue to take David's words seriously: "you shall not see me, unless you bring Michal with you." But the woman is kept out of sight by a rigorous ellipse. In this paragraph her omission signifies that the gentlemen cannot be disturbed whilst engaged in their masculine activity; business

[27] Even though *gam* occurs twice next to the name of Abner, both cases do not refer to the general but to his audience. After the elders of Israel it is now Benjamin's turn *as well*, 19a, and finally David is *also* to come to know of it.

before pleasure. And viewed as a whole the oppression of Michal after v.16 signifies a fate which provides, for the princess, an unexpected analogy with her brother Ishbosheth. He was only allowed to appear within his quality of "son of Saul", she gets no more chance to rise above the epithet "daughter of Saul". Her individuality is not considered worth one stroke of the pen, let alone her love of David which was so noticeable in I 18-19. I can explain this on the basis of another ellipse: that of David's reception. We hear nothing of gladness, or satisfaction, let alone of a loving welcome. For a short space of time the daughter of the king is promoted to the symbol of a radical shift, but the symbolism does not touch her individuality and now appears to go hand in hand with being downgraded to the level of a thing: she is, at the same time, reduced to nothing more than a pawn in the game of politics on a grand scale.[28]

In v.20b the delegation gets an official reception. The beneficiaries, Abner and the twenty, are neatly repeated from 20a, but are now placed in the middle. The carousal which David lays on occurs at the end of 20b and is, therefore, a postponed object, separated from predicate and subject.[29] So David's courtly care surrounds the group, which gets pampered in indulgence as it were.[30] Then Abner is allowed to speak. His speech in v.21 is the final one in this story, but also – for the unsuspecting Abner – the very last one in his life. The most important characteristic of this is that it consists of three lines which are reminiscent of the three lines in verse 12. That speech was also aimed at David, but via a messenger, and therefore indirect. Now Abner speaks of the same matters, but directly, face to face with David. The one speech is the counterpart of the other, according to the pattern ABC-CBA.

The symmetry is chiefly established by, and its recognition begins with, the axis B-B', the three identical words of v.12c and 21c. But within this great

[28] This also explains another ellipse, which I could have mentioned during my discussion of v.16: a report is actually given of how Paltiel experiences the compulsory separation, but none is given of Michal's reaction!

[29] There are twenty places in the OT where *'śh* + *mištę̄* occurs, including five in Genesis and twelve in Esther. In all these places *mištę̄* occurs either immediately after, or in very close proximity to, the predicate and/or subject (with the exception of Esther 1:5, which deviates by being overloaded with adjuncts).

[30] Its differing from v.20a underlines this. There the predicate is in the singular so that it agrees with the leader, not with the group, and the arrival of Abner is first completed by the mention of his destination, "to David, in Hebron". Only then is the subject amplified with a circumstantial clause which mentions the twenty. Leader and group are separated in v.20a, therefore, through David, whilst they are actually enclosed, however, by David's reception in 20b. Just one more detail in this connection: the words *'ănāšīm* and *'ittō* are grouped chiastically in 20ab.

resemblance a subtle difference has been introduced, which receives its full significance through the details of the correspondence C-C'. Abner had asked for a pact in 12c, which, in 13c, (the three words once again) he promptly received from David. But in spite of his slightly megalomaniac endeavours he is not God, and a pact with his person is apparently not enough. The people and its representatives, as fully-fledged negotiation partners, cannot be passed over. The political contract between David and Israel does not take place yet either, but only at the beginning of ch.5. In v.21b Abner implicitly recognises that another finalizing round of operations is needed on his part, before Israel actually goes over. We follow the transformation which 12d undergoes in 21b: "my hand" which has the task of "bringing Israel round to you" is transformed in the zeal, the will power and the great amount of effort of three verb forms, which are welded into a series by their rhyme with the cohortative ending, "I will arise, I will go, I will gather." The addressee changes from a simple "to you" to the revealing "my lord the king"; Abner already uses, therefore, the courtly style to address David. The object at the end of 12d and 21b is identical.

The 'I' and its hard work, taken over by 21b from 12d, disappear out of the text. The grammatical subject of the wishes in 12c and 21c (the B-B' axis) is complementary: first David, then his future subjects. Finally element C surveys the region over which David is to be king. The short and ambiguous "who has a country?" covered by label C, changes into the beautiful turn of phrase and the sweeping gesture of "so that you shall be king over all that your heart desires". If it is true that the referent of 'whom' in v.12b was Abner himself, then there is a polarity 12b-21d which intimates how the country of the one strong man becomes the country of the other strong man. Or ought we to turn the argument around and say: the C-C' connection argues that the ruler of 21d, David, is at the same time the possessor meant in 12b? The root *mlk* has now been used three times, solely by Abner, with a different audience each time (in v.10a Ishbosheth, in 17b the Israelites, in 21d David himself).

Straight after the speech "David sent Abner away." It is the fourth time we come across *wyšlḥ*.[31] It is now a culminating pi'el form, but I do detect a slight irony though, since the man who wanted so much to enter into a pact with David and therefore began to send messengers back and forth, now becomes an emissary himself; the strong man becomes the servant of the other strong man. The short clause which completes the whole is benevolent:

[31] Notice the varied way in which it occurs: twice with, and twice without, messengers, and always with a change in subject: Abner in 12a, David in 14a, Ishbosheth in 15a and once again David in 21e (with a personal name as object!).

"he went away in peace." Abner cannot know that this calm ending is to be intensified by the narrator, immediately afterwards at the beginning of the following unit, with a stylistic device which is to replace *b^ešālōm* and so anticipate his violent death. As the story's ending the word "peace" forms a frame together with the word "war" with which the story began.[32] This alternation, itself connected with the landslide which was the issue in the text, is a promising one for the nation. The civil war phase has given way to negotiations and peace is in the offing.

Now that we have interpreted all the sequences, and thanks to the pointers given to us by the style, we have received a well-founded idea of what is, and what is not, important and it is now possible to set down the structure of the story. The vv.17-19 paragraph was striking by being an analepsis. The campaign of Abner puts into operation what he announced, in an oath squared, as it were, so that vv.17-19 correspond with vv.9-10. The pattern ABC-CBA does more than link v.12 and v.21 to each other, it contributes to the composition at the same time. The divisions into three and into five parts, with which I began this section, remain correct and meaningful, but exhibit more aspects than the composition of the story. The structure or composition of the unit is covered by the following scheme of five members, which is formed in a partly concentric, partly parallel, way. All these parts offer one essential speech which is concerned with the transference of power.[33]

A	Abner versus Ishbosheth: power to David	vv.6-11
B	Abner to David: a pact is proposed	v.12
X	David to Abner: on one condition, Michal	v.13
	Abner and Ishbosheth extradite Michal	vv.14-16
A'	Abner canvasses Israel for David	vv.17-19
B'	Abner comes to David, pact discussed	vv.20-21

I have, of course, taken into consideration whether or not it is better to note a symmetry here which is consistently concentric so that B'A' follows the middle instead of A'B'. There are indeed arguments for this notation: they are the criteria of place and contact which I have employed at the beginning of this paragraph. But I am now looking for the structure which does thematic

32 The word *šālōm* often signifies something other than 'peace', and then forms oppositions with entities other than *milḥāmā*. But the war/peace antithesis is present in the OT, see Avishur, p.382. This author is mindful of the fact that a word pair can also function when its members are very far apart, for example, in the service of an inclusio.

33 No longer essential in this connection, are v.7c (Ishbosheth's reproach) and 16c (Paltiel snarled at to leave).

justice to the composition. And then there are two arguments which yield an ABXAB notation. The chief reason for writing A'B' after the centre is the relationship between v.12 and 21, which creates the B-B' pair. The A-A' correspondence is based on the fact that Abner quotes God twice on the destination of David; in vv.9-10 it is an oath which he backs up and will put into operation, in vv.17-18 an announcement of God about the liberator, his servant David.

For the middle also I have contemplated another arrangement. One might also divide X into C-C', and say: in vv.13-and-14 David demands his wife from Abner and Ishbosheth (element C), which is put into operation by both in vv.15-16. But there are two reasons for my preferring the label X when it comes down to it. The person of Michal is such a central symbol for the transference of power and is so much of a pawn on the political chessboard that she creates the unity of vv.13-16. In another way the speech of David in v.13 is also central, with its two points of agreement and demand. It fits better, therefore, in an arrangement which honours the pivotal function of the middle with an X, rather than a C which has a counterpart.[34]

§ 2. *The death of Abner*, 3:22-39

This text consists of two halves. The death of Abner is in vv.22-30 Joab's goal and next, in vv.31-39, it is a *fait accompli* which proves a handful for David. In the first half Joab is the main character, since he is the only one who acts, in the second half he is absent.[35] The murder which he has committed is the subject of much discussion, and the second half consists of four very different speeches all delivered by one and the same person, who at the same time manifests himself in this as new actantial subject, the king himself.

The unit begins with the coincidence that the two generals miss each other. The story gives form to this by means of an ingenious pattern of comings and goings which embroiders on the peaceful ending of v.21ef: "David sent Abner away and he went in peace." This piece of information is made into a motif, and appears in the text as a refrain in the lines 21ef-22d-23d-24e. This

[34] In addition I notice that the lay-out of the text around vv.12-13 cuts across the dialogic structure. The speeches of v.12 and 13 relate to one another as question and answer; they are, therefore, a pair, but are intersected by the scheme ABXAB. We might also consider referring only to verse 13 as C, and placing vv.14-16 under C' as implementation.

[35] Only in the first line does he have to put in a brief appearance as indirect object; from this order of David's onwards he is swallowed up in the group. He is the hidden target of the lines 39bc.

series, which closes a verse four times, is part of a taut quantitative regularity which still carries on, up to and including verse 27. For verses 22-27 form six quartets with their lines.[36]

The pattern of comings and goings consists of four clusters which begin beyond the scene boundary and are completed by an angry speech of Joab against the king. With his "sent" (or cause to be escorted away, *šlḥ* in the pi'el) David finds himself between two forces, the going of Abner and the coming of Joab.

verse	*coming*	*sending*	*going*
20a	wyb' 'bnr 'l dwd		
21e		wyšlḥ dwd 't 'bnr	wylk bšlwm
22a	hnh ... wyw'b b'w		
22b	... hby'w		
22d		ky šlḥw	wylk bšlwm
23a	... wyw'b ... b'w		
23c	b' 'bnr ...'l hmlk		
23d		wyšlḥhw	wylk bšlwm
24a	wyb' yw'b 'l hmlk		
24d	hnh b' 'bnr 'lyk		
24e		lmh zh šlḥtw	wylk *hlwk*
25b	ky lpttk b'		

David is constantly the grammatical subject in the centremost column. Abner is the object and immediately afterwards becomes the grammatical subject of the final column. Especially in David's column the forms exhibit many-sided variation. There is an abab pattern of verb tenses and an aabb pattern of voices. In 21ef the objective report of the narrator himself comes first with a

[36] My colometric ordering of the text makes this plain, with the exception of one point, v.24b. The *wayyōmęr* which stands alone, can either be added to 24a, or need not be taken into consideration for a moment, for the sake of the sets of four. The quartets are not only marked by the series with *šlḥ* and *wylk bšlwm* which reaches as far as 24e, there is also an instance of parallelism, 25d-26d, thanks to the contrast knowing/not knowing, whilst the cola of vv.26 and 27 are all syntactic units (clauses). Concerning vv.28-30: these can be grouped as 2 + 2 lines of report (4 lines of narrator's text, therefore) enclosing 4 lines of speech; but I cannot insist on the latter four, since my staggering the long summing up in 29bc into two lines has been done not for reasons of principle but of practice.

wyqtl form, subject and object. In 22d the personal names have disappeared and a motivating *kī* clause is used with a perfect. After these two instances of narrator's text two speeches of characters follow; in 23d anonymous informants report the departure of Abner to Joab, and this informing too employs wyqtl. Then the last word about it follows in 24e and David's general speaks. He adds a twist to the refrain which he brings to a climax. The variation at the end of the *wylk* column makes the nature of Abner's departure problematic in retroaction. It ensures the ominous disappearance of the congenial "in peace" and re-opens the question of Abner's departure with the abs. inf. *hālōk*, which is as beautiful as it is loaded. Or rather: Joab brings the matter up, since he is the speaker in vv.24-25, calls David to account and there is nothing he wants more than to reverse Abner's being gone. There is still something of amazement in Joab's voice as he lets fly at the king with the accusation: "Why did you let him go, so that he could depart *just like that*?"[37] His "why?" is the counterpart of the narrator's "because" of 22d and takes part in the abab pattern with the perfect.

The subjects change only in the column on coming. Joab arrives in Hebron and is in danger of shutting the stable door after the horse has bolted: Abner arrived in Hebron before him, and during his absence, and this infuriates Joab. I imagine Joab's hatred of Abner makes it impossible for him to believe that it was pure chance that Abner came greasing round David at the very time that he, Joab, was in the field. After v.23 attention shifts to Abner's earlier arrival. Since the lines are arranged in quartets we can work very strictly to rule and compare every line with its counterparts:

v.22a	23a	24a
b	b	c
c	c	d
d	d	e

Only at the level of the second lines is there no parallelism or significant contrast at work. The other series all exhibit parallelism. The 22a-23a-24a series follows Joab's appearance, the 22c-23c-24d series places the visit of Abner over against it, and 22d-23d-24e contains the refrain that the bird has

[37] The *šlḥ* in vv.21-23, means, as a pi'el, "shown out", but in 24e, in the reproach of Joab, the meaning does indeed change to "let him go". The use of the infinitive absolute of *hlk* is highly idiomatic: "he upped and went" or "he was able to take off" that is to say, "just like that" (which is unthinkable and unacceptable to the speaker).

flown – looking at it from Joab's point of view. A chiasmus on one square centimetre and the sound effects which *bā'* and *yābō'* create with the name *yō'āb* underline what happens in 22ab-23ab-24a; and, outside this sequence, the name *'abner* also contributes to the sound pattern. The little word with which it all began has the surprise at missing one another emerge: "Just then David's soldiers and Joab returned from a raid."[38] This *hinnē* is no longer purely spatial but functions, as notation of the surprise, temporally also.

In this way the series 22a-23a-24a containing Joab's appearance is opened. These lines display a development. Together with their context they exhibit this three course rotation: Joab comes and does not know; Joab comes and is informed; Joab comes to David and points out the "spying activities" of Abner to him. In 22a we learn where Joab comes from, in 23a no further information is given, and in 24a we learn where he is going to: to the king, to make his complaint. In 22a Joab is only part of a group. He is not mentioned until the second position, after "the servants of David". Their return from campaign is illustrated and brought to an end with an extra line, 22d, which puts the same verb into the hiph'il and honours the men as victors. The booty comes first, thanks to an inversion which unites the verbs and the military terms of 22a and b in a chiasmus *bā'ū mēhaggᵉdūd* and *šālāl rab ... hebī'ū*. This figure joins 22a and b closely and suggests that the picture of homecoming troops is now rounded off. But the completion is disturbed by the news item of v.23, which startles Joab. Now a chiasmus goes to work, which switches round him and the troop in 23a. The ambiguous "servants" is replaced by the much clearer term "the entire army with him", a collective character, and Joab comes first as leader. Then the soldiers disappear from the scene and we follow Joab alone, in his fury and lust for revenge. The opening verse is provided by the narrator alone. Joab is unobtrusively present, something which is to change already in 23a, the verse where he receives information about his adversary. As soon as this has taken place, Joab's involvement appears fully in the long speech of vv.24-25.

The military terms of 22ab and 23a remind us of the struggle in ch.2. But the official visit Abner pays David has brought an end to the civil war and that resounds in the word "peace" with which the previous unit ended. Now the new unit begins with an image which again links the person of Joab with conflict. But it is another front, and the narrator draws in the "peace" of Abner's departure from the other side of the boundary between the scenes. Which force is going to prevail in Hebron, the peace resulting from Abner's

[38] I quote "just then" from the JPS translation, a good rendering.

initiative, or the "pillaging" of Joab?[39] And I ask myself if David's relationship with each general and their contribution is a balanced one. I wonder about this because both the previous literary unit and this one each have the hiph'il of the verb *bw'* once. Joab brings much plunder, but gets no attention for this in Hebron; apparently it was taken for granted that this general could never be anything else but successful on the battlefield. On the other hand Abner had just contributed something to Hebron. What he came to "bring" (v.13 has this hiph'il) had been required by David; it was Michal! She can now be interpreted to mean the "booty" which the general had to surrender to David. As a political symbol she coincides[40] with the true spoil: the whole of Israel which is led to David. Abner receives all the attention and appreciation for bringing this about. So the question arises in my mind as to whether, between the lines, the nagging feeling of being neglected arises in David's own general. The imbalance that more attention is paid to the defecting general than to the loyal general who keeps on working is, without doubt, present (and it occurs much more often than just here, if we consider other professions). We would be surprised if Joab failed to be irritated by the discrepancy. This psychological aspect does not detract from the fact that for Joab himself the *talio* on account of his brother Asahel is shortly to be the chief motif.[41]

I would now like to take v.22c-23c-24d into consideration, the lines on the arrival of Abner earlier. The series cannot be separated from the lines which immediately follow on from them and consist of his departure escorted by David, the 22d-23d-24e refrain. In the narrator's verse, the circumstantial clause 22c occurs; simple information which unites three personal names. With the predicate on Abner "he was no longer there" the clause looks back and denotes absence. This void is now replaced in 23c by Joab's being informed of Abner's absence. The prejudiced listener Joab now experiences tension between the information "Abner had come to the king" and his peaceful departure. Through this the relationship between 23c and d is very different to that of 22c and d, where the quasi-innocent absence of Abner is

[39] The word *g^edûd*, which usually means "gang", sounds somewhat rough and informal to me, an impression borne out by Assyrian and Ethiopian cognates (see HAL *s.v. g^edûd* II). Its connotations contribute a coarsening of the atmosphere. *G^edûd* is soon to occur in 4:2, and we have already met it three times in I 30. In II 22:30 it stands for the enemies of David (in the traditional reading; see, however, HAL *s.v. g^edûd* I).

[40] "Coincide" is the literal translation of the Greek verb belonging to "symbol".

[41] This interpretation, which exploits the repetition of the hiph'il of *bw'*, seems a little less daring when one is aware of the fact that the verbs 'to come' and 'to go' each occur seven times exactly in the qal, from v.19 up to and including Abner's funeral; five times of which both occur in the part consisting of the refrain, vv.21-24.

seamlessly followed, and at the same time explained, by 22d. Then the third instance of Abner's arrival and departure follows in the speech of v.24sq. His movements pass through the centrifuge of Joab's anger and are accordingly marked by the scathing words of an enraged pointing out and questioning as well: *hinnē* and *lāmmā-zę̄* are, as the commencement of 24d and e, good examples of the emotive function of language.[42] In 25b Joab once more refers to Abner's coming. In the whole of v.25 he is busy slandering Abner and exposing his coming as spying; in 25b *lᵉfattōtᵉkā* expressly precedes "he came" whereupon Joab works out that "deceiving you" with two more infinitives in 25cd, entire clauses devoted to the disqualification of Abner. So the coming of Joab to Hebron has resulted in the paradoxical effect that attention has once again, and completely, become focused on Abner's coming to David. The shift of information on Joab's movement to Abner's movements is definitive and is marked by the fierce *hinnē* line with which the line on Abner (24d) corresponds to the *hinnē* line on Joab (22a).

Joab's speech to David is relatively[43] long and consists of seven lines. Three lines of anger and three lines of slander revolve around the pivot of verse 25a. Each trio begins briefly and grows quickly.[44] Joab is now very excited and there is no trace of court manners in his speaking to the king. The first and third clauses are reproaches in the form of rhetorical questions which relate to one another as general and particular, since 24e works out the short introduction "what have you done?" The 'what' and the 'why' questions enclose the deictic and equally emotional *hinnē* of 24d. The verbs follow each other rhythmically: do (of you) – come (of him) – send away (of you) – depart (of him). The post-axial lines get their coherence and their semantic centre of gravity from three infinitives. Subsequent to the conjunction *kī*, which is just as much motivating as it is asseverative, they claim to reveal the true but hidden goal of Abner's visit to Hebron: "for he came only to deceive you". Once again the beginning ("to deceive") is brief and general, after which *pattōt* is worked out in a double and anaphoral *lāda'at* (spying).

This "finding out" (literally "knowing") takes me back to v.25a first. *Lāda'at* is also an elaboration of "you know", *yāda'tā*, from the central line;

[42] I employ the term from Jakobson's communication model. *Hinnē* must be rendered in an unorthodox way here, for example by a free translation such as "nota bene"; *lāmmā-zę̄* formally introduces a rhetorical question, is a token of indignation and incomprehension and, as a term of cutting reproach, calls David to account.

[43] The force of 'relative' here is: measured according to the proportions (especially the ratio report/speech) of the stories in this Act and measured according to the utterances of the character Joab; the general rarely speaks for a long time at a stretch.

[44] Counts: 2 + 4 + 5 words or 4 + 8 + 11 syllables in 24cde, and 3 + 5 + 6 words or 7 + 15 + 12 syllables in 25bcd.

it is, moreover, a surprising reversal. In 25a David knows (not) Abner, in 25cd the same persons are present but "finding out" operates in reverse: Abner knows you like the back of his hand, maintains Joab. Verse 25 manipulates king David in the same way as the counsellors later work on the new king of Ammon and is a striking parallel of 10:3.[45] Joab now poses as the one who has seen through the low motives of the other and puts pressure on David by suggesting that one must be very stupid if one can't see that ... , etc. In contrast to v.23c, where the patronymic next to Abner's name is principally informative, and to 24d where it is still omitted by the speaker, Joab's reference to Abner's origins in v.25a is slightly reifying, a kind of scarcely-veiled disdain. He gave himself extra breathing space, as it were, before pouring out the slander of 25bcd in one breath.

According to Joab Abner is trying "to learn your comings and goings". Stated literally in Hebrew this is "your going out and your coming in" and is a merismus which wants to be inclusive.[46] It is synonymous with, and has the same referent as, "everything you do" in the next line, which English can hardly render with a merismus: 'your doing and failing to do'. David's "doing" at the end of 25d and the brief question of 24c frame the entire speech, as if David's behaviour is what actually must be justified. But a snake in the grass appears, introduced by the narrator. The movement *bā* of Abner (25b) and the fatal *wayyeṣē* (26a) of Joab enclose the words *mōṣā* and *mābō*. This "going out" of Joab leads the cluster of narrative imperfects which bring us the murder of Abner, "whilst David did not know it"! The thesis of Joab, who entertains the possibility of David's not seeing through *(yd')* the fact that Abner is spying on him (*yd'*), slanderously brands Abner as a source of danger, whilst in reality Joab himself is a source of danger for the one who is slandered and that is what David is unaware of (*yd'*)! By maintaining that Abner is up to something, Joab has diverted attention away from the possibility, indeed the reality, that he himself has got something up his sleeve. In fact it is his coming in (22a-23a-24a) and going out (26a) which are worthy of suspicion.

Verses 22-30, the first half of the unit, pursue a rhythmic course of two waves as far as their content is concerned and this is supported by the alternation of report and speech. The narrator provides the take-off which has a preparatory function (vv.22-23: return of Joab, he learns of Abner);

[45] The main *tertia comparationis* are: in both cases a delegation of the other side is maligned; it concerns an accusation of spying; the latter is elucidated by three infinitives. *Cf.* NAPS I *ad loc.*

[46] We are acquainted with this merismus in poetry too, for example Psalm 121:8 (as qal infinitives), a verse which, with its all-embracing terms, just like 121:7, makes for the climax of the poem.

then Joab takes over with his speech. In 26-28a the narrator continues the action and swiftly brings it to a dramatic climax, after which David takes an initial stand on the murder of Abner with a speech in vv.28c-29c.

After his speech Joab can only reach the goal of his quest as actantial subject by first removing an obstacle: the absence of Abner. Verse 26, another quartet of lines, is devoted to this. The first line is as follows: "Joab went out from David." This occurs exactly opposite to his appearing before David in 24a, so that the text really contains the "coming in and going out" of Joab. His departure already signifies, in the spatial dimension, that David simply loses sight of Joab's ways, and I also interpret this figuratively as a serious estrangement. Joab continues the action by sending messengers to his opposite. So we obtain a picture which contrasts with 3:7-11 where a general flew at his own king in fury too. But at that time Abner went on to send messengers "on the spot" to his opponent, something which Joab does not repeat here. He has something in mind which David must not catch sight of (and regarding which David, unlike the frightened Ishbosheth, would definitely have been up in arms about, if he had become aware of it in time). When his emissaries shortly afterwards succeed in overtaking Abner, even managing to bring him back to Hebron, what is stated straight away, with an inversion which focuses attention on the change of subject, is: "David did not know."

There it is, without an object. The verb, used in the absolute sense, painfully admits that David has lost sight of developments since his not knowing is not restricted by any adjunct or object. Yet another rhythm of two waves becomes visible. Joab appears and speaks of knowing in one way and knowing in another, whereupon he disappears and all that is actually left for David is the not knowing. The question of the king's being well-informed is put forward clearly in this chapter for the first time as a motif and has far-reaching consequences which become visible in the "King David" section. In the long run what it is all about is whether or not, how and how far, David is losing his grip on developments and is even a prey to continuing, fresh deception. After his two crimes in ch.11 this process of deterioration is to continue – intensified – and define him, as I have worked out in *King David*.

The general who, as a result of his own political initiative, saw himself forced to cut short the *wayyelęk hālōk* of a citizen and to force him to turn back, secured the trauma of a separation for this man. Now there is another general who regards the departure of Abner as a *wayyelęk hālōk* and gets him to turn back, with fatal consequences which mean a trauma for the politics of his superior, king David. What is driving Joab has already been discreetly indicated by the report, in v.26, that the messengers were sent "after Abner". Here we have the ominous preposition again which had the power of life and death during Asahel's pursuit of Abner! Are these messengers "behind Abner" a temporary disguise for Joab's pursuit, resumed after such a long time? Whatever the case might be, their words do fulfill this function. The narrator leaves to our imagination what the false pretences might be with which Abner is lured back to Hebron. He marks only the moment of turning back with a location, *mibbōr hassīrā*.[47]

Both the turning back and the designations of space are of importance in the quartet which brings the murder. Enclosing the line on David's ignorance a parallelism 26c//27a has come into existence. First Abner was the object of being brought back, now the same *šwb* occurs in the qal so that he becomes subject of a reversed movement which receives its own location: "Abner turned back to Hebron." (It's working, it's working! There he is! is the exultation in the heart of a Joab who has had to wait in suspense and now sees Abner approaching.) Without further ado the narrator has the murder take place, with two narrative forms which are so similar that they function like an anaphora: *wayyaṭṭēhū* ... *wayyakkēhū* .... In the meantime the adjuncts become more and more precise: after the name of the city in 27a the camera zooms in with a medium shot on "the middle of the gate" where Joab takes his colleague aside, 27b, and the close-up of 27c shows the belly of the victim, whilst the scene of the crime is fixed by *šām*.

The physical term is the climax. This line's connection with 2:23b where Abner finishes off Asahel (also *wayyakkēhū*, also in the belly) is known, and already indicates that we have to do with revenge in kind. The narrator confirms this straightaway with a separate line and a *bēt pretii* which establish the motive for the murder: "he died because of the blood [=on account of the violent death] of his brother Asahel." The reader accurately construes the meaning of this line straightaway, but is able to do so only because of his foreknowledge. But something is the matter, something strange. The apposition "*his* brother" creates a special kind of friction because the suffix does

[47] I do not know if it is possible to do anything with this name in the literary sense, the localisation of which cannot be identified by the historical geographer, but I expect that contemporary listeners did have options at their disposal. Does it mean, in this context, "the well of turning aside"? If so some kind of a connection would then arise to take us back to the "turning aside" which Asahel did not want. The name also occurs in a series with designations such as the pool of Gibeon (where the Joab/Abner conflict originates) and the Field of the Stone Knives. It is also possible to construe a contrast, in which the living water – supplied by the well I assume – is placed opposite to the blood of the murdered man. I also notice Joab's other assassination, that of Amasa in ch.20, which took place at the "the great stone in Gibeon". We must take distant connections into account.

not refer back to the line's subject, Abner, as the rules of syntax would actually lead us to expect! It is not Abner who is the antecedent, but the murderer of course! This curious shift is not negligence, but a token that reveals Joab's focalisation. The fact that Abner dies as retribution for Asahel is the way the murderer looks at it. Must we say: this is the way the murderer alone looks at it? More on this when we come to verse 30. The end of 27b is also concerned with a special focalisation. After all neither the narrator nor the reader believe that Joab's intention is "to be able to discuss things quietly with Abner" or "to talk to him privately" as he takes his victim aside in the gate. Therefore the close of v.27b follows for a moment the false pretext of the murderer, after which the surprise attack of 27c is all the greater.

If we place the report of Abner's death between its two counterparts, Asahel's end and Joab's murder of his colleague Amasa in ch.20, then it is striking how restrained this report is. The weapon with which Joab delivered the fatal blow is not even mentioned, let alone the gruesome details of being run through and entrails which are given us in chs.2 and 20. Reactions – such as those of passers-by who come to a halt, shocked by the dying body – are not depicted either. The belly is mentioned in v.27c chiefly for the purposes of supplying the *talio* motif. The contrast between Joab's preparations in 3:27 and 20:9, where he misleads his victim by cajoling him, and the honest words in ch.2 of Abner who fights openly, is great.

The lines 26d, 27a and b form a series by each time referring to another subject by its own name. They display the three men by means of revealing predicates: David as not knowing and Abner as returning, whilst Joab is the only one who is busy with transitive action, viz. "taking him aside" – which differs by not more than one letter from "striking him down" which follows immediately. What David and Abner have in common is the fact that they do not foresee the attack. The "taking aside" is once more a play on words with 2:18sqq., since Asahel too refused to turn away (the same *nṭh*) in spite of the urgent advice of Abner. Now Abner turns away at Joab's request and has to pay for it with his life. The one dies due to a stupid refusal after honest advice, the other because of a somewhat naive compliance after a deceitful approach. The *baššęlī* which Joab professes in the gate I associate with the *bᵉšālōm* which David accorded Abner. That "welfare" of Abner which was allowed to close the previous unit and which became a refrain in 22d/23d was, however, substituted in 24e by Joab himself. And now he gnaws off a root consonant, as it were, with his *baššęlī*; this erosion is an iconic sign for the corrosive activity of Joab. In this way Joab has already been busy undermining Abner's welfare twice in his utterances, before resorting to bloodshed.

The end of the first half is marked by v.30, since this is commentary of the omniscient narrator and is no longer a link in the series of actions. He shapes v.27 into a long compound sentence, which alone manages to unite five personal names. The sudden mention of Abishai, whom we have not seen taking part but whose presence here is in continuation of 2:24, is already a hint at the right focalisation. The verse states that the brothers had murdered Abner, "because he had killed their brother Asahel in Gibeon, in battle". We hear their view here and, at the same time, their justification. The question is, however, whether or not the narrator actually subscribes to this himself. I find this difficult to believe because the legal implications would be enormous. Are the rules of blood revenge also applicable to cases of violence which occur during civil war? Joab and his family stick to their guns. But they persist in a point of view which has terrible consequences. Just imagine: during a civil war x times one hundred or y times one thousand men are killed in combat, and that means a vital loss for x times one hundred or y times one thousand families. If these families really were to have the right to implement the *talio* in a post-war situation in order to make good their loss, that would entail twice as many calamities in the vendetta's first round alone and it would place, in addition, such a burden on the recently-won peace, that fresh escalation to full-scale warfare could not be turned back.

This exceptionally callous stance, reminding me of the *qiṣāṣ* which made it very difficult for Mohammed to manage when civilising the bedouin tribes, the narrator reproduces at some length in v.30. But there is a sting in the tail, and the final word throws the whole question open legally. That Asahel has been killed in battle is of importance for Abner's good name. Abner can fully appeal to the fact that he took action in a situation of war, and one of a *force majeure* at that. His killing Asahel was a regular act of war which comes under the elementary, undisputed, legal section on self-defence. The war is past, in the first instance through the political opening which Abner himself created. The narrator has ascertained the war's being over, marking it with his threefold *b^{e}šālōm*. When Joab meets Abner with violence this is an action which can no longer be judged according to the rules of warfare but to those of ordinary criminal law in peacetime. It would have been an entirely different situation if Joab had succeeded, during wartime in ch.2, in getting Abner within shooting range, or within sword's reach. Had he killed Abner on the field of battle then that would have been once again a regular act of war and he would not even have needed the justification of Asahel's fate. But now he has killed in peacetime and the cunning way in which he has set up the situation does not help his legal position very much. Joab appeals to the rules of the *talio*, and it is possible that he himself finds this position tenable, but the narrator undermines this claim: the *talio* is not in force "in war". His word *bammilḥāmā* is characteristic of the mentality of Joab who, in peace-time, continues his little private war and is, in this final position, the counterpart of Abner's peace (the final word of the previous unit).

The second wave of the plot leads to the speech which is David's first reaction to the murder. The key word "behind" has now been shifted into the dimension of time and is expressly added to the action of 28a, which itself has no object and which continues the characteristic feature of 26d. "And afterward David heard [it]". The line emphasises how much David is overtaken by events and can do nothing more than react. The position of the time adjunct is striking.[48]

The death of Abner has so many aspects that the narrator gives David no less than five speeches in order to deal with it in the first instance. The first occurs in half I and is not so much about Abner as against Joab. David utters a medium length sentence which is enclosed by two very long sentences. Due to its length the first speech is opposite the final one.[49] This purely quantitative aspect will be confirmed by the content of the speeches.

David begins with a nominal clause about himself and his monarchy, and his first word is the predicate: "innocent". The first thing which enters his mind after the news is, therefore, personal complicity, which must be emphatically denied. His office is the criterion of his first thought, and his "I" is, as subject, extended and doubled by "my kingdom". Rhyme and alliteration bind the core (P + S) of the sentence together: *nāqī 'ānōkī umamlaktī*. Then a burden of three adjuncts follows. Two exceed the boundary of here and now at once and are terms which are fitting for an oath; they mention the deity and the dimension suitable to him, eternity. Only then does the murder appear in the sentence, under the aspect of the blood of Abner which cries out for revenge, who is officially provided with his patronymic (for the third and last time after 23c and 25a). A double *min* betrays a parry: David immediately dissociates himself as emphatically as possible from the outrage. No wonder; nothing could politically embarrass his career and his policy more than this particular murder of the other side's strong man who was organising such an

[48] We are well acquainted with the combination up front in a line, and with the function of beginning a sequence (II 21:18), a subscene, a story (II 8:1, 10:1) or an Act (II 21:18, 13:1 and 15:1), introduced by *wayhī*. But it is unusual in this final position in the sentence, just as it is in II 21:14c (where it even occurs at the very end of a unit!); another unusual usage occurs in I 24:6, see NAPS *ad loc.*

[49] The speech of vv.28-29 has 11 + 8 + 12 words in its three clauses, a total of 31 words, therefore. The speech of vv.38-39 has 9 + 5 + 6 + 5 words, making 25 words in all. By way of comparison, the *qina* for Abner has 16 words, as does the oath of v.35. And Joab's speech of vv.24sq. consists of 30 words.

amazing about-turn. The death of Abner is only going to complicate the transference of Israel.

David's second sentence manages to keep our attention fixed on the shed blood. If there is to be a question of a blood feud then it will not be because of the death of Asahel, which was a "normal" incident on the battlefield, but because of the death of Abner, which is crime in peacetime. And the jargon of the sentence "may it return (lit. "go round") to the head of Joab" shows that David is calling down a blood feud and wishing it upon his general; "and all his family" adds David, since Joab acted on the basis of a mentality which is characterised in terms of ties of kinship and blood relationships and which forms a serious hindrance to the development of business-like politics for a young state. After the positive sentence, v.29a, a very long and highly negative sentence follows, which begins with a true *prohibitivus* and develops into a long summing up of various calamities which David wishes on the sons of Zeruiah. His fury is so great that he makes up a special variant of *kareth*, of the premature death as punishment from God which goes with certain crimes.[50] Not an "extermination" (*krt* in the hiph'il) of the criminal, but may a never-ending stream of woe strike this family. David mentions five concrete examples: he begins in 29b with two serious physical disturbances which take up one word each, "someone suffering from a discharge or an eruption", and continues in 29c with a trio of construct state combinations: "a male who handles a spindle", an expression which indicates the oppression of forced labour,[51] "or one slain by the sword, or one lacking bread". With this series David covers the most important predicaments in war and peace. I also notice that the second word of the s^{e}mikut pairs is a segholate form each time, so that the series assonates beautifully. The rhythm of 29bc is regular, both lines have three phrases each of which consists of two words. What David has pronounced upon Joab is a grievous curse.

Half II, vv.31-39

The narrator creates much space for the spoken word, and there is little action now. There is one more narrative cluster for the state funeral of Abner in v.32, and that is all. The lines of vv.36-37 have no proper action any more. The speeches are the main consideration and their extent is already a hint that they are closely connected with one another and want to be understood as

[50] An example of the *kareth* situation is to be found in the oracle of doom against the Elides in I 2. For a discussion of this occurrence and the talmudic punishment of *kareth* see M. Tsevat, "Studies in the Book of Samuel", Part I, in HUCA 32 (1961), pp.191-216.

[51] I share the view of S.W. Holloway in this matter. See "Distaff, Crutch, or Chain Gang: the Curse on the House of Joab in 2 Samuel iii 29", VT 37 (1987) pp.370-375.

being so. They all originate with one man, David. If we count his first reaction of vv.28-29, we see a series of 4 + 2 + 3 + 2 + 4 lines which consist of the spoken word.[52] There is, besides, a great quantitative regularity throughout the entire length of vv.31-39; once again there are quartets, and there are three quintets:

– 4 lines in v.31	centre: speech
– 4 lines in v.32	
– 5 lines in vv.33-34	centre: speech
– 4 lines in v.35	2 wyqtl lines + speech
– 5 lines in vv.36-37	
– 5 lines in vv.38-39	quotation formula + speech

If we now pay attention to the difference between narrator's text and character's text in half II, then we get this picture of simple alternation:

speech of David: commands a ceremony of mourning
  narrator: report of the funeral
2 speeches of David: a dirge on Abner and David's oath to fast
  narrator: the people recognise David's integrity
speech of David: evaluation and retribution

The unity of the piece does not only lie in the words of David, but also in his sounding board: his audience is continually present, takes extensive part in the display of mourning and is referred to six times, in 32d-37a, as "all the people". Prior to this, and subsequent to it, we find significant variations. Those of v.37-38a are quickly recognised. When, in v.37, it is stated "And all the people, even all Israel, knew in that day that it was not from the king to put Abner the son of Ner to death", it is better to have "all Israel" refer to the future subjects whom Abner was busy acquiring for David, as the successor of the reference in vv.12d and 21b (both out of Abner's mouth).

[52] The ordering of the cola of the speeches in v.29 and 31 is not compulsory, and I take the sensible course of not wishing to attach too much importance to the symmetry of these numbers. Nevertheless I think dividing the enormous number of twenty-nine words into two lines is justified, and to this end I appeal to the rhythm of the three pairs of words thus arising. In v.31 we notice the two concrete attributes in the plural which, in 31b, are the direct object of actions which go together as plus and minus, whilst 31c reveals the sense of 31b, has a completely different object (the dead man himself) and construes it in a different way (now as indirect object via a preposition). My structural argument in defence of the symmetry is that of the speeches' content. What they bring up is itself a concentric figure, as we shall see.

Then "all the people" implies the people in Hebron who are Judah, *pars pro toto*.

In v.38a David speaks "to his servants". At the end the collective audience is somewhat reduced, I think, to the proportions of the court.[53] But whom do we meet at the beginning? That is less easy to determine. In v.31 David gives a command "to Joab and to all the people with him" to go into mourning. The question is, to whom does "with him" refer? In other words does the suffix of *'ittō* refer to the latter-mentioned Joab or to the subject of the sentence, David himself? Depending upon the answer "the people" in v.31 get different referents: the army or just the people, those who are present. To clinch the matter[54] I choose "Joab and all the troops (that were) with him."[55] A short while later, when Joab has disappeared off the set, the phrase *kol hā'ām* gradually and imperceptibly takes on the meaning "all the people": via v.32d and its echo 34d to 35a//36a//37a. The fact that the narrator mentions the soldiers as addressees, in v.31a, does not yet mean though, that those who are also present do not take part in the process of mourning.

My preference has consequences. David now shrewdly summons that collective, which has always faced Abner in the civil war and has just been a witness to its leader's atrocity, to lead the way in a ceremony of mourning, and to walk in front of the dead man.[56] In contrast he himself walks behind the bier in the funeral procession; a spatial opposition which shows just how much David and Joab differ in their relationship to Abner, and one which is psychologically welcome to David, because he would hardly have been able

[53] Elsewhere the context is able to lend another kind of meaning to "servants": "the servants of David" are, in v.22a and *passim*, his soldiers.

[54] I do not think it is necessary to acclaim (or to doll up) this place as a case of indeterminacy. I do have arguments at my disposal, of course, which determine my choice. They are as follows. If "the people with him" were to refer to the subjects and David, it would be more than rather odd to allow another named person (in this case Joab) to precede them. The expression "all the people with him" is not as suitable for David as the choice of words "his servants" which we meet in v.38 and *passim*. It does go well with Joab, and has a predecessor in the *'ašęr 'ittō* of v.23a. Then there are many places elsewhere where "the people who were with him [both *'immō* and *'ittō*]" refers to the army and follows on straightaway, in the text, from its leader: see, for instance, Josh.8:5, 10-11, Judg.4:13, 7:1, 9:34, 48, I Sam.14:20, II 6:2, 16:14, 17:2, 16, 22.

[55] Some translations remain just as ambiguous as the MT – or should I say: do not commit themselves? The referents remain unclear in KJ, SV, LV, Buber, NBG, NEB, KBS and McCarter, for example. The following translations opt for Joab as antecedent: JPS, NBE ("Joab y sus accompañantes), JB. Goslinga gives David as antecedent.

[56] Driver, p.251, gives the following exact comment about *lifnē 'abner* in v.31c: "i.e. *preceding* the bier in the funeral procession". In support of this I observe that this *lifnē* occurs opposite to the *'aḥărē* of David in 31d.

to stand being at the side of the man whom he has just denounced as a murderer, in the procession.

David's decision that the army itself must take part in mourning and must lead the procession, is one step in his policy of keeping on maintaining publicly that he is the ally of Abner and of totally dissociating himself from the murder of Abner. Partly through the army's taking part the last journey of Abner has become a state funeral. The narrator inserts an ironic detail, and that is that he specifically puts Joab in front, as the first addressee of David's command to display mourning. Giving his general this order is a modest satisfaction for David, but I imagine that Joab, who now has to take part, *pro forma*, in the game, because the state so desires, feels that he is the victor: 'I've still managed to lay that traitor down'. The order is well-formed: two assonating imperatives in the qal, rhythmic phrases of 2 + 2 and 3 words; first two *concreta* in opposition (clothes versus sackcloth, rend versus put on), then the sense of the gestures in 31c: mourning before the dead. The preposition is more than a spatial definition, it marks a relationship too: the mourners relate to Abner. David himself is also officially present: v.31d is the only place in this chapter which unites the name "David" and the epithet "the king".[57] The way in which "king David" moves forward behind the bier is effectively painted by a participle giving duration and a circumstantial clause. David shows respect, the narrator has introduced an element of irony. The preposition *'aḥărē* is present, as a reminder of all that hunting after Abner which is now complete.

Verse 32 consists of the final links in the action and consists of four simple wyqtl-sentences which decrease from 10 via 9 and 7 to six syllables. Two sentences with a plural subject enclose the voice and lamenting of "the king", that is to say David in his official capacity. The word for bury, *qbr*, turns out to alliterate highly with the names "Abner" and "Hebron", so that their meanings are closely tied up with each other; 32c links "grave" anew with the name of the dead man. He is honoured with a state funeral and has not been given his last resting place in the family grave, somewhere in Benjamin therefore, but at the exact spot to which all his political influence had gravitated, the capital of David. The symbolism of *bitrōn* is replaced by unity with the crown of *ḥębrōn*. After "they" have buried, our gaze falls on one person, David himself, whose lamenting and weeping gets two lines, after which "all the people" follow his example in 32d. This alternation of

[57] In vv.8e, 10b, 12a, 14a, 18c, 19b, 20a, 21ae, 22ac, 26ad, 28a, 31a, 35a, only the name David occurs, in vv.21b, 23c, 24a, 31d, 32b, 33a, 36c, 37b, 38a, on the other hand, only the reference "the king" occurs. The two make contact in v.17b.

king and people is continued, since 33a-34c bring the king's dirge, after which "the people continued to weep over him". This line, viz. 34d, parallels 32d.

The *wayyeleķ hālōk* with which Joab had replaced Abner's "departure in peace" was anticipatory of the murder and now leads to the weeping of all, bkh, during which David follows the bier. The intense grief into which Abner's command plunged Paltiel, is, in retrospect the harbinger of the mourning for Abner himself:

v.16a *wayyeleķ hālōk ubākō*

v.24e *wayyeleķ hālōk*	31d/32cd ... *hammeļeķ* ... *hōlek* *wayyebk* ... *wayyibkū*

The king now bestows a special honour on Abner by composing a dirge for him and performing it personally. With this the general posthumously approaches his former lord: Saul too had received a dirge from David. The *qina* of 33b-34c has a striking structure, especially regarding the cola and their arrangement. Two monocola enclose a complete line of poetry (34ab) which also has two cola, but then in the form of a bicolon.[58] I note the scheme of the structure and put down a number of characteristic features next to it:

v.33b = A simile, question, repetition of intransitive verb[59]
v.34ab =B/B' two passive clauses on limbs, with negation
v.34c = A' simile, answer, repetition of intransitive verb

The poet alliterates a lot and chooses for this purpose exactly that word as motor which is the focus of his amazement at the murder, the word *nābāl*. Not only does this word alliterate immediately in 33b with the name of Abner, but returns in A', inasmuch as all its consonants can be found in the semantic counterpart thereof, *b^enē ʿawlā*. And then the consonants (with a slight alteration, i.e. the voiced labial becomes voiceless) take up all the remaining positions of 34c: n-p-l is mirrored by l-p-n and duplicated at the end, n-p-l.

[58] In Masoretic Hebrew the number of syllables in the poem, which consists of a single strophe, is striking: 9 + 20 + 11, i.e. the middle has just as many syllables as the monocola. The premasoretic Hebrew count hardly differs at all.

[59] To be specific: the root *mwt* occurs twice; firstly as a substantive in the construct state, secondly as a modal imperfect. Notice that in the closing monocolon a construct infinitive corresponds to the finite form *nflt*.

The structure of the opening line is aba'b'. This alternation of the monosyllable for dying and the substantives creates a parallelism which commences with the great similarity between the elements a and a' and, through this, makes for the suggestion that elements b and b' are to cover each other to a large extent. These are the name Abner and the substantive *nābāl*, "negative element"! But surely this is a grave insult to the deceased? Yes indeed, and this equation is exactly the impression of Abner (according to the poet) which Joab wanted to have take root, and which David wants to contest with all his might. The verb is loaded emotionally as it has a powerful modal aspect: "did Abner *have* to die the death of a villain?"

This question is the beginning of a strategy which is characteristic of the entire strophe and is rhetorical in the strict sense of the word, since the rules obey the aim to convince. Their content is a persuasive argument, in three steps, which is as follows: a shameful question is posed in v.33b, the drift of which is concretely refuted twice by "proof" in 34ab, after which the answer is given in 34c which, at the same time, forms the conclusion and contains a surprising about-turn. The "destructive element" qualification does not fit the dead man, but his murderers! David has suddenly inverted the point of the disqualification in the closing line. Even though that verse is the counterpart of 33b the structure is put together in another way; it is the short series cdc, and this order especially draws our attention to its centre. The elements c ... c are the same verb, "fall", which is the modest synonym of "die" in the opening line. Between them both are the "treacherous men" who are the point of the end. Suddenly a plural *b^{e}nē ʿawlā* functions as the opposite pole of the singular *nābāl* at the beginning. With this plural David makes a sharp attack on Joab and Abishai without mentioning them by name, but all the more effectively; on the brothers, who therefore together (and as representatives of the family taking its revenge) in v.30 were pointed out as the murderers of Abner by the narrator himself. The negative quality which they saw in Abner is true of themselves.

"Should Abner have died the death of a churl?" The hard facts of life are that Abner has met with such an end, but this rhetorical question, which presupposes the answer 'no', expresses that the poet is resisting the facts. After this line in the third person he switches to the second person and directs himself, in the remaining cola, to Abner personally. In 34ab the poet builds up his case with two pieces of evidence pointing to Abner's innocence. There are two pairs of limbs, "your hands and your feet", a simple and elementary word pair. The simple "bound" is filled out to, and varied by, "put into bronze [fetters]" and both get the negative.[60] The passive forms continue the a-u vowels of the crucial *yāmūt*. The denial contained in this bicolon I take to be an example of litotes: the non-chained condition of Abner is the discreet expression of his innocence. This is the only place in the poem which gives a positive picture of Abner, but only via implication. The limbs are metonymic for the person and are an example of the concrete in the service of the abstract, viz. the proposition that Abner is innocent. The chained body is a visualisation of the impotence of the criminal once he has been caught. He who was strong once must now, whether he wants to or not, surrender himself to what others are about to do with him, and it is this very kind of surrender which is so ignominious for such a free, and a strong (in the positive sense of the word) man as Abner. In other words, the central line of the poem also gives a compelling picture of the *fait accompli* which is forced on Abner. It is as if the poet himself feels chained by the hard facts. He tries, for a moment, to free himself, in words, from the compulsive and irrevocable quality of this death, with a simple negative. But the paradoxical effect is that Abner becomes only more intensely the object, indeed the victim, of the criminal action of others.

It is also necessary for a good understanding of the poem to be aware of everything which is missing. We do not hear the name of the murderer, and even less the details of the murder: no sword, no belly, or description of the location. The military fame and past of Abner do not join in. Political and religious aspects are also absent. The dirge regards the present as it has been determined by an act of violence, and the scale of values of the song is chiefly moral and legal. The focus of amazement is indicated already by the dominant alliteration, and is the criminal and the treacherous, by which the speaker is taken by surprise. His argument or strategy of persuasion finally consists of a radical about-turn: the immoral and the criminal do not stick to the victim – Abner must in no way be considered to be defiled by the enormity – but to the perpetrators. Having arrived at this point we see that

[60] Colon A in 34ab has seven syllables only, colon B is amplified to thirteen syllables. The amplification is slight in the difference between *yādẹ̄kā* and *raglẹ̄kā*, and especially lies in the change of predicate. The single word and passive part. *'ăsūrōt* (three syllables) gets six to seven syllables as a counterpart in *linḥuštayim huggāšū*. The choice of a perfect avoids the occurrence of rhyme. The interesting dual of the word "copper, bronze" with its meaning "chains" occurs six times in the OT, each time together with, and parallel to, "bind", *'sr*: it is also to be found in Judg.16:21, II Ki.25:7, Jer.39:7, II Chr.33:11 and 36:6, and each time it concerns the leader of Israel who, after waging war, is blinded and carried off in chains: Samson, Manasseh, Zedekiah, Jehoiakim.

this rhetoric, by being endowed with such a point, is the sequel to as well as a metonymy of David's first speech, the cursing of Joab. The proclamation of Abner's moral purity is also part of David's dissociating himself from Joab and contributes to the argument for his own innocence.

The lamentation of the people (v.32d) continues in v.34d. The parallelism of these lines integrates the dirge into the whole of the rites of mourning. The narrator completes the action by shedding light on one detail which concerns David personally and once again leads to a speech of his. The people regard the song for Abner also as a sign of David's personal involvement and bring him the bread of comfort. Such food and a similar gesture are also stated in 12:16-17, as David engages in proleptic mourning for his first child – by Bathsheba – who is about to die. Just as he refuses to accept the bread of comfort there and continues to fast, he does the same here too. This time, however, the narrator gives him the opportunity to speak and he even swears an oath on it. According to the form of the introductory line (35c) it is the formula of a curse on himself – the same with which Abner previously assured Ishbosheth that he would go over to the other side in accordance with God's oath (*šbʿ*). "Before the sun goes down", David assures his subjects, "I shall taste no bread or any other thing!" This abstinence is much more fitting than the tormented and fanatic Saul's forbidding his troops to eat (in I 14) at the beginning of a day of pursuit. So David commits himself to fasting. This is his personal contribution to the rites of mourning, which is the complement of the order to engage in the gestures of mourning which he had given to the army. David's speech to the collective and that on his own personal gesture are grouped around the song. The temporal adjunct, "the going down of the sun", forms a link with the day of warfare in ch.2 and attains, through this, a symbolical effect. The sun went down in 2:24 whilst Joab and his brother where still engaged in their pursuit of Abner.[61] The fall of darkness saved Abner physically that time, however, only temporarily. The sunset in ch.3 marks the completion of his decline. Joab has caught his prey and Abner's darkness is final.

In the actantial model the *destinataire* is often the receiver of the object. Sometimes, however, he is the party who judges the hero and his quest by

[61] The positive side of Abner, which is so difficult to demonstrate in the text, is, nevertheless, chiefly to be found on the level of communication; in the fact that a dirge is sung for, and about, him. David does this only for those who earn it.

giving or withholding his recognition.[62] Since v.31 David has been the subject of the quest which attempts to handle the murder of Abner. In the corresponding actantial model this time "all the people" is the receiver in the presence of whom David makes an appearance, leads the funeral and laments and fasts himself. The people has already been the sounding board of four speeches of David. In vv.36-37 the people gets the chance to play an evaluating role, and that is why these five lines are not so much a part of the action as a reflection on it. At the beginning of v.36 we can still see the people reacting to the personal action of the oath (David's decision to keep on fasting), but the narrator adroitly directs his report of incidental assent via 36c and the particle "as" to general assent, after which v.37 relates to the entire day of national catastrophe. In 36ab we find a parallelism of frank recognition, which is so great that even the object is omitted in 36a and the verb is used as an absolute. This popular assent joins in a much broader picture of the sanctioning of his policy, 36c. There is no exception to this, in view of threefold *kol*. The verse begins and ends with *all* the people; their presence and the judgement "good" flank "*everything* which the king undertook".[63] Looking back at the previous story makes us realise that the tribes of the northern kingdom have received a comparable part in the assent concerning Abner and his quest (to bring Israel under David); the text also states the term "everything which was good in the eyes of ..." twice. This was followed by the feast (the *mištę*) at which the trailblazer Abner was entertained in Hebron and which causes the host David to appear as an evaluating *destinataire* of Abner's political work. In v.35 the opposite extreme to that "drinking" occurs as the reception: now David is to abstain from bread in order to proclaim his final agreement to Abner.

Verse 37 continues with a double *kol* and no longer concerns one gesture of mourning, but the cardinal political fact of Abner's end. The recognition

[62] Examples of the reception which the hero receives from the *destinataire*: at the end of I 14 (prior to the list) the people recognise and defend Jonathan as the charismatic hero of the day; at the beginning of I 18 Saul recognises David, with a bare minimum of words, as victor against Goliath, whilst Jonathan does it from the bottom of his heart; in I 25 David recognises that Abigail, in her central speech, is right a) in so many words, and b) by marrying her: and in II 1:1-16 David's appreciation of the messenger turns out to be negative (and is a legal judgement), whilst he concludes by quoting the Amalekite himself.

[63] This concentric phenomenon can also be described in terms of two chiasmuses: "all the people" and "their eyes" at the beginning, and "the eyes of all the people" at the end, of v.36; and *wayyīṭab b*^{e}*'ēnēhęm* is mirrored in *b*^{e}*'ēnē ... ṭōb*. For the syntax see Appendix I. Just a mention of the people who are, as *destinataire*, in the position of being able to reciprocate approval and acceptance: we have had a good parallel of 3:36 in I 18:16, which is also at the end of a unit, also compare v.30 there.

which David harvests here implies that all consider him free from the slightest complicity in the act of violence. The denied *hemīt* of v.37b occurs exculpatingly over against the truth of v.30a, the *hārᵉgū* with which the narrator has established the responsibility of the sons of Zeruiah.[64] With this David has reached his goal which the first word of his first speech, *nāqī*, already gave away. His curse, the dirge and his abstinence have worked in a convincing way. This recognition (*ydʿ*) from everyone occurs in a healing and reassuring fashion over against the false and split quality of knowing in vv.25-26. The alternation of narrator's text with that of characters, which I have noted above already for vv.31-36, can also be formulated in actantial terms and is covered by the relation between David as hero and the people as receiver:

the subject, the king, speaks: command to mourn
 the people obeys, report of display of mourning
the subject, the king, speaks: dirge on/to Abner
 the people empathises, tears and bread of comfort report
the subject, the king, speaks: oath on his own fasting
 the people sanctions this, report on general agreement

After this David has the opportunity of speaking once more, vv.38-39.

The sunset which occurred as a temporal adjunct in the oath is the counterpart of "on that same day" of the people in v.35a. Three more temporal adjuncts follow v.37a which all have the same day as referent. Just like the judgement of the people they give away the fact that the unit is drawing to a close. In v.37a we sense the distance of the omniscient narrator in "on that day" and his survey of the subject matter also sounds in the inclusive nature of the entities "*all* the people" and "*all* Israel". Out of the mouth of David, who speaks just once more, proceeds the adjunct "on this day" (*hayyōm hazzę̄*, 38b) and finally, "today" (*hayyōm*, 39a).

In his closing speech David has assigned himself the task of evaluation. He attempts, in order to bring the crisis to a close, to define as correctly as possible the significance of "this day" and in the process arrives at a value judgement three times. A primary characteristic of this drawing to a close is that he pays attention to all three main characters and provides each one with a qualification in one sentence. Abner is first in v.38b, then David provides a thumbnail description of himself (39a) and "the sons of Zeruiah" (39b) in a nominal line, after which he devotes the closing verbal sentence to a desire for

[64] I glance for a moment at the verbs for 'kill' in v.30ab. In view of the fact that the meaning of a word is not a metaphysical or other pre-determined entity, but comes into being as a node in a relational network, I assume that the difference between **hrg* in 30a and *hmyt* in 30b is relevant. Does it not invest the *hārᵉgū* of Joab and Abishai with the connotation of murder?

retribution on the deity's part. So he ends with the person to whom he had addressed his declaration of innocence in his first sentence, v. 28c.

David has sought out a new addressee. Now that the official and mass ceremony is over, he addresses himself to a smaller circle, the court, with reflections which already reveal a certain distance from, and an initial coping with, the shock. He introduces the clauses with "do you not know?", formally a brief rhetorical question with the nuance: "you must become fully aware of". This form of *ydʿ* links up with the constructive knowing of v.37a, and the narrator now has David add conclusive elements.[65]

The line on Abner puts two words of esteem in front. The verb *nāfal* comes right from the alliterating heart of the dirge and forms a link with the song. David connects the loss of Abner with the whole country: "a ruler, a great man has fallen in Israel". At the last moment we learn, for the first time, of his positive qualities; they occur in opposition to the disqualification of the two brothers in 34c, which was enclosed by a double *nfl.* Verse 39a forms on the paradigmatic axis an antithesis, a pair therefore, with 39b by virtue of the opposition soft/hard. But on the syntagmatic axis the repetition of "today" brings with it a connection with 38b first of all. The lines 38b and 39a contain a scheme abc-c'b'a' which puts into order the words *śar wᵉgādōl ... hayyōm* and *hayyōm rak umāšūᵃḥ mẹlẹk* and relates them to one another in a surprising parallelism between general and king. The correspondence a-a' is evidence of the fact that David recognises and praises more than generalship in Abner himself.[66] Strengthened by the recognition of his greatness, the title *śar* says here, as counterpart of the word "king", that Abner has developed into a statesman. The b-b' pair now places next to Abner's greatness the "tender, mild" quality of David's side, and this final word is, in itself, extremely remarkable. Has a contrast been included in this synonymy-suggesting scheme abc-c'b'a'? What does David want to say about himself here? This is not immediately clear. And, reading sequentially, we are put on the wrong track besides, by the narrator for a moment. The *wᵉ* of *śar wᵉgādōl*

[65] It is not strictly necessary, but it is in fact quite possible to construe the syntax of 38b-39b in such a way that this *hălō tedᵉʿū* not only governs the nominal clause on Abner, but the two which follow also, viz. 39ab; doing a kind of double duty in prose. The patterns in the three lines which I describe above are, in any case, an argument for regarding the nominal clauses as of equal value, and as being attuned to each other. As far as the connection between 37a and 38b is concerned I notice, in addition, that the conjunction and negative undergo an interesting shift: first "all the people recognise (...) *kī lō*" and then David says: "*hălō tedᵉʿū kī ...*". First the negative is kept away from David, then the positive is ascribed to Abner.

[66] The word *śar* is mostly rendered properly (KJ, BJ, Hertzberg, Goslinga, and four Dutch translations: SV, LV, NBG, KBS) but the renderings of Buber, NEB, NBE, JPS, and McCarter fall short (commander ed.).

can be rendered in three acceptable ways, but in no case with an adversative meaning.[67] Through this we certainly do not initially get the idea, that the copula between *rak* and *māšūaḥ mẹlẹk* perhaps must be understood as being adversative.

Continuing on the sequential or syntagmatic axis, we get assistance in correctly defining the surprising *rak*. The opposition soft/hard, which arises between 39a and b and with which David marks himself off from Joab and his family, points the way to a solution in which *we* is still adversative. "I am weak at present, however, even though anointed king, and these men, the sons of Zeruiah, are too hard for me." It has been as recent a development as "yesterday or the day before yesterday" that Abner made his political about-turn which now causes him to bear the hallmark of statesmanship in the eyes of David; but shortly before he would have fitted exactly into the category of the hard military. Through this David stands rather alone, if not naked, between the great man of v.38b and the tough guys of 39b. The latter are too much for him, their cruelty has caught him off guard and confronted him with his own softness – are his own words. David has not yet become thick-skinned, and I remember that neither is he well-armoured later when (he is under the impression for a few hours that) his sons have been killed (ch.13) or, in ch.18-19, when he resists the political insight (which Joab has!) that a new pardon for the arch rebel Absalom is no longer a viable proposition, and abandons himself to paternal feelings. The dismay and bewilderment which Abner's assassination has stirred up in David bring him into contact with his own vulnerability. They make him conscious, so I imagine, of the fact that for him there is no way back out of the hard reality of war and politics; they give him the shivers at the idea that he too might one day be the target of a merciless attempt of which he is unaware, due to a certain amount of naivety which has just (v.26d!) played tricks on him. David's makeup does not involve his taking into account, at every moment, the worst that could happen. He now expresses the gap between his inner world, feelings of vulnerability and the very beginning of his divinely-willed kingship on the one hand and the harsh demands of politics and military matters, the calculations, the always being on the alert, on the other. The innocence of the individual disappears into this gap. I now speak of innocence because 39a is the counterpart of another 'I line', 28c; *nāqī 'ānōkī umamlaktī* was what was stated there, what is stated here is *'ānōkī ... rak ... mẹlẹk*.

[67] *We* can be regarded as a *waw explicativum* (as do the BJ and the JPS; and also the NBE: "un gran general"), or as a simple conjunction "and" (KJ and Buber); but it is also possible to read it as a climax: "a ruler, indeed a great one" – as does the LV.

With the disdainful appellation "these men" David once again dissociates himself from Joab and his family, v.39c.[68] Because he does not feel he can cope with them, he is forced to fall back on divine retribution for their behaviour. Concerning this he adds the asyndetic closing line. Here he does not mention their name any more, but wishes, in general terms, that "the doer of evil" shall receive divine punishment "according to his wickedness". This sentence and his first (28c) are the only lines in which the personal name of God occurs. No wonder, since there is clearly a connection between the first and the final ones of David's five speeches. Reading back from v.39c we gather that the catastrophes which David's curse calls down on the house of Joab can only be effectuated by God and are just as many applications of the desired retribution. The verb is well-chosen: *šallem*. It takes its place in regard to "war and peace", the words which enclose both the previous story (vv.6-21) and the first half (vv.22-30). The war appeared to be over and Abner left in peace; but both data are undermined and provided with a corrupting comment by Joab who has harshly violated peacetime with a personal act of war. Equilibrium can only return through retribution, through the *šallem* of God.

We have a survey of the closing speech and are now able to establish what its structure is. Subsequent to one sentence containing the recognition of Abner the lines 39abc follow, which become a trio thanks to a simple kind of logic: I am now vulnerable and I am not able to cope with these hard soldiers, let God punish them therefore. Looked at in this way the antithetical and nominal pair, 39ab, is information which prepares the closing sentence on retribution. The anti-Joab aspect is, therefore, dominant in this speech.[69] This brings us back once again to vv.28-29, the retribution of which David himself has already filled in with an extensive curse on Joab, and it contributes to discovering the structure of all David's speeches. I see a concentric pattern in the five speeches which compete with each other through the force of their emotive function. Cursing, swearing, commanding – the volitional aspect in each speech act is prominent, and the poetical function is heightened yet more in the middle because the speaker switches to poetry:

[68] I recall how David dissociates himself from this collective, when Abishai twice wants to use the sword against Shimei in chs.16 and 19. David retorts both times: "What business is it of mine and yours, sons of Zeruiah?" (in the BJ rendering 16:10b = 19:23b).

[69] McCarter is someone who destroys David's argument, and the double framework of war and peace at the same time, by simply deleting 39c.

A	curse on Joab	(4 lines)
B	command to mourn (all the people)	(2 lines)
X	*qīnā* of David to Abner personally	(4 cola)
B’	oath on fasting in mourning (David alone)	(2 lines)
A’	evaluation, retribution for Joab’s deed	(4 lines)

The centre is connected to the borders insofar as the point of the poem (the incrimination of *b^{e}nē ‘awlā*) has turned out to be a hidden attack on the sons of Zeruiah. These elements X and A-A’ can readily be distinguished from the rest thanks to the fact that the language in B-B’ stands out. The speeches under the label B are practical in nature and concerned with the rituals of mourning here and now, whilst the other speeches transcend the horizon of “today”. The David-Joab controversy is the framework within which David’s reactions to Abner’s *passio* are to be found. It is so intense that the dirge is encroached upon as a result. David could have decided, after all, to fill the qina with positive qualities of the deceased or with famous recollections from his career. This he has postponed, however, and limited to v.38, whilst the song is inspired by his own bewilderment and polemics.

The controversy between David and Joab, after this, is to be temporarily hidden from view, but is going to sweep on like a forest fire and, in its own time, is to flare up during the climax of the Absalom affair into a veritable feud, with which David is not yet finished on his deathbed. Here in the diptych of ch.3, in the meantime, a gruesome kind of parallelism has been created between the one king and his general in the Transjordan, and the other king and his general in Judah. The soldiers make history and bear the action: Abner defects and Joab murders. The kings can only conform to each *fait accompli*, at which the one is more petrified by shock than the other. Who is really the strong man? In a political reading we establish the fact that David is either not able, or not prepared, to correct Joab effectively. The venomous speech of his general in vv.24-25 should have already rung a bell in David’s mind, but he chose to listen to this slander and was insufficiently alert whilst doing so. David utters the gravest words possible for the dirty capital offence, but in actual fact he takes no action. This suspicious incongruity in word and deed has a serious backlash on the moral stature of David himself.

Chapter IV

One man's breath is another man's death

§ 1. *The fate of the house of Saul, II Sam.4*

The fourth chapter of II Samuel consists of two sequences, the assassination of Ishbosheth in vv.5-7, and David's reception of the perpetrators of the crime in vv.8-12. Everything prior to this is preparatory and informative. We recognise the division of the quest into two parts from the previous passage, in which David had to cope with another murder. The problem functioning as the background to the plot occurs at the beginning. Verse 1 reports on the panic in the northern kingdom. After this a new agent is introduced in v.2abc. It consists of the two brothers from Beeroth who serve in the army of Ishbosheth and who become the "hero" of the story. But before they get underway, thus setting the action in motion, two digressions are included in the text, one of three lines on the original inhabitants of Beeroth and one of seven lines on Jonathan's crippled son. This fragment on the handicapped Mephibosheth appears initially to have been given the wrong place, and we might be tempted to think that it would have been better if it had been included at the beginning of ch.9, to facilitate getting to know Mephibosheth better when he appears for the first time as a character. Nevertheless it is still possible to integrate this small paragraph into ch.4. This avenue is opened up when we manage, once again, to make a clear distinction between subject matter and theme. The chapter's subject matter is the death of Ishbosheth. The theme can emerge only after patient listening on our part, and should be unfolded by means of sound analysis.

Once again the narrator draws our attention to the other side. In v.1a and 2a Ishbosheth, still formally monarch of the northern kingdom, must undergo a certain amount of suppression again. His name is omitted and he is merely designated as "the son of Saul". Is this perhaps an early thematic hint? Upon learning of what has befallen Abner "his hands become feeble". Chapter 3:11 reported his fright after he was harangued by his general. This fear is now being exhibited through body language. Strictly speaking the said expression is metonymic, and we shall come to see that it has a special sense. An inversion inserts another subject in v.1c, but realises, at the same time, the northern kingdom's very close syntactic connection with the king's shocked reaction: "all Israel [still in the narrow sense of the word] was aghast." Of course the tribes are appalled. No sooner have they been convinced, by Abner himself, that it would be better for them to give up the Saulide project and unite with Judah under David, when their strong man gets treacherously murdered in the shadow of David's throne! This is bound to result in great confusion and shock; automatically a very threatening state of affairs for groups which have just embarked upon a spine-chilling transitional phase in which they are virtually stateless. Their national leader trembles, they can expect nothing from him. And the *de facto* leader, as has been stated in v.1a, is "dead in Hebron". This is not only the briefest of formulas for the most important event of the previous unit, it is also a crass understatement. And it is not going to be the only one in this story.

The opening verse has thus described the point of departure of ch.4 and posed the problem to which the plot will relate. No matter how summary, a complete picture is given, since three characters have been mentioned: the king, the general and his subjects. Their condition (death, fear, horror) makes for a sombre mood and arouses expectations in the reader: is this throne going to be rescued, or are everyone's premonitions of doom going to be abundantly confirmed by political developments? Will the two sturdy fellows, who are about to be introduced in v.2, perhaps be able to yet achieve something good for their lord? The narrator keeps us in suspense about this, since the two digressions which are next after the introduction of Rechab and Baanah ensure that the answer to this is postponed for a long time.

The first thing we are told about the two men is their function, the second the side they are on. They are "platoon commanders"; this designation is ambiguous due to the occasionally possible negative connotation of the word *g^edūdīm*, so that the gentlemen might just as well be "gang leaders". Might the going on raids associated with this word – compare 3:22 a moment ago – signify something of the mentality of Rechab and Baanah? At the moment there is nothing wrong with these two sergeants (as I will be calling them from now on). The same line, v.2a, establishes their duty to Ishbosheth as military personnel, before 2b divulges their names as Baanah and Rechab (in that order) correctly adding their patronymic and the name of their city of origin. Are these two men Canaanites perhaps, as were the original inhabitants of Beeroth according to the digression of v.3? No, v.2c prevents misunderstanding by stating that Baanah and Rechab are Benjaminites. "Aha", thinks the reader, "these officers are from the same tribe as Saul and Ishbosheth, they are bound to their master by ties of kinship".

The purpose of the two digressions I would like to discuss later. At this stage I monitor the thread of the plot which starts with the movement of v.5a. The first sequence is framed and delineated by the departure of the two Beerothites: in 5a they are on the way (*wylkw*) to the house of Ishbosheth, in 7f they leave it (*wylkw* once again). Within this ring one more verb of movement occurs twice, with the soldiers as subject: *wayyābō’ū* of v.5b and 7a. First the verb has the nuance of arriving, later that of entering the house of Ishbosheth. This form of consecution and of becoming specific can be seen from the way in which the destination is described each time: in 5b in full "to the house of Ishbosheth", in v.7 as briefly as possible, even without a morpheme of direction, "the house". Since the act of entering is not mentioned until v.7a, this line is not a flashback in regard to 5b, but a sequel; in addition it is the threshold for the denouement of the sequence, that is to say to the murder. The verse in between the double going and coming to, verse 6, is highly problematical. I approach it cautiously by first looking at vv.5 and 7 in more detail. Only after we have described how closely these two verses are attuned to one another, are we able to answer the question as to what we can, or want to, do with v.6.

The subject matter of v.5a manifests a double chiasmus in relation to v.2b.[1] This stylistic device and the quite extensive repetition of the four names themselves are a strong indication that the verse picks up the thread after the introduction of the agents. In other words: the double reversal of the order of appearance appears to presuppose the existence of the digression(s) and is then a warning not to label vv.3-4 as a later interpolation, so rendering it harmless. The lines of 5bc turn out to be an exact counterpart of the duo 7ab when we pay careful attention to the designations of space and time:

5b They came in the heat of the day to the house of Ishbosheth,
c whilst he was taking his afternoon sleep
(*w*^{e}*hū šōkeb ’ęt miškab haṣṣoh*^{o}*rayim*)
7a They entered the house,
whilst he was resting on his bed in his sleeping quarters
(*w*^{e}*hū šōkeb ‘al miṭṭātō baḥ*^{a}*dar miškābō*)

[1] First of all the word order of the names Baanah and Rechab is inverted in v.5, secondly these personal names occur after the references to family and city instead of preceding them.

At first glance the extent of the repetition is so great, that we see mainly similarity. And the circumstantial clauses 5c and 7b are so neatly parallel, that we might be led to believe that one *miškab* means the same as the other. But this is not the case. What counts now are the contrasts as they stand out against the background of similarities. In v.5 the arrival is especially linked to the time factor, which is represented by two word pairs in *s^{e}mikut*. On the other hand, in v.7, the action of entering is linked to the factor of space, which in the circumstantial clause is stated by two words twice.[2] In v.5c the meaning of the rhythmic word pair *k^{e}ḥom hayyōm* covers that of the datum "noon", so that the temporal data support one another.[3] The word *miškab* means neither the time nor the place of resting, but the 'act' of resting itself: Ishbosheth is taking a siesta because of the heat. In v.7b the word perhaps means, in itself, the same thing but functions as an adjunct of place because it is syntactically connected to "room". As the camera zooms in we see in the bedroom the bed on which the king is resting. We slowly become uneasy about the reason for so much attention to detail.

The subtle play of repetition and consecutiveness is now catastrophically disturbed if we leave the corrupt sixth verse as it is. I will soon be mentioning my insurmountable objections to this verse, but I would first like to monitor, for a moment, the completion of the plot. The complementary nature of the two lines, which occur twice and bring the two sergeants to their lord, is continued with two pairs of verbs in 7cde. The first two (together in 7c) have no syntactical complements whatsoever, so that the action is greatly accelerated precisely at its peak. Two hiph'il forms stand for the violence of the two men here, and both have "him" as direct object, in the form of a suffix, so that they rhyme. The following two verbs are also intransitive (in 7d there is a hiph'il once again) and their object is a substantive: "his head", the identical rhyme which makes 7de into a pair, is what remains of Ishbosheth in what follows, a horrifying *pars pro toto*. The sons of Rimmon have chopped it off and taken it with them to enhance the success of their next meeting, in Hebron. Immediately afterwards the movement of departure follows. The

2 The difference in nuance between arrival and entry works towards this. Entry is, by definition, a spatially-orientated movement, arrival is less so. The mention of the house of Ishbosheth in v.5b does not detract from space and time's being complementary, since it is the inescapable initial orientation of the reader after the digressions, and the name of the owner attracts more attention than the house as spatial reference. In 7a, on the other hand, nothing is added to the house: the spatial picture gets filled in now.

3 The word "noon" has another function, i.e. as a contrast to "the night" of v.7f, and as such contributes to the frame of the paragraph formed by the arrival and departure.

final line states, through the repetition of *wayyel^e kū*, that they are "simply" able to leave the building; there is no sign of haste which shows just how easily for the gentlemen the whole attack has run its course.

I would now like to approach the weaknesses of v.6, beginning at the end. The word *nimlāṭū* can only contribute to an attempt to save the verse so long as S.R. Driver's proposal to take the verb to mean "they slipped in" is uncritically accepted. The root *mlṭ* is, however, semantically speaking one of the most unequivocal forms in classical Hebrew and can mean only one thing, viz. "escape".[4] That is why verse 6c can only refer to the departure of Rechab and Baanah. Consequently the whole of verse 6 must be described and recognised as a coherent system in itself, a sequence which is very succinct but rounded off in itself: in 6a is the entry of the murderers, in 6b the murder, and in 6c the unimpeded departure. Well then, what can be said of all three parts is that they are intolerable, or much too redundant duplications which add virtually no information, and do a lot of damage, to the report enclosing v.6.

There are difficulties right from the start, viz. with the first word *hnh*, which can only be rescued by the revocalisation *hinnē*. In the Masoretic vocalisation it is *hénnā*, which means either the spatial reference "hither", or the feminine personal pronoun in the plural and is therefore unusable. In an amazing lapse the Comité Textuelle translates it, poker-faced, as referring to the subject, as part of an attempt to uphold the MT: "Et eux étaient arrivés [a masculine form twice! J.F.] jusqu'au milieu de la maison, en gens qui viennent prendre" etc.

Subsequently we hear: "they came to the middle of the house." Maintaining that piece of information in v.6 alters the quality of v.7a, which becomes a flashback with respect to 6a, and undermines the consecutive link between 5b and 7a. Moreover it disturbs the elegance with which 5bc and 7ab are attuned to one another, especially by making it more or less superfluous. Verse 6b continues with "they struck him in the belly" and is, of course, inspired by the blow to the belly of Asahel (2:23) and that to Abner's (3:27). But these two thrusts point to each other in the symmetry of the *talio* and have no need of a third. The same is true of the pair in 3:27 and 20:10 (Joab eliminates a rival). The datum "belly" mars the concentration on "his head" which is quite authentic in this chapter (see v.12 also). This is why I rate v.6b as an all too facile and insipid copy. The closing line is a non-functional prolepsis of the departure and employs a verb meaning "to escape", suggesting danger, and for this reason is incongruous. The mention of the names of both the murderers in v.6c is also suspect. It would be suitable to a closing line which brings a sequence to an end, or at a place where it is essential for the indication of a change of subject, but now that v.7 once again fixes our attention on the murder, the supplying of names half way through the completion is distracting and non-functional.

The only datum which provides really new information regarding the picture which we get from vv.5 + 7 is that of the "gathering of wheat", a participle

[4] For further details and justification see Appendix I.

in Hebrew. It is also striking as a *concretum* which an annotator would not invent so easily. It also occurs in the Greek text of v.6, which I have noted in Appendix I. The LXX has here: "And, behold the porter of the house had winnowed wheat; she had fallen asleep and was dozing, and the brothers, Rechab and Baanah, sneaked inside." This text is often followed,[5] instead of the MT, on the grounds of the consideration that "le *G est beaucoup plus satisfaisant que le *M, parce qu'il nous offre en une scène pittoresque exactement ce qu'il faut pour faire avancer la narration."[6]

I will not be undertaking an attempt to trace the Greek text back to, or employ textual criticism to link it with, the Hebrew original.[7] But I do consider defending the matter of the porter worthwhile, on grounds which, to my surprise, have not been put forward earlier, and which are narratological or structural. As I read *šōʿęręt* I hear the fascinating assonance with *'ōmęnęt* and I think: 'Well what do you know, another example of an anonymous woman as a functionary in a literary unit on Saulide misery.' In this passage there are, therefore, *two women*. In a systematic study of narrative art their appearance cannot be viewed apart from the wider context, and I am especially thinking now of the possibility that the characters who appear in an Act have their own order.

Well then, the group of units in II Sam.2-5:5 deals with women in its own way. In the beginning it was immediately noticeable that the two wives of David were expressly mentioned (2:2) without being functional in the opening sequence. They return with name and origins as leaders in the list of mothers in 3:2-5. Immediately afterwards two women from the Saulide side

[5] The LXX is followed in this by Thenius, Wellhausen, Driver, Budde, Kittel (in the BHK), Dhorme, Smith, Schulz, RSV, LV, BJ, NEB, NBE, McCarter. The MT is retained by Buber, NBG, Goslinga, KBS, and CT.

[6] CT, p.238; p.239 states: "Ce que 17,3 et 20,18s nous apprendront sur les qualités d'improvisation du traducteur grec, nous amène à nous défier de cette concierge mondant du blé, ..." CT calls this verse in the LXX "une scène pittoresque", whilst Goslinga (p.82) calls it "a graphic, almost romantic depiction". Picturesque I can only just accept, even though it involves more than that (as it so often does when the narrator is graphic), but I fail to see what is so romantic about it.

[7] CT, p.238: "On serait tenté de considérer les deux formes très limpides de 6a offertes par le *G et par le *M comme littérairement distinctes et de se refuser à voir là un cas de critique textuelle." And a little further on (in italics up to and including "personne"): "L'une des traditions textuelles semble donc avoir construit le début de son vs sur les ruines de l'autre. Mais, dans la suite de 6a, la tradition textuelle innovatrice a improvisé beaucoup plus librement puisque personne n'a proposé de relation convaincante entre le *M et l'éventuelle Vorlage de personne n'a proposé de relation convaincante entre le *M et l'éventuelle Vorlage de ἐκάθαιϱεν ou de καὶ ἐνύσταξεν καὶ ἐκάθευδεν."

appeared who are both crucial to the political earthquake of which Abner is the chief accomplisher; they are Rizpah and Michal. They have, as concubine and daughter of the king respectively, a special status, are referred to in the text by name and cannot be separated from one another structurally, as the triangle full of shifts has shown. And now we meet, in ch.4, two female functionaries on the side of two unfortunate sons of Saul! Their anonymity has a point of contact with the suppression of the personal name of Ishbosheth and functions as a sign of the decline of the house of Saul now underway.[8] Their contributions are, in themselves, unfortunate. In her haste to flee with Mephibosheth, the wet nurse has the terrible misfortune of crippling Jonathan's little boy, and the porter, when it is her turn, is unable, through tiredness, to help her master, Ishbosheth, by sounding the alarm for instance.

The parallel between both women, which, through the assonance of their job designations is underlined on the level of sounds, fits therefore in the order of the characters and is a strong, because structural, argument for conceding the female porter a place in the text. At the same time this datum can do duty as material for justifying Mephibosheth's trauma being situated here, and nowhere else, in the text. In addition there is the striking rhyme which makes the personal names of the Saulides into a pair, and consists of the theophoric element, irrespective of whether it is -bosheth or -baal.[9] The *'ōmẹnẹt* and the *šō'ẹrẹt* are the company of Mephibosheth and Ishbosheth, whose names appear in this order in the text (v.4f and 5b). Fate has the Jonathan branch, which is held in esteem by David and which is here embodied by Mephibosheth, crippled, making it thus unsuitable for the succession to the throne at the very moment in which the first king of Israel kills himself; and via the destructive variant of the two assassins the political development cuts off Saul's son, his first in line, who has, it is true, felt the velvet, but only of a nominal and transitory throne. The narrator has not included Mephibosheth's accident in his own text, i.e. in narration time, at the place which tallies with the chronology, i.e. with the order of the time narrated. He has postponed it to ch.4, so that it has become an achronism. It

8 What anonymity first of all means, as is so often the case elsewhere, is that the character's being individual is not important enough to be disclosed or to warrant a name.

9 Current opinion, viz. that the element *-bšt* in the names Ishbosheth and Mephibosheth is a later hybrid ("un leçon débaalisé" to quote CT) of names which end on "master, lord", *ba'al*, has been subjected to scrutiny and rejected by M. Tsevat in "Ishbosheth and Congeners", HUCA 46, (1975) pp.71-87. I myself have not finally made up my mind either way on the forms ending in *-bšt*, but I do not understand why Tsevat's article has so seldom been taken into account, in CT for instance (which includes him in the bibliography, but omits a review of the relevant pages, i.e. 228-230) or McCarter.

was his choice to place the analepsis or flashback 4:4 right in front of the attack on Ishbosheth. He made this decision on thematic grounds. I said that Ishbosheth's end is merely the subject matter of the story, but as the vile assassination of a Saulide it supplies material for the theme. The theme of II Sam.4 is the adversity of the house of Saul.

I now return to v.6 in the recension with the female porter. The only place, two lines in all, which she gets is underlined by the initially occurring *hinnē*. Her working with the corn explains why she has now fallen asleep – the circumstance which Rechab and Baanah make grateful use of, but which the murderers will not find very surprising, since they have fixed the time of their action to coincide with the siesta of the others. But the line on her work has a special status: in the middle of verses 5 and 7, with their adjuncts of time and place, it is a modest analepsis. It has that temporal characteristic in common with v.3 and the verse on the unfortunate nurse. This is not a good sign. Shortly before we encountered another *hinnē* plus analepsis which introduced a fatal sequence: the return of Joab in 3:22. The action of the porter is her sleeping, 4:6b; this forms an opposition to the over-activity of the nurse which turns into a disaster.[10] In sleep she is the same as her master.

The entry of the two soldiers takes place next; the first mention of this in the reconstructed text is 7a which relates consecutively to v.5b: the entry comes after the arrival. Because v.6ab had another subject, the woman who filled in her own outline, and was a temporal interruption adding colour to the background of events, the (restored) verse 7a gives the names of the brothers.[11] The circumstantial clause which follows is not only the spatial complement of its equal, v.5c, but also has one more focalisation alternative. One might interpret the line as what the brothers come across and what they see with their own eyes after their entry. The reader, who has gradually become uneasy, can almost feel, between the words, the vulnerability of the man who lies asleep, and who is about to become the target throughout the entire length of his armourless body.

The murderers waste no time and attack – thanks to the fact that the narrator halts his description and quickly takes down a series of verbs. With the rhyming duo in the hiph'il *wayyakkūhū waymītūhū* it is quickly over. The narrator allows us one visual detail, the head of Ishbosheth is chopped off in 7d and taken away as proof in 7e; once again the object takes care of the

[10] Seven out of a total of eight words on the accident in 4:4cde are verbs.

[11] In this way the words "Rechab and his brother Baanah", which occur in the MT of v.6c, have managed to get a good function and can be retained, albeit in another line.

rhyme, which is now so extensive that it forms an epiphora. The theme of the story is backed up in a special way, and made visible, by the *isotopy of the parts of the body*. First the hands of Ishbosheth were feeble, as an image of his great fear; following on from this we saw the legs of his nephew, characterising permanent impotence by being crippled; and now the misfortune of the Saulides is completed by the severed head which, as an image of horror and death leaving us speechless, is to pursue us for another five verses. In the following sequence there is still more to come.[12] The parts of the body are chiefly metonymic in relation to the theme of Saulidic disaster, but through repetition they back each other up and also gain metaphorical power conveying death and decay. The head of the Saulide state has now been eliminated and the dynasty itself has become crippled.

The murderers have no trouble in getting away. The narrator refers to this by a simple "they went away" which completes the ring with v.5a.[13] This departure makes me think of the *hālōk* which the angry Joab used for the safe departure of Abner: "has he been able to go away *just like that*?" The final answer was: at first, yes, but because of Joab's personal intervention, in the long run, no, as a matter of fact. The question now arises concerning these two assassins: can such an easy getaway as theirs actually be brought off? Are they going to succeed completely? They direct their steps to Hebron. The words on the route they took, viz. "the way of the desert" and "went all night" put their journey alongside that of 2:29, but in the opposite direction. Both journeys are moments in the decline of the northern kingdom. But there is yet another parallel, which is even more surprising. "They went all night" plus a crossing of the river Jordan was also the case of the men of Jabesh at the end of I Sam.31! With their loyalty to Saul, and their courageous swift journey through enemy lines, they are, of course, the opposite pole of the treacherous Benjaminite duo and their cowardly attack. And then there is the isotopy of the parts of the body, which already appears to begin in I 31 with the mutilation of Saul's body. The antithesis here earns detailed examination in § 3 below.

The attack on Ishbosheth was, in the first sequence, the actantial object of the two sergeants; the death of Ishbosheth now becomes an issue which David must settle. The narrator wastes no time and makes skilful use of the

[12] We noticed a largely metonymic isotopy of weapons in the dirge of David at the end of NAPS II.

[13] As has been previously mentioned, the ease with which they get away is an essential datum in the overall picture of sleepiness on the part of the other side; I would like to repeat that the form *nimlāṭū* does not fit here.

verb "to come". He puts it into the hiph'il, "bring",[14] and has the men reach David with their hideous trophy in the very first line of the second sequence. The official notation consists of four personal names and gives away the focalisation of these two who want so much to show David "Ishbosheth, the son of Saul". From the narrator's point of view the precision of this notation also has a function: like a clerk of the court he establishes the bringing of a corpus delicti and so prepares the verdict which the judge, David, will shortly pass.

The gentlemen arrive in Hebron, never to return again. At the end they get their own line with Hebron (v.12c), after which the very last line (v.12e) is reserved for the grave in which the head of Ishbosheth ends up: also "in Hebron". The two parties, who were still together in 8a as perpetrators plus victim, are thus set down in different lines, but are united in death.

The perpetrators address two long and well-worded sentences to David in v.8cd. It is the sirens' song of enmity and vengeance which is all too well-known to us – and David. David's men spoke in this way in I 24:25, and David's comrade-in-arms, Abishai, in 26:8, after they had stalked the hunter Saul, whereupon David could have struck him down if he had wished. In both cases David forcefully rejected this temptation with an oath.[15] The selfsame thing is about to take place here, since David says in 9c *ḥay yhwh* with a fine relative clause as introduction. But first let us listen in to the men of Beeroth. Their first word marks their point of view, then five words come next which follow exactly v.8a, "the head of Ishbosheth, the son of Saul." The speed at which the gentlemen get down to business is amazing! They speak of "your enemy who sought your life" all in one breath. This apposition refers to Saul, it is true, and not to Ishbosheth, but the gentlemen make the connection so easily that they do, in fact, manage to suggest that Ishbosheth has been a dangerous enemy of David's.[16] The name Saul is at the centre of the line; straightaway a link arises with the axial word of the following line.

The murderers combine piety with the court style in their second sentence. They proclaim the seductive interpretation of the facts that God (here

[14] In this way a new pair of hiph'il forms has yet again been completed after the attack of 7c: the *wayyāsīrū 'ęt rōšō* is now complemented by *wayyābī'ū 'ęt rōšō 'īš bošęt*. I notice, in addition, that this is the last act of the sergeants to receive a mention.

[15] In I 26:10 the exordium of David's oath indeed reads *ḥay yhwh*, in 24:8 it is the formula of rejection *ḥālīlā lī*, but here too it is connected to *yhwh*, via the preposition *min*.

[16] The apposition follows the name Saul and refers to Saul, since the word *'ōyibkā* did this too in I 24:5 (where, moreover, the formula of extradition is used which Rechab and Baanah employ here in 4:8d) and 26:8 (*idem* with *sgr* instead of *ntn*), and the phrase *bqš 't npšk* is likewise typical of the Saul of "The Crossing Fates".

designated by his personal name; which is almost transformed into blasphemy in the mouths of the murderers) "has given vengeance this day to my lord the king". This is not the formula for extradition but is, however, in view of the precedents in I 24//26, an actual variant invented by the gentlemen for the occasion and supercharged with "vengeance".[17] The last word occupies a central position in the sentence and regulates the rhythm.[18] It has been embellished by being put into the plural; if it is not a 'plural of intensity' then it is one of diversity, because the act of revenge is at the expense of "Saul and his descendants".[19] As a well-chosen turn of phrase this word pair reminds us of the many positive places in which "seed" figures as a word for being blessed with many children, such as the blessing of God on the patriarchs. The content here, of course, is antithetical. The two words *hayyōm hazzę̄* are more solemn than the ordinary "today" (*hayyōm*) which would have been adequate. Everything points to the fact that the gentlemen have done their best with their speech.

David gives them what is due to them in a very long speech of forty-eight words. The introduction to this, i.e. v.9a, also has the air of being the official minutes. Once again the narrator is busy recording information, like the clerk of the court; information which will shortly be required in a court case. He notes down not only the personal names of the two visitors, but records their origins using two terms, the patronymic and the place. The completeness of the description of David's addressees in 9a is ominous for the two men.

The structure of David's speech is as follows:

– v.9c	solemn introduction	1 line
– vv.10a-11a	the content of the oath	6 lines
– v.11bc	conclusion	2 lines

[17] The formula of extradition (mostly with *ntn* as the verb, but sometimes alternating with *mkr*, *sgr*, and *nkr*) occurs approximately seventeen times in "The Crossing Fates" but, with the exception of 4:8 and 5:19 (*bis*), is virtually absent from II Sam. (compare, however, 16:8b and 21:9a). The references in I Sam. are 12:9, 14:10,12,37, 17:46,47, 23:4,7,11 (*bis*), 24:5,11,19, 26:8,23, 28:19 (*bis*), 30:23.

[18] The clause has a special, fine kind of rhythm. To put it like this, the word *nᵉqāmōt* is preceded and followed by two word pairs: wytn yhwh / l'dny hmlk / *nqmwt* / hywm hzh /mš'wl wmzr'w. We might even go so far as to say that the semantic weight in each of the four pairs of words is so apportioned that a) prior to the axial word the weight rests on the second word (i.e. *yhwh* and *hmlk*), but b) after the axial word on the first (i.e. on *hywm* and Saul); which suggests the idea of centripetal force. Two personal names occur in the outermost pairs. The first line, v.8c, has eleven words (of which Saul is the most central) and the second has nine, making a total of twenty.

[19] I quote §136 of the "Grammaire de l'hébreu biblique" by P. Joüon; in §136*f* the *pluriel d'intensité* occurs, in §136j Joüon himself mentions our reference 4:8 as an example of his *pluriel de généralisation*. Compare the *pluriel d'extension* in paragraph c.

At least this is the rhetorical build-up, which is determined by three considerations. The *'af kī* line of v.11a corresponds to the *kī* line with which the content of the oath begins; this is a correspondence which rounds off the oath. In v.11b we read *w^e'attā*, the hinge which normally marks a volitive ending and prior to which a description of a state of affairs took place. This is also the case here, vv.10a-11a contain information on events which have already taken place. Their five preterits are replaced, after the hinge, by two futures bearing a decision.[20]

This rhetorical order differs from the legal one, which is also weighty. In this the position of 11a as the point of a *qal waḥomer* argument is different and this line comes under the conclusion:

- v.9c introduction to the oath
- v.10a-e description of a capital crime as precedent
- v.11abc applied to the present via an a fortiori argument

In the legal draft the asseverative *kī* of the oath is the introduction to recounting a previous legal case, viz. the one against the Amalekite messenger in ch.1, and the line with *'af kī* concerns a new question; yesterday's attack on the agenda for today.

The exordium with "as the Lord lives" is amplified by the relative clause "who has redeemed my soul from all adversity". So David places his own *nęfęš* line as answer opposite the *nęfęš* line of the visitors. The correspondence is a subtle hint that the gentlemen do not need excite themselves about the enemies of David out for his blood, because he is already under the protection of the Lord and does not need any henchmen. At the end of his life David is to use the relative clause once more, in an oath which finally clinches the question of the succession, I Ki.1:29.

Underlined by *kī* the content of the oath is next. Its syntax is fascinating. Because, in the long run, only one thought is put into words covering the precedent, in the sense of 'I have executed that messenger of Saul's end', it is very striking that 10a-e is divided into five or six clauses. This apparent fragmentation creates the impression of spontaneity and the vernacular. Upon closer inspection there is much more order. I observe a six-cola-long alternation up to the climax of v.11a: messenger/death/messenger/death/messenger's wages/death, after which the speaker is determined not to abandon capital punishment for the Beerothites in his conclusion, 11bc. Architectonic artefact and quasi-confused vernacular do not adversely affect

[20] Notice that the two perpetrators of the crime are still in the third person in v.11a, next to their deed in the past tense, whilst they are addressed as "you" (plural) in 11bc and are held responsible.

one another. The syntax shows wide variety: a *casus pendens* up front in 10a and second degree direct speech in 10b, followed by our expectation of a redeeming predicate. But no, this is postponed for we must first deal with a parenthesis, 10c. At last, the predicative core of the sole statement with the chief announcement occurs in 10d; it is a double action which cruelly ends the messenger's suspense and makes him a victim: an object of execution. By loosely adding a relative clause David delivers a stab of irony, before formulating the point of his *qal waḥomer* in a very lengthy, eleven-word sentence in v.11a.

In ch.1 the messenger was denoted three times by *hammaggīd lō*. Ch.4:10a contains the echo of the significant trio. The messenger is enclosed by the antithesis of death and life. Life occurs only in the pro-David line, the 9c exordium, after this the lexemes of death (*mt, hrg* and *dm* + *b'r)* are interwoven with the *mgd-mbśr-bśrh* series. In 10b an embedded speech occurs, which David uses to quotes the Amalekite. But his quotation is a free one, placing, moreover, the little word *hinnē* in front of the information "Saul is dead". In this way a parallel with 8c arises and we come to understand that, for David, the death of Ishbosheth is, in one way or another, a counterpart of the death of Saul. This is bound to already arouse a certain amount of suspicion in his two listeners.

David obviously considers it unnecessary, in this context, to repeat all kinds of details from the death report he received in Ziklag. Those who are not acquainted with ch.1 cannot determine in ch.4:10 what the messenger was actually guilty of. David's free and condensed summary goes so far that not even the incriminating *mōtattī* of the messenger, through which he became witness for the Crown in his own capital case, is copied. The simple *met* masks the refined dialectic of lies and eyewitness account which occupies the centre of 1:1-16.[21] David connects up with the brief version of the Amalekite in 1:4 and his own choice of words *met šā'ūl* in 1:5, leaving aside the complexity of the long version (1:6-10). At the same time there is a parallel with the quasi neutral *met 'abner* of v.1a, so that we come to realise that the text contains a whole series of understatements. As if only one of the three has been able to die a somewhat ordinary death! The parenthesis in v.10c is an interesting novelty since David gives his interpretation of the messenger and reflects the self-image of the Amalekite which masks his greed. In ch.1 David, as prosecutor and judge, had kept to the main point only, viz. that the messenger had killed Saul. He took the man at his word and

[21] See, of course, the analysis of the story in NAPS II, or my article in OTS xxiii (1984), pp.39-55, entitled: "A Lie, Born of Truth, Too Weak to Contain It. A Structural Reading of 2 Sam. i 1-16".

could not have known, at that moment, that Saul's death took place in another way. He did not, in charge and verdict, refer to the possible motives or mentality of the messenger. Things are different now, however. I imagine David is currently in possession of more facts on the final hour of Saul on Mt. Gilboa, and has more insight into the profit motive of the messenger. He characterises him with a new word, *bśr*: "And he, he was as a bringer of good news in his own eyes." In 10e he mentions the messenger's wages which he owed the man[22] and ironically admits that the messenger had earned every bit of this *b*ᵉ*śōrā*. It has taken the form of the death sentence, according to the preceding line, 10d.

David might have said that the Amalekite "was a bringer of good news in his own eyes", but what he actually does is to tag on *k*ᵉ to the participle *m*ᵉ*baśśer*: the man was "*as* a bringer of good news." This is a subtle addition, which has an undermining effect. The Amalekite was not a bringer of good news in his own eyes, but merely pretended to be. The preposition says, therefore, that the David of today, no longer bound by the exclusive information of the scoop, has seen through the Amalekite's enacted role of bringer of good news whilst his real objective was the pursuit of gain. This snake in the grass has been missed by the modern translations.[23]

The participle *mbśr* is the successor to *mgyd* found in 10a, and is the point at which the precise alternation *bśr/hrg/bśr/hrg* begins which takes us on to the point of the legal argument. This is contained in v.11a: "how much more [ought the death sentence to be in force] when wicked men kill a man of integrity in his house on his bed of rest!" The verb occupies a central position, surrounding it appears the pair of opposites *r*ᵉ*šāʿīm* versus *ṣaddīq*, which is sharp in its polar value judgements and is reinforced by the difference created by the plural versus the singular with the connotation of "can you manage with two against one?" Enclosing the subject and the victim are the words stating the qal waḥomer, the formulaic introduction with *'af kī* at

[22] Driver listens carefully to the relative clause of 10e and detects (in the first five lines of p.256) a possible gerundival aspect in *l*ᵉ*tittī* (he translates it: "to whom it was for my giving"). He commences by rendering the entire clause: "to whom I ought, forsooth, to have given a reward for his good tidings". But he creates confusion on the focalisation and on *'ašęr*, see Appendix I. For the function of the infinitive see Ges.-K. §114 *l*.

[23] Because they are, to a large extent, literal the older European translations such as the KJ and the SV reproduce the preposition "as", without our knowing whether they understood its subversive effect. The modern versions (JPS, NEB, NBE, KBS, NBG, LV, BJ, McCarter, Hertzberg) all have freer renderings which understandably smooth out the syntax, but unfortunately miss out the preposition: e.g. "the man who thought to bring me good news" in BJ and "creyendo darme una buena noticia" in the NBE. Buber was probably aware of the snake in the grass: "und in seinen eigenen Augen war der doch einem Freudenboten gleich".

the beginning and at the end the specifications as to place, which reveal how absurd this violence was and that the real issue is an assassination.

David reaches his conclusion now that the *a fortiori* has been formulated which makes the first death so different from the other. After the hinge introducing the closing word pair 11bc he poses a rhetorical question with *hălō* which makes its content unavoidable. In answer to the two men and their almost sentimental line with *bqš* (seeking) on his own life David now asks (*bqš*) with a well-known legal formula for [compensation for] the life of Ishbosheth.[24] The terms "his blood" and "your hand" make us attentive to the isotopy of the parts of the body.[25] He ends with a forceful term, "purge you from the land", since he is now faced with the task of indemnifying the community from [the consequences of] a serious case of bloodguilt.[26] This term for cleansing in the final line is exactly opposite to the term for liberation in the first line.

The narrator himself takes responsibility for the final verse with a cluster of five narrative clauses. Viewed objectively the first line, v.12a, is parallel to 1:15 where David ordered one of his soldiers to thrust the Amalekite through. There David was allocated direct speech for the order, here the narrator himself reports it. The verb *hrg* is inspired by 10d which used it for the previous execution. The harsh sounds in *qaṣṣeṣ* in 12b underline the first of two extra punitive measures which the criminals must undergo, so that their souls will find no rest in a decent grave. Their hands and feet, the parts of the body which have carried out the murder and the defection, are chopped off – a mutilation of the extremities which is an answer to, but not the reflection of, the mutilation which the gentlemen performed on Ishbosheth by chopping off another extremity.

The isotopy of the parts of the body exhibits a certain equilibrium: after what happened to the hands of Ishbosheth and the feet of Mephibosheth which 'embody' the impotence of the house of Saul, the amputated hands and feet of the brothers are an act of revenge in miniature for the crime which had 'cut' such a ghastly opportunistic covenant with calamity. The second measure is that the perpetrators of the crime are hanged in public. In this way

[24] "Demand blood at the hand of" occurs right away in Gen.9:5 (where the verb is *drš*), where the taking of a human life is adjudged by God to be a capital crime.

[25] In the units 1:1-16 and 3:22-39 on the victims Saul and Abner what is of central importance in David's sentence and his curse on the messenger and on Joab respectively is that the shed blood be upon the head of the killer. Here in ch.4 both head and blood belong to the victim.

[26] The term *b'r* in the pi'el occurs in the juridical paragraphs Deut.19:13 and 21:9 which discuss homicide (and not manslaughter) as well. They attend to the interests of the community ("out of your midst") and the divine standard of the legal measure.

they are exposed to the elements and have become carrion for the wild animals.

An inversion introduces the last two lines and marks the contrast of the treatment which the head of Ishbosheth receives. As far as possible he gets a respectful burial in Hebron. His head is buried in the grave of Abner.[27] This is the general who had exposed Ishbosheth in all his weakness by defecting, but who had subsequently and unexpectedly had to pay the highest penalty for this decision. The irony of the situation that both adversaries of the Judaean throne are united in the city where the throne of David stands, in an emergency grave, is nevertheless almost unbearable.

David has become a receiver (*destinataire*) of the visit of the two Beerothites, in a completely different way to what they had planned. His reception is an evaluation of the attack and has contrasted villainy with innocence. The two mutually exclusive quests of the sergeants and the judge-king are linked by an unemphatic, but recognisable symmetrical articulation of the plot; a scheme ABC-CBA the centre of which is the only dialogue in the passage, so that C-C can also be replaced by the label of the axis, X:

A	a) initial data: death of Abner > Ishbosheth's panic; the two Beerothites, vv.1-2
	b) their journey and arrival, vv.5a-7b
B	murder of Ishbosheth and departure with trophy, v.7c-f
C	arrival at David's and seductive speech, v.8
C'	answer: David's long speech, precedent + verdict, vv.9-11
B'	execution of the perpetrators, v.12abc
A'	burial of Ishbosheth in Abner's grave, 12de.

The symmetry is very far from perfect, and does not need to be either. The extensive part b of segment A has no counterpart; the size of this piece of text and that of C' differ greatly from that of the other segments. There are, though, enough instances of correspondence to confer a relative validity on the scheme. One of these is that the framework now receives its importance which connects v.12de with the opening verse. A' does not have the whole member A as counterpart, but only part a. The death of Abner is now duplicated, as it were, by the burial of his former lord. Ishbosheth's fear has been shown to be an adequate reaction and has been outstripped by the horror of reality. The name Hebron has been strategically placed at the

[27] What I have said about the alliteration in 3:32a also holds good for the closing line, 4:12e, with its words *qbr* (*bis*), *'abner*, *ḥębrōn* and twice *b*ᵉ.

beginning, middle and end, always occupying the final position of the relevant line (1a, 8a, 12ce). And there is a certain balance between the first and the second half of the series, insofar as half of the deed receives a long piece of action (part b of A) and half of the evaluation has a long speech, C'.

§ 2. *David king over Israel,* 5:1-5

The close of the Act is only one sequence long and in the first instance does not even reach v.5, but v.3 only. It contains little more than a speech of six lines and a cluster of three narrative lines in which Israel and David reach an agreement on his second throne. The first line is parallel to v.3, which is often mistreated but which I make use of in a positive way:
1a All the tribes of Israel came to David in Hebron
3a All the elders of Israel came to the king in Hebron
The two variants make the lines into each other's complement. The tribes in Hebron – these are not one or two million people but their representatives. Their host is David, that is to say the king. It is probably not even necessary to consider the arrival in v.3a to be a different one from the one in v.1a. In other words: all the referents in v.3a are exactly the same as those in v.1a and the action is identical; only the two parties (the man and the nation) are presented with another aspect.[28]

The interlacing which first introduced a division in the pairs tribes/elders and David/the king is completed by the linking of function and name in v.3b: *hammęlęk dāwīd* and the chiastic reflection of this in the final line: they anointed *dāwīd lᵉmęlęk*, 3c. With the linking of function and name the business of the new throne is settled. The line on the covenant, 3b, not only registers the place name of Hebron once again, but ends with another personal name, that of the witness Yhwh, whilst the final line also finishes on a personal name, that of the nation. The frequency of names in 3bc lends an official note to the report. In the whole of v.3 seven names occur and in the entire sequence "Israel", the name of the people involved, occurs six times in the narrow sense, whilst the name occurs for the seventh time in v.5b

[28] The identity of (all the referents of) vv.1a and 3a can be conveyed in translation by rendering v.3a as a flashback: "So all the elders *had come*". Several translations meet this decision half way by using the word "so" (without the pluperfect): KJ, SV, BJ, LV. Compare also "dus" (= thus) used by the NBG and "pues" by the NBE.

I also notice that the counterpart in ch.2, the verse in which Judah comes and anoints David in Hebron, chooses an in-between variant: neither "the whole tribe of Judah", nor "the elders of Judah", but "the men of Judah came and anointed David". Finally a remark on *šbṭy* in 5:1a. This word can be taken as a metonym for "staff bearers", i.e. tribal leaders. See the discussion in ch.VI §1 on a similar *šbṭy* in 7:7b and also Appendix I on this reference.

where, accompanied by *kol*, it has the tendency to take on the broad sense which, from now on, becomes possible under David.[29] The names of both David and Hebron occur 3 + 1 times in the segmented piece of text consisting of vv.1-3/4-5, the root *mlk* is associated 3 + 4 times with David.[30]

Hebron is the political centre of gravity of the whole country and exercises an increasing centripetal force. The first line is highly parallel to the first line of the previous sequence:

4:8a *wyb'w* [a hiph'il] ... to David in Hebron
5:1a *wyb'w* [a qal this time] ... to David in Hebron

The first arrival is the nadir of the downward curve of Saul, the second is the terminus (in this Act anyway) of the upward curve of David. Both are illustrative of the pull exerted by David's throne.

The tribes address a great speech to David, which is divided up into three plus three lines.[31] Two characteristics are quickly to be noticed: as a political and rhetorical piece the speech is inspired by the preparatory work of Abner, *in concreto* even by his speech in 3:17sq. And the dominant person in the speech is referred to as "you".[32] During his tour of the tribes Abner had to use the third person for David in his speeches *to* the tribes. The speech *of* the tribes is directed to David himself and relays the general's arguments to the king: which proves just how far Abner's analysis has penetrated those involved; his arguments are even elaborated on and spruced up. Both 3:17-18 and 5:1-2 are made up of a first degree speech which culminates in a second degree speech of God himself on David's election.

The great similarities between the speeches make the differences and, therefore, the unique quality of each of them stand out clearly:

similarities:	lacking a counterpart:
3:17b and 5:2ab	5:1c
3:18b and 5:2c	3:18a
3:18c and 5:2de	

[29] The added word *kol* raises the question, does it not, as to the precise difference in meaning between "Israel and Judah" and "all Israel and Judah".

[30] In v.2a the root *mlk* occurs one more time, in the flashback on Saul's reign.

[31] Two marginal notes: v.1b is remarkable insofar as it fails to mention the addressee. The grammatical second person in the speech reveals, however, that David has this role. Instead what meets the eye is a highly redundant *l'mr* (immediately after *wy'mrw*!). The arrangement of 3 + 3 lines is in order if we count the quotation formula of 2c with the content of 2de.

[32] This second person is morphologically represented by the suffix *-kā* in v.1c and 2c, by a threefold and quasi-redundant *pronomen personale separatum* immediately preceding the verbal predicate in 2bde: *'attā*, and three times as an element of that predicate (as afformative and preformative, therefore).

The amplification consists of the single line of flashback and the single line on election both being replaced by double lines. These pairs, v.2ab and 2de, are very closely connected to one another by anaphoras and epiphoras. The subject of the complex sentence, 2ab is the same as that of the simple clauses of 2de: David in the second person. All four lines end on the same referent, Israel.[33] The point of the quartet is continuity: 'you've already been leading us well, keep up the good work'.

The tribes' speech is alive with pairs. Not only are the halves, the degrees, and the times discussed neatly divided and not only does the 2de pair, qua content and chronology, link up with 2ab, but there are also all kinds of pairs on the level of the choice of words. The most important are the two merismuses, "your bone and your flesh", "yesterday and the day before yesterday", with a double *gam*, and the double movement of the general in *ḫammōṣī* and *ḫammebī*. The mass of pairs show all kinds of unification and continuity: 'we are your kinsmen, we want to be your subjects, Israel and Judah belong under one king, your leadership of today and tomorrow was already unmistakable yesterday, and besides, it was ordained by God'. The tenor of unity comes into relief even more due to a moment of dissent. In the flashback political and military power were separate, Saul was king and you were general. But the separation is now a thing of the past and is lifted in the parallelism of 2de. I interpret this pair of lines as having a poetical structure; 4 + 4 ictuses and a maximum of word pairs which make the parallelism between the verse halves complete.[34] It is the decisive pronouncement of God exactly, and catches the eye as a quotation.

The opening line, 1c, is unique in the speech. It lets us see at once how much the speakers want unity. "Behold, we are your bone and your flesh" is, strictly speaking, and judged according to the standards of actual consanguinity (in a manner of speaking) only one per cent accurate. It is, in fact, a hyperbole and, as such, a strong expression of the *longing* to join up with

[33] Three times out of the four a line ends on the name itself, whilst the "over us" of v.2a points to the same thing. I notice another chiasmus of direct and indirect object, since preposition and *nota objecti* vary concentrically: *'al* + *'et* in 2ab, *'et* + *'al* in 2de. This figure confirms just how much 2ab and 2de form a quartet with each other. Compare the resemblance between *'attā ḫāyītā* with *'attā tiḫyȩ̄* and their positions.

[34] The first and the final words are identical in 2de, the predicate *tir'ȩ̄//tiḫyȩ̄* is a word pair due to different aspects of sound and form and the remaining duo *'ammī* and *nāgīd* becomes a pair due to a complementary meaning (leader and led), if not a merismus.

David.[35] In v.2a the monarchy of Saul is peacefully accommodated in a temporal adjunct which does not occur until the second position, as a subsequent explanation of "yesterday and the day before yesterday". In this speech there is no place for the tensions and conflicts of the time. David and Saul complement each other rather, as king and general in 2ab. This complementariness in the version of the tribes is considerably more subtle than the one line, 3:17b, in Abner's version which already ignores Saul and which both reaches far back in time and anticipates the tribes' going over to David by limiting itself to the desire for David's kingship.[36]

The connection between 3:17 and 5:2 is arresting because of the repetition of the merismus yesterday/the day before yesterday with a double *gam*, but also because of the fresh use of the periphrastic construction in v.2b. The roles are reversed: in 3:17b "you have been seeking David", whilst in 5:2b David actually provides leadership and the people report as his subjects. The twist that it was David who was the one who (literally translated) "caused [Israel] to come in and to go out" uses the roots *yṣ'* and *bw'* as merismus, in the hiph'il here. Through this it is a reminder of, and a sequel to, I 18:16 (a verse which ends a story) where the same pair occurs in the qal and the general David is loved "by the whole of Israel and Judah". The line opened, therefore, with the same merismus which the II 5:1-5 passage worked towards: "all Israel and Judah" occur at the end of v.5b, and finally united under David draw the whole Act to a close. The merismus of coming in and going out has another opponent in the vicinity: Joab had used it in the nominal form to slander his opposite number Abner, 3:25c. But this episode of dissension is now over as well. Nobody spies on David's comings and goings, his leadership is accepted without reservation. This reception of David by the people as *destinataire* of political developments is in accordance with 3:36c which, apart from that, mentions the approval of the Judaeans.

Abner's call to action in 3:18 has no counterpart here, in keeping with the fact that such action is undertaken now and that it coincides with the present development. The similarity between the two quotations of God supplies contrast especially. In 5:2de there are two parties in very close fellowship; the

[35] Notice that the later division of Israel and Judah, in the situation of David's return from the Transjordan in ch.19, is marked by the question of real consanguinity: in 19:12 David wants to accord preferential treatment to Judah with the argument: "you are my bones and my flesh", which has the disastrous effect that Israel promptly secedes (again). See further NAPS I *ad loc.*

[36] The two cola scan in exactly the same way, and no wonder: it is the metrical appearance of maximum parallelism; which is one more argument for regarding the pair as a line of poetry:

2d oó oó ooó oooó

2e ooó oó ooó oooó

shepherd and his flock who are destined for one another – a state of affairs fitting in with the acceptance of David's power. In 3:18c, when the people have yet to be won over by Abner, the focus is quite different. The general appealed to the self-interest of his audience by making "my people" the object of rescue and enclosing it with divine help ("my servant David") and liberation (**yšʿ*) versus two phrases full of enemies. There is no longer any question of threat versus rescue in the hemistiches of 5:2. Politics' and waging war's complementing each other in 2ab – tasks which were, at that time, divided between two men – is repeated in 2de, with the difference that both tasks must now be fulfilled by the same leader. I view the metaphor that David is to "pasture" the people as an image of his monarchy and political responsibility therefore, whilst the sacral title *nāgīd* is connected with the military protection of the nation.[37]

In 5:3 the time has come for the matter to be settled. Contrary to what Abner foresaw in 3:21c it is not the elders or the people who make a covenant with David but the other way around. And it is not merely the individual David who makes a covenant with the people. The narrator is very meticulous in his choice of words in v.3b and conveys, by different means, the official nature of the contract which now takes effect: "King David made a covenant with them in Hebron in the presence of the Lord." The name of the man and his function are now brought together, after their still being apart in vv.1a and 3a. The fact that he has become the subject reveals his power and is the realisation of 3:12c//13c where David was likewise the only one who could bring about the covenant, in his own view and in that of Abner. The mention of place-names and, more strongly, the inclusion of the name of God, are the act of a writer who, as clerk of the court or notary public, must attend to the official registration and laying down of a transaction. That the sentence ceremoniously draws to a close with the personal name of God is inspired by the words of the people, who have just explicitly appealed to his decision in v.2c. God is the witness and the patron of the contract between this king and his subjects. The word covenant is unique, insofar as it is neither

[37] But I am not going to deny that the two titles partly cover one another! The basic passages in which the word *nāgīd* occurs for the first time have to do with the most urgent task facing the first king: the liberation of the country from the enemy. Twice the title applies to the young Saul who is chosen by God, I 9:16 and 10:1, but the title quickly passes to David in two places which both say that *yhwh* "has commanded" David to be "leader (*ngyd*) over Israel", I 13:14 and 25:30. See after this in addition *nāgīd* (two more times linked with God's *ṣwh*) in 6:21, 7:8 and I Ki.1:35. A recent dissertation on the term by Campbell, pp.47-61.

applied to the first king's acceptance of the throne nor to any later kings.[38] I imagine that it presupposes the Torah as background and that it implies divine promise or destiny, and the mutual obligations of the partners.[39] In any case it underlines the special nature of David's monarchy. The narrator's brief report ends with "king of Israel", the same words on which the people ended as did the embedded speech of God. We immediately recognise 3c as parallel and complementary to 2:4b – when "they anointed David king over the house of Judah". But that acceptance of the throne was not coupled with the making of a covenant! One might construe, on the basis of this, a subversive suggestion on the part of the narrator to this effect: at the beginning of the Act there are no clouds in the sky for David, and at the end it is, in fact, overcast. At the beginning, supported by an oracle, he returns to his place of origin and receives the throne as a matter of course. The men of Judah had no need of a covenant with their leader. The second throne was not only an issue requiring much effort, but it falls to David in spite of two heinous political murders, so that the new subjects do very much want a well-defined contract before marshalling themselves under his authority.[40]

David has scarcely been anointed when the narrator switches to the numbers which draw the Act to a close. The location of the annalistic data in 5:4-5 is almost more interesting than their content. They are the successors of 2:10 and occur as a counterpart opposite to king Ishbosheth's figures. The comparison teaches us that David was ten years younger than Ishbosheth when he became king and reigned twenty times longer. The mention of his age and the number of years he reigned invite us to count them. The sum of thirty plus forty is ten times the sacred number seven. This backs up the surmise that the numbers referring to the length of David's reign are principally of a literary and symbolical nature, and do not need to be taken literally or as being exact. The sum of the figures in verse 5 is itself just over forty in fact.

[38] The twenty-one references in I and II Ki. which contain the word *b^erīt* almost all concern the covenant between God and the people, and none of them concerns the ascension to the throne.

[39] The word and the concept *b^erīt* are dealt with by Moshe Weinfeld in the "Theologisches Wörterbuch zum Alten Testament", Vol.I 1973, columns 781-808.

[40] The tension between literature and historiography is great at this point. The speech which the narrator allows the people to say is full of willingness and trust. But the historical reality behind it – a field to which literature, due to the ambiguity and artificiality of its linguistic symbols, never directly refers – must have been otherwise. We become conscious of this as soon as we switch over to a historical evaluation of the textual data and there are elements in the text which give away the fact that David's authority over "all Israel" is not a bond which arose quite smoothly.

The construction of the annalistic ending is that of the double application of *parallelismus membrorum*. The lines 4a and b begin with a number which occurs in front as the real predicate,[41] and end on *mlk*. The lines 5a and b invert the word order and introduce their half of the chiasmus so formed with a spatial phrase. The two cities' names occur up front because they state the two phases of David's reign and they form, at the same time, a complementary parallelism. Another chiasmus occurs in the second half of these lines. Whilst the reign of seven and a half years in 5a follows the name of the region governed, Judah, in v.5b the order is the other way around. The number thirty-three is now less surprising, insofar as the reader can now work it out for himself by subtracting the figures in 4b and 5a, and the region "all Israel and Judah" gets a place at the end of the sentence. This inclusive expression has thus become the fitting close of the paragraph and that of the entire Act.

The formula of age plus number of years reigned is well-known to us from the book of Kings. Here, in verse 4, it is applied to David. But what is special about it at this point is that the formula is duplicated by the sequel, 5a and b. That verse analyses and divides up the figure forty; it turns out to be the sum of two phases which are distinguished by a change in the seat of government. And now, all of a sudden, seven years of David in Judah have passed and thirty-three are to follow in Jerusalem. But the city of this name has yet to be conquered and that brings us to the narrator's treatment of time. The lines 4b and 5b survey the entire reign of David and both are, as statements of the omniscient narrator, a prolepsis. The specific function of the short annalistic passage is also revealed by this temporal aspect.

§ 3. *The integration of Act IX*

The texture and the structure of the individual stories have kept us busy for so long that it is advantageous to pause here and formulate their connection once again. The analysis of the details has, in many ways, established that the

[41] Hidden behind this choice of words is the insight that 5:4b has a peculiar predicate and has only the appearance of a verbal clause. It is not the verb *mlk* as one might, out of habit, think but is, in actual fact, the number which occurs initially. A minor and simple transformation provides us with the deep structure and shows the true nature of the report, viz. the kingdom of David lasted for forty years. Another operation which lets us see what the predicate is repeats 4b, but adds, in brackets, a certain amount of explanation: "forty years [was the period during which] he was king."

systematics of the events, whose number differs on one point from the literary units, is concentric and governs the Act as a whole:

A	David is anointed king over Judah	2:1-7
B	Abner makes Ishbosheth king in Mahanaim	vv.8-11
C	civil war, battle of Gibeon; Abner kills Asahel	vv.12-31
X	Abner-Ishbosheth conflict, Abner defects to David	3:6-21
C'	Joab kills Abner because of his brother Asahel	vv.22-39
B'	Ishbosheth, lacking Abner's support, is murdered	ch.4
A'	David is anointed king over Israel	5:1-5

Abner is the great initiator at Act level (level ten in my staircase model of textual hierarchy). If it had been up to him he would have become king maker for the second time. Afterwards he could have boasted that he had emerged as a great statesman, and he could have laid claim to making history in, and beyond, the vacuum left by Saul. That there are arguments which could be brought to bear against this is now beside the point. After the second anointing it would have been difficult for David to have given Abner anything less than the position of chief of general staff. At macro-level regarding the plot, and at level ten of the actantial model, Abner is the hero and the subject. David's second anointing narrowly escaped being the object with which Abner could have proudly completed his quest, bringing it to a satisfactory conclusion. But Joab's attack upsets all possible claims we can imagine Abner making, and precludes him from completing his political endeavours. Two levels higher this has its good side. On the level of the composition of the books of Samuel (that is, level twelve) David has, for a long time (especially narration time) been the hero of the chief quest, and he is, after his ascending the throne, to be so for a long time (both in narration time and in narrated time). At this level it would have been extremely undesirable if Abner had had the chance to maintain that the latest king on the throne of Israel was also his political creation! Or to put it yet another way: Joab's lust for revenge is, at this level, an instrument of Providence which has guided David on the way to the throne and wants to see him get there without too much moral damage. After all David is, on this level, not only the hero, but also the receiver of the object which God (the *destinateur*) grants him.

David takes virtually no initiative in II Sam.2-5:5 and is, at this level, viz. level ten (that of the Act itself) not the hero, but the receiver. This is even visible at level eight at the start. In the first paragraph he *gets* anointed as king, information which is quickly repeated twice more (in 2:7d and 11). He had sought advice earlier, but only with respect to his removing to Judah, and

God's answer finally made him the receiver of the oracle. His message to the Jabeshites keeps to the plane of events lacking an outcome. After this everyone is busy working for him. Joab serves him on the battlefield, the women give him a potential dynasty in the form of sons, Abner organises the transfer of Israel. David is constantly the beneficiary of all this effort and also the addressee *(destinataire)* in the sense of having to determine his political and moral position in three cases in which he is receiver: when Abner comes to negotiate, when the latter's body is brought into Hebron and when the sergeants arrive with Ishbosheth's head.

David does not need to do anything almost. This does not mean that he is powerless. On the contrary, his throne in Judah has such charisma that the initiative of others and events adapt themselves to it. And in the case of the two assassinations, which can easily be explained to the detriment of David, what is actually recognised is the fact that David was not behind them – an exceptional example of non-action. All that is left for David to do is define his position publicly and pronounce a judgement. For the rest his non-action acts like a magnet which determines a force-field, making particles behave in an ordered fashion. Finally he *gets* asked and anointed by Israel as king over the nation as a whole.

Whilst the upward curve of David stops at nothing, the downward curve of Saul runs its own course. Nothing turns out right any more for the Saulides. It was a long time ago, in terms of narration time, that the two lines crossed each other and the distance between them keeps on and on increasing. In this way they continue the course of the "crossing fates". This development can also be seen from the treatment of women in the Act. The part they play in chs.2-4 takes place in three phases. First we learn of the women of the winning side. There are two of them. They are mentioned by name along with their origins in 2:1-3:5 and their number increases to a series of six mothers who bear David six sons, thereby embodying the coming dynasty. In phase two we meet another two women. This duo is also mentioned by name (in 3:6-21) and is initially part of the losing side. Their position is at the centre, i.e. in the story of the great about-turn, and is a mediating factor. One of the women, someone who was at one time the possession of Saul himself, is taken away from the born loser, Ishbosheth, but she remains in the northern camp; she is sexually possessed by the man who personally defects and who sets the about-turn in motion. The other woman, Michal, is more suited as a mediating figure because her previous history is ambiguous through and through. She is the daughter of Saul, but she had become the spouse of David; after this she was taken away from him by her own father and given in marriage to another, so that she now (at the beginning of ch.3) lives in the territory of her parental tribe. Her extradition is the issue at stake in the negotiations between David and Abner, and her going over to the other side – she too is taken away in ch.3 – is the condition and symbol of the political landslide. The story which employs the displacement of Rizpah and Michal as a metonym for the great about-turn, and in which the fall of the house of Saul becomes inevitable, is the exact centre of the composition and the series of events.

Phase three of the women's part occurs in ch.4. Once again there are two women and again they belong to the losing camp. But these two are given no name and they are simple functionaries. Anonymous though they may be they have a special part to play in the lives of the two sons of Saul: through misfortune and inattention they contribute to disablement and death. In this unhappy role the two mark the calamitous decline of the dynasty. The contrast with David's leading ladies and their motherhood is indeed very sharp. We conclude that the treatment of this small group of characters, three pairs of women, exhibits its own systematics which operates in the service of the theme and is developed along the extended lines of the "crossing fates". In the section concerned the women have an anonymous predecessor, with a special profession, who was consulted by Saul in this capacity: it was the medium of Endor who lent him succour when he had to drink the cup of damnation to the dregs. In this way the aspects of death and calamity have already been brought up in I 28 by a woman side by side with Saul himself.

The crossing lines have brought the highest levels into view, where the group of stories in 2:1-5:5 occurs alongside other groups and so contributes to the sections and to the book. A part of this integration can be dealt with at the end of ch. VI, as we survey the section "Throne and City". But we ought now to be discussing the two series of data which allot Act IX its place next to the previous Act which completed the second section. The first is the isotopy of the parts of the body, the second consists of parallelisms which link the passages on Saul's death with the stories of Abner's death and that of Ishbosheth.

The isotopy of the parts of the body made the calamities of the house of Saul harrowingly visible, but is not limited to ch.4. It has already been prepared for at least as far back as I 31. All occurrences of this are mentioned under the following note; only the main ones will be discussed here.[42] The

[42] In I 28 Saul "falls flat", in anticipation of his death. In I 31:9a and 10b the Philistines chop off his head and hang his body on the wall of Beth Shan. In II 1 the diadem on the head of Saul and the band on his arm (v.10c) are surrounded by the head of the messenger (earth on it at the beginning, and blood on it at the end). In 2:7a there are the hands of the Jabeshites, in 16a/b the

head is continually linked with death or a curse. Prior to the beginning and at the end of the Act there is the severed head of a king, first that of Saul and then that of his son.[43] In addition the head of the Amalekite appears in II 1 and in ch.3 that of Joab, who were both cursed by David.[44] Such company adds nothing to the reputation of the general! Hands are strong or feeble.[45] They appear twice in ch.4 next to legs at different moments of terror.[46] This pair forming directs us to a surprising piece of information. Re-reading the dirge of 3:33-34 we come across a sentence on the hands and feet of victim Abner which, in gainsaying its own negatives, expresses the utmost impotence of the assault victim. In retrospect we now know that there was also a structural reason for the appearance of these parts of the body in a song which had, as its point, David's indignation at Abner's dying as if he were a criminal. They take part in the Saulide isotopy of calamity and are a prelude to ch.4, where the hands and feet of "criminals" (a word used by David himself, in the dirge) put in an appearance to mark their proper punishment.

Ishbosheth's severed head and the execution of the two sergeants reminds us of the mutilation of Saul's mortal remains and the execution of the Amalekite. If we compare the second half of I Sam.31, in which the Jabeshites take down Saul's body from the wall of Beth Shan, with II Sam.4 we find a whole series of similarities and significant contrasts, numbering at least seven:

head/the flank of the champions, in v.18a Asahel is fleet of foot. Chapter 3 is concerned with 8b (dog's head), 8d/12d (hand of David/Abner), 18c (the hand of the enemies), 29a (the head of Joab) and 34ab (the hands and feet of Abner). The climax follows in 4:1b,4b,7de,8ac,12bd.

[43] The heads of the champions also belong to this series in 2:16a which occurs next to their "side" in the text; a demonstration of their destruction.

[44] Notice that there is a balance between Abner and Joab in ch.3. Before David curses Joab in v.29 has not Abner rhetorically cursed himself in 3:8b: "am I a dog's *head* from Judah?"

[45] Strong in 2:7a, 3:8d and 12d (of David and Abner respectively), 3:18c (*bis*, of the enemies). Feeble in 4:1b.

[46] One pair consists of the hands of Ishbosheth in the process of becoming feeble and the crippled legs of Mephibosheth (4:1b and 4b), the other consists of the severed limbs of the murderers in 4:12b.

data from I Sam.31 and II 1	*and counterpart in II Sam.4*
1) In 31:9 the body of Saul is mutilated by the the uncircumcised, he is decapitated: *wayyikr*^{e}*tū 'ęt rōšō*	In II 4:7 the head of Ishbosheth is chopped off by the two assassins, *wayyasīrū 'ęt rōšō*
2) The headless body of Saul is removed; the text is silent on the fate of the head.	Only the head of Ishbosheth is taken to Hebron; the text is silent on the fate of the body.
3) *wayyel*^{e}*kū kol hallaylā* is a token of courage and loyalty.	4:7c repeats this from 31:12 and exhibits treachery and desire
4) The place name *yābeš* means "dry".	the place name *b*^{e}*'erōt* means "springs".
5) The funeral of 31:12 is a posthumous tribute (a gesture which attempts to eradicate desecration).	The funeral of 4:12 is a posthumous tribute (a gesture which attempts to compensate crime).
6) King Saul is the father	King Ishbosheth is the son.
7) II 1 continues with a messenger who brings good tidings (*mgyd – mbśr*),	4:10-11 expressly calls this incident to mind (*mgyd – mbśr*),
8) and ends in an execution (*hrg*)	and ends in an execution (*hrg*)

These components have created a parallelism between the close of the previous Act and the ninth Act, and this figure of equivalence[47] exhibits or underlines certain meanings in its turn. In their ends father and son are brought very close together. The two sergeants from Beeroth are placed in sharp relief against the Jabeshites and their loyalty; their mutilation of Ishbosheth's body and their motive clearly classify them amongst the execrable, somewhere between the Philistines and the Amalekites.

[47] Equivalence comprises similarity and significant contrast. It is the key concept in Jakobson's fundamental recognition of the importance of repetition in wordcraft and occurs in his definition what is literary: "The poetic function projects the principle of equivalence from the axis of selection into the axis of combination." The speech of 1958, published in 1960, which puts forward the definition is entitled "Linguistics and Poetics" and is now also available in the volume brought out by his widow, "Language in Literature", Harvard University Press, 1987.

Act IX is framed by the double anointing of David as king, which occurs in the first and second sequences. Within this ring there is another in which he appreciatively relates to his opposite number. In the penultimate sequence (4:8-12) he pays posthumous tribute and recognition to Ishbosheth by giving him a grave in Hebron, in the first but one sequence he recognises the courage and loyalty of the Jabeshites who have posthumously brought back Saul and given him a funeral fitting to his station. The grave of Saul gets its parallels at the end of II 3 and 4, the dirge on Saul and Jonathan receives a counterpart in the lament on Abner.

INTERPRETATION OF ACT X
(II SAM.5:6-8:18)

והגיד לך יהוה כי בית יעשה לך יהוה

Chapter V

Jerusalem: The City of David?

§ 1. *Introduction to Act X*

The double notation of David's reign in 5:5 serves as an intermediary between two Acts. Its first half, v.5a, looks back to Act IX and its second half, v.5b, looks ahead to Act X (and its successors). Act IX is not only cordoned off by its own closed structure, but is, moreover, more than any other Act in Samuel, marked by spatial terms. There is every good reason for calling it the Hebron Act. In contrast to this Act X stands out as the Jerusalem Act. However, this is not by virtue of a fresh dissemination of spatial references. The narrator now adopts another strategy. He makes the city of Jerusalem thematic by bringing it to the fore in various kinds of ways. In the short, introductory passage, 5:6-12, the city enjoys prominence as an actantial object of David's conquest and subsequent civic development, whilst the status of crown land is conferred upon the "fortress of Zion", as the special term in v.7a puts it. In ch.6 much attention is paid to the sanctification of the united Davidic state's capital by the arrival of the Ark; this act of consecration bestows upon the city the extra dimension of religion, which increases and perpetuates the significance of Jerusalem enormously. The city is absent in not one of the surrounding passages.[1]

The importance of Jerusalem is bound up with the most important aspect of II Sam.5:6-8:18, namely that the entire Act is of a sacral nature. This is not

[1] The analyses which follow will trace the functions of the city. The name Jerusalem occurs twice in the list of 5:13-16. Once the city is designated in a special way in the war story in 5:17-25 (as we shall see), forms the setting for ch.7 (revelation and prayer) and is also present in ch.8 (with its name, in v.7).

difficult to demonstrate; we need only examine God's role here. Whilst the designation *'ĕlōhīm* is only in limited use,[2] the proper noun *yhwh* emerges strongly.[3] And this lexical observation really comes into its own on the narratological plane. In the previous Act YHWH occurred only once in the narrator's text, when he assented to a question of David's.[4] But here in Act X he continually takes part in the action: the Lord is present twice in each literary unit as a real agent. This is a remarkably systematic distribution:
– in 5:6-12 "the LORD, the God of Hosts" is on David's side (v.10b), whilst David himself appreciates, in v.12, the fact that the creation of his monarchy is an act of Yahweh. His activity is named twice in a *parallelismus membrorum* (the object clauses of 12a//b) which prevents our missing the point.
– in 5:17-25 Yahweh is so good as to answer twice, via an oracle, David's request for guidance. In his speeches (vv.19ef and 23c-24c) He lets himself emerge both times as the true agent behind David's prospective victories against the Philistines.
– in ch.6 the Lord manifests Himself as He did in the previous Ark story (I 4-6) as *numen tremendum* and interrupts the solemn procession, which is carrying the Ark into the city, with a fatal blow, v.7. Months later the procession can be completed after the explicit report in vv.11-12 that God has blessed the custodian of the Ark. A negative intervention of God calls a halt, therefore, to an undertaking which the king dares resume only after a positive act of involvement by God.
– in ch.7 the Lord governs the background and the foreground. The background is that He "has given him rest from all his enemies all around" (v.1b), after which David conceives the plan to build a temple for God. Then the Lord appears in the foreground in verse 4 through his word, and by

[2] The word *'ĕlōhīm* chiefly occurs in two clusters: seven times in ch.6 as part of the phrase "the ark of God" (plus an eighth time in 7:2), and eight times on the lips of David, in his prayer in 7:22-28, particularly in order to say that YHWH has become the God of Israel. In conclusion it occurs in 5:10 (overshadowed, because surrounded by, the name *yhwh ... ṣb'wt*) and then just one more time as the subject of an action in 6:7b.

[3] Just imagine, the proper noun, *yhwh* itself, occurs twenty-six times in the narrator's text of this Act, in 5:10b,12a,19a,d,23a,25b, 6:(2d),5a,7a,8a,9a,11ab,13a,14a,15,16a,c,17a,c,18b, 7:1b, 4b,18b, 8:6c,11a,14d. In eleven of these references YHWH is subject, or in twelve if we add 5:23b. The name occurs seven times in the phrase "the ark of Yahweh" (each time in ch.6). In character's text the tetragrammaton occurs twenty-four times: 5:20d,24c, 6:2d,9c,12b,21b,c,d, 7:3c,5b,8b,11c[bis],18d,19a,c, 20b,22a,24b,25a,26b,27a,28a,29b.

[4] In II 2:1bdh YHWH answers David positively twice via the oracle. Afterwards the tetragrammaton occurs only in character's text (speeches which are uttered with varying intensity and purpose), viz. in 2:5c,6a, 3:9b,18b,28c,39c, 4:8d,9c, 5:2c,3b, a total of ten times therefore. The word *'ĕlōhīm* occurs in Act IX three times only in character's text, each time in the introduction to an oath: 2:27b, 3:9a,35c.

according David an extensive oracle with exceptional content (vv.5-16) via a prophet.
– finally in ch.8, where an enumeration of David's conquests is given to us, the narrator points out the true agent with the sentence: "And YHWH gave victory to David wherever he went." The exact repetition of this line (v.6c) in v.14d duplicates the presence of the Lord and articulates all the material of ch.8. The analysis of the successive units should shed more light on these cases of the prominent presence of Yahweh and link them to their context. It is necessary to point out, and suffice it to say, that this is what makes Act X show up against its surroundings. There is indeed no other Act in the books of Samuel which so clearly puts God forward as agent as this one does.[5]

The sacral nature of II Sam.5-8 makes it the apotheosis of David's long rise to power.[6] Taking in the unity of I and II Samuel at a glance I would even go so far as to say that Act X is the sacral centre of gravity of the entire composition. This sort of quality also has its consequences for the treatment of time in this part of the text. On the surface of it the stories' order of appearance in narration time suggests that their referents observe the usual chronological course of events: first conquer Jerusalem and push back the Philistines, then bring in the Ark and receive the oracle. But a close reading discovers several achronistic details already visible at the beginning of the Act; cases of prolepsis in the short run with which I will be dealing in § 2. Next we may notice more far-reaching cases of anticipation. I am silent, as yet, on the historical events of 5:17-25, which a diachronic diagnosis assigns to a previous stage of David's rise.[7] But what I would like to do is refer us to the beginning of ch.7 and ch.8. In 7:1 we read "the Lord had given him [*sc.* David] rest from all his enemies all around". I do not wish to play off this information against the promise of such rest which God gives in v.11b. But I

[5] There is one exception apparently, that of I Sam.4-6, i.e. the major part of Act II, plus the neighbouring chapters 3 (God calls Samuel to the office of prophet) and 7 (the judge Samuel is supported by God). I notice, however, that the subject in I 4-6 is chiefly the ark, that is to say a thing, whatever numinous significance it might have, and not the deity of whom it is the footstool. Further consideration of this is one of the tasks of NAPS IV.

Nevertheless it is striking that this is a comprehensive Ark Narrative which can and must be considered as predecessor and background to II Sam.6. I do not mean diachronically, among other reasons because I do not believe in the separate existence of an Ark Narrative which could have contained both I 4-6 and II 6, or earlier forms of it. A synchronic search for parallels such as the destruction and blessing polarity (in II 6 contra Uzzah and pro Obed-Edom, In I 6 contra Beth-Shemesh and pro Abinadab) which occur when the ark is on the way, will meet the case.

[6] That is why it is natural that many exegetes speak of the *Aufstiegsgeschichte* of David; mostly they allow it to begin in I 16, sometimes in I 15, and to continue up to and including II 6 or 8.

[7] According to N.L. Tidwell in "The Philistine Incursions into the Valley of the Rephaim (2 Sam. v 17ff.)", SVT 30 (1979), pp.190-212.

do maintain that the link, or the difference, between 1b and 11b makes the initial announcement, i.e. 7:1b, relative, persuading the reader to interpret the announcement in v.1 as an advance on permanent security. This question is also subject to the influence of ch.8. Reading this chapter we gather that its summary of victories is detailed evidence of David's security: these triumphs are the fulfilment of God's promise to David.

Chapter eight is, however, itself also proleptic. The military campaigns of David mentioned did not all take place at the same time, shortly after the receiving of God's word. Several of them must have been undertaken in the period covered by II Sam.9-20 (i.e. by the largest part of the fourth section, "King David", which also contains I Ki.1-2). The treatment of time in ch.8 is special in that military highlights are compiled from a whole period whose overall length remains unspecified; say at least half of David's total reign.

The moments of anticipation will now be read from back to front. Successes from around the period of II 9-20 are brought to the fore and classed under ch.8. Why? Apparently because the narrator aims at completeness here. He gives the entire list as it functions in Act X as well as in Acts XI-XIII. During the creation of "King David", the section which is to show the fall of David and its consequences, he cannot, and does not want to, keep to the duties of a historiographer wishing to report the hero's conquests at the right time. The second half of David's reign, and particularly the development of David's dark side, may not be disturbed by the military successes. In *King David* I have shown that the same consideration, one level lower, already occurred to the narrator. During the development of Act XI, the middle of which relates David's two capital crimes, he does not want to divulge the final victory of Joab and David against Rabbath-Ammon. For thematic reasons he postpones the mention of this until the end of ch.12, even though the event took place long before the birth of Solomon.

Alongside the negative reason for keeping the successes of David out of the "King David" section, the narrator also has a positive reason driving him to insert the list in Act X. Bringing the campaigns to the fore in ch.8, he includes them under one thematic denominator which is stated in the key sentence "so Yahweh gave David victory everywhere where he went". In line with this the whole Act is occupied with presenting God's sanctioning David. Reading back once more, I notice that the result of all that Davidic triumphing has again been brought forward and placed at the beginning of ch.7, "rest from all enemies around", in a form which expressly gives God credit for it: "*yhwh* gave David rest". And God's making history here is, if not actually anticipated, then certainly prepared and already indicated in its early stages, by the beginning of the Act. The narrator does more in 5:10 than merely note the sober facts, he interprets and reveals the germ of a historical view when, in an initial conclusion after the taking of Jerusalem, he explains the "David became greater as he went along" of 10a, using v.10b and its extra epithet: "for Yahweh, the God of Hosts, was with him".[8]

The moments of preparation and anticipation are but a part of the entire Act's treatment of time. Another part is the narrator's forgoing a clear time scheme for the single-event occurrences of Act X and their possible succession. No explicit time adjuncts have been included in chs.5-8 which would enable the reader to ascribe the cardinal passages on the Ark and the oracle a reference point on a time scale. This observation in itself has negative connotations and needs to be assessed. The Act's content seems to avoid susceptibility to simple chronology. Such an uncomplicated ordering of events in time is difficult to separate from the transtemporal importance, or, what is more, the transcendental dimension, of these events: the choice of the city of Jerusalem, its sacred status and the promise of a lasting dynasty, given by a deity whose blessing rests upon Zion, appear to rise above the compulsory chronology of consecution which dictates that ordinary events should appear in their allotted space in the text.

§ 2. *David's conquest of Jerusalem and his prosperity there,* 5:6-16

The report of the conquest of Jerusalem, 5:6-12, is not really a report of the conquest of Jerusalem. The event itself is, for an educated person from Judaeo-Christian civilisation, of outstanding importance and he would very much like to hear a lot about it. But the text thoroughly frustrates our historical curiosity. We are told nothing about the course of events, nothing about the armies, almost nothing about the siege. We obtain no insight into the political motives of the hero who has set his sights on this enclave, or into the way in which his choice is viewed in Israel.

Besides, the city's capture is covered by only half the text, i.e. verses 6-8. This part is not characterised by deeds but words. Action is restricted to an absolute minimum. "The king advanced" and "David captured the fortress" is all that is offered to us, in 6a + 7a. Furthermore, these two acts are couched in such simple terms that even the poorest in spirit would be able to think them up if he wanted to say that the hero conquers a city. In other words, even these verbs are barely specific. Such observations caution us to seriously ask ourselves where the text's uniqueness does in fact lie. Not,

[8] Notice that the doubling of the root *hlk* in 5:10 (itself the iterative continuation of the momentaneous *wayyelęk* from v.6a) enters into a collocation with the double *hālak* of David in ch.8 (v.6c//14d).

apparently, chiefly in the nature and the details of the city's capture. The speed with which the siege is over is a textual fact too, whose value must be assessed. It reveals how prosperous the hero is in this undertaking.

The unit as a whole displays a strong quantitative balance. The first half is, in the main, a dialogue between the enemy parties, the second half contains, on the other hand, not one single spoken word and has been given the features of a summary by the writer. The centre, v.8de, leaves the narrative flow through an expression current among the narrator and his original audience. In the space of a moment the framework of the past, the time narrated, breaks.[9] The surrounding two pairs of clusters are of the same dimensions, having five lines each.[10] Thus we get the following composition:

A	arrival, speech of Jebusites to David: derision	v.6a-e
A'	capture, David's speech against Jebusite derision	vv.7a-8c
x	saying (temporal framework broken)	
B	David takes up residence in the city; enlarges it, he is prosperous, with God's support	vv.9-10
B'	Tyrus aids building work David owes his kingdom to God	vv.11-12

This arrangement is in itself a signal as to where we must look for the theme: the prosperity of David and the support of God. But first a stylistic analysis has the right to its say.

The verbs bearing such elementary action are tuned in to each other by means of an alliteration which underlines the way in which one thing stems from another: *wylk* becomes *wylkd*. The initial movement of the hero is opposite to the Jebusites' being seated at the end of the opening line. The alliteration in the series *yᵉrūšālayim – yᵉbūsī – yōšeb* makes the city adhere more strongly to the non-Israelite tribe in residence there, so that the question arises whether the newcomer can lever the two apart. The Jebusites want to talk about

[9] As far as the latter is concerned, a time adjunct such as *'ad hayyōm hazzę̄* could have followed the present tense of *yōmᵉrū*, as for example is the case with parallels such as I 5:5, 6:18, 30:25 and II 6:8, 18:18, without causing a problem. Notice that I give the saying a minuscule not a majuscule x in the scheme which immediately follows.

[10] Generally speaking the cola of my typography of 5:6-12 follow the change of clauses. However, I have divided the long sentence on Hiram's work force and consignment, in v.11, into two. Notice that there is an enumeration of four objects and that the series is interrupted by the placing of the receiver, David, after the first object (the emissaries or diplomats); through this the groups of craftsmen become somewhat isolated, in 11b. In the meantime the length of the objects has continued to grow: from one to two and from another two to three words.

exactly the same thing in their diatribe. But the static singular *yōšeb* is relieved in v.9a, as David "takes up residence in the fortress", that is, by his action *wayyešeḇ*. And the name Jerusalem from v.6a is, as it were, corrected or re-evaluated in v.9b by the hero himself: "and he called it the City of David" (following in the footsteps of the narrator for that matter, v.7b!). It is striking how, temporarily, the name Jerusalem is very infrequently used, if not avoided, even though the city is present clearly enough as the setting for the various stories which are to come in II Sam.[11] In this Act the name is outdone by the telling epithet "the city of David",[12] which intimately and inseparably joins together what the derision of the Jebusites tries to keep apart. Moreover, the name is put into the shade in 5:6-12 by a double *meṣūdā* and by the exclusive name Zion. The twofold introduction of a construct state combination which ends in a favourite proper noun lends importance and cohesion to the lines 7ab, which become a parallelism in the process. As an aside and as a noun clause 7b is the first short interval.

The designation of the hero is also interesting. Following on from his anointing in the sequence 5:1-3, and from the official figures of his reign in vv.4-5, the opening line refers to him once as "the king" during his advance, but that is enough. Subsequently he always, and with striking frequency, appears under his own name.[13] This state of affairs is going to continue for the time being as well.[14] What we are concerned with, therefore, is the highly personal experience and the highly personal new possession of the individual David.

[11] The name Jerusalem occurs in 5:13a and 14a (unavoidably so in view of the connection with 5:5 and the express change from Hebron to Jerusalem), is avoided in 5:17-25, and does not occur either in ch.6 or ch.7 (a feat!); it does not return until 8:7b (the sole occurrence in this chapter). Prior to the conquest the name occurred only as a gloss in I 17:54 (a curious anachronism which has crept into the text) beyond II 8, in the "King David" section therefore, it occurs six times in chs.9-14, becoming frequent only in chs.15-20 (viz. fifteen times).

[12] The phrase and title "the City of David" occurs in II 5:7b,9b and 6:10,12,16, five times therefore. After this Act it does not occur anymore up to and including I Ki.1. In I Ki.2:10 David is buried in his own city; a sequel to this is that the expression occurs another twelve times in I-II Ki. during the funeral of a Judaean king; finally it occurs in I Ki.3:1, 8:1, 9:24 and 11:27.

[13] The proper noun David occurs not less than thirteen times in the brief passage 5:6-12, then twice in v.13. The designation "the king" disappears after 5:6a!

[14] Chapter 5:17-25 also states David every time (totalling nine times), referring not one single time to "the king". As a rule ch.6 also has the proper noun of the hero, viz. eighteen times, and when "the king" does appear it is significant: initially in 6:12a ("and it was told to King David"), then in v.16c in the field of vision of "the daughter of Saul", the contemptuous princess Michal, who thinks she is behaving in a way that befits royalty (she reviles "the king of Israel" in v.20d). Only in ch.7 does the nomenclature change: the hero is included as "the king" in vv.1a, 2a, and 3a, in anticipation of the theme.

The Jebusites imagine that they are safe in their compact fortress, the walls of which fit into the slopes of a mountain chain on three sides. They look down on the besieger and mockingly drive home to him that he will never succeed in penetrating their fortress. The singular *wayyōmęr* with which v.6b lets them have their say links up well with the singular (but collective) form, "the Jebusite", from 6a. Their speech appears to take up three lines. But the introductory word *lēmor* is repeated between 6d and 6e which gives 6e a status of its own. First we listen to their actual words in 6cd: "You shall not come in here; on the contrary, the blind and the lame will turn you out!" During a siege it is not something shocking when well-barricaded defenders call out to the attacker that he will not get in. The derision of the Jebusites is, however, shocking when we realise that it is part of one of the Israelite texts which has been written generations, if not centuries after David, doing duty for a community which finds the unity of David and Jerusalem self-evident. We should try to imagine how the original audience received the text, and then the shock is indeed great: was the most famous king of Israel unable to stand up to a bunch of invalids from a small and forgotten people!? And one of the tremendous implications is the message to David: you don't belong, and you never will belong; keep on roaming outside as war lord with your gang, and forget settling down somewhere.

The narrator redoubles the indignity with the extra *lēmor* which gives 5e a place of its own, as the explanation of the derision, and especially by repeating 5c in 5e, so that the "not coming in" forms a ring around the invalids. The tone in which 5e is put, that of providing an explanation, and the change of the second person to the third for David are both means of distancing oneself from the attempt of David. He is objectified here, as the butt of a war of nerves by the Jebusites. And the omission of an addressee for the second *lēmor* suggests that the message which they proudly send into the country shall resound on all sides: David will never be able to carry off his attempt on our impregnable fortress. Presently the saying will pick up the scornful predicate and immortalise it with rhyme and all: *lō yābō*. But the brunt of his attack is going to point in the other direction.

The fast narrative tempo ensures that no problems arise for David and that the spear point of the derision can be turned round. The city falls without our learning a single detail of the operation involved; a token of David's superiority of course. And as soon as the city has been taken the narrator appears in the role of the faithful notary who enters the new property in the records: verse 7b says in an informative aside "this is the city of David". The narrator once more allows us to feel the distance between his own present time and the reported event as he now gives David his say in 8a and adds the time adjunct "on that day". What David says reveals the point of view of a conqueror who, in looking back, gives the game away on his trick in one gesture, subsequently repudiating the insult. Opposite the alleged impossibility of penetrating the speaker places his solution, as if he were concerned with the solving of a compulsory riddle: "any one who wants to defeat the Jebusite[s] has to hit him on the pipe."[15]

Without now contending that this translation or its explanation is certain I interpret this pronouncement as follows. I take the word *ṣinnōr*, "drain-pipe, water-pipe",[16] to be a reference to the largely vertical shaft within the Ophel, through which the Jebusites, in time of war, could draw their water from the Gihon spring – named "Warren's shaft" after the Briton who discovered it 120 years ago – at the foot of the hill. He who manages to conquer or cut off the source of supply, severs the main artery of those besieged and quickly brings to them to their knees. On a metaphorical level the shaft is the throat or wind-pipe of Jerusalem; the sensitive spot where David has hit "the Jebusite" (the singular consistently links up with that of 6ab).[17]

Verse 8c is a new sentence, and I slightly accentuate its contours with this rendering: "and those lame and blind of yours – David abhors them with all his being".[18] Thanks to this rendering David directly relates, at any rate in this line, to the previous speaker: this is structurally highly desirable due to the regular composition of the paragraphs, and it is encouraged by a chiasmus,

[15] The same syntactical interpretation and a comparable rendering are to be found in RSV, Buber, NBG, KBS, JPS, and McCarter. See also App.1 ad loc.

[16] The word is primarily known from mishnaic Hebrew, occurring only in the plural, as "streams of water", in the Bible in Ps.42:8; see HAL p.972 and its reference to Stoebe, ZDPV 1957.

[17] The text is silent on precisely how we are to visualise this; it was not relevant to the intention of the writer of II Sam., therefore. He who would still like to form a historical opinion is directed to the later variant in I Chr.11 which points to Joab as the man of the surprise attack. Perhaps Joab climbed the shaft with an elite band of men, or took it from above. Our author can hardly pay the general this tribute after the clash between David and Joab in ch.3, and David's cursing the general here – data which do not occur in the Chronicles rewrite.

[18] The Masoretes too recognised a new clause, as is evident from the strongly separative accent above *ṣinnōr*. I reject the syntax of LV, NEB, and CT which reads on, making the invalids the direct object of *yiggaʿ*. With *you* I reproduce the emphasis with which "the lame and the blind" occur initially, which emphasis is also created by the double *'ęt*. I don't believe the Qᵉre *śōnᵉ'ē*, as a proposition it is too superfluous after 5d. The various translations which render *śn'w nfš dwd* as an apposition sound weak on this one. See also App.1.

between 6d and 8c, of the two groups of invalids.[19] David flatly contradicts the Jebusites and in so doing parries their derision. It is a real riposte. The "you" in my rendering makes for a situational interpretation: it applies to the relationship to the enemy underlined by the symmetry A-A'. I do not hear David pronouncing or proclaiming generic prejudice against invalids.[20] What he does is to introduce a reversal. First he was the one who was excluded, now he is in a position to curse, or at any rate to exclude, the forces which were directed against him. His pronouncement occurs as an intermediary between the derision (6e) and the saying (8e). Only when we reach 8de do we leave the situation and end up at a saying which generalises. Now the two groups of invalids are directly linked by "not being allowed to come in". Once again they chiastically join up with their previous appearance, and the gnomic nature of the sentence appears from the singular in which they now occur, and from the absence of the article: "blind and lame comes not into the house", is how abrupt it sounds.[21] What the social function of the saying might have been is something about which we can only speculate impotently. What is more important is to specify how the line relates to the unit in which it has been preserved. In addition to this the importance of its central position within the structure must be assessed. More will be said presently on the saying, as we trace the motif of "the house".

The five lines of vv.9-10 form the third paragraph. Its beginning has clearly been construed parallel to v.7:

7a David captured the fortress of Zion	9a David took up residence in the fortress
7b – this is the city of David	9b and called her the city of David.

The connection between 7a and 9a is that of the simple passage of time, one is made possible by the other. The name Jerusalem is still suppressed, the quality of the word "fortress" impresses upon us the reality of David's keeping on his guard. Military security must come first followed by political

[19] For the sake of curiosity I would also like to mention that the KBS ascribes v.8c to another speaker; the narrator himself is supposed to be the one who tells us: 'David has taken a dislike to the blind and the lame'.

[20] Apparently Buber was afraid of a reading in which David discriminates against the invalids, for he reverses the sense of v.8c by turning it into a rhetorical question: "sollen Hinkende, sollen Blinde Dawids Seele verhasst sein?"

[21] I notice, in addition, that this present tense of 8d puts *y'mr* into the plural for the first time.

and religious development. It is not surprising that a new war story follows at once.[22]

The 7b-9b connection takes us, for the first time, to the treatment of time. The information in 7b is slightly achronistic. The narrator steals a scoop right from under the nose of the hero by divulging the title "City of David" before its *auctor intellectualis* gets round to giving the name! In other words, what happened first of all in narration time, is that the writer quotes from the self-evident knowledge of his audience that Jerusalem *is* the City of David, before the hero can claim it. In its immediate context, vv.6-7, and in the mouth of the narrator, the "City of David" is primarily a well-known essential characteristic of Jerusalem, an objective historical quality which adheres to it thanks to, and since, the annexation; and we are incidentally reminded that the title originates with the hero himself. Alongside this there is a difference between 7a and 9a which is worthy of mention: the narrator speaks of Zion, David does not. This special name is, perhaps, a narrator's hint to his audience concerning the holy mountain, which they know will be crowned, say about forty years later, with the temple of Solomon.[23]

The paragraph vv.9-10 does not only have the same beginning as vv.7a-8c thanks to its first two lines. The following three lines, 9c + 10ab, make sure that it especially forms a parallelism with the paragraph vv.11-12:

(9ab	the hero takes up residence in the City of David	11ab	King Hiram of Tyre lends him carpenters and masons)
9c	David built on all sides, inward from the Millo	11c	and they built a house for David.
10a	David became greater and greater	12a	David recognised that Yahweh had confirmed his kingship over Israel.
10b	and Yahweh (...) was with him.	12b	and that He had lifted up his kingdom for the sake of his people Israel.

In paragraph B (= vv.9-10) the continuous growth of David's power is, via a simple parataxis, traced back to God's support: 10b follows on from 10a. The closing line is boldly underlined, since not only does the text include the title "the Lord of Hosts", but it also reinforces it with a word in between, to *yhwh 'ĕlōhē ṣᵉbā'ōt*. This combination is exceptional in Samuel. Moreover,

[22] The double *mᵉṣūdā* of 5:7-9 is a prelude to "the fortress" in v.17d.

[23] II Sam.5:7 is the only place in the entire composition in which the name Zion occurs.

the title "Lord of Hosts" is characteristic of this Act.[24] Here, in the brief period of war with which the Act opens, it occurs for the first time. This suggests that the miraculously swift and simple surprise attack on the Jebusite fortress is furthered, if not brought about, by invisible powers on David's side – the militant angels of God Himself. I would like to link this with another observation, viz. that the entire Act does not pause at any hero or general from David's army or even give them a mention, in sharp contrast to Act IX where we time and time again ran into commanders, and kings did hardly anything at all. Here in 5:6-10 we see first David himself in action, then the force behind and above him. The connection with his initial movement (*wylk* of 6a) is made by the fine paronomasia *wylk hlwk* which serves David's power (*gādōl*, via fine assonance the continuation of *hālōk*). We can also describe it in another way: the pair *wylk – wylkd* which forms the bare bones of the action ends in, and culminates in, *wayyelęk hālōk w^{e}gādōl* of v.10a, under the supervision of the transcendent power of 10b.

The parallel between 9c and 11c is greater in the original than in translation, since 9c ends on *wābaytā* whilst the Phoenician efforts of the whole of v.11 result in a *bayit* for David. I now take into consideration whether *baytā* of v.9c is just such a prolepsis in regard to the palace in 11c as the title "city of David" in 7b was in regard to the giving of the name in 9b. And, in addition, I expect that these two cases of *byt* itself are once again anticipated by the closing word of 8e, so that the house in the saying may well refer to the royal palace.[25] In narrated time we may assume the building itself was, after all, begun quite soon after the capture of Jerusalem, whilst the saying gains status only through generations of use. Using the guideline of narration time we now get the following series.

The people, not David, took to using the saying "lame and blind shall not enter the palace". In their experience it is connected with the capture of Jerusalem, long ago, when the famous king David had to verbally defend himself against the Jebusites and was abused by them with "lame and blind" who would be able to take him on. The context of 4:4 and ch.9 shows that the line ought not indeed to be ascribed to David. The mutilated state of the

[24] The word *ṣābā*, "army", occurs fourteen times in the secular sense in Samuel, of which ten times as part of the phrase for commander-in-chief (sc. for Abner, Joab and Amasa). The title *yhwh ṣb'wt* occurs only five times in I Sam. (in 1:3,11, 4:4, 15:2 and 17:45, largely programmatic references, of which three in connection with warfare) and six times in II 5-7, viz. 5:10, 6:2,18 and 7:8,26,27.

[25] In any case I reject the designation "temple" for II Sam.5, because nothing prepares for it and it is more or less in inconsistent with the play on *bayit* (temple? no, dynasty! and only later a temple) in ch.7.

house of Saul, illustrated in various ways in ch.4, is not over, but the reader becomes conscious of it in ch.9, when a crippled grandchild of Saul, brought in from somewhere far away, does obeisance to the king. David gives the lame a permanent place of honour in his palace.[26] Subsequently 5:9c tells us how David enlarges the city: "from the Millo", some bulwark or another which formed a distinct part of the fortress walls, "towards the palace",[27] i.e. up to the place in the centre of the small city where he plans to have his own house. With the assistance of craftsmen recruited from abroad he gets his palace. The B-B' order means, amongst other things, that David's own people can manage to fill the city with buildings, but that his palace requires special craftsmanship. Thanks to the alliance with Hiram king of Tyre he now had Phoenician craftsmanship at his disposal; it must have been a splendid construction. In v.11 the language itself is the product of craftsmanship.[28]

Just how much the saying, the motif of the palace and the invalids are connected with one another becomes apparent on the basis of two further observations. The word *bayit*, the verb "to enter" plus negative, and the lame/blind pair all occur exactly three times in our text, and they are all excised from the rewriting of the event in I Chr.11.

The parallel between v.10 and v.12 is obvious. Against the background of similarity two shifts are noticeable: the perspective, and the factor of Israel. In v.10 the narrator himself reports David's power and God's support. For this he uses words which make David the successor of Samuel.[29] The relationship between God and David returns, it is true, in v.12, but is much more specific. It concentrates on the royal office (*mlk*; in 12a and in 12b) and is linked with God's own people: with Israel (also occurring twice, as epiphora). This is now subordinated to the point of view of the hero. The narrator begins with "David recognised" and establishes the fact that David himself acknowledges and feels at home with the origin of his power and monarchy. The two object clauses give evidence of being a *parallelismus membrorum* which is broadly based on three word pairs and which, as the climax to a careful choice of words, brings the unit to a close in an attractive way:

[26] The word *pisseᵃḥ* occurs only in 5:6-8 and along with Mephibosheth.

[27] The min *hammillō wābaytā* construction is of the same type, for example, as the phrase on the height of Saul who "was taller than everyone *miššikmō wāmaʿlā*".

[28] The kings and their project are linked by the sounds -īr: *ʿīr (dāwīd)* – *ḥīrām* – *qīr*. There is a chiasmus in *ʿăṣē ʾărāzīm* + *ḥārāšē ʿeṣ*, in view of the guttural series + reš + sibilant between the forms for "wood". And the double *ḥārāš* alliterates with the name of the of the sender, *ḥīrām*.

[29] See I Sam.2:26 (as the climax of the 2:11b – 2:18 – 2:21c series) on the growth of the young Samuel and how acceptable to God he is.

12a ...	kī hę̆kīnō	yhwh	l^{e}męlęk	‘al		yiśrā’el
12b	w^{e}kī niśśē		mamlaktō	ba‘ăbūr	‘ammō	yiśrā’el

The syntax of both clauses is also drawn parallel. The word *mamlākā* has resonances reaching far back.[30] But it is, at the same time and together with the name of the people,[31] a prelude to the solemn words of the crucial text of 7:8-16, the oracle of God favouring a Davidic dynasty. Both there and here the throne of David is a phenomenon in the service of a much greater project: the history of God and his people. And the divine election of David, glorious though it is, is only a means used to benefit the covenant between Yahweh and Israel.[32] David recognises this himself at this point.

The parallelism of parts B and B’ is so great that I would like, for a moment, to look at what happens to our reading if we switch them round. This is not a difficult operation and it also results in a configuration with an attractive ending to its unit, viz., David’s peaceful residence, the completed city and the sanctioning, solemn verse 10. But we observe that the narrator spurns this option. He would rather have the construction of the palace for an ending, and in particular, David’s recognition of the blessing of God resting upon him. Thus the palace has become the tailpiece and culmination of all the work of building and, supported by the *bayit* motif (three times), at the same time, the token and confirmation of David’s prosperity. Furthermore the B-B’ order means that the unit, thanks to the final rhyme on the name of Israel, closes with the national dimension giving David his proper place. Now for the overall survey, the wording of which I have altered slightly:

A	attack, challenge of the defenders	speech
A’	capture, the attacker nullifies the challenge	speech
[the saying from a later period used for the axis]		
B	taking up residence, city building, God’s support	report
B’	craftsmen from Tyre, palace construction, David acknowledges: God makes me king on behalf of His people	report

[30] The previous references to "monarchy" favouring David (and contra the doomed Saul) are I Sam.13:13-14, 15:28, 20:31, 24:21, (28:17) and II 3:10,28. Those yet to come are a cluster in ch.7: in verses 12,13,16.

[31] "The/your people Israel" is an ideologically important phrase, which we meet in I 2:29, 9:16, 13:13-14, 15:1,30, 27:12, II 1:12, 3:18,37, 5:2,12, 6:21, 7:7,8,10,11,23,24, 16:15, 19:41 and 24:4. Notice that of these twenty-one references not less than nine occur in our Act X: a concentration.

[32] The words of the covenant formula are indeed shortly to appear in the text, in David’s long prayer of thankfulness for the oracle in 7:18-29.

Due to the parallelism of 7ab and 9ab I am, for a moment, tempted to classify the labels as AB-BA. But I will not, in fact, do so. Nevertheless, this concentric scheme does enable me to find a few oppositions which clarify our view on the supporting roles. In the first and last paragraphs two groups and two individuals occur in polar opposition and can easily be allocated the actantial positions of helpers and opponents. Facing "the Jebusite" (as consistent singular!) is the Phoenician ally, king of another city state, Tyre. The one party hurls abusive but impotent jeers at David, the other furnishes constructive deeds. The Jebusite sends the paper tiger of "the lame and blind" into the ring against David, Hiram sends David skilled craftsmen and supplies him with stately accommodation.[33]

The treatment of time prior to the saying differs greatly from the way it is dealt with afterwards. The AA' flank has a minimum of action and a high narrative tempo. In our example here these features cover the instantaneousness of the event and the limited scale of narrated time. After the saying the BB' flank conveys acts of a chiefly durative nature: residing, building, growing, being settled. The completion of the city and the construction of the palace themselves easily take some years. This length of time is an effective transition to yet more summary and overview, with which the omniscient narrator makes himself felt in *the separate paragraph formed by vv.13-16*: the rapid enumeration of eleven births in vv.14-16 covers still more years, and is, being offered here immediately after David's removal to the definitive capital city, fully proleptic.

The function of 5:13-16 is highly determined by its position in the text. Once again procreation is the sequel to the reports of David's power and a manifestation of his prosperity and prospects. The paragraph is, of course, the counterpart of 3:2-5, the birth of David's sons in Hebron.[34] It has its own structure. The double *yld* which formed a ring around the names in ch.3 has now been placed in the initial position (5:13b + 14a), the mothers' names no longer receive a mention, and a line (13b) is devoted to the male/female balance: "and again sons and daughters were born to David" – a registration

[33] I notice another semantic nicety. Paragraph B' seems to be framed by the parallel that in v.11a *mlk* borders on *-rām*, "high" (the predicative element of the original theophoric name Aḥiram) whilst in 12b *nś'* "to lift up" occurs next to *mmlkh*.

[34] Several details in the text to support this: the double *'ōd* in 5:13ab presupposes the former paragraph; the Hebron/Jerusalem switch is expressly indicated by the temporal final clause of 13a and the mention of both place-names; after which the final word of 14a marks the difference once more.

which makes us think of genealogical notations in Genesis.[35] The names of eleven sons then follow in vv.14b-16 in a uniform parataxis without any extra qualification.

Here is the position of this list once again. We recognise a parallelism of not less than four elements, preceded by a chiasmus which makes up part of the concentric structure of Act IX. Firstly I would like to give the chiasmus in IX:

David anointed over Judah *versus* Ishbosheth king

[axis: Abner defects]

Ishbosheth eliminated whereupon David anointed over Israel

Next I would like to single out two elements concerning David from this quartet, because they fit in at the top of the list of parallelisms. I allocate a place for them there, along with the description in italics:

	Act IX		end of IX and beginning of Act X
David anointed king	2:4 > 7	//	5:1-3
formulas of reign	2:10-11	//	5:4-5
war story	2:12-31	//	5:6-9
David "stronger all the time"[36]	3:1	//	5:10 > 12
list of sons born in Hebron and Jerusalem respectively	3:2-5	//	5:13-16

These correspondences produce the insight that Acts IX and X have a highly similar start and are closely connected.

We are now in a position to determine the theme of 5:6-12 (and vv.6-16

[35] See Genesis 5 where, after the birth of the firstborn, who is mentioned by name, "sons and daughters" follow continually, at the end of vv.4,7,10,13 etc. The same procedure in the second half of Gen.11.

[36] This parallel can especially be discovered via the double and figurative use of *hlk* in 3:1 and 5:10.

respectively). As I already said it was not the capture of Jerusalem. That unexpectedly rapid conquest occurs as a instantaneous element in the service of the length of time in 9-12. And the length of time is a temporal datum in the service of the meaning: stability. The message is one of settling down and safety, consolidation for David and the protection of God. The narrator has given himself surprisingly little room to say all this, a mere 109 words (in vv.6-12); thus forcing himself to make the most of every word. As a consequence his vocabulary here is unusual and concentrated. It opens or closes the collocations of several key words.[37] I would like to single out just one detail by way of example. The words *kwn* and *bayit* both occur twelve times in Samuel, both concentrate half of their occurrences in this Act and both begin the last series in 5:9-12.[38] The word *mamlākā* also occurs twelve times in Samuel and these cases form an important series; this word and several others in v.12 make our 5:12b location, among other things, the opposite pole to the important passage of I 13:13-14 (the first blow Saul receives).[39]

§ 3. *David beats the Philistines,* 5:17-25

The design of 5:17-25 is transparent: war with the Philistines in two rounds each of which take up a part of the text, part A = vv.17-21 and part B = vv.22-25. The material can be described in three steps: the Philistines attack, David asks for and receives an oracular answer from God, David wins the battle. In accordance with this each half opens and closes with reports from the narrator, whilst consulting God produces speeches in the middle.

This comprehensive parallelism forms the background against which a series of differences between the halves stands out. The first half concerns the way in which the two conflicts are introduced. I observe that the beginning of 17b is extended into 22a (the advance of the Philistines becomes an "again

[37] First of all see notes 2-4, 8, 11-14,24,30 and 31 above. Moreover I would like to mention that "cedars" only further occurs in 7:2,7, that various alternatives for *bayit* are thoroughly explored in ch.7, that the name-giving element returns in 6:2,8, and that the word *yᵉbūsī* further occurs only twice in II 24 (v.16,18 – and cf. next note on *bnh*).

[38] The root *kwn* occurs in I 7:3, 13:13, 20:31, 23:22,23, 26:4 and II 5:12 and 7:12,13,16,24,26. The verb *bnh* occurs in I 2:35 and II 5:9,11, 7:5,7,13,27 for building a "house", in I 14:35(bis) and II 24:21,25 for the building of an altar (in II 24 on mount Zion!). In note 24 we saw that *ṣᵉbā'ōt*, in the sacral sense, also occurs *six* times in Act X beginning with flank BB' in this unit.

[39] The word *mmlkh* occurs six times in I Sam., viz. 10:18, 13:13,14, 24:21, 27:5 and 28:17, and six times in Acts IX-X, viz. in II Sam.3:10,28, 5:12 and 7:12,13,16. Six of the twelve references are connected with David's election, three with the rejection of Saul. The *kwn* + *mlk* combination occurs in I 13:13, 20:31, II 5:12a and 7:12,13 (and cf. vv.16,25).

came up"), whilst 18b + 19a recur in exactly the same way in 22b + 23ab. This technique repeats the introduction of A by rigorously condensing it, but at the same time it is clear that 17a remains outside of this. The opening line contains, therefore, the datum which gets the enemy on the move and applies to both halves. I render the line with a pluperfect because it is a flashback in respect of what has gone before.[40] "Now the Philistines had heard that they had anointed David king over Israel." This opening reaches back over the unit 5:6-16 to 5:1-3 which tells of the anointing of David.

I value this flashback in two ways. The first is obvious: in v.17 the narrator reaches back to vv.1-3 in order to show that the Philistines react at once after receiving the report of the coronation in Hebron. The power politics aspect is clear, if the Judaean newcomer is not dealt with now it might never be possible to bring him to heel again. However, the flashback has yet another side to it; it does not occur until v.17, or to put it another way: the same narrator who wanted to indicate the close connection of v.17 with vv.1-3 has nevertheless chosen to put the unit of 5:6-12 (and what is more: the anticipatory short paragraphs of 5:4-5 and vv.13-16) in between.[41] He seems, therefore, to have created a synchronism. The capture of Jerusalem and the Philistines' advance eastward have (if we take the text in the form in which it has been handed down to us seriously – and this is just what I try to do) taken place at approximately the same time.[42]

I now see the grouping of the lines at the opening. There are three pairs and they display the symmetry of the war dance. The Philistines hear and move, then David hears and moves. There is auditive contact, and the proper point of departure is sought in order to deliver the decisive blow when physical contact takes place. The quest of the Philistines is expressed as straightforwardly as possible lexically, with the naked words that they advanced "to search for David". This choice of words is highly reminiscent, together with the double "hear" enclosing it, of I Sam.23 and the situation facing Keilah.

[40] 5:17a is at least a flashback in respect of vv.9b-16 which take up a sizable amount of narrated time (after the capture of Jerusalem); the possibility of its being a flashback in respect of 5:6sqq is not precluded – but only on condition that "the fortress" of v.17 is not Jerusalem, which I contest below.

[41] This is a synchronic not a diachronic exercise. He who wants a diachronic view of II Sam.5 at all costs can replace "the narrator" with "the redactor" in my sentence. Presently I will be giving reasons as to why I find it difficult to believe in the prevailing assumption that 5:17-25 originally belongs to the early David, the condottière of the [narrated time of] I 22-23.

[42] This very assertion leads to the interpretation of *m^e^ṣūdā* which is next and reads: David withdraws into the fortress of Zion.

In this passage too David faced the Philistines and here also he obtained the solution twice by consulting God via the priestly oracle. But during this phase of his life he was the target of the doomed Saul's searching. Now the national enemy attempts to give him back the taste of being hunted for one, then two times, but this hunt too has no chance of succeeding.

I render v.17d as: David "entered the fortress" or "withdrew himself[43] into the fortress", meaning Jerusalem itself! My hermeneutics argues strongly for, among other things, the reader's submitting to the directives of the style, part of which is the guiding function of the key word. If, therefore, in the immediately preceding and very brief passage, the word *m^eṣūdā* refers to Jerusalem as many as two times, then I must be consistent in my obedience to the style and be bold enough to recognise the recently acquired stronghold in v.17.[44] This interpretation has its implications for the treatment of time, it makes the synchronism more compelling. Reading between the lines I perceived that the conquest of Jerusalem ran its course miraculously quickly due to the efforts of an invisible, but decisive army – remember how II Ki.6:15-18 worded such a presence – which is enlightening as to why the quick capture: this is how David obtained the stronghold which he needed right away in the sight of the enemy advancing from the west!

The lines alternate in pairs. In 17cd David replies to the enemy initiative of 17ab. Lines 18ab are once again devoted to the enemy. The iconic message of this switch is that David must beware of getting surrounded. "The Philistines forced their way in and fanned out in the Valley of the Rephaim." The lines are not lacking in menace and bring impending danger in the southwest

[43] Sometimes *yrd* does not mean "go down" but its opposite (see II Ki.2:2 and 6:18) or actually "withdraw" with a possible defensive nuance, in Judg.11:37 and 15:8 (*yrd* + *sl'* and then *wyšb*, just as in:) I Sam.23:25. See HAL p.415a which offers a whole series of references, not all of which are equally convincing. Another application of *yrd*, it seems to me, is "enter into battle" in I 26:10, 29:4 and 30:24. Notice that *yrd* in II Sam.5:17-25 occurs in opposition to *'lh* each time, whilst it is not about the high/low distinction, but about a military move.

[44] Some, such as NBE and McCarter, believe in a "fortress of Adullam" pointing to I 22 or II 23:19, but this is not convincing. Firstly "the fortress of Adullam" is foreign to the text, which refers to "the cave of Adullam" in I 22:1 and II 23:13. That David "remains in the *m^eṣūdā*" in I 22:4-5 is probably just as indefinite as the plural *m^eṣādōt* of I 23:15,19 and 24:1 which requires a place-name each time for further elucidation. Secondly the Adullam region is probably too far west for our text, the confrontation taking place much closer to Jerusalem – see McCarter's sketch, p.524. Thirdly, the datum "in the fortress" of II 23:14a is not identical to "the cave of Adullam" in v.13, but occurs here because of the very fact that it is different (according to Goslinga, p.103, who also renders this *m^eṣūdā* as indefinite: "in the region of the (natural) hiding-places and mountain fortresses", pp.103 and 463). Fourthly, the occurrence of the name Adullam is too far removed from II 5 to be able to be inserted here just like that.

to Jerusalem.[45] The name of the lowlands where the Philistines fanned out[46] bodes no good, "the Valley of the Titans". I detect a mythical undertone here backed up by the connotations of "the Rephaim" in Deut.2-3, and especially by the indirect comment in II Sam.21-24. Here we encounter yet a few more ogrish giants, petrifying to all mortals except David and his heroes and forming the sons of Rapha in a row, 21:15-22. Even the valley returns once more, in a short paragraph which wants to be taken as a counterpart of ch.5 (and has a polar mention of water!), 23:13sqq.

Once again the camera swings round to the other side. Following on from the somewhat receptive *wayyišma'* of David is his more active *wayyiš'al*, David consults God. Keeping to the auditive level the centre of half A is taken up by a dialogue: the words of David's question and those of God's reply. Both speeches take up two lines again and their verbs mirror each other. Moving on ahead for a moment I can see the proportions of the outcome. After the speeches the enemy is finished off in two lines (20ab). David's pronouncement on God's intervention (20d) is immortalised in a name (20e) and follows the two-line pattern. Then another duo rounds off passage A with a report on booty. If we count the solitary *wayyōmęr* of 20c with its content, we can clearly see that the whole articulates in terms of six-line groups:

exposition:	3x2 lines	the two parties take up positions
development:	2x3 lines	dialogue: oracle consulted
denouement:	3x2 lines	David wins, name given

The first series is report only, the centremost one consists of speeches, and the final series is itself concentric insofar as two brief lines of report occur twice around two long lines of utterance (David on *prṣ* > name giving).[47]

Situated around the centre, the arrival of David (20a) corresponds to that of the Philistines in 18a. The place designations contribute to this: they rhyme, assonate and apportion the same stresses over an identical number of sylla-

45 The Emeq Rephaim has not been identified with complete certainty, but I consider McCarter's little map (p.524) a likely reading. Apart from this I question the persistent need of historical-critical scholarship to historically and topographically identify the data of a notoriously literary construction. Does the text permit this kind of pegging things down, or require it? It is more important to follow the play on words: from *p*^{e}*lištīm* to *p*^{e}*rāṣīm*, from *r*^{e}*fā'īm* to *b*^{e}*kā'īm*. The artefact exists in a way peculiar to itself.

46 For *nṭš*, "fan out", see Appendix I.

47 I notice another detail which establishes this concentric order. It is the position of the little word *šām* in the lines of report which border on the *prṣ* matter, it occurs both in 20b and 21a immediately after the wyqtl form.

bles of a s^emikut: the threatening of the *'emęq r^efā'īm* is answered by the blow at *ba'al p^erāṣīm*. Notice that the final place-name, put in 20a, anticipates the name giving of 20de – in exactly the same way as v.7b did with "the City of David" which did not get its name until 9b. This correspondence to the previous unit is amplified when we notice how v.8de corresponds to v.20e: a pronouncement (here name giving, there a saying) which, with its present tense's attainment of the public's present day, makes for a frame-break regarding narrated time.[48] The two details of the treatment of time themselves are a subtle hint that the 5:17-25 unit has been created for this place and has not been attracted from anywhere else. Also regarding the proper noun *yhwh* and the twofold divine intervention this passage is an exact fit in the Act's overall pattern.

The blow at the place "Baal of Breaches" is the blow delivered by the Master of Breaches. The victor himself, David, points to the hidden but true agent in v.20d. My reading of the name is a double one therefore, and I let it refer to the deity as well. This literary recognition of ambiguity can be justified by observing that the beginning and end of the 20de pair are chiastic.[49] The singular of the verb acknowledging a unique act is amplified and elevated beyond the punctual in the generalisation of the noun plural: *pāraṣ yhwh* changes into *ba'al p^erāṣīm*. The speaker David gives us a two-sided image of water: the flash flood – for this is what the *pęręṣ mayim* of 20d is – means life for him but his opponents are unexpectedly dragged to their deaths, past saving. The words are carefully ordered in an interior and an exterior duo:

pāraṣ yhwh   *k^epęręṣ mayim*
         'oy^ebay l^efānay

The interior duo (bearing in mind their *-ay* rhyme) offers us the confrontation of mortals; they are surrounded by the forces who decide on their fate, God and water. The Jebusites were outmanoeuvred via their water conduit, the *ṣinnōr*, and now it is the Philistines' turn to be subjected to the

48 Even though David cannot be precluded as the grammatical subject of v.20e (SV and KJ have this), I render the line with an impersonal subject in line with the present consensus: "that is why one calls this place Baal of Breaches".

49 An indirect justification from the field of the history of religion is that the name/the word *ba'al* used in early Israel was still in use for the God of Sinai, as is apparent e.g. from several theophoric names which retain the element *ba'al* without our needing to doubt the yahwistic soundness of the bearer or his parents. Think about Jerubbaal, Eshbaal etc.

surprise attack of a flash flood. In their way they too had been mindful of supernatural aid but their gods did not come to the rescue.

The end informs us of the enemy ignominiously being forced to abandon his idols there and then (21a), so that they become a prey to the victors (21b). The latter are designated in just the same fashion as on their way to Jerusalem in v.6a: "David and his men". The fate of the idols matches I 31:8 when the king of Israel was the loser and his head was sent round the houses and temples as good tidings.[50] Their location at the end is ironic: we learn of the gods only after the defeat of their worshippers has supplied proof of their impotence.

In half A the Emeq Rephaim threat was met by the Master of Breaches, who came to help David by way of a flash flood – we count three construct state combinations. Half B also has three which require stringing together. Attacking through the same valley once again, the enemy is now designated by the combination *maḥănē p^{e}lištīm* (24c), and this time is defeated by the force(s) which come(s) marching up "over the tops of the baka bushes" (24a).[51] In this way the threat is parried with *p^{e}rāṣīm* in one part, and in the other with *b^{e}kā'īm*: both are natural forces which God uses to defend David, and both also rhyme with and reply to *r^{e}fā'īm*.

The composition of half B uses two, not three, series of six lines. Two small groups of three lines of report frame one long, central speech of six lines. Just as 22ab is the shortened form of vv.17-18, so 23ab condenses the lines 19abc. As a corollary David's questioning of the oracle need no longer be included, leaving God as the sole speaker in B. What mainly characterises B now is that God speaks for a very long time, 23c-24c, and gives precise instructions on military strategy. Afterwards no more names are given. However, place-names as such do occur, this time in the narrator's text in 25c. They are two in number, both are segholate forms which alliterate, *gęba'* – *gęzęr*, and they are successors to the word pair at the end of v.20a=e. Something else specific to B is the formula of obedience applied to David in 25ab. We are more accustomed to these words as applying to Moses, and they substantially add to the portrait of the David of Act X. He is the obedient servant of God who is to

[50] Notice that I 31 has the same combination of plur. plus suffixes, *'ăṣabbēhęm*, and that the strongly alliterating verb of II 5:21a, *'zb*, also occurs here with the loosing side (v.7, also of the wyqtl type). On the basis of this observation with respect to verse 21 I reject what N.L. Tidwell, SVT xxx (1979), "The Philistine Incursions into the Valley of Rephaim (2 Sam. v 17ff.)," pp.190-212, does with the idols, explaining them away (p.210sq.).

[51] Notice that all three cases of s^{e}mikut are introduced by the same preposition, they rhyme with each other and occur, with a final s^{e}mikut in 23e, at the end of their line. An additional comment on *mḥnh*: this word can be viewed as an echo of Act VIII, where it often occurs; this establishes the connection I just made with I 31.

call him "my servant" two units further; an honorary title with which, once again, we are more familiar in reference to Moses. In this way the reciprocity of the king and his God becomes great and intimate.

The long speech of God appears to far transcend the binary scheme of the priestly oracle – which responds with yes or no via the Urim and the Thummim. The first counsel David receives is that a different kind of strategy is now needed to defeat the Philistines. The "do not engage in a direct attack" of 23c is the successor to 19e and occurs exactly opposite it. An alternative which is further elucidated by a local detail in v.23e immediately follows the prohibition, 23d. David has to make an outflanking movement and attack the enemy from behind. The mention of the *baka* bushes is a prelude to the set of three forming the denouement, 24abc. Each line of the initial set of three mentions a movement of David, 23cde. In the decisive v.24 the "striding forward" and "marching out" of God occur around David's part, 24b. The extent to which these two verbs are synonymous is illustrated in the poetry of the theophany: they also occur as a word pair in Judg.5:4 and Ps.68:8 which shows Yahweh's military intervention to give his people victory.

The proportions of the six lines reveal where the decision is taken, with a striking interruption. There is a regular increase in magnitude which is sharply disturbed by the brief v.24b, which I render with "strike!" in the sense of "take decisive action!"[52] The series alongside it has 2 + 3 + 4 + 7 + 8 words. The word *'āz* marks zero hour and creates, by occurring in duplicate, a synergism between David's attack and God's military participation. Just as the conjunction itself shows, the long line 24c explains what the mysterious sound in the tops of the trees of 24a means. Once again there is the suggestion of heavenly hosts coming to the rescue. Thanks to the preposition *lpny*, the proper noun of God and the enemies as object, 24c becomes the counterpart of 20d (more than of 19f). But now God Himself speaks in advance, in 20d it was the king who looked back in thankfulness. Their synergism also lies in the fact that *l^{e}hakkōt* is ascribed to God as his aim in 24c, whilst it is realised by David in 25c. The "hearing of steps (*ṣ^e'ādā*)" by

[52] This "act with decision" is the good rendering offered by BDB. This dictionary mentions our passage under *ḥrṣ* I, and does not recognise *ḥrṣ* II – different from and better than Ges-B, KBL and HAL which all have a rendering to the effect "eifrig hinter etwas her sein" and here "pass auf!" The aspect "resolved" is important in many references, see Dan.9:26sq, 11:36, Is.10:23 and 28:22 for the niph'al, and I Ki.20:40, Job 14:5 for the qal. The participle *ḥārūṣ*, which in I Ki.20 is said of *mšpṭ*, refers in Is.10:22 to *klywn*, after which *nḥrṣh* (ibid. v.23) is almost synonymous with *klh* (destruction, = v.22). "What is determined" in Job 14:5 is also *in malam partem*.

David is the sequel to his hearing and the *m^e^ṣūdā* of v.17. His *ḥrṣ* is the extension of *prṣ*.

In 6:13 the striding onwards of the procession follows on from the striding onwards of God and bears the ark into Jerusalem, also *ṣ'd*. In 6:7-8 a new *prṣ* incident occurs which is once again immortalised in the giving of a name. It is apparently the opposite pole of, and a warning after, the pro-David breakthrough in 5:20. These forward-looking links and the various details which point backwards from 5:17-25 in common with the sacral dimension of the piece and God's double action convince me that this unit has been written for the place in which it occurs and that the analysis of its style and structure makes the diachronic diagnosis (that the unit originates elsewhere) superfluous, if it has not demonstrated the latter's inaccuracy.

§ 4. *The ark is transferred to the City of David,* II Sam.6

The composition of the whole; quantitative symmetries.

The plot of chapter 6 is simple and largely coincides with David's aim of fetching the portable sanctuary to his new capital. The ark had long ago accompanied the Israelites during their desert journey and had subsequently taken its place in the temple of Shiloh. But since then it had been captured during the war (I Sam.4) and, after peregrinations throughout Philistia, had ended up finally in Kirjath-jearim (at the end of I 6). However, in his resolve to move the ark David gets involved in two serious incidents. The first of these is the Uzzah affair which halts the undertaking for three months, the second consists of his own wife taunting him. Both cases end up in a specific death the details of which will be described later.

The text of II Sam.6 is, therefore, a passage in four parts: the record of a great national procession (vv.1-5) which is interrupted (vv.6-12) and only achieves its objective after resumption (vv.13-19), after which a personally-delivered bucket of cold water awaits the king at his homecoming (vv.20-23). This closing sequence is the only place where dialogue occurs; the rest of the chapter consists almost exclusively of narrator's text. The lay-out of ch.6 is obtained quite quickly, except for the middle. I have long hesitated as to the position of 12c, which verse runs: "David set out and brought up the ark of God out of the house of Obed Edom to the City of David with joy". Does this long line go with what has gone before or with what follows? We can see that it supplies two spatial references. The first points back to the ark's delay after the Uzzah incident, the second looks ahead to the objective. These spatial data do not make our decision any the easier, therefore. And what happens when we turn to the key word *'lh*? The only thing the line has in common with the very long sentence of v.2 is that it commences with two wyqtl forms and has David as grammatical subject; his bringing up of the ark (no more than an infinitive in v.2!) appears to be realised in v.12. However, shortly afterwards we read v.15 where this movement becomes more than a report: it is depicted by a durative clause which places David, for the first time since (the just as durative and festive) v.5, next to "all the house of Israel". The fact that the actual entry of the ark occurs in vv.13-16a bestows an anticipatory quality on v.12c.

The line 12c can, therefore, be read as the end of the long interruption and as the beginning of the resumption of the procession. The question as to where v.12c belongs gets a curious and very ambiguous answer when we count the words of the four parts of the chapter. I use the letter P for the rite's getting underway and its completion – the p stands for procession and for positive – whilst C stands for the conflicts which form, for David, such a nasty disturbance of the sacral proceedings and revolve round Uzzah and Michal. As is common practice at the boundary of verses 3 and 4 I delete six words, an easily recognisable dittography, and in the final clause of v.2 I delete one *šm*, for the good of the syntax, as various commentators do also.[53] Verse 12c takes up a seesaw position and I note its number of words separately:

P_1	C_1	[v.12c]	P_2	C_2
72	107	[12]	107	72

If we include v.12c in what has gone before, the middle has 119 + 107 words, and if we classify it under what follows then we get 107 + 119 words. That is why my answer to the question as to whether v.12c is a part of C_1 or of P_2 is: both and neither one of the two, at any rate on this level, where I am to divide the text as a whole. A step lower, on the eighth level of my text model, there are good reasons for regarding v.12c as a part of C_1, as we shall see.[54] But in respect of the story as a whole the line fulfils the quantitative and qualitative[55]

[53] In my colometric typography I have put both dittographies in square brackets. There are more good reasons than just the syntactic one for dropping the short dittography in v.2c, see Appendix I.

[54] This model, which distinguishes six layers in the texture and, above it, six layers in the composition (reaching from sequences and speeches via the literary unit of the story or the "scene" to sections and the whole book), is discussed in NAPS II, ch.1.

[55] What I mean by quality is meaning and narrative function; I have mentioned the spatial data and the anticipatory (v.15) and retrospective (vv.2 and 5) links.

function of a Janus type of parallelism,[56] or perhaps, still better, of a roof tile construction.

Is it not possible that the symmetry of 72-107-[12]-107-72 is just a coincidence? And does not the assumption of a dittography in the text handed down to us cast a slur on this series? These objections can be eliminated because, one and two levels lower, we again encounter different quantitative symmetries. But first I would like to comment on levels seven and eight. I refer to corners P_1 and C_2 (i.e. vv.1-5 and vv.20-23) as sequences because of their strong internal cohesion. The larger parts C_1 and P_2, which take up much room in the middle, are organised in a different way. The first piece can still be well divided into sequences, there are two: vv.6-9 with the incident at the ark and vv.10-12 on the delay. But vv.13-19 is less susceptible to a natural articulation of sequences.[57] In this part of the trajectory there is a loose kind of succession on the syntagmatic axis and further analysis of the texture makes me prefer to speak of several series of short links rather. These small units are also visible in vv.6-12 where each verse constitutes such a link.

New quantitative series govern both the level of the links and that of the corners. The initial and final sequences each have their own tripartition. The opening, vv.1-5, is articulated into three links: an introduction, vv.1-2, which defines the king's aim and the special status of the sacred object, a close-up of the cart with the priests next to it (vv.3-4), and, as closure, a long durative clause full of festivity, v.5, half of which is a long list of musical instruments. The end, vv.20-23, has as primary characteristic the presence of dialogue, which implies the elementary distinction between report and speech. Here the threefold division consists of a speech of Michal versus a speech of David, with the narrator's text as the cement which keeps the dialogue together and frames it. The figures for the words adding up to seventy-two in both cases are:

[56] For the Janus parallelism, primarily a poetical term, see Wilfred G.E. Watson, "Classical Hebrew Poetry, A Guide to Its Techniques", Sheffield 1984 (JSOT Supplement Series 26), p.159. An example is the word *zāmīr* in The Song of Songs 2:12: occurring in the middle of a tricolon, it means "pruning" with respect to colon A, and regarding colon B, "singing". Notice that in 2:12 and 14 the balance between the auditive and the visual is important.

The roof tile verse 12c covers the end of half I and the beginning of half II. In poetry this kind of double function is sometimes made explicit by a redoubled writing of the connection in a so-called "terrace pattern": see Watson for this kind of overlapping, ibid. pp.208-213.

[57] Notice that a small preparatory link on Michal (four clauses, v.16) occurs between two longer series of sentences. If necessary these can be called sequences: vv.13-15 at last the ark's entry into the city, vv.17-19 closing ceremonies (but preferably three links: 17ab the installation of the ark, 17c18ab offering and blessing, 19ab food for the people who return home in 19c).

	P_1			C_2		
verse nos.	1-2	3-4	5	Michal	report	David
words	31	26	15	15	26	31

and the reader now understands why I cannot put matters down to chance here.[58] The quantities on two levels not only assume (the deletion of) the minor and the major dittographies, they support this ruling as well.[59] At the same time the numerical precision carries a warning against further deletion and addition because this would disrupt the proportions, and it prevents the interpreter from disconnecting the Michal incident from the body of the story for fear of its being secondary material.[60]

Finally the block of vv.6a-12b itself consists of three parts, each of which displays its own quantitative symmetry and the first two parts of which consist of exactly the same number of words. The first consists of two links, Uzzah's deed plus his death at God's hand, v.6 + v.7.[61] The second too is a pair of links and consists of David's reaction to the incident, viz. anger and fear, v.8 + v.9. The third part consists of three two-line links on the alternative, a three month stay somewhere half-way along the way, in the house of a Gittite, vv.10-12b. Notice at this point the small survey of the 2 + 2 + 3 links which coincide with the verses (minus 12c):

verse number	6 and 7	8 and 9	10 11 12ab
number of words	4-5-5 and 4-5-5 subtotal 28	8-8 and 6-6 subtotal 28	17 + 17 + 17

[58] The location of the final number 26 is arbitrary and I do not put forward an abc-cba symmetry in the series of six numbers.

[59] Note well, I do not say that evidence is provided by the numbers alone. I remain cautious and say with respect to the deletion of one *šem* in v.2c (the small dittography) that this decision is supported by a combination of semantic, syntactic and quantitative arguments.

[60] Against McCarter and every commentator who attempts premature diachronic diagnosis.

[61] Verse 6c and 6d may be taken together in order to aid the count. In point of fact 6d is the motive for the deed in 6c; it is a *kī* clause with a qtl form, and by joining it up with 6c not only does the advantage arise that three wyqtl lines from v.6 are answered by the three wyqtl clauses of v.7, but it also appears that the systematics of the initial wyqtl are well maintained to the end of C_1.

The articulation of the remaining passage, where the ark receives its place and the celebration is for the refreshment of all, P_2 = vv.13-19, is not so simple and is the only one not governed by numbers.[62]

We have now reached the level of word choice. The name of David occurs twenty-two times and that of Yahweh twenty-one times, much more frequently than the word *'ĕlōhīm*. Except in v.7b the word "God" serves only as a modification of the ark in the set phrase "the ark of God", and occurs only in vv.2-7 and 12, seven times to boot. From v.9 onwards the set phrase is relieved of duty by "the ark of Yahweh", which remarkably enough occurs the same number of times. The dominance of the tetragrammaton commences majestically in v.2 where the proper noun of the God of Israel is inserted in doubly solemn words, the moment his footstool comes into view: "the ark, over which is called the Name of the LORD of Hosts enthroned on the cherubs". So much emphasis is rarely to be found during narration. After this "Yahweh" fulfils syntactic functions which usefully and attractively vary. He is the grammatical subject in vv.7a, 8a, 11b/12bc, He is feared and is, therefore, the grammatical object in v.9a, and He is the one who vis-á-vis David is ever present in the key phrase *lifnē yhwh*. As well as its seven combination occurrences with *'ĕlōhīm* and *yhwh* the word *'ārōn* occurs once on its own, in v.4b. The name Jerusalem has been clearly avoided, and systematically replaced, by "the City of David" (in triplicate; vv.10a-12c-16a). This stresses the personal aspect of the removal led by the king: he finds that the ark ought to be housed in the crown lands, and so be permanently connected with them.

I would now like to provide a short record of seven frequent words on the basis of which we can see immediately just how much their occurrence is correlated to the arrangement of the chapter into four blocks.[63]

[62] See also my analysis of the texture of vv.13-19 below. It is difficult to know whether to classify v.17c in a link with 17ab, or if this line goes with 18ab. If we count the enumeration and the fullness of 19ab as one long sentence, then perhaps the grouping of the lines is 2 + 3 + 4 for the arrival (report given by the narrator and focalised by Michal, respectively) in verses 13-16, after which it is celebration and completion in verses 17-19: 3 + 2 + 2 lines.

[63] The nine most commonly occurring words are, apart from particles etc.: David twenty-two times, Yahweh twenty-one times, the ark fifteen times, *kol* twelve times, house ten times, God eight times, *lifnē* and *'ālā* (qal/hiph.) each seven times, Israel six times. I count v.12c as part of C_1 in this record.
The heading O (for obstacle) is identical with C.

	P_1	O_1	P_2	O_2
David	3	8	8	3
Yhwh	2	8	8	3
the ark	4	7	4	-
God	3	5	-	-
lifnē	2	-	3	2
'ālā	1	1	5	-
Israel	2	-	2	2

What meets the eye is that the king and God are on an even footing. This selection of seven words is striking because of their interrelationship. We see three, four names which bring king, people, and the God together; they are grouped around the sacred object, of which the movement (*'ālā*, the going up to the capital city, v.2b-12c-15) is concluded with burnt offerings, and peace offerings, a different ritual application of the same key word (17c//18a). The series has its own variations and rounding-off:

wayyeleֽk dāwīd ... l^{e}ha'ălōt ... 'ărōn ... šem yhwh ṣ^{e}bā'ōt v.2bc
wayyeleֽk dāwīd ... wayya'al 'ẹt 'ărōn ... v.12c

w^{e}dāwīd w^e..yiśrā'el ma'ălīm 'ẹt 'arōn yhwh v.15

wayya'al dāwīd 'ōlōt lifnē yhwh uš^{e}lāmīm v.17c
waykal dāwīd mēha'ălōt hā'ōlā w^{e}hašš^{e}lāmīm v.18a
...... b^{e}šem yhwh ṣ^{e}bā'ōt v.18b

The infinitive states David's aim at the beginning and at the end its attainment. This framework is put into the shade by another one close by: the full name of God as "Lord of Hosts" occurs in exactly the same verses, 2 and 18, and nowhere else in the chapter, including the word *šem* itself. One step inside and we find a new ring, marked by the apocopate form which reports the implementation. In the middle the narrator takes time to depict the solemn arrival of the ark by means of a durative participial clause, which unites "David and all the house of Israel" as in v.5a. The lines 12c and 15 correspond also with their close. The modifier "with joy" which concludes the long sentence of 12c flows on and gets a say in the modifier "with shouting and the sound of the ram's horn" which completes the long sentence of v.15. In this chapter full of modifiers and details we can see how the key word *'ālā* keeps things moving in order, to switch over after the arrival and placing of the ark, in a fitting way to a concentration of four occurrences

(17c-18a) which bestow even more verticality and sacral value to the movement: the sacrifices ascend in smoke. Each line in the series has the name of the king as grammatical subject.

David's commitment to Yahweh is essential in this chapter and is particularly expressed by the key phrase *lifnē yhwh*, which occurs six times[64] in fascinating variation: twice David plays and dances "before the eyes of Yahweh", in vv.5 and 14, which is closely watched by Michal with a cold look on her face in 16c; in 17c David offers burnt offerings "before Yahweh", after which the series grows to a climax and this *lifnē yhwh* has to be shouted by a wrathful king in the ears of someone who does not want to understand, v.21bd.

The chapter consists of somewhat more than fifty sentences which take up almost two pages of the BHS version, and that is more than elsewhere.[65] It means that the average sentence here is considerably longer.[66] I would like to put forward two explanations for this phenomenon. Firstly, the average length of the sentence is highly magnified by the simple presence of five exceptionally large sentences which consist of 22, 15, 17, 15, and 19 words respectively. The first is the heavyweight at the beginning, verse 2, which by formulating the aim and by characterising the ark so broadly already establishes the tone for a ceremonial whole. In vv.5 and 19 the length is brought about by enumerations which, touching the senses of hearing and taste, spell out ritual and celebration for us. The two sentences which remain fight each other in the dialogue. In v.20 the stinging scorn of Michal is expressed in an eloquent period; David's rebuking her in v.21bc is even longer, whilst the violent emotions dent it as it were (the kink between 21c and d).

[64] The first time that *lifnē* occurs is in v.4, the significant line in which we see the priest walking "in front of the ark". There are four lots of seven among the frequently-occurring words: *lifnē* and the verb *'ālā*, and the phrases "the ark of God" // "the ark of Yahweh". Elsewhere in II Sam. the phrase *lifnē yhwh* occurs in 5:3 (the covenant before God, between king and people!!), 7:18 (*lpnyk* in vv.26,29) and 21:1,9.

[65] A few figures for the sake of comparison. In my colometry II 6 gets sixty lines for practical reasons; the "normal" units, I 28:3-25, II 13:1-22 and II 20:4-22, which may be called representative for Hebrew narrative art, have 96, 87 and 69 lines respectively in NAPS I-II, and take up one and a half pages only in BHS. A text such as II 10, which has as limited a number of speeches as ch.6, also gets one and a half pages in the BHS and in NAPS I 64 lines.

[66] I would not be surprised if a scholar with diachrony on his mind declares this aberration to be direct proof of another hand or source.

But even without the contribution of these verses the average sentence length is greater than normal.[67] The chapter gives a weighty and very full impression. My second explanation is accordingly to be found on another level and is an interpretation which touches both the top five sentences as well as the others: the fullness of the text (created by so many long lines) is called for by the subject matter and the weight which the narrator assigns to the transfer of the ancient sanctuary. The solemn and ritual nature of what happens is mirrored in sentences with many people, many objects and modifiers of all kinds. That this has not deteriorated into amorphousness is, amongst other things, thanks to and to be judged by the numerical precision with which the parts have received their proportions.

What happens on the P_1-P_2 axis is, certainly as far as the master of ceremonies, David, is concerned, not very exciting, and thus far the plot is not powerful or very interesting. But the king learned a hard lesson which also had to be learned when the ark entered the country after its wandering through Philistia (I 6, end). The Uzzah incident makes clear that the treatment of the holy object is a tricky question which requires the utmost accuracy. The "Breach of Uzzah" lends depth to the development in one stroke and manages to create suspense, so that a certain amount of plot does arise. Divine intervention makes the implementation of David's plan for the ark doubtful and difficult. The resulting anxiety of the participants in the rites is quite palpable in v.13 where breaths are held at the resumption of the procession. After six steps a sacrifice is offered to God in order to placate Him; only after the acceptance of the victim is the ban to be broken and can the celebrations continue after a delay of three months.

[67] After the subtraction of the dittographies ch.6 has a total of 370 words. If I put the top five sentences with their eighty-eight (!) words in brackets, about forty-seven clauses remain in my colometric impression for 282 words. The sum 282 divided by 47 is precisely six! Sentence length is tabulated below:

words –	lines	words –	lines
1	2	7	2
2	1	8	5
3	5	9	3
4	7	10	1
5	8	11	2
6	9	12	1
		13	1

The median is six words per line, and this itself is higher than elsewhere (where the median is four to five words per line); the upturn after seven words per line is also striking: a further thirteen long lines follow.

The syntactic profile of the chapter points to a solemn celebration as well, as the climax towards which the series of clauses work. It is not anomalous but actually informative. The outline is as follows:

P_1	four wyqtl(w) clauses + 3 participial clauses
C_1	fifteen wyqtl clauses, almost without interruption[68]
P_2	two wyqtl clauses + 3 participial clauses
	wqtl & inversion + qtl in 16ab, then wyqtl series resumed, seven wyqtl clauses in vv.17-19
C_2	four wyqtl clauses as frame round the dialogue,
	final clause of v.23 has inversion + qtl

This profile teaches us that the backbone of Hebrew narrative art, the concatenation of narrative imperfects, is also dominant here, in spite of the special nature of the subject matter and the aura. We also see that inversion is the means used twice for bringing Michal to the fore, so that the relation between v.16b and 23 is reinforced. But the main thing is that the flow of the narrative forms is strikingly interrupted twice by an island of durative clauses on ceremonies. In this way the celebration and the special event are firmly activated: verse 5 and vv.14-15 are centres of gravity, introduced by priests and sacrifices. They are separated by the incident and its aftermath. But at the same time the mediation of C_1 makes it possible to double the amount of lines devoted to playing and dancing.

Analysis of the first half, vv.1-5 and 6-12

"David again assembled all the picked men of Israel, thirty thousand strong." This is the way the story starts. David was not born in the city in which he now lives, neither has he inherited it from his father. He has had to conquer it, and shortly afterwards not far from his walls he has had to withstand the Philistines. His present position is due to military means, and the narrator has given us to understand that the troops of David did not fight alone but were supported by heavenly hosts. The little word *'ōd* of v.1 points back to the efforts of ch.5. David considers the presence of his best troops essential to his plan for the ark, and no wonder after ch.5. The number 30,000 I value as a round, literary figure which wants to show that the number of troops is

[68] There are three slight variations. After the third wyqtl clause there is a motivating *kī* clause with qtl in v.6d, direct speech occurs in 9c (with x + yqtl) and the negative prevents a wyqtl form in v.10a (which must therefore use qtl).

somewhere between a standing army and a massive people's army.[69] The organiser is called David in verses 1 and 2 and his proper noun remains dominant throughout the story: it is his personal undertaking which is reported for the length of a chapter.[70]

The exceptional verse 2 begins with two predicates and two grammatical subjects. The verbs give momentum to the start but remain singular in honour of the organiser, even though David is accompanied by "all the people who were with him" – a term reminiscent of his period as fugitive and placing the armed forces close by him. The "going" of "David and all the people" receives its counterpart at the close of the undertaking as the parties disperse: notice how 19c and 20a end parallel but separate too with the rhyme *bētō*. Now people are on the way to Ba'lat Jehudah, that is to say to Kirjath-Jearim, the place where the ark has been located for decades, more or less because of embarrassment.[71] This is several hours march away to the north-west of Jerusalem, in territory which has just recently been drawn away from the power or the influence of the enemy in the west. On their escape route from the watershed in the hill country (in 5:23 designated as Geba) to Gezer and further westward, the Philistines pulled out through the Kirjath-Jearim region.

David wants to transfer the portable sanctuary to the recently chosen centre of power, according to v.2b. This plan establishes the quest of this chapter and attracts a series of hiph'il forms which are to carry the development. It begins with *ha'ălōt* itself, the realisation of which – via a narrative imperfect and participial clause – I have already mentioned. It quickly

[69] David used to be a war lord with 600 men, which we find in chs. I 23, 27 and 30. I imagine that David, during his rise to power in Judah and with a view to the expected expansion of his kingdom to Israel, increased his standing army to several thousand men. Second Samuel 15 gives some idea of its later extent, where the Gittite mercenary contingent alone is 600 man strong and makes up not more than a third (during the battle against Absalom three columns function under the same number of generals, ch.18) of David's faithful followers. Opposite the standing army forming the regular backbone of David's military power is the total number of able-bodied men who in time of need can be called up and must fall in as massive people's army – compare the masses whom Absalom mobilises following Hushai's advice, and think of the census of II 24 which was carried out by the military and had, amongst other things, military implications.

[70] As opposed to the twenty-two occurrences of David "king" occurs three times only, chiefly because of the view of Michal, "the daughter of Saul", on the course of events: v.16c and 20d. "King David" occurs only in v.12a.

[71] See I Sam.6:21-7:2 It is well-known that names of the place Kirjath-Jearim vary. Apart from "the fields of Ja'ar" (Ps.132), which could be a case of poetic licence, there are the variants Ba'ala and Kirjath-Ba'al from I Chr.13:6 and Joshua 15:9sq,60 and 18:14sq.

receives initial realisation in the "caused ... to ride" (*wayyarkībū*) of v.3a. Then, after the incident, there is the removal of the ark (*hāsīr*, 10a) which David does not dare to attempt, so he deposits it temporarily (*wayyaṭṭēhū*, 10b) along the way. The objective is attained with the row of four hiph'il forms in v.17-18a: the ark is taken into the city and placed in a tent (*wayyābī'ū ... wayyaśśīgū*), after which sacrifices conclude the journey (*wayya'al ... ha'ălōt ...*).

The narrator lets David go "from" and not "to" Ba'ala, "to remove the ark from thence". The first of this double *min* is a subtle token of David's haste; the centre of his attention does not rest in the starting point, but makes towards the journey's destination which is also understood by the infinitive. The name of the destination is avoided for a full nine verses. A third *min* quickly follows, in v.4a. For the time being the ark receives the least striking description, with the relatively neutral word "God" as modifier. This is going to change just when the incident is taking place. Verse two itself prepares for this insofar as the usual designation is immediately followed by an explanation of the narrator's in v.2c. For a moment he leaves the narrative flow with information in a heavily loaded relative clause which is to reveal the true (and, as becomes apparent later, the dangerous) status of the object. The word "God" is replaced by the proper noun plus modifier. "Yahweh of the powers", that is to say the God who backed up David's settling in Jerusalem (5:10), and the tetragrammaton is enriched with an extra apposition, "who is enthroned upon the cherubs". This addition points back to I 4:4 and accentuates the holiness – might I say at this point, in anticipation of v.6: the untouchability? – of the object.[72] Its owner is indicated by the turn of phrase which says that "the Name of Yahweh was proclaimed over" the ark.

The ark is placed on a new cart drawn by cows. This is the means of transport with which we became acquainted in I Sam.6, the return of the ark from Ekron to the west of Judah. But is it actually desirable to repeat this form of transport? It was an idea of the Philistine diviners! I wonder whether the alliterative connection *krb-rkb* wants to raise doubts about it, especially when I see how the hymn of II 22 plays on these roots in the context of a theophany, also indicating by this God's unique way of travelling, 22:11a.[73] There are two more remarkable details. The cattle which have to do the

[72] At the same time I Sam.4:4 is the only place where the addition of *yšb hkrbym* occurs as well, and which is a part of the first passage where the ark plays a role in Sam. This passage is I 4:3-4; the ark had been mentioned once in a relative clause: 3:3.

[73] I also wonder whether the verb *rkb* close to the end of v.2 with the *krbym* has been placed using a ὕστερον πρότερον: the lifting up [and carrying away] out of the house of Abinadab precedes the causing to ride.

pulling in this text, unlike those in I 6, are at some distance from the cart – they do not occur until the end of v.6 – and after the incident we do not hear any more about this form of transport. Verse 13 speaks of "the bearers of the ark" and that implies that at the task's resumption the Levites themselves have shouldered it – in a way in which touching is apparently permitted as concerns the cult and thus occurs in opposition to the hand of Uzzah.

The link of vv.3-4b presents two concrete operations which are report (wyqtlw forms) supported by two circumstantial clauses. The latter introduce two priests, sons of the man who has meanwhile been the host of the ark "on the hill", at or in Kirjath-jearim. They are both mentioned by their proper nouns. These data remind the reader for a moment of the priests at the beginning of I Sam., a duo also mentioned by name (I 1:3 – the very first occurrence, moreover, of the name *yhwh ṣ*^{e}*bā'ōt*) and engaged in cultic duties in I 2 in the temple of Shiloh where the ark was accommodated at the time. They were the sons of Eli, and their relationship with the ark received a fatal outcome in I 4, on the grounds of their corruption. Is this an omen for Ahio and Uzzah?

The third link is verse 5, a very long, independent participial clause.[74] It is the climax of the exposition. After this the entire entry could have been concluded in five lines,[75] if there had been no disturbance. But perhaps there is a subtle hint of doom hidden in the preposition itself which makes 5a parallel with the line on Ahio:

v.4b	w^{e}'aḥyō	hōlek	lifnē hā'ārōn
v.5a	w^{e}dāwīd w^{e}kol bēt yiśrā'el	m^{e}śaḥăqīm	lifnē yhwh ...

The priest is not placed in front of "the ark of God", but in front of "the ark", and this is the only time, out of a total of fifteen times, that the object occurs *tout court*, with the article. God does appear, on the other hand, under his own name and for the first time as participant, only in the line on David and the people. Moreover the key word *lifnē* begins its series of seven occurrences in this pair of lines. The difference in partner contains subversive suggestions: does the priest pay more attention to the object than to its sometimes highly demanding owner? Does he have in this situation less

[74] A brainteaser for grammarians: how are we to accurately distinguish between the circumstantial clause and the independent clause with participle? In v.5 and vv.14-15 I see independent clauses not because of markers which the circumstantial clause is supposed not to have but through recognition of the narrator's broad depiction. Compare NAPS I on II Sam.15:18 and 23.

[75] These five lines can simply be borrowed from the narrator and one can add this series to vv.1-5 without any problem: 17abc, 18b, and 19c.

contact with Yahweh than the others, with their exuberant music? After the single "before the ark", which is allocated to the priest and has no more than a spatial significance, a "before (the eyes of) Yahweh" follows six times and is given to David each time, having a contactual rather than a spatial significance: it points to a living relationship.[76] Has the generation under Abinadab perhaps become rather routinist at the expense of a certain amount of alertness? Whatever the case might be, in verse 5 the joy of the people as a whole and that of their master of ceremonies is carefully documented in the form of a lengthy enumeration of various musical instruments. In front there is, in addition, distributive *kol* in 5a, "they played on *all kinds of* musical instruments of cypress wood", after which a meticulous series of five elements follows, "on lyres and harps and tambourines and sistrums and tinkling bells".[77]

Block C_1 begins with a pair of verses in the ratio action (v.6) to reaction (v.7) and they are made up of 4 + 5 + 5 words each. After the long sentences of the exposition the complication now makes its appearance with the laconic style and the short clauses with which we are familiar as soon as dramatic action takes place. Uzzah stretches out his hand to the ark and grasps it, apparently because it is in danger of slipping due to an unexpected movement of the oxen.[78] The priest who wants to support "the ark of God" and must die right next to it is killed by God, after Yahweh has become angry – a remarkable variation. Line 7b is the only place where "God" is more than a modifier; He is now the subject who acts. It seems as if this passage wants to link the general term 'God' to Uzzah (just as the previous one withholds the specific *yhwh* from his brother in 4b) so as to suggest that this priest no longer had any insight into the uniqueness of the God of Israel. Then 6b and 7bc repeat the focalisation of Uzzah, whilst the narrator in 7a actually does have an eye for what is specific about this God and designates him by his own name, as does David immediately afterwards in vv.8-9. The victory of the name of Yahweh has become a fact after this blow.[79]

[76] I would, moreover, like to recall that in all kinds of places the expression *lifnē yhwh* means (in my paraphrase): "under the approving eye of Yahweh", indeed "with Yahweh's permission", or "with Yahweh as witness". See, for example, such references as I 7:6, 11:15 (bis), 12:7, II 5:3, 21:9. This aspect also carries weight in II 6.

[77] This *ṣęlṣęlīm* makes an onomatopoeic impression on me, and reminds me of the tingling of ears (*ṣll* in the qal) of which the old Eli was notified in I 3:11 (via an oracle given to Samuel).

[78] McCarter's translation (whose Nodan I replace with Nacon, by the way) is especially worthwhile in v.6cd: "When they came to the threshing floor of Nacon, Uzza put his hand on the holy ark to steady it, for the oxen had let it slip." I agree that *šmṭ* is a transitive verb.

[79] Only during the transition from the first to the second half do we still hear the term "the ark of God" used, in v.12bc.

What did the priest do wrong? There is no simple answer to this one. The repetition of the preposition *'al* in 8a makes it likely that the uncertain expression *'al haššal* at the end of 7b is also causal. This gives some support to the old view "because of his negligence" providing us with an interpretation of Uzzah's flaw.[80] Perhaps his transgression lies in his touching the ark during transport, and perhaps the divinely acceptable alternative was that he should have trusted that God, or better: Yahweh!, could look after His own footstool Himself, assisted by his four-footed creatures. I am prompted to suggest this by the consummate behaviour of the draught animals in I 6, cows with calves who hold their Creator in higher esteem than their maternal instinct (to echo Is.1:3). Another option is that transport per cart is ritually undesirable or disagreeable to God – because it was a solution first thought of by the uncircumcised for instance – and that the priest's touching the cart is the last straw for God. As one of similar references I Ki.8:3 suggests that the lifting and bearing of the ark by the Levites was the only proper way to transport it.

The following two verses are also a pair and they offer two reactions of the organiser David. First there is the spontaneous and especially emotional reaction, then comes a deeper one with a religious aspect. "David became angry", says v.8a. Of course he is angry, his celebration has been utterly ruined.[81] He has to discover that his celebration is, in a radical sense, not *his* celebration, not his moving house, and not his procession. The whole enterprise has to be cancelled and David must slink away in complete suspense as to a possible sequel. Something like this does not please any kind of ruler.

The key word of v.8 with its balance of 8 + 8 words is *pāraṣ*. It occurs three times exactly, as many times as in 5:20, and is once again linked to a name giving kept outside the action. What David finds so difficult to swallow, namely that Yahweh has "broken out against Uzzah", he personally immortalises in a place-name – honest as he is – and the narrator honours this by putting it on record.[82] Once again the deity has broken loose, with a numinous power and unexpectedness which petrifies a mortal, and this time not in favour of David's undertaking, but to its detriment. One Perez passage is the

[80] See also Appendix I on this crux.

[81] The rendering of *wyḥr* with "displeased" and "distressed" and suchlike is a half-hearted form of avoidance, and a false kind of prudishness; see also Appendix I.

[82] A frame-break does not take place until the end of v.8b. Notice that there is temporal friction between "he called that place" (a momentaneous past tense on David) and "to the present day" (the present of the original audience) which occur in one clause. Of the four elements (there and then plus here and now) the outermost two are present in the demonstrativa.

obverse of the other.[83] The dialectic arising between the two creates space for a better awareness of Yahweh's freedom which passes human understanding; God does not allow Himself to be organised. The about-turn in the Perez motif, which takes place here at short range, has something of the two sides to the astonished exclamation: "is Saul one of the prophets too?" which are just as numinously loaded and which punctuated the election and downfall of the first king.

In v.8b of the four co-ordinates (there and then plus here and now) the two outermost were connected. Verse 9a joins in by referring to the 'then' dimension. "David feared Yahweh on that day", conveying a spiritual depth which becomes possible after the emotional letting off steam of a moment earlier. It is the existential-religious and desired reaction to the *numen tremendum*. It is accompanied by the mortal's bewildered, almost distraught question: "How shall the ark of Yahweh come to me?" With this the hero himself opens the series of seven times *'ărōn yhwh*. Different from the priests he has understood perfectly that the God of Israel has shown Himself in His uniqueness. Note the "to me" which is again personal, instead of "to the capital" or the name of the city. It joins up with "the city of David" in the following line, with the designation of the hero by his name each time instead of the more objective "the king" etc. Verses 8 and 9 are not only a pair of links quantitatively, they are also balanced qua content. This pair is an ABAB symmetry, since 8a/9a relates what David is going through whilst 8b/9b allows him to put it into words (in a name / in an occasional speech).

The sounds of *yābō 'elay* are picked up at the beginning of v.10 by *lō 'ābā*, which reinforces the lines' coherence. David's fear of God prevents him from "removing the ark (sure enough: the ark of Yahweh) to himself" – a dangerous verb, a negative link in the hiph'il series, after which the suffixed preposition *'elāw* is the sequel to the *'elay* in v.9c. This is even more striking because the line has its own spatial mention of the aim, and relates at the end: "to the city of David". This substitute for the suppressed name Jerusalem co-operates with the verb "remove"; the duo forms a framework with v.12c:

10a David did not want to transfer the ark to himself in the City of David
12c David went and brought up the ark (...) to the City of David.

These lines of almost identical length are, moreover, equally peculiar as far as, as a result of the formulaic nature of this city's name, the name David gives a top and tail to both. The framework consists of the polarity of stagnation and

83 The root *prṣ* neither occurs in the immediate context, nor in II Sam. in its entirety. (The forms in I 28:23 and II 13: 25,27 do not count since they are a metathesis of *pṣr*.) A hithpa'el occurs in I 25:10 and an important niph'al in I 3:1, having to do with contact with God.

new movement, and at the same time guarantees the integration of the hinge line, 12c, which at level eight (the grouping of subscenes into a story) found itself in the seesaw position. On level seven, where sequences (and short links here) join up into subscene C_1, v.12c gets its proper place as counterpart to v.10a. There is also an opposition between the beginning of 10a and the closing word of 12c: the fear on which the refusal is based makes way for the joy of resumed movement. Therefore, by reason of the framework, the word *śimḥā* does not mean "festivity" but "joy".[84]

The lines of vv.10-12 allow themselves to be read on the syntagmatic axis as three pairs. That is why we might consider classifying the quartet 10a-10b-11a-11b as an AA-BB pattern, in view of the subjects.[85] Or we might follow the content: in 10a David's plan to transport the ark has failed, 10b provides the alternative; 11a the ark stays at Obed Edom's and attracts God's blessing there (11b); after which David hears of this in 12ab and takes action in 12c.

In the six relevant lines (12a is a variant of the quotation formula) the name of Obed Edom occurs five times, too frequent to retain its powers of discrimination and indicate a pattern. Nevertheless after 11a the use of his name and house differs every time. In v.10 and 11a his house is a designation of place and, because of this, the alternative for the spot which 10a must relinquish. In 11b "house" means something new however: it is the *familia* of the man from Gath who enjoys the blessing of God.[86] It is his enterprise, his people, in short, as 12b puts it replacing the word house, "everything he has". We can observe another pattern of pair forming on the paradigmatic axis which is more productive for a proper understanding of this sequence:

A	David does not want to transport the ark to his city	10a
B	David deposits the ark: designation of place	10b
B'	the ark remains there: place and time designations	11a
C	The Lord blesses the Gittite and his house	11b
C'	King David hears that the Lord has blessed etc.	12ab
A'	David transports the ark from thence to his city	12c

84 McCarter has "with festivity", NBE "haciendo fiesta". I still hesitate about "with much/ great rejoicing" of NEB and BJ, cf. the JPS and LV. SV and KJ are correct ("with gladness"), KBS and Buber as well ("in Freuden").

85 In v.10ab the subject is David + David, in 11ab the ark of Yahweh + Yahweh Himself.

86 Compare the shift, discussed a short while ago, from the spatial to the contactual which *lifnē* undergoes in vv.4-5.

The narrator could easily have omitted 12ab, after which 12c joins up with 11b and can be understood without any problems. The reverse would have worked as well: omit 11b and only admit the blessing to the text in the form of information for David. But the narrator chooses something else, the above parallelism CC': report it himself and reflect it once again in a message. The people who pass on the news may include their interpretation at the same time: this blessing has come "because of the ark of God", is their view, and David does not doubt it.[87]

The pair BB' is about peace and the alternative location. David is apparently forced to leave the ark in the vicinity of Uzzah's accident. It is curious how things revolve around the house of a Philistine, a man from the city of which David was a pseudo-vassal some ten years ago. Perhaps he belongs to the contingent of mercenaries under the command of Ittai the Gittite in II 15? Even odder is the fact that his name seems to be theophoric without honouring a Philistine god; the name Edom points in another direction. How far the name "servant of Edom" assumes another cult I do not know. But in any case an irony has come about; the God who has just been an extreme stickler for detail and very demanding of his priest now tolerates the housing of his ark in an uncircumcised man's residence thus behaving like a moderate towards, and even blessing, a man from another religion.

We are now able to survey the block C_1 in its entirety (= incident 1 plus delay). Does it consist of three parts which articulate as 2 + 2 + 3 links?[88] Or are there two halves, i.e. vv.5-9 and 10-12? Once again a problem solves itself thanks to a clue of style and structure. Not only is the vv.10-12 part delineated by an inclusio but verses 5-9 are too. This passage is framed by the verb "to come" which receives throughout the entire chapter a significant series of 2 + 2 occurrences.[89] The first two occur as an opposition in v.6a and 9c:

6a they came to the threshing floor of Nachon
9c "How can/shall the ark of Yahweh come to me?"

The procession made such promising headway and was surrounded by such a richness of musical sound! And now they come to a threshing floor: a place

[87] Two more details: as regards ordering in a pattern 12a does not count as a variant on the quotation formula and can be taken quite well with its content, 12b. The CC' segments are different from the rest since they both have the little word *kol* which marks the sequence's centre of gravity, after which David is able to decide in 12c to resume the procession after all.

[88] For the sake of clarity I would like to repeat the arrangement for a moment. Verses 5-15 are articulated as follows: a = 3 + 3 sentences (= v.6 + v.7), b = 2 + 2 clauses (=v.8 + v.9), and c = 2 + 2 + 2 clauses (=vv.10-12 according to the paradigmatic order ABBCCA).

[89] The series occurs in vv.5a, 9c, 16a and 17a. The last two references are a consecutive answer to the question in 9c and as a closing form the hiph'il of 17a is a culmination: this bringing immediately changes into the hiph'il of the placing, 17b.

full of the promise of fulfilment and fruitfulness. But there of all places the greatest of undertakings founders, as if it were struck by lightning. The only thing left is a rhetorical question on the impossibility of progress, posed in the despair, shock and bewilderment paralysing the organiser and master of ceremonies, David.

Therefore I prefer, in the long run, a two-part division of the vv.5-12 block. Two pictures now clearly face one another: the swaying cart and the punished hand of the priest Uzzah over against the accepted accommodation and the Gittite with a blessing; the rage and fear of David leading to the impasse in 9c versus the alternative (10b), and the relief (v.12) which makes renewed movement possible. The proper nouns Uzzah and Obed Edom, which do not occur after this, establish the bipartite division and its internal equilibrium, they occur five times exactly.[90] The polarity of these two persons is not by chance but flows from a substitution which dawns on us if we recall the events of I 6. The house of Abinadab (the father of Uzzah) fulfilled, after all, the same function (as emergency accommodation for attending to the ark after a terrible blow from God) which the house of Obed Edom has here in II 6!

The presence and absence of David is, in the two halves of block C_1, complementarily distributed. This is linear in the first half because of David's absence in vv.6-7, whilst vv.8-9 on the other hand are full of his reactions. Verses 10-12 function concentrically: at the edges the shocked David who is forced to leave the ark behind, versus the informed king[91] who sets out once again, whilst the middle (v.11ab) is kept apart for the three-month period of peace, the whole "house", and the blessing.

Analysis of the second half, vv.13-19 and 20-23

Just as the first half is completed by v.12c so the resumption of the procession is launched by v.12c, which, as has been previously mentioned, is a verse which functions like a roof tile. The announcement that "David brought the ark up" is a prolepsis, for this event does not really take place until v.15 which depicts this "bringing", based on the same root in the participle, and in

[90] The first occurrence of the name Uzzah is anticipatory: in v.3c; the name is then concentrated in vv.6b and 8. The name Obed Edom occurs in five lines in succession, being even more concentrated therefore: 10b-12c (12a and b are pushed together once more). In the whole of ch.6 only four words occur five times. The other two are "people" and "day".

[91] The fact that David is also called king in v.12a is the only time this occurs in the narrator's text of ch.6. It may reproduce the focalisation of the Israelite subjects who pass on the news. David himself views the ark's transfer in a highly personal way, but the people cannot but see him primarily as king.

vv.16a//17a which report the arrival at the city. The prolepsis can be sensed especially due to two data: the fact that v.12c not only indicates the beginning but also the destination of the journey,[92] and the fact that v.13a goes back a step in time through its precision look at the beginning of the resumption. These observations lead to the consideration that v.12c lends itself well to the reading that it is prior summary of what happens in vv.13-19: the line is a kind of heading for the block. The phrase "the ark of God" is used one more time in order to retain the link with v.2b (and the standard use of the phrase in the first half), and to express that the original enterprise is being resumed at last, but afterwards the word 'God' is finished with and the proper noun, Yahweh, reigns.

How much the "roof tile" or hinge line, 12c, stands alone is something I can also tell from verse thirteen's own temporal introduction. This kind of *wayhī kī* marks a new sequence, and this particular example of it gets a new echo in the *w^{e}hāyā* which introduces v.16 and helps to set this interruption apart. Verse 13 does something very interesting, and as I note the translation here I am initially inclined to include 14ab as circumstantial clauses: "And it came to pass, when the bearers of the ark of the Lord had gone six steps, that they slaughtered an ox and a fatling,[93] whilst David played with all his might [lit. snapped with his fingers[94]] before the Lord, girded with a linen ephod." Verse 13a is so special because the detail of the six steps brings together the co-ordinates of space and time and renders them concrete and visual at the same time. So all attention is drawn to the resumption, which was probably perilous for the participants. The bearers were doubtlessly qualified personnel, Levites we assume, but after the Uzzah affair the launching of the holy object had really become a very sensitive business! Will God actually permit a fresh effort or is a new catastrophe to take place? This was the great strain under which the participants, with David leading the way, had assembled themselves after three months. In the picture of David dancing and playing "with all his might" for God I also sense his curiosity as to the outcome, and his fear of the numen: in all that movement the priest-king can at once express

[92] If v.12c had solely reported David's bringing up of the ark from the house of Obed Edom, *wayya'al's* being an inceptive imperfect could have still been defended; this is now difficult to maintain.

[93] The first fifteen translations which I glance through here all give David as the subject of 13b. Do they do this unthinkingly? I notice that David is explicitly designated as subject in the next three lines via a striking anaphora, and it is quite possible that the subject of 13b is the impersonal "they" (in French "on"; in German "man").

[94] For this rendering, which follows Avishur and Ahlström, see Appendix I. McCarter, impressed by the Greek, interprets *mkrkr* as "strumming (with his fingers)" but to that end he alters *bkl* 'z; unnecessarily so.

his release and strain. In this way the dance has a warding-off effect for himself also.

The sacral steps of the ark's consecrated bearers are also connected with 5:24a, where the "striding" stood for Yahweh's own advance against the enemy (v.24c). Now victims are brought to placate God in connection with the resumption of the procession. His mercy is hoped for, but his terrifying intervention is also taken into account. In this way the datum on the steps is a window on the same ambiguity which has been introduced by the double use of the Perez motif, and which connected this chapter with the previous one as well. The number six I take to mean "one less than the sacred number seven", in the sense that the imminent post-six matter is going to end either favourably or catastrophically. Breaths are held after the six steps: now, at the next step it will become clear whether God ... etc. Nevertheless a sign had taken place, and it has been interpreted as a good omen: the blessing which has fallen to the family of the man from Gath.

The six steps are the threshold of the second half, and now this has been stepped over the text breaks out into durative depiction. This depiction is marked by a striking trio: the name David takes the lead as anaphora in the participial clauses of 14ab + 15a, all of which, secondly, I take to be independent clauses. First the sketch shows David only. In v.14a he is putting an enormous amount of energy into dancing,[95] thereby resuming what he did in v.5; his addressee, the deity himself, is once again present, for "he plays before the eyes of Yahweh". He does so in the temporary office of priest, since 14b adds that he "is girded with a linen ephod". As a character in a literary context David has thus become the successor of the divinely acceptable Samuel: he too was introduced as "girded with a linen priestly garment", in I 2:18b, and was going to exercise yet another holy office. Verse 15 closes the first sequence of this block and carefully places verse five's "all the house of Israel" right next to the master of ceremonies. The durative description of how all "bring up the ark" is, at the same time, the fulfilling of the programme of 2b, together with, or via the mediation of, the anticipatory report *wayyaʿal* of v.12c. They go forth "with shouting and with the sound of the horn", auditive data which supplement the visual ones of v.14. The parallelism with 12c ensures that we understand them as a variant and a shaping of the modifier "with joy" in the title sentence.

The whole sequence is now summarised by the words "the ark of Yahweh arrived in the city of David". This is the way v.16a puts it, as it introduces a

[95] We gather this by looking down over Michal's shoulder and, with help from v.16c, completing the "handiwork" of the *mkrkr* with the footwork of David's *mpzz*.

mini-sequence next to the great event and gets its own small threshold with *whyh*.[96] The verse on Michal has two main, related functions. It prepares for the closing sequence in vv.20-23, and as a disruption to the progress of vv.13-15 > 17-19 it is an iconic sign that Michal is to provide a disturbing contribution to David's homecoming, in an attempt to spoil his day. The epithet with which the princess is introduced, and which is consistently maintained in 20b and 23, is in keeping with her own point of view. She is not referred to as "the wife of David" in v.16, neither is she allowed to become so in 20 and 23, but she is the "daughter of Saul" and this is the way she feels: of royal blood, from a different tribe and family to David. She now looks down, in two different meanings of the word. She looks, moreover, "through the window" and this attribute has approximately the same function in the modern sense: have a coloured view on something. The window symbolizes her special frame of mind, which prevents her from empathetically and joyfully taking part in the sacred festivities and everybody's rejoicing. She is presently given the floor to explain this, her husband is the "guilty one". In 16c the narrator follows her perspective, for the king's daughter "sees King David leaping and clapping before the eyes of the LORD". Pointing to the feet and the hands of David, the participles are a merismus for the ruler in a total movement which stands for total surrender, and Michal cannot experience this. The doubling of the participles (in regard of 14a) is a token of her vexation. The designation "king David" reveals, as focalisation of Michal, an objectifying view which is a sign of lack of personal involvement, and already contains a hint as to why she censures his behaviour – more on this at v.20. "She despised him deeply." Looking down at and on her husband she considers herself to be above him, but at the same time places herself outside what is happening and is isolated from everyone.[97]

[96] In the rendering of de Boer, who correctly keeps to the form (instead of making *wyhy* of it) and pays much attention to the function of this consecutive and summarising perfect:"Well, thus it was, the ark of the Lord coming into David's city, and Michal, Saul's daughter, looking down the window ..." in Festschrift E.A. Nida 1974; see also Appendix I.

[97] Michal, says v.16d, despised him *b^{e}libbāh*, and this is almost universally rendered "in her heart". This sounds like a stopgap and is, moreover, not so self-evident, because she blurts out her disdain, letting it rain down on David's head, thus externalising it as quickly as possible. Further research on references with *b^e* + *lb(b)* + suffix produces a number of places where the complement denotes inclination and/or intensity: Ex.4:14, Hos.7:14, Ps.15:2, 78:18, 125:4 and perhaps Lev.19:17. A proper understanding of our reference, it seems to me, is that Michal despised him *deeply*. (This verse does not go with the group in which "in his/her heart" is complementary with expression, e.g Deut.30:14, or actually has a polar relationship with the expression of negative thoughts, such as Job 1:5 and 2:10.)

After the pair with the verb "to come" in 6a + 9c, this block also completes a pair: the hiph'il in v.17a concludes the series, and collaborates with the qal in 16a. In 16a the third and last mention of "the City of David" occurred to conclude the journey through the province. This general term of place is now replaced by greater spatial precision in 17ab and the privacy of a consecrated tent specially put up by David for the ark. This detail occurs at the end of the journey, the moment when the ark finally comes to rest – a psalm would indeed use the word *m^e^nūḥā* – "in its place". The arrival at the city is completed with the "bringing in of the ark" in v.17, and the assonance of the *wayyābī'ū – wayyaśśīgū* forms has the arriving flow into the positioning. An internal rhyme underlines where the reverence and the effort go, to the portable sanctuary: ... *'ōtō bimqōmō ... nāṭā-lō*. The arrival of (16a and) 17a also faces the coming of v.6a as success opposite failure.

The concatenation of hiph'il forms reaches its climax in 17c-18a, whilst the key verb *'ālā* which opened the series earlier gets a second meaning at the same time and is excessively present: in four forms which fill a double paronomasia. David performs his final ritual before Yahweh by bringing burnt offerings and peace offerings.[98] To prevent our underestimating this ritual as the conclusion of the procession, the sacrifices receive an extra line, 18a, under the common denominator of completion, *waykal*; a word which prepares us for the encircling *kol ... kol ... kol* of the celebration's closing verse, v.19. If we may call the subsequence of *wayya'al dāwīd* and *waykal dāwīd* anaphora, and observe that the name of David in the surrounding two pairs of lines does not occur after the opening wyqtl form, a group of six lines in pairs arises:

– 17a and 17b arrival and positioning of the ark, hiph'il forms in the plural,
– 17c and 18a the two lines on the sacrificing in the singular with David as subject and an identical rhyme at the close, and
– 18b and 19ab two clauses with a pi'el in the singular.

The actions of David in 18b and 19a are mutually explanatory. First he turns to the procession's participants and spectators with a blessing, which he gives "in the name of the Lord of Hosts", a formula which is to be found only in v.2 in this chapter and takes us back to this solemn beginning. It was linked with the ark here, and that is why it fits in well at this point too, at the moment when David's enterprise is successful. After the spiritual side of the blessing, guaranteed by the Name, a distribution of celebration fare follows in v.9 which involves everyone physically in the positive outcome. The

[98] Notice that the final *lifnē yhwh* in 17c has been placed prior to the peace offerings in order to get an epiphora on *š^e^lāmīm* in 17c//18a.

emphasis on "all" and the richness of the distribution are so great that next to the threefold occurrence of *kol* there is also a threefold addressee of David in v.19,[99] and that the diversity of food is mirrored in a threefold enumeration which gives the numeral "one" a multiplicational significance in fact.[100] The words *'īš* and *kol* which regularly face each other in polarity support each other in the closing line 19c as well, as, literally, "all the people [each man] go(es) to his house". This clause is the counterpart of 12c which opened with another *wayyelęk* and *bayit*. The same two Hebrew words make for a contrast[101] between 19c and the movement of David in 20a, who returns "to his house", and with the next dialogue in which one woman is alienated from all and ensures a negative close.

The David-Michal clash is placed in an easily-recognised framework of narrator's text; except for the quotation formula in 20c and 21a there are two lines at the beginning and two lines at the end. The lines 20a and b have the man and his wife as subject and show how their movements cut across each other, which is not a good sign. David returns "to bless his house" – the very last little stone in what he has built today, which completes what 18b had to say on blessing. But Michal goes outside. "Michal, the daughter of Saul" and not "his wife, Michal". She does not keep waiting for David to enter the room in which she finds herself, but is much more active: she gets up and goes outside to meet him. She can't wait to vent her spleen! This also implies that she meets him in or in front of the gate when, I assume, he is not yet alone. This also means that she spits venom at David more or less in public. Perhaps she finds this justifiable from her point of view for she attacks the way he exercises his royal duties. But from David's point of view, and that of the courtiers with him, this is nothing less than tactless.

In v.16 "she saw King David", now she hurls stinging abuse in the face of "the King of Israel", making out that she, not he, is the one who knows what royal dignity is. She compares her husband to the plebs, since this is how she characterises the people with an expression of contempt squared: "the slave girls of your slaves". Her first word (after *ma*) is "worthy, honourable", but her last is "empty" and brings a despicable group to the fore out of the

[99] The first address is "to all the people", initially specified by the apposition "to all the multitude of Israel" and subsequently illustrated via a merismus: "from man to woman", i.e. from every man to every woman.

[100] One could also point to more phonetic means, for example the *me'īš w^{e}'ad 'iššā* combination which is echoed by *'īš ... 'ęšpār ... 'ašīšā*.

[101] The contrast is marked with an epiphora: both lines (one with the movement of all, the second with the movement of one) end on *bētō*.

public.[102] The tension between the two words is the scope of her scorn. Her whole speech is one long, well-formed period which administers in three clauses the selfsame number of lashes. She begins with a rhetorical question on the "dignity of the king today", followed by a quasi-factual pointing to his "nakedness today" and ending with a four-word comparison of which some parts are more vitriolic than others. All her clauses end on terms for the people with a decrease in merit each time: ... Israel, ... his slaves ..., ... layabouts, a parallelism which demonstrates in its own way how the king has degraded himself in Michal's opinion. Our ear picks up another trio which regulates her three clauses and shows that she herself is quickly looking up the opposite of honour: a systematic selection of niph'al forms creates the effective alliteration of *nikbad ... niglā ... niglōt*. The final root is in triplicate as well, and its semantic value pinpoints what is making Michal so furious: David's shamefully "exposing himself". She starts in v.20 with the quasi-neutral observation of the "fact" that David has exposed himself "before the eyes of the women". This dig is all the more painful for David because the only garment which he still had on to cover his shame was the linen ephod. Michal mocks him in the exercise of his priestly office and insinuates that his religious surrender to God is something quite different. Moreover, her pronouncement is so embarrassing because it touches the realm of sexuality with a suggestiveness which David cannot consider refuting. We onlookers can take the clause to be a poorly-disguised sign of sexual jealousy.[103]

Michal reinforces the point by repeating what is galling her, during which she fashions a unique combination of construct infinitive plus absolute infinitive in the simile: "as to uncover oneself openly like one of the layabouts". At the same time their ending -ōt rhymes with that of the word "slave girls", making for the action's closer involvement with this group of spectators and posing the question as to which word has the most contaminating effect: *'ămāhōt* on the action *higgālōt*, or vice versa. Finally Michal classifies David amongst the scum of the nation by comparing him, via a second preposition *k*ᵉ, to "one of the *rēqīm*". At the same time she herself has answered the question she posed at the beginning, "how honoured is the king?" thus leaving no room for further discussion. Another means used to closely connect the three clauses is the so-called staircase parallelism.[104]

[102] The form *nkbd* is, for the rest, a perfect. See on this, and on the reading *ryqm* (instead of the emendation *rqdym*), Appendix I.

[103] My assessment of the combination is that it is, in fact, still permissible within the framework of Michal's rhetorical and vitriolic design and I do not, therefore, drop one of the two infinitives. Cf. Appendix I.

[104] The words "day" and "uncovered himself" occur in an a/ba/bb pattern spread over three clauses.

It is now David's turn. What can a person do when so much aggression and venom heads straight for him? There are not many options. One can choose a form of evasion, such as denial or flight. On the other hand one can decide to engage in a confrontation, in two ways: one can allow oneself to be affected by the fury of the person to whom one is speaking, which boils down to hitting him back – something which very often happens since fury is a highly infectious emotion and a contagious form of energy; or one can decide not to react on the same level as the other, but to try and let the venom run away like water off a snake skin, for example because of the insight that the other is at odds with himself, giving away more information on his own problem than the actual matter in hand.

David gives two answers differing greatly in tone and content. His speech is usually not rendered in the proper way, so that I will first analyse its structure to arrive at a correct order and translation, before going on to a deeper exploration of content and of the question as to what David does to Michal. The narrator gives David twice as much room for a speech than his wife. It consists of thirty-one words (of which fifteen are directed at Michal) in approximately six clauses. It is essential to rediscover how well the Masoretes understood the whole by placing their *sōf pāsūq* at the end of 21d. David utters two main clauses; both are clearly cordoned off by the stylistic means of the framework and consequently stand out well against one another. The first period occurs in v.21, has about three clauses and carries the key phrase *lifnē yhwh* to its climax by placing these two selfsame words both at the beginning and at the end. This inclusion is based on identity. The second period is to be found in v.22, consists of three lines, and is marked by a fine framework which is founded upon antithesis: "lowly" versus "being honoured" in the first person. This inclusio is the successor to the one employed by Michal in v.20: the figure joins up chiastically with her *nikbad* versus *rēqīm* and the meaning is synonymous. The function of David's chiastic hook-up with the words of his wife is a simple one: this is how the style effectively shows that David parries her assertion that he has degraded himself.

The double framework guarantees a double answer from David. This structure, consisting of nineteen words in v.21 and twelve words in v.22, requires an order and translation which does not consider the parataxis with which the clauses are connected, after 21c, as being the most important.[105] That is why I argue for a rendering such as the following:

105 The JPS, apart from this a very good rendering, places the division between 21c and d: "It was before the LORD who chose me instead of your father and all his family and appointed me

"[It was] *before the Lord*,
– [the Lord] who chose me instead of your father and all his family
to appoint me prince over the Lord's people in Israel, –
it was *before the Lord* that I played! (v.21)

And if I earn more disgrace than this,
so that I will be base in my [own] eyes,
[even then] among the slave girls that you speak of,
among them I will be honoured." (v.22)

The different content and tone now stand out well. In v.21 David utters words of principle, whilst keeping his integrity intact. He was genuinely engaged in performing a rite which was glorifying to God from start to finish, and Michal's false criterion ricochets. The narrator has ensured that his concatenation of six times *lifnē yhwh* is completed in the hero's speech, repeating here the combination of the verb "to play" from v.5. The speaker mirrors the narrator, and vice versa: earlier in the chapter the narrator chose words which are preparatory to, and mirror, the king's speech.[106]

The double "before the Lord" is an envelope. Wrapped up inside it is a relative clause (six words) which throws light on what the person of God means to the speaker in this connection, and which is extended by an infinitival clause with another eight words (= v.21c). David refers his wife to the divine ruling to which his office goes back: he is chosen. He does not confine himself to recalling the fact of this election, without measuring it against, or comparing it with, something else. As early as v.21b David cannot resist the temptation to contrast his being chosen with the fate of his predecessor. "The Lord has chosen me instead of your father and all your family" as the JPS rendering correctly puts it. But the comparative *min* can also be rendered "in preference of" as in the English BJ, and from behind the election of David the rejection of Saul slips into view. David's addressee, his own wife, is a part of "all his family", thus implicitly taking part in the doom. He cannot resist linking a lash for "the daughter of Saul" with his

ruler over the LORD's people Israel! I will dance before the LORD [22]and dishonor myself even more, and be low in my own esteem; but among the slave girls that you speak of I will be honored." The division between v.21 and 22 is also ignored by the LV, BJ, Buber, NBE, NEB. For details from the speech such as "my/your eyes" of 22b see Appendix I.

[106] This mirroring of the *śḥq lpny yhwh* from v.5 and the framework of the 21b-d speech are strong arguments for upholding the MT. The quantitative balance between blocks P_1 and C_2 and that of their components argue against the addition of one or more words such as *'rqd* (against Driver) and *brwk yhwh* to 21b on the basis of the LXX. Contra BJ and McCarter.

own election. The dignified and sincere words on his playing before God, which represent David's true self, conceal a barb at the same time, revealing the fact that David's ego too wants to have its little say to Michal. Which only goes to show that she really has touched a raw nerve.

David recovers himself in 21c and explains the nature of the election is "to appoint me prince over the Lord's people, over Israel". This is the formula we recognise from different references, such as I 13:14, 25:30 and recently II 5:2. With such words the speaker joins the parties in an intimate association: king-people-God, and there is scarcely any room for Michal in the triangle. David's choice of words implies several corrections. Michal had called him "the King of Israel", which invites comment from David. Again he feels obliged to sharply and conscientiously define what this involves. His word "prince" ("appointed by the Lord", what is more) is a sacral term which sets before her: 'I'm not an ordinary monarch of the kind present all around'. David tells her, using the term "the people of God" placed before the name Israel, that he does not just simply rule over a people who happen to be called Israel, but governs God's own people.[107] Moreover, the contract between people and king was concluded "before Yahweh", according to 5:3b; here the narrator has already prepared the *lifnē yhwh* series of ch.6, therefore. The closing word *bētō* of v.21b plays along with the closing word *bētō* of 19c//20a, so placing the house of Saul outside the relationship of David's house with that of all his subjects. Finally, the syntax of v.21 has a remarkable profile which is the expression of great emotionality. The period does not begin with an elementary component such as subject, object or predicate, but with a two-word adjunct which, via two clauses, is increasingly extended, so that the speaker is in danger of getting out of breath. After the completion of v.21c he draws breath again, as it were, – it seems as if he simply drops or forgets the entire construction which he has put together up to now – and he utters a clause, 21d, no part of which reveals any connection with 21bc. Then after all this there is a predicate at last for the reader to go by. Or, to put it another way: the fact that the last two words of the dented period repeat the first two indicates that the speaker wants to close the circle, but where can he put his predicate? He has no choice but to place it prior to the key phrase.

After the religious dimension of his behaviour has been maintained and the sacral origins of his office have been recalled, David changes his tone, moving into another area. The first half was about "today" and former times, the

[107] The term "the people of Yahweh", which is not placed as an apposition next to the name Israel, is much more than an epithet in 21c and anticipates, together with other terms on election such as the word *nāgīd*, the vocabulary of the praying David of ch.7.

second turns towards the future with two wqtl forms and an imperfect (in the cohortative, expressing a firm belief).[108] Michal gets a taste of her own medicine for now the king decides to deliver a replica using terms which originated with her: honour – women – disgrace. Verse 22 is the half of the speech which actually goes into her reproach. But its framework, from *n^eqallōtī* to *'ikkābedā*, two niph'al forms again, itself reveals what the speaker is aiming at: he stands his wife's inclusio on its head. Michal began allegedly with David's honour, but arrived at his lowering himself. David begins in 22a by assuming the humiliation of his own free will, and ends with his honour intact thanks to the loyalty of his subjects. It is a splendid rhetorical tour, because David manages in 22ab to aggravate the debasement motif twice, inciting it against himself, before rescuing his honour from the very jaws of hell! There is an exact balance of six words on disgrace (22ab) versus six words on honour (in 22c). In 22a he first anticipates the possibility, that he is to undergo further humiliation, with *'ōd mizzōt*, and chooses the word which is the very opposite to *kbd*: *qll*. Its form, *n^eqallōtī*, is at the same time an ingenious echo of Michal's venomous pair *higgālōt niglōt*. Then he goes a step further and foresees the ultimate disgrace, things are going to go so badly for him, that he will loose all his confidence in, and all his contact with, his own dignity: "perhaps I will be vile in my own eyes". This line lives off the contrast with two other evaluations: in your eyes I am this already, but not yet in my own. Then the climax comes: the moment my self-image is dashed to pieces, says David, then I can still rely on the least of my slaves: they will not desert me. David has adopted the word for slave girls, *'ămāhōt*, from Michal's attack and turns it against her. This proud closing line soundly aggravates the inciting of her sexual jealousy. And there is another implicit comparison at work against Michal. The painful implication of David's point is, after all: your abandoning me makes you less worthy than the plebs you have such a low opinion of. So David trumps her both with the brilliant rhetoric, and the venom, of his final line.[109] How eloquent is the goaded ego!

[108] Driver would like to drop the -ā ending of the cohortative from David's final word, because he could not link it with the expression of conviction. The cohortative can, however, express particular nuances of certainty, see, for example Gen.46:31, Is.38:10, Jer.4:19,21, and cf. Joüon p.308, note 2. The conviction aspect is not to be found in the modern translations (KJ, SV *et seq.*), but at least Driver has caught on (on p.273 he wrote "conviction is what the context requires").
[109] Three more details: the "in my eyes" of 22b is more penetrating and more personal than the "before the eyes of" of 20e, and, moreover, the speaker lets it follow in 22c through a double *'im* [Driver: resumption for the sake of emphasis] – an intimacy between David and the women which must enrage Michal.
Finally the syntax of 22a and c is chiastic; predicate + complement and vice versa; which is underlined by the rhyme and alliteration of *'ōd mizzōt* versus *'im hā'ămāhōt*.

Apart from this there is an antecedent to the apparent (over)sensitivity of David to humiliation vis-à-vis Michal. In the first Michal passage, shortly after his admission to the court, in I 18, David uses forms of *qll* and *qlh* for not accepting, for the time being, Saul's proposal that he should marry ... sure enough, Michal.[110] This connection which stretches far back brings to light the fact that, in relation to the previous royal house of all things, David has been put under a spell by a low or degrading position. Deep in his heart he wrestles with the emotions of a parvenu now and again.

What has come over Michal to make her let fly at David so sharply? We do not need to long for information from lost sources, if indeed they ever existed, to obtain an answer to this question; it is methodologically necessary to call the previous Michal passages to mind and to trust solely in their data and context. I would like to repeat the question, formulating it in another way: what prevented Michal from wholeheartedly taking part in the celebration of all? Her earlier moments of appearance, usually in a supporting role, are informative enough. There is not one single mention among them of David's ever having loved her. What was, however, mentioned is the fact of her loving him in I 18, which love she proved in I 19. Circumstances dictated a long separation. During this period she experienced with Paltiel what receiving love is like. But this tender affection was rudely taken away by politics. An agreement between the big bosses Abner and David resulted in her being reduced to a pawn on the chessboard of power, and she was robbed of Paltiel's ardour without being welcomed by David. It appears that she has ended up in a cold or non-functioning marriage with the new king, which must have been all the more painful because of her previous love for David. I assume that this original love had aroused expectations as to the quality of their living together again, after which his indifference wounded her deeply. Her frustration comes out in II 6.[111] She really cannot open up her heart and take part in the celebration. Her misfortune forces her to hold off the festivities and, with a negative view on things, to look down on the abundant energy of her dancing husband.

[110] It is v.23 of I 18. Here too it bears upon a speech of David himself, the play on words *qll-qlh* also occurs in the niph'al and forms a framework, "in the eyes of" occurring here as well.

[111] Robert Alter gives a fine portrait of Michal; it serves as an example in "Characterization and the Art of Reticence", ch.6 of "The Art of Biblical Narrative", New York 1981.

My interpretation involves my rejecting the following ideas of Anthony Phillips in "David's Linen Ephod", VT 19 (1969), pp.485-487: "David was *evidently* engaged in a ritual dance which may well have been intended to culminate in sexual union with Michal," and on the latter: "As a loyal Yahwist, she took exception to the king's participation in a ritual *no doubt* associated with the Jebusite cult in Jerusalem" (italics mine, JF). This opposition (her loyalty versus his religious corruption) is baseless.

The narrator himself closes with a line which leaves the scope of the narrated day far behind. He surveys the entire life of the woman whom he again characterises as "the daughter of Saul", and he observes that she has borne no children. The message is deliberately ambiguous, so that the reader's task is to ask whether her childlessness is to be explained by David's subsequent abstinence from intercourse, or because "God had closed her womb" (as the formula goes in Gen.30 and I Sam.1). Perhaps both these solutions are right, the reader is not in a position to choose either one of them. What he can and must do, after recognising that the writer intentionally keeps to the middle of the road, is to work out several implications.

There is a dynastic aspect. If Michal had borne children to David a synthesis between the house of Saul and that of David might have arisen to benefit the nation and the monarchy. Such a birth would have aided David in a policy of conciliation towards the Saul family and the tribe of Benjamin; a policy which, after his fair attitude to Saul's death and towards Abner and Ishbosheth, is in keeping with expectations. The splicing would have healed many wounds. But it may not be like this. Michal's childlessness is now in the text as the opposite number of the list of children which have been borne to David in Jerusalem, 5:13-16. The mention of "the day of her death" is also significant. This datum has the creeping rot set in for the rest of her life as it were. Now that her womanhood may not taste a fervently desired fulfilment of maternity, she is in terms of social psychology a marked woman, doomed to isolation. So the woman undergoes a slow death in life in the new palace, and is to be compared to the ladies of 20:3, who, as grass widows "to the day of their death", get exactly the same formula.

The lexicalisation of her end, in the word *mwt*, also creates a parallel between blocks C_1 and C_2. The Uzzah incident produces the sudden death of the priest, and in a hair-raising variant a vegetating Michal may experience how a creeping kind of death gradually turns her life to stone. The light shed by the paragraphs on procession and music receives some of its brightness through the darkness of numinous violence and the chill of isolation.

Chapter VI

God grants the kingdom a future

§ 1. *II Sam.7:1-17: David receives an oracle concerning his "house"*

As a rule this chapter is dealt with in a framework rampant with prejudice. It is particularly discussed by that branch of historical critical scholarship which collects diachronic syndromes. It is high time for a fresh and open-minded analysis of the text. I feel the need to re-establish my points of departure. What is necessary and natural is a working hypothesis based on the soundness of the text and its being an integral part of a composition stretching beyond two pages. It merits internal analysis by a meticulous interpreter tuned in to the density of style and choice of words, the high level of religious and historiographic reflection and the special ideological load of ch.7; next it should be properly linked to its II Samuel environment; a context to be continually taken into consideration whilst interpreting ch.7.

II Sam.6, a long chapter, consisted almost entirely of narrator's text and only at the end did it devote a paragraph to true dialogue. Chapter 7, which is even longer,[1] is a photographic negative of this as it were: only at the beginning is the narrator at the helm (vv.1-4), what follows consists exclusively of two speeches; they articulate the whole into two parts and are exceptional qua size and content. Only in v.17a-18c does the narrator come between them for a moment to attend to the transition from oracle to prayer. Both chapters begin with a cultic initiative of David's.

Due to so much spoken word there is hardly any story line to speak of in the usual sense of a well-maintained development spread over and borne by many links and contributory acts. But insofar as the plot can be formulated

[1] II Sam.7 contains 461 words, versus 370 in ch.6.

using data from this text, its basis is provided by the narrator's opening report. According to the introduction in vv.1-4 the issue is David's desire to build a temple for God; the reader is under an initial impression that the actantial subject, object and the quest binding them, have already been given. Our expectations are quickly upset, however. In an even more radical way than its predecessor this chapter scrubs David's hero status; once again Yahweh is the one to quickly manifest Himself as agent and ensure a great surprise. Offering the prophet a revelation via his nocturnal intervention, he stands the king's quest on its head. The mortal who thought the initiative was his, and adopted the stance of a sender (*destinateur*) by giving God a temple (*bayit*), becomes the beneficiary (*destinataire*), and gains a certain immortality through the receipt of a lasting dynasty (*bayit*) from God. We shall come to see that the prophet too is subject to a curious shift. Even though ch.7 gets by with little plot the verbal drama is a sign of great dynamism. It marks a reversal which compels a drastic rearrangement of the whole actantial scheme. All mortal David can do is thank and praise.

The opening sequence is carefully composed of five duos.[2] The simplest pair is that of the quotation formulas in v.2a//3a, which have the king and the prophet converse with one another. Both characters utter two sentences, their dialogue being the middle of the paragraph. The narrator himself attends to its framework with an introductory pair before, v.1ab, and one behind, v.4ab, which completes the short exposition and also introduces the body of the chapter. The first lines of both pairs have a temporal designation, their second lines point to the Lord's action. The inclusio is also to be found on the word level. The chapter's first word, the articulatory as much as purely serviceable form *wayhī*, returns twice in v.4. Initially having the same temporal function in v.4a, it obtains a main function[3] in 4b, and thus completes the exposition with a climax: the vision crucial to the chapter. Whilst "it came to pass" in 1a needs the commencement of action in v.2, "it came to pass" in v.4 remains itself and becomes the main event.

Verse 1 is the introduction to the exposition and runs: "As soon as the king was settled in his house and the Lord had given him rest from his enemies on all sides, [the king said etc.]." The first line refines and extends the data of the seizure story, when "David went to live in the fortress" (5:9) and

[2] The little imperative of v.2b, a call for attention, is the only exception to this and can be considered in the analysis as a part of v.2c. Notice that the phonetic layer provides justification: the full alliteration of *rᵉ'ē nā* with *'arōn*.

[3] I refer particularly to semantics and style: in 4a the verb sustains the temporal introduction, in 4b "to be" has the importance (in translation) of an independent verb: "the word of the Lord *came to* Nathan".

"a palace was built for him" (v.11). The place becomes more precise in 7:1a, which now confirms that David does indeed live in that palace. And the second line immediately finishes with the element of strife so prominent in ch.5. David need fear no enemy activity whatsoever anymore, and owes this to the same person who made him conqueror in ch.5. From now on his settlement is in the constellation of security. The term for this concept stems from the book of Deuteronomy; the passage's first sign that God structures His relationship with David in terms of the original covenant reformulated by Moses.[4] The peace under David is, therefore, a special fulfilment of God's ancient promise of giving the people rest in the promised land. His living in security contrasts sharply with his years as a war lord, when he "moved about from place to place": *wythlkw b'šr hthlkw*, words employed in a figura etymologica (I 23:13) of which the words of God Himself (II 7:6sq) are soon to remind us. David himself is consistently referred to in vv.1-3 as "the king", and this choice is determined by the theme of the lasting dynasty.

His partner Nathan appears for the first time in v.2, but fails to get an introduction of his own. He is referred to as "the prophet" and the withholding of further information on him suggests his more or less self-evident presence at court. The king's initiative is presented in the form of a speech to Nathan. The king utters, if we may include the signal for the prophet's attention with his beginning, two clauses:

2bc r^{e}'ē nā, 'ānōkī yōšeb b^{e}bēt 'ărāzīm
2d wa'ărōn hā'ęlōhīm yōšeb b^{e}tōk hay^{e}rī'ā

We see a carefully formed parallelism which results in a contrast. The initial words exhibit maximum alliteration. Afterwards "I" and "God" occur next to one another as subjects.[5] They too have many phonetic links; their aleph and the vowels ō-ī. There is even more similarity in the third position, for God and David now have an identical participle as predicate. Then an adjunct of place follows, which in turn suggests identity by starting both phrases with *b^{e}* plus a contracted segholate form (*bēt/tōk*). The contrast supplying the point does not occur until the final word.

David's sentence on himself is linked to "live in a house" in v.1a, and increases it significantly by one word: David now lives "in a house/palace of cedars". So the house of 5:9c/11b is combined, for the first time, with the

[4] See for example Deut.12:9-10 and 25:19. Verse 8 of Deut.12, with its idiom "everyone does what is right in his own eyes" goes well with the end of Judges, whilst the "rest" in vv.9-10 gains an implementation under the established David. Deut.12:11a and 14 go well next to II Sam.6-7. When Solomon has finished the temple there is "rest" in I Ki.8:56.

[5] This is not a linguistic statement, because the ark is the subject of 2d; but the thing itself represents God and the word *hā'ęlōhīm* determines the construct state combination.

cedar wood of 5:11c which was supplied by the Phoenician ally. This luxury now faces the sober tent canopy of v.2d. The shift from plural to singular also contributes to the contrast. The adjunct "under [literally: in the midst of] a tent canopy" is striking. It is a sequel to, and the metonymic substitute of, the adjunct in 6:17, where the ark was permanently installed "in the midst of the tent (*bᵉtōk hā'ohẹl*) which David had pitched for it". The fact that this is a substitute is given away by the preposition "in the midst of", which fits "tent" perfectly there but links up poorly with the literal "tent canopy" here.[6] I assume the narrator wishes to reserve the word "tent" for God himself who makes a striking pair, *'ohẹl umiškān*, out of it in his first oracle, among other things by combining it with movement and *not* with "sitting" (v.6b). The metonymy, or rather synecdoche, consisting of a *pars pro toto*, has its own positive function. The word *yᵉrī'ā* is much more sensory than "tent", so forming a more effective contrast with its equally tangible material counterpart in 2c, cedars.[7] The king, who had roamed about as a guerilla for years, sees how settled he has become and almost seems ashamed of his God's nomadic trait.

David does not literally say: "I [also] want to build a house [therefore], in this case a temple, for the Lord." His speech offers "only" two facts which are placed next to one another for the sake of comparison. The conclusion which can be drawn from this juxtaposition is something which David leaves to the listener. It seems so self-evident that the prophet does not speak of a temple in his approval either. So the whole exposition is a virtuoso avoidance of the term which, on the one hand, shows the king's objective the best, but on the other is to be severely criticised in the oracle speeches and stood on its head.

Nathan himself is won over at once by the obviousness of David's (unspoken) conclusion and plan. His reaction is highly empathic. In his capacity as man of God he thinks he can give the king *carte blanche*, v.3b. He motivates it with a *kī* clause, "for Yahweh is with you", and so far he presumes to dispense, or at least to know, God's position on this matter. The prophet's attitude is not surprising; recent developments all point to God's blessing – as the narrator himself said in 5:10b "the Lord is with David".

[6] The phrase "*under* a tent canopy" seems much more likely, i.e. we first expect the word *taḥat* to be used. This is in fact the selfsame word with which the parallel passage in I Chron.17 chooses to replace the original preposition.

[7] An additional remark in connection with the substitution. The word *yᵉrī'ā* occurs fifty-four times in the Hebrew Bible, and is mainly to be found in Exodus at the construction of the Tabernacle of the Congregation. It occurs throughout Ex.26 and 36 in contact with the word *'ohẹl*, and in Ex.26:1 and Num.4:25 it stands in contact with the word *miškān*.

Nathan's two sentences are brief and to the point. His initial word *kol* excludes any reservations he might have and he speaks of "your heart". This word activates a series of references: I 13:14, which anticipates David's election and calls him "a man after God's heart" without releasing his name; I 16, its confirmation, where the God "who looks on the heart" points out the youngest son of Jesse as his favourite to the fallible Samuel; and also the encouraging reaction which the charismatic Jonathan gets from his shield bearer in I 14:7.[8] Moreover, a comparable *carte blanche* had already been given by the first prophet who faced a king in I 10:17.[9] Nathan has a succinct, because asyndetically lined-up, "go and do it" follow the key word "heart" with its connotations of the proper attitude, intrinsic quality and destination. A series of phonetic means draws the speech's eight words even closer together. Besides the anaphoral alliteration which opens the lines, *kol* ... *kī*, and the fact that 3c also ends on a kaph, there is a threefold play on the consonants l and k in v.3b: *kl* 'šr b*l*bb*k* *lk* 'śh.

Nathan thinks he is properly in keeping with reality. His pair of clauses, 3bc, exhibits the same alternation as the 1ab introductory pair of the narrator and David's pair, 2cd. All these duos first have predicates on David (who sits, *bis*, but wants to act and is stimulated to do so) and then speak on God, whose protection (1b,3c) encompasses David, even though he himself is a mere tent (canopy) dweller. So the question has been posed three times as to how far the king's situation is tuned in to the reality of God. Are they parallel? Analogous? Do they contrast with one another? Whatever the case might be the king's strong resolution is the foundation of a true quest. The prophet thinks he will take on the position of helper in the actantial scheme evoked by the king's plan. The last thing he expected was to pass through two startling shifts in one day. God's declining David's plan proves Nathan wrong and entails a new actantial model and an opposite quest (God promises a house = dynasty) in which David is merely to take up the position of receiver. The consent with which the prophet hailed the king's idea makes him, for a moment, into an obstacle to the true quest, which is still hidden on the day of the king-prophet talk and whose terms do not become clear until the double oracle. Nathan's error briefly places him in the position of opponent. But God is merciful to him, even though he was wrong about his Sender, and accepts him as helper in his own undertaking by giving him the nocturnal vision that contemplates the king's future.

[8] This reference in I 14 has the same phrase "all that is in your heart", and makes that the object of *'ăśē* too.

[9] The I 10:7bc reference itself says literally: "do what your hand finds, for God is with you", and Saul's legitimisation is indicated by the datum of his getting "another *heart*" (*lb* in v.9).

Nathan too is a fallible human being and God intervenes. The lines which report this, 4ab, are again a pair, but they break through the king/God alternation which governed (the subject of) the previous pairs (1ab, 2cd, 3bc). Now God is the one who acts in an all-powerful way, takes the initiative, and decisively alters the mortals' situation, choosing a vehicle which is numinous, suitable to his decree and promise (*dbr*): a vision in the night. The auditive term rounds out the visual one, with a complementariness repeated in v.17 where it is much more noticeable.

The narrator could have reported at the end of his exposition: God appeared in the night to Nathan and put words into his mouth; afterwards the prophet went to David, passing on the vision with the words: "thus says the Lord", – whereupon the narrator would have recorded the passage which now occurs in vv.5-16, as Nathan's speech to the king.[10] And sure enough the narrator does pursue such an option in chs.12 and 14, where the king, as judge, is confronted with situations he does not yet know are parables of the real issue. This also takes place via extensive speeches, of Nathan (once again!) and the wise woman of Tekoa respectively, and the reader learns of their words at the same time as the king, not earlier. In ch.7, however, he chooses the other option, so that we learn of the oracle at the same time as the prophet, i.e. *before* David. With this the narrator increases Nathan's prestige, and in harmony with this we also observe that God does not admonish His prophet or be hard on his mistake, even though there is room enough in his long speech. He takes him in his service in order to get down to business as quickly as possible and to go into David's plan.[11]

The bestowing of great prestige on Nathan is functional. Thanks to the fact that the prophet, as spokesman, accepts God's word expressly and without criticism, and, through this, is thoroughly committed to the divine promise of a Davidic dynasty, he is able, in ch.12, to enter the palace as an outstanding man of God, and this is once again functional in Nathan's purpose of first having to put David on the wrong foot in order to hit him even harder with the revelation: "you are the man", after which he can deliver the long oracle of doom with authority to the overwhelmed king. I would to like recall my

[10] In other words, and on the practical level: the narrator could have switched round the report of v.17 and the speech of vv.5-16.

[11] Notwithstanding, the term "Nathan's oracle", which many historical critics give to the chapter, is simply a misnomer; it not infrequently generates erroneous ideas. Examples of this are the three elementary mistakes which Heinz Kruse makes in one sentence on p.142 of his article "David's Covenant", VT, 35 (1985) pp.139-164: "In 2 Sam. vii 5-7 (...) we find that Nathan, as an interpreter of God's will, is opposing the king's plan to build a temple." On the contrary, the story states that Nathan was *for* it, v.3, that it is God who does not accept David as builder, and that Nathan does not interpret but flawlessly passes on what is said to him, v.17.

analyses in *King David* which have demonstrated that the judgement of Nathan, pronounced after the parable, consists of *two* oracles of doom, due to their connection with the two capital crimes committed by David. One is very short, 12:9-10a, the other longer, vv.10b-12. They were introduced by a historical preamble on David's election, 12:7d-8. The points of contact with ch.7 are plain. Here too the oracle is in two parts, with a short and a long passage. After the refusal it turns out to be an oracle of salvation in vv.8-16, the beginning of which (three lines with preterits, vv.8c-9b) is a flashback to the divine appointment of David and his success.

We can now look over the appearances of the prophet Nathan. There are three in all and they occur in II Sam.7 and 12, and in I Ki.1. They all are highly important and contain long speeches. All are concerned with the dynasty and Davidic continuity:

II Sam.7 double oracle, positive: the promise of a lasting dynasty.
II Sam.12 double oracle, negative: catastrophes will eat away at the house of David.
I Ki.1 political handiwork: via Bathsheba the prophet manipulates the aged David who cuts the knot of the succession.[12]

After the fundamental passages with which Nathan was twice sent to David by God Himself, and which are in polar proportion to one another as protection to doom, the prophet throws himself into practical politics and the factions' competitiveness, on his own initiative. He is not scared of getting his hands dirty in ensuring the safety of the Davidic line and helping the candidate preferred come to power. The aim of I Ki.2 is a strong Solomonic throne and the key clause completing the entire "King David" section runs: *w^e hammamlākā nākōnā b^e yad š^e lōmō*. Immediately preceding this Solomon had uttered, to an opponent, another clause whose every word has indeed been inspired by II Sam.7:

I Ki.2:45b *w^e kissē dāwīd yihyę nākōn lifnē yhwh ʿad ʿōlām.*

There are thus lines of communication from our chapter, the climax of Act X, to the following Act (which founds the "King David" section and puts it in a minor key) and they carry on to this section's end; the completion of the books of Samuel. These data turn II Sam.7 into a key unit. But the first to do this of course is the intrinsic weight of the chapter; in particular the speech of vv.5-16 now demanding our attention.

[12] The name which Nathan himself, once more sent by God, took to Solomon ran *ye dīdyā*, "beloved of Yahu", II Sam.12:25!

The long bipartite speech of God: the refusal in vv.5-7

The long speech of God in vv.5-16 is divided into two oracles. Verse 5 begins with a tiered double introduction which takes us away from the narrator's text and leads us down to third-degree direct speech. The first line is the messenger's commission (first-degree speech), the second line is the messenger's formula (idem second-degree) which marks the oracle proper. This procedure is, however, repeated in v.8ab, with minor adaptations, so that we have two separate words of God: a short passage in vv.5c-7c and a long one in vv.8c-16b, with 48 and 131 words respectively.[13]

The prophet had said to the king: "go, act!". This is now swept away as the king must now receive (God's) words from Nathan. The messenger is sent on his way with a simple "go!". His addressee is designated twice, with words which, immediately after the exposition, greatly alter the tone and make it very personal for the rest of the chapter. Up to now we had seen "the king" three times vis-à-vis the prophet, and that sounded rather formal. Now God utters the proper noun David, which remains the case in 8a. But what is even more important than the king as an individual is his quality, and this appears earlier than his proper noun, in the designation "my servant". So the relationship between God and the mortal occurs first, with a remarkable title.[14] The name David is now merely an apposition for identifying the servant. David is seen as the obedient one who knows that the norm is above and beyond him in the God he must follow. This title has seldom before been conferred by God. Only two great men from the Torah, Abraham and Moses, were so designated.[15] It sounds intimate, issues from a close relationship, and witnesses to God's care and recognition. Shortly afterwards David is to respond to it ten times by uttering "your servant" in his prayer. The word is also a sign of great trust: God expects his servant to run things properly. Right from the start what God wants to get across is dominated by

[13] God utters a total of 197 words to Nathan; David gets to hear 186, for he hears the two oracles and twice the messenger formula, but not v.5a//8a. The 197 words which the narrator and God share with Nathan and the reader are in equilibrium with the second half of the chapter, where David is to utter 198 words.

[14] This is not completely new, because the title has already been quoted in 3:18, where it was placed after the proper noun by Abner.

[15] The title "my servant" for Abraham: in Gen.26:24, for Moses: in Nu.12:7, 8, Josh.1:2,7, II Ki.21:8, Mal.3:22.

David's election and God's (covenant) love for him.[16] Just how important the title "my servant" is in reference to David, appears later on in the Bible, where it regularly appears in passages of different genres and centuries.[17] The ideology of II Sam.7 has become common property in biblical Israel.

The highly personal tone assumed by both parties blossoms when the chief oracle begins, and is not prominent in the initial part, which I call the oracle of refusal. A scrutiny of the key words and the proportions of the lines reveals the compelling and symmetrical structure of v.5c-7c:

A Are you the one to build a house for Me to dwell in?
  B I have not dwelt in a house
      from the day that I brought the people of Israel out of Egypt
      to this day,
    C but I kept moving about in Tent and Tabernacle.
    C' As I moved about wherever all the Israelites went,
  B' did I ever speak a word with any of the leaders of Israel
      whom I appointed shepherds of my people Israel, saying:
A' "Why have you not built Me a house of cedars?"

Two questions in the 'you' form and the key word "build" frame this unity, A-A'. Two long sentences of the same size[18] look back in history with perfects, to the period between the exodus and the monarchy, and deny that during this long period there ever was a single time when God needed or spoke of a permanent residence, B-B'. They do this in a polar manner: verse 6a is an indicative clause in the negative which is forcefully underlined by *kī*, whilst 7b, on the other hand, begins with the interrogative particle *hă*, but, as a rhetorical question, does presuppose negation. In this ring correspondence C-C' occurs, brought into existence by durative and iterative specifications and the repetition of *hthlk* in the first person.

[16] The pre-eminent poetic equivalent is the title "my servant" which God gives to "Jacob" in the Book of Comfort, by which I mean the book of poetry of Deutero-Isaiah. The oracle of salvation is prominent in this composition (Is.40-55).

[17] "David, my servant" occurs the most often (after II Sam.3:18): four times in I Ki.11 (vv.13,34,36,38), II Ki.19:34, 20:6, Is.37:35, Jer.33:21,22,26, Ezek.37:25, Ps.89:4,21, I Chron.17:4; but "my servant David" occurs in I Ki.11:32, 14:8, Ezek.34:23,24, 37:24, and in the parallel text I Chron.17:7.

[18] Verse 6a is made up of thirteen words, as is verse 7b, if we leave aside the little introductory word *lēmor*. With the exception of v.23 these lines are the longest in the whole chapter; only 8c can approximate them with twelve words.

The concentric construction's virtuosity can particularly be observed in noticing how much the articulation in 3 + 3 lines exhibits an interesting friction with the syntax, whilst managing to remain plain. In the first half each line coincides with an independent clause, but in v.7 this is very different. Here one long compound sentence takes up the entire CBA series. Its nucleus, the question "did I ever reproach one of the tribal leaders?" is "clad" with three clauses, each in its own way independent.[19]

The polemical question with which the first oracle opens contains two scoops. It introduces the word "build", showing that God wishes to immediately express his opinion on David's plan. He had not enunciated this plan in v.2, but, for the good listener, it was the conclusion of his two observations. The question also combines for the first time "my dwelling" with a permanent residence, *bayit*. But because the speaker has made a rhetorical question out of it he appears to reject dwelling in a temple. However, the refusal is not fundamental, but provisional, since the emphasis falls on the extra pronoun prior to the finite verb form: do *you* want to build a house for me? A surprising and postponed answer to this question is to be indirectly given in the second oracle, with another pronoun indicating David's male issue as alternative:

v.5c	ha'attā	tibnẹ̄	lī bayit l^{e}šibtī
v.13a	hū	yibnẹ̄	bayit lišmī

It is true Solomon is to be allowed to build the temple, but after the polemics against residing God's speech in II Sam.7 is not to connect the verb *yšb*, or his residing, with that edifice.[20] In this pair "my Name" follows "my dwelling" rhyming with it but at the same time being a subtle correction of it. The real resident of the temple is not to be God in person, but the Name, and another representative of "the Lord of Hosts enthroned (*yōšeb*!) on the cherubs", i.e. a thing: the Ark, which is still "housed under a tent canopy". What God does in the vv.5-7 part is not exclude or reject the building of a

[19] Verse 7a is merely an adjunct of place which, for the rest, becomes longer than average by being changed into a relative clause by *'ăšẹr*. Likewise verse 7b has become much longer, being prolonged by a relative clause explaining what "the scepters of Israel" (literally) are, and verse 7c is, solely linguistically speaking, an independent clause, but in its context it is an embedded speech filling in *dbr dbrty*.
The term "clad" is inspired by, but different from, the terminology in the "Hebräische Syntax" of Brockelmann, who speaks of the "einfache bekleidete Satz" versus the "zusammengesetzte Satz".

[20] The verb *yšb* occurs five times at the beginning of ch.7, but afterwards nowhere else (except v.18b in which it means "to sit").

temple in principle, but turn down David as its builder and deny his own need for a temple.[21]

We are to encounter yet more initial pronouns so that a complete I-you-he series arises; one of the contours of the speech, vv.5-16. Here the singular of the "you" wanting to build (A) quickly merges into the leaders of Israel, you (plural) who have not built (A'). The speaker leaves his baffled question (Do *you* want to build? Can you really mean this?) via various oppositions. He places the past over against the future: I have never lived in a house (the *bayit* of 6a against the *bayit* of 5c). "My dwelling" in the present (5c) is replaced by the negative next to the perfect, *lō yāšabtī* (6a). The entire passage, vv.6-7, looks back in time. The mortal in the singular in 5c quickly drops out and is replaced by a human partner in the plural: first "the Israelites" in 6a//7a, then their leaders in 7b, who get to hear a special reproach, in 7c, which has a unusual status: it has never been uttered against them. Finally, the most interesting opposition is that of 'moving' versus 'residing'.

Moving is designated by a hithpa'el of *hlk* which has a certain iterativeness as such.[22] But in C-C' the element of duration and repetition becomes plainer via other means. First there is the periphrastic construction, not often used, in v.6b, then the spreading out of "all the places where" with the little word *kol*, which exhibits another distributive aspect in its echo "*all* the Israelites". The adjuncts of place complement each other well: in 6b God always accompanies them "in tent and tabernacle", – a splendid duo which is perhaps a hendiadys or in any case a flower of style – in 7a the adjunct occurs in the same place and begins with the same preposition, "among/with all the Israelites". The similarity of 6b and 7a is so great that the halves of the oracle join up seamlessly, even flowing into one other.

[21] André Caquot has examined the correspondence of v.5c with 13a in more detail. In his article "Brève explication de la prophétie de Natan (2 Sam 7,1-17)", pp.51-69 in "Mélanges bibliques et orientaux en l'honneur de M. Henri Cazelles", = AOAT 212, 1981, he writes on p.54: "quand le verbe d'une interrogation rhétorique se trouve repris dans une assertion positive qui lui sert de réponse, la négation impliquée par le tour porte sur le sujet du verbe et non sur l'action qu'exprime celui-ci". At the same time he rejects the correspondence of 5c with 11c (second half), considering the difference in verb and construction. As does M. Noth, "David und Israel in II Samuel 7" in Festschrift André Robert 1957, pp.122-130, = Gesammelte Studien zum AT, 1960 (2nd ed.), pp.334-345.

[22] I had already mentioned the repetition of *hthlk* in I 23:13 previously, and I also recall the expression *hithallek lifnē* X (often *yhwh*), which reproduces [the iterativeness of] conduct, or even rules of life; e.g. of Samuel in I 12:2(*bis*), or of Abraham (Gen.24:40), or of Noah (Gen.6:9) and Enoch (Gen.5:22,24): see also Ps.56:14 or 116:9. And in Sam. itself once again, I 2:30,35.

I would now like to compare the tails of the long sentences, that is the second half of B-B'. Both point to an entire period, but in a different way. In 6a two centuries are enclosed by the merismus *yōm ... yōm*, which takes us from the exodus to the present day. What lies between the temporal extremes is exactly what is shown us in 7b: "the leaders of Israel whom I had commanded to pasture my people." This clause's similarity with what is stated in v.11a is so great that identification with the Judges is plausible: they are the ones who fill up the period between *yōm* and *yōm*. We also recognise the time adjunct at the beginning of 11a, it is inspired by the *miyyōm* from (the counterpart of v.7b, i.e.) verse 6:

v.7b ... šibṭē yiśrā'el 'ăšęr ṣiwwītī lir'ōt 'ęt 'ammī 'ęt yiśrā'el

v.11 l^{e}min hayyōm 'ăšęr ṣiwwītī šōf^{e}ṭīm 'al 'ammī yiśrā'el

We also see a chiasmus (*šbṭy – 'šr ṣwyty = 'šr ṣwyty – špṭym*) which backs up the judges identification. The word "staffs" or "sceptres of Israel" in v.7b is a metonym for "tribal leaders" (as the JPS renders them) and needs no emendation.[23] It is not only supported by the chiasmus and further parallelism between 7b and 11a, but also by an isotopy. The first oracle has a whole series of pastoral terms in common with the opening line of the second which qua length, syntax and content follows on naturally from 6a//7b: staffs and pasture my people from 7b, "from the pasture" and "from behind the sheep" from v.8c. This isotopy has a remarkable predecessor in 5:2. It was not the elders who spoke here, "but all the tribes of Israel" (*šbṭy* therefore!) and their words culminate in a speech, not of "God", but of Yahweh, which is an eye-catching *parallelismus membrorum* whose terms are completely tuned into 7:7b/8c:

5:2d 'attā tir'ę 'ęt 'ammī 'ęt yiśrā'el
5:2e w^{e}'attā tihyę̄ l^{e}nāgīd 'al yiśrā'el

Furthermore the idea of "pasturing" (the verb *r'y*) goes back to I 16:11 and 17:15,34,40, passages which introduce the man from Judah *as shepherd.*

Now that v.8c has come into the picture we see the leadership topic unfold in three stages: in v.6a it is God himself who leads the Israelites "up out of Egypt", in v.7b he has already delegated authority to the judges who "must pasture my people Israel", and just now God has narrowed down this delegation to the election of the shepherd David who is "to be a ruler (*nāgīd*)

[23] The JPS rendering retains, therefore, the word *šbṭy* of the MT. As does Buber, who renders it "Stabhaltern". There is a careful examination of the metonymy "sceptres" in CT, cf. Appendix I.

over my people Israel" – the third step, which comes in 8c. In accordance with the merismus of v.6 this series draws attention to two cardinal events as points on the time scale, which encompass a period of two centuries: between the Exodus and David's blessed monarchy lies the period of the Judges.

Meanwhile the parameter of God's interest has become plain; the welfare of this nation, mentioned as many as four times in the space of a few lines.[24] He loves Israel, doing the same thing with its name as he does with David's in the messenger's commission. In 7b-8c-11a as speaker, God puts the sign of his commitment first: the word "my people", *'ammī*, which is connected to *'abdī* via alliteration and assonance (including the rhyme via the suffix). Only afterwards does the proper noun Israel appear: another apposition again, added only for the sake of identification. The first oracle sheds a broad circle of light, in which the entire people of Israel appears as the chosen partner of Yahweh. The second oracle directs a laser beam on one family, by making David the founder of a blessed dynasty. So the intimate relationship of God and His people is made current and concentrated in His blessing on this monarchy. At the same time David's place in God's view becomes plain: he is in the service of the people and not the other way round.

The first oracle ends subtly by allowing a long rhetorical question to end in, and be surpassed by, a new, short rhetorical question looking back to the opening line as its counterpart. The interrogative word "why" we know to be a rhetorical vehicle of reproof. Insofar as the answer to 7ab is understood to be negative and God has indeed never asked for a house from former leaders, 7ab, as a long introduction to 7c, can be called an *irrealis* which imparts its own quality (of never having happened) to the question at the end. It is indeed an apparent reproach. There is one more nicety deserving attention; it arises out of the comparison of 5c with 7c:

A ha'attā tibnẹ̄ lī bayit lᵉšibtī?
A' lāmmā lō bᵉnītẹm lī bēt 'ărāzīm?

The enacted astonishment of v.5c has now become an enacted reproach needing a negative to indicate indignation and deprivation. The scoop which connected "my dwelling" to the word "house" in A, is succeeded in A' by another scoop with *bayit*. The phrase "house of cedars", itself a new combination in v.2c, was used by David to show the luxury of his own palace, in the clauses of his unspoken resolution. Now God takes over the metonym and applies it to *his* supposedly coveted accommodation! But as a good listener to David's plan he not only renders explicit what has been concealed,

[24] The word Israel occurs eleven times in ch.7; seven times in the double oracle and four times in David's prayer.

he undermines it at the same time by holding it up to ridicule. The word "my dwelling" from element A is replaced in A' by the "cedars", which, moreover, occupy the end of the first oracle. The serious message lying behind the ironic shift ("house of cedars" as a temple instead of a palace) is that the existence of God is really not analogous to that of the well-intentioned mortal, and that he wishes to withdraw from the veiled assimilation ready to pounce should he let himself be tied down to the same sort of accommodation as the king. That is why the final word of v.13a is no longer *l^ešibtī*, but *lišmī*: "he is the one who will build a house *for my Name*." When all has been said and done can a positive characteristic of God's mode of existence be mentioned on the basis of the first oracle? Yes, he himself has shown that nomadic mobility and dynamism suit him, whilst mortal man cannot, in the long run, do without the security of a permanent location. He comes back to this in v.10, once again for the good of the nation.

The second half of God's long speech: the promises to David, vv.8-16.
The lines of 8ab, as first and second degree embedded speeches, do not take part in the revelation proper. They resume the messenger's commission and the messenger's formula, but exhibit variations compared to their example, v.5ab. First of all there is the hinge word, *w^e'attā*, which is as serviceable as it is far-reaching. It does indeed mark a great change, since the words of refusal which draw on the past are now relieved by promises and otherwise positive lines on the imminent and the distant future.[25] Unusual though the text of ch.7 be, due to its unique subject matter, there are still points of contact with other oracles, regarding genre characteristics. Consider the oracle of doom with its bipartite structure. After an accusation concerning yesterday's crime (with verbs in the perfect, therefore) comes the messenger formula as pivot, with or without the reinforcement of *lāken* or *w^e'attā*, followed by the proclamation of imminent judgement in future verb forms (yqtl, sometimes a participle).[26] These characteristics apply *mutatis mutandis* to the unique oracle of salvation too, in II Sam.7. It devotes six negative and three positive lines to the past (vv.5-7 plus v.8c-9b, which, for the rest, has been placed *after* the pivot as preamble to the main part) and the main part devotes twenty

[25] The first oracle had five sentences, in which two explicit and two implicit negatives are at work. The main part in vv.8-16 contains *c.* twenty-five clauses, in which the negative occurs only three times, and only then in order to fend off what is negative: 10cd and 15a.

[26] Even though the messenger formula takes up the pivot position in the pure form of the oracle of doom, there are in fact many oracles to be found which also begin with the formula. Presently I will take this datum into consideration when dealing with the question of whether there are one or two oracles in this chapter.

lines, in vv.9c-16, to the future. The messenger formula is also the pivot between one flank and the other. In terms of genre 8b is the primary messenger formula, indispensable to the oracle, whilst 5b is secondary. This is established by the observation that God is referred to by his full title in v.8b: "thus says the LORD of Hosts". The context (i.e. the sacral Act X) also has the title occur in ch.7; essential, as this chapter is the climax of the whole Act. On the level of words this makes the proper noun of God, *yhwh*, into the most frequent word in ch.7 (appearing eighteen times).

The comparison with oracles of doom points to enough real similarities to produce another insight. Up to now my terminology has been somewhat ambivalent; I spoke of one long speech but a double oracle. We can put the question pointedly: do verses 5-16 form one oracle or two? Perhaps it is wiser to remain ambiguous, but I tend to favour one in the long run. When we are on the level of texture and see not only the repetition of the messenger formula but also that of the messenger commission, it is useful to speak of two. But on the level of structure, viewing the speech as a whole and all God's words facing David's words in the space of the chapter, it is better to speak of one oracle. The formal fact of God's words occurring in one speech, under the heading "the word of Yahweh" in v.4's introduction, probably clinches it.

The positive main issue is articulated into four in 3 + 7 + 6 + 7 lines, which are distinct due to factors of both form and content. An initial description might read:

a) vv.8c-9b	David's past: *I* have chosen and protected *you*
b) vv.9c-11b	security for my people Israel
c) vv.11c-13b	proclamation: your house and throne are secure
d) vv.14-16	a strong bond between *him* and *me*

Part a) is the only short one and it alone tells of the past. This little passage forms a preamble summarising David's history in three lines: he is appointed by God – God was always close by him – and saved him from the enemy. Three 'I' forms occur first, so that we do not overlook God's initiative. The very first word is an extra pronoun which stresses: "I am the one who took you from behind the sheep". The 'I' forms are all parts of predicates focussed on David and he is present solely as beneficiary, in the form of the suffix.[27] Each line has an I-you kind of contact, so elucidating the intimacy which set

[27] David is the subject of a relative clause once, at the end of 9a, but he is represented by *-kā* four times.

the tone from "my servant" onwards. This speaking is intimate, but not private, since God's interest in David has a broad goal which is expressed straightaway in 8c in an infinitival clause. There is a link with the end of 7b which becomes even stronger through the pastoral terms flanking the 8ab hinge two by two:

v.7b	... ṣiwwītī lir'ōt	'ęt 'ammī	'ęt yiśrā'el
v.8c	l^{e}qaḥtīkā ... lihyōt nāgīd	'al 'ammī	'al yiśrā'el

The double complement denoting the national dimension is preceded by a complement of place which is also double and depends on *min ... min*, so that we do not miss the humble origins of David and are reminded of his exceptional start in I Sam.17: I have taken you "out of the pasture // from behind the sheep". But the same chapter on Goliath's defeat with sling and stone showed us that being one kind of shepherd can turn into being another kind, and be elevated to a higher plane. The sacral term *nāgīd* ties in precisely with, and wants to recall, the solemn sentences which have already named, by this word, the task of the elect; the series I 13:14, 25:30, II 5:2, and particularly 6:21 which has just been mentioned. I notice that our passage, which is hard to overestimate ideologically, makes a distinction between the judges and the bearer(s) of the *nāgīd* title.

The second line also ties in with the refusal prior to the hinge:

v.9a	wā'ęhyę 'imm^{e}kā	b^{e}kol 'ăšęr hālaktā
v.6b-7a	wā'ęhyę ...	b^{e}kol 'ăšęr hithallaktī

Besides, the keeping on moving through the desert was also God's constant escort of the tribes. Now the career of David is described in similar terms, so that his phase as roaming war lord is a continuation of the exodus. At the same time this "I have been with you" (*w'hyh 'mk*) of v.9a is a subtle correction of the prophet's rather easy, *yhwh 'mk*, in v.3c. Furthermore it reminds us of 5:10b where the full title *yhwh ṣb'wt* also occurred. God's protection is shown by the little word *kol* which returns in 9b, giving me the insight that the line on the extermination of enemies is the other side, but also the realisation, of the positive clause of 9a. In the centre line, 9a, we meet me-and-you alone, whilst the flanking lines add a collective, the polarity of my people versus your enemies. Finally 9b also looks back to v.1b: the exterminating is the establishing of "give rest", but it is also its reverse side and much more violent. Both lines have a proleptic aspect because the defeat of all enemies is not reported until the enumerative unit, ch.8.

Once again I inspect the initial position pronouns. The broad *'ānōkī* of the royal planner opened as early as v.2c a quest which was quickly abandoned. It was put into perspective by the mockery of *ha'attā*, the very first word of the vision in 5c which also referred to David. God goes on to place his 'I', mighty and autonomous, over against the well-meaning mortal: *'ănī* is the first word of the main part, 8c-16. Finally he is to enter into a new reciprocity with the son of David's body, so that the 'I' of 8c gets a sequel in "he – I – he", a series which we have yet to pass in vv.13-14.

The past tense of "I took you" had to become a form of the perfect in 8c, in view of the x-qtl syntax, and two wyqtl clauses followed. The waw now systematically remains *Satzweiser* for the space of eleven lines (up to and including v.12c). After this there is a consistent alternation; the waw is an index of parataxis four times and five times it is not.[28] A subsequent detail is that the narrator stops using imperfect forms after the preamble of David's election and changes to clauses (once again up to and including v.12) which in principle open with wqtl. There is a considerable minority of modern experts who take 9c-11b to be in the past tense and are of the opinion that the wqtl forms of this passage consist of a copulative waw plus an "ordinary" perfect.[29] An approach like this is inadvisable it seems to me, because it implies flatly ignoring the change from the typically narrative form wyqtl to the polyvalent wqtl. Can we reach a ruling in this discussion? I pussyfoot around at first by gathering a certain amount of data. There is a total of ten verbs from the wqtl conjugation (with a sequel in 14c and 16a), and they do not stop after v.11b. In principle the series of wqtl forms continues undisturbed even as far as up to and including v.12c. Nobody can deny that the wqtl lines in v.12 refer to the future.[30] It is incontrovertible that the 10cd lines also refer to the future, with their x-yqtl scheme which is unavoidable because of the negative. Furthermore – for the first time I employ an argument based on content – the fame which David is to receive, amongst the great men of the earth, has not yet been brought about in so short a time since the conquest of Jerusalem. Or, keeping to matters of principle and not appealing to events which, strictly speaking, have an extratextual status, I remain true to the literary signs and formulate the following: prior to the

[28] This holds good on condition that my colometry is accepted. In 14c and 15b we are concerned with subordinate clauses which begin with *(k)'šr*.

[29] The series vv.9c-11b is put into the past tense by the SV, Keil, Rost in "Die Ueberlieferung von der Thronnachfolge Davids", 1926, p.59sq., Ernst Kutsch, "Die Dynastie von Gottes Gnaden", Zeitschrift für Theologie und Kirche, 58 (1961) pp.137-153, Buber, Goslinga, Ridout (in PCP) and KBS. On the other hand the series is translated in the future by the KJ (only after 9c), LV, Wellhausen, Driver, Carlson, NBG, Goslinga, BJ, NEB, NBE, JPS (about the only one to have a new paragraph begin in 11c). See also App.1.

[30] There are at least two, 12bc, and in my view three, because I re-locate the redundant *yhwh* from the end of 11c to 12a, reading *whyh*, a textual alteration which requires only a transposition of consonant signs.

report of his military triumphs in ch.8 David is not yet a star on the international stage.

I now go on to confront myself and the reader with the wqtl question, first of all checking the material in Samuel.[31] The so-called copulative perfect (wqtl as a past tense) is rare and limited to isolated cases and special circumstances, both in narrator's text and character's text.[32] It is never the continuation of a wqtl form in a speech. Cases involving a completely different wqtl function, repetition in the past tense, need not be considered.[33] The great majority of cases concerns wqtl in speeches. The form is a wish or a command in c.twenty-eight cases, or the continuation of such a volitive form (an imperfect for example), and in around two hundred cases wqtl is a future tense. As fortunate coincidence will have it, exact figures are available on the text shedding the most light on our situation (wqtl forms in an ideologically-loaded speech which looks at the past and to the future).[34] Moses' long speeches in Deuteronomy contain 595 wqtl forms and 192 wyqtl forms.[35] But

[31] Rudolf Meyer had shown that wqtl forms should be accepted as narrative perfect tense in classical Hebrew and not emended, and that they have not been subject to Aramaic influence: "Auffallender Erzählungsstil in einem angeblichen Auszug aus der 'Chronik der Könige von Juda'", pp.114-123 in Festschrift F. Baumgärtel, Erlangen 1959. Apart from this the cases in report form are incidental and presumably have a special function, such as summarising and resumption: I have discussed this in Appendix I at the *whyh* of 6:16a and have quoted De Boer in respect of it.

[32] Here is a list of all the references with wqtl as perf. cop. in reports: I 1:12a, 5:7b, 10:9a, 17:48a, 25:20a, II 6:16a, 13:18d,19d, 15:30d, 16:13d, 19:18c-19a and 23:20c. It is conspicuous that five of this series of thirteen cases are an introductory *whyh*, and that II 13:19d, 15:30d and 16:13d have a descriptive and/or expressive function, and are not in the least momentaneous.

The places with wqtl as perf. cop. in speech are even scarcer and occur in special cases: I 12:2b (a synonymy of intransitive forms), 24:11b (*w'mr* has a special function, but which? Repetition in the past tense not excluded!) and II 6:21d (end of a virtual anacoluthon).

[33] There are forty-seven references with wqtl as an iterative past tense, and it is striking that these forms of the perfect almost all appear in clusters; see e.g. I 2:14-16, 16:23 (six times), 17:34-35 (eight times in a speech of David's), I 15:2,5 (six times altogether).

[34] Lenart de Regt, "A Parametric Model for Syntactic Studies of a Textual Corpus, Demonstrated on the Hebrew of Deuteronomy 1-30", Studia Semitica Neerlandica, Assen 1988, with a Supplement of 91 pp. with one-way and two-way frequency tables. An important characteristic of this study is that de Regt does not study verbs atomistically, but keeps a constant watch on their succession, in an attempt to arrive at forms of Hebrew *consecutio temporum*.

[35] In Deut.1-30 de Regt distinguishes 237 nominal, and 2903 verbal (including participial), clauses. Of these 791 are in the imperfect and 595 are in the consecutive perfect (all in "subdomains", i.e. in speech).

in this extensive material wqtl is often the foregoer of another narrative imperfect or an ordinary perfect, but not of wqtl.[36]

These linguistic data do not favour a reading with past tenses in II Sam.7:9c and following; they make such a rendering highly improbable. In addition, the argument must be put forward that the wyqtl-wqtl sequence in 9b-c may not be viewed as the transition from one separate or isolated form to another. In reality it is the transition of a series of three preterit forms (from the preamble) to an exceptionally long series of wqtl forms in parts 9c-11b and 11c-13b. And because the point-blank ignoring of so outstanding a kink is, in my view, unacceptable, my choice falls on a reading of the wqtl forms as futures; which is in terms of statistics already the most natural situation in the case of a speech. In this way I do not find myself in the predicament of having to account for my seeing one half of the wqtl series as past tense and the other as future, without the transition in between being marked by anything whatsoever. Finally there is a quantitative aspect which as a whole must be weighed in connection with the genre of the speech. Six + three lines have already been devoted to the past, and it would upset the balance of the passage as an oracle of salvation if the retrospection were to continue for another seven lines. The promises would then be in the minority. In my reading the ratio of past to present is much more credible: nine lines of retrospection followed by the main matter, twenty lines of announcement and promise.

What objection could there be to reading the consecutive perfects of part b (= vv.9c-11b) as future forms? The content of lines 10ab perhaps? If one should come across them separate from their present context then it is indeed better for the "planting" of Israel by Yahweh to refer to the time of the arrival in, and conquest of, the promised land. But the fact that up to now Israel has not been able to live in rest and security in its place does ideologically belong to the very core of this exceptional chapter. Evidence of this is brought up at once in 10cd and 11a. From time immemorial (*ka'ăšęr bārīšō-nā*, the end of 10d) and through the entire period of the judges until now there was unrest and oppression. Only now, with the coming of David, will the blows of tyranny and crises cease, and the nation, unified under one crown, receives the "rest" which makes putting down roots really possible. Or, to

[36] The narrative imperfect is the foregoer of another narrative imperfect 139 times, of a normal perfect fifty times, of a constr. infin. fourteen times, and of an active participle eight times. There is one exception to the absence of a wyqtl-wqtl sequence, according to the cross-reference table on p.35 of de Regt's Supplement, and that is (the author writes to me) Deut. 5:28b + 32a. Here in Moses' speech *wy'mr yhwh 'ly* stands first, followed by a second-degree speech in vv.29-31, and then *wšmrtm* etc. This wqtl form is, however, a commandment not a past tense.

put it another way: the promise of land and offspring which constituted the primary concern of the first covenant, that of God with the patriarchs, and which were also taken up into the Sinaitic covenant (with the balance of "you my people/I your God") are no longer relevant two centuries after entry and God decides in II Sam.7 to adapt and renew his covenant with Israel.[37] To this end God commits himself to Zion and David's dynasty, which he promises to maintain. In the speaker's view the election of the people of Israel requires, at this juncture, a new form of realisation in which he widens his preference for David and brings it onto a higher plane by committing himself to this monarchy.

I resume the literary analysis, considering b = vv.9c-11b with respect to its own style and structure. This passage's usefulness to the whole lies in its bringing up the national dimension. David and his government are in office on behalf of the people of Israel and not the other way round. My heading for the paragraph is: "Israel gets a safe place". The people have already been clearly mentioned in the refusal of vv.5-7 but chiefly as a witness to God's accompanying them on their travels. Now Israel becomes the direct object of God's concern; even the subject. It takes up the body of the paragraph, the five lines between 9c and 11b, and the placing of the proper noun, at the end of 10a and 11a, outlines the contours. Surrounding it is an envelope of two I-you lines, 9c and 11b.

In 10ab Israel grows from an indirect object which receives a place to a direct object planted with loving care, and subsequently gets to stand on its own feet with *šākan taḥtāw*. God does not exert himself for his own house (6b, *miškān*), which meant mobility, but for the stability of his own people: "they shall live on their own", is my rather close rendering of the preposition.[38] In the centre one short clause occurs in which Israel remains the subject, "it will tremble no more", after which it is the object again as it was formerly; the object of continued oppression which, however, is prevented by the negative. The adversaries are not identified by their name or country, but fall under the denunciation "evil men", *bᵉnē ʿawlā*, so receiving the same disqualification as Abner's murderers.[39] First God goes far back into the past at the end of 10d with "in the beginning", a temporal designation which the

[37] It is worth considering calling the agreement in Josh.24 the third covenant and that of I Sam.12 (the statute of a heteronomous monarchy) the fourth; II 7 is then the fifth covenant.

[38] The root *škn* fails to occur elsewhere in Samuel.

[39] The word *ʿawlā* (fem.) is found only in II Sam.3:34 and 7:10, and nowhere else throughout the entire length of Gen. through Kings. The masculine form *ʿāwęl* occurs twice in Lev.19 and twice in Deut., being absent in the Early Prophets. A parallel of our reference in v.23b of Ps.89, a long poem which processes many key words of II Sam.7.

reader, appealing to the 6a connection, might flesh out with 'bondage in Egypt'.[40] Then he adds the entire period of the Judges[41] in v.11a, a long complement of space filling a whole colon and running parallel to the penultimate clause of the refusal (the second half of 7b). So two positive acts of God (placing and planting) are followed firstly by the people's settling down and secondly by two negations of what is destructive. Prior to the centre (10c) the co-ordinates of space are prominent (10ab), after it the co-ordinates of time.

The opening line is on the activity of God towards David, linking up well with the preamble. It takes us further too: up to now God had chosen David and protected him, now he is going to put him in high places. The symmetry of 9c is emphatic. It begins with the care of the I-you words, then mirrors "a great name" in "like unto the name of the great men" and finally looks round in the world; "the earth" is the spatial term which makes contact with what follows, where "the place" of the small nation is assured.[42] The final line ensures a parallelism on the paragraph level (level seven in my text model) which helps delineate the first and the second part: 11b is, as it happens, the equal of 9b, the final line of the preamble.[43] They interact with each other resulting in a new distribution on the time scale. The pronouncement that the enemies are destroyed now refers to a past which is redoubled: in the future too God is going to keep repulsing the dangers. The 9b//11b pair – with the complementary nature of its past and future which, without jamming, join up with one another – gives the full content to the prolepsis of the narrator, who had said in v.1b by way of introduction: "Yahweh had given him rest from all his enemies all around".

The promise that the people shall dwell in security is the background against which the chief announcement, vv.11c-13b = part c, stands out. This paragraph foresees a lasting Davidic dynasty and is the oracle's centre of gravity. The beneficiary is David himself, as an intensive series of suffixes in 11c-12a-12b makes known, *-kā* 2 + 2 + 3 times, whilst the 12c-13a-13b series

[40] The verb *'nh* III "oppress" is indeed the term for what Egypt did to the Israelites in Ex.1:11,12 (*cf.* the niph'al in 10:3, with polar content.)

[41] Together with Buber ("und noch vom Tag an" etc.) and Carlson, p.107, I do not interpret the waw in front of *lmn hywm* as a waw explicative, but as the ordinary conjunction "and". Notice that, as an introduction to a colon-filling complement, it joins the long queue of waw as *Satzweiser*.

[42] The reflection in the centre is of interest because the underlying syntax is *not* symmetrical. "A great name" is an attributive relationship, whilst the "fame of the great" is a s^e^mikut.

[43] Notice that 11b's relationship with the preceding lines is assured because 11c is a commencing line which indicates a new theme and is perhaps not even on the same level as its surroundings (maybe being first-degree speech, not third).

considers the son with three 'he' forms. The start, 11c, is marked by two stylistic means. Its wqtl form is a declarative perfect this time, which can best be rendered by a present tense.[44] Even more striking is the fact that the line speaks *about* Yahweh by putting him in the third person twice. God's long speech is embedded language for which the narrator is ultimately responsible. He is also responsible for the third person which makes v.11a catch the eye amongst the long series of 'I' clauses. This deviation can actually be naturalised. Its consequence is that the line operates like a heading formulated from the messenger's point of view. It is the prophet Nathan who sums up the centre of gravity of the oracle which comes next, its new and surprising part moreover, in a title: "Also Yahweh discloses to you that, as for a house, he will make one for you!" Everything which is still to come can be seen as (not more than) an elaboration of this pledge.[45] The special status of 11c can be made visible by having it printed in colometry with second-degree direct speech, not third, thus indenting it just as much as the lines of 5b and 8b, which also speak in the third person of Yahweh and imply that the messenger is the speaker.

The rendering with "as for a house" makes the syntax of the object clause of 11c expressly visible. I see a connection between this order, O + P, and the issue of 9c, which has the order P + O with *w'śty lk šm*. The two lines form a parallelism which indicates the beginning of successive passages, and places God's activity opposite that of David as the prophet saw it in 3b. With a royal gesture Nathan had said here: *'ăśē*! This strong encouragement was not restricted by its object (an all-embracing *kol 'ăšęr bilbābᵉkā*), but the speaker understood full well that it was the king's wish to build a temple, and that is why I now render his imperative with "make!" In the body of the oracle God answers with an inversion this time; it is the play on words which manages to carry the dynamism of the whole chapter of revelation. *You* are not going to make a *bayit* (= temple) for me, *I* am going to make a *bayit* (= family = dynasty) for you. This creation of a dynasty is, in the long run, also

[44] The following also have the present: KJ, SV, Keil, LV, Buber, NBG, Hertzberg, NBE, KBS, JPS, McCarter. The emendation which reads *whgdylk* for *whgyd lk* ("he shall make great", according to Klostermann, Schulz, BJ) is unnecessary. An interesting parallel of *whgyd* is *whgdty* from I 3:13a, if its interpretation as performative is correct.

[45] On p.205 McCarter writes that v.11c "is to be read as a rubric intervening between major sections and introducing the dynastic promise in vv.12ff." The translation "as for a house" is his; unfortunately he changes the MT's *y'śh* into *yibnę̄*. Kutsch means 11c when he says in his summary (art. cit. p.150):"Das Kapitel ist um einen Satz als älteren Kern herum komponiert." His qualification on p.140, viz. that v.11c is "ein Fremdkörper in seiner Umgebung", I find too judgemental.

the foundation of the great name which David is going to acquire through God's blessing.

After the syntactical inversion what strikes us is the balance of the two clauses round *kī*. They have the same number of words, and not only does the subject remain the same, but the indirect object does too. This is David, just as it was at the edges of part b: *lᵉkā* twice. This suffix reaches its peak of frequency in 11c + 12ab by occurring seven times. The personal tone returns with it and what is additionally indicated is that it is systematically David's turn as beneficiary.

What he is to receive is underlined by the syntactic inversion: a "house". And the special nature of this "house" is already revealed by the accompanying verb. The choice of "he shall make" is, at the same time, an avoidance of "he shall build". By using *ya'ăśę̄* God stands outside the much discussed plane of "I build, you build" and the material object which goes with it; he had already mockingly turned round on such building in the envelope of the oracle of refusal. As far as this is concerned the decisive reversal, brought about by the play on words, is not symmetrical. What God is about to give is not a tangible material object.[46] The choice of "make" as opposed to "build" is connected with two more verses. It cannot be viewed apart from v.13a, when God holds out building prospects for a brief moment: David's son will be allowed to do this later. It is not 11c which should face the amazed "do *you* want to build a house for me to dwell in?" of 5c, but 13a. The choice of "making" also ensures that God, as builder, is not in line with 5:11c where the Phoenicians "built a *bayit* = palace for David".

In v.12 the threshold of personal death is stepped over and God sees two, three decennia into the future, beyond David's end. The line 12a has two clauses as temporal protasis and is completed by two clauses, 12b and c, which present God's activity as main clause and begin almost anaphorally: *wahăqīmōtī* // *wahăkīnōtī* – the narrator has, therefore, chosen two hiph'il forms and created a phonetic connection which cannot fail to be noticed. The swing from the temporal line to the main clause covers that of the generations before and after David. In 12a he rests with his forefathers, in 12b "his seed after him" appears. The formulation of 12a implies that David will not come to an untimely end. The expression "rest with your fathers" indicates a natural and peaceful death, and I hear in the words "when your days are full" a suggestion *that* David's life is to serve a full term, as a kind of rebound.

[46] In the long oracle of doom against the Elides, with which II Sam.7 has interesting points of contact (such as *hăqīmōtī*, *hithallek*, *bayit*, *nę'ęmān*, etc.), God does in fact say: "I shall build him a lasting house", I 2:35.

"I will set up thy seed after thee, which shall proceed out of thy bowels, and ...." I quote from the King James version because the Hebrew choice of words counts once more. The combination "your seed after you" itself takes us back to the Torah and God's promises to the patriarchs, and the idiom denoting "the offspring of your body" becomes even more specific. It stems from Gen.15, its sole occurrence except for here and 16:11! There are more points of contact with Gen.15, making the chapter of important background relevance.[47] Here too a nocturnal vision is the vehicle of revelation, and a son of the body is at the centre of attention, albeit in a way which is more painful and more loaded with fear and hope, in the cycle of a man who has to wait ninety-nine years for a child.[48] The chapter is exceptional in many respects; one of which is that it sees far, and with precision, into the future and foretells four hundred years of "oppression". Why should we not link this *'nh* to v.10d? It guides us to the consideration that II Sam.7 sees the Davidic dynasty as the decisive phenomenon (*deo volente* of course) meaning the end of (four?) centuries of Egyptian and Amorite oppression. Be this as it may, the coming of Solomon, whose monarchy and throne are to be safe due to God, is set against the background of Gen.15 due to the choice of words. So the Davidic covenant becomes the counterpart, and the fulfilment, of the first covenant made with the patriarchs.

Chapter 16 verse 11 waits in the distance. The rebellion, triumphing at that moment and putting David to flight, is a realisation of the oracles of doom in ch.12. The leader is indeed a male offspring of David: Absalom. Tormented by the dust and the stones thrown up by Shimei, David says, at the moment of deepest mortification having come to himself at last and open to God's rulings: "Behold, my son, which came forth of my bowels, seeketh my life," and prevents the Saulide's being punished. The terms in 7:12bc can be fully made to cover Absalom's dash for power, even though the reader thinks that

[47] The points of contact in Hebrew are: Abraham gets a *maḥăzę̄*, II Sam.7:17 speaks of a *ḥizzāyōn*; Gen.15 also uses the term *dbr yhwh* for the advent of a revelation; Abraham has to try and count the stars in the sky, which gives away the fact that night is the time for contact with God; *bayit* and *zar'ăkā* occur in Gen.15:2,3,5,18; the unique designation *'ăšęr yeṣē mimme'ę̄kā* occurs in 15:4; a double designation of getting old and a peaceful death for Abraham stands in v.15; I am struck by the Rephaim and the Jebusites in the list of the peoples of Canaan in vv.20-21, in view of David's military contact with them.

[48] In an article published in the autumn of 1989 in OTS 25, and entitled "Time and the Structure of the Abraham Cycle", I show that a special series of temporal designations, and the relationship between narration time and narrated time, are the keys to the composition. The long central passage, Gen.17-21, covers the hundredth year of Abraham's life, in which birth and death are announced to him by God, and the arrival of Isaac and the destruction of Sodom and Gomorrha do indeed take place.

these lines initially have Solomon in mind. In the actual course of David's life the negative variant of God's prediction gets a chance first, as a highly dangerous threat to his throne. The second half of David's life, when he is an established authority, thus deviates from the direct line linking the dynastic oracle to the Solomonic succession in I Ki.1-2. David is driven off course by his capital crimes and encounters dangers jeopardising even the realisation of these unconditional promises.

The pair 12bc is followed by the pair 13ab. This is particularly due to the synonymy of 12c and 13b:

12c wahăkīnōtī 'ęt mamlaktō
13b wᵉkōnantī 'ęt kissē mamlaktō 'ad 'ōlām

The word monarchy appears in v.12c for the first time in this chapter. In 13b it becomes more concrete by the addition of the throne, whilst the verb undergoes a minor change (from hiph'il to polel). The expression for an indefinite period of time (*'ad 'ōlām*, initially comprising the son's life and not much going beyond this) is a good ending for the whole part, and a favourable element after 12c. The son is special enough to interrupt, for the first time, the long series with the initial waw, and the expressly initially placed *hū*, together with its successors, I-he in v.14, completes the series of pronouns. Nevertheless it is important to recognise the true quality of 13a: a line merely spoken in passing, and encapsulated by 12c//13b on God and his confirming the Davidic throne. Only in 13a does *bayit* mean temple for a moment, and nowhere else for the rest of this long chapter. Solomon's building a temple is an element of secondary importance compared with the promise of a dynasty.[49] In its context it is only a result, and evidence, of the strength which God is going to grant this monarchy.

Just as parts a and b (preamble and paragraph on the people of Israel) were concluded with a parallelism, parts c and d are too. In particular the end of the 13b and 16b lines, the gesture "for ever" reaching on into the distance, brings me to the arrangement in which vv.14-16 form the final paragraph. Now that v.14a has the position of commencing line we see that the quasi-redundant "I" with which it begins is the counterpart of the "I" with which v.8c opened part a, and the principal part as a whole. The commencing lines of the four parts have their own systematics and indicate contours as well:

[49] Against Carlson, p.120, who says of v.13a: " ... the D-group have incorporated Solomon's building of the temple as the crowning motif of the dynastic promise in 2 Sam. 7."

a) I am the one who took you ... and I was (*wā'ęhyę̄*) with you 8c
b) wqtl: I shall make a name for you 9c
c) wqtl: the Lord ... shall make a "house" for you 11c
d) I am the one who will be (*'ęhyę̄*) a father to him 14a

In addition there are two small chiasmuses on both sides of the boundary of c and d, contributing to a reciprocity which itself creates, with a larger chiasmus, the concatenation of the last two paragraphs. In verse 13 we see an equilibrium arise which takes place via he-mine – I-his and is grouped around the objects of temple and throne. In v.14 the reciprocity gains perfect balance, via the I-him plus he-me series. For the concatenation of the four lines we are alert to the alternation of the subjects:

13a he is the one who shall build a house for my name
13b and I shall establish his royal throne for ever
14a I shall be a father to him
14b and he shall be a son to me

The balance in 14 is so great that not only the number of syllables, but even the number of true consonants are exactly the same in both lines. God's electional love gets a new form here, that of a father/son relationship. But the element of asymmetry which also lies in this relationship (the one being brought up should obey the one bringing him up) now gets a chance in its own line of seven words, 14c. Again there are two hiph'il forms, but this time one (the reproving father) answers the other (the sinning son), and they are followed by two synonymous expressions which denote means of punishment. Punishments doled out (the rod) or received by men will guarantee Solomon's not forgetting his place as a mortal before God.[50]

After this critical line, not without menace, the speaker returns to the side of love, this time seen from within the solidarity context of the covenant, *ḥęsęd*. Its presence is stated by disaffirming something negative (this solidarity's giving way). Once again there is a *'šr* line of seven words which provides an explanation by talking about painful experiences: v.15b, and once more a

[50] It is feasible to allow the relationship between the first and the second member of the s[e]mikut constructions to remain ambiguous in both cases and to read them both ways: as an objective and subjective genitive at the same time. The absence of the article in front of *'ănāšīm* // *'ādām* has both phrases speak of people in general. The word pair rod//plagues is taken over by the poet of Ps.89 in v.33 (MT).

double hiph'il comes into play. Strictly speaking there is a sentence of comparison which begins with *k'šr* and is subsequently made more profound by a second degree subordinate clause with *'šr* which speaks of abandoning once more:

15b ka'ăšẹr hăsīrōtī – away from Saul
'ăšẹr hăsīrōtī – away from your eyes

After the successor's chastisement mentioned in the preview the doom of the predecessor is recalled, but happily in favour of a negation. The painful disjunctions of yesteryear make way for a close-knit conjunction. The verb *swr*, still a qal in 15a, is an echo of what happened to Saul in I 16, when "the Spirit of Yahweh departed from him", with a qal form in verse 14.

The paired use of hiph'il forms commenced in the middle of paragraph c. Now we see that it also takes up the middle of paragraph d. The concatenation of vv.13 and 14 occurred between these centres. If we now take a look at the beginning of part c and the end of part d, then we see how the 'you' form returns. Verse 15c itself ended on *kā*, after which the two lines of v.16, with the same suffix four times, address themselves entirely to David, as counterpart of the *kā* which occurs seven times in 11c-12b. As far as this is concerned there is a concentricity keeping parts c and d together as complements, which together shape the oracle's core formed by the promise of the dynasty. But parts c and d plainly end in a parallel way at the same time: their final verses both have a series of not less than five key words in common.[51]

The word *bayit* occurs in verse 16 in the third, decisive meaning of "dynasty" and, referring back to 11c, forms a framework for the nuclear passage. At the same time it is so closely connected with the word monarchy in 16a, that both words form a kind of hendiadys and are the subject of a verb form in the singular: "your royal house shall stand secure (shall be confirmed)". This "appointment" of the house of David as an enduring dynasty, thanks to the word *nẹ'man*, is in line with passages I 2:35(bis), 3:20 and 25:28. The effect of this is that, in the composition as a whole, a "trustworthy" priesthood is first announced and pursued by God (as an alternative to the corruption of the Elides), subsequently a staunch prophet is appointed (Samuel, I 3:20) and not until much later, after the unsuccessful Saul project,

[51] In v.13 as well as in v.16 we come across: house, throne, kingship, forever.

is a "trustworthy monarchy" finally appointed and recognised by him.[52] In particular the bond with the staunch priesthood is clearly laid down. How many words does I 2:35 – part of an oracle which also looks exceptionally far into the future! – not have in common with the oracle of II 7! I quote the majority:

I 2:35 a	wahăqīmōtī	lī	kōhen	nę̄'ę̆mān
c	ubānītī	lō	bayit	nę̄'ę̆mān
d	w^{e}hithallek	lifnē	m^{e}šīḥī	kol hayyāmīm

The similarities are striking.[53] Looking back on this furnishes the insight that the Davidic dynasty is already implied as early as I 2-3 and that the priesthood which God had in mind here is reserved for this house.

The trustworthiness of the dynasty becomes even more concrete through the security of the throne. At the end of the previous paragraph throne and kingship were joined in one phrase and subsequently combined with the predicate "make secure" and the word *'ōlām*. Skilful variations of this occur in v.16. This time the abstract and the concrete each have their own line, they are both connected with *'ad 'ōlām*, and the root *kwn* appears again as well, in a third variant this time. We see a chiasmus of the predicative niph'al forms and their subjects arise, which is backed up on the phonetic level by alliteration on the consonants n, m and k:

16a	w^{e}nę̄'man	bēt^{e}kā umamlakt^{e}kā
b	kis'ăkā	nākōn

This device makes the diagonal synonyms emerge well.[54] The form of **kwn* is the sequel to the series I 13:13 (where the alternative, an established monarchy of Saul, stuck in the *irrealis* mode), 20:31 (the monarchy which Jonathan

[52] The writer has allowed two persons to anticipate this recognition: first, the priest Ahimelech who calls David "faithful" without reservation (I 22:14) and has to pay for it immediately with his life, and later the woman Abigail. Her choice of words in 25:28b is a striking preparation of the key clause II 7:11c (and the framing with v.16), for she says: *'āśō ya'ăśę̄ yhwh ladōnī bayit nę̄'ę̆mān*! A burlesque and ironic variant is Achish's *wayya'ămen* regarding David in I 27:12.

Here is another modest speculation (against my usual practice) on the mind of the writer: I think he has been guided by the word pair *ḥsd w'mt* so that, after the *ḥsd* verse v.15, he continued with a line based on the root *'mn*. Or to put it the other way round: for the sake of the connection with I 2:35 he wanted to arrive at *n'mn* and decided, inspired by the word pair, to create a *ḥsd* line as well.

[53] Notice that the hiph'il of *qwm* is used in the same first person wqtl form, that the king has already explicitly been mentioned, that God's building activity is spoken of, that the hithpa'el of *hlk* occurs as a term for a lasting relationship (such as in II 7:6sq) and that the temporal designation *kol hayyāmīm* is a variant of *'ad 'ōlām*.

[54] Another chiasmus becomes visible if we put 13b next to 16b (both being after all the close of a paragraph): "I establish ... his royal throne // your throne ... shall be established". It does its bit for the integration of the crucial passage.

himself no longer aspired to) and especially II 5:12. Our passage now means the full development of what David perceived then, "that the Lord had established him as king over Israel".

The term "for ever" contributes to the climax, not so much by being doubly used, as by reaching much farther into the future. In v.13 it could still be understood to mean "for life". The pledge of v.16 goes further than Solomon, however, encompassing many generations, and the fact that the term allows no precise delineation does not detract from this. This reaching deep into the future is now possible because the final lines are no longer about "his" (i.e. Solomon's) position, but *your* royal house. With this the end of the whole oracle has fittingly returned to the person who is the beneficiary of the promise in 11c, and, what is more, is the addressee of the oracle as a whole, David.

The final paragraph appears to be composed of sets of two through and through. Yet another one of them is worthy of mention. It is a kind of double rhyme with an ingenious shift. The lines of 15b and 16a end in the same way, with *l^efānę̄kā*.[55] But amongst the components of this rhyme the beginning of the magnificent gesture on the distant future, *'ad 'ōlām* in 16a, already appears and this too returns unchanged, in 16b, in the significant position, moreover, which is to ensure the closure of the entire oracle. Thus both halves of the nuclear passage 11c-16b end in a look forward, whereby revelation far transcends the boundaries of the present. Both final verses, 13 and 16, refer to the national dimension, within which David knows his place. With their positive content they have taken over from the negative lines, 9b and 11b, which also completed two paragraphs but were concerned with the past and the near future of David, and were about the destruction of "your enemies". Destruction is one of the preconditions which make lasting construction possible.

The last time it was the narrator's turn to speak he called the long speech "the word of the Lord", using an auditive term. Immediately afterwards he uses the visual term as complement, in a poetic variant: "this vision".[56] What has come to the prophet Nathan is both a visionary experience and the

[55] The correspondence of the word *mpnyk* from 9b (end of the first paragraph) with the *lpnyk* at the end of 15b//16a can be used as an argument for retaining the last *lpnyk* and not changing it into *l^efānay*. This then contributes the following to the interpretation: now that the enemies have disappeared, a magnificent panorama of lasting power unfolds before David's eyes.

[56] As a rule the word for vision in prose is *ḥāzōn* or *maḥăzę̄*, see the headings of several prophetic books, or Gen.15:1 or I Sam.3:1 (and compare in the same chapter *mar'ā* of v.15, and the complementary nature of the auditive and the visual in vv.15-18 and also in Gen.15:1). The word *ḥizzāyōn* occurs elsewhere only in poetry (eight times). I Chron.17 has *ḥāzōn* for our reference.

receiving of a self-contained text. He passes on the content of the oracle without changing one jot or tittle of it. This is expressed by the conclusion "as ... so" of verse 17 and is reinforced by the doubling of *kᵉkol* and the double referring back with the demonstrative. The conclusion is now justified that the prophet does not interpret God's word at all, but passes it on verbatim – in keeping with his function as already indicated in the messenger's commission and formula: he is just a messenger of the deity.[57]

§ 2. *David responds to the oracle with a long prayer*, 7:18-29

The second half of this chapter is not framed by narrator's text, but only introduced, by two short clauses of report. When David has received the exceptional message of God, he goes straight to him and "sits down before Yahweh". The verb of movement ends in rest which takes over from it. The phrase *lifnē yhwh* occurs in 18b only, but at the same time is applicable to 18a and does double duty: it also informs us where David appears. We should understand that David goes to the tent where the ark is. This visit is complementary with respect to ch.6 in which *lifnē yhwh* was a key phrase. At that time David danced exuberantly before the ark, now he humbly seats himself to pray, next to the ark.[58] This sitting is the dignified replacement of the sitting in v.1 which had inspired David into thinking he could be a giver (*destinateur*); now he knows better and has his hands full with reacting in a fitting way to all the divine gifts which are now his as *destinataire*, receiver. Immediately after the message of the lasting monarchy has sounded, the narrator refers to him officially with two words: "king David"; it is the only time these words are linked together in this chapter. Both as monarch and as private person David turns to God.

The special prayer follows the ordering of God's long speech, by discussing the past in its first half (the seventeen lines of vv.18d-24b), and the future in its second half (the fifteen lines of vv.25-29). These parts convey different attitudes of the speaker at the same time. In the first half David employs

[57] The fact that Nathan does not interpret holds good for the character in a narrative. This is different on the level of human reality, that of the history of religion and dream research. Since Freud we have come to realise that the dream experience has another mode of existence than its report. The report is a text, i.e. a linguistic product of ordering and selection, and the report on a dream is for this reason itself an interpretation, viz. by the dreamer.

[58] I do not know for certain whether he entered the tent and could/was allowed to see the ark. The "sitting before the face of the Lord" which is a prayer, is in any case not unknown, thanks to Judg.20:26 and 21:1, where *lpny yhwh* also concerns the ark.

several rhetorical questions and many indicative clauses, in which past tense verbal forms dominate. The second half has the nature of a request since it has four imperatives and *c.* four other volitional forms.[59]

A word unique to Samuel, *'ădōnāy*, occurs seven times in the prayer.[60] Each time this plural of majesty appears as a vocative and is connected to the proper noun *yhwh*.[61] The word means "my Lord" and forms a pair with its obverse, the word *'abdᵉkā*, "your servant", which appears ten times in the prayer. Together with the narrator we see "your servant" as a fitting and humble answer to "my servant" which God has uttered twice in his messenger's commission. But the character David is not conscious of the connection with v.5a//8a because the lines do not constitute a part of the actual oracle and he has not heard them. God's word "my servant" had an intimate sound, David's "your servant" must firstly be literally heard, as an expression of subjection, obedience and humility. And these aspects are again reinforced by God's continuously being called "my Lord", etc.

The proper noun Yahweh is used as a vocative in ten out of the eleven times it occurs and we can therefore expect many clauses in the second person. It cannot be interchanged anywhere with the word for God or deity, *'ęlōhīm*, which did not occur at all in the oracle, but occurs eight times in the prayer, having the highly specific task of demonstrating that Yahweh is the true God via the fact that Yahweh has made himself the God of the people of Israel.[62] A fifth key word which I would like to mention by way of introduction is the root *dbr*. This word too has a specific usage. It occurs fourteen times in the chapter and each time it concerns the history-making utterances of God or his promise.[63] First it bears the framework of the oracle by occurring in 4b as the title ("the word of God") and by its double occurrence in v.17. And it is thereupon put into three clusters (of three occurrences!) by the praying

[59] Apart from that the request plainly depends on what God has already accomplished, because there are several syntactic cores (especially v.27) with preterits, where a fourfold "thou hast spoken" (25b-25c-28c-29b, and cf. the synonym in v.27a) runs throughout like a *leitmotif*.

[60] I mean of course the word so written and vocalised, not the well-known Qere for the tetragrammaton. The word *'ădōn* occurs ninety times in Sam. (primarily in I 25-26 and II Sam.) with regard to a mortal, often in the form *'ădōnī* and addressed to the king.

[61] The word *'ădōnāy* occurs in 18d-19a-19c-20b-22a and after an interval in 28a-29b. The tetragrammaton ibidem, plus the vocatives in 24b-25a-27a and the subject of 26b.

[62] The word *'ęlōhīm* stood alone in v.2d (as part of the phrase "the ark of God"), with the article. It returns in 22c-23b-23d-24b-25a-26b-27a-28a.

[63] Words from the stem *dbr* occur in v.4b-7b(bis)-17a-17b-19b-20a-21-25b (bis)-25c-28b-28c-29b.

David in his text.[64] So the kind of speech which already so strongly characterised II Samuel 7 as a duet of oracle and prayer, is intensified by its being made thematic and thought through in the prayer as well.

The halves of the prayer can themselves be divided into two. The first half is made up of the parts consisting of vv.18d-21 and of vv.22-24 which qua genre can be both linked up with and distinguished from one another. The first part is thanksgiving, after which David changes to language desirous of elevation to a higher class: a hymn of praise. The acknowledgement concentrates on all the good which God has done and shall do to David, whilst the hymnal part is much broader in scope and envisages the uniqueness of God and his people. The difference in subject matter also contributes to the distinction between thanksgiving and praise therefore.

In the first part the most noticeable phenomenon of style is the regular use of the double vocative, "my Lord Yahweh". It occurs at the end of a line each time and is a strong indication to group the lines in pairs, other than the traditional division into verses. The fivefold repetition of this reaches as far as into the line after the thanksgiving, v.22a, so that the transition from thanksgiving to praise runs a fluent course. When the thanksgiving is composed out of four pairs, other repetitions also fall exactly into place.[65] Here is the first part, which I initially consider as being articulated in pairs:

18d mī 'ānōkī *'ădōnāy yhwh*
18e umī bētī kī hăbī'ōtanī ‘ad hălōm

19a wattiqṭan ‘ōd zōt b^{e}‘ēnę̄kā, *'ădōnāy yhwh*
19b watt^{e}dabber gam 'ę̄l bēt ‘abd^{e}kā l^{e}mērāḥōq

19c w^{e}zōt tōrat hā'ādām, *'ădōnāy yhwh*
20a uma yōsīf dāwīd ‘ōd l^{e}dabber 'ēlę̄kā

[64] In vv.19b-21; it does not stand in the centre, vv.22-24; in v.25bc it occurs three times, and finally in 28bc + 29b. Of all the fourteen references only v.20a has David as the subject of "speak", but in a negatory sense; and in v.17b Nathan has become the subject of "speak", but he does not utter a word of his own! In other words each of the two references where a mortal speaks point away from himself, to the greater glory of the revelation.

[65] In what follows I will refer to the first line of each pair with small letter a, and the second with a small letter b. The key word *bayit* occurs in the second line of the first two pairs, *zōt* occurs in the a lines, 19a and 19c (but once again in 21), and in particular the three occurrences of the key word *dbr* in successive b lines are of interest: a narrative imperfect and a substantive for God surround the refused, because superfluous, speaking (now an infinitive) of David in 20a.

20b wᵉʾattā yādaʿtā ʾẹt ʿabdᵉkā, ʾădōnāy yhwh
21 baʿăbūr dᵉbārᵉkā ukᵉlibbᵉkā ʿāśītā ʾẹt kol haggᵉdullā hazzōt
lᵉhōdīªʿ ʾẹt ʿabdẹkā

The first and the third pair are mainly about the reality of David, which is determined by God (and his speaking). The second and fourth pair contain God's acting and speaking; each time as subject. All the b line endings also contribute to the forming of pairs. The end of the first two pairs exhibits the opposition "thus far" – "far off" and the end of the final pairs contains an infinitival phrase on the God-mortal contact, in which the direction of speech is turned round (I speak to you – you inform me) as a reflection of the dialogic situation.

The first pair can easily be scanned and read as a strophe with two bicola. There is a sixfold rhyme on -ī, which becomes the sound of humility as ensured by the meanings of 18de. Two short rhetorical questions of four syllables each are A cola and look to the speaker and his family. God is addressed in the B cola where his activity is situated. The phonetic similarities between *ʾānōkī* and *ʾădōnāy* underline the contrast between powerful Lord and amazed mortal. The 'I' is extended to "my house" and this word now counts twice, for God has ensured by his promise that *bayit* does not only mean house or family, but also has the potency of "dynasty". Its consonants return in *hăbīʾōtanī*, God's powerful action.[66] The clause "You have brought me thus far" initially allows a figurative reading, as a pronouncement on the blessing and protection which David up to now (*hălōm* having thus become temporal) has enjoyed from God. But a literal reading is also feasible. The words house and bring (*bwʾ* in the hiphʿil) take on a connection with the narrator's introduction (in v.1a and) v.18ab. David has left his fine palace behind him and sits in prayer near the ark. God's promise has brought him here, spatially and then symbolically (as one who prays bringing thanksgiving). And he has received another house, i.e. a dynasty, as a gift.

Between the words *mī* and *yhwh*, which enquire about identity (viz. that of the mortal) and then establish it (that of God), the words *ʾānōkī* and *ʾădōnāy* occur with clear, "long" *ā-ō* vowels. On the sound level they continue the a-o combinations of v.16: *nākōn* and *ʿōlām* were the magnificent gesture on which the oracle ended and the key words of the promise. They receive a sequel in words such as *hălōm* (which, as the end of a line, marks a boundary and signifies a boundary itself), its counterpart *rāḥōq* (the word which clearly

---

[66] This is, together with the poetical aspect, the reason for my classifying the *kī* clause together with the second *mī* question as one colon in the colometric text. This decision is backed up by the alternating appearance of the double vocative.

lexicalises the future in the prayer), the important *tōrā* and monosyllables such as *'ōd* and *zōt* which are characteristic of this thanksgiving.

The answer to the question "who am I?" goes something like this: an insignificant mortal who is surprised that he of all people continues to enjoy God's favour. The rhyme's cheeping sounds stand for his insignificance, but they are also preparatory to the isotopy governing the entire thanksgiving. It is the polarity insignificant/great, which is present in different forms. The mortal of v.18 is small, but sees how great he is being made, and that is the first piece of evidence on the greatness of the deity who has chosen him. I have been brought "thus far" he says, and that implies that he has been placed at the head of a unified kingdom with good prospects.

The second pair amplifies the isotopy small/great with a surprising paradox. "But this was too small in your eyes" says David, and his little word "this" stands for the greatness already bestowed upon him. The line which the end of the 18de pair drew with the expression "thus far" now appears to be a preparation for the leap into the future. Your speaking "with respect to that which lies far off" (= the future, *mērāḥōq*) leaves the boundary just mentioned far behind it, and as the promise of a dynasty it is fresh and even greater evidence of God's greatness. The *bētī* and *hăbī'ōtanī* of the first line b are succeeded by *bēt 'abdᵉkā* in the second line b. This clause of 19b combines the first of the *dbr* trio with the first of the three cases of "your servant" and in so doing links the beneficial speaking of God to the one who subjects himself and prays. Accordingly the latter is to declare, in the second place (v.20a), that he himself, face to face with so much mercy, has nothing to say; which is also paradoxical in regard to the extent and eloquence of the whole prayer.

The blessed present (v.18) is surpassed by the rose-tinted future (v.19ab = pair 2). The little words ("yet" and "also") which mark this surpassing seem insignificant themselves before obtaining the attention they deserve. But whilst the first *zōt* is relieved by a second and surpassed, they are carried on in the third pair by the *yōsīf* ... *'ōd* of v.20a. This line brings a third paradox by being a rhetorical question on (the possible content of) David's speaking and by calling it unnecessary at the same time. The little opening word "this" refers back to God's speaking on the distant future. This is so powerful and normative (*tōrā*) that the speaker, in his third pair of clauses, speaks of "man" in general[67] and subsequently, from within this broad perspective, is enabled to be objective about himself as is apparent from the

[67] The noun clause, v.19c, is interpreted as a volitive sentence by the JPS translation, which is an interesting (and grammatically totally acceptable) alternative: "May that be the law for the people, O Lord GOD."

word "David" in 20a. This speaking about himself in the third person[68] reveals that 20a goes with 19c and that the speaker now classifies himself simply as an example of "man". His "adding" (saying more) may be dropped, now that God has granted a safe present time and a dynastic future on top. The thanksgiving gives all honour and space to the merciful adding which God does.

The theme of God's history-making word got one line in the second pair, took up both lines of the third pair (insofar as "instruction" or "law" is also the word of God) and becomes a centrally placed nominal form in the fourth pair; surrounding it is a development of "know" (*yd'*, qal) to "have know" (*yd'*, hiph'il) which refers the conversing partners to one another and constitutes the unity of the pair at the same time:

20b "And you, you know your servant, ...

21 For your word's sake ... making it known to your servant."

What does the speaker actually want to communicate in that "you know me"? The core of v.21 says that "you have already done all this greatness according to your (heart, = decision, or) will". This *k^{e}libb^{e}kā* itself alludes to I 13:14, the text's very first hint on David as the man according to God's heart (*kilbābō*). It stretches very far back therefore, which suggests the great continuity and faithfulness of God towards David. Then there is the line from I 16:7, "the Lord does not look at the eyes, but at the heart." We can also have this lesson, which Samuel receives when looking for the new candidate at Jesse's, refer to the inner qualities of the one chosen. So two references from way back also throw light on v.20b. The man at prayer suggests that the revelational activity of God (v.21) links up perfectly with his own qualities of which God is well aware; they were also the reasons for his being chosen at that time.

The complement "according to your heart" connects up closely with "because of your word", and together these adjuncts, expressly placed in front of the predicate, are part of a network. It is the isotopy of the normative which imbues the thanksgiving. The expression "small in your eyes" is of the type which reminds us of "good/evil in your eyes" and is, apart from this expression, also a sign of God's view which is the norm and is recognised by the praying mortal. Next the promise of God is characterised as "law for the people", and his activity is, in v.21, tied to the doubly expressed norm of "your word and your heart". This final application of the isotopy gains importance when we see that v.21 has the characteristics of closure. It is a

[68] Afterwards David speaks one more time in the third person about "David": in v.26c, combined with "the house of your servant".

very long and very full sentence, and its object, "all this greatness", is a phrase which sums up God's blessings and characterises them with a word (*gdwlh*) which finally mentions the positive pole of the small/great isotopy, completing it at once. So the final sentence places the idea "great" explicitly opposite the "small" of v.19a.

I said that we might initially read the thanksgiving as four pairs. After doing this I see, however, another possibility which returns for the most part to the Masoretic verse order. In the second instance I read three sets of three. They make the "this" of v.19c emerge well as a reference back to 19b, from which it does not want to be separated, and effectively ensure that 20b can be read as a kind of answer to the rhetorical question of 20a. The speaker then creates this association: it is entirely unnecessary for me to add anything, because you know me through and through! This alternative grouping of 18-21 can be appreciated as I now offer the text in sets of three:[69]

What am I, O Lord GOD,
and what is my family,
that You have brought me thus far?

Yet even this, O Lord GOD, has seemed too little to You;
for You have spoken of Your servant's house also for the future.
May that be the law for the people, O Lord GOD.

What more can David say to You?
You know Your servant, O Lord GOD.
For Your word's sake and of Your own accord You have wrought this great thing, and made it known to Your servant.

This grouping forfeits several parallelisms which became visible through the paired ordering, but allows others to come to the fore. Now the double *'ōd* occurs in the commencing line of both sets of three, where it underlines the contrast between "little" and "more". The third lines (19c and 21, then) place the notion of *tōrā* and "your word" parallel to each other, and both have the demonstrative *zōt*. As final lines they indicate how "the people" and "Your servant" respectively are beneficiaries and receive God's revelation. Further on David is to point to revelation several times: especially in 22c and 27a, but compare also with 28c and 29b. Each time the promise of God appears in a form of the perfect. That is to say, the solid ground upon which

[69] I follow the JPS translation, giving it a colometric form here.

the speaker takes up his station every time has been laid down by the giving of the promise.

The hymn which now strikes up celebrates the uniqueness of God in three lines, and that of the people of Israel redeemed by God in six lines. With his opening line 22a David joins up closely with the thanksgiving because each of its elements has a link with what has gone before. The double vocative occurs again, as an echo of the systematic series in 18-20. The very first word "therefore" renders the logical relationship with what has gone before explicit. The same blessings for which I have just expressed thanks now make me praise you, says the speaker. The connection culminates in the predicate. The thanksgiving ended with the nominalising phrase "all this greatness". In the hymn this summary is turned into a verbal form which praises God. "You are great" now looks to the timeless quality of God himself and is therefore a telling commencement of the hymn of praise. (In the second paragraph, vv.23-24, the "doing of *haggᵉdullā*" returns when Israel is the beneficiary.)

In v.22bc even the verb disappears. Two short noun clauses which can be retraced in poetry as a bicolon express the uniqueness of God in a negative manner. They are the effective and well-known formula, underlined by *kī*: "truly, there is nobody like you, there is no God besides you", after which a relative clause makes the whole grow into a tricolon. This clause runs "according to everything which we have heard with our own ears" and is not in the least a set formula, but is inspired rather by the concrete situation.[70] It is already the third constituent of the sentence (after v.19b and the end of 21) to point to revelation as people's source of knowledge. Immediately preceding a paragraph on the nation David does not say "what I have heard", but takes his place in the midst of Israel by using the plural "we". From the outset the blessings of God have been aimed at the collective, and they are always accompanied by his word. The complement "in our ears", which for a while seems to be redundant, establishes that these messages sounded very clear. They have been received and by including the complement in his text David acknowledges the responsibility which arises for "us" from listening carefully.

The second part of the hymnic paragraph occurs in vv.23-24 and concerns the national dimension. First there is a long and complicated period filling four lines or more, followed in v.24 by a two-line variant of the covenant formula. Due to his activity God has entered into an exclusive relationship

[70] In the BHS, which follows the Leningradensis, stands b*kl ’šr šm‘nw b’znynw* but the apparatus mentions that "a great many manuscripts" have k*kl* etc., a variant usually preferred.

with a certain nation, which nation takes up "a unique position on earth" because of it. The speaker begins with this in v.23a. It is a rhetorical question on Israel which, thanks to the comparative preposition *k^{e}* (bis) becomes a complement of 22b, the line on the incomparableness of God. At the same time the question beginning with *mī* is in opposition in two different ways to the *mī* question with which the prayer opened as a whole. Line 18d assumes an "I am small after all!" kind of reply. The question "who is like your people?" also assumes a negative answer it is true (no nation can be our equal), but relevant potential space is taken away by another answer's continuing positively on Israel ("as a unique people on earth") and by holding the attention through a whole chain of increasingly dependent subordinate clauses. The opening "who is like your people, like Israel?" functions like a peg upon which message upon message is hung. I represent the seven clauses of v.23 as a staircase, in which the number 1 points to the interrogative main clause and the numbers following indicate the degree of dependence of the connected clauses:

umī k^{e}ʿamm^{e}kā k^{e}yiśrā'el, gōy 'ẹḥād bā'ārẹṣ (1)
'ăšẹr hāl^{e}kū 'ḝlōhīm (2)
lifdōt lō l^{e}ʿām (3)
w^{e}lāśūm lō šem
w^{e}laʿăśōt lāhẹm hagg^{e}dullā w^{e}nōrā'ōt
lahărīṣ^{e}kā[71] mipp^{e}nē ʿammẹkā ...[72] gōyīm wēlōhāw
'ăšẹr pādītā l^{e}kā mimmiṣrayim (4)

The numeral "one" means "unique" here, just as it does in the Sh^{e}maʿ or in The Song of Songs 6:9. Everything which follows, i.e. 23bcd, is meant to furnish evidence on the uniqueness of this people. Its core is an almost breathless salvo of infinitival clauses to the honour of God who gives Israel its place at the centre of history. This series of third-degree clauses has received an envelope of relative clauses (in the second and fourth degree). The first is just a run up; it is the only clause which may be called inconspicuous: *'ăšẹr hāl^{e}kū 'ḝlōhīm*. The final relative clause uses, as predicate, the verb *pdh*, "redeem", the same as that which opened the series of infinitives and their striking enumeration. The enormous complex which depends on the relative pronoun *'ăšẹr* of v.23a is kept together by yet another envelope. It is of the

[71] I read the MT's *l'rṣk* as *lhrṣk*, "by your putting to flight", see App.1.

[72] The relationship between the object and the predicate in the last infinitival clause is interrupted by the relative clause with the second "redeem". I illustrate the third-degree clause first, and below it the *'ăšẹr* clause.

abc-cba pattern since the words "gods, redeem, people" from v.23b return in a reversed order of appearance in 23d. One half of the series is positive (the true God sets Israel free), the other (cba) is its negative obverse as the god*s* and nation*s* are ousted in 23d.

The repetition of the idea of "redeeming" points to the origins of the people of Israel: it is an act of God, which grants slaves freedom. In this ring on "redeeming" the favoured and the disadvantaged complement each other in a balanced way: in v.23b God himself is the beneficiary (*lō*: a 'dativus commodi') and *lᵉʿām* stands succinctly for "his own chosen people as covenant partner" (see v.24), whilst the end reveals from whose grasp the people have been snatched, "from Egypt". Due to this division there are initially three to five clauses with a purely positive content.[73] Their final word *nōrāʾōt* contains, however, the seeds of negativeness; it denotes awe on the part of Israel, but chiefly fear and dread of this mighty deity on the part of other peoples. This leads on to 23d, two clauses full of opponents. First Egypt is mentioned by name as an exemplary, or number one, enemy; the apparently invincible super power. Bordering on to it, as object of God's expulsion, are "the peoples [each] with its own god(s)", and we may assume that the neighbouring peoples are being thought of here, those who had for the most part been obstacles during Israel's journey to (and settling in) the promised land. God himself drives them away; fear is their lot.

On the threshold of negativeness the tone of the verse changes too. In 23b David commenced a quasi-neutral review by employing the ordinary word *ʾẹ̆lōhīm* which had just done duty for (other) gods in 22c, and by giving it the predicate *hālᵉkū*: a plural! At the end of 23a he glanced at the whole earth, in order to determine what is unique about Israel. The requisite detachment is maintained well, up to the end of 23c, and is apparent from the fact that it is only in this passage with its prayer chock full of second person forms that David speaks of God in the third person. But immediately after the critical word *nōrāʾōt* he breaks with this aloofness and in the clauses full of resistance (23d) he resumes his talking *to* his Lord: 23d has four 'you' morphemes for the true God. The period ends with a freshly used "gods" which once again refers to the idols of the other peoples. With the aid of the quasi-neutral *ʾẹ̆lōhīm* of 23b this word, *ʾẹ̆lōhāw*, forms a second ring round the flashback.[74] Two lines further on I see that the same word in 24b completes the hymn. At the same time it is, as a part of the covenant formula, the terminus of the

[73] There are three positive infinitive clauses in 23bc; if we count 23a and the relative clause at the beginning of 23b then there are five.

[74] This can be backed up by observing a chiasmus: *ʾẹ̆lōhīm* + *lifdōt* are a conjunction in 23b and are turned round in 23d, the disjunction *pādītā* + *(gōyīm wᵉ)ʾẹ̆lōhāw*.

development which the word of God undergoes in 22-23. It is, as it were, taken away from the nations and their polytheism and receives a specifically Israelite tint. That is why it may stand, in a brotherly fashion, next to the irreplaceable proper noun Yahweh – a new sign of the said development.[75]

The first two infinitives are acts which God undertakes "for himself", *lō* (bis), and their clauses have many monosyllables; the rhyming consonant 'm' links the *'am-śūm-šem* series to *'ęlōhīm*. An amplification follows these two sets of five syllables: a clause with four words and fourteen syllables. The beneficiary is now "them" (the people) and what has been received from one's God and liberator is (literally) "this great and terrifying [deeds]". The plural completes the singular, elucidates it and demonstrates the tenet of God's greatness. There is a connection with 21 and 22a. "All this greatness" David has received is now in historical perspective. It is a blessing of God, a link he adds on to a chain of formidable acts long in existence. The old and the new *gᵉdullā* surround and demonstrate together the predicate *gādaltā* which gives God praise.

This repetition of the stem "great" reinforces the close relationship of thanksgiving and praise. At the same time there is a connection with the oracle, owing to v.9c, where God doubly linked his "making" with "name" and "great":

9c w^e'āśītī lᵉkā šem gādōl kᵉšem haggᵉdōlīm 'ăšęr bā'āręṣ.

The *bā'āręṣ* of David which, horizon-like, makes Israel's uniqueness visible, is thus inspired by this line too. Whilst God announces just as much fame for him as the earth's great men enjoy and uses **gdl* twice, David goes one step further in a *combat de générosité*: looking round *bā'āręṣ* he ascertains the uniqueness of the people and does not ascribe it to a quality inherent in Israel, but to the intervention and election of God, and he reserves the words of the stem *gdl*, which has now been used three times, solely for God.[76]

The hymnic part reaches a conclusion, v.24, which states that both God and the people of Israel have been changed by the deliverance from the house of bondage. This takes place by means of the bipartite covenant formula which is varied interestingly here. We encounter the balance, but not the

[75] Now compare the use of *'ęlōhīm* in v.26b and 28a. A similar development is undergone by *gōy*. It occurs once, surprisingly, for Israel in 23a, but it is quickly swamped by *'ām*, which appears five times in vv.23-24 (twice predicatively in "to [his own special] people" and twice in "your people"); in 23d the plural occurs, destined for the surrounding nations, as an opposition to *gōy 'ęḥād* in 23a after which *gōy* fails to occur in the text.

[76] He is to combine the words "name" and "great" once more in v.26a to the glory of God.

symmetry, of the well-known reciprocity "I will be your God, and you shall be my people".[77] This does not come about due to the formulation of 24b, but through that of 24a. And the order is reversed in addition; the new or true identity of Israel as God's people now occurs first, so joining up directly with the point of v.23.

Verse 24b states in the usual way that "Yahweh has become their God", but puts this clause in the second person because of the genre of the whole speech, which consists of nothing but speaking to God. An extra initially placed *'attā* works towards this. This pronoun is preceded by not less than four morphemes for "you", with which v.24a underlines the intimate divine relationship Israel obtains.[78] That which is special about this line is to be found in its head and tail. Words inspired by the oracle appear here. What attracts the attention is the occurrence of a transitive verb, "establish Israel as his people", with a stem we became familiar with in vv.12-13 and 16, viz. **kwn*, instead of the intransitive *hyh* used elsewhere. The status of people of God does not originate with Israel itself, it is not a quality inherent in this nation, it harks back rather to a decision and an act of God, of which Israel is the object.[79] The end of the line makes the permanence of this form of election explicit with an *'ad 'ōlām* which rhymes and alliterates with the preceding word, *l^e'ām*.[80] This makes for the prayer's orientation to the Davidic throne's strength and permanence just promised by God. There is, however, a significant shift at the same time: in the prayer these two qualities go with the older relationship between God and Israel, and David makes no mention here of his monarchy or his throne, only of "the house of your servant". The hymnic paragraph thus ensures that David's house and its blessing keep within the national framework, the humble speaker implying that his monarchy is purely in the service of God's people.

[77] The covenant formula occurs in the quoted order in, amongst other references, Lev.26:12, Deut. 26:17sq., Jer.7:23, 11:4, 24:7, 31:1,33, and Ezek.37:27; the order is turned round in Ex.6:7, Deut.29:12 (with the verb *lhqym*), Jer.32:38, Ezek.11:20, 14:11, 36:28, 37:23, Hos.2:25, Zach.8:8.

[78] This emphasis on "you" goes so far that 24a employs a second and completely redundant *l^ekā*, placed after the name of Israel.

[79] The stem **kwn* in the polel is also used in the poetry of Deut.32:6 and Ps.119:73, verses where establishing is a divine act of creation. In the parallel text I Chron.17 the *wtkwnn* has been flattened to *wttn*, v.22a.

[80] The lamed which is present four times in the second half of 24a continues effectively at the end of v.24b, *lāhẹm lēlōhīm*, underlines the semantic connection and, in so doing, reinforces reciprocity.

The thanksgiving and the hymn have cleared the way for the prayer's point, the petition in vv.25-29. Their content also offers the grounds of David's asking. Their extent was 9 + 9 lines. The petition has 9 + 6 lines and the hinge word *w*^{e}ʿ*attā*, occurring three times, helps us determine its composition:

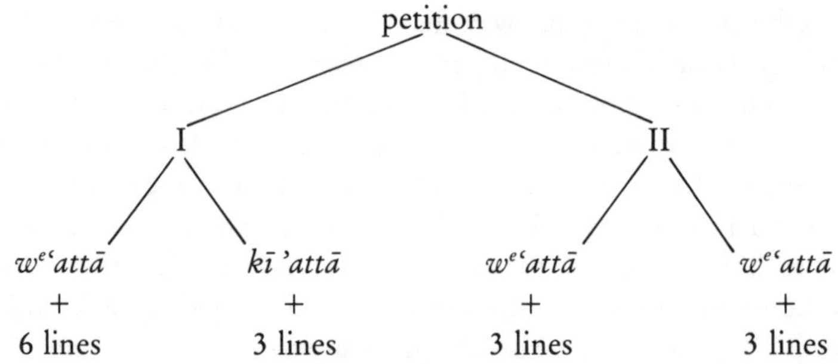

There is a binary composition on two levels therefore; I call vv.25-26, Ia, and v.27, Ib, whilst v.28 and v.29 are IIa and IIb respectively. Broadly speaking these quarters exhibit a petition-determination / determination-petition alternation. This can be quickly seen from the verb forms: in v.27 and v.28 no volitional forms occur, but the main indicatives do, whilst the surrounding parts (i.e. Ia and IIb) are governed by the imperatives and volitional forms comprising David's petition.

Actually this request does not exceed the promise of God; on the contrary, it repeats and varies its terms as we shall see. And this means that David asks for nothing more than God's sticking to his promise of a lasting dynasty. The fact that David's petition carefully covers the content of the promise has positive aspects.[81] It shows that David has listened well and that he can, and wants to, wish for nothing more than what God has already bestowed (in the form of a speech). He does not wish to go out of bounds and defines himself, after receiving the promise as well, as a humble and obedient servant keeping to the position of receiver or beneficiary.

Just as the hymn commenced with the adoption of an immediately preceding key word from the thanksgiving, so the beginning of vv.25-29 dovetails into the hymn's conclusion. A special concatenation technique is applied,

[81] According to some authors he may not do this, because it would be unsuitable after a pledge from God himself; Tsevat, for example, in his "The Steadfast House: What was David Promised in II Sam.7:13b-16?", HUCA 34 (1963) pp.71-82, and idem, "The House of David in Nathan's Prophecy", Biblica 46 (1965) pp.353-356. I fail to see any objection. The fact that the request covers the content of the promise may not be explained in such a way that the one praying doubts the promise in any way whatsoever. This is contrary to the spirit of the chapter.

which 26b + 27 are also to use in connecting parts Ia and Ib of the petition. Twice something is placed in an address which has just been expressed with a predicate and "evidence" – insofar as the prayer is determined by a persuasive strategy and offers the arguments of a religious conviction. From 24b onwards we see the vocative for God grow from one through two to four words, after which IIa and b both fall back on the *'ădōnāy yhwh* pair which was characteristic of the thanksgiving. An overview of the amplification and alternation is as follows:

vocative:	... *yhwh*	24b
predicational:	you, *yhwh*, have become *'ęlōhīm* to them	24b
vocative:	*yhwh 'ęlōhīm*	25a
predicational:	*yhwh ṣ^ebā'ōt 'ęlōhīm 'al yiśrā'el*	26b
vocative:	... *yhwh ṣ^ebā'ōt 'ęlōhē yiśrā'el*	27a

This series shows that we have a continued strategy of persuasion here which, as an abiding theme or background, has the link between the God and the people of the covenant, whilst in the foreground the genre characteristics alternate from thanksgiving to praise to request.

After the exordium in v.25a the request proper appears in the form of two frank imperatives – the first of two pairs.[82] Next come imperfects of the 26abc trio plus their consequences, followed by a retrospective motivation in the 27abc trio. These sets of three are construed round a second-degree direct speech with a fundamental utterance: in 26b – a constative nominal clause which is almost a creed – the full name of God and the range of his power gloriously appear whilst in v.27b the divine promise occurs at its briefest. In other words, the 25abc trio is the main matter followed by an elaboration (26) and the grounds (27). The imperatives of 25bc are chiastically intertwined with the prayer's second cluster of a threefold *dbr*:

25b	haddābār 'ăšęr dibbartā (...)	hāqem 'ad 'ōlām
25c	wa'ăśē	ka'ăšęr dibbartā

At the same time what characterises the prayer as a whole is the linking of volitional forms and indicatives in that past tense covered by the chiasmus. The crux of the asking occurs here: the promise given is reflected in declaratives, the requested implementation, in interrogatives. The form *hāqem*, which primarily and adequately does duty as an expression for being as good

[82] The other pair of imperatives also stands next to one another, in v.29a. There are no further imperatives in the prayer.

as one's word, is also inspired by God's *wahăqīmōtī* in v.12b, whilst the imperative *'ăśē* is an echo of the 'making' promised in 9c and 11c. The positive figura etymologica of "speak" in 25b faces the negative (rhetorical) figure of the speaking that never was in v.7b. Both cases revolve round 'building'. In one case building (a temple) is refused by God, in the other the building (a dynasty for David)[83] is the hope of the man at prayer.

The resumption, in 25a, of the words *yhwh* and God from 24b (in 25a) is part of a larger concatenation which relativizes the boundary between hymn and request, at the same time causing it to appear as an axis around which reflection takes place; I now note the words forming the ends of 24ab and 25ab:

24a (long clause, 9 words)	... 'ad 'ōlām
24b (short clause, 5 words)	... lelōhīm
25a (address, 3 words)	... 'ęlōhīm
25b (long clause, 10 words)	... 'ad 'ōlām

David places the duration of his dynasty, for which his prayer now asks, within the framework of the permanence which God conferred upon his relationship with the people (24a). Should God do this, continues David with a third *'ad 'ōlām* line, "your name shall always be great". He suggests that the best guarantee for God's renown is his continued support of David's house. And he implies, moreover, (I take another step back, to the "forever" of 24a): so Israel shall be saved at the same time, as the people of God. That is why a proud combination of the full name of God and his presence in Israel sounds in 26b: "The LORD of Hosts is God over Israel." The same guarantee is suggested by the connection between "making Himself a name" in v.23b and the final clause of 26a. God uttered the word renown twice for the benefit of David and David employs it twice in favour of the deity.

The petition is enclosed by the 25b-26c connection. "The word which you have spoken in favour of your servant and in favour of[84] his house" briefly keeps us guessing as to its content, until it is filled in by line 26c, which not only chiastically repeats the words servant and house, but also links them: "and may the house of Your servant David be established before You." Four of these words are inspired by the end of the promise, verse 16.[85]

[83] Notice that the combination of 'build' and 'house' in the sense of dynasty is visible for the first time in 27b; v.11c had "*make* a house".

[84] In v.25b the preposition *'al* (bis) means both "about, with regard to" and *in bonam partem* "for the benefit of".

[85] The words house, servant, *yihyę* and *nākōn*.

The *ā-ō* combination of the threefold *'ōlām* is continued in the powerful *ṣᵉbā'ōt* – by which David shows he remembers the official name from v.8b very well – and leads to the key word *nākōn* at the end of the promise. *Lᵉfānękā* too refers back to it. Arriving at verse 26 we have now reached the prayer's climax. The climax consists of a fusion of loyalties which mutually reinforce one another, not according to the laws of logic but in obedience to rhetorical rules such as that of parallelism.

The eternal renown of God is marked by an embedded speech, and its importance is apparent from its careful location in the massive address of the motivating verse 27. This trio itself is also built around an embedded speech, as two very long clauses round a very short one: 11 + 3 + 11 words. Their chronology curves back to the promise and David's venturing to respond. Line 27a stands for revelation, 27c calls the speech now uttered "this prayer", so that the man who is praying has given us a genre appellation for his words in his own text. The reciprocity (in the activity) of deity and mortal is plain and is made explicit by the particle *'al ken*. "The ear of your servant" takes us back to the other phrases on revelation; firstly, to 22c (our ears), then v.21 and 19. Verse 27b implies a form of self-interpretation on the part of the text, and is as such a narrator's hint: the subject, David, goes on ahead of us, indicating the core of the oracle in a mere four syllables, viz. *bayit 'ębnę lāk*. The object's location again concentrates the message on the dynasty as a surprising gift. The figura etymologica (praying this prayer) is the counterpart of the one in 25b: "the word which thou hast spoken" has given me courage "to pray this prayer".

The concluding passage, IIa+b = vv.28+29, is chiefly a mirrored reiteration of the first half of the petition. It gains its unity through the following elements: it contains the prayer's third cluster with a threefold *dbr*, it has its own double *wᵉ'attā* for the combination of facts plus wish, and its own double vocative (the *'ădōnāy yhwh* pair again) besides, its own variant, *lᵉ'ōlām*, for the idea of "forever" and the key word *brk* three times in its final verse.

After the hinge and the address there are two clauses which form a *parallelismus membrorum*:

(28a) ... you are [the true] God, (28b) and your words come true.

They sound like a creed thanks to the nominal quality of the clauses which renders their content timeless.[86] The first colon fixes and completes the well-maintained theme in the rhetorical layer, viz. that the God of the

[86] Of course *yihyū* is, in itself, a verbal form, but it has the same function as *hū* in 28a, indicating the copula. This is why such clauses with *hyh* count as nominal clauses in some linguistic theories.

covenant is, as such, the only true God. Something like this also applies to the words of God: your words *are 'ĕmęt*. Then the speaker hastens to give a concrete example: the revelation just conveyed which brings him salvation ("this goodness").[87] This "thou hast spoken" is the sequel of, and has the same content as, the "thou hast spoken" of 25bc. We might also make the following connection: a double *watt^edabber* (19b-28c) encloses a double *dibbartā*. In any case "the good", with its *ō* and *ā* vowels, covers what the future (*mērāḥōq*) has in store for David.

For the space of three clauses v.28 has been emphatic and indicative. This is the foundation upon which one more request is built. It is verse 29, where everything turns on one word: "bless me", requests David. The stem *brk* has virtuoso variations with a pi'el imperative in 29a, plus a figura etymologica which pairs a substantive with a pu'al in 29c. Just as the professing nominal clause, 26b, was amplified in v.28, so 26c (the content of David's entreaty) is repeated in 29a.[88] The imperatives *hō'el ubārek*, the prayer's second pair, are the assonating successors of *hāqem ... wa'ăśē* from v.25.[89] The two clauses which ask for a blessing, thus having a volitional form, surround the final indicative, yet another "thou hast spoken", which justifies the asking.

The oracle and the prayer

Now we can survey the two long speeches. I would like to provide an overview of their parts, giving its extent in lines. First there is the oracle proper, without the messenger's commission and the messenger's formula:

verse	5c-7c	8c-9b	9c-11b	11c-13b	14-16
	refusal	preamble	Israel safe	promise I...	and II
	6	3	7	6	7

In my colometric arrangement it is tempting to change the two sevens into sixes, e.g. by including the subordinate clauses 11a and 15b after their main clauses. But for fear of becoming system-obsessed I have not done this.

[87] Notice that the nominal clause with *dbryk*, 28b, is relieved by a verbal clause with the punctual tense *wtdbr* and the deixis of "*this* good". The preposition *'ęl*, which functioned in 19b just like the double *'al* in 25b, is the ordinary "to" in 28c.

[88] Line 29a has, exactly like 26c, "the house of your servant", the verb *hyh* and the end *lpnyk*, whilst *nākōn* is varied with *l^e'ōlām*.

[89] One more pair of imperatives occurs outside the prayer and that is ironically enough the *canard* of Nathan in v.3b.

Nevertheless, groups of three, six and nine are plainly normative as the figures for the prayer show:

verse	18d-21	22	23-24	25-27	28-29
	thanks-giving	hymn I	hymn II	petition I	petition II
	9	3	6	9	6

The final series can be re-written in the same way, if we classify the material in three genres: thanksgiving, nine lines, hymnic paragraph, nine lines, petition nine lines plus a repetition of six lines.[90]

On the level of paragraphs there are clear parallelisms between oracle and prayer. The hymnic part, especially vv.23-24 on the constitution of the chosen people, is the historical counterpart of the "Israel safe" paragraph (vv.9c-11b) which refers to the future, but is also as a flashback to origins, a discreet variation on the paragraph of refusal 5c-7c (which showed God as present but mobile); discreet because David does not include the negative and reacts with praise. The promise of a dynasty, which is the core of the oracle, is answered by the request which is the prayer's centre of gravity.

Several remarkable symmetries emerge when we start to count words.[91] If we divide the oracle so that 5c-11b (minus 8ab again) is half I and the promise to David half II (vv.11c-16b), then half I has precisely the same number of words as vv.18d-24, the first half of the prayer: 107 words. This is remarkable because the two large passages in ch.6 have the same number of words, viz.

[90] The numbers of lines in this prayer are based on my colometric arrangement, with one alteration: I have counted the two clauses of 18e as two cola. The arrangement is objective in the sense that the majority of lines (c. 23) consist of one simple clause each; but a few decisions inevitably had to be made on the grounds of taste and other factors which are difficult to measure. Giving every infinitival construction in v.23d its own colon has too fragmentary an effect. There are two objections to this: the embeddedness of the relative clause in v.23d prevents splitting the clauses into two lines; and the three lines 23abc are strongly rhythmical, so they can easily be scanned as bicola. (Moreover 23d can be read as a tricolon). Another point is 28a compared with 25ab. Both have the same introduction, but I also include the short nominal clause in 28a, whilst I have given the longer verbal and ascending clause after 25a its own line. This is supported by the chiasmus of the final words of 24ab + 25ab. The question of the duos and trios in the thanksgiving makes me hesitate as to the colometry of 18de.

[91] The main figures for the whole are:

verse	1-4	5ab	5c-7d	8ab	8c-9b	9c-11b	11c-13b	14-16	17	subtotal
words	48	9	48	9	22	37	34	38	11	256

and in the second half of the chapter:

verse	18abc	18d-21	22	23-24	25-27	28	29	subtotal
words	7	50	15	42	57	15	19	205

107. Subsequently there are three paragraphs of fifty-seven words each: the hymnic part, vv.22-24, and the first petition following it, vv.25-27, but also everything prior to the oracle, the introduction of vv.1a-5b.[92] It is too early to attach far-reaching conclusions to these figures, but they do illustrate the precision proportions of the constituent parts and suggest, just as in ch.6, that large parts of the text are sound. This is a pleasant endorsement of the utter superfluousness of adding or deleting a single word of the text.[93]

§ 3. *II Sam.8 appears to be a survey of David's military successes*

The structure and theme of ch.8 can easily be discovered since they are determined by three implementations of the repetition phenomenon.

I would like to begin by looking at the end. The vv.15-18 paragraph, which I provisionally call "the state's officials", returns – not without significant variations – at the end of ch.20. This is an extensive repetition which not only completes the chapter, but also ensures the closure of the entire Act. Moreover a parallelism has arisen on a still higher level. The section on the fallen David and Absalom's rebellion gets rounded off in the same way as the section "Throne and City".[94]

In ch.8 it is striking that two lines are completely identical: v.6 = 14d. Forming a refrain which articulates the body of the chapter (vv.1-14) in two parts they have some special characteristics. They disclose the divine dimension transcending David's military campaigns and introduce Yahweh as agent, who "gave David victory everywhere he went". So their duality inserts the annalistic chapter perfectly into the sacral Act where "the Lord of Hosts" continually intervenes in favour of the chosen king.

[92] Another two combinations provide the subtotal fifty-seven: if we include 18abc in 18-21, and if we put together 5c-8b. More quantitative symmetries: the oracle of refusal vv.5c-7c contains the same number of words as the narrator's text 1a-4b, both have 48 words. The paragraph on "Israel safe" of 9c-11b has thirty-seven words, and the shaping of the promise in vv.14-16 has thirty-eight. Petition II consists of thirty-four words, the same number as promise I.

[93] I have made two extremely minor alterations to the text. At the boundary between 11c and 12a I have changed *yhwh* into *whyh* and the *lkm* of 23c into *lhm*. See also Appendix I.

[94] The repetition of the "government chiefs" in ch.20 is a phenomenon on level 9 (literary units or "scenes"), level 10 (Acts) and level 11 (sections). The latter holds good provided that the "King David" section also includes I Ki.1-2 (as fourth Act of the fourth section). But the repetition of David's government chiefs does not fit any more after the succession and has therefore been placed after the third Act of "King David".

Another characteristic of 6c//14d is that, as a refrain, they are part of an extensive parallelism which makes the anti-Edom paragraph the counterpart of the one against Damascus.[95] Four of the five lines of vv.5-6 return almost identically in vv.13-14. The narrator ensures we do not miss the connection by expressly linking up, in v.13a, with the campaign against Damascus. The time adjunct "at his return from the battle against Aram" refers back and, together with the core of the sentence "David made a name", depicts the campaign against Edom as no more than a detour or excursion of David on his way home.[96] This has fascinating consequences for the way in which time is dealt with and for the chapter's theme.

Even though the narrator has thus reduced the battles against Damascus and Edom to the halves of one campaign, he has also separated them by interposing vv.7-12. This paragraph, designated as the chapter's centre of gravity from now on, is by far the longest in the unit and concentrates on what David does with the booty in Jerusalem. In terms of time this means that vv.7-11 form a drastic interruption of the Aram-Edom connection, that they are proleptic in respect of vv.13-14 and, the other way round, that the paragraph against Edom is a flashback with respect to the centre. These phenomena sketch the unique importance of the central paragraph. The passage's point is the way in which the thankful king David "sanctified to the Lord" the "silver, gold and bronze vessels", which he had received or conquered from various quarters, i.e. how he devotes tribute and booty to the deity. The fact that David's answer to the decisive *wayyōša' yhwh* has become the centre of gravity of II Sam.8 also shows just how much this chapter suits the sacral Act X. The long chapters on the ark and the oracle too were applications of the two-sided theme: God blesses – David gives thanks/dedicates.

Round the centre of gravity the (body of the) chapter is an enumeration of campaigns on the level of sequences. The end is (after v.15) an enumeration on the level of sentences. And there is also an enumeration on the level of

[95] The refrain is a phenomenon on level 6, that of sentences. The parallelism of vv.5-6 (against Damascus) and vv.13-14 (against Edom) is a phenomenon on the level of sequences, level 7 of the text model which I have discussed in NAPS II, ch.1.

[96] As coincidence will have it the names of Aram and Edom are very similar in their written form (both in Old Hebrew and in the square alphabet); the difference between daleth and resh is minimal. This has led to a certain amount of misunderstanding in ch.8. The MT has v.12 begin with *m'rm*. Part of the tradition reads it as *m'dm* (not only LXX and Peshitta but also several Hebrew manuscripts – "nonn MSS", according to BHS app.) and is mistakenly followed by Driver, CT and McCarter. See also my own Appendix I.

words formed by the names of the six losing parties who are all placed in v.12, i.e. at the end of the central paragraph. If, in order to clarify the issue, we now assume that David has booked all these successes after removing to Jerusalem, and during the first half of his forty-year reign, ch.8's narrated time takes up about twelve years.[97] The enumeration of the subdued nations in v.12 is both the closing of this narrated time span and its further condensation. The series is a closure seeing that vv.13-14 are a flashback. We can see more plainly how true this is by recognising that the names' enumeration is a summary of the series of campaigns, and by reminding ourselves that the chapter itself is largely a prolepsis whose task is recording the might of David's kingdom, so that the fourth section (mainly II Sam.9-20) can devote itself entirely to the internal troubles of David's monarchy.

Now that we have grasped the chapter's structure it is time for a more linear run through the text. First I would like to follow verses 1-6. The military handiwork takes place entirely within the narrated time of this passage. There are four very short to short paragraphs with a schematic set-up. Each one offers a campaign and in addition they have the following fixed components: the name of an enemy (people), a salient detail of his defeat, but first the decisive factor *wayyak dāwīd*. This core, "David defeated" plus a direct object, comes first each time so there can be no doubt about who is superior. Everything prior to the clash – circumstances, motives – is omitted.

The four campaigns are arranged in duos due to fresh repetition on the level of sentences. The lines of 2d and 6b are identical and form a refrain articulating both the extremely concise opening, vv.1-2, and the longer sequel, vv.3-6. They mention how first Moab and then Aram "become slaves of David, bearing tribute". For a while I detach the lines v.1a and 6c.[98] Now we can see the proportions of the campaigns against the Philistines, Moab, Zobah and Damascus respectively: a series of 2-4-5-4 lines, or 12-21-33-25 words. This makes a total of ninety-one words, exactly the same number as in the centre, i.e. vv.7-12!

[97] Years 8-20 of his reign. Notice that the campaigns against Hadadezer and Ammon come up for discussion later in chs.10-12 where, as acts of war, they form the significant framework for David's corruption – see NAPS I. Another temporal consideration: imagine that Solomon was born two years after David's adultery with Bathsheba and that he was twenty at his coronation, then the campaign of David against Ammon, requiring at least two seasons, took place approximately between the years 17 and 18 of David's reign. This date is a *terminus ad quem*.

[98] Verse 1a is a temporal clause in the service of the whole chapter and it determines the relationship with ch.7. Verse 6c functions together with 14d one level higher than the repetition 2d//6b and marks the two halves of the body of the text.

The temporal opening, v.1a, is a separation and a link at the same time and loosely governs the relationship with what has gone before. "Afterwards [the following] came to pass." The taut series of military success reports in ch.8 is the fulfilment of the proleptic or promising clauses 7:1b-9b-11b. Verse 1 deals with the Philistines as quickly as possible. They had already been given a beating twice in Judaean territory in ch.5 and now they are subdued in their own territory. The crucial word *wayyak* is ignominiously amplified to *wayyaknīʿem*. Whereupon this follows as a salient detail: "David took the bridle of the mother city" – if indeed this is what it actually says.[99] In any case one might surmise that it is an idiomatic expression for some form of curbing or humiliation. The word *mętęg* is backed up by another segholate form, the *ḥębęl* which decides on the gruesome fate of the defeated Moabites in the following verse. The semantic fields of these words touch each other; something I cannot divorce from their textual proximity. The report that David took the reins "out of the hands of the Philistines" means the roles are reversed from now on; the enemy finds himself in *his* hand, sc. in his power. This consideration supports the reading that *mętęg* does indeed mean 'bridle' here and functions as a metaphor for (severe) oppression.

The paragraph against Moab is set out in the form of a quartet, viz. ABBA. The name of this people occurs only in 2a and 2d. These two lines at the far ends send word on war and political consequences. David's victory is stated briefly in a mere five syllables, much more space – two predicates – being allotted to the subjection of the Moabites. The centremost lines, 2bc, become a pair due to the anaphora of the verb *mdd*. Verse 2b broadly speaks about the measuring line and the enforced lying down together – data which bode no good. The concrete act of cruelty follows in 2c with exact figures and the spine-chilling opposition of *lᵉhāmīt* and *lᵉhaḥăyōt*. The conqueror poses as lord of life and death here, and twice as many Moabites are put to the sword as are spared. The A lines of the quartet are in proportion to the B lines as general to particular; 2a+d uses general terms, words returning in later paragraphs, whilst 2cd reports the unique treatment undergone by (the army of) Moab.

The paragraph against Zobah introduces us to the one who gets the blame in the passage. He is called Hadadezer, a name which occurs not less than eight times in the chapter – the same number, incidentally, as the conqueror's verb *nkh*. By way of exception verse 3a mentions a person rather than a people, someone who makes his appearance in full regalia, as it were, with the

[99] This rendering is tentative. The uncertainty has much more to do with the word *'ammā* than with *mętęg*. I follow Driver, who adds to his translation: "i.e. the authority of the metropolis or capital", as do Buber, BJ, NBE (Alonso adds the name Gath for the capital), NBG.

phrases of his patronymics and his function. This happens again, the last time he is mentioned, in v.12 of all places; the verse with the enumeration/ summary. Here too the personal name is thrown into relief by the row of national ones, and the full designation "Hadadezer, the son of Rehob, the king of Zobah" has even to serve as a climax, not only for verse 12's series but also for the complex, ever increasing period, 11ab12ab.

This ruler appears to be the chief obstacle to the northward growth of David's power. Anyway this is how I interpret the linking of the time adjunct in 3b to the defeat of 3a. "David defeated (...) Zobah, when he [went, =] advanced to make his influence felt in [the region of] the River." In this paragraph and the next we hear almost the same figures on the defeated. In 4a there is a contrast between cavalry and infantry, after which the salient detail of the Zobah campaign follows in v.4bc. It concentrates on enemy cavalry, which is paralysed. A hundred chariots are spared, to the greater honour and glory of the conqueror I take it. Of the five lines which make up vv.3-4 the centremost is very long. Two pairs surround it; 3a and b end on geographical names, 4bc rhyme thanks to the chariot epiphora. The central line stands out therefore, which might have something to do with the treatment of enemy soldiers. Of this army alone it is said: "David captured it". There is no slaughter, but what does happen to it then? Did David perhaps incorporate these soldiers as mercenaries as time went by?

At the beginning of the fourth campaign the name Hadadezer occurs once again, this time with one apposition. He gets one more chance insofar as an ally hastens to assist him. This fact and the identical close of v.3a and 5a are internal means which keep vv.3-4 and 5-6 together as a pair. The Aramaeans of the city state Damascus are the ones who intervene. At the hands of the narrator, however, their intention of "helping" becomes an ironic undermining of Zobah's ruler, whose theophoric name says that his help is in Hadad. This god has been able to accomplish nothing for his vassal, and Damascus suffers the same fate. The full name Aram-Damascus appears in lines 5a//6a, the shorter name occurs as part of the David + Aram / Aram + David chiasmus in lines 5b//6b. The four lines can be read as an ABAB series. It then becomes plain that Hadadezer's influence on Damascus is replaced by David's authority; an about-face which is expressed in a new chiasmus:

5a	Aram-Damascus	Hadadezer, the king of Zobah
6a	David ... governors	in Aram-Damascus

This device embodies the parallelism of the A lines. The B lines (5b and 6b) have exactly the same relation as v.2a and d had in the Moab quartet. This time David does not subject his victims to cruel treatment, what he does do is introduce figureheads through whom he can keep the Aramaean state under control. Their defeat too results in the fact that they "become slaves, bearers of tribute".

This line on slavery does not return in the counterpart, the settling of the score with Edom in verses 13-14. Instead the supervisors' report is doubled. Verse 14b underlines the thoroughness of what is stated in 14a and is not a mere duplication. The asyndetic link and the inversion of the word order make 14b into a more detailed elaboration or explanation of 14a.[100] In this paragraph which has recourse to what has gone before, two more matters catch the eye. Everything is immediately dominated by "David made a name", inasmuch as this short clause occurs initially. The statement links up with the promises God gave in ch.7, so we gather the whole chapter to be the realisation of "I shall make your name great as [that of] the great men of the earth."

Another characteristic of the Edomite paragraph is that it too becomes the counterpart of the Zobah campaign through the connection of v.13 with v.3. The two lines of v.13, which we regain by restoring a homoioteleuton,[101] have a chiastic correspondence with 3ab. The diagonal line from the set "he defeated" (3a + 13b) is intersected by a much more striking repetition of two infinitives with a rhyme in 3b and 13a concerning the strength and the marches of David: *bᵉlęktō lᵉhāšīb yādō* versus *bᵉšūbō mēhakkōtō*. On the phonetic level these duos form their own chiasmus, of which the innermost half is a play on the root *šwb*. These subtleties are the umpteenth token of the stylistic refinement which makes ch.8 so much more than the writing of annals. They also make us ponder the relationship of their sequences; which is that they indicate the northernmost and southernmost positions where David establishes his power. The contrast is also borne by the geographic data of the great River (sc. the Euphrates) and the Dead Sea (present in v.13 via the Plain of Salt). They almost form a merismus encompassing the map of ch.8.

Five campaigns, six peoples, seven names of the defeated – all this diversity obtains a centre, when the gravitational centre, vv.7-12, displays the conqueror in his capital Jerusalem.[102] The paragraph is framed by the booty which

[100] Verse 14b is not a doublet. A stylistic hint on this is the fact that the designation "*all* Edom" of 14b returns in 14c, whilst this *kol* is not used in the parallels v.2d and v.6b.

[101] The homoioteleuton has happened because of the similarity in writing of the names of Aram and Edom; see also Appendix I.

[102] The five campaigns each have their own paragraph. The six nations are Edom and Zobah plus the names of v.12a. The seven names are Edom of vv.13-14 plus the nations in v.12. The Amalekites have come into their own so much in I 15, 30 and II 1, that the narrator does not grant them another paragraph, it is the turn of the Ammonites in chs.10-12.

David carries off from Hadadezer, heard in the alliteration of *šlṭy* in 7a and *šll* in 12b. This enemy's name appears six times, he is apparently the exemplary loser. This gains depth now that another ruler, mentioned three times, makes his appearance as a foil for him. This Toi follows the recipe: the enemy of my enemy is my friend. His joy at the subjection of Hadadezer is great and flows over in good wishes for David which his son must pass on. Verses 9 and 10b give us his point of view, so that the defeat of Zobah is mirrored with emphasis in the central paragraph. That "David had defeated him" is stated twice, taking it in turns with a form of *lḥm* which also occurs twice and is linked to Hadadezer's name.

The passage opens with two long clauses, vv.7a and 8. They surround the very short clause, 7b, which releases the name of Jerusalem for the first time since ch.5, and an inversion in their syntax creates a chiasmus at the expense of Hadadezer:

7a David took the shields of gold / from the servants of Hadadezer
8 from B and B, the cities of Hadadezer / David took very much copper.
The precious metals surround him, but he loses them.

In v.9 someone appears for the first time who, just like Hadadezer, bears the title of king, the ruler of Hamath. But he is overawed by a greater king: the full title *hammęlęk dāwīd*, which in 10a so designates the hero for the first time in this chapter, is not only the address to which the prince is sent, but reveals at the same time the respectful point of view of Toi, who is not desirous of a trial of strength with the king of Israel. The narrator had preceded him in this in v.8 and sticks to the full nomenclature in 11a.

Verses 9 and 10 begin anaphorally. When Toi hears that the army of his arch enemy is defeated, he acts, *wayyišma' – wayyišlaḥ*. Verse 10 grows into a period of three lines. In the first David is honoured with a double infinitive, in 10b a subordinate clause of cause points at the occasion and it strikes us by repeating the object clause of v.9. A varied trio has thus arisen: the defeat of the king of Zobah occurs in the points of view of the narrator (in 3a) and Toi, in which it is news (9) and a good reason for entering into a pact (10b). Verse 10c is a fresh motivating clause which explains just how much Hadadezer had been a nail in Toi's coffin. The parallelism of 10b and c creates the contrast that Toi never could manage to shake off the enemy whilst David wins in one fell swoop.[103] Toi's relief is expressed in a series which, as a trio, carries with it

[103] Verse 10c nominalises and fixes all the warfare between the two and has an iterative aspect; it describes a trait of the enemy. Verse 10b, on the other hand, has momentaneous verb forms which give Hadadezer short shrift.

the idea of perfection: the silver vessels, the golden vessels, the bronze vessels. They symbolize that there could be no better ally for David.

The narrator handles this ironically. He commences an even longer period of four lines (11ab12ab) with the little word "also" which has the fatal consequence of the friend's gift falling into the same category as the booty of so many enemies. This link seriously undermines the friend/enemy contrast and raises questions: to what extent does Toi want to avoid conflict and, with his good understanding of political developments, did he really have any other choice but to present himself as an ally? He has become just as much a "bearer of gifts" as the defeated.

In v.11 the key word is 'sanctify' and it is solemnly accompanied by the full title "king David" plus the proper noun Yahweh. Here we have the heart of the matter as far as the middle paragraph is concerned. The transition from 11a to 11b connects, in a suspiciously loose way, the vessels of ally Hamath with the precious metals of the others, after which the key word is repeated and a parallelism, 11a//11b, is created. At this stage the narrator might have brought things to a full stop, but he cannot get enough of it and makes his period twice as long. Via the adjunct "of all the peoples which he had subdued" he makes room for launching the long chain of v.12 (six names of nations, with Hadadezer as an extra face). The closure of the centre of gravity is also a summary of (the wars) of the whole chapter.

We are approaching the final paragraph now. Does 15 go with the main part or is it the introduction to the government chiefs? It is not difficult to first of all read these sentences on David as the sequel to v.14d. The successful conclusion to military violence abroad culminates in harmony at home, created by so righteous a king. I now note the little word *kol* which first underlines the subjection of the southern neighbour in 14bc, and is then found in the general adjunct of space in 14d, thereupon marking a completely different relationship than that of conqueror/slaves:

14d The Lord gave David victory wherever he went
15a David was king over all Israel
15b and David executed true justice among all his people.

During the 14cd-15ab series David grows from an indirect object and beneficiary to subject. Lines 15ab are a notorious parallelism which ends on the same referent: the whole people. The nation is designated by a word pair which joins up with God's terminology of love in the oracle, "my people Israel". The quality of David's rule is divinely acceptable. The middle of 15b offers a striking phenomenon in so highly enumerative a chapter lacking the spoken word, it is the poetic expression *mišpāṭ uṣ^{e}dāqā*.[104] This pair of words really characterises the activity of the king, since it occurs in a periphrastic construction which ensures that David is permanently occupied with this quality. The line fills in what David's kingship in 15a consists of[105] and is, at the same time, a value judgement revealing the narrator's point of view. Now that everything is in order, at home and abroad, it seems as if heaven on earth has broken loose. Where to now? What more is there to experience? The answer is given in the section of II Sam.9-20 and I Ki.1-2. Not morally pleasant it is psychologically and narratively fascinating, thanks to the outbreak of vice.

Secondly, verse 8:15 also goes with what follows. Together with the line on David's sons, 18b, it forms the head and the tail of the final paragraph. The core consists of the highest ranking army officers and government officials, six men in five lines, vv.16-18a. This part alone, in an altered order of appearance, is repeated at the end of ch.20. I deduce from this that v.15 + 18b are specially meant for ch.8. The reason is simple: these statements on David's righteous rule and the priestly office of his sons[106] belong, as positive elements, in Act X as the sacral centre of gravity of the whole composition, and their omission in ch.20 is the umpteenth sign of David's moral bankruptcy which has crushing consequences after ch.11. But perhaps the datum of David's sons becoming priests is itself a stick of dynamite placed by the narrator under the perfection. It is conceivable that we ought to assimilate v.18b as the first hint of David's approaching *hubris*. In which case the priesthood of his sons is a sequel to the corruption of the sons of two former

[104] According to the concordance of Eben Shoshan *mišpāṭ uṣ^{e}dāqā* stand next to on another twenty-seven times in the Bible, each time in poetry except for the solemn spoken word of Gen.18:19 and I Ki.10:9. There are also other references with the same roots such as Prov.12:5 and 21:15, or where the word pair is spread over cola, e.g. Ps.72:2; the masculine noun *ṣędęq*, in amongst other references, Eccles.5:7, and via inversion initially in Prov.1:3 and 2:9.

[105] The *wymlk* of v.15a is an interesting example of a durative wyqtl form. The parallelism of 15a//b makes the reign in a precisely as lasting as the behaviour in b. I also notice that a qal imperfect of *mlk* is rare for David; elsewhere it occurs only in I 23:17 and 24:21 (in the mouth of Jonathan and Saul respectively). As a rule a narrative imperfect such as *wymlk* means "he became king", as in the case of Hanun in II 10:1.

[106] The priesthood of David's sons is a well-known problem, because the fact is they are not Levites or descendants of Aaron. What is to be done with this datum? One might, embarrassed by the matter, try to a) artificially stretch the meaning of the word, as some do in the footsteps of the parallel reference of I Chron.18, the Aramaic Versions and the LXX, or b) emend the word *khnym* like Wenham who, in ZAW 87 (1875) pp.79-82, "Were David's Sons Priests?", proposes *sknym*, "administrators (of the royal estates)". I hesitate on the latter. I would rather put forward above another alternative which retains the MT. In 20:26 the priesthood of Ira is the replacement of 8:18b.

people of integrity in Samuel, Eli and Samuel. Besides, looking back from section IV one might see this office as something which the sons have appropriated without their father's correcting them (just as in the case of Absalom and Adonijah later).[107]

The five lines of vv.16-18a are so ordered that the two generals, who together take up the initial position in 20:23, are separate and situated at the edges.[108] Within this the two highest ranking officials of the civil service are mentioned, in 16b and 17b. The Zadok and Abiathar duo occupy a central position with their cultic office.[109] A repetition of the *špṭ* + *ṣdq* tandem arises from their joining up with the Jehoshaphat line and 16b and 17a have the element *'aḥī* three times in their patronymics. The concentric organisation of the lines in vv.16-18a gives 18b an air of being an outsider. These priests do not occur next to *the* priests, a fact which, in itself, might suggest that the office does not go with the sons of David.

§ 4. *Act X and its context: integrations 1-3*

After so much analysis several pointers will be sufficient to establish the relationship of the literary units of II Sam.5-8, subsequently according them their place, as Act X, in the whole composition. I would like to do this in three steps; on the levels of Act, section and book.

Integration I takes place on level 10 of the semiotic staircase which covers the hierarchy of the text and concerns the proper extent and order of Act X. Of late Flanagan has suggested viewing 5:13-8:18 as a group consisting of two lists, two war stories and two passages on legitimacy.[110] Brueggemann

[107] Perhaps the intransitive *hāyū* denotes this appropriating. The sons have *become* priests, not: made or inaugurated by David.

[108] As I have already written in Volume II, in the Corrigenda, I should have included 20:23-26 in the Hebrew text at the back of *King David*.

[109] The switching round of the names Abiathar and Ahimelech seems to me unavoidable. Abiathar served David as a priest before he became king and probably survived him in that office; in any case he was still relevant enough in I Ki.2 for (Zadok and) Solomon to be exiled. In his office Abiathar occurs in 15:29, 35, 36, 17:15, 19:12 and occurs in the counterpart 20:25 on the same level with Zadok.

[110] James W. Flanagan, "Social Transformation and Ritual in 2 Samuel 6", pp.361-372 of "The Word of the Lord Shall Go Forth", Festschrift for D.N. Freedman, 1983. The definition of literary unit he holds is erroneous in the first place; he calls II Sam.5:13-8:18 "a single literary unit", while, without the two small lists, there are at least four. On the other hand a word such as "compilers", for example, reveals the fact that Flanagan underestimates the level of integration.

adopted this shortly afterwards.[111] Perhaps it would be useful to start with a negative exercise, explaining first of all why this division does not work. I see the following objections. Firstly, the proportions raise objections. Flanagan's proposal treats so brief a text unit as 8:15-18, with its mere thirty-nine words and mainly enumerative function, as if it were on the same footing as such long and completely different passages as ch.6 (the story of the ark in 370 words) and ch.7 (promise and prayer taking up 461 words). He sees the paragraph on the government chiefs, moreover, as a counterpart of 5:13-16 because both short passages consist of lists. But because their contents differ highly and the natural counterpart of the end of ch.8 is the end of ch.20, I find this similarity too formal; it is not a felicitous one.

Secondly, having an Act begin with an enumeration – cutting its content off from what has immediately gone before at the same time – leaves much to be desired aesthetically. Verses 10-12 in ch.5 establish David's settling in Jerusalem and the blessing of God resting upon it; the births underline this in their own way and may not be separated from it. The natural counterpart of 5:13-16 should not be sought in ch.8, but has already been given earlier by the narrator in 3:2-5 (children in Hebron). This correspondence wishes to contribute to the equilibrium between Acts IX and X which have such a striking spatial connection, to Hebron and Jerusalem.[112]

Thirdly, we have seen that 5:6-12 goes with Act X because of Yahweh's special contribution to the action. Fourthly, this passage cannot be part of the previous Act because that group of units was shown to have a concentric structure, the hermetic nature of which rejected alien elements.

What positive comments can we make on the organisation of the properly delineated tenth Act? There is a tendency to set out the subject matter in an AB-BA scheme, but this concentric symmetry is neither forcefully nor compellingly carried through. We encounter various acts of war in chs. 5 and 8, in passages which have the tendency to become fragmentary and consist of paragraphs which, being rather easily distinguished, are relatively independent. The two great designs of chs.6 and 7 are to be found in between and bring the sacral aspect to its peak.

The double *wayyōša'*, so strategically placed in ch.8, now corresponds with God's double intervention pro-David in the Valley of the Rephaim. The

[111] Walter Brueggemann, "2 Samuel 21-24: An Appendix of Deconstruction?" in CBQ 50 (1988) pp.383-397. Brueggemann follows Flanagan's order so eagerly (I might say: uncritically) because it construes three pairs in different genres, which links up perfectly with his own subject, the three pairs of units in chs.21-24.

[112] Besides Flanagan has not considered the parallelisms which I have noted above in ch.V § 2 (p.168).

Philistines beaten back there are first in line for a definitive subjugation in ch.8 and encircle, as losers, the pair II Sam.6-7. Another characteristic of chs.5-6-7-8 is that they exhibit a regular alternation in the use of report and speech by having much/little/very much/no spoken word.[113] It is striking that the clash with Michal occurs approximately in the centre of the composition, particularly as we remember that the extradition of the princess was the pivot of the previous act. As level 9 phenomena I give the chapters capital letters; as a level 8 phenomenon paragraph 6:20-23 gets a minuscule letter x:

A	five brief passages, speeches of David and Yahweh, topic: war	ch.5
B	long report, procession and ark, the sanctification of the city	ch.6
x	clash between the daughter of Saul and king David	
B	long speeches of Yahweh and David on the lasting dynasty	ch.7
A	five paragraphs of enumerative report, topic: wars and punishment	ch.8

Apart from this David's settling and prosperity in Jerusalem take up a central position between his military successes in ch.5.[114] The corresponding counterpart in ch.8 is that the rich booty from the various campaigns streams into Jerusalem and is devoted to God there, according to the broad centre of the text.

However the ABBA scheme does not show important characteristics of the Act and that is why I am not strongly attached to it. These characteristics, pointed out regularly during analysis, are i) the sacral aspect of the whole Act, of which the appearance of Yahweh as an agent in the foreground is only a part, and ii) the tendency to achronism, of which, amongst other things, the major and minor anticipations are signs.

Integration 2 is a movement taking place on level 11 of the semiotic staircase and concerns the relationship between Act IX and Act X. One Act is the group of units tied to Hebron, the other is tied to Jerusalem. They form a close pair in various ways. This is already revealed by the barely marked transition from one Act to the other, which becomes visible only through structural analysis. As regards the treatment of time II Sam.2-8 differs from what has gone before. In part II we saw that Act VIII (= I Sam.27-31 + II 1) had a half-hidden, but very precise time scheme of exceptional thematic

113 The number five for the chapter is a shortened notation of 5:6-25 here.

114 The five short passages which I refer to under label A are: 5:6-8 (the conquest of Jerusalem), vv.9-12 (prosperity, God's support), vv.13-16 (list of births), vv.17-21 and 22-25 (the two battles against the Philistines).

importance. In Acts IX and X, on the other hand, there are few designations of time. The synchronism of the reigns of Ishbosheth and David evades our grasp. The content of David's seven year reign in Hebron is entirely omitted. His policy's focus lies outside Judah to be precise, insofar as the stake in II Sam.2-4 is constantly that of power, and nothing but power, over all Israel. That is why Act IX concerns itself with the struggle for this throne. The long time the civil war took, disclosed by an iterative note in 3:1 for example, is given form only by making the act of war in ch.2 exemplary; subsequently chs.3-4 already concern themselves with the end of the period in the form of three affairs: that of Michal (extradited), Abner (murdered) and Ishbosheth (ditto). We hear nothing more on Judaean politics. After this when the unified kingdom comes into being, Act X continues to be vague in its treatment of time. Its achronic and proleptic aspects witness to the influence of God on the terrestrial plane. They are signals of the transcendental, which becomes visible as a fourth dimension and ensures the apotheosis of David's long rise. And if we move over to II Sam.21-24 for a moment, we can see that chronology and time scheme are vague, and more often even totally absent.

The connection between IX and X is reinforced by the parallelism of a number of paragraphs from the beginning of both Acts and from the end of Act IX, which I have already noted on p.168:

	beginning of Act IX		end IX, beginning X
David anointed king	2:4 > 7	//	5:1-3
reign formulas	2:10-11	//	5:4-5
war story	2:12-31	//	5:6-9
David "stronger and stronger"	3:1	//	5:10 > 12
list of sons born in Hebron and Jerusalem resp.	3:2-5	//	5:13-16

Subsequently there is a conspicuous joining of the axis of IX to that of X. Paragraph 6:20-23 is the sole place within Act X where a woman is mentioned and also the only place where David continues his relationship with the house of Saul. On the level of interpretation where we are now, I indeed argue in favour of the pivotal position x of the hostile Michal-David dialogue, because it follows naturally from 3:6-21 and is the unit which is the middle of Act IX, and which itself revolves round the return of Michal. We observe that the narrator has accorded a subversive place to the painful clash in the apotheosis of II Sam.6-7, as a discord in the harmony of the arriving procession and the divine promise of a lasting dynasty. The clash is heated enough to disturb the illusion of perfection which one might get during the completion of the Act in ch.8.

Naturally Acts IX and X also form a pair because of their subject matter: David comes to power and consolidates his position. I have tried to capture this in the subtitle of this volume, *Throne and City*. Their unity is, finally, marked by several effective oppositions. In IX David hardly acts at all, in X he is the sole mortal protagonist. In IX the generals are doubly prominent, in X, on the contrary, they are not allowed to do anything. In Act IX the presence of women is subject to systematic distribution, in X, by way of an exception one is permitted to appear in a subversive paragraph, but her fate is that she is put out of action. In Act IX national disunity proves merciless, in X David forges national unity.

Integration 3 moves a level higher by envisaging Act X and the II Sam.2-8 section as part of the entire composition. On level 9, that of the single unit such as ch.7, the prophet Nathan was little more than a vehicle for the Word of God. However, his true significance becomes visible on level 12. The overview this position furnishes us enables us to compare his presence in II 7, as receiver of the dynastic vision, with the two later crucial interventions in ch.12 and I Ki.1. In so doing we are at the same time able to avoid hyperanalysis and an atomistic exegesis of ch.7, which lead to fatal consequences with an author such as Tsevat who, taking umbrage at the unconditional nature of (the promise which is the basis of) the Davidic covenant, goes on to stigmatise the heart of the passage as an interpolation.[115]

The bipartite oracle of salvation which Nathan receives in David's favour may not be read without relation to the twofold oracle of doom he delivers to David as God's reaction to the king's double capital crime, and this intervention of punishment and pardon cannot be viewed apart from I Ki.1, where Nathan plunges into practical politics to safeguard the throne for the "beloved of God" (= Solomon).

The transition from Act X to Act XI is the most dramatic contrast between Acts to be found in Samuel. David's long march to the top has received its climax in ch.7, but is quickly followed by a tremendous anticlimax: the fall of David in ch.11, which commences with his looking out of the same palace which was present in various aspects in chs.5-6-7 and with a *yšb* which stands in ominous opposition to the *yšb* of 5:9, 7:2, etc. Nathan is present both at the peak of Act X and that of Act XI and he makes an essential contribution with

[115] Matitiahu Tsevat, "The Steadfast House: What Was David Promised in II Sam. 7:13b-16?", in HUCA 34 (1963) pp.71-82, and by the same author, "The House of David in Nathan's Prophecy", Biblica 46 (1965) pp.353-356.

the extensive speeches of his Sender. The covenant with David is unconditional for a short space of time, but is disgraced by the receiver of the divine promise, so as to become permanently frayed. The positive nature of Act X has become the background against which all the criminality and calamity of Act XI emerge all the more sharply.

The *'ad 'ōlām* which triumphantly marks the extent of God's choosing this dynasty turns against "the house of David" which from now on is to be visited by the sword *'ad 'ōlām*. The verb *swr* which occurred in a litotes favouring David (7:15) turns against him, because it is now (12:10) used for the sword, with the same negation. The preamble of previous events, which initiated the positive turn in 7:8-9 and indicated David's election, gets a counterpart in 12:7-8 in a comparable preamble; this too points to his special office but now prepares the charge and the announcement of punishment. In addition there are various contrasts to be sketched on the level of words.[116] Also an obvious thing to do is construe an antithetic parallelism between David's thankful prayer as his response to the promise, and his confession of guilt (plus other words in reaction to Nathan, such as the verdict of 12:5-6) as his reply to divine judgement.

The unconditional nature of the promise in 7:11c-16 ought therefore to be read in interaction with the oracles of ch.12. But it is striking that the promise is not nullified in this dialectic. David gets a personal reprieve in 12:13 and the third appearance of Nathan, at what is almost the deathbed of David (I Ki.1), functions in the service of Davidic continuity. His zealously advocating Solomon as successor cannot, once again, be viewed apart from the covenant of II Sam.7.

Consequently the tension between election and rejection which appeared in the first monarchy, tearing apart Saul's body and soul, now takes control of the soul and body of the man who had received everything in order to escape from such a struggle. We have studied the dramatic consequences and externalisations of this in *King David*.

[116] Place the *miyyad šā'ūl* of 12:7 opposite 7:15b, or the pair little/add of 12:8 opposite 7:19sq,. or the positive *heqīm* of God in 7:12 and 25 opposite his negative *meqīm* in 12:11, or the peaceful *škb* of 7:12a opposite its dubious and criminal implementations in chs.11 and 12.

INTERPRETATION OF ACT XV
(II SAM.21-24)

ירעם מן שמים יהוה   ועליון יתן קולו

Chapter VII

Two crises of crime and punishment flank the champions

§ 1. *Bloodguilt and atonement, II Sam.21:1-14*

A story which starts off with a problem normally has a plot aiming at the solution. The same is true of this passage. There is a great famine, and the cause is numinous: God is furious because of Saul's earlier violation of a treaty the Israelites had entered into with Gibeon plus its surrounding districts, of which treaty he, the Israelites' God, is the patron deity. Josh.9 relates the Gibeonites' craftily managing to insist on a protected status from the people whom they see is about to dominate Palestine.[1] 'Joshua established friendship with them; he made a pact with them to spare their lives, and the chieftains of the community gave them their oath.' The tribal leaders explain the gravity of the agreement in a speech with a characteristic ring composition: 'We swore to them by the LORD, the God of Israel; therefore we cannot touch them. This is what we will do to them: We will spare their lives, so that there may be no wrath against us because of the oath that we swore to them.' My reason for such extensive quotation is that various words from Josh.9 obtain key positions in II Sam.21.

During a calamity such as famine ancient thought asks itself whether the deity's wrath has been kindled. David asks God himself what has provoked his fury (v.1c) and is plainly told (1ef). From his ensuing talk with the Gibeonites (vv.3-6) a plan emerges to ritually execute seven descendants of Saul who do indeed get hanged (v.9). The end of the sequence vv.7-9 could have functioned well as the end of the story: 'They were put to death in the first days of the harvest, in the beginning of the barley harvest.' Additionally

1 The English quotations which follow are from the JPS rendering of Josh.9:15 and 19-20.

the narrator could have underlined it with the very last line (v.14c) of the passage, 'God responded to the plea of the land thereafter', and that would have been that. As a strategy seeking the solution to the problem posed at the start the plot is already complete in v.9, and lines 9cd do indeed reveal the narrator's overview proper to this. In 9c he counts, and in 9d he allocates a place on the time scale to the execution. But the story is not over yet; five more verses follow!

This line of reasoning sheds light on the special nature of the sequence of vv.10-14. It has the quality of surprise, vouchsafing a wholly new and unexpected dimension to the plot. All this is indebted to the quite unforeseeable appearance of a woman. The determined intervention of a mother, as despairing as she is courageous, arouses the ruler to take equally unpredictable steps. Rizpah's and David's initiatives in the final sequence enrich the plot, elevating it to a different and higher plane than the bare symmetry of bloodguilt and atonement, as we shall see. Rizpah's wake induces activity in David which brings about a drastic change in the theme of the piece.

The structure of chapter 21:1-14 is rather simple. There are four sequences; the first is alive with disjunctions which almost all change to conjunctions in the fourth. With this about-turn the final sequence's content, though surprising, is still integrated and the unity of the piece is given.[2] Verses 10-14 really do belong to the design. Here are the paragraphs:

– introduction:	the problem and its explanation (v.1abc and 1def) background information on the Gibeonites (v.2bcd)
– exposition:	dialogue between David and the Gibeonites (vv.3-6)
– realisation:	the ritual execution of seven Saulides (vv.7-9)
– surprise:	Rizpah's wake inspires David to conjunctive measures (vv.10-14).

The disjunctions active in this chapter are as follows:

1) God versus Israel, a gulf already yawning in the first three lines. The nation's life is being threatened by a chronic famine and the king, who feels responsible for the well-being of the people, suspects that the catastrophe is a sign of God's anger. This is why he seeks out God as a supplicant, consulting him in v.1c. His suspicions are confirmed; without beating about the bush God himself tells him the reason for his wrath. This piece of information

[2] That is why marking the final sequence with extra white as a separate paragraph, and printing it with its own heading, as McCarter does, are so unfortunate. Besides, his title, 'Rizpah's Vigil', inadequately covers the content since the woman's active presence is restricted to v.10 and the sequence devotes much more space to the consequences of David's part.

enables David to devise a policy which can neutralise the deadly disjunction. David's acting in v.1c is only a reaction to the emergency, but can be valued at the same time as adequate action. This proper initiative of his already gets the plot going in the chapter's third line. The narrator wastes no time!

2) God versus the house of Saul; a disjunction found in v.1e and resulting from God's being the patron deity of the Gibeonite treaty broken by Saul.

3) This is preceded in time by the gulf given with the enmity of the first king towards this Amorite enclave. This disjunction is covered by the first motivating clause, v.1f, whose predicate is highly incriminating for Saul: 'he has killed the Gibeonites.'

4) David has little choice within the God-given parameters, he must seek some form of atonement which itself implies or brings about a disjunction between David and the house of Saul. Gradually the form this disjunction is to take emerges from the dialogue with the injured party. David allows the Gibeonites to kill seven Saulides by way of expiation. He does this, not out of personal enmity or for reasons of political expediency, but because he now has his back to the wall: taking the emergency situation of his own country into consideration and finding himself more or less under duress in the presence of God. This disjunction appears in words in vv.5-6 and becomes reality in vv.8-9.

5) It is intriguing to describe the relationship between Gibeon and its minor sister cities and Israel in terms of dis- and conjunction. In v.2 the barometer of this relationship goes up and down. In 2a the king invites the injured community for a talk, which is a second aspect of conjunction after his consulting God. Interrupting the progress of events for three lines, a notable analepsis follows whereby the omniscient narrator supplies his reader with depth information on the Saul-Gibeon conflict (disjunction 3). In 2b there is an immediate contrast between dis- and conjunction, for 'the Gibeonites were not part of the Israelites, but of the remnant of the Amorites'. Straightaway the contrast plumbs the ambivalence of their existence as an enclave. Do they belong or not? No, not to begin with, or even: essentially no, as v.2b points out in regard to their Amorite blood. 'But the Israelites had sworn to them', continues v.2c, and that means: in the second instance the Gibeonites do belong, as resident aliens it is true, but with a protected status nevertheless.

Lines 2bc have had recourse to the distant past, to the time of the Exodus. They recollect what Joshua 9 reported on the relationship with Gibeon and its surrounding districts. Line v.2d follows chronologically, on the one hand taking us on at least one-and-a half centuries by speaking of Saul, and on the other looking back ten or twenty years (in respect of the reigning David) by staying an analepsis. However, the line's information is fresh; we did not know about Saul's persecuting this enclave near his residence. The predicate of 2d occurring in its usual place, i.e. initially, conveys a dramatic disjunction for the Gibeonites: 'Saul had tried to wipe them out.' The words the narrator has follow on from this, 'in his zeal for the people of Israel and Judah', appreciate the motives of the first king to a certain extent. There is a difference therefore, between this reading and the one given by God in v.2f. What the narrator says ('he had tried to slay them') sounds almost extenuating if we contrast it with the simple and hard *hemīt* of which God accuses Saul. We now gather that not all those suffering persecution have been liquidated. The difference becomes even greater if we construe a chiasmus between motive, deed and result in the said lines:

1e the bloodguilt of Saul	1f because he has killed the Gibeonites
2d he tried to slay them	in his zeal for Israel and Judah

Saul's good intentions are now face to face with God's assessment of them. Notice that the order of result, deed and motive runs exactly counter to the chronology, so that the series begins with God's assessment, bloodguilt. It is not for nothing that we first learn of Saul's Gibeonite persecution from the lips of God. The treaty's patron deity is hard and clear, the narrator introduces nuances; but that does not necessarily mean that his own point of view on the violation of the agreement is a different one. – In the mean time v.2d has taken us back to gulf no.3, the disjunction of death.

6) When the Gibeonite's proposal meets with acceptance by the king the disjunction of death has to be answered by another disjunction of death. David fully agrees to their idea and separates seven male Saulides who are handed over to Gibeon. They are two sons and five grandsons of Saul who are cruelly parted from their mothers who are both mentioned by name. I say cruel because one really does wonder just how many had reached adulthood; a minority I fear. Their being taken away from their mothers is put into an even harsher light by v.7 which places the exception in the initial position: one grandson is spared for a special reason. In long sentences so full of names that the gruesome outcome becomes inevitable we encounter the numerical series of one (saved), and two (sons of Saul) plus five (grandsons) is seven. The series ends with the appearance of the root for 'one' in the text, the *yaḥad* of v.9, but only to indicate one and the same death for all: 'all seven of them perished at the same time'. The boys' being irreversibly torn away like this from the family of Kish and Saul, from the tribe of Benjamin and from the nation are variations of the same disjunction.

7) The final disjunction is of a positive nature and is sustained for a long dry season by the conjunction bringing the real about-turn (which did not appear until now) in the story of catastrophe. The heroic conjunction of Rizpah, consisting of her keeping watch over those hanged, gets the form of a disjunction at the same time through her driving the animals away from the corpses day and night. Only after a period of months does it become apparent that her wake has not been in vain, and that her appearance has stimulated a series of conjunctions which seal those gulfs which can be sealed.

First I would like to run through the text of vv.1-9 looking for characteristics to define the picture given and for textural details worthy of assessment. The first line itself is of immediate significance. The temporal adjunct 'in the days of David' is so general as to reveal the considerable distance between narrator and subject matter. This adjunct is so vague that there is not a single story in the rest of Samuel for which it can do duty. We did, it is true, detect a tendency to achronism and instances of prolepsis in Act X, but those characteristics could not detract from the principle that the life of David is related at close range and, in the main, chronologically. The vagueness of the time adjunct in 21:1 betrays the fact that this story has never been a part of the overall composition. Moreover the piece cannot be inserted without force anywhere prior to this point in II Samuel. This is out of the question now I have demonstrated the typical coherence of the various Acts and sections. The solitary position of 21:1-14 is itself able to serve as part of an argument maintaining that chs.21-24 are an appendix.

The story starts quickly. It does not say: 'it came to pass in the days of David' – followed by another wayyiqtol form reporting some action or another. The *wayhī* of v.1a is more, and line 1a is as a whole more, than just a temporal introduction, because the verb is given a subject straightaway which takes us to the heart of the matter: there is famine. And 1b reinforces this by introducing duration at once: 'three years'. In harmony with this figure the narrator succeeds in getting the word *šānā* into the line three times, by saying 'year after year': without interruption.

In 1c David responds to the emergency's failure to cease by putting a laconic and very direct question to God, literally: 'he sought the face of God'. Due to its transitive aspect this expression is more powerful and more immediate that the *wayyešęb lifnē yhwh* I recollect from 7:18. The narrator forgoes a standard sentence for the asking for an oracle, and wishes to lose no time reporting the way David sought contact and obtained an answer. Moreover he gives the answer straightaway. 'The Lord said to him' and then a two-line speech on the bloodguilt regarding Gibeon follows. Even though still occupied by the introduction, the narrator has thus decided not to report the cause of the calamity himself, but to leave that to the wrathful deity. This is meant to be read as a form of objectivity. The narrator does not toy with his omniscience, he avoids the accusation that he himself is occupied with a theory on the meaning of the famine and prevents potential criticism of the hero, which might run: David, you are trying to appropriate the assertion that God is angry in order to use it as pretext for liquidating growing young rivals from the previous royal family. By having God himself speak the narrator prevents this kind of anti-David claim of false self-legitimisation.

God's information gives David insight into a possible way out of the crisis. He summons and addresses the injured party at once. The quotation formula in v.2a is, however, only an anticipation; the narrator inserts a three line aside for his readers as background information on the peculiar position of the Gibeonites. He postpones the opening of the dialogue until v.3 where he has to begin by resuming the quotation formula.

The 2bcd complex, going way back in history, begins with a timeless nominal clause recording Gibeonite origins. Following this the history of their initial contact with Israel, at the time of the entry under Joshua, is represented by one clause only. Moreover this short line merely reports the other party's committing itself by means of an oath. Again the narrator loses no time; he says nothing on the nature of their first contact or the content of the treaty concluded. This indicates that he assumes his public's acquaintance with the subject matter or text of Josh.9.

The narrator takes a great step in time. In his aside's final clause he himself speaks on Saul's violation of the treaty. Saul's passionately treating the enclave as enemies gets repercussions in the phonetic stratum. There are three verb forms close together, each with a doubled consonant in its centre as in the pi'el,[3] and agreement in vowels and hard plosives. The impression of intensity they create is underlined by the consonants which have these words plus the name of Saul flow into one another in a case of sandhi; notice the 's', the 'l' and the labials at their boundaries: waybaqqe*š* *š*ā'ū*l* *l*^{e}hakkōtā*m* *b*^{e}qannōtō. There is also a semantic similarity between 'to try' and 'to work for'. It is hidden, it is true, in Saul's black and white picture of his world where the life of one collective appears to be served by the death of the other. The fact that the name Israel is now suddenly part of the 'Israel and Judah' duo and has thus received a slightly altered meaning, might be a hint of the narrator's that the unity Saul wants to serve is itself not particularly well-

[3] The first and the third forms are, in fact, true pi'el forms, whilst the infinitive in between is a hiph'il.

forged; disquieting in view of the originally apparently comfortable dichotomy of Israel versus the Amorites. The successor to the zealous Saul is at any rate going to behave very differently towards these resident aliens! He politely sends for them and relates to them as the inquiring party. The contrast between David and Saul can also be seen from the differences between the *waybaqqeš* of one (v.1c, entreating God) and that of the other (which is out for death 2d).

The explanation of the famine as God's wrath turns the tables radically indeed. Saul's dedication to his people meant, he thought, killing the Gibeonites. Over the years this leads to a development whereby David can do his best for his starving people only by choosing, respectfully, to take sides with the Gibeonites and abandoning descendants of Saul to death. With a telling and loaded word the king calls this atonement.

The second sequence systematically consists of the spoken word. The talks alternate with each other such that David begins as the inquiring party, gives an undertaking in the middle, and at the end voices his consent. The Gibeonites speak twice in between, first two then four lines. Here is an overview of the alternating series:

– David: two questions plus one goal	3 lines, 3bcd
– Gibeonites; two negative nominal clauses	2 lines, 4bc
– David transforms his question into an undertaking	1 line, 4e
– Gibeonites: a bitter period, the decisive proposal	4 lines, 5c-6b
– David agrees without reservation	1 line, 6d

When the tribal leaders in Josh.9:20a spoke of 'what we will do to them', it indicated the oath's protection and the importance of preventing 'wrath'. Now that wrath has burst out anyway the David of v.3b has to use similar words in a very different sense (that of atonement): 'what shall I do for you?' One *ma* question is explained by the other, 'how shall I make expiation?' And the line on his objective, v.3d, reveals how much the ruler has to give way before the resident aliens: 'so that you may bless the LORD's own people'. The damage and persecution the Gibeonites have suffered lie as a curse on the nation which they are part of.

The Gibeonites do not yield straightaway. Noticing Saul's successor adopting a positive attitude is a big change for them. Negotiations are now underway and having listened to the ruler's question they do not commit themselves at once. Their reply to the two *ma* questions is evasive, having nominal clauses dominated by a double *ʾēn lānū*. This negative anaphora makes 4bc into a parallelism. In both cases the negative is used succinctly; the Gibeonites are not concerned about property they do not have, but about having a claim, and this involves a special use of the word *’ayin*. The proper rendering is not simple, because the second negative functions very differently from the first. A good translation, it seems to me, is: ‘To us this business regarding Saul and his house is not a question of silver and gold, and it is not for us to kill anyone in Israel.’[4] Their first line speaks of ‘Saul and his house’ as God did in v.1e, but using the pair ‘gold and silver’ states that it is not a matter of loss of property and compensation. The following negation functions in a different way. In 4c they make it seem as if they have no need of revenge against any Israelite whatsoever. For it is politically judicious and a token of circumspection, to begin by saying to a king of a different people: we do not want to kill any of his subjects. First we will just wait and find out what he, David, does next, think the Gibeonites, and then we shall see.

There is little David can do with these denials. They force him a step further. If he wishes to draw the resident aliens out and receive a practicable answer, he will have to make concessions or take measures which will give them a feeling of security. The narrator makes a virtuoso move: he has David apparently put the same question as in 3b, but two words have now been added, transforming the question into something quite different:

4e *ma ’attęm ’ōm^{e}rīm ’ę‘ę̆śę̄ lākęm*

3b *ma ’ę‘ę̆śę̄ lākęm.*

The criterion is no longer David’s wanting to do something, but what the interlocutors have to say on the question. Their opinion is now the point of gravity according to the speaker. With this 4e has been made into an assent. The proper translation recognises the shift in David’s position and runs: ‘Whatever you say I will do for you.’[5] With this the Gibeonites get the opportunity to put forward their conditions for the return of good relations – what David in 3d still called ‘blessing Yahweh’s inheritance’. What the king says borders on the granting of a mandate. This is apparent from the sequel; this one sentence is enough for the Gibeonites and now they fire away.

Quantity is a reliable indication of where the dialogue’s centre of gravity lies: in vv.5-6, the Gibeonite’s second turn to speak. It consists of four loaded lines, two on the great collective suffering of the day before yesterday, two on

[4] According to the NBG. Still shorter, but having the same interpretation of (the difference between the one and the other) *’ayin* is the KBS with: ‘We do not want silver and gold, and we cannot put someone to death in Israel.’ Notice how the *’īš* of 4c is placed opposite Saul in the JPS rendering: ‘We have no claim for silver or gold against Saul and his household; and we have no claim on the life of any *other* man in Israel’ (italics mine, JF). I find this too specific.

[5] According to KBS, NBE, JPS. For the question as to the syntax of 3b (is it interrogative? One or two clauses?) and different renderings of it, see App.I.

the deadly compensation of tomorrow. The lines from 5bc and 6a are, it is true, kept together under one syntactic arch, but the relief or the progress of this period is halting and fragmentary, under pressure from great emotion and an indignation which is alive and kicking. Verse 5b is a *casus pendens*, 5c succeeds it asyndetically and is the fleshing out of Saul's heinous plans (the *dmh* of 5b), but can be understood totally apart from its immediate context. The passive nature of this clause is the exact complement of the active forms of 5b, which stand for Saul's policy of persecution. The change comes with the main clause 6a, which is also still uttered in the passive and continues the internal rhyme of the suffix for 'us'. But once the Gibeonites get their hands on the representatives of the house of Saul their only active form follows in 6b, the very verb denoting the horrifying execution, a special and ritual form of hanging.[6]

In their first reply the Gibeonites had answered David's *lākęm* with the term *lānū* (twice). Their second answer prolongs this and transfers the negation to Saul. Their first line, 5b, succeeds in a virtuoso way in having *lānū* heard twice, in *killānū ... dimmā lānū*. These verbs, an assonating pair thanks to the pi'el, are the core of the two short relative clauses, which, themselves a striking parallelism within the *casus pendens*, characterise the previous king. The Gibeonites are still so shocked and pained by his persecuting that they avoid mentioning his name and temporarily refer to him scornfully as 'the man who'. His name does not appear until the end of the speech, but it is then subjected to sarcasm. What Saul has caused and launched in the way of destruction, is, as it were, frozen in a perfect on *-nū* in 5c which is factual and reportorial and is illustrated by a negative complement (*min* is exclusive): 'we have been exterminated, so there is nowhere for us to live in the territory of Israel'. In 5b the speakers were the grammatical object, now their status as victims is to be found in the passive form of the verb. Instead of a perfect the reader had expected an infinitive linking up with *dimmā* here. The choice of the finite form and the past tense underlines the fact that the suffering has actually been inflicted; it is a fact which is not to be gainsaid.

A third (fifth) *lānū* now follows which is the only positive one; it is going to decide the case, v.6a. The Gibeonites want to get control over a number of

[6] The material of the root **yq'* is too scarce for more exact pronouncements. For example it cannot be determined whether this form of execution implied impaling or crucifixion or another specific and torturing form of hanging. The most relevant parallel is the reference in Num.25:4, with the designation of the public nature of the punishment, the adjunct *nęgęd haššęmęš*. The qal produces the well-known reference in Gen.32 on the spraining of Jacob's hip joint. The three references to revulsion (qal imperf. *tq'* + *nfš*, Jer.6:8 and Ezek.23:17sq.) offer no key.

descendants of the treaty's violator and ask for seven men – apparently a round figure to underline the seriousness and sacral nature of the matter. As satisfaction this plural of *'ănāšīm* alone can make up for the crimes of *hā'īš* (sc. Saul). The final line exhibits precision by having three proper nouns and an adjunct of place. The proper noun of the God of Israel even appears twice; firstly in all seriousness as the witness of the execution, then in the sarcastic adjunct which calls Saul 'the chosen of Yahweh'. The Gibeonites know that they have been included in the inheritance of this deity for generations, but hint at ambiguity towards him with this scathing qualification of their murderer occupying the sensitive position of the end of the speech. The term *b^eḥīr yhwh* is unique to the Former Prophets and probably originates from poetic diction.[7] These aspects only make the sting in the tail sharper. The proper noun Saul has been relegated on the lips of the speakers insofar as it merely functions as part of an adjunct of place. It is true, nevertheless, that this phrase, 'in Gibeah of Saul', together with 'on the mountain of Saul', does contain a vengeful sting. The injured party does not want to hold the execution on its own territory, but on the site of their persecutor's previous residence of all places. This causes the retributive aspect to become apparent in the punishment. The execution has, moreover, nothing to do with their own cult or with the sanctuary in Gibeon.[8]

The element *'īš l^ehāmīt b^eyiśrā'el* from the end of their first speech has undergone a reversal in the first part of their second speech to '*hā'īš* / who destroyed us / in the territory of Israel'.[9] These lines, 5bc, (with 6 + 5 words) are in the past tense. The second half, v.6ab (with 5 + 6 words), has the future forms of tomorrow and contains the compensatory reversal which is a form of sacral *talio*. The request for men to be hung also enters into a relationship

[7] The phrase 'the chosen of the Lord' is unique. The word *b^eḥīr* occurs twelve times elsewhere, exclusively in poetry and each time with a suffix referring to God: six times in Deutero-Isaiah, five times in the Psalms and in I Chron.16:13 (which is inspired by Ps.105). Barthélemy writes in CT p.301 on the intention of v.6b: 'Il s'agit, dans la bouche des Gabaonites, de l'expression sadique du mépris ajoutant aux délices de la vengeance.' And somewhat prior to this, on the designation 'Gibéa de Saül l'élu du Seigneur': 'S'ils nomment cette ville sous son titre le plus orgueilleux, c'est pour dire que ce sera la gloire de la royauté abolie de la famille de Saül que ce supplice doit flétrir à jamais.'

[8] That is why it is not true to the text to trot out elaborate data on Gibeon's sanctuary and cult, and to give a Canaanite ritual reading of the chapter in other respects too as H. Cazelles does in 'David's Monarchy and the Gibeonite Claim' (II Sam. xxi, 1-14), Palestine Exploration Quarterly 1955, pp.165-175.

[9] The reversal can readily be observed in the contrast between the highly indeterminate *'īš* of v.4c, and the highly determined *hā'īš* referring to one man in v.5b.

with v.4c. It enables us to determine the special nuance of the *'ēn lānū* there. The Gibeonites' negation does not refer to a claim, but states their not being in a position, or having the right, to kill. Upon being offered the chance by the king, thus gaining the position of being able to execute after all, they really do turn out to have a claim. But for David this is no surprise, since he had been able to gather as much from God's word.

David answers as shortly as possible with 'I shall give'. The ellipse of the object is a sign of complete agreement. The choice of *'ętten* reveals how important the word *yuttan* was in the v.6ab proposal. At the same time the king replaces the Gibeonite's hoph'al with his own qal form. The passive form, since it does not name the subject who gives, fails to lay down responsibility. This is a diplomatic avoidance of the speakers. David is so frank as to take the responsibility upon himself, and the quasi-redundant *'ănī* before the predicate serves to underline this. The narrator confirms the position of David with the predicate of v.9a: 'he delivered them (*wayyitt^{e}nem*) into the hand of the Gibeonites'. But he concurs still more with the other party, because the succession of 'he gave them ... and they hung them' in 9ab copies this verb combination from the Gibeonites' speech, in which the forms were volitive. The wish of 6ab is mirrored in the realisation of 9ab.

Verses 7-9 form sequence no.3: the implementation of the proposal, the execution. We observe that it is not up to the king to enforce the actual punishment. The fact that the Gibeonites, the party who requested satisfaction, do the hangman's work themselves underlines the case is a matter of *talio*. The only factor David can exert influence upon now is the extradition. This is particularly perceptible because the exception in v.7 occurs first: the spared Mephibosheth. The prepositions *'al ... 'al* of being spared plus reason create a contrast between this verse and the negative pair, v.1ef, in which the same prepositions served an accusation plus reason. Using an adjunct (v.7b, eleven words) longer than the core of the sentence (v.7a, eight words) the narrator ensures that the pro-Mephibosheth choice is not the personal arbitrariness of a David who has to do the horrible work of a life or death selection. It is carefully established that he is bound by the contract with his close friend Jonathan, of which I 20 had reported.[10] The sacral nature of that agreement is laid down by means of the name *yhwh* (and resumed from I 20),

[10] At the same time this Gibeon-Saul affair gives depth and existential relevance to the proviso stipulated by Jonathan that David was not to leave his line in the lurch when he became king. This proviso from I 20:15 (where the positive content of the *lō takrīt 'ęt ḥasd^{e}kā* masks the alternative of the *hakrīt* of other Saulides by David) comes into operation and binds David.

in combination with the word 'oath'. This root and the status of v.7b as an express reminder form a link with the swearing in v.2c in the heart of the extensive first analepsis. The link creates an analogy. Just as the Gibeonite enclave has become a minority in post-entry political reality and is protected by an oath of the surrounding majority against arbitrariness or persecution, so the Jonathan branch (and in concrete terms mainly Mephibosheth), as part of the dynasty which has lost, is protected by an oath of the new king. But at the same time the contrast is given that Saul broke the first oath, whilst David honours his covenant with Jonathan and applies it. David's ruling, to give the Gibeonites their satisfaction with regard to the house of Saul, leads to the diminishing of that contrast.

The honouring of the second oath (which oath was mentioned in 7b) is part of the restoration of the first. That is why I draw the analogy somewhat more, developing this association: just as Mephibosheth became crippled in an accident which was tied in with the downfall of his father and king Saul, his grandfather, on Mount Gilboa, so the Gibeonite enclave is crippled through Saul's doing. One could also express the analogy in terms of relationships. To the left of Mephibosheth stands Saul whose doom spreads metonymically to Mephibosheth (in the form of paralysis); on his right stands Jonathan whose intimate friendship with David saves Mephibosheth's life during the Gibeon crisis. This person's analogue on a community level is the Gibeonite enclave. To the left are the persecution and the losses which the enclave suffers due to Saul's side and which one could read as a metonymy of the doom resting on the king. On the right stands the chosen king David who, thanks to divine information, returns to the terms of the treaty which protected Gibeon. The sparing of Mephibosheth is analogous to the indemnification of Gibeon, both acts are required by an oath.

The identical ending of the lines in v.7 underlines David's gauge, 'Jonathan the son of Saul'. After these two lines of saving follow two lines of being earmarked for death. Actually they form one vast sentence (of 27 words!), but it can easily be shared out between the two sons of Rizpah and the five sons of Saul's oldest daughter Merab.[11] We now hear two mothers mentioned by name, and they receive even more attention in relative clauses with *'ăšer yālᵉdā* plus the name of the husband. Partly as a result of this four successive lines (vv.7-8) bristle with proper nouns. In this way the narrator creates the impression of accurate chronicling.

[11] Like so many others I too see myself forced to restore the name Merab at the place where the MT has Michal; see also Appendix I.

Verse 9ab is, as has been mentioned, the implementation of 6ab and contains, in view of the subjects, the co-operation of David and the Gibeonites. This pair of lines with the seven as object is quickly followed by pair 9cd, in which two intransitive predicates shed light on the seven's becoming victims: 'they fell ... they were put to death.' The place adjuncts of 9b are variants of and sequels to those of 6b, in which the locations and the addressee (i.e. the patron deity) alternate chiastically:

6b we want to hang them / *lyhwh* / on the Hill of Saul

9b they hanged them / on the mountain / *lifnē yhwh*

Lines 9b and 9d are also complementary because they attend to the execution's co-ordinates of place and time, adding these adjuncts to their predicates, which have the complementariness of hoph'al and hiph'il. The contrast between the numbers seven and one (in 9c) impresses upon us how unanimous and unnaturally simultaneous the final hour of the seven young men is.

Excursus on the relationship between 21:7 and ch.9

Does the story or the subject matter of II 21 belong before or after the chapter in which Mephibosheth receives a place at the court of king David? Or is there a third alternative? A variant of the first question is: can we accommodate this text somewhere else in II Samuel where it has its natural place?

a) Suppose that the event in II 21 and the sparing of Mephibosheth according to v.7 go with Mephibosheth's admittance into the court in ch.9. This option can be easily disputed. Chapter 21:7 presupposes that Mephibosheth is in the vicinity or is available; and something similar to this applies to the children of Rizpah and Merab. These circumstances are scarcely concordant with David's question opening ch.9. The king looks around him and for the time being there is no sign of a Saulide anywhere. Via (the knowledge and assistance of) someone else Mephibosheth has to be fetched from afar. The question 'is there anyone left of the house of Saul?' is conceivable, albeit cynical, after the blow of 21:8-9, but it is not conceivable after the sequence 21:7-9. According Mephibosheth a place of honour in ch.9 in view of the covenant with Jonathan would also be a peculiar duplication in regard of the sparing according to 21:7. Could it be that one overlaps the other in some way or another?

b) Suppose that the chronology was: first II 9, then II 21. This is more troublesome to rule out. Nevertheless in 21:8 the availability of the seven is no problem and this is something which hardly links up with David's searching in 9:1. There is a temporal aspect which raises a problem. Mephibosheth was five years old when his father fell in battle according to 4:4. Nothing in ch.9 points to the fact that he is still a child; what he says reveals a certain political maturity which indicates adulthood rather, and if the note on his son Micha in 9:12 is not a prolepsis, then this verse proves he has been sexually mature for some time. Now suppose that Mephibosheth was 20 years of age and had a little boy of two years old when he was taken to Jerusalem. This would mean he arrives fifteen years after the battle on Mount Gilboa. This is hardly in line with the Gibeon crisis which has been inherited from the previous reign and broke out early, rather than later, in David's reign. The Hebron period is already over since we may assume that the whereabouts of Saul's family during this period was in the kingdom of Ishbosheth. It is therefore hazardous to date the Gibeon crisis after the establishment of Mephibosheth at court.

c) Such historiographical arithmetic does not lead to great certainty. A more reliable method is to look at the passages themselves, at their style and structure. The organisation of sections III (I now refer to II Sam.2-8) and IV (or rather its Acts in II 9-20) is such that there is no room for the story of II 21 anywhere else. Act IX is hermetically closed, its concentric structure averts insertions. Act X links up closely with it and has its own thematics which are just as intolerant of the inclusion of II 21. Such considerations also hold good for Acts XII and XIII. Only between chs.9 and 10 are we able to include the subject matter of II 21 if the worst comes to the worst. But the distance implied by the data of v.1ab and v.12cd prevents this, and v.7b would be redundant immediately after ch.9.

d) It is not wise to let ourselves get caught up in the false dilemma of whether the Gibeon affair took place before or after the lame man's arrival at court. I suspect that we must adopt an entirely different course, maintaining that II 21 is an independent passage forming no part of the great design. In 11 21 we find a national crisis report standing by itself, peopled by many characters and drawing a number of lines that represent the ambivalent relationships between the house of Saul and the house of David. It is conceivable that the subject matter was known to the writer of sections II and III. I imagine he extracted one detail out of all that material, i.e. the sparing of Mephibosheth, because he could superlatively open a subplot in section IV with it. He allows only the meeting between David and Mephibosheth in ch.9 to be seen, omitting entirely the historical background – the national crisis resulting from the Gibeon affair. Whatever the case might be it is a fact that section IV, 'King David', opened and closed in an ingenious way with two scenes which themselves are the beginning and ending of two interwoven trios, as worked out in my *King David*. One series of three units deals with the positive theme *ḥęsęd* and is manned by David, Ziba and Mephibosheth; the other series of three units is the negative series David versus Shimei. Intertwined with one another in II 16 and 19 the two series provide a complete picture of the ceaseless ambivalence characterising David's relationship with the previous royal family. It consists of personal moments and unique encounters. In contradistinction to this the aim of II 21 is national from the outset. The chapter – according to the end of my § 1 – results, moreover, in another view on the relationships between the two royal families and in a definitive atonement. That is why its place towards the end of the books of Samuel, in an appendix, is correct, or at least better than any other position.

Line 9d bears signs of the overview which the omniscient narrator enjoys in his flashback. It is striking that one moment in time has to be mentioned three times, with increasing precision. The beginning is vague, 'days of harvest', and the plural 'first' which follows does not yet reveal which harvest it is; after which the three words of a double semikut provide elucidation: 'at the beginning of the barley harvest'.[12] This elaboration is not a sign of unwieldiness, but is out to say something. What? Paradoxically the end of the story is not the end but conceals a beginning. Let me explain this.

[12] He who takes the similarity of 'first' and 'beginning' seriously, will detect a certain symmetry throughout the six words; if not an abc-cba, then in any case an ab-ba, of the four words in the middle.

As I mentioned previously the plot has come to an end with the final line of v.9. If vv.1-9 was all that had been handed down to us we would have looked upon it as self-contained unit. The surprise Rizpah is to give David and the reader cannot be predicted beforehand. If we subject v.9d to close reading, we do, however, notice signs which point beyond the completion. The words 'in the days of the harvest' enter into a chiasmus with the opening clause of the story which also gives a quasi-date, 'famine in the days of ... '. Initially this cross ways construction appears to be the framework of the unit and, as a figure of inversion, to point to the end of the emergency. But this barley harvest is, at it were, vacuous, because the land still groans under the regimen of the chronic draught. The term 'barley harvest' is reduced to the purely temporal, since barley grains have been absent from the fields for a long time. The choice of this term for the execution's entry in the calendar is nasty regarding the starving people, a cruel joke almost. And after nine verses we are still in the grip of uncertainty – there being no evidence in the text itself that God's wrath really does cease after the expiation demanding death. The passage is not as rounded off as it looks.

Nevertheless the striking contrast between famine and harvest suggests a ray of hope. There is more text to come – an entire sequence – and the term 'the beginning of the harvest' has returned quickly to be linked to the unexpected appearance of the mourning mother. But what is even stronger than this is the reference in the same line, v.10b, to water and heaven; in Hebrew one word is completely taken up into the other. How and when will God's abode (the *šāmayim*) release life-giving water (*mayim*) again? Amplifying 'harvest' metonymically I wonder: can there ever be fruitfulness in and for the land? Has Rizpah got something to do with the promise of bread hidden in the notion of harvest?

Verse 10, and v.10 only, is for this mother: three out of a total of thirty-seven lines. But what a surprise, what an intensity, and what a gruesome spectacle. First there is a short line, in which the narrator shows the woman with the attribute which characterises her best at this time: the cloth of mourning. She is active: she takes it and spreads it out. The place is now called 'the rock', and we gather: this stay is going to be hard, very hard. Rizpah places herself, for a long period, in a pure hell. The moment we allow our imagination to dwell on the details of her situation, we recoil: the bodies just hang there, exposed to the elements. The stench and the sight of decay can hardly be borne by an outsider let alone a relative – and Rizpah is a mother who, day in day out, week in week out, is forced to experience this with her own children! The horror defies description, and the narrator does not describe it either.[13]

What is driving Rizpah, or better: what is enabling her to keep up this stay whilst hardly getting any sleep because of constantly keeping the animals away? I do not think her keeping going is due to solidarity and motherhood alone (as the closest form of kinship), but to an iron will as well. She is not only motivated by the forces of yesterday and today (motherhood), but also by the decision to defy the present (the animals!) with an eye to the goal of tomorrow. This aim is a decent burial for all seven Saulides, their guarantee of true repose. Otherwise they would be dumped in a ravine as carrion for the wild beasts; a natural sequel to execution and one which threatens day in day out. To be thrown away and torn apart just like criminals would mean no rest for the soul, the *nęfęš*, in the underworld. This is the final end looming over the lives of the seven, which is why Rizpah has come to fight for essentials.

I ascertain that she does not dare, shortly after her arrival, to take down the dead from their stake or gallows, in an attempt to give them a grave of some kind herself. If Rizpah had had a chance to do this then she would surely have done so. But her failure to take such action reveals her knowing it is out of the question. We can thus infer that a special expiatory procedure peculiar to this execution was the bodies' having to be exposed to the elements for a long time. Rizpah accepts this as the final limit beyond which she may not go. At the same time, however, her intervention is somewhat touch and go. Perhaps it was even a calculated risk of hers to hope that the government or the Gibeonites would not prevent her from keeping away the animals and scoring out the stigma of criminality. After all's said and done this undertaking of hers took the authorities by surprise. How far could they afford to let her go? They did not dare to make a scene with a screaming and kicking mother being rudely dragged away from her children.

After the concise opening, 10a, I see two very long sentences; they derive their length from a series of three or even four merismuses which have not yet been considered in the discussion on rain from heaven:

[13] The hard and gruesome side of the spectacle is got rid of and smoothed over in the reading of N. Poulssen, 'An Hour with Rispah, Some Reflections on II Sam.21,10', pp.185-211 of AOAT 211, = Festschrift for J.P.M. van der Ploeg, Neukirchen-Vluyn 1982. The horror and cruelty is ruined by high but unreal ideas on 'womanhood and motherhood' to which he imputes the monopoly of 'depth of feeling'. Poulssen almost waxes lyrical on the 'chtonic essence of her being' and 'the telluric sensibility of the mother image', too easily employs oppositions such as 'the man's world and the woman's world' or 'the sphere of ethos as opposed to the sphere of pathos' and even goes so far as to write (p.201) that 'she is in her element there on the mountain top'. Fertility, archetypes, 'the inescapable forces of water, blood and earth' fascinate Poulssen in a Jungian way; he also is of the opinion that Rizpah is performing a rain ceremony.

10b wattaṭṭēhū lāh ’ęl haṣṣūr mitt^{e}ḥillat qāṣīr
'ad nittak mayim 'ălēhęm min haššāmayim
10c w^{e}lō nāt^{e}nā 'ōf haššāmayim lānū^{a}ḥ 'ălēhęm yōmām
w^{e}’ęt ḥayyat haśśādę̄ laylā

In the last line the complementary pair 'the birds in the air' and 'the wild beasts of the field' works smoothly with the merismus of time, 'by day'/'by night'. But there is a pair from nature in 10b too, viz. the rocks versus the water. They enter into an opposition with each other and both take on associative and symbolic relationships with their surroundings. The rock stands for hardness, death and barrenness, the water for softness, life, harvest and growth. Once more the careful work of the narrator becomes apparent; this pair forms a chiasmus with the heaven and the field of v.10c.

I have not mentioned the most important merismus yet. It consists of two time adjuncts in 10b. They require so many words that line 10b becomes recognisable as the successor to 9d, the provisional ending; but at the same time we notice that the barley harvest, which stood alone in 9d, has now received a complement: the coming of the rain. The merismus is marked by the prepositions *min* and *'ad* which create an arc of tension 'from the beginning of the harvest until the water poured itself out over them from heaven'. In two fundamental aspects there is a lot of confusion on the latter term. Whose point of view is covered by the clause on water? That of the narrator or that of the character Rizpah? And does this temporal adjunct refer to the rains which do not set in until October/November, or to an exceptional shower in the early summer, which Rizpah wrests from God because her behaviour quickly mollifies him? I see many signs in the passage which, in both cases, argue in favour of the first and against the second option.[14]

The long time designation requiring eight words in 10b is, just as in 9b, a sign of the kind of overview enjoyed by the omniscient narrator. The mention of the rains is not Rizpah's point of view. She is not sitting on the rock in order to extort rain through magic power but, as the passage itself says, to make sure that the dead are left intact. It is neither her responsibility nor her concern nor intent to turn back the country's affliction.[15] This is a matter for the king; it is his task. If one views the adjunct of the coming of the rains as a sign of Rizpah's perspective, then her act becomes strongly associa-

[14] If the end of 10b were to represent Rizpah's point of view, it would require the rendering that she stayed on the rock 'until such time as the water would pour down', etc.

[15] Against Poulssen, art.cit. pp.198-206. The text of 21:10 does not mention a single act which might have the faintest chance of being part of a rain ceremony. The cloth which she spreads out is an attribute of mourning, and the fending off of animals is the protection of the relatives.

ted with David's policy; she could have been hired by the ruler to speedily complete the procedure by magic for the starving country. This interpretation does serious harm to the unforeseen, the original, and the highly surprising nature of her deed. Rizpah really is not an instrument of the king's policy or of a collaboration between David and the Gibeonites. Neither is it a matter of performing a rain ritual. Her responsibility is first to her own two sons and the five relatives. This area of responsibility is exactly covered by the field of her attention, for months on end.

When did the rain fall? If one says: early, then Rizpah's wake lasted only a few weeks, if one says: in the autumn, then she spent the entire stretch of the dry season on Mt. Gibeah from *c.* May to October! I do not believe that just because isolated showers of rain *might* actually sporadically occur in May or June one is to be found in our passage. If the narrator had really wanted to say this he could have, and should have, chosen plain terms for it, and they fail to appear in the text. I also notice that the narrator does not use such language as: then God gave rain and lightning, as in I Sam.7 or 12. Instead we encounter the niph'al of *ntk*, a reflexive-passive form which draws attention rather to the natural rhythm of the seasons and the normal time of rain. Moreover 10bc is swarming with terms from nature. Rizpah's wake is encircled by rock and field, air and birds and animals, and on the time scale is delineated by the natural terms (the qualifiers of a farming community) of the (empty!) harvest time as the beginning, and the coming of the life-giving water in the autumn, as the end. Besides, the water which after all 'normally falls' during the autumn, is a gift of God, and its coming is (of course) for David a sign that the atonement for the blood-guilt incurred against Gibeon has been accepted by God. But the narrator does not position the end of divine wrath after verse 9 or 10 as it so happens, but at the end of sequence vv.10-14 in which David has resumed his role as actantial subject. The significance of this late report we shall see presently.

It fits within the great succinctness and sobriety of that single verse devoted to Rizpah, that the narrator summarises the entire duration of Rizpah's wake by means of the merismus of time in v.10b. Her presence is the most staggering conjunction of the story and ensures, a hot season long, the preventive disjunction (the warding off of the animals) which is the final instance of disjunction. Surveying the whole I allot to Rizpah's single verse the place or link with, or introduction to, the final sequence which turns to David again.

As unforeseen and original as it was, the mother's appearance formed no part of the agreement reached by the king and the Gibeonites. But it does in turn inspire *David* to doing something which is equally unexpected and is even less conceivable as part of the atonement arrangements. He has the bones of Saul and Jonathan who perished in battle fetched from the city which had taken the trouble, and summoned up the piety, to remove their bodies from the Beth-Shan zone after the catastrophe. He also has the bones of the seven collected and sent along[16] as part of a new and definitive interment for Saul and Jonathan which he gives the extremely suitable location of ancestor Kish's grave. David devotes the utmost care to this burial, as the words 'all that the king had commanded' of 14b imply.

The transitiveness of his effort completes a series of the verb 'to take' which places life and death, decided upon by men, around the mourning of a woman:

8sq.	'the king took the two (...) and the five ...' and delivered them up to death
10a	'Rizpah took a cloth' and with it marked the rock as the place of her mourning
12sqq.	'David took the bones of Saul and Jonathan' and gave them, together with the seven, their real resting place in the family grave in Benjamin.

The many place adjuncts from v.14a ensure rest, completion, and satisfaction after the place adjuncts of 6b//9b which documented so precisely the place of the gruesome deed. After long wanderings Saul finally lies between 'his father' and 'his son' who are both so designated in relation to the first king, but also keep their proper nouns in v.14a.

Then the final line follows, along with the remarkable timing of its content: 'God responded to the plea of the land thereafter.' Firstly the very last clause, together with the very first, attends to the framing of the whole. As designations of the catastrophe and the about-turn of God they mark at the same time the outermost limits of the plot. Secondly it is important to be aware of where this divine forgiveness of, or compassion towards, the nation does *not* occur: not at the end of v.9, where it would have been a response to the execution, and not at the end of v.10, where it would have signified a direct response to Rizpah's wake and a reward for her courage. The fact that the narrator does not put this playing hard to get [of God] until after David's series of acts, and that he underlines this special location with the unique placing of *'aḥărē ken* at the end of the clause, leads me, thirdly, to the conclusion that God did not actually decide to end the period of punishment

[16] I am of the opinion, therefore, in respect of 13b plus 14a that the remains of the seven hanged are placed next to the bones of the king and his son, even though the text of 14a on this is elliptic. If one assumes another use of the grave the transport from Jabesh would then be a separate operation, which would seriously affect the sense of the final sequence. See also App.1.

of the famine until there was the added weight of David's creative and conjunctive act as his response to Rizpah's wake. I thus arrive at the following reconstruction of the temporal ordering of what happened in the autumn: a) Rizpah kept up her wake just as long as the bodies on the mountain swung there, far into the autumn, b) the autumn rains fell, so that David, who had of course been aware for a long time of what Rizpah was doing knew that God's anger had really subsided and that the atonement procedure was successful and complete. He had perhaps been appalled and deeply impressed by Rizpah's dedication, but as long as the nation suffered he could not take any measures himself yet. But now the rains had come he could c) blow the final whistle on the phase of exposure, and even though he might have confined himself to this he went one step further in honour of Rizpah and d) organised one solemn and comprehensive state funeral for the nine. The plot had the appearance of being finished at the end of v.9, in reality the denouement is not possible until the humane policy of David, which bestows recognition and compassion on the whole house of Saul.[17]

All the disjunctions from the beginning which could possibly be repaired have now indeed been replaced by conjunctions. David has taken the adversity and the accusation of the Gibeonites seriously. This enclave has obtained satisfaction and can take its place in the nation as a whole again, for the oath and the agreement have demonstrated their validity. God is reconciled with all parties and gives the country rain. And the disjunction between the house of David and the house of Saul, inherent in the original situation and a given in the necessity of David's action concerning the blood-guilt can now, by an even greater conjunction, be dismissed as a pluperfect tense. David has understood the message of atonement and also applied it to his own alternatives and policy, even though not obliged to do so. For him the catalyst was the unique step of Rizpah the woman and mother, her iron will and passion-

[17] This is my interpretation, since this is what (the style and structure of) the text says. In this way I keep analysis and exegesis separate from ideological criticism. Walter Brueggemann confuses these two in his 'suspicious reading' (the words are his) of II 21, in his article '2 Samuel 21-24: An Appendix of Deconstruction?', in CBQ 50 (1988) pp.383-397. He construes an opposition public data/private information and with it undermines the omniscience of the narrator, who has something cleared up by God himself in v.1 which, as far as human beings are concerned can never be anything other than an interpretation (blood-guilt > famine). So Brueggemann undermines the oracle and puts forward 'the possibility that in fact David kills Saul's family, but provided a rationale by blaming Saul, for which there is no public evidence'. Brueggemann also confuses literary observations and historical conjectures in a sentence like: 'the blame, attribution, and justification all rest on a private communication to David, which at the most came to him through his hired priestly functionaries' (both quotations from p.386).

ate faithfulness. These factors inspired him to pay tribute to the deceased Saulides together: the conjunction of the family grave.

The relation between the first and the second royal house is assigned more importance in the text than the Gibeon affair. A final round through the chapter, which starts at verse 12, indicates a third case of analepsis, and ends up in a network stretched out by a series of analogies. When the narrator has told us of David's contact with the city of Jabesh, he systematically keeps on going further back into the past, via a first- and second-degree relative clause, 12cd, and an extra temporal adjunct in 12d. If we read v.12 from back to front the original chronology emerges: the Philistines defeated Saul on Mount Gilboa, hanging him up with Jonathan up on the wall of Beth-Shan, but at night his body was secretly removed by the Jebusites who now, at least ten years later, are approached by David. In terms of genesis this comprehensive recall effected by 12cd does point to the chapter's being an independent passage and not a part of the great design. But the analysis uses the terms of poiesis and its task is to define the structural place and contribution of the flashback of Saul's downfall. The connection with the two other cases of analepsis is then of importance.

A series of analogies now arises as a sequel to the first (the exceptional positions of Gibeon and of Mephibosheth) which has already been discussed.[18] Analogy no.2 says: just as the uncircumcised enemy has hung king Saul and his son publicly and ignominiously on the wall of Beth-Shan, so the non-Israelite enclave of Gibeon, which has been treated with hostility by Saul, has got the chance to publicly punish seven Saulides with a special, ritual and ignominious form of hanging. So the fate of the seven is a posthumous sign of the doom of king Saul, since it becomes a part of Saul's adversity, thanks to metonymy, within the real webs of meaning stretched by this story's own means. The report of the name Gilboa, which occurs in the Bible only in connection with the death of Saul in battle, creates a series of three names with a common root: Gibeon, Gibeah, Gilboa. The trio invites the reader to consider the relationship between the catastrophes which these three, all of them high, places get to see and on the Saulidic meanings of this correlation. Restricting myself to one exercise I rewrite the series in chronological order: Gibeon, Gilboa, Gibeah. The hidden suggestion emanating from the analogy of the hanging is that the Philistines' sacrilegious treatment of Saul's body can on a providential level be partly reduced, and is a retributive response, to Saul's bloody violation of the treaty which protected

[18] The systematic character of the narrator's use of analepses and analogies in this text makes me extremely suspicious of the usual ukase of a large number of exegetes, as if v.7 could be secondary – see for example McCarter p.442, who throws verse 7 out of 'the original account'.

the Gibeonites. But the analogy particularly shows Saul's adversity is not over at his death, being a monster which looms up unexpectedly years later to throttle his descendants in the iron grip of retribution.

A smaller but more attractive analogy which arises thanks to the analepsis of v.12c is the treatment of the maltreated bodies by the Jabeshites and Rizpah. The Jabeshites have to slip through enemy lines to take away the maltreated bodies of Saul and Jonathan; a perilous journey which reveals their loyalty and dedication. Rizpah accomplishes the impossible by protecting the maltreated bodies of the seven a whole hot season long on her own. But that action was just as open to danger, for by this she systematically chipped away at the exposure of the bodies, which was an indispensable part of the punishment. I suspect that both the Gibeonites and David originally watched closely and with great anxiety what the woman came to do and I explain the fact of their leaving her alone in spite of everything as something partly due to embarrassment: it would now be all too cruel to tear her away, in addition, from her already so terrifyingly executed children. Anyway the analogy creates a metonymic relationship between the figure of Rizpah and the inhabitants of Jabesh. It is as if the courage of the group appears once more, but is now concentrated on one woman who is as vulnerable as she is courageous.

The final analogy is the culmination of all the conjunctiveness evoked by the catalysis of Rizpah's intervention. It consists of a third party's concern for the Saulides' earthly remains who wants to show them honour and piety through this. He is David and he attends to the seven plus the royal two. The analogy has emerge how he, inspired by the impressive mother, switches to an *imitatio* of the Jabeshites and at the same time gives back the seven their honour and repose. By doing this he achieves what Rizpah wanted to do but could not. David completes her pious work and that is an amazing and an atoning form of conjunctiveness. This completion consists of the interment of all nine in the family grave and together with v.14c attends to the closure of the story.

§ 2. *Heroes: two series of paragraphs and a list*, 21:15-22 and 23:8-39

Between the two stories of crime and punishment, but surrounding the poetry of the long and short songs, are two passages on heroes. Because they occur in the appendix and hardly influence the narration outside of it it is tempting to skip them, deeming them enumerative fragments in an annalistic style. However I refuse to label them like this since it would do little justice to the text. The arrangement of the subject matter is, it is true, annalistic and both the characterisation and use of a developed plot are reduced, in comparison with the 'standard' stories in Samuel. But upon close inspection both passages turn out to be well-organised units and much literary attention has been paid to the shaping of the parts and their whole.

That the influence of composition is no less apparent here than it is elsewhere can be seen from the fact that the passages in ch.21 and ch.23 are tuned in to one another. Their very place in the concentric ordering of the appendix as a whole is a prior clue. The passages can be recognised as each other's counterpart by their subject matter and their organising principle. The material is homogeneous and bounded by clear co-ordinates of place and time. We get to see incidents and pictures from the clashes on the Philistine-Israelite border which occurred in the early years of King David. For the rest exact dates are lacking, which can be ascribed to the scope of the narrator: he wants to celebrate victories and honour the heroes by recording their *res gestae* and that is enough. The word for 'war' used regularly by the narrator here approximately stands for 'fighting', and generally gives the impression of being a mere denominator handy for raking into one entity various intermittent hostilities spread out over a number of years.

The organising principle of the two hero passages is complementary. In ch.23 we encounter forty prominent fighting men grouped in a special way in the text. The position according to which they are organised is, of course, that of the side of Davidic Israel. But the obviousness of this is only apparent for 21:15-22 has chosen a diametrically opposite position in order to report four incidents in the same theatre of war. The piece groups the adventures of four champions from the house of Rapha and as far as this part is concerned transfers the structural principle to enemy territory, the Philistine city of Gath.[19] These Gittites, who are mentioned by name, lose to four warriors from David's side who also are mentioned by name. In ch.21 the attention paid to names and details is evenly divided between friend and foe. In ch.23 on the contrary this balance is not present. Here the text is much more extensive and uses in the paragraphs of vv.8-23 (i.e. before the pure enumeration of names in vv.24-39) an opposition of name and fame versus anonymity in respect of David's men, but totally avoids mentioning a single enemy proper noun. In 21 we meet only individuals and that which strictly appertains to their duels; nothing is mentioned about their military ranks. More individual warriors appear in 23 but now with an eye to their military rank and status each time, and systematic attention is paid to at least two groups at

[19] The point of view is another matter! This is not Philistine in ch.21, but stays of course Israelite (which does not yet automatically mean: totally pro-David).

the top of the military hierarchy (in the traditional reading: the Three and the Thirty), whilst the enemy appears as a collective which perishes *en masse* several times. Not just the strong similarities, therefore, but also the striking differences between the units 21:15-22 and 23:8-39, are what make them into a diptych around the poetry.

The verses with which they border on the poems are also complementary. The last verse of the first passage, 21:22, is a final summary, an afterword with a 'these four were born' flashback to the enemy. On the other hand the first verse of the final passage, 23:8, is as a heading an opening which, with its demonstrative pronoun, looks forward to its own side: 'these are the names of the heroes of David.'[20]

The four men of Rapha, 21:15-22

The balanced attention paid to the fighting parties and the criterion that the four incidents group the fate of champions from one enemy school are immediately reflected together by the opening line, v.15a. Both national names are mentioned and touch each other; there is equilibrium so far. But the passage does not say that there was war with the Philistines, as in v.18b//19a, but shifts the centre of gravity in the opposite direction of all things by saying 'the Philistines were at war with Israel'.[21] This about-turn serves the organisation principle.

The second line pays attention to 'David and his servants'. They also occur with this designation, and only, in v.22b. The repetition helps us recognise a framework in 15ab and 22ab. A linear reading of the unit might still find the characteristic 'descendant of the Rapha' at the end of 16a and in 18c-20e a coincidence, but at the last moment it appears essential to adjust this impression. The final verse reveals the organisation principle[22] in 22a and has an interesting temporal aspect. Its two halves are a merismus and an envelope, because they offer the four's life and death polarity. This opposition occurs initially in the sentences, but is followed by another: 'Rapha in Gath' versus

[20] Perhaps we ought to go even a step further and enhance the translation by highlighting *'ăšęr l^e* more, in a rendering which goes something like this: 'These are the heroes who belonged to David['s side].' In other words: maybe *'ăšęr l^e* does more than avoid a double semikut (in itself by no means unwanted) and has been chosen with an eye to the oppositions and complementariness of the two units.

[21] The point is to be found in the various prepositions: *'im* in vv.18-19 does something entirely different than the *l^e* of v.15a. Also notice the detail that the word 'war' in v.15a (and 20a) has no article, but that pair 18b//19a on the other hand does.

[22] A fascinating detail is that not before 22a, and only through this line's content, do we conclude that the enemy of incident three, Goliath, was also 'one born with Rapha'; a datum, by the way, which ch.17 of I Sam. had not given away either.

'David and his servants'. Even though the latter are the winners they do not receive the syntactical position of subject. The predicate 'perish in battle' saves this for the victims – the final token of the organising principle. The merismus is a form of derision because it says: the only thing worthwhile determining after this Gittite rabble's birth is that they have now been exterminated by David and his men. The rest – growing up and becoming strong, being trained from youth[23] to become the city's prize fighters – amounts to nothing. That was a pile of illusions; in the text there is only a gaping lacuna between 22a and 22b.[24]

Incidents 2-4 all have a tidy place adjunct for the struggle, the beginning does not. This is a hint that makes me suspect that lines 15abc do double duty, being the introduction to the whole passage rather than the first incident. The distribution of the two parties over 15b and c still continues the balance of their names in 15a for a while. Afterwards the balance seems to tip towards the Philistines, because Rephaite no.1 appears in close-up in v.16, where two out of the four lines focus attention on the armour of the champion. The great weight of his spear shows we have to do with a giant[25] and the warrior's threat is doubled by the datum which opens the first incident, v.15d. This concise clause reports: 'David grew weary', a datum which presupposes lines 15bc and draws their information into incident 1.[26] The datum obtains its negative importance, and is exploited by the enemy in 16d, where the Philistine 'announced he would defeat David'.[27] But things turn out differently. This Ishbi-benob had received three nominal clauses and a wyqtl clause which reports only what he said.[28] Now the narrator has him eliminated in two wyqtl clauses containing the transitive acts of Abishai. The first involves David: 'he helped him' which means there is no chance of a reprieve for the Philistine. His own intention 'to defeat' (the infin. *l^e^hakkōt*) is no match for

23 From youth, *minn^e^'ūrāw*: that was the experience of Goliath in I 17 as recognised by Saul in v.33 of the same chapter. All that training, as we saw in *The Crossing Fates*, could not offset the *na'ar* [also in I 17:33!] David.

24 A modern rendering of the terms might run: these youths have been destined from the cradle to be canon fodder.

25 The data of 16bc and its parallels in 19c and 23:21b should, after all, be valued as a literary motif in combat stories; that is why there is also a relationship with passage I 17, which exhibits extreme expansion of the various details, first of all in the catalogue of Goliath's weapons but later too.

26 Line 21:15d mediates, therefore, between the general and the particular and, as far as this part is concerned, offers a transition from v.15abc to v.16.

27 See also App.1 for the rendering of 21:16d.

28 Strictly speaking v.16a is a *casus pendens* and the lines of 16ab together form a parenthesis, after which 16d finally brings the predicate. Then the subject appears; the hero introduced in 16a.

the deed of David's comrade, *wayyak*, 17b. In order to avoid ambiguity regarding the outcome the narrator adds: 'he killed him'.

All the words in v.17b are exactly the same as those in I 17:50b where David finishes off Goliath. Even greater is the identity of I 17:7a with v.19c, because the same Goliath appears before us here. If we count the datum from v.16b (the weight of a piece of armour) and the element 'the deriding of Israel' (v.21a; *cf.* 23:9c) then we already have at our disposal five such elements which are points of contact between I 17 and II 21. The most striking of course is the fact that Goliath's vanquisher is called Elhanan here. The contradiction between the two texts, brought about by the fact that this hero is the one to whom the victory is ascribed and not David, is in my view less salient than the fact that the editors of the books of Samuel have allowed it to remain. This fact is proof that the editors/writers of ancient Israel had no problem in handing down contradictory material; food for thought for that branch of historical criticism that is diachronically preoccupied with Bible study! The producers of literature in ancient times had a completely different view on tensions and duplications. This must be connected with the fact that they did not need, by a long chalk, to keep to a strict criterion of logical or historical consistency such as pleases the strict and priggish schoolmasters of source criticism.

I am not going to attack the genetic solution to the contradiction of the double ascribing of the victory against Goliath.[29] It is not conceivable that, if David was the real victor, succeeding generations would have taken the honour away from him, ascribing it to one of his soldiers. The reverse – the historical fact of Elhanan's killing the giant being later attributed to David – is, on the other hand, conceivable indeed and has parallels elsewhere. Upon the appearance of a great man in history the normal procedure in the history of the reception of his greatness is to extract some triumph or another from a contemporary in the background and award it to the national hero. The editors of the books of Samuel have not deleted Elhanan's triumph. By not retracting the event they put the reader onto the track of the origin and intention of I 17: that enormous chapter wants to celebrate the hero David in spite of the fact that (and whilst it is not disputed that) the victory against Goliath is 'not historical'. It follows that during the creation of stories historical reliability does not need to be a decisive criterion. The values and the truth of I Sam.17 are, for the narrator, not linked to the question of whether or not the David-Goliath fight 'really took place'. The values that

[29] I argue against even trying to harmonise the two texts. A childish attempt at this was made by the Chronicler, who twists it into meaning that Elhanan killed a brother of Goliath, I Chron.20:5.

did motivate the story I have patiently attempted to trace in *The Crossing Fates*.

Returning to 21:17 we see that the first clash has received an intense ending qua form and content. It is an oath taken by the men and the narrator suggests to us that he is quoting their utterance by embedding two lines of spoken word in his text. Their importance is formally marked insofar as one can scan the lines as a bicolon with two times four ictuses. The designation *'āz*, which is the introduction to the men's shocked response and strikingly occurs initially, gives the moment a solemn touch, elevating it beyond contingency; a historical decision follows formulating a ruling. The words occurring at the end of 17de form, together with 15a, a framework for the paragraph. The negative content of the oath explains why we are not going to see David in incidents 2-4. Their urgent message is that 'the lamp of Israel' may not be blown out. Should David unexpectedly perish in battle, then night will fall on Israel. Only his permanent presence can prevent this. As far as this part is concerned the metaphor shifts into an indirect designation of David himself; the eloquence of his men pays him tribute. Their wish is the counterpart of the perilous situation at the beginning of I Sam. when the corruption at Silo endangered the nation and the lamp of the temple almost went out – at the very hour Samuel was to receive his call from God himself, during the night.[30]

Verse 17 has four elements in common with the moment when David deploys three columns in order to defeat the arch rebel Absalom, at the beginning of II 18.[31] The text which appears somewhat later in narration time places the insight that David may no longer be exposed to the dangers of the battlefield much earlier in narrated time, saying that people already wanted to keep the early David out of harm's way.

The incidents of 21:15-22 are governed by a tight scheme, which is embellished and dressed up in the first and fourth instance, but is visible in its naked form in the concise short passages in the middle, v.18//19. Even though incidents 1 and 2 contain only three lines each, the scheme still contains six components:

1) each short piece begins with 'there was war again', and
2) three cases are accompanied by: 'with the Philistines'.
3) In incidents 2-3-4 the place where the fighting took place is mentioned.

[30] More on I Sam.3 and the symbolism of lamp, night, and blind eyes is to be found in NAPS IV.

[31] These elements are the prominence of Abishai (one of the three generals in 18), the root *'zr* (animated on the lips of the men, at the end of 18:3, but pointing the other way), the commandment 'you may not go' and the formulation of David's unique importance (in 18 by means of a comparison with 'us' and a number).

4) In the short pieces 1-3-4 there are terrifying details on the size or the armour of the relevant champion from Gath.
5) That does not help him, because in all the pieces a *wayyak* follows with, as subject, a hero from David's side, who is mentioned by name each time: Abishai-Sibbechai-Elhanan-Jonathan.
6) Three defeated are mentioned by name, the fourth receives only a qualification, the expression *'īš mādōn*, which could mean 'expert in derision, agitator' here.[32] The location of the name is interesting. In the middle (vv.18-19) its bearer stands next to, but also after, the name of his vanquisher. In the outermost paragraphs, which have attained the proportions of a vignette, he appears initially however, supported by the boast of his exterior: Ishbi-benob with his heavy spear and new armour (v.16) and the 'man of strife' with his grisly surplus of fingers and toes in v.20.

The centremost pieces are, for various reasons, a pair which stand out against the outermost two. They have one full line in common, 18b = 19a. They are the only lines to contain the name of the unidentified place Gob and the only ones which mention the men who duel next to one another.[33] Goliath is the only one who is not called a *yᵉlīd hārāfā*, but 'the Gittite'.[34] This is done the moment the struggle at last begins to approach the source of the 'Raphaite' threat, Gath itself, now the place adjunct in 20a of the continued 'war'. This initiates the fourth incident.

This final anecdote dresses up the bare scheme with several nominal clauses which occur in the middle of the paragraph and render the fearsomeness of the Rephaim physical this time. The 'man of strife' coming into view now has a total of twenty-four fingers and toes, something which might arouse a mixture of terror and abhorrence in the other side. The mention of 'war' of 20a is given a binary explanation and completed in 21ab; one line looks at the

[32] This phrase *'īš mādōn* is familiar from Prov.26:21 (where it is about wrangling in every day life) and Jer.15:10. Because there the stakes are higher, I think the term might also refer to a champion. I Chron.20:6 has the variant *'īš middā*, 'a man of (great) stature, a giant'.

[33] Nevertheless incidents 2 and 3 each have their own line. I see 18a as a division which separates the short passages 2-3-4 from the paragraph in which David was almost finished. With this verse 18 has received the extent of three lines. Due to considerations of balance the narrator also gives three to v.19 by adding the description 19c (notice that the nominal clause on the spear does not go with the subject but with the object of 19b!).

[34] As has already been written about by other authors the fighting men of Gath are not called *the sons* of Rapha. I too think this is significant; we must look at, and render, the expression *yᵉlīdē hārāfā* in a different way. I assume that the word *yᵉlīd* here is short for *yᵉlīd bayit* (a term we are acquainted with from Gen.14:14, 17:12,23,27, Lev.22:11 and Jer.2:14; compare also the *yᵉlīdē hā'ănāq* in Num.13:22,28 and Josh.15:14) or at least must be explained in this kind of way, e.g. McCarter's 'the votaries of Rapha'.

enemy and the other grants victory to a nephew of David. In 20b and 20e there are qualities of the champion from Gath. The short passage is thus concentrically designed:

20a	introduction: war against Gath
20b	'a man of strife appeared'
20cd	the sets of six fingers and toes are reported and counted
20e	'he too was born [in the house] of Rapha'
21ab	content and result of the duel: derision and death.

The fourth victor's being a full nephew of David is convenient. It enables the series made up of four incidents to end on the name of the man who is, after all, being celebrated. The bearer himself was in incident 1, and the unit is now rounded off with a pair which looks at both camps but leaves the decisions 'in the hands of David and his servants'.

I now draw a connecting line from this unit with four short paragraphs to unit 23:8-39 with its four long paragraphs. The final verse of the first unit has a formula with *’ellȩ̄ yull^{e}dū* which looks back, whilst the first verse of the final unit is a formula *’ellȩ̄ š^{e}mōt* ... which points forward. The same figure was to be found in 3:5b (with the same pu‘al!) and 5:14a (with the same 'names'!) in the enumeration of children of David. That is why I do not believe that the symmetry joining 21:22a and 23:8a is coincidental, but is rather one of the signals which show us that their units are just as much a pair as the short lists of 3:2-5 and 5:14-16.

The heroes of David, 23:8-39

The text is plagued by dubious details and notorious corruptions, but they cannot prevent my observing, upon close inspection, that a mature literary structure is quickly to be identified in it. This insight serves as my point of departure whereupon I re-establish my hermeneutic stance: the whole is more than the sum of its parts. This principle is, in turn, to act as guideline in an attempt to establish a text – particularly at the points where the root **šlš* is used – and to understand or explain it satisfactorily. *Ad hoc* solutions based on an atomistic fiddling around with isolated problems are both undesirable and outdated. What is needed is a structural approach in which main lines are being thought out to support the search for the right answer to the said problems and corruptions. Some of these are so knotty that they cannot be disentangled but have to be cut open – a procedure nobody can avoid in this passage.

I would like to note several fundamental considerations here, which will hopefully be of use in getting acquainted with the passage. Let us begin with the Three: it is not *a priori* certain that a man who makes a formidable champion is able to lead troops too, or can be automatically assured of such recognition. I notice that the paragraph on the Three (vv.8-12), who are not mentioned elsewhere, does not end on an appointment or mention a rank in the military hierarchy, whilst the paragraph on the well-known commanders Abishai and Benaiah (vv.18-23) does in fact do this.

Observing this difference brings me to a second consideration, that of the occurrence of oppositions. It looks as though this passage is no less characterised by operating with this phenomenon than so many others. Attention to oppositions is potentially of great investigative importance within the hermeneutic horizon of this large unit and can hand us the keys to a sound interpretation of its parts.

One recent discussion makes it seem as if the men who undertake their perilous journey through enemy lines in the intervening paragraph of vv.13-17 are the same three honoured by vv.8-12.[35] But the passage offers no clues, and we must take into serious consideration the possibility that these three ('of the thirty high-ranking officers') are not *the* Three. Their identity is kept from us of all things; a new and relevant opposition thus arising between permanent anonymity and the greatest fame of six men, all equally true to David. However, each of the famous Three do that in their own way whilst the anonymous three perform a stunt as a trio.

As far as the list from v.24 onwards is concerned I do not want to force the data into an arithmetical straitjacket. The fact of its probably being a list of Thirty does not banish the argument from reality that under the pressure of warfare and the ravages of time people drop out and alterations take place in the list. But quite simply because it is not necessary to dogmatically to keep to the precise total of thirty – in line with the fact that the end of the list itself has the information: 'thirty-seven in all' -, it is accordingly unnecessary so to take heed of precise proportions that one finds one must take recourse to a radical intervention, re-punctuating the word 'thirty' almost everywhere as *šālīšīm*, 'high ranking officers'.[36] The choice between *šᵉlōšīm* and *šālīšīm*

[35] According to CT, which listens carefully to the Targum and follows in the footsteps of Isaiah of Trani. Keil and Goslinga are clearly against this view; the latter (p.438) still refers to this opposition: 'The Three mentioned in vv.8-12 did not in fact operate together but singly (...).'

[36] This was put forward by Thenius (in the second edition of his commentary, Leipzig 1864) for vv.8,9,13,18,22,23,24. It has been adopted to a large extent (for vv.8,13,19a,23,24) by Nadav Na'aman in 'The List of David's Officers (*Šālīšīm*)', VT 38 (1988) pp.71-79. There is an

produces thin ice I will not skate on until I have drawn the solid main lines of the composition. I follow the text.

The unit has a simple main division into four parts: vv.8-12 and 13-17 on the Three and another trio, 18-22, on two generals, and finally the pure list vv.24-39. There is a clear balance qua length: 88-75-94-95 words. Moving down one level I would like to study the internal structure of the passages prior to the catalogue.

Part I does indeed have a structure of its own which is indicated by two series of indicators. We have the order of the first hero with the name X, then there is 'and after him' + hero Y, followed by another 'and after him' + hero Z, which makes for the start of the three short paragraphs: 8/9-10/11-12. There is also a refrain at the end of the second and the third paragraph, which via its content and a double occurrence (v.10d//12c) is strongly reminiscent of the refrain on God as deliverer in ch.8.[37] The difference is that there David was mentioned directly as beneficiary, as grammatical object of the verb *yš'*, whilst the construction of 23:10d//12c concentrates on God's involvement without mentioning beneficiaries: 'the Lord wrought a great victory (that day)'.

The first paragraph is the most concise and this tallies with the feat of arms of the hero, Esh-baal the Hakmonite, who has managed to eliminate[38] 'six hundred men in one go'. This strongly worded report forms a bridge between two very different numbers and that is how it is.[39] So with one stroke of the pen it has become plain that this brave man was indeed 'the head of the Three'. Whether his weapon was a battle-axe or a spear does not affect line 8c's being the counterpart of 18b in which Abishai sees to 300 enemies on his

extensive article on the term by B.A. Mastin, 'Was the *šālīš* the Third Man in the Chariot?', SVT 30 (1979) pp.125-154.

[37] Another similarity is that the second refrain, here and in ch.8, does not yet coincide with the end of the chapter.

[38] For the philological problems at the beginnings of both v.8b and 8c see App.1.

[39] We find a similar bridge at the beginning of Judg.9 also, where the monarchy of Abimelech is founded on the one stone upon which he has his seventy brothers slaughtered. The immediate context there makes more of the numbers, see for example the election speech the relatives have to hold in Sichem, and the seventy pieces of silver for the murder. *Cf.* an article of mine in the Festschrift for Sh. Talmon, (Eisenbrauns, Winona Lake) 1990, on Judg.9 and 19. An example from Sam. of a bridge between numbers is to be found in I 11:7f and 8bc where 330,000 soldiers advance 'as one man' (whilst the latter is the counterpart of the enemy's dispersal in v.11, so that 'no *two* of them are left together [*yaḥad*]').

own. This takes place in the third passage, in which *c.* five sentences are occupied with the relationship between the Three and the Thirty and where fights of individuals mentioned by name are noted in addition. Because there are no fights and no names of brave men in vv.13-17 a certain kind of relief occurs. The anonymous trio's part, with its stake of water brought from the House of Bread which has been cut off, forms a digression which interrupts all the clash of arms placed around it.

The second paragraph of part I contains nine lines and shows the second of the Three, Eleazar. The ridicule of David and his men goads the enemy (v.9c) who musters an army of such strength that the Israelites have to withdraw (9cd). The individual's sudden appearance, and his surplus of courage and strength, is now marked by word order and asyndeton as the start of v.10: *hū qām*. Straightaway he reaps victory, 10b. The hero is now characterised by two clauses which zoom in on his hand, depicting indomitability in an oxymoron of exhaustion and not knowing when to stop (v.10bc). No matter how tired he gets from mowing with the sword, his hand cleaves to the hilt – spattered with the blood of his victims I imagine. When the narrator puts down his refrain in v.10d, with an 'on that day' revealing how he overlooks the battlefield, one of this line's implications is that the other combatants take heart and complete the turn of the tide in the battle brought about by Eleazar. Their withdrawal in v.9d is nullified by their attack in 10e. But just how much the strength of Eleazar is the standard emerges from the choice of words: 'the soldiery returned after him', upon which the sentence is not yet complete but surprisingly gets another adjunct on top: 'but only to fleece'. The fact that this reaping victory is obviously a sheer result of Eleazar's action is expressed iconically by means of the line's location after the refrain. At the same time a modest framework with the word *'aḥărāw* has arisen.

The third paragraph repeats set components from the previous one: the formula of introduction, so that 11a meshes with 9a; the Philistine muster; the army's losing ground, now even called 'fleeing', 11d; the hero's holding his ground (now with the root **yṣb*); his defeat of the Philistines, and finally the refrain on God. This makes a total of not less than six elements and illustrates how people are able to tell anecdotes according to a fixed pattern. The special nature of the Shamma paragraph lies in the object of concern this time: there is a field of lentils and the enemy sees it will yield a good harvest. Now there are two lines with the word *ḥẹlqā*, one during the threat (v.11c) and one on the triumph: the hero stands there as steady as a rock, v.12a, and the narrator turns the field itself into an object of his rescue: *wayyaṣṣīlẹhā*. The setting at Lehi can be read as an allusion to Judg.15: a second Samson is fighting against the same enemy here.[40] There is a strict alternation of Philistines – field – Philistines – field – Philistines in 11b-12b. If we make a comprehensive record of the hero's being on hand, we arrive at the following pattern for the whole paragraph:

A	the personal details of the hero	11a
B	the muster of the Philistines	11b
C	the field of lentils	11c
B'	fleeing before the Philistines	11d
A/C	the hero saves the field	12a
A/B	he defeats the Philistines	12b
A'	God adds to the victory	12c

In this notation the hero and the contribution of the deity are complementary; they form a ring of allies round the turmoil of battle.

Part II covers vv.13-17 and is well marked by a framework. In 13a the scene is ushered in by the movement of a trio of officers, whilst 17e ensures closure with the flashback: 'this[41] is what the three heroes have done'. The piece stands by itself through its having a proper and complete plot. After a relatively comprehensive introduction (vv.13-14) v.15 formulates the problem: David's thirst, to which v.16abc offers the intrepid action of the three bringing the solution: water from Bethlehem, and the end ensures a big surprise in 16d-17d.

The movement of the descent is continued in the 'they came' of 13b, which is an arrival. There are now four clauses which form an ABAB series and indeed consist of two sets of two, 13bc and 14ab. They take alternate looks at the two camps and all end on an adjunct of place. The order is David – Philistines – David – Philistines. But whilst the individual David is in the west on one spot, first called the cave of Adullam and then the fortress (13b-14a), the enemy consists of two collectives which are more to the east in two places (13c-14b). An entire Philistine regiment is encamped in the Valley of Rephaim, cutting David off from his tribal territory. In addition the enemy have a post or base high in Judah, N.B. in the very city where David was born. A

[40] The combination *t^{e}šū'ā g^{e}dōlā* also occurs in Judg.15. After Samson has raged fiercely with the jaw bone of an ass, he becomes thirsty and a spring is mentioned. In II Sam.23 an anecdote on David's thirst follows, and a spring/cistern in his home town is mentioned.

[41] Note that the demonstrative pronoun is not in the singular: not *zōt* but *'ellę̄*. Interesting question: what does this tell us? Possibly this is the way the end of part II wants to be seen, i.e. as a continuation of 21:22a, 23:8a and 22a.

re-reading of 13a, in which three of David's heroes 'go down' with the resolve to reach Adullam, leads to the conclusion that their route probably led from the mountains of Judah to the Shefelah and in particular that this journey itself was full of danger.

The alliteration of the words *m^eṣūdā* and *maṣṣāb* is part of the chiasmus David/fortress // post/Philistines and together with this device underlines the difference in military position: the first is defensive, the second a sign of occupation. Whilst duo 13bc had verbal forms, pair 14ab consists of nominal clauses each of which has the time adjunct *'āz*. I now link the first adjunct of the whole quartet, 'for the harvest', which occurs in a line on David, to the very last, which occurs in an enemy line, 'Bethlehem'; this name does not necessarily mean 'the House of Bread' but can be read so in this literary context.[42] The link marks the striking long introduction as a framework and is of semantic value. What is being suggested is that the harvest and bread are threatened, and an anticipation arises insofar as the next verse, v. 15, asks for water. Besides, water and bread, both in reality and in a work of art, usually signify more than matter. Food often stands for (emotional and psychological) nourishment.

David is in danger of being cut off from his roots and even before he himself mentions the word water the narrator has already stated his yearning for it. There is no pi'el with a tidy definite object up front in 15a, but a hithpa'el without (the restriction of) any complement, so that the reader understands: David is full of longing. The special nature of this thirst is also marked by the narrator's allocating a speech to it. It is a stark question, 'who will give me water to drink?' David is thinking of the cistern at the gate of his birthplace and cannot tear himself away from the idea.[43] He is longing for the living water from the true spring. The heroes have grasped this, for they are now going to undertake something no ordinary mortal would dare to do. They are once again to pass through enemy lines and draw water from under the noses of yet more enemies.

[42] The systematics of the spatial terms in 13b-14b is itself already an indication that the early complement *'ęl qāṣīr* is not a place adjunct (and in view of the double *'āz* of v.14 neither is it a time adjunct). I interpret it as an adjunct of aim in which *'ęl* has the meaning of *'al* (*cf.* Chron.) – see also Appendix I *ad locum.*

[43] The distance between Adullam and Bethlehem (vice versa) is so great and takes so much time to get there (obstacles not included) that, on the grounds of the time factor itself, it is not possible to put forward its simply being a matter of quenching one's acute thirst and that is all. David is willing to manage for a couple of days on water from the neighbourhood, but the day after tomorrow he is prepared to carry on with, and thanks to, the true water, that from the one genuine spring (which he localises on the map and which the good reader 'reads' psychologically as well as geographically).

The strong verb with which v.16 opens relates that they do not sneak past, but cut their way through, the enemy: the root *bq'* is applied expressively here.[44] Six words have 16b run tidily parallel to 15b. This near-identity indicates that the heroes do exactly what David has said. They make a dream come true and that is an unforgettable event. When they reappear before David – the form 'they came' of 16c is the successor of the form in 13b – the plot seems to be complete and everyone can be pleased and proud. But what happens now is so unexpected that the narrator redoubles line 16d. Exactly the same thing occurs in 17d: 'David did not want to drink it [the water]', the repetition framing the denouement, (the six lines of) 16d-17d.

The shock of this refusal must have been great for the three and the spectators. The originality with which David goes against all expectations is great and recalls the scene from ch.12 where he sent his whole court barking up the wrong tree in a matter of life and death. That too concerned a refusal: the king refused to mourn for the dead baby. This case is concerned with David's realising what his wish entails after it has been granted. Only after the completion of the march does it dawn on him what he has actually asked for: not water, but the blood of the three, for they had staked their lives. The line which was formally a question ('*who* is going to do such and such for me?'), but sounds like a desire for refreshment ('oh how I wish I could get something to drink') was perhaps never meant to be a real wish, but was merely an *irrealis*, the airing of a dream. Now that the dream has become reality David recoils. The act of drinking would make him fully responsible for a life-endangering wish so he feels, and with a cursing word (*ḥālīlā*) he forcibly flings away the fatal alternative, as far as he can. Once again the narrator decides to create a speech for this, this time one of two lines. First there is the outright refusal in 17b, with God as a witness, and then a new question. It too has a rhetorical quality, only this time a re-established contact with reality is served: 'Can [I drink] the blood of the men who went at the risk of their lives?' Then the narrator repeats the refusal in 17d; which can motivate the reader to do some gap-filling: after his 'no' his men try to get him to drink, but David maintains that the water would thereby become blood. He compensates the negative aspect of the refusal *myhwh* with a positive address *lyhwh*, he offers to God as a libation the water first offered to him, v.16e, so as not to waste it.

Part III covers vv.18-23 and has one short plus one long paragraph. The paragraph on Abishai has two long clauses and four short ones. These four,

[44] There are a few other places in which this verb 'split' is used as a military term to mean 'enter (a country or city) by force' or 'to break a way through'; see II Chron.21:17, Is.7:6, Jer.39:2, Ezek.26:10, 30:16; and compare in particular II Ki.3:26.

18c and 19abc, form an extensive parallelism with the end of Benaiah's paragraph, so that there is structural support for reading 'the thirty' in 19a. I also link the *rōš* of 18a with the title *śar* of 19b, so that the first line introduces Abishai to us as head of the thirty (or of the high ranking officers, the *šālīšīm*). The long line 18b has the same structure as v.8c and the same position immediately after the personal details, which establishes the leading position of Abishai in part III. The number of those defeated by him is lower and has not reached during one day of warfare, since 'on one occasion' has now been omitted.

The four short lines consist of two sets of two whose syntax is chiastic. The chiasmus in v.18c and 19a is: 'name' – number 3 // number 30 – 'honoured'. The cross ways construction includes a complementariness of two honourable contentions for Abishai. He enjoys fame with the Three, and of the Thirty he is the one enjoying the most prestige. The office he obtains, the command of the Thirty, links up with 19b. Just like 19c this line has a verbal predicate and enters into a chiasmus with it which marks a difference. 'He became their commander, *but* did not attain to the Three.' If we keep the four lines together, we can see that their relationship is concentric:

A He won a name among the Three;
B since he was the most highly regarded among the thirty,
B' he became their leader.
A However, he did not attain to the Three.

In the following paragraph the elements AB-B'A' are repeated with respect to Benaiah, but with a change of places, so that the lines of v.22b and 23abc exhibit the pattern ABA'B'. The result is that the final duo 23bc at the end contains the opposition 'not a member of the Three, but a commander of the body-guards'. This time the strong man does not *become* this (compare the *wayhī* for Abishai in 19b), but receives the office from David.[45]

What is typical of Benaiah? Two of his *res gestae* are each mentioned in a separate line, 20bc, there being, in addition, an anecdote in v.21 which honours him as fighting man in five lines. But he receives two epithets as early as v.20a, the moment he is introduced. He is called 'a brave soldier' and, in the same breath, 'of many exploits'. The pieces of evidence which follow in 20b, 20c and in the anecdote all begin with the pronoun denoting him, *hū*, a striking anaphora which is amplified by the predicate *hikkā* each time. The fact that he defeats [the two sons] of Ariel of Moab is reinforced via a play on words. In v.20c 'on a snowy day', when wild animals hungrily searching for

[45] The Hebrew of 17c lacks a predicate; in the parallel text this is the form *'ęštę̄* which is filled in by JPS with a good understanding of David's utterance.

food risk deeper penetration into the human world than usual, he dares 'to go down into a pit' and 'kill a lion' there, *'ęt hā'ărī*. Four words precede this animal and the same number follows. Facing the *yārad w^e hikkā* pair are two word pairs with their alliteration and a continued ō vowel; mentioning place and time they exhibit quantitative balance, *b^e tōk habbōr // b^e yōm haššalg*.[46]

Just like the Shamma vignette the incident with the Egyptian warrior is ordered concentrically:

A	He killed an Egyptian, a man of striking appearance.[47]	21a
B	A spear was in the hand of the Egyptian,	21b
C=X	yet [Benaiah] went down against him with a club,	21c
B	snatched the spear out of the Egyptian's hand	21d
A	and killed him with his own spear.	21e

Elements B-B' exhibit a chiasmus of spear and owner, which places a static nominal clause opposite the verbal clause of Benaiah and the dynamism of his skilful robbery (*gzl*). The device reinforces the pattern's aspect of symmetry and reversal. The intervention of the winner occurs in the middle. This line does indeed earn being called the turning point, because the Egyptian is subjected to the insult of being met by someone carrying only a club. It gets even worse for him, for he is not felled by the said 'club' but by his own weapon which has just been snatched away from him. The parallel with David versus Goliath is plain. In I 17 everyone believed in the power of 'sword and spear', and the bewildered Goliath, who saw a shepherd boy entering the arena, was to find that the Israelite 'was making for him with a stick'. There too a champion of striking appearance was eliminated with the means of a shepherd and finished off with his own weapon.

The preceding summary itself, which is 21a, suggests the Egyptian's not having a chance against the formidable Benaiah. The specification of this element A (the verb *hikkā*) follows in A' (with *hrg* and the shame of 'his own spear'). The central movement is 'he went down' and is, through this choice of words, the successor to the previous making a bee line for the lion. The repetition suggests that a wild animal has been defeated once more.

[46] I note the premasoretic form of the word for snow here: this was monosyllabic. Fascinating question for the grammarian: why does 20c have the perfect *w^e hikkā*, after *yārad*, rather than *wayyak*? The form is, after all, neither an iterative in the past nor a future! The answer of the stylist (who took the trouble while dealing with 7:9-11 to pay proper attention to the *w^e qātal* phenomenon!) is: for the sake of the threefold anaphora of subject and predicate.

[47] I read the word *'īš* with Qere therefore; it is linked to a *mar'ę* which one must interpret pregnantly (a good or large form); it is not necessary to replace it by the Chronicler's *middā*.

Part IV is a pure list, but has special edges. The first and the last man are the only ones from amongst the Thirty (-seven) whom we know from the stories. Asahel and Uriah are fascinating characters who are both allowed to appear in the foreground once, but who have to pay for it with their lives. Part IV opens with Asahel, which is striking for various reasons. First of all v.24a is the counterpart of v.18a. A parallelism puts the two brothers of Joab in the same position and links the opening of III and IV.[48] Subsequently the name *'ăśā'el* itself attracts attention, 'God has made'. It occurs in the first position, but recalls the endings of all three previous parts.[49] Part I ended in v.12c with 'Yahweh wrought ... ', *wayya'aś yhwh*, part II finished on *'ellę̄ 'āśū* ... in v.17e, and part III commenced its conclusion in 22a with *'ellę̄ 'āśā*. What is now noticeable about v.24 is its containing another theophoric name with the component El and that its bearer appeared for a moment in 21:19. His name is 'God has shown mercy' and is, as Goliath's victor, the literary double of David himself of all people. The structure of the play on words with the verb 'make' at the boundaries of the four parts has an ABBA pattern: it is true some bruisers do marvellous heroic deeds, but they are surrounded by the God who makes the victories great (*bis*, v.10d//12c), who is the creator of all the champions on David's side and through his mercy (formulated by parents in Bethlehem, and given to a child as a name) protects the existence of Israel and the Davidic dynasty, and provides them with a future.

§ 3. *The census: God's punishment and compassion*, Ch.24

Who is the hero of this story? This elementary question, occurring in every analysis, is here of special importance because the answer to it is perilous. At first it is tempting to say: that's David, isn't it? Isn't the king the one who organises the census, confesses guilt and chooses the punishment, adopts a protective attitude to his sheep and finally builds an altar? All true of course, but not enough, and that is because of the little stick of dynamite which is verse 1. If the chapter had been preserved without this opening and without v.25cd, we still would have had a superb story in front of us. In this kind of a text verse 2, that is to say the king's decree to take a census which is offered in direct speech, would have occurred in the initial position. With this initiative David would have firmly registered his candidacy for the position of hero

[48] Asahel belongs 'to the Thirty' says v.24a. The line's being parallel to v.18a is a stylistic argument for Abishai's leadership of the Thirty, i.e. for the emendation 'thirty' at the end of v.18a.

[49] With the minor modification that although v.22 summarises, just like v.17e, it does not quite occur at the very end of part III.

and actantial subject on the axis of the quest. And not until verse 13 would the reader begin to inquire as to whether another quest is being enacted, on a higher plane and in secret. The verses in which God allows the plague to rage but calls a halt at Jerusalem out of compassion, vv.15-16, are to subsequently induce him to formulate a plot on a higher level. The actual text undermines David's candidacy as hero from the very start and does that radically.

Verse 1 and the final two clauses, 25cd, frame the chapter together. These two boundaries themselves create a parallelism between this literary unit and that of 21:1-14 which has similar limits (the wrath of God and, in the end, atonement) and once more a collective death plus a horrible punishment at its centre. The very first word of ch.24 brings the final chapter in line with 21: '*once again* the anger of the Lord flared up against Israel'. Through their subject matter as much as by various formal means, among which their limits, the two stories around the heroes and the poetry are each other's counterpart.

Verse 1 opens right away with the broad perspective of God versus the nation in the first line. In the second line it reveals that David is the instrument of a God who has something up his sleeve. God aroused in the king the desire to count the people. The wickedness of this is not something which is indisputable right from the word go. But the narrator's radical and frank choice of words prevents doubt on our part: 'and He *incited* David against them saying: Go, number Israel and Judah!' Without (being able) to see through it, David becomes an accomplice in a nefarious plan. The taking of a census is the infringement of a taboo and counts as a sin in this story. The implication of the revealing verse 1 is that God makes sure David commits a mortal sin against him, the creator and the protector of this chosen people, and that 'thanks to' this royal lapse, he can subsequently lash out with punishment against the nation. Let us not mince words: intriguing behind the scenes God creates a situation which provides him with the excuse to afflict his people with the plague. He needs an excuse therefore. This conclusion takes me back to the beginning: just why was God angry with his people?

Having arrived at this point we can exploit a difference between the beginning of ch.21 and that of 24 which stands out against the background of their similarity. In ch.21 the reader quickly gets – after a few lines of narration time – the explanation of God's wrath which David, kneaded into a supplicant by the famine, does not obtain until after a long period of narrated time: God himself reveals an old sore to him, the blood-guilt of Saul. All at once the various responsibilities are plain: that of God as claimant and creator of history, that of the Gibeonites who are also claimant and have a right to serious satisfaction, that of David who as ruler can create the conditions for compensation, etc. How different the state of affairs in ch.24! Here the reason for God's wrath is actually kept from us. And the Satanic behaviour of God now creates the alarming and subversive impression that he is unable to dole out the plague until he can point to a good excuse. The Satanic behaviour of God? This is not a mischievous formulation of this writer, but of the Chronicler who has included II Sam.24 in his work (in I Chron.21) and *mir nichts dir nichts* changed the subject of the inciting in verse 1 from Yahweh to 'the Satan'![50] So an intertextual discussion arises to produce the interesting question as to the one to whom mortals should ascribe everything which is painful or nasty: to God or to Satan. The dialectic of the Satanic verses II Sam.24:1 and I Chron.21:1 submits the provocative motion: it does not make much difference, what *is* in fact the difference between the two? In the case of David and his census we cannot keep the two apart! And if there is one party who can summon up sympathy for this reversal in the image of God then it will be the 70.000 who die miserably in a single day.

The importance of all this freethinking – or heresy, some readers might say – which attempts to do justice to the radical nature of verse 1, is that this opening introduces a splitting in knowledge levels which persists until the end. The omniscient narrator has his readers notice right away that he has insight into divine reality and furnishes us with extra knowledge; from the outset we see more than David can. He has no insight whatever into the level of providence and is allowed to labour under the illusion that his sin, confession and compassion are important factors in the development. He is particularly under pressure because he thinks his transgression has caused a national catastrophe and that the people are suffering because of his guilt. He is subsequently allowed to cherish the illusion that his repentance makes some, or a lot of difference, and that his repetition of the confession of sin (in v.17) moves God to prematurely halt the plague. But the narrator's audience know better in fact, and in the story there is nobody who comes and opens his eyes.

God is the hero – or the villain, if we transpose the word of the Chronicler into the term of narratology – of the first quest and that furnishes us with both the first and the fundamental actantial model which governs this story, on the plane which David does not get to see. God destines doom for Israel, using for this purpose the king who really does want to quantify his own power and the general who has to carry out the count; he has but one opponent: the same general, who before being overruled raises his voice in a

[50] A striking sign of spiritual freedom, and proof that a writer at a late date still had the possibility of taking drastic action with his subject matter. Which latter sheds light on the writers' creativity which remained uncensored until a late date in full recognition of its value.

mild protest against David's resolve. The critical Joab of v.3 I call Joab[1], and the performer who has to get started anyway, Joab[2]. One is a helper, the other an opponent, of the quest of the wrathful subject and the scheme which goes with it:

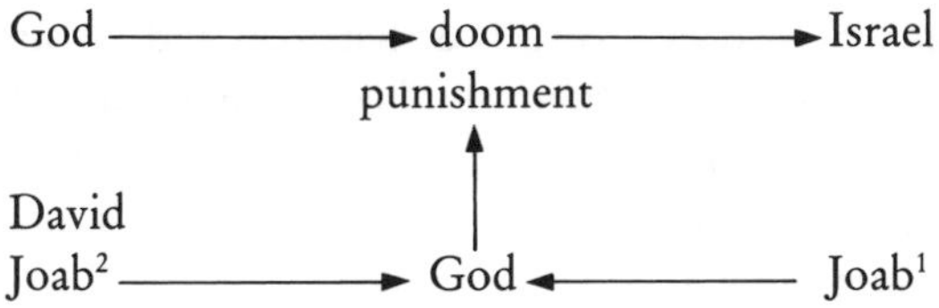

This scheme goes with the underlying truth, unknown to David, of the events up to and including v.15ab where the extent of the catastrophe is measured in figures plus the co-ordinates of time and place. This verse has a strongly articulating function in the progress of the story, as becomes apparent if we think away the rest: we are then left with a text which is still completely intelligible and has been rounded off well. The raging of the plague points back to v.1a and makes up the deficit which is given with the wrath of God at the beginning. After God has got his satisfaction the operation of another actantial model is now needed. The hitch after v.15 in the plot of ch.24 is comparable with the hitch which occurred in ch.21 through the unexpected appearance of Rizpah and, enriching the plot, took it on to atonement.[51]

I would now like to follow the first part of the text, vv.1-9. God's stirring up trouble is animated, for the narrator has a line of direct speech available for it along with two swift commands and the names of Israel-and-Judah which, as a pair, mirror and respect the composition and the uneven start of the unified kingdom. The temptation is hidden in the imperatives perhaps: David now thinks that the census is divinely acceptable, because his 'go and count' is commanded by God himself. A dialogue between David and his chief of staff follows at once. Throughout the whole passage vv.2-8, David is designated as 'the king' each time, perhaps as a sign of his pride and desire to measure the power of his kingdom. In part B, vv.10-19, where the forces of guilt and punishment rest upon him, he feels personally responsible and is now going to be systematically designated by his proper noun.

A project such as a census requires spatial terms and we are about to get a generous measure of them. This starts to occur, in duplicate, as early as David's first sentence where 'all the tribes of Israel' are geographically

[51] The similarity quickly becomes plain when one compares 21:9 with 24:15. In the first verse the co-ordinates of time and place occur also for closure and there is also a form of the root **mwt* predicate with the victims as subject which contributes to the rounding off.

recorded in the merismus 'from Dan to Beersheba'. These two names, standing for the northern and the southern boundaries, return as a pair in v.15b to indicate that the whole country is covered with the plague. But they already occur earlier, and separately, in the description of the route taken by the soldiers who have to carry out the census. Here too they indicate completeness, v.6b and 7b, in order to record that Joab and his men are inspecting the country from top to bottom. They even form part of a chiasmus. This device, whose other diagonal is occupied by a verb which itself has the spatial meaning 'to cross', marks the fact that David's command from v.2b is fully completed in v.8:

2b	šūṭ-nā b^{e}kol šibṭē yiśrā'el	middān w^{e}'ad b^{e}'er-šęba'
6b/7b	... dānā ... b^{e}'er-šęba'	wayyāšūṭū b^{e}kol hā'āręṣ (8a)

Around this device there is a ring which indicates the limits of part A and so completes the piece of vv.1-9. The command 'count Israel and Judah' which God gave David is passed on to Joab by David with a variation, 'take a census of (*piqdū*) the people', v.2c, and another short clause on 'the number of the people', v.2d. When the soldiers return with their figures David obtains from Joab 'the number of the census' in v.9. But the number is only available divided between 'Israel and Judah', the names mentioned at the beginning: the 800,000 of 9b and the 500,000 of 9c.[52] The ring has arisen due to the reflection of three elements, and the axis upon which they turn occurs in the phrase with the infinitive which states Joab's assignment in v.4b:

Israel and Judah	(1c)
piqdū 'ęt hā'ām	(2c)
'ęt mispar hā'ām	(2d)
....	
lifqod 'ęt hā'ām 'ęt yiśrā'el	(4b)
....	
'ęt mispar	
mifqad hā'ām	(9a)
Israel and Judah	(9bc)

David's three lines are answered by Joab with another three lines, a good balance. The middle contains a formula in the language of the court, 'my lord the king'; Joab really knows hows to put things very politely. He even begins

[52] The verb *wayhī* of 9b does double duty by also being in force in 9c. Its absence in 9c is compensated for by the addition of the initial word *'īš*. The two names and the two numbers get to stand exactly underneath one another after all. The final three words of 9b also do double duty. The consequence for 9c is that this line now ends as it began: on *'īš*.

with a fine wish about increasing power for the king and a long life, but that does not detract from the fact that his criticism is a matter of principle. His protest is covert, but he begins with God which itself gives away the fact that the speaker is aware of moral or religious objections to a census. A number of different barbs are well hidden in the magnanimous gesture of this wish: 'May the Lord your God increase the number of the people a hundredfold, while your own eyes see it!' Behind the quasi-redundancy with which Joab adds 'your God' to the proper noun Yahweh lies the question whether David is still obedient to the divine norm. (But David would answer without hesitation 'yes': God himself put him in the way of this idea!) Irony is concealed in the fact that Joab – under his own steam, far ahead of the actual count and right away in his first sentence – introduces a number. He points out that God can ensure enormous growth. The silent criticism is, given this alternative, the figures provided by the random picture of a count like this would be very quickly outdated. David might live to see such growth himself; the circumstantial clause on his eyes (3c) is, at face value, Joab's wish that his sovereign might live that long. But the message behind it is: enjoy the look of it, don't try to work it out. (David is not going to listen, however, and what his own eyes are to register almost ten months later is a gruesome reduction: see the *bir'ōtō* of 17a.) The number Joab mentions, 'a hundred-fold', is so great that it must be called a hyperbole. And as a hyperbole it ridicules the desire to count and measure.

After so much circumspect courteousness the truth finally comes out in v.3d: the critical 'why' question, attenuated by the repetition of the vocative in the court style. This line is ambiguous. One could maintain that the question is exploratory and probes for motives. But it has the most forceful effect as a rhetorical question perhaps, and the interrogative 'why' turns into a pointer, the hint: it is prudent to relinquish your plan. In this way the line borders also on the well-known situation of a 'why' question actually being the vehicle of a reproof.

Joab's criticism is to no avail, David presses ahead with his plan: 'the king's command ... remained firm' and not only applies to Joab but to other generals as well.[53] This line on 'the word of the king' and his military audience co-operates with 2a so that the two lines, as a framework, round off the talk. The first half of part A, which is actually all dialogue, is therefore complete. The second half, vv.4b-9, stands out against this by not having a single spoken word. It is a report which concerns itself exclusively with the

[53] There is a small shift thus in v.4a with respect to 2a. There 'Joab' was 'the leader of the army', now the title is extricated from him and given to other top brass: 'Joab and the [other] army leaders'.

journey of Joab and his colleagues throughout the country. The relation between the two halves is simple: that of command and performance. I draw attention to the fact that they both have twelve lines. Let my reader himself decide how much value is to be attached to this. I myself volunteer the possibility that this number iconically refers to the twelve tribes of which the people ideally consist; this is fitting in the context of a census.[54]

The report on the count consists of 3 + 3 + 3 lines on the operation and ends with three lines (v.9) which hand in the result to the king. I would first like to look at the nine lines of 4b-8b, in which I observe a certain amount of concentricity. The centremost trio is marked by the anaphora of a threefold 'they came' and draws three main lines on the map of Israel. In 6a the military goes northwards into the Transjordan, in 6b westward to the Phoenician coast, and in 7a they go, after calling in at Tyre, quickly southward; a movement through the heart of the Cisjordanian region which, remarkably enough, is indicated only by the non-Israelite enclaves or local majorities. The fourth region on the map stands in 7b and points to the south pole of the Dan-Beersheba merismus. This part of the journey is sketched as a movement from the centre to the periphery, by means of the verb 'go out'.

The same verb dominates v.4b, the line bringing Joab's departure from Jerusalem and so commences the report of the census. But this 'going out' of Joab 'from the king' is, at the same time and primarily, the counterpart of v.8b, 'they came [back] ... to Jerusalem'. The rounding-off function of this line on homecoming is apparent from the information on place and time, being the evidence of a narrator who commands a view of everything. He measures the time span for us: counting all the way the men have traversed the land in nine months and twenty days, and he has the line end on the sparingly-used proper name of the city of David. Also lines 5a and 8a, noticeable by being very short, (a mere three words), can be viewed as each other's counterpart because their action is not a part of the actual count. The movement of 5a leads to the start at Aroer, whilst 8a looks back and is a summary.[55]

The description devotes much attention to the start and to the eastern and the northern boundaries and, due to its stating so many geographical names,

[54] This quantity of twelve lines does not only occur in A. The numbers after it do not follow rigidly but appear to orientate themselves to the holy number: vv.10-12 has twelve lines, vv.13-15 thirteen; vv.16-17 also has twelve lines but is only a part of vv.16-19, all in all seventeen lines. The final scene between David and Araunah has twenty-four lines. This means that both part A and part C of the composition have twice twelve lines!

[55] Notice that the wyqtl of this clause, v.8a, is not consecutive any more for this reason. May we call this summarising verb *wayyāšūṭū* a flashback, viewed strictly temporally?

is of an enumerative nature. It is not primarily a result of narrating just for the fun of it, it responds rather to the need for documenting the kingdom of David and the task of historiography. Many names appear in sets of two. Here is a survey of the composition:

Joab and the generals departed from before the eyes of the king + task (4b)
They crossed over the Jordan (5a)
They started in[56] the wadi of Gad – two city names (5b)

They came – two names of regions (6a)
They came – two names of cities[57] (6b)
They came – one city name, two series[58] (7a)

They went out – one regional name, one city name (7b)
[In this way] they traversed the whole country (8a)
They came [back] to Jerusalem + time taken by the task (8b)

It will be clear by now that an apparently dull text enumerating geographical data can also be an object of literary concern and careful composition. The movement of Joab and his men across the map is in an anti-clockwise direction. Suppose there were feelings of resistance to the census among the people – a point of view comparable with that of the characters God and Joab, and which has parallels in our time. Then the route of Joab can be 'read' as an encircling. It is conceivable that he regularly left a sentry post behind in the east and the north whilst the count was in progress, with a view to cutting off reluctant subjects who wanted to temporarily leave the country. In the west and the south the natural barriers of the sea and the desert came to his assistance. These considerations fit in with a primarily military interpretation of the census. The fact that David first of all wanted to be represented by an efficient administration over his people, with the object of being able to draw effectively on a reservoir of able-bodied fighting men whenever he wanted, is revealed by the designation of those counted at the end of 9b: 'the strong men who can handle a sword'.

Does the central part of the chapter go up to and include v.15 or farther? Various authors have the final part begin at v.16, chiefly with a view to God's

[56] 'They began' is what the LXX have; the 'they encamped' of the MT does not make any difference to my argument: v.5b stays the start, on the tributary of the Jordan.

[57] This is correct if one interprets Dan as the name of a tribe and district, after which Iyyon and Sidon are the rhyming city names; it is also correct if one follows the JPS, 'they came to Dan-jaan and around to Sidon.' For the problematical condition of the text see Appendix I.

[58] The first phrase of 7a mentions the name Tyre; this is followed by a long phrase which unites 'Hivite and Canaanite cities'.

about-face; and we saw that v.15 itself appears to be a closure. Others see a new beginning in v.17. But an appeal to theological or diachronic arguments or to those regarding content is not a strong one. As always I advocate the primary importance of properly observing facts of form and proportions, serious study of style and structure, and the suspension of interpretative conclusions.

In vv.10-19 (as a part of a story a phenomenon on level 8) I notice an extensive parallelism which organises sequences and speeches (phenomena on level 7). It becomes visible as soon as we observe, in v.17, the striking repetition of David's confession of sin in v.10 and reflect on its structural contribution. Both cases are answered by a revelation of God which is made known to the king via the prophet Gad. Parts vv.10-14 and 17-19 have a complementary relationship. The first passage stands for guilt and punishment (= three days of plague), and after the reversal of v.16 (God already takes pity on the first day of punishment) the second passage stands for compassion (in the repeated confession of guilt by David) and the premature halting of the punishment (one day of plague only).

Furthermore I observe that the main matter is covered by speeches, of which there are seven in number. They are interrupted once by a report cluster (in four, five wayyiqtol clauses, vv.15a-16c), but for the rest they are consistently concatenated by means of six pairs. Each pair reports a movement in its first line[59] and the second line is about speaking and/or is itself a variant of the quotation formula.[60] Here is a summary:

David's conscience smote him afterwards	10a
and David said to the Lord:	10b
speech (three lines)	10cde
When David rose in the morning	11a
the word of God had come to Gad (...):	11b
speech (three lines)	12cde[61]
Gad came to David,	13a
he told him and said to him:	13b
speech (four lines)	13cdef

[59] This obtains literally for v.11a-13a-18a-19a; in 16f the position which the angel has reached after one day's work is involved, and in 10a the movement takes place in David's feelings.

[60] I note two small deviations which detract virtually nothing from the systematic alternation. In 14a only one clause occurs, purely the quotation formula, and the 'he said' with which 17a opens is doubled by 17b.

[61] Paying attention to the actual message of God in v.12 I leave the formalities (12a the messenger's assignment, 12b the messenger's formula) aside for a moment.

David said to Gad:	14a
speech (4 lines)	14bcde
[the narrator's cluster follows here, 4 wyqtl lines, and:]	15a-16b
He said to the angel who was destroying the people:	16c
speech (2 lines)	16de
The angel was then by the threshing floor of Araunah.	16f
When David saw the angel (...), he said to the Lord:	17ab
speech (4 lines)	17cdef
Gad came to David the same day	18a
and said to him:	18b
speech (1 line)	18c
David went up, according to the word of Gad,	19a
as the Lord had commanded	19b

The unity of the passage, vv.10-19, can be supported by still more arguments. There is the appearance of the prophet in vv.11-18, which is the indispensable link between heaven and earth. The piece follows step for step a spectacular growth process in David, so that his second confession of guilt exhibits fascinating differences with respect to his position in v.10 and v.14. And finally there is the organisation of time on the basis of a whole series of temporal signals distributed throughout the text.[62] The second of these is so strikingly placed, in v.11a, that we must not neglect the time scheme.[63] I conclude that part B goes up to and includes verse 19. This does not get in the way of recognising a change in v.16. Just like part A the central passage has two halves; I call vv.10-15 B_1 and vv.16-19 B_2.

The quantitative balance of the speeches in vv.10-14 invites us to investigate their relationship. On thematic grounds I see a concentric pattern in the series of 3-3-4-4 lines:

[62] Even though A. Schenker, 'Der Mächtige im Schmelzofen des Mitleids', Freiburg and Göttingen 1982 (= OBO 42), does not set out the text properly as a consequence of preoccupation with theology and content, he has rightly stressed the aspect of time, dealing with it correctly. He sees (in common with the rendering 'the same day' in v.18a by various translations, from SV to JPS) that the plague is already stopped after one day [see my following note] and retains the word *mō'ed* at the end of v.15a with its usual meaning, here 'a time appointed [by God]'. See his p.7 and note 11 on pp.61sq. Also correct regarding this term are Carlson, p.215, and Goslinga pp.468sq.

[63] Notice that the word 'morning' from v.11a returns in the merismus of 15a. Schenker writes on p.7 about this expression: 'es handelt sich um einen Zeitpunkt an diesem gleichen ersten Tag des Ausbruchs der Epidemie, da 'von Morgen an bis Zeitpunkt X' verlangt, dass X noch in denselben Tag fällt'.

A David: confession of guilt, asking for forgiveness
B God: Gad has to make David choose a punishment
B' Gad specifies the three punishments
A' David speaks of distress and compassion

The *ṣar lī me'ōd* of v.14b is an echo of David's *ḥāṭātī/ niskaltī me'ōd* from v.10 and the idea of forgiveness gets a sequel in v.14d. This is the correspondence between A and A'. There are three speakers and the addressees move up; only vv.13-14 have a pure dialogue. In v.10 and v.17 David speaks directly to God, but God (after v.1) no longer speaks directly to David anywhere, he uses Gad twice as spokesman. This furnishes a special speech of God to the prophet the first time, vv.11-12, but not the second, v.18. Only from the subordinate clause v.19b are we able to infer that what Gad says to David in the second place, the task of building an altar, does not originate with himself but comes from God.

The remarkable location of the datum that 'David rose up in the morning' enables us, on the one hand, to conclude in retrospect that David's remorse (his speech of v.10) came on in the night, and is on the other hand the basis against which v.11b takes off, so that this line can easily be seen to be a flashback – which is yet another retrospective element. The combining and deducing to which this passage has put us furnish a fascinating synchronism: in the same night David's conscience plays up Gad receives, through revelation, God's reaction to the king's guilt. At that moment David does not know what has fallen to Gad's share, and the prophet does not know that remorse is making the king ready to hear the announcement of punishment. Moreover David has no insight whatsoever into the fact that his position as a sinner is at the same time that of a puppet. We know that, since we have already been told about the puppeteer. The synchronism raises the question of causality, leaving at the same time the answer open: does God decide to set the prophet on David because [and not until] he sees David's conscience in operation? The same question of simultaneity which perhaps implies, or maybe does not imply, a causal link is to crop up presently in vv.16-17.

The very first sentence of the central part hurls David into an acute and spectacular protest of violent emotions. 'His heart hit him' – this formulation is inspired by I 24:6 and the connection with this reference assures that David now realises and feels that he has broken a taboo which could cost him his life.[64] There in I 24 he threatened to invade the sphere of the sacred by touching the anointed one with violence, here the invasion is of the kind – so David discovers after the deed – that the holding of a census means an infringement of a divine prerogative. His speech has a simple structure a-b-a. The first and the third line relate his achievement via perfects: sin and folly, whilst the middle addresses God himself with the vocative of his proper name and in an urgent imperative begs for forgiveness. Line 10e motivates this by being a *kī* clause, but inflects back with the rhyming perfects *niskaltī* and the repetition of *m*ᵉ*'ōd* to the perfects *ḥāṭātī* ... *'āśītī* of 10c. The self-disqualification in the middle has been frozen into the noun 'sin'. The well-known hinge word 'and now' at the beginning of v.10d marks the contrasts of past/present, observation/wish and sin/forgiveness. From previous events we remember David's most painful hour, when the prophet exposed David as a merciless egoist and criminal and David stammered the same words 'I have sinned, forgive me', in ch.12.[65]

In v.12 God answers David's 'having done' (*'āśītī* in 10c) wrong with what 'I will do to you' in 12e. It is a punishment. This is not necessarily a refusal of the plea for forgiveness. The fact that David stays alive and can choose between three punishments probably already implies partial clemency. It is, however, an irony at the expense of David, once chosen by God to replace Saul, that God orders him to '*b*ᵉ*ḥar l*ᵉ*kā*', with such an object. The narrator has taken the option in v.12 of not yet including what the punishments are. He postpones them until David himself gets to know of them from the lips of Gad. In vv.10-12 he does not allow us, for a moment, to share in his omniscience. We hear them itemised at the same time as David and not before. This might possibly signify we are supposed, during part B, to go deeply into David and his emotional condition.

Gad not only gets the title of prophet in v.11b, but also that of 'seer of David', in a line on 'the word of the Lord', an auditively transmitted revelation therefore. This recalls the combination of *dbr* and *ḥzh* in ch.7, where the revelation also came to the prophet at night. This revelation received a pointed introduction with a first- and a second-degree direct speech which formally included a messenger's assignment and a messenger's formula: 7:5ab. The same is the case here in v.12ab. The similarity bears the importance of this moment.

[64] It is very striking that the formula *wayyak leb dawīd 'ōtō* is linked to the time adjunct *'aḥăre ken* in I 24 also.

[65] The syntax of 12cd is a chiasmus of predicates and numbers: 'three [punishments]/ I am imposing upon you, choose for yourself / one of them'.

Gad appears before the king in v.13 and utters four lines. The narrator allows him the honour of specifying the three punishments, so that David and the reader are put in the picture at the same time. Each one of the lines 13cde mentions a punishment. They are connected by the interrogative particles *hă ... 'im ... 'im* initially and the rhyme on 'your' at the rear. The sixth word of all lines (which is also the final one in 13c and e) forms the series *b*^{e}*'arṣękā – ṣārękā – b*^{e}*'arṣękā*. 'Your country' does not quite occur in the line on fleeing, but an addition on 'your enemy', viz. that 'he pursues you', does. Because *ṣārękā* has spatially ousted *'arṣękā* from 13d, a line which in spite of this evokes space the most through its being continued and the complementariness of flee/pursue, I read the flight as a leaving the country. In the middle of the sentences there are the shrinking periods of the three catastrophes: seven years – three months – three days. This decrease is inversely proportional to the gravity of the punishment. If this were not so then the choice would hardly be a choice. The two lines with six words which end on 'your land' are, qua word order, strictly parallel: first the predicate, then the period of time. But this is the other way around in the central line, 13d, so that two syntactic chiasmuses arise:

13c	13d	13e
hătābō l^{e}*kā*	three months	*w*^{e}*'im hęyōt*
seven years	*nūs*^{e}*kā lifnē ṣārēkā*	three days

In 13c and e there is a catastrophe which overtakes David, in 13d he himself becomes the subject and has to flee. The opting for his movement ousts the word 'sword' as peer of the alliterating words for famine and plague.

He who has read the whole book of Samuel thinks back, at the famine, to ch.21, which is indeed the counterpart to this story, and at the fleeing before a pursuer, to the Absalom episode. No wonder David does not want to repeat the experience. But if this piece of the appendix refers to an event of the early David, as does so much of the material bordering on to it, then there is a snake in the grass. What David manages to avoid here – the only punishment to be performed on him by the hand of man – is lying in wait for him and has yet to take place, after he himself has put the evil mechanism of sex and violence into operation which is to produce the loss of four sons!

The speech ends with the powerful line 13f. It is a conclusion in search of a conclusion: marked by the hinge word 'now then' and via two short but powerful imperatives which insist on a choice ending with the dependent question 'what sort of an answer I am going to give my sender?' The question points to David's answer and his answer is the conclusion. The choice of words ‘know and see’ is an ironic counterpart of the knowing which David wants in 2d and the seeing [of a vastly growing people] which Joab wishes on him in v.3c. The ‘I’ of v.13f and the designation ‘my sender’ make clear to David at the last moment what we have already listened in on in 12cd. It is God who gives David the choice, being the mighty one who is able put such hair-raising alternatives into operation. Gad is purely and simply one who, being sent, passes on a word of God. The narrator finds the repetition of a messenger formula no longer necessary at the beginning of the speech.

David’s answer contains the same number of lines and its structure is determined by the intertwining of two, more significant, chiasmuses. The first is that of 14b and 14d, in which the idea ‘much’ (*m*^{e}*’ōd* and *rabbīm*) is encircled by the sharp contrast of my distress versus his compassion. The diagonal device creates a balance: my very difficult predicament can only be counteracted by his great compassion. The resh of *ṣar* rolls on in the alliteration of *rabbīm raḥămāw*. There is a rhyme *lī – kī*, and the repetition of the word ‘very’ places the observation with which David commences in 14b in line with his initial confession of guilt (which had *-tī m*^{e}*’ōd* twice).[66]

The second chiasmus occurs in 14c and 14e and deserves an outline:

14c	Let us fall	into the hands of the Lord
14e	but into the hands of men	let me not fall.

The second chiasmus counts as two. What immediately hits the eye is the inversion of the syntax; but there is more: the cross exhibits an ingenious linking and alternation of singular and plural. In 14c a collective is brought under the power of one person, God himself. But the legitimacy of the speaking about ‘us’ is unpleasantly undermined by the reversal which is a chiasmus and is succeeded by a ‘me’ which stands for the speaker personally and is potentially more honest. But here David is, in fact, very much thinking about his own skin, he does not want to fall into the hands of men (plural!).[67]

His ego also makes itself felt in an ellipse. The composition of the speech is, it is true, a simple ABA’B’, in which one chiasmus works within the A-A’ relationship and the other refines B-B’.[68] But the syntax adds something else. The ‘we’ line on falling obtains a fine motivation, that of the nominal, almost

[66] Furthermore I call to mind I 26:21, where king Saul uses the words *ḥāṭātī* ... *hiskaltī* ... *m*^{e}*’ōd*; in the same story in which David speaks of the *hesīt* of God (as Carlson remarks, p.208-211) the negative effects of which can be atoned for by a sacrifice.

[67] I interpret *’ādām* of v.14e as a collective.

[68] There is also a quantitative balance which underlines the same alternation: v.14bcde has 3 + 4 + 3 + 4 words.

hymnal, *kī* clause on divine mercy in fact. That is why we now expect a motivation once again after the 'I' line on falling, but it fails to arrive. The ego of David has blue-pencilled away something very nasty, a statement of the kind: people are implacable. This could be political realism but this repressed implication of/after v.14e raises the question as to the amount of projection in such a blatant generalisation. He who so wishes can discover part of the answer in the treatment which David himself metes out to his political enemies and upon which ch.8 has supplied us with implacable information.

Has David made a choice between the three options? Yes and no. The only option which he has crossed out is the second one; political defeat plus having to start again from scratch, which v.13d carries with it. What remains is: famine or plague. The choice between them ought to be looked at on two levels of communication. Within the story there is the character of David who refuses to give his opinion on this. One can read his shifting the choice between famine and plague back to his God in a sympathetic and an unsympathetic light. Is it respect for the deity, or David's unwillingness to take full responsibility for an unequivocal decision upon himself? Or both? On another level, that of narrator-reader contact, the answer is easier: in ch.21 we have already had a famine, so that it is now the plague's turn.

The series AB-B'A' of the four speeches on guilt and punishment is now complete and is followed by the only cluster with imperfects which part B has: vv.15-16c. Verse 15 is a verse of overview, with its death toll and the merismuses of time and place which are both regulated by 'from ... to ... '. The verse would have been a closure, where it not for the fact that in v.16 attention's camera zooms in on the slaughter in progress and the figure performing it, 'the angel'. The inclusion of the name of the capital changes the spatial aspect. The repetition 'from Dan to Beersheba' in v.15b means that the punishment has a *talio*-like symmetry with sin: with the census which had to go from Dan to Beersheba according to David's own utterance.[69] With v.16's naming the capital, a picture of periphery and centre arises and the ravaging of Jerusalem becomes the climax of the first day of destruction. But this climax is too much for God and he cancels it. He 'has repented as to the evil' in harmony with (a variant of)[70] the poetical-liturgical creed which he himself once formulated in Ex.34:5-7. The *nḥm* of the text sides with the *rḥm* for which David had hoped. David is proved right in his trusting in the compassion of God. Does this now mean that God has been

[69] This correspondence has been observed by Schenker, *op. cit.*, p.8.

[70] The phrase *niḥām 'al hārā'ā* does not occur literally in Ex.34, but it does, however, in the variants Joel 2:13 and Jonah 4:2.

influenced by his chosen king's statement of faith? That remains to be seen![71] The narrator avoids the use of indications upon which a causal connection between David's clause of hope and God's repentance might be founded. The suspension of causality becomes even more compelling in a moment when we place v.17 (and 21f) next to v.16 and God's 'halt!'.

The hand in which David chose to fall is the hand of the angel. This hand frames 16a-e and changes from an instrument of destruction into a hand which is lowered and allowed to stop. This ring of a stretched out and a lowered arm is part of a regular alternation of destruction and compassion which has its point in God's about-face:

wayyišlaḥ yādō
  hammal'āk ... lešaḥătāh
    wayyinnāḥem 'ęl hārā'ā
  lammal'āk hammašḥīt
rab! hęręf yādękā!

after which the angel is mentioned for the third time in v.16f. This line curves back, as a specification of position and via the element of 'the Jebusite', to the beginning, v.16a, with the name of the city.[72] Now that God has changed his mind, and not before, the content of *mō'ed* in 15a is laid down. This word should not be made more problematical than it is. It forms part of the merismus 'from the morning to the time of the *mō'ed* [appointed by God]' and contains a slight prolepsis, insofar as the adjunct that it is enough has yet to follow in v.16b-e.[73] This connection is reinforced even more when we notice that the specificative little word *'et* which accompanies *mō'ed* has a counterpart in the speech which says 'stop': in the word *'attā* which marks the cessation with its 'now'.

If David had heard the command to the angel at this point, he could have uttered a speech of thanksgiving. What he actually does, however, is utter a new confession of guilt. How does this come about? One of the surprises of v.17 is that he does see the angel, but does not hear the words addressed to him. He does not know that God has already ordered an end to the plague. The narrator has him say the further line 21f, which unambiguously proves that the king, during his negotiations with Araunah, is still under the illusion that his cultic activity or his sacrifice is affecting the raging of the plague.

[71] Against Brueggemann, who in his article in CBQ 50, p.393 note 15 writes: 'David relies on the compassion of Yahweh, *which causes* Yahweh to repent and save the city.' (Italics mine, JF.)

[72] The name Jerusalem is to be found only in v.8b and here in 16a.

[73] One may render the prolepsis, in translation, as follows: 'from the morning to the time which God *was to* determine'.

David's not knowing is thus established. And that has major consequences for the question of causality. God's cancellation of the catastrophe is an autonomous event which has little or nothing to do with the mortal's squirming. It takes place according to a circuit of its own upon which David, with all his good intentions, has no influence whatever. There is no causality, but there is an intriguing synchronicity. At approximately the same time as God calls a halt to the angel David observes the angel and utters his second confession of guilt.[74] When he is informed by Gad a little while later that he must build an altar he naturally interprets this, in his ignorance, to mean that he must make an expiatory offering, and that this cultic activity is necessary for halting of the plague.[75] But the reader does know better thanks to the additional knowledge the omniscient narrator supplies him in v.16.[76]

The line which opens David's verse has two striking characteristics. The report that David sees the angel standing there makes 17a into a reflection of 16f which gave information on the position of the angel, but was destined for the reader. The datum of David's view is, however, pushed into the background, being 'only' an infinitival phrase tacked on after the core of the clause, as if its content were nothing special. There is therefore no *wayyar* of David following on consecutively from v.16. This means that the angel's becoming visible is the second time the omniscient narrator treats us in the same way as David, as far as the obtaining of information is concerned.[77]

[74] I differ with Schenker who has failed to detect the entire problem surrounding knowledge and the lack of it, and who contradicts himself on the temporal relationships of v.16 and 17. The following sentence on his p.7 forces v.17 into the role of a flashback: 'V. 17 ereignet sich ... am ersten Tag, *vor* dem Zeitpunkt, and dem JHWHs Reue dem heimsuchenden Engel Einhalt gebot.' On pp.8-9, however, Schenker rightly refuses 'V. 17 in V. 16 einzuschieben' and admits: 'Dabei ist Davids Fürbitte nicht *die Ursache* von JHWHs Erbarmen.' (Italics mine, J.F.). Schenker comes close to the synchronism with the following kind of sentence, p.8 'Die Bitte Davids fällt mit dem Willen JHWHs in eins.'

[75] For the record: I do not deny by this that the altar, the first sacrifice upon it, and the cult which follows have their validity and importance. David's burnt offering is, however, a seal of – thus an act after – the staying of the plague, and in no way a ritual cause or adaptation of it.

[76] At this point the difference between 24:25c and 21:14c becomes interesting. Line 25c actually omits the temporal phrase *'aḥărē ken* which was so aptly placed in ch.21 and this is not for nothing. This temporal adjunct may not stand in 24:25 because there is no causal connection between v.25ab (altar plus sacrifice) and a divine answer. But I would like to point out once again: David fails to notice this.

[77] Because the participle is neutral regarding time the *makkē* of the source language in v.17a is not unequivocal. What is of importance is to render it properly in the target language. It does not state (but neither does it deny) that the angel had destroyed, nor that he wanted or was to destroy. I advocate the translation that David 'saw the angel who smote/destroyed (etc.) the

Verse 17a is a flashback which does not stretch so far that the report comes earlier than v.16 (God's repenting), but moves David's observation and speech (approximately) next to God's command to halt in narrated time. Now David too is moved by compassion, but the point of the ingenious manipulation of time is that the two circuits remain completely separate.[78]

David sees the angel of vengeance and is speechless for a moment.[79] Then he utters the four-line speech which is the climax of his growth process and reveals a completely different mentality from his centremost speech (of v.14). There are two pairs: first two observations with perfects which form a *parallelismus membrorum*, 17cd; and then an interrogative clause answered by a volitional clause, 17ef. The first pair is a double admittance of 10c's 'I have sinned' with a synonym (*hę'ęwētī*) echoing the noun 'sin' from 10d. But the confession of guilt now becomes really personal through the double addition of the pronoun *'ānōkī*. It seems linguistically redundant but it performs the important stylistic and psychological function of David's entirely mastering his own responsibility by means of it.[80] This is also due to the occurrence of a double 'I' in an opposition to 'these' of v.17e (*sc.* the subjects). This opposition serves the innocence of the people. Line 17e with its initial *casus pendens* has a double brokenness which reveals spontaneity and emotion placing the sentence as a specimen of the vernacular: ' ... but these [people], the poor sheep, what have they done?' The rhetorical question

people' which is to be found in the KJ, SV, LV, and Buber. The rendering 'who *was* strik*ing* down the people (according to the English BJ, NEB, NBE, and JPS) is temporally more specific than the Hebrew and implies that David also observes the action of the angel; actually the original language does not speak out on this with the attributive *hammakkę*. This kind of rendering makes the flashback characteristic of v.17a very (or too) plain.

[78] Schenker does not study and formulate the synchronism in temporal terms. What he does do is to try and forge it into a nice connectedness: 'David und JHWH kommen zusammen im gleichen Mitleid mit den schwer leidenden Volk!', p.9. This is only possible if one has suppressed the satanic moment. His conclusion which immediately follows is euphoric and untenable: 'Das ist der Grund, weshalb JHWH gerade David zum Stifter des sühnenden Kultes durch den Propheten Gad einsetzt!'

[79] The fact that he deserves a moment of astonishment I deduce from the striking repetition of *wayyōmęr* which opened 17a and fills the whole of 17b. To a certain extent comparable are the places in which one character delivers two speeches one after the other, the narrator managing to squeeze a 'he said' in between. An insertion like this is usually done for a good reason. We saw in I Sam.26:9-10 and II 16:10-12 that the practical/fundamental difference or refusal + explanation was marked by this.

[80] We can now see the difference in centre of gravity between 10c and 17c. In 10c *m*^{e}*'ōd* stresses the act (even though the first person is not absent), but in 17cd the centre of gravity lies in the subject, the first person (even though the act is not absent).

uses the verb *'āśā* once again, but now in order to place the people outside the context of guilt (*'āśītī* of 10c) and punishment (*'ę'ęśę* of 12e). The contrast between asking in the service of innocence and admitting one's own guilt is still accentuated by the *hinnē* which underlines the 'I' clauses. The plea that the people are innocent is a token of good intentions, but it is put in an odd light by the information of v.1, in which the nation, not the king, had aroused God's anger. This datum effects irony and undermines the good intentions of the uninformed David a long time in advance.

David is now aware that he ought to have been a shepherd instead of a dictator who makes the fate of his subjects secondary to his need for power, having put them through the bureaucratic mincer.[81] Finally, in the third instance, he formulates his personal responsibility without reserves. The purity which he reaches in v.17 reveals at the same time that the first person singular of v.14e is still not so very different from the 'we' in 14c and is still mainly egoistic. Now, in v.17f, David asks God that the burden might exclusively rest on him and his family, simple alliteration underlining this: *bī ub^ebēt 'ābī.*

The narrator does not say that God answers David when he sends Gad to him twice in v.18. This is only simulated by the progress of narration time, by the fact that Gad's coming is placed after v.17. But David is sure to fall into the trap of thinking there is a causal connection between his definitive confession of guilt and the command to build an altar. Something like this had overtaken him earlier when he got up full of remorse (vv.10-11) and a short while later the prophet entered with a message of punishment. One of the reasons for drawing the parallel is the fact that the four words of v.13a are repeated exactly in v.18a. But the addition in the final line is also of importance. The adjunct 'on the same day' is a mainstay of the underlying time scheme and confirms that David's being assigned an atonement ritual is given on the day when God repented and David saw the angel.[82]

The prophet does not say 'go, make' to the king but 'go up, raise an altar'. The verticality of one supports that of the other imperative. The threshing floor of Araunah is, if we take *'lh* seriously, higher than the city of David, thus on the mountain which is later to bear the temple. The pair of impera-

[81] The one word, 'the sheep', already makes the function of shepherd sufficiently clear. I do not rectify the verb of 17d with the *hr'h hr'wty* of 4QSam[a], *cf.* the *hr' hr'ty* of Chron. – to begin with because the MT is sound and secondly because 'the shepherd', *hr'h* is a bit too much of a good thing and adds a sentimental touch to the argument.

[82] The original text has *bayyōm hahū*, which is literally 'on that day'. But the proper interpretation of this is to my mind indeed 'the same day', as in the SV, LV, NEB, JPS, McCarter, and GNB. (The KJ, Buber, NBG, BJ, NBE, KBS stay neutral, 'on that day'.)

tives is a welcome alternative after the fatal horizontalness of the pair 'go, count' from the beginning and the punitive 'know and see' of v.13f. The assignment covers, like v.1c, only one line and does not add anything cultic to the datum 'an altar for Yahweh'. The David of v.25 looked on it as a hint to the good listener and sacrificed burnt- and peace-offerings immediately after the purchase of the ground and the building of the altar. The prophet's instruction mentions the proper place for the altar; it turns out to be exactly the same place reached by the angel of vengeance. The threshing floor of Araunah is the spatial marking of the temporal boundary given by the about-turn of God, who found the destruction 'enough!' The Israelite public giving ch.24 its first reception must have realised with a pleasant surprise: our God has called a halt to the angel on the exact spot where the temple now stands!

Verse 18 does not say that God has spoken to Gad again. But there is no doubt about the authority of his second appearance before David. Verse 19 has a striking parallelism between 'according to the word of Gad' and 'as Yahweh had commanded', so that we know for certain that Gad was a messenger again and are aware of the identity of his Sender. Part B ends on a note of obedience which is diametrically opposite to the opening in v.10 on sinfulness. Not only does the clause 'as the Lord had commanded' say this but also the indicative *wayya'al*: David does indeed climb the mountain at once; a good ending to the series of lines in the sparse narrator's text which had reported various movements of getting up and coming in. – In the sequel this upward movement is, as it were, to be subject to involution; the hiph'il forms *w^eya'al* and *wayya'al* in v.22b and 25b make the verb transitive and report the cultic culmination of David's journey. This can be compared well with the qal/hiph. alternation of the same root in II Sam.6.

Part C covers vv.20-25 and has been effectively delineated in two ways. It is a scene which concentrates entirely on two figures and their dialogue and, by means of 3 + 5 wayyiqtol clauses, it is first shown in and then shown out by the narrator. A total of eight lines of report frame five speeches which each have a simple quotation formula and together offer eleven lines of spoken word. The boundary with the middle part is also finely indicated by the camera's turning through 180 degrees: at once we look over the shoulder of the Jebusite towards the approach of the king and his retinue. Not only is there a *wayyar*, but a *wayyašqef* prior to it, in a clause of its own and used absolutely. The word recalls Abraham in Gen.19:28, who also looks out over destruction,[83] and the approaching negotiations can be compared well with

[83] Abraham's 'look out over' in Gen.19 is, moreover, the successor to the vista (also *šqf* in the hiph.!) the angels of destruction have of Sodom in ch.18:16.

Gen.23, where the patriarch drives a hard bargain with the Hittites and, poker-faced, paid an unheard-of price for a piece of land in which Sarah was the first to be provided with a grave. Initially the application of *šqf* to Araunah simply says that he is situated at a high point: apparently he is present at his threshing floor or at work. But it also symbolises the dignity of this interlocutor and David is to fully respect this.

The consideration with which the narrator treats Araunah is not only apparent from the fact that his perspective (20ab) is allowed to offer insight at the meeting, but also the fact that Araunah is allowed to open the talk with an informatory 'why' question, even though David is the inquiring party in the negotiations. The Jebusite knows his place as resident alien, but he also has good manners, for upon recognising the king he leaves his place and goes to meet him, *wayyeṣē* 20c. He nullifies his originally high position, moreover, by immediately performing a careful[84] prostration. He bows to the one whom he sees, and that is not the individual, let alone the sinner David, but 'the king', a term which has not been used since v.9 (the close of part A). At this moment 'the king and his servants' are "*ōbᵉrīm 'ālāw*'. This surprising choice of words for an approaching movement arouses my suspicions that the beginning of part B and the passage vv.18-20 (thus the end of B + the beginning of C) have been placed parallel – having more to do with one another therefore – by the following chiasmus:

10d ha'ăbęr-nā 'ęt 'ăwōn 'abdᵉkā	wayyāqom Dāwīd babboqęr (11a)
18c hāqem lyhwh mizbeăḥ	hammęlęk wᵉ ... 'ăbādāw 'ōbᵉrīm 'ālāw (20b)

Is this device in fact a chiasmus? I think it is, in view of the ingenious change of qal and hiph'il which each determine both roots once. David's awaking, suffering an agony of remorse, concerns the special twenty-first day of the tenth month[85] which is to end with the setting up of an altar and a rite which seals the atonement. This diagonal (11a-18c) thus covers the substitution of the ruler's despotic autonomy with heteronomy: listening to God. On the vertical line (10d + 18c) we find the imperatives of complementary speeches and speakers. One hiph'il speaks of forgiveness, the other is a sign of expiation. On the other diagonal (10d-20b) we see that the solemn approach

[84] The idea that he makes a careful or reverent bow is implied by the full formula *wayyištaḥu 'appāw 'arṣā* which adds two adjuncts.

[85] Schenker wants to give the day added lustre by making it into a Sabbath. This sounds too good. There is no datum in the text to suggest that Joab departed on a *yōm rīšōn*.

of the official group with the king in their midst is busy making forgiveness a reality.

Just like Joab Araunah twice utters the courtly 'my lord the king', and in his opening question the word with which he classifies himself, 'his servant', is complementary to 'my lord'. David continues the syntax of the question by having the immediate infinitive clauses link up with the predicative core of Araunah's sentence in 21de. These lines form a rigorous *parallelismus membrorum*. They begin with various verbs which are an anaphora all the same by being just one sound different, *liqnōt/libnōt*. Then there is a chiasmus which symbolises the change of owner: 'from you' becomes 'to Yahweh' and these adjuncts are linked crosswise to the concrete threshing floor and altar which are both grammatical objects. The aims indicated by the infinitives are themselves in the service of a higher aim, which is stated by the final clause of 21f: the cessation of the plague. The line is virtually a copy of v.25d and reveals both David's idea that the plague is still raging and his illusion that his cultic contribution is necessary for its halting. Apart from this the parallelism with the ending goes further, turning out to be 3 + 3 cola in length. Lines 21def relate to lines 24d-25a-25d as striving for or wish, and their realisation.

In answering Araunah ignores the question of buying and selling. He skips this stage, courteously offering his material at once for a sacrifice in the way the king wants it. But there might be a problem attached to this omission. It is not improbable that Araunah wants to keep his land, the inheritance of generations, and tries to keep the question of ownership off the agenda with a great show of generosity. But David does not allow this point to be brushed aside, stating expressly in v.24 (with an absolute infinitive), and in a way which cannot be got round, that he wants a real sale and will gladly pay the full price.[86] And so it happens.

The generosity with which Araunah wants to distract David goes from the magnanimous gesture 'that which is good in his eyes' in v.22b to the all-inclusive *hakkol* of 23a which emphatically occurs initially in an official sentence. Here Araunah refers to himself in the third person, as subject of a performative perfect which attempts to create a *fait accompli*; he manages to double 'the king' thanks to the extra use of the vocative. Between them, in 22cd, Araunah further stuffs his speech full of concrete things: 'the oxen for a burnt offering' and the 'threshing sledge and the yoke of the oxen as pieces of firewood'. The speaker's quasi-giving and the king's taking frame this speech, which is the centremost and the longest of the five. Araunah inter-

[86] The context makes us gather that *bimḥīr* from v.24b pregnantly means 'a large sum', 'the full price'.

rupts the regularity of the alternation of the speeches, moreover, in an extra attempt to win the king over, and now utters another fine wish (23c) which has been set apart by the narrator himself, by means of an inserted quotation formula (23b). Here Araunah respects his sovereign's deity – who in any case was originally not his own – with a double designation: 'May Yahweh your God have mercy upon you!' Through this wish with its two words for the subject, God, his contribution is in balance with what Joab said at the beginning.

The five speeches have, through the surplus of Araunah, the following speakers in their order of appearance, and I add their content in a few key words:

21b	Araunah: the object of your coming?	(1 line)
21def	David replies: (2 +) 1 aim	(3 lines)
22b-23a	Araunah: a princely offer of sacrificial necessities	(4 lines)
23c	Araunah again: wish	(1 line)
24bc	David insists: buy *bimḥīr*, not sacrifice *ḥinnām*	(2 lines)

The double designation for God is taken over by David in 24c, but then by way of a subtle correction determined by a plain 'no'. He has the final word, in the relationship king-subject, just as with the narrator, and utters two parallel sentences which begin with the anaphora *lō* and end on a semantic rhyme: the virtuoso contrast of 'the full price' versus 'for nothing'.[87] David insists upon a change of ownership. The difference between 'from you' and 'to the Lord' in 24bc is adopted from 21de. The pair of verbs from that verse, buy-build, now becomes buy-sacrifice and their point now lies in the adjunct at the end of the lines: the synonymy of 'for the [full] price' and 'not ... free'.

Araunah says nothing more and David gets what he wants. The anaphoral objectives *liqnōt // libnōt* of v.21de now become reality in the just as anaphoral imperfects *wayyiqęn // wayyibęn* of v.24d and 25a. The narrator honours David's emphasis on an honest price by omitting in the first line of his final cluster the name of the previous ȯwner but including the considerable sum of fifty shekels of silver. In this way no slur falls on the legitimacy of

[87] The contrast has to do with the function of the negation which is different in 24b than in c: in 24b it occurs independently initially, in 24c it determines the sentence up to and including 'gratis'. Put in another way: the combination 'not ... free' is the counterpart of 'for the [full] price'.

the conveyance and the new owner of this historical piece of ground.[88] The series 'he bought – built – sacrificed' ensures that the report on implementation fuses the acts from 21de with those of 24bc. The report in 24d still mentions the threshing floor and the price. The place dwindles in 25a to the monosyllable 'there' and we see an altar emerge which is devoted to the heavenly owner whose proper noun is repeated. The third line is shorter still and mentions two kinds of sacrifices. Whereupon David's share is complete.

Two narrator's clauses remain whose content and position is of structural importance. Verse 25d is the fulfilment of David's plan in v.21f and the name Israel links up with the very first verse. The connection proceeds, however, particularly from v.25c where God allows himself to be entreated. This datum occurs exactly opposite to his wrath from v.1 and now rounds off the plot. It is, at the same time, a striking repetition of 21:14c which contributes to the stories' becoming a pair within the appendix II Sam.21-24.[89] Lines 25cd are actually a parallelism. Their verbs instantly ensure this impression by being a niph'al in both cases, which creates so much assonance that we are close on a fresh anaphora: *wayyē'āter // wattē'āṣer*. The positive side of this allowing oneself to be entreated emerges from the minus times minus is plus of the final report, 'the plague was stayed'. The passive aspect of the pair creates a certain detachment suitable to the closure of the story. The succession of the five imperfects in v.24d-25d suggests the consecution and the causal connection in which the benighted king believes: *now* I have built and sacrificed, yes, *because* I have sacrificed on the new altar, God has stayed the plague. But the reader knows, having been adequately informed by the narrator, that the change in reality already occurred one or two hours earlier, and can read the cultic act 'merely' as a sealing of the atonement. If this altar really marks the site of the future temple, the close of the books of Samuel gives food for thought. The beginning of the temple is then – in the form of this predecessor, the altar built by David with its corresponding cult – connected to a crisis between God and his people, in which the Lord has wielded the classic catastrophes of famine, the sword and pestilence.

[88] It is after all probable that the altar marks, on the ex-threshing floor of Araunah, the place upon which the temple of Solomon is to be built later. But the reader does not hear me joining in with Schenker and others to say that ch.24 is a *Gründungslegende*. If it were then it would be very important; and if it is so important why is there not a single sign of it in the text? Even the Chronicler, who has made considerable changes in the parallel text, does not insert such signs, but creates the threshing floor > temple ground identification only through its sequel I Chron.21:28-30 and ch.22:1-4 (particularly v.1).

[89] Notice that in ch.21 the deity is denoted by *'ẹlōhīm* and here by *yhwh*. The whole of ch.24, including the Jebusite, consistently speaks only of Yahweh.

Chapter VIII

The great hymn of thanksgiving and a short poem of the king

§ 1. *Praise and thanksgiving of the triumphal king*, II Sam.22

A good poem deserves rigorous study.[1] It is so complex that we can make solid pronouncements on *what* it says only when we know *how* it speaks and is construed. Not until we have gone the whole way out of respect for the text – the way of linguistic, stylistic and structural research – can we interpret it adequately. Recognising the contours and proportions – of which an empirical and verifiable description can be given – provides us with the frameworks within which responsible semantic production can develop. This process of assigning meaning is two-sided and intersubjective. The text divulges its meanings whilst and because the educated reader assigns meanings in a self-controlled manner during the act of reading. A mysterious and intimate interaction takes place, for the meanings 'in' the text do not live and work outside our receptivity. This responsiveness is an active and extremely sensitive attitude of mind, and every moment of the reader's competently giving meanings is inspired and governed by the signs and the instructions of the text.

The poem in II Sam.22 has 53 true verses[2] and in its form of Psalm 18 is one

[1] I am indebted to Joke van Maanen, Dirk Leenman and Dr. Phons Rodrigues Pereira for their contribution to the inspiring seminar I led in the seasons '85-'87 on Hebrew verse structure and which also tackled Ps.18 for a term.

[2] There are 50 masoretic verses *sc.* vv.2-51, both in Sam. and Ps.18), but vv.7 and 16, with their two bicola, count twice, and with Van der Lugt, p.501, I read v.31c as a monocolon.

of the longest poems in the Psalter.[3] Because of its size it is interesting to ask how the poet remained master of his subject matter above the level of strophes and to pose the related question of whether we readers can generate a grasp of these higher units. On the ground of my own experience with Hebrew poetry and supported by recent theoretical developments in The Netherlands[4] I am of the opinion that almost all the material in the Psalms and many poems elsewhere (in the chokma and the prophets) are covered by the following model. Two to four feet form a colon, usually two or three cola group themselves into a complete verse, two to four verses form a strophe, and two to four strophes make a stanza.[5] In long poems such as Psalms 18 and 68 there is another layer on top: stanzas join up with each other into sections.[6]

The poem of II Sam.22 consists in the masoretic version[7] of 365 words distributed over 110 cola which fill fifty-three verses. The verses join up to

[3] Only two Psalms are longer: 119, of course, the acrostic which accords an eight-verse stanza to each letter of the alphabet (a total of 176 verses therefore) and Ps.78 (with seventy-two 'verses' taking up almost eighty lines of poetry). Ps.89 (with fifty-two true verses) is as long as Ps.18 – which makes me wonder if, at this rarefied altitude of such very big numbers, chance does in fact account for it. (After 'the big four' a couple of Psalms follow at a distance: 68 and 69 – with thirty-six and thirty-seven masoretic verses respectively), and the quartet 104-107 (with thirty-five, forty-five, forty-eight and forty-three masoretic verses respectively).

[4] Various articles by J.C. de Moor, including a series in 'Ugarit-Forschungen' 10, 12 and 18 (of 1978, '80 and '86). From his pupil Pieter van der Lugt a thick book: 'Strofische Structuren in de bijbels-hebreeuwse poëzie', Kampen 1980 (deals with Psalms). In addition Harm van Grol, 'De versbouw in het klassieke Hebreeuws, fundamentele verkenningen deel een: metriek', KTH (Roman Catholic Faculty) Amsterdam, 1986 (deals in detail with a corpus of twelve poems of different genres, somewhat more than two hundred lines of poetry altogether). A volume from De Moor's Kampen circle has appeared very recently: Willem van der Meer and Johannes C. de Moor (eds.), 'The Structural Analysis of Biblical and Canaanite Poetry', JSOT Supplement 74, 1988. Their work has clear points of contact with my text model which I have explained in NAPS II, ch.1.

[5] Compare Van Grol, p.240. Once in a while a monocolon can fill a verse, one verse can be a strophe and one strophe a stanza.

[6] I give as complete a justification as possible of verses (requiring it) and of all (boundaries of) strophes, stanzas and sections of those two Psalms in a short work to appear in the near future entitled 'Two Great Psalms: Hermeneutics, Structural Analysis and the Poetics of Hebrew Verse', Leiden 1991. I refer the reader to this study for extra information and considerations outside the scope of NAPS III; they offer a theoretical basis for this section and contain the full argumentation for the arrangement I give here of the parallel text of Ps.18.

[7] One word has been deleted in my text, at the beginning of v.39a. Many commentators delete the final two words of v.12 as a gloss, and one of the two verbs in 43b. During the count I have not, of course, included the heading of v.1 and the *wayyōmar* of v.2.

form twenty-four strophes. The first of these stands by itself as the introduction. A pair of strophes forms a short stanza three times: in vv.5-7 (four bicola) and vv.17-20 (*idem*), and at the end vv.47-51 (with 2.3.2. and 2.3 cola). The short stanzas surround and alternate with three long stanzas which from now on I will call sections for intrinsic reasons[8]: vv.8-16 (five strophes), vv.21-31 (*idem*) and vv.32-46 (seven strophes). The theophany described in vv.8-16 is the path God takes to alleviate the poet's distress and deliver him from his enemies. To put it another way, the two pairs of strophes prior to and after it are complementary qua content and form the framework of section I. Here is an overview, with several brief indications as to meaning:

	no. of strophes	nature	no. of verses
introduction: hymnic anticipation of themes	1	3 bicola	3
stanza A: the speaker in distress	2	2x2 bicola	4
SECTION I: theophany from heaven	5	2 tricola 4x2 bicola	10
stanza B: God saves the poet	2	2x2 bicola	4
SECTION II: God rewards purity	5	3+2+2+3 bicola 1 bicolon + 1 monocolon	12
SECTION III: triumph in the fight	7	6x2 bicola and 2 bicola round 1 tricolon	15
coda: stanza C, hymn and thanksgiving	2	bi+tri+bicolon, bi+tricolon	5

The five or six tricola receive well thought-out positions.[9] The majority help in marking the stanza boundaries quantitatively. In this way the strophe opening the theophany section consists of two tricola, the end of the second

[8] By intrinsic reasons I mean the criteria which can be derived from the poem itself. The psalm creates and employs a clear difference between three short stanzas (with twenty-five, twenty-eight, and thirty-nine words respectively) and three long ones (with sixty-nine, eighty, and a hundred and three words, also an ascending series thus).

[9] In my notation there are five tricola: v.8, v.9, 44c+45ab, 48ab+49a and v.51. But a sixth arises if one does not write v.31c as a monocolon, but situates it as a proper C colon after 31ab as many do (LV, Buber, NEB, NBE, N.H. Ridderbos in BZAW 117, Van der Ploeg, Kuntz).

section is perhaps a tricolon and the final strophe of the third section is conspicuous by having three verses which are arranged as 2.3.2 cola.

We also encounter quantitative marking one level higher. The majority of the strophes, nineteen out of the twenty-four, has two verses per strophe. The rest are tristichs and are found in boundary positions. First of all there is the single strophe with the task of opening the poem. The central section is framed – and thus bounded – by the tristichic strophes of vv.21-24 and 30-31c. Finally we find two such strophes on both sides of the boundary between section III and the coda: vv.44-46 and vv.47-49.

According to Hebrew standards the metrics of the poem is regular. Approximately two-thirds of the cola have a rhythm with three ictuses.[10] About twenty cola have two accents and a much lower number, *c.* ten cola, has four accents.[11] This produces a rather uniform picture, and an average of just under three ictuses per colon.

The poem has a tiered construction, insofar as it begins with a single strophe as introduction, moves up to a stanza with two strophes and then develops a section of five strophes which is the first climax. Stanza A of vv.5-7 gives the necessary drama by introducing a problem: the hero is in distress. The answer to the affliction and the solution to the problem occur in vv.17-20; they form stanza B which corresponds to A. God is the saviour here and the whole of section I is devoted to how he gets ready for the fight and leaves his heavenly dwelling. The cosmos quakes under his wrath.

Strophe 1 is a unique beginning thanks to vv.2-3. There is an exuberant row of nouns which describe and qualify God, and seven of them are metaphors. Not until the end of two long series (the first two verses) do verbs appear, but they function only in short and asyndetic relative clauses. However these

[10] Cola which can easily be assigned *three* ictuses are, in an unemended text: v.3a- 4a - 5a - 5b - 6a - 7a - 7b - 7c - 8a - 8b - 9a - 9b - 9c - 10a - 10b - 11a - 11b - 14a - 14b - 15a - 16b - 17a - 17b - 18a - 18b - 19a - 19b - 20a - 20b - 21a - 21b - 22a - 22b - 23a - 23b - 25a - 25b - 26b - 27b - 28a - 28b - 29a - 29b - 30a - 30b - 31a - 31b - 33a - 33b - 34a - 34b - 35a - 36a - 37a - 37b - 38a - 38b - 40a - 40b - 41a - 42a - 42b - 44a - 44b - 44c - 45b - 47b - 48a - 48b - 49c - 51a- 51b - 51c – seventy-three cola already. Scanning according to the rules of an accentuating metrics which Van Grol has attempted to further objectify one can add v.6b-8c-45a-47a, and also v.39a and 43b after deleting an imperfect form. Then we arrive at almost eighty *Dreier*.

[11] Non-controversial cola with two ictuses I would like to call v. 4b-7d-13a-13b-15b-16a-16c-16d-24a-24b-26a-27a-36b-41b-46b-49a-49b-50b, eighteen cola thus; with v.39b and 43a included, in which the segholate form can be counted as a monosyllable, we arrive at twenty *Zweier*.

Plain cola with four ictuses are 2a-3c-31c-32a-32b-39a-43b-50a; probably we can also add 35b and 47a, which then produces a total of ten *Vierer*.

ends of the verses do exhibit the I-thou complementariness of which the whole poem is full, and these acts, which through alliteration on ...*ḥ...s* become more involved with one another, have a telling content: 'I take refuge in him – Thou savest me from violence'. The core of the semantics is hardness which produces protection. The hardness of God is expressed in two words for rock and two for fortress. Words like 'crag' and 'fastness' remind us of David's time and condition as a fugitive, as does the word 'escaping'. Words such as 'shield' and 'horn' recall verses from the qina and the psalm of Hannah. This is not by chance, for the two poems mark, together with II 22, the beginning, middle and end of that magnificent conception, the books of Samuel.

The words for rock are both monosyllables and enclose, in the first verse, two long words which have *mem praeformans*. In 3b it is the other way around: the words *maginnī* and *miśgabbī* occur around the monosyllables **qarn* and **yašʿ* which are joined into a semikut. Rhyme and internal rhyme are the dominating phonetic means: in vv.2-3 -ī sounds eleven times. The poem is opened by the holy name, after which four predicates follow in the first verse. They grow from a bisyllabic *salʿī* via *mᵉṣūdātī* into two words, *mᵉfal[lᵉ]ṭī-lī*, after which 3a is one compound predicate of four words (two nouns in semikut plus relative clause). Two words begin with mem in v.2, as do two in 3b and three in 3c.[12] The final word of this series is no longer a divine quality but introduces the first threatening moment, 'from violence'; God saves, however, *min* is fortunately separative. From the second verse the idea of salvation which God brings the poet comes strongly to the fore, thanks to the threefold use of the root *yšʿ*. It is linked each time to the rhyme 'me', but is varied at the same time: noun in 3b, participle and imperfect in 3c.

The words rock, my salvation and violence are to return combined with the pair Yahweh/my God at the end, so that, as a form of *inclusio*, they contribute to the closure of the great design. There David has become the Anointed One and a great king. At the beginning, however, the poet is merely a 'me' and it is going to take a long time before his position and qualities appear in the text.

Verse 4 brings movement. Were it not excluded by the sequel, where the strophes in stanza A have a hermetic structure, we would have failed to accept it as a part of the opening. The content is different, the cola are now verbal and all of a sudden the length is strongly decreased. I scan vv.2-3 as 4 + 3 and

[12] If we interpret the second word as a premasoretic monosyllable *qarn* and count its semikut as a unit of stress, then the quantity of syllables in v.3bc is strikingly regular: 3-4-3 / 4-3-3-4.

3 + 4 stresses (a balance which itself creates an impression of being self-sufficient), whilst v.4 is without doubt 3 + 2.

The positive content and the trio of ictuses in 4a join up well with the nominalising exuberance and the hymnic tone of the preceding. But v.4b opens with a *min* of fear and points to menace: violence is now present in 'my enemies' – the first plural in the poem. With this the introduction borders on strophe 2 which keeps exclusively to danger. In other words: v.4b's task is to prepare for and lead to negativity. The verse's content is still positive. The parts have an order which reverses the chronology, for the praising of God follows the salvation. The Lord and my enemies border on and clash with each other in the middle. The idea of salvation is at work just one more time: the *'iwwāšeᵃʿ* of the hard-pressed self is the form which, as niphʿal, brings the complement of the transitive act *tōšīʿenī*. The void which gapes now that v.4b has no third ictus is iconic; it opens a space of fear, in which catastrophic expectations struggle with the hope of divine intervention. But there is no easy or instant solution; first the following strophe is to deepen the fear with merciless perfection. The cry for help is to broaden out into an entire verse (v.7ab) and not until v.7cd, another complete verse, is there to be an answer.

Stanza A comprises two strophes with a pair of bicola each. Strophe 2 is (together with strophe 18) the only strophe in the long poem in which God does not appear at all and has such a hermetic structure that I have written out the text in full:

kī 'ăfāfūnī mišbᵉrē māwęt	P	Ss
naḥălē bᵉlīyaʿal yᵉbaʿătūnī	Ss	P
ḥęblē šᵉ'ōl sabbūnī	Ss	P
qiddᵉmūnī mōqᵉšē māwęt	P	Ss

This notation shows a chiasmus on the strophe level. Not only do the four clauses enter into an AB-B'A' symmetry through the repetition of the word death, but through a syntactical switch too: in the outer ring the verb occurs initially but, contrariwise, follows in the inner ring. Each time the subject is a construct state combination with a concrete plural plus a word for destruction; hence the Ss notation. The negative forces in the middle are denoted by words which have more or less become proper nouns, Belial and Sheol; at the edges the simple word death occurs twice, itself a segholate form again. Whilst mem dominates the alliteration here, lamed leads in the central cola and ties in all the nouns there.

The poet's subtlety also extends to the lower levels, right down to the sounds. He is engaged in a fresh alternation of segholates and words with a *mem praeformans*. The short words (torrents//cords) occur initially in the middle, the long words move up a position in the outermost clauses, but are extended by the alliterating word for death which gives them their *frappe*. These phonetic aspects endorse the chiasmus. But at the same time an aba'b' arrangement is intertwined throughout and attends to the ordinary *parallelismus membrorum* of an A colon with its neighbour, the B colon. This we can discover by following the subjects: the waves-torrents in v.5, the cords-snares in v.6. This order is supported by the qal-pi'el alternation in both verses.

At verse level verse we can see two chiasmuses of a syntactic nature. Verse 5 places its predicates around the broad subjects, in verse 6 it is the other way round. This syntax of inversions creates a picture of movement and encircling on the levels of verse and strophe. One moment the predicates press forward to stifle or startle the poet, at another the forces of death. Above and below, before and behind, these powers lie in wait for him. One can also find the 'snares of death' in Proverbs (13:14 and 14:27). The combination 'the streams of Belial' is, however, unique. The word pair is a paradox of depersonified personification.[13] Elsewhere the label Belial is attached to people, which reveals the fact that the torrents and cords of this strophe are themselves images for persons: the enemies in 4b and about to appear. The suffocation waves and torrents threaten to produce (*'pp*) can later be turned back only by the wrath (*'appō*) of God who exposes the sea beds (*'ăpīqē yām*) in v.16, the close of the theophany. But now the poet is only victim: 4x *-nī*, and appears to stand hopelessly alone. The metrical regularity, probably 3 + 3 and 3 + 3, suggests that the front facing him is not to be beaten. The poem has, after a handful of verses, reached a dramatic all-time low.

Strophe 3 already ensures a favourable development and brings two verses of response which usher God back into view. The extremities mark the contrast between affliction and answer: *baṣṣar-lī* versus *b*^{e}*'oznāw*, both space adjuncts. At the exact centre of the strophe calling and hearing border on to each other: the 'he heard' with which 7cd begins links up immediately with the 'I called' upon which 7ab ended. Line 7cd is enclosed by terms of auditive reception, 'he heard' ... 'in his ears'. 'My voice' and 'my calling' touch each other within this. Thus the whole is, semantically and syntactically, a new chiasmus. This is also the case with everything after 'my distress' in line 7ab.

[13] The word *b*^{e}*līya'al* is always combined with designations for people: *bat/ben*, *'ādām*, etc., (and in two places with their speaking, *dbr*).

The redoubled[14] *'ęqrā* is the polar, since negative, successor of the happy 'I call: Yahweh is praiseworthy[15]!' of v.4. Its 'aleph carries over into 7b and begins each of its three words with alliteration.

The stanza's metre is very regular and, just as in the introduction (the two ictuses of v.4b), gets shortened only at the end: 3 + 3 and 3 + 2. In the corresponding stanza B the regularity is complete and each verse half has three ictuses.

According to my arrangement the poem chiefly consists of strophes which are short because they comprise two verses only, and not sets of four.[16] One of the best proofs of this is provided by the structure of section I, which has not been ascertained yet, but clearly follows a concentric scheme on the basis of strophes made up of pairs of verses:

A	creation shakes, fire indicates God's wrath	vv.8-9
B	God approaches, flying low out of heaven	vv.10-11
C=X	he lives in light and darkness	vv.12-13
B'	he thunders and fights with lighting from heaven	vv.14-15
A'	the foundations of creation are revealed by his roaring and wrath	vv.16a-d

I begin with a circular reading which follows this pattern and lays it down. Strophes 4 and 8 which take up elements A-A' are parallel with each other through their verses: abab. In their first verse, v.8//16ab, parts of the cosmos form a merismus which, as a word pair spread over the first and second colon, already ensures the *parallelismus membrorum*, getting seconded in this by the verbs which also form a word pair: shaking in v.8 and becoming visible in 16ab. The second line of both strophes, v.9//16cd, subsequently states the cause of these spectacular natural phenomena. It is the heat of God's wrath (*'appō* in 9a/16d).

[14] The second 'I called', that of 7b, is replaced in the Psalm by the form *'ăšawwēᵃ'*. The result is that the B cola there have the pair and the verb/noun variation on the root *šw'*. This alteration is a slight embellishment which hints at the desire to polish. However two extra verbs occur in 7d, *lᵉfānāw tābō*, of which there is at least one too many: the first, a chiefly visual term which does not fit in well in an auditive line. Besides, it is metrically undesirable.

[15] The pu'al participle *mᵉhullāl* does not only mean 'praised', but can also be rendered as a gerundive, which I prefer here.

[16] Against Van der Lugt, who forcefully pursues what he calls proportionality, ('evenmatigheid'). On p.473 he arranges Psalm 18 into 3.15.16.16.5 verses (he sees fifty-five lines of poetry therefore), i.e. vv.2-3/4-16/17-31/32-46/47-51. According to him the number of verses on strophe level are: 3/3.4.4.4/4.4.4.4./4.4.4.4./3.2.

The elements which create correspondence B-B' keep exclusively to God's acting, differing in this from the other three strophes. They have many verbs, of which they also have the same number: five. These verbs are complementary, since there are four intransitives in strophe 5 : they reproduce God's movements, and in strophe 7 four are transitive: God now subjects the earth to all kinds of projectiles because he fights. Both strophes expressly point to heaven as the place in which God prepares himself for battle and from where is going to shoot (*šāmayim* in 10a/14a).[17] Another complementariness which supports scheme B-B' is the fact that vv.10-11 chiefly make a visual impression, whilst v.14 is completely auditive.

Thus a single strophe remains in the middle as axis. This unit X, the poem's sixth strophe, vv.12-13, has only two verbs and they are less in the service of an act than in the description of the dwelling of God himself. It is about a paradoxical designation of heavenly space which is able to succeed only via a dialectic of light and darkness. If we accept the irregular text of the Samuel version – and that is neither lexically nor syntactically at all impossible – we hear three pairs of words in the verse devoted to darkness: 'darkness as [his] pavilions', and probably joined to it as appositions, v.12b: 'a thick mass of water, the cloud layer'.[18] After the heavy weight of this verse a light line of poetry follows with only one predicate, making for enjambment between colon a and colon b. I take v.13 to mean: 'because of the brightness which went out from [and before] him coals of fire were kindled'. The picture fits in exactly with v.9. And as a consequence the storm of fire which startles the cosmos and makes it shake is essentially tied in with, if not emanating from the centre of the divine sphere. To put it another way: verse 13 sanctions anew the earthquake and the accompanying phenomena of fire as the wrath of the creator.

[17] This correspondence of 10a and 14a on the matter of heaven's location has, as obverse, that the word 'heaven' fails to occur anywhere else in the section, even though this is to be expected from such an extensive and systematically composed theophany. That is: here is a structural argument for reading, with Psalm 18, 'mountains' in v.8b instead of 'heaven'. Was a tired copyist thinking of the merismus 'heaven and earth' when he wrote down v.8? See also note 25 below.

[18] The main problem with v.12 and 13a is that they disturbingly stand out against the metrical regularity which, for a long stretch of text, appears to argue for a norm of three ictuses. Verse 12 is definitely 4 + 4 ictuses. This is just permissible even though section I has no other colon with four ictuses. But then 13a follows with only two ictuses. This is such a reduction that the longer text of Ps.18 (+ *'ābāw 'ābārū*) obtrudes itself as alternative. A possible solution for reducing v.12 is to rearrange the goo of seven (!) successive nouns without *wᵉ* into a tricolon : 'He made the darkness his surroundings, / his cover the dense mass of water,/ the thick blanket of clouds.' But does the taut composition admit a stray tricolon here?

I round out my circular reading with a linear one now, going through the theophany section once again. Its beginning, strophe 4, is striking due to its quantitative aspect: it consists entirely of tricola. Pair 8ab has a chiastic syntax, whilst the number of nouns and verbs changes: in 8a two imperfects plus singular subject, in 8b two nouns in the plural plus an imperfect. The phonetic effect of the opening – *wattig'aš* + *wattir'aš* differ by only one consonant – suggests the mighty shaking and this is transmitted in *yirgāzū*, a qal again.[19] A colon C is piled on top of this which, with its hithpa'el of *g'š*, probably intensifies the initial verb, and finally reveals the cause of all the tumult. With this motivating *kī* clause on God's wrath the colon leads at once to the subject of v.9. The three cola of that verse are all more slender. In 9ab too the subject and predicate alternate chiastically. There are various phonetic means connecting these verse parts.[20] In 9ab, which only have 7 + 6 syllables, short words for nose and mouth occur in the singular, in the fatter colon 9c (with 3 x 3 syllables) we come to God himself (in *mimmęnnū*) and a plural occurs. The wrath of God is shown in concrete images, with a smoke-fire-coals series which goes against the chronology of physics, from the rarefied to the tangible.

Then God inclines heaven and descends. This movement is continued in 'he mounted' and 'he was seen', says the alliteration in the series *wayyeręd-wayyirkab-wayyērā*. There is fine play on words, *rkb-krb*, which suggests that it is good to ride upon a cherub. The semantic contact which the 'he flew' of 11a enters into with 'on the wings of the wind' states precisely that it is the light and swift movement of flying. After the wyqtl forms the parallelism rests on the space adjunct which is activated by many phonetic means. He who notices the similarity between *'al k^e^rub* and *'al k... rūăḥ*, remembers at once that a cherub himself also has wings. A feather-light impression arises of the co-operation between the mount and the wind.

The glowing coals of 9c and the 'thick cloud' of darkness of 10b return chiastically in the special centre, where they each get an entire verse. Here the poet approaches the mystery of God's being. But it is no more than an approach, for he limits himself to describing his dwelling. One can read these spatial designations as a metonymy which, through its opposition of light and darkness, wants to touch the mystery of God's existence for a moment. In the prose of Exodus a narrator has been engaged in a similar way. He

[19] The form manages to exactly repeat the consonants resh and gimel which took turns in colon A and has a sibilant once again.

[20] After the two 'ayins and qameṣ four times in *'ālā* and *'āšān* there is the 'aleph which connects *'appō* and *'eš*; in the space adjuncts (which state divine organs) four labials are in operation: *b^e'appō* // *mippīw*.

manages to create a true chiasmus of light in darkness and darkness in light at the supreme moments of the actual Exodus and of God who reveals himself on the mountain.[21] Here in the poem the density of matter is not only suggested by the piling up of nouns, but also of various phonetic means once more.[22] Verse 13 continues the smoke-fire-coals chain further back and reveals that the brightness of God is the beginning. The poet is to come back to this in v.29.

The point of the description and the aim of God's starting to move are still hard to deduce from the strophes which occupy vv.8-13. This changes now. Strophe 7 first offers a very balanced line in v.14 which completes our visual impressions with auditive ones. But then a line follows with four verbs which are the point of God's activity and reveal what was intended all the time: harassing and scornfully dispersing the enemies.[23] Because the noise of v.14a is directed below, this half verse is the counterpart of 10a (also listen to how *wyrd-wyr'* continues in *yr'm*). The identical syntax of 15a and 15b, the clear rhyme on 'them' and the suspicion that the arrows of God are identical with the flashes of lightning suggest that the two half verses have to do with the selfsame thing. This idea gets support from the strophe's other half: the referent of 14a is identical to that of 14b, both cola speak of the thunder. Apart from that verse 14 is a counterpart and an amplification of a colon from the psalm of Hannah (I Sam.2:10b) via the technique of inverted quotation. The normal metre has recovered in this strophe, 3 + 3 and 3 + 2, with a shortening at the end as in v.4b and 7d.

In the middle of the section there are many clouds and water masses, at the edges fire and heat make their appearance. In the final strophe of the theophany the foundations of the world are exposed through this.[24] Verse 16 stands out in relief from what has gone before through the phenomenon of dependence, a kind of syntax which presupposes enjambment from one verse to the other. There is one predicate only (repeated twice through verse

[21] I have written about this in the chapter 'Exodus' in 'The Literary Guide to the Bible', edited by Robert Alter and Frank Kermode, Harvard University Press, 1987.

[22] The main phonetic means in v.12: the alliteration of *ḥšk* and *šḥq* at the extremes and *ḥšrt* in the middle, rhyme and alliteration of *s^{e}bībōt-sukkōt*. In v.13a the doubling of nun + gimel is conspicuous.

[23] I say four verbs because the form 'he sent' in v.15 does double duty: God sends arrows *and* flashes of lightning. For the presence of enemies (the suffix *-em* without antecedent) see note 28 below.

[24] The *mōs^{e}dōt tebel* of 16b remind me of the *m^{e}ṣūqē 'ārẹṣ* in the song of Hannah: these 'pillars are the Lord's', she says. The theophany in II 22 is an application of that insight.

technique, in 16a and b) for the whole strophe, the niph'al form *yērā'ū/ yiggālū*. After v.16ab only adjuncts follow. The passive is reduced to its origin in 16cd: the wrath and the hot breath of God which repeat v.9 and in so doing point back to the beginning. Once again what the first cola say is identical to what the second cola say. The choice of words *ga'ărā* is not only connected with the auditive line v.14 and its *r'm*, but also with the *g'š//r'š* of the beginning. Then the feminine plus the proper noun of God (*b^e ga'ărat yhwh*, two ictuses) are replaced by the two ictuses of another feminine plus organ (as bearer of and metonym for wrath), *minnišmat rūăḥ 'appō*.[25]

We now survey the theophany section. In a narrative text we could have expected approximately the following sequence from a writer: (a) God hears David's cry for help (b) and becomes angry with his enemies; (c) description of his dwelling (light and darkness), (d) after which God prepares for battle and descends; (e) against a background of fire-spitting mountains he causes a thunder storm to rage so that (f) creation shakes. Then (g) he wipes out the enemy with his arrows. The text of II Sam.22 is, however, a lyrical text which stylises the phenomena and brings them into a state of equilibrium through a circular technique rather than keeping to a chronological course. All the same I suggest that the outermost ring restricts itself to the shocking phenomena on earth, whilst the complex BXB' is, on the other hand, occupied with heaven.[26] The middle is the shockproof equilibrium of God's dwelling, where the phenomena of light and darkness balance each other, surrounded by the preparations in, and the fighting from, heaven.

The theophany separates and connects the short surrounding stanzas. The separation can also be formulated using a textual characteristic which I have not yet mentioned. Our poem bristles with morphemes for 'me'.[27] There are ninety-one of them, but the 'I' of the poet is totally absent in this part of the

[25] In exactly the same place the text of the psalm has the suffix for 'your' twice. This address stands alone in the section and I suspect that amongst other things the second person has to serve in marking the end of the series of five strophes.

[26] This arrangement is a new structural argument for reading, along with the Psalm, 'mountains' in v.8b! Another solution is this: perhaps the combination 'foundations of heaven' was an acceptable term in which case they *are* simply the mountains (on earth). In this case the colon of the Psalm and that of Samuel still have the same referent and the arrangement earth (AA') versus heaven (BXB') sticks to its guns also.

[27] There are 49 occurrences of *-ī*, 22 of *-nī* and 20 of *-ay*. To this total of 91 one can add: 3 times the afformative *-tī* with perfects, and the preformative for the first person with imperfects 19 times. God, however, receives a suffix for 'him/his' 20 times and the morpheme *-kā* only six times! The suffix for 'them', the enemies (*-em/-ām*), occurs 9 times, in vv.38-46 only.

text. And this is also the case, more or less, with the other side: the enemies.[28] The depiction of the theophany really concentrates only on God, his place and his intervention, and this remarkable limiting gives him the glory. The obverse of this is that the poet, after the centre in the long section III, becomes the great hero who strikes and destroys. The enemies are needed here as his victims, and are therefore present in large numbers in vv.38-46.

As a lyrical report on God's intervention the theophany passage connects the stanzas on the poet's distress with the quartet of verses, of the same length, on his being saved. This is already apparent from the fact that strophe 9 does not even find it necessary to mention its subject; it is abundantly clear that this is the deity who has come down. There is a swift series of transitive verbs with which God saves the poet. Suddenly the 'I' is present in each colon through *-nī*. This is continued, and heightened by, other endings with *-ī* in the strophe of vv.19-20.[29] The consonant mem is prominent in vv.17-18. The many occurrences of alliteration contribute to placing the enemy opposite God and the poet. In v.17 *mimmārōm* occurs straightaway opposite *mayim rabbīm*. These 'mighty waters' ensure the first unmistakable link with stanza A and its streams of death. Mem continues in v.18b and the 'I' stands alone opposite the strong enemy, *miśśōnᵉ'ay kī 'āmᵉṣū mimmẹnnī*. But the first *min* means 'liberation from' of all things and continues the *mē'oyᵉbī* of 18a. The enemies' strength comes too late and is not able to bear all the activity from up above. The 'I' is 'taken out of the water' like a Moses redivivus. The fact that 'from mighty waters' is followed by 'from my strong enemy' and its amplification which is allowed to fill the whole of 18b is a new argument for viewing the waves and streams as a metaphor for the enemy.

The opponents get one more colon, and their verb creates another link with stanza A: the pi'el of *qdm* occurs in the metaphor of v.6b and is

[28] There is something odd about the enemies and their suffix. The suffix *-em* appears twice in v.15, as end rhyme of the cola, and it refers to the enemies – but they are nowhere to be found as antecedents. This becomes plain when one studies other references with **hmm*. Many of these references have as subject God who destroys Israel's enemies: Ex.14:24, 23:27, Deut.2:15, Josh.10:10, Jud.4:15, I Sam.7:10, Ps.144:6, II Chron.15:6; with another subject, but also in war, are Jer.51:34, Esth. 9:24; only Is.28:28 falls outside the series. That is why I am of the opinion that the suffix *-em* of Ps.18:15 and our reference is a more or less formulaic turn of phrase in a word pair like *hpyṣ//hmm* and points to the enemies. Moreover, as a consequence the Ketib (identical with *wyhmm* of Ps.18) does not need to be changed.

[29] In strophe 9de *-nī* occurs twice in the middle, but in v.18, contrariwise, at the edges. Then comes strophe 10 with the vowel -ī eight times: *-nī ...dī / ...hī ... lī* in v.19, and in v.20 ... *'ōtī / -nī kī ... bī*.

non-metaphorical in v.19a. God's support wins and occurs in 19b as a noun with *mem praeformans*, *miš'ān* – the first since the overwhelming hymnic enumeration in the opening verses. It is followed by *męrḥab*, 'space', which describes the reality of the poet and is the semantic opposite pole of his straits (*ṣar*) of v.7a – the third link.[30] All consonants of *yaṣṣīlenī*, 'he saved me', from 18a return in v.20 (in *wayyōṣē la-* and in *yᵉḥallᵉṣenī*) and we notice that 18b and 20b finish in a parallel way by both having a *kī* clause with polar content: strength of the enemy versus God's delight in me.[31] Just as the wrath of 16d prepares for God seizing in 17, and just as 18b leads on to 19a, so the clause 'that he delights in me' is the transition to v.21 and the subject matter of the central section vv.21-31.

Section II is the compositional and ideological centre; the platform from which the poet looks at the dramatic run up of vv.5-20 and to the triumphal end of vv.32-46. Before this he is in danger and has to be saved, afterwards God makes a strong hero of him so that the victories are his. Before and in the central section there are hardly any enemies, afterwards they appear in many verses as victims of the triumphant hero.

Section II contains the same number of parts as I: five strophes. The centremost (strophe 13) can be properly delineated but the verses around it are not easy to arrange. I organise them into 3.2 and once again 3.2 verses. The set of five verses, 21-25, is about 'my integrity' which is requited by God and framed by four repeated words. The set of five in vv.28-31 is more varied as it speaks of God's light and purity. The transition of the third person for God in 21-25 to the second person in v.28 plus A cola from 29-30 takes place in the centremost strophe which addresses God. An important characteristic of those two verses is, moreover, that there is no room for an 'I' in addition. So the issue is generalised to a rule, to a wisdom formula.

Two, three strophes long we seem to end up in the aura and genre of wisdom. The poet shows himself as honourable (*ṣdq*) and with clean hands (*br ydy*) and he gathers that his salvation is a reward which God gives to him for his honesty and his respecting the God-given rules and laws. The purity of the poet is described and confirmed by the latter in vv.22-23. These verses are determined by an anaphoral pair: *kī* ... / *lō* which is followed by a positive

[30] This connection has also been seen by Kuntz, p.28.

[31] This form of vertical parallelism is one of the scarcely important arguments for making vv.17-20 into two strophes. Their subject matter and semantics are so similar that drawing a boundary is hardly possible. But I bear in mind that far and away the majority of strophes can be properly delineated and that a length of two verse emerges as the norm.

and a negative clause each time. The strophe in vv.24-25 mirrors verses 21 and 22.[32]

Verses 26-27 (strophe 13) are the centre of the centre. The poet narrows down his own experience of God's repayment here to general wisdom, to a 'gnomic quatrain'.[33] He reproduces the precision of God's contact with people by repeating the root in a verb with which he qualified, in the same colon, a person as faithful or foolish.[34] At the same time he creates polarity and equilibrium between both verses by devoting one to good people (*ḥasīd* and *tāmīm* – effective assonance) and the other to bad. What God does is to mirror therefore. He ensures that everyone gets precisely his due, for better and for worse. This gnomic point of the poem occurs, moreover, quantitatively in the centre.[35] The most important word of the strophe, *tāmīm*, is the centremost of the poem; no wonder it occurs three more times. The concept 'perfect, unblemished, honest' is therefore a key one for the poet. He is going to join it once to 'the way of the Lord' and once to his own way – which is not made 'perfect' by himself but by God, in v.33b.

The poet continues by saying 'you' to God, but only gradually does he introduce his 'me'; it does not occur yet in v.28, forms a suffix in 29, and becomes the subject in 30. The You for God is now so important that he makes it into an anaphora which unites vv.28-30 into a strophe and under-

[32] In v.25 the expressions 'he rewarded me' plus 'according to my merit' are a reflection of v.21. The combination of *šmr* (qal) and *drk* from 22a is followed in 24 by *tmym* and *šmr* (now a hithpa'el), whilst the only negative in strophe 11, *rš'*, receives a synonym *'āwōn* in 24ba, the only negative of strophe 12. (Notice that *drk* and *tmym* are linked in 31a and 33b.) In their final verses both strophes have the word *nęgęd*, connected first with 'me' and then with God (23a=25b).

[33] Cross and Freedman used these two words in JBL 1953, p.21. They think that the strophe is a quotation of 'an old gnomic couplet with sing-song rhythm and anthropopathic conceptions', and Kuntz (p.12, 'an ancient gnomic quatrain') follows them in this. Why these two verses should be regarded as being written by a different hand escapes me.

[34] Only in the fourth colon does he deviate: he does not put perverse opposite 'perverse', but 'wily' treatment of God. With this the bad guy is sent barking up the wrong tree and the poet has still brought a certain amount of variation in the doubling. The *gibbōr* of 26b (which functions there with the broader meaning of *gębęr*) protrudes inconveniently and I cannot see any function for it.

[35] Verses 26-27 are the 27th and 28th line of poetry of the 53 verses; in other words v.26 comes exactly in the middle. There are 54 cola in front of it and 52 cola follow v.27; thus the middle of the 106 cola lies between v.26 and v.27. The centremost word of the total of 365 words, word no.183 thus of the unemended Masoretic text, is the word *tāmīm* which is not only doubled immediately, but bears a chain by also occurring in 24a, 31a and 33b! It stays at the centre if one deletes from the first half the two final words of v.12 and from the second half *'ăkallem* from 39a and one of the two imperfects at the end of v.43.

lines it two or three times with *kī*.[36] In v.28 the initial 'thou' honours God as liberator. A 'poor people' faces the 'haughty'. The first group is liberated, God looks down on the second group.[37] The balance between 28a and b is furthered by both verbs taking the hiph'il, and the combinations 'ayin-nun and 'ayin-mem of the first colon return in the second. Verse 29 is important due to its utilising the antithesis light/darkness with which we have become acquainted from the heart of the theophany. The roots *ngh* and *ḥšk* are a chiastic offshoot of the contrast between v.12a and 13a. They are distributed over half verses, but not symmetrically over the characters. God is the lamp of the poet and spreads light in his darkness. He gets the two words for light and his own proper noun, also used twice and placed in the verse as a pivot, borders onto it. In order to be able to see his way the 'I' relies on the light of his God. In v.30 the idea of battle which was re-introduced returns in v.28 and is further elaborated. Strengthened by God the poet can do everything. He runs over gangs and defensive walls as though they were not obstacles; his movement is that of a hart in the hills: a prancing.[38]

The reintroduction of the element of war via strophe 14 is not expected by the reader who allows the poem to revolve around the axis of vv.26-27. The idea of battle does not join up with the words or the subject matter of vv.21-25. I explain its presence as being preparatory to section III which makes the transition from section II to section III via vv.31 and 32 less sharp. The final strophe of the central section goes on to honour God and resumes for this purpose the diction of wisdom.[39] With this v.31 joins up well with strophes 11 and 12 (vv.21-25). The third *tāmīm*, said of God's way in v.31a, creates a balance: prior to the pivotal strophe 'I was blameless before him' (24a), at the centre of the centre 'You deal blamelessly with the blameless hero' and afterwards 'the way of God is perfect'. This strophe's rounding off function is apparent from various aspects: the praise genre, the divergent length (a mere 3 cola), the transition to speaking on God in the third person and the connection which the words 'shelter with' and 'shield' make with the

[36] This observation is opportune for the variant in Ps.18, in which v.28a also begins with *kī 'attā*. Even if we do not wish to include a *kī* in v.28 of Sam., it is nevertheless inviting to read the first short word as a misspelt variant of *'attā*, and I do indeed so read it; as do Cross and Freedman, JBL 72 p.28 note 62.

[37] There is no compelling reason to alter 28b according to the psalm. The occurrence of *-kā* and *'al* in the Samuel version gives the sentence another direction it is true, but the bosses stay victims. Translate the preposition pregnantly and *in malam partam*, and compare for *tašpīl* in combination with own eyes Ps.113:6.

[38] The Song of Songs 2:8-9a also uses the verb *dlg*. 'Hark! My beloved! There he comes, leaping over mountains, bounding over hills. My beloved is like a gazelle or like a young stag.'

[39] One can even find two of the three cola in the book of Proverbs, in ch.30:5.

beginning by being an inverted quotation from v.3ab. The above-mentioned aspects of praise, the third person and the key word 'perfect' ensure, for the rest, a good link-up with verses 32-33 which form the beginning of section III.

Verse 32 joins up closely enough for various commentaries and translations to set out wrongly, and to fail to observe, the new beginning.[40] But it catches the eye due to length, tone and content. For the first time in a long while[41] the verse receives a length of 4 + 4 ictuses. The balance of 'Yahweh // our God' becomes a broad symmetry through repetition of the long word *mibbal'ădē*. The tone is that of the hymn and the poet sings the incomparableness of the God of Israel by means of two rhetorical questions. Hannah had already said it in I 2:2, 'there is no rock like our God'. In turn the words *'el* and *ṣūr* point back to v.3a.[42] There is a new addressee, because for the first and only time the poet speaks of 'us'. He is part of a community which knows itself to be the inheritance of God and places the 'I' experiences of its third section, which are radically to prove the incomparableness of God, within this context.

With the words *mā'oz* and *ḥayil* of 'my mighty stronghold' in v.33 the poem begins to deviate from the description strophe 1 gave on God.[43]. Those substantives were of a more defensive nature: 'refuge' and the like. However, the lyrical 'I' is now taken up with quickly growing into a hero and king. The theme changes, it becomes his strength – but each time he recognises that he receives it from the deity. I suggest the following free rendering of verb and object in 33b: 'he has cleared the way for me' and also put forward not degrading the key word *tāmīm* to an adverb[44] but to take it as a predicate: 'so that my course is impeccable'.

Section III is the longest and gives the hero a clear path to prove *that* God is his strength and is everlasting, via many images. Here are a few data of the extent, for the sake of comparison:

[40] See, for example, LV, NBG, Kraus (BKAT), NEB, JPS, GNB, Vesco, McCarter; the majority make v.31 into a start. Buber, KBS (in the Psalm), Cross and Freedman, Weiser (Psalmen, ATD), Van der Ploeg, J. Ridderbos, Nic. H. Ridderbos (BZAW 117), Dahood (AB), Kuntz, Van der Lugt, Craigie have a new beginning in v.32.

[41] If one has put the problematical verse 12 in brackets or felt obliged to shorten it, we will have to go back as far as the opening strophe for the 4 + 4 metre.

[42] An abc-cba pattern thus arises which connects the elements from v.3a plus 'shield' from 3b with v.31c and v.32.

[43] The fact that the words *mā'oz* and *ḥayil* once again come from the group of segholates and that of nouns with *mem praeformans*, as do many words in strophes 1 and 2, is an argument for not changing *mā'uzzī* (according to the Psalm) into the participle of *'zr*.

[44] Against CT which, apart from this, retains *wayyatter* like I do. See also Appendix I.

	section I theophany	section II purity	section III victory
words	69	80	103
ictuses	*c*.62	*c*.65	*c*.94
cola	22	23	31
verses	10	12	15

Judging the piece purely on the ground of content, one can distinguish three phases. In vv.34-37 the hero is trained by God himself and strengthened for war, in vv.38-43 the battle rages and the poet gains great victories, in vv.44-46 he is recognised as the great ruler.[45] Because this succession of phases is chronological, there is a certain narrative development in this section, and that is also in force for the piece of text vv.4-20.[46]

A correct analysis of form, a sound division into strophes and a proper view on their context is more important for understanding the text. An important criterion here is the appearance of the characters, and especially the grammatical person they are accorded. In this way one can organise the two strophes of vv.32-35 into one stanza which speaks on God in the third person. Then in principle the four strophes which follow are regulated by the alternation Thou-me (36-37), I-them (38-39), Thou-me-them (40-41), they-them-I (42-43) and Thou-me plus they-me (44-46). Now it is a matter of seeing properly who the subject is, who the object of God's help or on the other hand of his enmity is, and who among the people is the one trampling who into the mud. For five cola the people are the subject at the end (44c-46) it is true, but only to hobble along in their chains and submit to David. A comparable reversal takes place in vv.42-43 where they get no help and have to bite the dust before David.[47]

Verse 33 appears to link up as an apposition with the double hymnic question on everlastingness. And the verses 34-35 too still have a similar form

[45] Compare Nic. H. Ridderbos who in BZAW 117 calls vv.4-31 'erster Hauptteil', vv.32-46 'zweiter Hauptteil' and arranges it as follows: 33-37 'Zurüstung/Uebung des Königs', 38-43 'Sieg über die Feinde', 44-46 'Herrscherstellung'.

[46] The narrativity is not the main thing, but it does have to be taken into consideration in some texts. Robert Alter has devoted a chapter to this in his 'Art of Biblical Poetry', New York 1985.

[47] It is now possible to link the strophes after v.35 also into stanzas. But how? The number of repetitions (e.g. of the idea 'under', or feet/hands) is so great that different combinations contend for priority. I mention two possibilities: 32-33 hymnic opening, then vv.34-39 one stanza (on strength and victory in particular; with six words for hands/feet of the poet) of 3 strophes, and 40-46 another 3 strophe stanza (primarily on subjection); or 32-37/38-41/42-46.

of dependence by creating a fine quasi-anaphora at their beginning (pi'el participles plus rhyming body parts which form a merismus vertically): *m^{e}šawwē raglay ... m^{e}lammed yāday ....* Moreover by keeping on speaking about God in the third person, they link up closely with 32-33. Not until the beginning of v.36 does a series of independent verbs begin; they are unambiguously finite forms and carry on up to the end, v.46.

For two strophes God is busy training his hero. It is not surprising that the poet compares his speed to hinds (34a) after the 'prancing' of v.30b; and we recall Asahel. In 34b God ensures 'I stand on my high places'. The picture is a positive counterpart of the high places which *had* become a place of catastrophe and where the gazelle (Jonathan) died in battle – in the dirge of David in II Sam.1. In the situation of II 22 the falling (*npl*) is now reserved for all enemies (v.39b). Opposite the high-spirited standing on the high places (in colon b of the 'feet' verse, v.34) is the bending of the bow[string] (in colon b of the 'arm' verse, v.35). In 35a and b battle and bow are a word pair – again a long noun with the mem versus an original monosyllable. The bronze of the bow is a hyperbole for strength and splendour.

The God who was 'my horn of rescue' in 3b and 'the rock of my protection' in 47b hands the proper weapon to the poet in 36a: 'the shield of *your* victory' – so that we have read together three facets of the key word *yęša'*. Insofar as we must imagine the shield with the arm of David, verses 36-37 now mirror the parts of the body which received a strophe in 34-35.[48] At the same time we see the connection between the proud and sturdy standing (34b) with the free and strong steps of v.37. The strength of the legs complements the speed of 34a. In the strophe which says 'You' the taw is busily occupied with alliterating.[49]

The attention paid to the legs receives a special implementation because the poet is now going to repeatedly provide us with images of the underlying enemies: they cannot get up // they lie under my feet (v.39ab), they have to offer their necks [to my victorious boot] in 41a, they are trampled like dust and mud, v.43ab; moreover the word *taḥtenī* appears three times in rhyming position and extends into the coda (37a-40b-48b). The enemies tried to gain height (*qāmay* 40b-49b, and *cf. rāmīm* 28b), but their fate has already been decided in 39b: *lo y^{e}qūmūn*, they rise no more. This is a form of revenge (*n^{e}qāmōt*), says the coda with a play on words and a poetic plural. How high and low are divided leaves nothing to guesswork. The decline of the enemy

48 Furthermore I notice that the second line of both strophes uses two words: in 35ab the ordinary words my hands//my arms, in 37ab a metonymy plus a rare word: my steps//my feet (the hapax legomenon *qrsl*.)

49 Seven taws in vv.36-37: *titten, 'ănōt, tarbenī* and *tarḥīb* straight after one another, *taḥtenī*.

peoples (48b) occurs once more opposite the ascent of David, 'you raised me clear of my foes', v.49b.

In the strophe where 'I' becomes the subject and the winner, vv.38-39, the 'aleph is busy alliterating; in the unemended text six words begin with it of which five form a chain of imperfects for the triumphant hero. In v.38 swift horizontal movements of his occur, in v.39 the enemies' vertical descent into the standstill of death takes place. Strophe 20, vv.40-41, basically speaks about the same battlefield scene, but transforms the images in the sense that God as second person is the ruling power once again, whilst the 'I' changes into the beneficiary: the suffix 'my/mine' six times.[50] The taw is frequent again, seven times. The only enemy part of the body brooked in the text is the neck they must ignominiously bare as a sign of capitulation.

Strophe 21, vv.42-43, closes the David-enemies-God triangle by describing the link between the enemy and God: but it does not come about. A play on words has the void of no help (*mōšīăʿ*) immediately follow the enemy's despairing looking round (*šʿh*). His fate is the opposite to that of the poet (3c/4b). He stands alone, God does not respond. Two clauses per colon create an animated syntax, which answers expectation with disappointment. The final verse on the war uses a simile twice and the breadth of two semikut expressions in order to secure the end of resistance completely. Encircled by the poet – the great phonetic similarity of *'ęšḥāqem ... 'ęrqāʿem* underlines a syntactic chiasmus – they are pulverised. In the unemended text the suffix *-em* occurs four times for the victims in strophe 19 and four times in strophe 21.[51]

The section closes with an extensive strophe of three verses whose centre is a tricolon. In v.44 the poet is the thankful object of God's care, in the central verse he is the surprised addressee of the obedience of those subjected, and v.46 restricts itself to a picture of their decline. The winning of the battles is now called 'thou hast caused me to escape' by the poet. He has emerged 'from the disputes with my people' as victor and God embodies this in the position 'head of the nations'.[52] On top of that a procession of slaves enters which gets the honour of filling a tricolon. We hear a note of amazement from

[50] The word strength is a repetition in respect of 33a, the word war in respect of 35a, 'thou hast given' is, as a perfect, a variant of *wttn* in 36a, and 'my enemies' looks round to 38a and 49a.

[51] Precisely stated the object suffix is *-ām* once, the end of v.38 and the end of v.42, and *-em* three times in the unemended text.

[52] The *ʿammī* of 44a is not plain. Completing it to *ʿammīm* to make the cola rhyme is the line of least resistance. But a few Mss have the singular *ʿām*, as does the Psalm, and I therefore retain the singular. The poem mentions no internal difficulties or discord, so that the translation 'from the disputes of my people' is not to be recommended. I propose reading the *genitivus objectivus*: conflicts with my people, fights against my people.

the poet as he reports to us: 'peoples I had no knowledge of now serve me as slaves'. The unfamiliarity not only continues in the quickly recognised synonym *b^enē nekār*, but also in 'at the mere report of me': v.45b states that people bow before they have even seen David. This series of elements on the unknown ones (who receive 2 ictuses each time and stand in front of an imperfect) and the rhyme on 'me' indeed ensure that 44c and 45ab have to be grouped into a tricolon. The new slaves do not make contact in v.46, they are absorbed totally by their impotence: collapsing 'they hobble because of their chains'.[53]

The body of the poem is complete. A stanza of two strophes and five verses remains which connect praise and thanksgiving: vv.47-51. The poet begins animatedly with two exclamations ('live!' and 'blessed') which receive a short clause each within colon A. He places his God-liberator high, 47b, since he has given him a high place (*rwm* again, now factitive), away from the fighting horde, 49b. That was being snatched away from violence, *taṣṣīlenī*, 49c adds to this, with a recollection of the saving hand of God in 17a//18a (*yaṣṣīlenī*). All cola from strophe 23 rhyme with 'me'. In v.47 there are only the characters he-mine, after which 48a continues as an apposition in the same way as 33a after the hymnic verse which opened section III and spoke of the Rock as well. In vv.48-49 the mighty deity once again arranges, for the space of five cola, the relationship between 'me' and 'them'. The virtual anaphora *mōrīd//mōṣī'* gives 49a its third place in and through a tricolon governed by participles.[54]

The start of the final strophe is marked by the demonstrative 'therefore', the vocative, and 'I want to thank you'. I read this verb as an indication of genre and it is a direct expression of what the poet wants with God and from his relationship with him.[55] He now takes on another relationship with the peoples, by singing the praises of the Name before them. It seems as if the final verse wants to spell for us the epithets which fill in the name.[56] Who is the power who has accorded this jubilant and grateful king a name among the great – I quote now the promise of II Sam.7? He is 'the tower of victories for

[53] This seems to me, and CT, to be the correct rendering of the unemended **ḥgr* and v.46b. The NEB also has 'limping', and Buber 'hinken sie herbei', after which the usual 'from their strongholds' is made to follow. This rendering is plausible in itself, but only in combination with the translation (rejected here) 'come outside' or 'tremble' for the verb.

[54] Verse 49a is also placed as a C colon after v.48 by Van der Lugt and Craigie. Compare in addition to the two hiph'il forms the two pi'el participles which open vv.34-35.

[55] In this chapter 'the poet' is not to be understood genetically as the original, historical creator or writer, but each time in poetical terms as the lyrical 'I', the implied author.

[56] I value the fact that Buber, the NBE and the JPS place a punctuative colon (i.e. ':') at the end of v.50.

his king' and the one 'who shows grace to his anointed'. The word *ḥęsęd* refers back to the heart of the psalm, the gnomic strophe on requital. As a short segholate form it is contrasted in this hymnic final verse with the long form *migdol.* As noun, metaphor, and high-rise concrete entity the word 'tower' refers back to the various excellences of God fixed into the nouns with which the poem began and whose majority were also the metaphors making a fortress rise in the mind's eye.

The closing stanza is more or less framed by 'the Rock of my deliverance' who becomes 'the tower of victories'. The combination of *yišʿī* and *yᵉšūʿōt* also refers back to the first strophe, which applied this root twice in vv.2-3. Not until the final verse does the lyrical 'I' reveal his royal status. He changes into the third person at the same time – a transformation which signals the end of more than a hundred 'I' morphemes. The vowel *-ō* of the rhyming pair *malkō//mᵉšīḥō*, but also their m and l sounds are continued in the words which, as apposition, identify the king and fill in the protruding colon C. The strength and highness which King David has received from God shall be transferred undiminished to the heirs, confides the poet. This thought too recalls the crucial text with the promise of a dynasty.

The words 'his king' and 'his anointed' carry us back to the song of Hannah once again: her final cola ended on the same rhyming pair! If, still impressed by David's great psalm and its careful composition, we re-read this woman's song of thanksgiving, only then are we able to fully see how many similarities there are. They stretch from entire cola (the Highest who thunders in heaven, I 2:10b; his incomparableness, v.2 there) to a veritable concatenation of key words.[57] The most significant of these are *rūm*, *qęręn*, *'āzar ḥayil*, *tebel* and *šᵉ'ōl*, *ḥošek*. The large number of words the poems have in common require our making an explicit connection between the poetic opening and the poetic close of the books of Samuel. The song of Hannah, which does not necessarily have to be an original creation, but partly a fresh arrangement of verses already in existence, obtains via the introductory word the hallmark 'prayer'.[58] This does not become clear until the end, when the woman looks further than the present and wishes the future king power from God. The narrative sections of Sam. tell us that this happens to David. His great song of thanksgiving shows him at the peak of self-awareness and

[57] These are the words which the song of Hannah has in common with II 22: *yhwh*, *rwm* (qal and polel), *qęręn* (bis), *rḥb*, *yšʿ*, *ṣūr*, *rbh*, *yṣ'*, *pę̄*, *'el*, *qęšęt*, *gibbōr*, *'āzar ḥayil*, *mwt*, *šᵉ'ōl*, *špl* (hiph.), *ʿāfār*, *wayyāšęt*, *tebel*, *ḥasīd*, *ręgęl*, *šmr*, *ršʿ*, *ḥošęk*, *ryb*, *ntn*, *šāmayim*, *rʿm*, *'ęręṣ*, *ʿoz*, *malkō*, *mᵉšīḥō*. That is to say: more than 30 words, which take up *c.*40 of the 114 places in her song – too large a number in common with II 22 to be called 'chance'.

[58] The quotation formula in I 2:1a begins with *wattitpallel.*

strength. God is a Rock for him also; when David calls him 'the horn of my deliverance' this is a fulfilment of Hannah's prayer for the anointed. Both speakers depict God as the one who has laid the foundations of creation and for this reason gives power to whom he will. The reader is now able to travel this path under his own steam. In short, the strength of the thankful king forms a framework with the poem of Hannah and is its fulfilment.

§ 2. *An oracle on good government*, 23:1-7

The poem of 23:1-7 has received a very short introduction from the editor which is easy to translate and difficult to interpret: 'These are the last words of David.' The last words in his life? This is not likely. The aged David's most important dicta on the succession to the throne and the settling of several scores occur in I Ki.1-2 and are in place in the composition of 'King David', as we have seen in NAPS I. What the king says in II Sam.23 fits in well at this point, immediately after the great and royal song of thanksgiving, and not at the end of his life. This song's content, with its point on the morality of government and on the God-given covenant, joins up well with chs.7 and 8, thus with the powerful finale of the section proper, 'Throne and City'. This prompts me to accord this heading the interpretation: 'this utterance of David is the last to be included in the books of Samuel'.[59]

The poem has a clear and simple organisation. The eighty-six words which go to make it are included in eleven verses consisting of twenty-three cola. The verses are grouped into five strophes consisting, in principle, of two lines each. Only the centremost strophe has three verses. This is a hint of the quantitative to us: the point of the message is to be found here probably, in the three bicola going from v.3c through 5a. With respect to this boundary the text is often organised differently. My own arrangement of the half verses has the fourth strophe (v.5b-e) emerge well in its partly being determined by the asseverative[60] particle *kī* in the position of an anaphora. It also highlights how the heavier *kī lō* combination, thanks to a play on words ever shifting in meaning, opens a B colon three times (5a, 5e, 6b).

[59] Besides, 'words' must be understood pregnantly as words of elevated style, poetry, in order to exclude the direct speeches of David in ch.24 which, on the syntagmatic axis, are his last words.

[60] As far as the rendering of this *kī* is concerned I concur with an alternative of Del Olmo Lete's in VT 34, p.421: it may be 'given an explicative-completive value that enhances such an emphasis'.

The metre is fairly regular. The majority of cola have three ictuses, three have two ictuses, and five have four ictuses.[61] The cola with four ictuses occur only in marking positions: in the final verse of the central strophe and in the final strophe. For the reader who does not believe in Hebrew metrics I note the distribution of the words amongst the strophes:

strophe	1	2	3	4	5
verse	1bcde	2a-3b	3c-5a	5bcde	6a-7c
words	4 + 4	4 + 3	3 + 3	5 + 3	4 + 4
	3 + 3	3 + 4	4 + 3	5 + 3	3 + 4 + 4
			4 + 6		

Once more the surplus of the centremost strophe is conspicuous. The six words of its final colon are almost all monosyllables. The fourth strophe has its own pattern too. The remaining cola work with three or four words each time. The balance of the figures at strophes 1 and 2 is striking. The totals per strophe show that magnitude increases after the second strophe; the series is as follows: 14-14-23-16-19 words.

In a sense the poem begins by not beginning. Within the poetic space is a heading which swells into a complete strophe. After this the utterance proper does not begin yet, as strophe 2 is a new introduction. In this way it takes four verses and eight cola before the poet gets down to business. He postpones this moment by applying a double envelope. The first (v.1b-e) is entirely nominal, the second (v.2a-3b) verbal. The first appears to underline his own status of being charismatically gifted, the second reveals that his 'oracle' has been prompted by God. On the one hand this is a shift of the authoritative word, on the other hand an authorisation of the lyrical 'I' as speaker of a sacral text.

The first envelope or strophe announces the 'oracle of David' in v.1b and

[61] The cola with two ictuses are v.2b, 4b, and 5e; the cola with four ictuses are v.4c, 5a, 6a, 7b, 7c. The rest (15 cola thus) have three ictuses, at which I am not certain of the accuracy of the following scans:
v.2a ó oó ooó (with the stress on *rwḥ* for emphasis)
v.3b ó oó oooó (initial *ly* is stressed)
v.5d oó oó ooó (if the MT is retained the half verse ends on a segholate form which can be reduced to a monosyllable).

The short word *kī* has in my scansion a metrical accent in 5a owing to emphasis, but it is proclitic elsewhere (so that I note oó for the *kī lō* and *kī kol* combinations).

doubles the title with 1c. The cola continue the synonymy of *n*^{e}*'ūm dāwīd* // *n*^{e}*'ūm haggẹbẹr* with appositions which probably have a complementary relationship. One states David's origins, he is from such and such a family.[62] This 'son of Jesse' is, it is true, a unique datum, because it is not applicable to any one else (except his brothers), but does not yet guarantee historical importance. The other apposition which describes David as 'the man who is highly placed' does ensure this. And in order to secure the uniqueness of this position the following colon adds the word 'anointed' which proves that the stake is the function exercised by one sole person, kingship. The entire second verse further amplifies the appositions which supply more detail on the position of David.

The choice of the word *n*^{e}*'ūm* already indicates that the lyrical 'I' presents a charismatic David: a speaker who is acquainted with divine inspiration. The entire introduction, i.e. both strophes 1 and 2, whose extent already runs to one third of the complete poem, is from a literary point of view inspired by the oracles of the seer and authoritative utterer of curses Balaam; this process even goes so far that its two-step character refers to his 'sayings' in Numbers.[63] But at the same time David places his own emphases, which have to do with his status as king and poet.

The halves of his second verse begin with a virtuoso assonance of words which qualify him as ruler and speaker and have the same kind of formation (qatīl type): *m*^{e}*šīḥ*//*n*^{e}*'īm*. They end with the pair of words Jacob-Israel, whose charm lies in the fact that they are and are not synonymous. To begin with Jacob denotes the patriarch himself, which is reinforced by the vertical parallelism with the name Jesse.But the name is often used in poetry too, as a designation of the people. The nation itself is designated by this name which originally – according to the cycle of stories of the *heros eponymos* in Gen.25-35 – was given to the patriarch by God himself at a moment of rebirth. A chiasmus of individual and people is thus hidden in the word pair Jacob-Israel. The vowels of the singular forms *m*^{e}*šīḥ* and *n*^{e}*'īm* are continued in the plural *z*^{e}*mīrōt*. With this word, which must be understood in the

62 I do not, therefore, believe in the antithetic parallelism which Del Olmo Lete envisages here; he thinks that 'son of Jesse' alludes to humble origins, VT 34 p.415.

63 Both the third and the fourth poem of the series in Num.23-24 open with a bicolon of exactly the same cut as II Sam.23:1bc and mention, as the source of Balaam's 'oracle', the words and the vision which originate with the God of Israel. The emphasis on the theme 'speaking with authority' is also present in the first two poems. See Num. 23:7-8 and 23:19, 20 and 23.

traditional way[64] to mean 'songs [accompanied by stringed instruments]', and once again pointing to the theme 'authoritative word', the end of the strophe reverts to the beginning, the double title word 'oracle'. A vertical parallelism in the layer of sounds contributes to this: the B cola open with *unᵉ'ūm // unᵉ'īm* (and looking ahead to strophe 2 for a moment: the following B cola open with 'his word' and 'he spoke to me').

Just as the first strophe is in proportion to v.1a as direct speech (in the first degree), so the second is also in proportion to v.1bcde as direct speech, but this time in the second degree. One can continue to peel away or remove envelopes in the central strophe: the said strophe is part of 'David's last words' to the same extent as the others it is true, but can at the same time be read – and marked by further indentation in print – as third degree direct speech, because these verses (3cd and 4a-5a) are the content and the long-awaited revealing of what God's word actually says, according to the announcement of strophe 2. The consequence of this tiered construction is that only this centremost, third strophe is God's word in the narrow sense.[65] In the fourth strophe the perspective of the speaker David returns quite plainly.

The difference between the first and the second introduction is that strophe 1 about David is in the third person, whilst he appears in strophe 2 as 'I' in the text. The cola of v.2 are synonymous and have an alternation of verbal plus nominal clause. Their syntax is chiastic. The speaking of God occurs with a verb and a noun in the middle, enclosing them we find the complementariness of his 'spirit' or breath and 'my tongue'. Now that the proper noun of God appears I observe a chiasmus in the treatment of the two characters throughout the introductions. David is quickly and simply referred to by his name, after which he is described by a series of appositions. The other is first called 'the God of Jacob', v.2a has the proper noun Yahweh, then v.3ab changes to epithets once again and exhibits a parallelism with

[64] I take colon v.1e to literally mean: 'and the pleasant [as concerns producing] songs of Israel [which honour God]'. I see a literary metonymy here, because the quality of the songs (they are congenial) is shifted to their maker; this is no surprising shift. See the material which S.R. Driver offers (I follow what he refers to as option a), not the view that David is the object of the songs). Compare already the KJ: 'the sweet psalmist of Israel'. Del Olmo Lete revocalises to *zimrōt*, sees the word as a divine epithet and translates, inspired by amongst other things Ex.15:2, the Amorite name Zimri-Lim and the Ugaritic root *ḏmr* with 'the Favourite of the Defence of Israel', pp.416 and 425.

[65] Nevertheless the 'original text' which the 'seer' David has received from God is interpreted by the lyrical 'I' David and spoken from his own position: God is the third person in 3d and the human speaker is, at the last moment, the first person in v.5a.

v.1de on strophe level.[66] The verse halves of v.3ab run parallel owing to their order predicate plus subject. If we draw a diagonal line from 3b to 2a we can see that these two cola exhibit an abc-cba symmetry which hermetically closes off the strophe:

v.2a	rūăḥ-yhwh	dibber	bī
v.3b	lī	dibber	ṣūr-yiśrā'el

We recognise both the quality of the spirit (wind, breath, storm) and the epithet Rock from the great song of thanksgiving. There the spirit of God was a hot wind which made the sea bed(s) dry, here however it is about the inspiration of David.[67] The ū sound joining them is a good continuation of the authorised *n^e'ūm*. The double *dbr* is this, of course, from a semantic point of view and belongs to God as the source of the oracle.

The first person disappears temporarily. When it returns, at the end of the central strophe and not before, it is preparatory or transitional to strophe 4 where the suffix for me occurs twice and is solidly supported by the internal rhyme of a threefold *kī*. The disappearance of 'me' is connected with the level of wisdom to which the poem now ascends. A line is formulated in the central strophe with the tone and diction of wisdom literature. It is v.3cd which is subsequently supported by two images: a shining morning and lush growth. In v.5a they appear to be metaphors of the relationship which 'the house' of the poet has with God – and coming from ch.7 we gather that it concerns his dynasty.

The first verse of the centre, v.3cd, is determined by an anaphora and asyndetic balance. This enables us to read colon A plus colon B as subject plus predicate, but the other way round no less. Whilst both solutions are conceivable I prefer the following: 'he who governs the people righteously, governs in awe of God'. But there is more than just this indicative speaking. Is it not to a certain extent a lesson which is first drilled into David by God and which he subsequently passes on as an oracle to his audience, his successors for instance? One might translate it jussively as: he who wishes to be a ruler of integrity must ever proceed in the fear of God. And equally: he who wishes to govern with integrity can succeed in this only if ... etc. The oracle is a) centred in the morality of governing properly, b) shows with images from nature how benevolent this is, but c) then departs from the general by applying these insights to the government of David: v.5a and the entire

[66] The same rhyme on 'Israel' which 3a and b have is less fine than a Jacob which can be restored at the end of 3a, is supported by the parallelism of the strophes, and occurs in the Lucianic recension.

[67] The great song of thanksgiving ended on the royal status and quality of David, the minor oracle begins with it.

fourth strophe (v.5bcde). The terms which buttress motif a are the second word pair through which 3cd is determined: the adjective 'sincere' and the combination of substantives 'the fear of God'.

The syntactic co-ordination of the following verses is not easy. I make a link between the first metaphor, because it is introduced by k^e, and the strongly stressed final clause which has a corresponding *ken*. Then the translation in which v.4c, the second image, has become a parenthesis runs: 'Just as the light of the morning, when the sun rises shining, of a morning without clouds – thanks to such a radiance [as well as] rain the grass [comes up] from the ground – so is my house with [the help of] God?!'

The equilibrium between 4a and b is plain. The subject[68] morning is repeated as the words 'oracle', 'he spoke' and 'ruler' were earlier. It is then explained by two words, in colon A by a short verbal and relative clause, in colon B by a negated noun (of the same syntactical status). The new verse picks up the start of 4a by varying the combination preposition + light with preposition + radiance, and adds the opposite pole rain in sharp asyndeton, not unlike the English expression 'come rain come shine'. Perhaps we ought to read the combination 'grass from the ground' along the lines of vertical parallelism as a successor to 'the sun rises'. Then the application in colon B, v.5a, follows – which probably wants to join up with both images: just as the light rises irresistibly and vegetation grows in a natural way, so the ascent of the Davidic dynasty is just as glorious and natural. Looking forward we notice that the vegetation as metaphorical range – so prominent in the love poetry of the Song of Songs – is used again at the end of strophe 4 to be broadly expatiated upon in strophe 5, where the opposite of the good ruler is portrayed.

Just as the vegetal term 'grow' of v.5e is preparatory and transitional to the final strophe, so the two parties of v.5a are preparatory to strophe 4, and the final colon 5a is a transition to the quartet of cola following. The content of the fourth strophe (v.5bcde) entails decentering. The centre of gravity in the poem shifts from strophe 3 as compositional centre and away from the general sapiential speaking, and comes both psychologically and ideologically to rest in the two verses of the covenant: strophe 4.

Verse 5bc has only one predicate, the second colon consists of two appositions which further qualify the object of 5b. It revolves round the 'eternal covenant' God has given to David and which is 'orderly in all things'. Chapter 7 answers to these terms extremely well with its extensive bipartite

[68] The term subject is justified insofar as it is possible to interpret the word *'ōr* not as the substantive 'light' but as a constr.inf. of the verb *'wr* with 'morning' as its subject.

oracle. The word *'ōlām* does not occur in narrator's text, is rare in speeches, but reaches a peak in the revelation of ch.7 and the divine promise. The second half of that chapter, the extensive text of thanksgiving and prayer, one might call, as David's first attempt at a worthy reply to God, the first token of *š^emūrā* here in v.5c; at any rate a first token from the receiving party. To begin with the word 'secured' looks at the faithfulness with which God upholds his covenant. In 5c two participles enclose the short word 'in all things', in 5d there is a doubling of substantives together with *kol.*[69] The term *yiš'ī* is ambiguous and can stand for 'save' as much as 'become saved' of David.[70] So quickly after the great song of thanksgiving, in which the root indicated each time that God saved the poet, the second alternative takes a certain preference, whilst the first does not preclude God's help. The syntax of 5de is parallel to 5bc, via the order of object + predicate with God as subject: 'Will he not cause all my success and [my] every desire to blossom?'[71] With both its verses the poem's ideological centre of gravity makes clear that the well-being was initiated by God and can proceed through his blessing.

The final verse causes all this to emerge extra sharply by developing a contrast. The disqualification Belial is used in an original manner[72] as a term for the alternative, a ruler like the thorn bush which at the end of Jotham's fable is also linked with devastating fire. The plural which appears further on gives away the fact that the poet speaks of *b^enē* b^elīya'al. Using 'all of them' he lumps them together. They ought, moreover, to be removed; taking the vowels into account no less than the consonants their *mūnād kullāham* occurs opposite the *hūqām* of the man in the singular from strophe 1.[73] Opposite their crackling destruction in the fire are the pleasing sounds of the songs David composes, and facing the holy oil with which David is anointed stands the untouchability of these thistles. You had better arm yourself well against them if you want to seize them. In this way the negative image of the sons of Belial faces the four positive qualifications of the beginning which

69 Del Olmo Lete's opinion that *bakkol* 'spoils the rhythm of the passage' (p.421) does not, therefore, convince me.

70 Del Olmo Lete, p.422, opts for the 'objective sense': 'as an expression of the ruler's function ('all my saving activity ...').

71 This is the JPS rendering. I wonder if we may also read the hiph'il intransitively as grow, sprout; then 'everything I undertake' is subject, as sequel to 'my house' of v.5a (with the same underlining of the positive with the combination *kī lō).*

72 The term occurs here personified; elsewhere it is always dependent upon a carrier such as *ben/bat*, *'anšē* etc. See, however, Deut.15:9, Nahum 2:1, Job 34:18.

73 In addition I observe that the highly defined *haggębęr* from v.1 – provided with the article sparingly used in poetry! – occurs opposite the indefinite *'īš* of v.7a. It seems as if it is approaching the meaning 'the hero'.

ABBREVIATIONS AND BIBLIOGRAPHY (continued)

AB	The Anchor Bible, ed. D.N. Freedman, New York
AOAT	Alter Orient und Altes Testament, Veröffentlichungen zur Kultur und Geschichte des Alten Orients und des Alten Testaments, Neukirchen
ATD	das Alte Testament Deutsch, Göttingen
CTCA	Mlle A. Herdner, ed., Corpus des tablettes en cunéiformes alphabétiques, 2 vols. Paris 1963
GNB	Groot Nieuws Bijbel, 1985
HUCA	Hebrew Union College Annual, Cincinnati
KTU	M. Dietrich, O. Loretz, J. Sanmartín, Die keilalphabetischen Texte aus Ugarit, Band 1, Neukirchen 1976
OBO	Orbis Biblicus et Orientalis, Freiburg and Göttingen
UT	C.H. Gordon, Ugaritic Textbook, Roma 1965
UF	Ugarit-Forschungen, Internationales Jahrbuch für die Altertumskunde Syrien-Palästinas, Neukirchen
WUS	J. Aistleitner, Wörterbuch der ugaritischen Sprache, Berlin 1974 (4th ed.)

Y. Avishur, Stylistic Studies of Word-Pairs in Biblical and Ancient Semitic Literatures, AOAT 210, Neukirchen 1984

A.F. Campbell, S.J. Of Prophets and Kings, A Late Ninth-Century Document (1 Samuel 1-2 Kings 10), CBQ Monograph Series 17, Washington D.C., 1986

R.A. Carlson, David, the Chosen King. A Traditio-Historical Approach to the Second Book of Samuel, Stockholm 1964

A.L. Laffey, A Study of the Literary Function of 2 Samuel 7 in the Deuteronomistic History, An Extract of the Thesis, Roma 1981

in connection with the poetical texts:
P.A.H. de Boer, Texte et traduction des paroles attribuées à David en 2 Samuel xxiii 1-7, SVT iv (1957), pp.47-56
P.C. Craigie, Psalms, vol.1, Word Biblical Commentary, Waco, Texas
F.M. Cross and D.N. Freedman, A Royal Song of Thanksgiving: 2 Samuel 22 = Psalm 18, JBL 72 (1953), pp.15-34
M. Dahood, Psalms I-III, AB 16-17, New York 1965-70
S.A. Geller, Parallelism in Early Biblical Poetry (Harvard Semitic Monographs 20), Missoula, Montana 1979
H.W.M. van Grol, De versbouw in het klassieke hebreeuws, fundamentele verkenningen, deel een: metriek, Catholic Theological Faculty of Amsterdam, 1986
J.K. Kuntz, Psalm 18: A Rhetorical-Critical Analysis, JSOT 26 (1983), pp.3-31
P. van der Lugt, Strofische Structuren in de bijbels-hebreeuwse poëzie, Kampen 1980
T.N.D. Mettinger, The Last Words of David. A Study of Structure and Meaning in II Samuel 23:1-7, Svensk Exegetisk Årsbok 41-42 (1976-77), pp.147-156
M. O'Connor, Hebrew Verse Structure, Winona Lake, Indiana 1980
H.-J. Kraus, Psalmen I-II, Biblischer Kommentar XV.1-2, Neukirchen 1978 (5th ed.)
G. del Olmo Lete, Mitos y leyendas de Canaán, según la tradición de Ugarit, Madrid 1981
idem, David's Farewell Oracle (2 Samuel xxiii 1-7): a Literary Analysis, VT xxxiv (1984) pp.414-437
S. Pisano, S.J., Additions or Omissions in the Books of Samuel. The Significant Pluses and Minuses in the Massoretic, LXX and Qumran Texts, OBO 57, Freiburg/Göttingen 1984
J.P.M. van der Ploeg, Psalmen I-II, Roermond 1971-74
H.N. Richardson, The Last Words of David: Some Notes on II Samuel 23:1-7, JBL 90 (1971), pp.257-266
Nic.H. Ridderbos, Die Psalmen. Stilistische Verfahren und Aufbau. Mit besonderer Berücksichtigung von Ps.1-41, BZAW 117, Berlin 1972
R.J. Tournay, O.P., Les 'dernières paroles de David', II Samuel, xxiii, 1-7, Revue Biblique 88 (1981), pp.481-504
J.L. Vesco, O.P., Le Psaume 18, lecture davidique, RB 94 (1987) pp.5-62

Appendix I
philological justification

The promiscuous use of *'ęl* for *'al*, noted before, is also to be found in the text this volume is about. In 2:9 first *'ęl* occurs three times, then *'al* three times – the regularity of the alternation is curious. The same alternation occurs once in 24:4a.

The cases in which *'ęl* is to be understood as *'al* are: 3:17b (end), 3:29a (first *'al*, then *'ęl*), 3:32c and 33a (versus 34d and 1:17); 6:3a, 7:19b (also according to S.R. Driver, p.276), 21:1e (bis), 10b, 24:3b, 16b.

I would now like to go through the text in the usual way:

- 2:2b — *hyzr'lyt* is a defective spelling just as in I 30:5b (the entire double apposition is exactly the same as this reference).
- 2:2b — therefore do not alter *hkrmly* either, see explanation also.
- 2:4c — introduces a new subject, indefinite and plural.
  Material with respect to *wayyaggīdū*, mainly in Sam.:
  a) direct parallels of our reference are I 17:31b, 19:21a, II 3:23b and I Ki.2:39c which have *wyg(y)dw* and another wyqtlw clause in front of them;
  b) an X + qtl clause or wyqtl clause followed by *wayyaggīdū* with unmarked change of subject occurs in Judg.4:12, 9:42, I Sam.14:33a, 23:25b and II 11:10a:
  c) *wayyaggīdū* with unmarked and indefinite subject after another kind of clause occurs in I 24:2b, II 3:23b, 10:5a and I Ki.1:22c.

d) *wayyaggīdū* without a change of subject and after a wyqtlw clause occurs in Judg.9:7a, I 11:9, 25:12c and II 17:21c.

– 2:4d *’šr*: my rendering: ‘The men of Jabesh-Gilead were they who buried Saul.’

– 2:6b *hz’t ’šr*: once again I refrain from altering, *pace* S.R. Driver who in his Notes argues for emending the demonstrative to *tḥt*. Analysis shows that both the demonstr. and the initial position of *’šr* are structurally correct and necessary.

– 2:7d This clause is not necessarily governed by the *kī* of 7c; other references with a *kī* clause and subsequently a clause beginning with *w^{e}gam* are Gen.40:15, Ex.12:39, Josh.2:24, Jer.10:5, Ruth 3:12, II Chron.24:7.

If 7d is not dependent on *kī* in 7c, 7d relates to 7ab; approximately as follows: Do not lose heart, and [an encouraging fact for you in addition is that] I have just ascended the throne.

– 2:8 The flashback indicated by inversion is correctly rendered by the NEB (‘Meanwhile Abner had taken ... ’), the JPS (‘But Abner had taken ...’) and McCarter (‘Now Abiner had ... ’ etc.).

– 2:9 *h’šwry* of the MT must be repunctuated to *ha’ăšerī*; the series has its own north-south pattern, the Assyrians are obviously superfluous. McCarter wants to read Geshurites. There are different arguments against this: the datum that Geshur is not an Israelite tribe, that it was still an independent kingdom under David and that we might expect some name or other connected with Galilee between Gilead and Jezreel, whilst the enumeration follows a counterclockwise direction on the map.

– 2:15b *wl’yš-bšt*: the waw after Benjamin is a *waw explicativum*, as it also is further on in v.31a.

– 2:17 my analysis indicates that the verse is the end of a paragraph; so also LV, NBG, Buber (see his ‘Dann ... aber’ in vv.17 and 18), KBS. It is the beginning of a paragraph in the typography of the JPS, BJ, McCarter, Hertzberg, Goslinga, NEB.

– 2:25c *’ḥt* has the pregnant value here of ‘one and the same’ hill. Because the semantic field of ‘one’ is very broad in Hebrew (it actually has the indefinite meaning of ‘such and such a one’ in II 15:2), I suspect that parallels are to be found for this ‘one and the same‘. The famous *’ęḥād* of the Shema‘ comes close; compare the explanation of that ‘one’ by Gerald Janzen in

VT xxxvii (1987) pp.280-300.

– 2:27cd *lwl'* and *hbqr*: This verse is dealt with in a strange kind of a way:

a) there is a willingness to retain *lūlē*, but also to erroneously make *mhbqr* into the *following* morning: LV, S.R. Driver, Bible de Jérusalem, NEB, NBE, McCarter, JPS.

b) or there is a wish to end up with 'this morning' and a consequent feeling compelled to emend the conditional particle to *lū* (and if necessary to interpret it as a wish): so Buber, BHK3, NBG, the KBS;

c) the reader who has the JPS rendering should take the initial conditional clause in the main text and the main clause from the alternative rendering in the note; then the correct text is as follows: 'As God lives, if you hadn't spoken up, the troops would already have given up the pursuit of their kinsmen this morning.' SV, KJ and Keil were right. For arguments for my reading see my own analysis and Goslinga Vol.II p.54sq. CT is silent at this point.

– 2:28cd *yrdpw*: The parallelism of c and d is a strong argument for having *yrdpw* fall in line with the perfect form *yspw*, to read *rdpw* thus.

– 2:29c *btrwn*: The proposal to take this word to mean 'cleft' is highly tenable. We are sufficiently familiar with the verb *btr*, 'cleave', and the noun *bętęr* (a sacrificial piece of meat) from Gen.15 and Jer.34, see HAL p.160; the *hārē bātęr* in the Song of Songs 8:14 (HAL erroneously gives 8:4) are 'cleft mountains'. Up to now the word here in 2:29 has been interpreted as a geographical name by KJ, SV, LV and the modern JPS; and as 'morning' (see the arguments of Arnold in S.R. Driver) in the Jerusalem Bible, NEB, NBE and McCarter and *cf.* NBG, whilst the translation 'cleft' occurs in Gesenius, BDB, Buber, Hertzberg, Goslinga, KBS.

– 2:31a Initially the reader thinks that the 360 men are the object of *hikkū*; but then he gets stuck, there is another intransitive verb, and the *atnāḥ* warns. He has to reconstitute the syntax and makes the 360 subject of *metū*. There is, therefore, a curious telescoping of the syntactic units. I have two reactions to this:

a) there has been an accident in the tradition, perhaps v.31a originally had an internal object such as *makkā gĕdōlā*, or we must presuppose the virtual presence of such an expression; b) or does the difference also occur elsewhere? To a certain extent similar are: Ex.7:7 and 12:28 and 50 where in a the verb *'āśā* is used in an absolute way, and in b it is explained and repeated by a *ka'ăšęr ... ken* scheme.

– 3:3a Read, along with the Q, *wayyiwwāl*^{e}*dū*.

– 3:6b The correct meaning of the hithpa'el participle of *ḥzq* must be stated with emphasis, because the form is misunderstood here and there. In this way HAL gives 'treu halten zu' – a deterioration in respect of Ges.-B and BDB; the same notion is found in NBE: 'Abner fue afianzándose en la casa de Saúl' and in the JPS: 'Abner supported the House of Saul.' The KJ slips up at the preposition: 'he made himself strong *for* the house of Saul'. For the correct rendering see analysis. Amongst those correct are SV, LV, Buber, Driver, NEB, KBS, NBG.

– 3:7b in the MT, at any rate that of the BHS, the subject of 'he said' is absent. This leads to misunderstandings in the act of reading. Even though it would fit in with my interpretation by calling the absence of 'Ishbosheth' an ellipse I find it goes too far. From the information angle an explicit mention of the new subject is vital. Therefore at this point I follow the few Mss (BHS app.) having Ishbosheth, and *cf.* 4QSam[a].

– 3:10b I do not know for sure whether in classical Hebrew the hiph'il of *qūm* in fact suits an object like 'throne'. Further investigation shows that this hiph'il occurs elsewhere only once, in I Ki.9:5 // II Chr.7:18. The word *kisse'* is, as direct object, chiefly governed by the hiph'il or the polel of *kwn* (or is the subject with the niph'al or hoph'al of this root), and verbs such as *'śh*, *śym*, *ntn*, *rwm* (hiph.) and *bnh*. I wonder if the combination *hqym* + throne is perhaps a slight contamination of *kwn* (hiph. or polel) + throne and of a *hqym* that has for example a word or promise of God (sc. that he will put someone on the throne) as object and means 'keep one's word'.

– 3:12a *taḥtāw* = 'where he was', but the question is: who is this 'he', the general or his king? The first, and linguistically the simplest, option to be considered is to have it refer back to the subject of the sentence, to Abner thus. But perhaps it does not even make much difference; in any case Abner wants to intimidate and browbeat Ishbosheth with this high-handed act under his very nose. The proper rendering begins with the idea 'on the spot' but does not stop there. The word exhibits a shift from the spatial to the temporal, which we find quite normal with *qdm* or *lpny* or *'ḥy*. 'On the spot' shades into 'immediately' as in Dutch ('ter plekke' > 'terstond') and English. One can see the beginning of this kind of development, if one so desires, in 2:23d, where Asahel dies. Many translations fiddle about with *tḥtw*; Schulz *et al*, LV and BJ delete four words in this way, Hertzberg emends the preposition to *taḥtay* and NBG has the suffix refer to David ('in the place where he was'). Admissible and conceivable are the KJ 'on his behalf' = SV and Goslinga 'for him', NEB 'instead of going to David himself', KBS and McCarter 'as his representatives'. Just like I do these five voices have the suffix refer back to the subject. However I do not follow them in translating because I find this rendering tautological on closer analysis: he who sends messengers allows himself to be represented and has others look after his interests, by definition. Other translations are more outspoken. Buber has 'vom Platz weg' and the JPS is even better with 'immediately', – which brings us back to the oldest translation, the LXX, with παραχρῆμα: instantly, at once.

– 3:12b *l'mr* can be properly rendered here and understood, thus accepted in addition as 'in other words' or 'that is to say'; idem in 5:6d. So Buber, NBE, CT as well.

– 3:13efg Driver is as telling as he is concise here. Repeating that *kī 'im* and *lifnē* preclude each other and backing up his preference for the former, I add that the plus *lifnē* of 13f is perhaps a dittography having arisen because 13f is located between two lines which already have a *pny* each. This plus has made an infinitive out of the original finite verb form 'you bring'. Driver wants the form *habe'tā* after 'unless', whilst I myself think that the conjunction requires an imperf. after it; which calls for somewhat more emendation sad to say: *tābī'*. In addition I observe that 13g is a specifying time adjunct (that, together with e, creates an inclusio), so that a temporal *lpny* in 13f is too much of a good thing. The somewhat inelegant bulkiness of the construction 13efg is effectively taken care of in the JPS: 'Do not appear before me unless you bring Michal daughter of Saul when you come before me.'

For 13e, however, I prefer a nuance of warning or refusal: 'You will not get to see me personally, unless ...' etc.

– 3:15b The end of the line has 'her husband' and reading the word plus suffix is unavoidable it seems to me: *'īšāh*.

– 3:17a another flashback, observed well by the LV, Driver, Buber, NBE and McCarter, and best of all by the BJ and the JPS (which give 17-19 their own paragraph). Contra Schulz and Goslinga.

– 3:22a *wᵉhinnē* is skilfully rendered 'Just then ...' by the JPS. The KBS begins with 'thereupon' which gives the undesirable impression of consecution.

– 3:22a the MT has the sing. *bā'*, but this is not possible in the position after the two subjects; read therefore the plur. *bā'ū*, with the Sebir and 2 Mss (as mentioned in BHS app.). If necessary one can get round the question by dividing 22a up into a short nominal clause for the servants and a verbal clause for Joab. But this solution is inadvisable in view of the division of the text into quartets of lines and the chiasmus which 22a and 23a have.

– 3:24e the absolute infinitive is nice here and used very idiomatically. KJ is rather awkward: 'he is quite gone'. KBS and NBE are good: 'how could he go just like that?' and 'dejándolo marchar sin más'. Translations such as the SV, NBG and the BJ opt for an adjective like 'zoo vrij, ongehinderd, unmolested'.

– 3:25c Retain the K *mbw'k*, which becomes the vocalised *mᵉbō'ękā* and *cf.* S.R. Driver, Notes ..., *ad loc.*

– 3:36b I begin at the telling analysis of the syntax that Driver *ad loc.* has given. The preposition *kᵉ* is not the conjunction *ka'ăšęr*, and we are able to render the MT of 36c in one way only: 'Like all that the king did, *it* (viz. his conduct on the present occasion) pleased all the people' (*ṭwb* being the *verb*, as in v.19) – according to Driver on p.252. But the oddness of the text is in no way diminished. I observe that the result of this rendering of 36c is that 36b still has no subject, which is almost unbearable after the ellipse of the object of 36a. Put another way: the object, omitted but understood, of 36a must have the same referent as the omitted subject of 36b! An extremely problematical shift. That is why I suspect, all the same, that we are concerned with some contamination or another on the syntactical level, or with a conflate reading. Perhaps an older, intact text had the following link: 'and all that the king did was good in their eyes' – whereby *kl 'šr 'śh hmlk* has thus become the subject of *wyyṭb* and the last four words of 36c can be cancelled if so desired.

– 4:2 The absence of a preposition like *l*ᵉ in 'two men ... *hāyū bẹn šā'ūl*' is a phenomenon that also occurs in 8:18a (*bnyhw ... whkrty* has the meaning of the *bnyh ... 'l hkrty* of 20:23b), in I Sam.14:18c ('the ark *wbny yśr'l*') and I 18:6, where *whmḥlwt* occurs in the sense of *bmḥlwt*.

– 4:6 see first of all the excursus in small print in ch.IV. The Greek of 4:6 is as follows: καὶ ἰδοὺ ἡ θυρωρὸς του οἴκου εκάθαιρεν πυροὺς καὶ ἐνύσταξεν και ἐκάθευδεν, καὶ Ρεκχα καὶ Βαανα οἱ ἀδελφοὶ διέλαθον.

– 4:6a in the alternative text, which is obtained by retroversion from the LXX, the verb *šql* (which Wellhausen and Driver argue in favour of) is unsuitable. Like McCarter I opt for *lqṭ* which has two of the three radicals in common with the MT *lqḥy ḥṭym*. However, it cannot be a participle, as vocalised by McCarter and as Wellhausen and Driver punctuate their *šqlh*, because her action is a flashback: *now*, i.e. the moment the two men come in, she is asleep, after she *had* gathered grain earlier. This requires vocalisation as a perfect, *lāqᵉṭā* thus.

– 4:6c *nmlṭw*: Since S.R. Driver argued in favour of 'slipt in *or* through' (a form of entering therefore!) this rendering has unfortunately become in vogue, or, to tell the truth, has been indiscriminately adopted by, for example, Smith, Schulz, LV, BJ, NBE (?), JPS, McCarter. Driver's assertion that this is 'according to the primary meaning of the root' and that 'escaping' is 'the special sense' is baseless and untenable. The verb *mlṭ* has, in fact, a semantic field of exceptionally clear simplicity and means 'escape' everywhere. The rendering 'slipping in/by' is a desperate attempt to make something of the disrupted Hebrew. The short clause 6c actually refers to the disappearance of the murderers (*cf.* also CT p.239 point 3 – there is an unwillingness to be blinded by the διαλανθάνω of the LXX like Driver) but Buber and NBG (who make v.7ab into a flashback, a good solution), Goslinga, KBS, and Hertzberg (with an inconsistent rendering) rightly retain the 'stealing away'. The word διαλανθάνω in the sense of slip by/through is, *pace* Smith, Driver and McCarter, impossible as a rendering of *nmlṭ*. CT rightly rejects this, referring to Judg.3:26 and II Ki.19:27 as exact parallels for the niph'al of **mlṭ*.

– 4:7a I have transferred the subject from the MT of v.6c to v.7a where it belongs: the narrator takes up the thread of the action, whilst v.6 had another subject and was an analepsis. We can also read in v.7a X + qatal, thus *rekāb uba'ănā bā'ū habbayit*. I have a slight preference for the syntax of wyqtl + X, because 7a is a consecutive continuation and complement of v.5b.

– 4:10e Driver is of the opinion that this clause cannot be reconciled with David's point of view and has to therefore dissociate himself from the RSV and Keil who have heard the irony in it. He writes that *'ăšęr* cannot be 'namely'. However I have come to the conclusion that this word ensures a loose tie and neither requires nor excludes a gerundival understanding of *ltty*; subsequently that we must first determine who or what the antecedent of *'ăšęr* is; and finally that the rendering of this relative pronoun is highly dependent on the context so that it is purely a question of translation as to whether we can put 'namely' to use somewhere. My own view is that *'ăšęr* does not necessarily refer to the messenger (present twice as object suffix in the immediately preceding 10d) as Driver and Goslinga want, but can refer back to a) the entire (double) clause 10d, or b) to the final predicate, 'I killed him' thus, with the intention of adding another short comment or modification to the crucial action. The final clause 10e can include both the focalisation of the messenger (I deserve a messenger's wage) and the irony of David (I owed him a messenger's wage). McCarter's translation is subtle but due to the *irrealis* too much of a good thing: 'a man to whom it would have been suitable for me to give a reward!'

– 5:2b the Ketib has placed a *he* wrongly and has undergone a haplography; follow the Qere and write *'th hyyt hmwṣy' whmby' 't yśr'l*.

– 5:6d the form *hsyrk* is in the singular; this is possible because the verb occurs initially in the clause and it is not necessary to repunctuate the form to a (defectively spelt) plural *hęsīrūkā*.

Keil and Goslinga are right here.

– 5:8b some translators dare not begin the main clause with *wyg*ʿ; so KJ, SV, BJ, NBE, Goslinga, and *cf.* Ulrich p.83 who thinks that *wyg*ʿ is not a jussive. This results in their leaving an empty space where the main clause should be, an ellipse thus (so NBE, BJ, Goslinga; both KJ and SV fill the gap with a clause borrowed from Chron.) or their making a link and construing 8c as a subsequent object of *yg*ʿ: so SV, NEB, CT. Because the construction ***kl mkh ybsy*** is the equivalent of a relative clause (*'šr ykh* ... – *cf.* Josh.15:16) and a temporal clause (*kī ykh* etc. – compare Ex.21:20 alongside 21:12), I see no objection to interpreting the waw in front of the imperf. as a *waw apodoseos*; a similar waw + imperf. also occurs in Prov.23:24b (mentioned in Brockelmann, 'Hebräische Syntax' § 123g) and Num.23:19, Hosea 14:10 (mentioned in BM § 118.1). For the waw at the beginning of an apodosis see also Ges.K. § 116w and Joüon §§ 156kl and 176i. The waw of 5:8b is supported by Aquila and Symmachus.

- 5:8b the verb *ng*ʿ usually means 'to touch' it is true, but there are also clear examples that it means touching in the sense of 'hitting': Gen.32:25, Josh.8:15, and Is.53:4 (where *ngw*ʿ is a synonym for *mkh* and *m'nh*!). References such as Josh.9:19, II Sam.14:10, Ruth 2:9, Job 5:19, 6:7 form the transition between the two meanings, and compare the verbal *ng*ʿ of Gen.12:17 and II Ki.15:5 with the nominal of *ng*ʿ II Sam.7:14. See also point 2 in HAL p.631b.

– 5:8b we can already take 'the pipe' to mean the prepositionally governed object of *ng*ʿ. I myself prefer a somewhat different alternative, which says that the object *bw* ('him', sc. the Jebusite) is understood self-evidently and omitted: so that *bṣnwr* becomes purely an adjunct of place in 'he should hit him in/on the throat/pipe'.

– 5:8c a) the Q *śĕnū'ē* assumes (on condition that we read 8c as an independent clause) that the double *'ęt* functions as a *nota subjecti*, which is not out of the question: it seems implausible to first expressly mark the subject with *'ęt* and then utter a passive participle as a predicate on it, which becomes particularly clear if we consider option c.

b) the K *śn'w*, which requires the vocalisation *śān*^{e}*'ū*, also presupposes (on condition that we read 8c as an independent clause) that the double *'ęt* functions as a *nota subjecti*, which is not impossible, but does not seem very probable. Besides, the statement which arises on the ground of K seems so redundant in respect to verse 5d that I do not support this reading. The same holds good *mutatis mutandis* for the form *śōn^{e}'ē* which we gain by retroversion from the LXX. CT supports the K as an asyndetic relative clause: 'eux qui ont haï', but views in addition the lame and the blind as the object of *yigga'*.

c) The variant *śn'h* of 4QSam[a] has recently been placed at our disposal here, an active form which does not hedge about responsibility and unambiguously recognises the person of David as subject. (Passive forms gladly want to tone down, palliate and so on, the agent's responsibility for his action.) I am enchanted by the fact that this *śān^{e}'ā* had already been put forward by S.R. Driver, p.260, Schulz, Kittel (in the apparatus of BHK3) and Goslinga, before the Qumran datum came to light, and I follow Ulrich, p.136 and 148, and McCarter in their preference for this variant.

– 5:13a the meaning '*in* Jerusalem' is indicated three times around this line by the preposition *b^{e}* (also used for this line in the variant I Chron.14:3); but this fact does not exclude the view that the first preposition *min* in II 5:13a means 'in'.

– 5:18b here and in 22b the verb *nṭš*, whose semantic field is difficult to understand, means 'fan out', just as in Judg.15:9, I Sam.30:16 and perhaps I 4:2 (an intransitive qal?). McCarter is right in saying that it does not revolve around a spreading out 'for purpose of plunder' which BDB and Tidwell (SVT 1979 p.196) want; the references in I 30 and Judg.15 prevent this. I see no root **yṭš* such as G.R. Driver (in JTS 1933 p.379) and Tidwell (p.195) want.

– 6:1a the reverse, a *wy'sf* which we must interpret as *wysf*, occurs in I 18:29, and the *wtsf* of Ps.104:29 is *wt'sf*. Ad I 15:5 Driver gathers a series of references where the first root consonant aleph has dropped out.

– 6:1a the text is further in order, with the *status absolutus bāḥūr*. We are also able to read a construct combination with a patach in *baḥūr-b^{e}yiśrāel*; *cf.* 10:9b and NAPS I app.I *ad loc.*

– 6:2a the form *mibba'ălē y^{e}hūdā* has had curious echoes in Ms.B and the Antiochian text of the Greek: τῶν ἀρχόντων Ιουδα, whilst 4QSam[a] explicatively adds 'that is Kiryath Jearim'. There is a good discussion of this reference in Pisano pp.101-104 which ends with: 'Whether MT contains simply a hurried narrative which speaks only of the place *from* which the ark was brought without specifying that David went *to* Baal-Judah, or whether a correction must be made according to the seeming logic of the narrative, it may be said at least that there is no *textual* basis for correcting the MT reading, which is surely an old one, as its indirect reflection in LXX's *Vorlage* indicates.' I myself see the yod of *mb'ly* as a dittography and consider the remaining word *b'l* as a variant of *b'lt*.

– 6:2c the MT has a double *šem* in the relative clause here. This text form has three or four disadvantages; the redoubling is neither fine nor functional, that the first *šem* has no article is unpleasant, and the preposition at the end of the verse dangles unattached, without it being clear what its suffix refers back to exactly. All these unpropitious matters disappear outright if we delete one *šem* as a dittography. Language and translation flow now: ' ... the ark of God, over which the name of the Lord of Hosts has been proclaimed who is enthroned on the cherubs'. In ch.V § 4 I have shown that this decision receives a double confirmation, moreover, from an unexpected quarter: quantitative symmetries on the level of sequences and corner parts. These symmetries mean for the entire chapter an important restraining effect on the desire to emend: they are disturbed by the addition or deletion of one word. For the dittography see also Ulrich p.66.

– 6:3c/4a A fine example of a dittography through homoioteleuton, whereby the *ḥdšh* at the end of v.3 and the first five words of v.4 can be deleted without the slightest loss of information. *Cf.* Ulrich p.66 and Pisano pp.272-277.

– 6:6a the most natural thing after a spatial detail like 'threshing floor' is that the word is followed by the name of the owner. The data of the parallel reference I Chron.13:9 (*kīdōn*), the LXX (Nachon and Nodab) and now Nodan from 4QSam[a] differ it is true, but they all appear, nevertheless, to vary a name. On the ground of I 23:22sq. and 26:4 (*cf.* NAPS II, App.1 on this) I considered, in addition, whether *nākōn* might be an adverb, but this leaves me with the indefiniteness of *grn*. The quantitative symmetries which I have just mentioned prevent me from adding a single word. That is why I keep to the first option and view Nachon as the name of the owner. See also the thorough discussion of the data and the alternatives in Carlson pp.77-78. The location of the threshing floor remains obscure.

– 6:6b *šlḥ* is elliptical for *šālaḥ 'ęt yādō*.

– 6:6d the meaning of the verbal form *šāmᵉṭū* is uncertain here and whether it can be retained. Those who fail to opt for 'slip away' might consider whether an emendation *šm nṭw* fits; two words thus, *šam nāṭū*, 'because they turned off there' – exactly what the cows in I Sam.6 did *not* do. NB *šām* in v.7bc, and *cf*. *nṭh* in 2:19 and 21. But the word counts argue against this proposal.

– 6:7b *'al haššal*. The Versions can be backed up insofar as there will turn out to be a causal adjunct: 'because of the/his ... '. If we do not wish to round out the text to *'al 'ăšęr šālaḥ 'ęt yādō* (a suspiciously ingenious solution against which CT effectively lodges an objection) we might consider an extra waw (which had disappeared via haplography): *'al haššālū*, 'because of negligence', assuming that Biblical Hebrew had this word at its disposal as Biblical Aramaic had. CT observes on p.244 that 'aussi bien Aq[uila] (...) que Saadya (...), Abulwalid (...), Rashi et Radaq l'interprètent à partir du sens araméen de la racine *šlḥ* comme signifiant 'négligence, faute par inadvertance'. Le hifil dérivé de cette racine est en effet utilisé en 2 R 4,28 et Abulwalid rapproche la formation du substantif *šal* de celle de *qaw*.' Pisano gives a good discussion of this reference on pp.104-106, and states at the end of it: 'The reading in MT here is either irretrievably corrupt or else the meaning of the word has become unintelligible. Because of the difficulty in seeing how it could be a corruption of the longer text of I Chr and 4Q, which appears rather to be an expansion, MT seems to witness here to the older form of the text.'

– 6:8a what is written is written, 'David became angry', and we must not, because of half-heartedness or religious cold feet, translate away this *wyḥr* as 'he was displeased/vexed/distressed' and suchlike (as do KJ, BJ, LV, NBG, NEB, NBE, KBS, and JPS) or even worse, change it to *wyṣr* as do KBL and HAL (HAL: unmutig werden; in three places?). The same holds good for I 15:11 where Samuel becomes angry, and see

NAPS II App.I *ad loc.* Keil, Smith, Goslinga, Hertzberg, Buber, McCarter are correct.

– 6:13a the iterative reading that a sacrifice was offered each time after six steps is persistent and rears its head again with modern authors such as Carlson, Miller and Roberts, and McCarter. This opinion, already effectively rejected by Driver, Goslinga and others, appears especially to appeal to people who are either more cultic than the ancients or have a weakness for ancient eastern parallels. It has, however, particularly poor credentials, for the Hebrew of the MT with its two wyqtl forms does not allow it and is itself as right as rain so that changing this (as for example McCarter does, p.171) is altogether wrong. The divergent text of the Greek is no ground on which to build.

– 6:16a there is no reason to change *whyh* to *wyhy*, because a preterit wqtl is not uncommon in prose: we also find a similar *whyh* in Sam. in I 1:12, 10:9, 13:22, 17:48, 25:20, and *cf. w'mr(w)* in I 5:7b and 24:11b, *wśbty* in I 12:2b, *wz'qh* in II 13:18d, and *wṣlḥw* ... *w'brh* in II 19:18sq. See also P.A.H. de Boer in the Festschrift E.A. Nida 1974, M.Black and W.A. Smalley eds., pp.43-52: 'The Perfect with *waw* in 2 Samuel 6:16'. Referring to A.B. Davidson, 'Hebrew Syntax', 3rd ed. 1902, Edinburgh, who writes on p.85: 'The perfect with *waw* seems occasionally to resume and restate briefly an event previously described in detail,' De Boer arrives at this rendering: 'Well, thus it was, the ark of the Lord coming into David's city, and Michal, Saul's daughter, looking down through the window ....' Carlson p.86 writes on this reference: 'it is evident that this is a strongly marked consecutive form, intended to stress an important phase in the procession (...).' Ulrich p.196sq. speaks of a mistake in too easy-going a manner and wants *wyhy*.

– 6:16c *mkrkr* is an interesting pilpel and is discussed by Avishur and Ahlström in Short Notes in VT of 1976 and '78 respectively, by Avishur once more in his book of 1984, 'Stylistic Studies of Word-Pairs ...', pp.719-723 and by McCarter p.171. Taking everything into account I too think that the verb refers specifically to an activity of the fingers just as in Ugaritic (a passage in the Ba'al cycle, CTCA 4:IV:27-30, = KTU 1.4 IV 27-30) and perhaps in Rabbinic Hebrew (Avishur 1984, p.722), so that our passage shows the total dance of the celebrant by means of a merismus: with his hands (*krkr*, snapping with his fingers) and feet (*pzz*).

– 6:20d Driver draws our attention to the fact that *nkbd* is a perfect with the meaning of the middle voice, 'how the king hath got him honour today ...!'

– 6:20e the doubling of *hglwt* with *nglwt* is discussed by Driver p.272 who chiefly speaks about the second *-ōt* instead of *ōh* and does not turn against the combination. The combination *is* rejected by Ges.-K. § 75y and Talmon in Textus I (1960), and is considered suspect by McCarter. I see the absolute form *niglō(t)* as stylistic emphasis made in anger and as grammatically conceivable.

– 6:20f the word *ryqym* must not be changed, because of the LXX, to *rqdym* (contra McCarter). The MT is superior because a) it exhibits a framework 'worthy – empty' which serves the drift of the speech well, b) this inclusio is answered by David with a synonymous framework in v.22 and c) *ryq* is, moreover, a part of the series of words at the end of 20def which judge more and more negatively.

-6:21d the form *wśḥqty* can be taken and accepted at the point it occurs, at the end of a period, in at least three different ways:
a) as a consecutive perfect requiring a translation such as 'I shall play'; not a very attractive alternative because in v.21 David actually speaks rather on the reality – the procession – of today (and adds a complement by just speaking on a future possibility in v.22);
b) another reading is the declarative interpretation of the perfect (in which the waw exerts no influence), 'I play', *c.f.* *'āmartī* of 19:30, 'I herewith say/decide'.
c) I prefer the third reading. In this the waw is purely copulative as in v.16a and does not detract from the preterit character of *śḥqty*. I see the waw rather as an expression of emotion, a form of emphasis. Translation: 'yes, I have played [sc. on this holy day, as priest and as anointed one] before the Lord'.

– 6:22 is translated by Avishur, in 'Stylistic Studies of Word Pairs ...', p.239, as follows: 'I will make myself more contemptible than this, and I will be abased in my eyes; but by the maids of whom you have spoken, by them I shall be held in honour'.

This syntactical interpretation is correct, *cf.* the JPS which I quote during my analysis in note 105, and KJ and SV (which still begin with 'and' in 22c, not with the preferable 'but' that gives the period a fine relief). I myself tend to see a conditional period at the beginning, according to the model which is unavoidable in I 16:2c; the translation then runs: 'And if I am going to get even lower than this time, so that I am low in my own eyes, then I will still be held in honour by the girls you have mentioned.' But a hypotaxis like this in aid of more contrast in the period is a matter of the receiving language rather than the giving language.

– 6:22b the LXX has 'in your eyes', followed by Driver, Kittel (BHK3), Smith, Schulz, RSV, NEB, BJ, NBE. This reading ruins David's point and is, as CT explains, probably based on a mistaken understanding of the syntax in the original. Compare for *w*^{e}*hāyītī* such and such *bĕʿēnay*, 'in my *own* eyes', the construction of Num.13:33b *wann*^{e}*hī b*^{e}*ʿēnēnū* [thus: in our own eyes] *kaḥăgābīm w*^{e}*ken hāyīnū b*^{e}*ʿēnēhęm*.

– 7:7b the form *šbṭy* does not need to be emended, it is a metonym for 'tribal leaders'. So also Buber and JPS. See my arguments in ch.VI *ad loc.* and the data in CT which makes reference to Deut.29:9 (compared to Josh.23:2 and 24:1) and Gen.49:16. So P.V. Reid, '*šbṭy* in 2 Samuel 7:7', in CBQ 37 (1975) pp.17-20 also retains *šbṭy*. His arguments for 'staff bearers' are so good that his proposal for repunctuating the form as a denominative participle *šōb*^{e}*ṭē* (followed by McCarter) is unnecessary. D. Murray, 'Once again ’T ’ḤD ŠBṬY YŚR’L in II Sam. 7:7', RB 94 (1987) pp.389-396, wants to emend by inserting the short word *mkl* after the numeral, but this is rightly rejected by C.T. Begg, 'The Reading of 2 Sam 7,7: Some Remarks', RB 95 (1988) pp.551-558. The proposal of Robert in VT 21 (1971) pp.116-118, to interpret Yhwh as subject of the infinitive *lrʿwt* must also be rejected.

– 7:9c after a series of three preterits a very long series of *wqtl* clauses is opened by *wʿśty*. This transition may not be ignored. In my interpretation I go in to, at great length, the rendering with past versus future of the paragraph 9c-11b and further; q.v. the arguments there in ch.VI which lead me to futures. Rudolf Meyer's argument for accepting the *perf. copulativum* as good Hebrew in various passages, in 'Auffallender Erzählungsstil in einem angeblichen Auszug aus der 'Chronik der Könige von Juda', pp.114-123 of the Festschrift F. Baumgärtel, Erlangen 1959, is applied by Oswald Loretz to II Sam.7, in a short contribution, 'The perfectum copulativum in 2 Sm 7,9-11', CBQ 23 (1961), pp.294-296. But he provides scarcely any arguments. The correct argument that wqtl *can* be an ordinary past tense is not the same as the argument or evidence that wqtl *must* be a preterit in a given reference (for example here in II Sam.7).

– 7:11a the waw with which the line opens is usually skipped or interpreted as waw explicativum respectively: Driver, LV, BJ, NEB, NBE, NBG, KBS, JPS, Hertzberg, Goslinga, McCarter. I support Carlson, however, who retains the waw as copulativum, and recognise in 10d + 11a two periods of time which agree with 6a + 7b: slavery in Egypt and the time of the Judges.

– 7:11b changing the 2nd person suffixes into the 3rd person (as do Driver and McCarter) is baseless and is refuted by stylistic analysis (by pointing to the connection with v.9b and 1b).

– 7:11c *whgyd* is a declarative perfect and the waw can be rendered by ('voorts' =) 'furthermore' (Goslinga) or 'und namentlich' (Ges.-K § 154a note b) or 'also' (McCarter): 'furthermore the Lord declares to you that he will make you a dynasty'. See note 44 of the analysis in ch.VI, where the emendation *whgdylk* is rejected at the same time. The whole line 11c can, as I have explained in my interpretation, also be printed as second degree – instead of third degree – direct speech.

– 7:11c/12a the tetragrammaton at the end of 11c is totally redundant, and it does not have any stylistic function either. Conversely the syntax at the beginning of 12a requires a *whyh*. We obtain this by shifting and transposing the consonant signs *yhwh* from the end of 11c. As in the LXX, KJ, Driver, Schulz, NEB, NBE, McCarter. The double *yhwh* in 11c is retained by, amongst others, SV, NBG, JPS, KBS. In the parallel text I Chron.17:10-11 *yhwh* occurs prior to the verse divider as much as *whyh* occurs after it; here the proper noun is, however, indispensable as the subject of 'to build' because the line 10c begins with the first person hiph. of *ngd*.

– 7:23c the MT has *lkm* instead of *lhm*, but this form does not fit. The reading *lhm* which I follow is very obvious and enjoys the support of some Mss (according to BHS app.). It cannot refer to the plural *'lhym* because in the meantime a double *lw* has been used which refers back to this quasi plural. Therefore the form *lhm* alludes to 'the people', which is a collective.

– 7:23d a word for 'to your land' (MT *l'rṣk*) does not fit at all here. The context, especially the staccato of infinitives with acts of God which are all for the benefit of his people, urgently requires another *l*^{e} + infinitive. The form *lgršk* of the parallel text in I Chron.17:21 is a good candidate but requires a fairly major operation. I follow a suggestion of M. Rehm's in 'Textkritische Untersuchungen zu den Parallelstellen der Samuel-Königsbücher und der Chronik', Münster 1937, pp.64 and 74, and interpret *l'rṣk* as a variant of *lhrṣk*. The latter can be interpreted as a hiph'il of **rṣṣ*, 'shatter', but better as a hiph'il of **rwṣ* which both here and in Jer.49:19, 50:44(Q) means 'drive away' (< lit.: 'cause to run'). This variation aleph/he is well known in classical Hebrew, *cf.* forms such as *l'dyb* for *lhdyb* in I Sam.2:33, *'aškem* for *haškem* in Jer.25:3; *cf.* also the appearance of the he in the niph'al imper. and infin. (hiqqatel for *'inqatel or the elision of the he after the preposition l/k/b in various hiph'il infin. forms, see BL § 25a'. Compare the easy switch of 'af'el and haf'el in Biblical Aramaic.

– 7:23d after the plural 'peoples' the suffix in 'and his gods' is an irregularity. Nevertheless, on the ground of suspecting that a formulaic turn of phrase or fixed expression 'a people and its god(s)' existed, and that its ending has been adopted unchanged I hesitate to emend. I read the text as 'peoples, [each] with its own god(s)'.

– 7:26 I interpret the imperfect after the imperatives of v.25 as an indicative and consecutive *w*^{e}*yiqtol*: 'then your name shall be great' is thus the result of God's acting pro David and Israel. I also read the x-yiqtol construction in 26c as indicative. Idem on both matters: NBG, Goslinga, BJ, KBS, McCarter. Both verse 26a and c are translated as a wish in KJ, NBE, Keil, Smith, Buber, JPS. With only v.26a as a wish: SV, LV, NEB, Ridout PCP p.220.

– 8:3b The Q has added the name of the Euphrates at the end, it is true, but the K is possible as well since the reading '*the* river' or 'the River' means the most outstanding river, viz. the

Euphrates. This is also the case with the word *(han)nāhār* in Gen.31:21, 36:37, I Ki.5:4, 14:15, Micha 7:12 and Zach.9:10.

– 8:7b Has this information 'he brought them to Jerusalem' inspired the glossator in I 17:54? The Greek (Ms.B and the Antiochian text), but now also 4QSam[a], have after this an extensive plus which anticipates I Ki.14:26 (the datum that Pharaoh Shishaq takes the gold from the temple). The various texts and the relevant data occur in the detailed discussion which Pisano accords this plus on pp.43-47. On p.46 he says: '4Q's longer text certainly indicates (...) that there existed a Hebrew text containing the plus which constituted the Palestinian text of Samuel (at least in the first century A.D.). This may be a good indication that the plus was present in LXX's Hebrew *Vorlage* as well.' Pisano's conclusion (p.48) is that 'the shorter MT is to be preferred as the more original text, into which the historical note on the destiny of David's bronze was inserted.' I agree, because the datum on Shishaq is not only an excessive but also a non-functional anticipation, which disturbs, moreover, the chiasmus (of *lqḥ* and its objects) which I have discussed. See also Ulrich, p.45.

– 8:8 the name *bṭḥ* is in I Chron.18 *ṭbḥt* and data from elsewhere, such as the Amarna letters (see HAL s.v. *ṭbḥ*), argue for implementing a metathesis and reading Tebach. In Ms.B and the Antiochian text the Greek again has an extensive plus which is discussed by Pisano on pp.47sq.

– 8:10a the name Joram is an Israelite-Yahwistic adaptation of the theophoric name which in Aramaic (and in view of the LXX rendering) probably runs Hadduram.

– 8:13 The victory which David gains at the Dead Sea is, in view of this adjunct of place and the immediate sequel of v.13, clearly the fruit of a campaign against Edom. The paragraph on Edom vv.13-14 is a counterpart of the paragraph on Aram in vv.5-6. In the tradition the text has been subject to at least a switch of *'rm* and *'dm*, and perhaps a homoioteleuton. In the first case we can, along with Rehm, op.cit. pp.74sq., read *ub^ešūbō hikkā 'ęt 'ĕdōm b^egē męlaḥ* etc.; this is the minimal operation which is necessary. The following deal with the text in approximately the same way: Buber, NBG, BJ, NEB, KBS and JPS, in keeping with the LXX.

I retain MT *mehakkōtō* as sound, find that the name Aram

goes with, and can remain where it is after, 'his return' and assume that a homoioteleuton has taken place. Like Keil, Driver, LV, Hertzberg, Goslinga, NBE, CT and McCarter (who for the rest includes Abishai as subject – something I think goes too far and fails to take into consideration the theme of ch.8 as part of Act X) I read a second form of *nkh*, now a finite form: the *narrativus* which gives the battle against Edom its own line. See also I Chron.18:12 and the title of Ps.60. In my analysis I refer to the chiasmus of wyqtl plus b[e] + inf. + suffix and vice versa which creates a link between v.3 and 13 – an argument for the restoration of the second line of v.13. In saying all this I now look back to the first word of v.12:

– 8:12a Instead of Aram a few Mss have Edom (app.BHS). The *mē'arām* of the MT is impeccable and there is no reason whatever to alter it (with the LXX and the Peshitta) to *m'dm*; contra S.R. Driver, NEB, CT and McCarter. On the other hand there are two good and simple reasons for retaining Aram in v.12. One reason is positive: the name refers back to vv.5-6, the paragraph devoted to Aram as one of the peoples subjugated by David (compare 5b with 13b and v.6 with v.14). The other consideration is negative: it is not yet Edom's turn in v.12 – it gets its own paragraph as conquered nation in vv.13-14.

– 8:14b I do not look upon this line as a variant or duplication of 14a. The asyndeton, the emphasis on *kol* (now that this occurs initially) and the placing of the complement of place in front are just as many signs that 14b already presupposes 14a. The line therefore wants to underline the thoroughness with which Edom is brought under control.

– 8:17a Benaiah has no function in the MT and the foreign legion is merely attached in a vague kind of way. Inserting the preposition *'al* is unavoidable, along the lines of the counterpart at the end of ch.20; unless one can prove that the conjunction *w[e]* sometimes has a similar pregnant meaning.

– 8:18b 'priests', is that what the sons of David were? This statement is surprising and, so quickly after the professionals of 17a, doubtful. It is understandable that G.J. Wenham, 'Were David's Sons Priests?', ZAW 87 (1975) pp.79-82, has proposed reading *sknym* as 'administrators (of the royal estates)', but McCarter rightly points out that it is difficult 'to think of the surprising designation of David's sons as priests as having arisen by corruption from an uncontroversial text'.

-21:1e The MT word order *byt hdmym* furnishes us with no predicate in v.1e. A different allocation of the he provides the solution: we read *byth*, which is a variant spelling of *bytw*, and recognise *dāmīm* as subject. What is stated, therefore, is: 'On Saul, on his house [rests] bloodguilt.' The motivating clause which follows, v.1f, explains why. Compare, in addition, the combination 'Saul and his house' in v.4b.

– 21:4e The syntax of this line is rendered in three different ways. The translations of Buber, BJ and McCarter presuppose two independent clauses; an interpretation which we can neither forbid nor refute. Then there is the option that the line is a compound sentence. This interpretation can be realised in two entirely different ways. One group of translations opts for an interrogative sentence: 'what wouldst thou have me do for thee?' According to SV, Smith, Hertzberg, NBG, Goslinga, NEB. The other group sees *ma* as an introduction to a dependent question which is an object clause, and reads a main clause after it. As a consequence the point of gravity comes to rest on the promising part of all things! 'Whatever you say I will do for you.' According to KJ, Driver, LV, NBE, KBS, JPS. The latter interpretation deserves preference because David had already posed the question in v.3 and had received an evasive (and formally negative) answer. He must therefore, in the second instance, go a step further to draw the Gibeonites out and he does this in v.4e by giving carte blanche to these injured partners to the treaty. The line is a commitment, and sure enough the Gibeonites put forward a proposal after this which is put into operation without fail by the king. The quotation of the line from 21:4 in Ges.-K. § 120c also implies the interpretation that it is a compound sentence. From a stylistic point of view v.4e is an ingenious extension of 3b.

– 21:5c I see 5c as the content, if not the object, of the *dimmā lānū* in 5b. Reading through Ges.-K. § 120 gives me the idea that such an asyndetic syntax is possible, see especially § 120g. In addition I notice that v.5b is a *casus pendens* and that the main clause finally appears in v.6a.

– 21:6a The Qere has the form *yuttan*, an internal passive of the qal; but the Ketib *yntn* is not erroneous and presupposes the vocalisation of a niph'al imperf.

– 21:6b The MT is sound and makes good sense. For this reason alone the drastic changes which different commentators have put forward in imitation of Wellhausen and Driver (read Gibeon, delete Saul and read *b*ᵉ*har*) are superfluous. Moreover one is now able to read in CT p.300 that the reading Gibeon is not supported by the Greek translations, except one doubtful scholium. Furthermore CT p.300sq. has good arguments for *b*ᵉ*ḥīr yhwh* and good arguments against the alteration *b*ᵉ*har*.

– 21:8b At the beginning of the line the MT has 'the five sons of Mikal'. This motherhood is not only at variance with the data on Michal which we have from I 18, the end of I 25 and II 3 (the marriage with Paltiel), and especially the end of II 6, but also with the fact that we have already become acquainted with the father, Adriel, in I 18 as the husband of Merab. The name of this elder daughter of Saul is supported by two Hebrew Mss (app. BHS) and the Lucianic recension.

– 21:9cd Here three small blemishes occur in the MT which are rectified or completed by a Qere each time. The first is *šb'tym* from which the yod must be deleted; the second is the form *hm* which, placed in front of the verb *hmtw*, is a haplography of *hmh*; and the third change is the addition of a *bēt* to the word 'beginning'.

– 21:11a It is clear that 'what Rizpah had done' is the object of information which David receives; it is preceded by *'ęt*. Now that the verb **ngd* is in the hoph'al this particle can be entitled nota *sub*jecti. It does not need to be deleted, neither does the verb need to be transposed into a hiph'il; see J. Hoftijzer on this situation, pp.14-22 and p.90sqq. in his 'Remarks Concerning the Use of the Particle *'t* in Classical Hebrew', OTS xiv (1965), pp.1-99. Other references with the hoph'al of *ngd* and the so-called *'t nominativi*: Gen.27:42, Josh.9:24 and I Ki.18:13.

– 21:12d The form *tlwm* in the MT is changed by a Qere and the order of the words *šm hplštym* is improved by a Qere, so that we get *tl'wm šmh plštym*.

– 21:14a A spontaneous reading of this verse views 'the bones of Saul and his son Jonathan' as the direct object of 'they buried', all the more since the wyqtl forms of 12b and 13a have the same extended object. But now the question arises as to whether the bones of those hanged, gathered in 13b, were *not* interred in Kish's grave. It is difficult to say no to this, so that Smith, Buber, Hertzberg, Goslinga and KBS interpret the particle *'ęt* of v.14a as the preposition and translate as follows: 'They gathered together the bones of those hanged (13b) and buried [them] *with* the bones of Saul and his son Jonathan in (...) the grave of his father Kish (14a).' This solution is sympathetic and not impossible, but I still get the impression of artifice. After we have heard three times within a short space of time *'ęt 'aṣmōt* in 12b-13a-13b which is a direct object (whilst 12cd also have transitive verbs, with the same object), it is unpleasant to have to suddenly see the fourth *'ęt 'aṣmōt* as preposition plus substantive. Two alternatives remain. One is that we assume the writer does not want to overburden the long clause 14a (with a five-word object and a double place adjunct of six words) with an extra object 'and the bones of those hanged' and leaves it implicit. The LXX adds this object and some modern translations follow its example (LV, BJ, note in JPS). Finally we can take the omission of those hanged in 14a to be a discreet hint that they have received their own grave elsewhere which the narrator does not want to pay any special attention to here. But this reading undermines the conjunctiveness of the final sequence too much, and this solution of *two* graves also encroaches upon the sense of v.12 which would then mention a separate transport.

– 21:14a the rendering which takes *ṣelā'* to be a proper noun of a place gives me the impression of being a solution to a quandary. I put forward the alternative of interpreting the word as the designation for a ridge in the wall of a grave in the rock or of some protruding ledge, upon which the urns or ossuaries were placed.

– 21:14c That the adjunct 'afterwards' occurs right at the end of a story, is remarkable; but there is no linguistic objection to it. Moreover we can find clauses elsewhere which end on *'aḥăre ken*, see Gen.41:31, Josh.10:26, I Sam.24:9a and Jer.34:11.

– 21:16b HAL gives *s.v.* **qayin* the translation 'Lanze, Spiess' for this hapax legomenon. The LXX has 'spear' here.

– 21:16d the JPS gives a simple rendering 'tried to kill David'. NEB:

'was about to kill him'. NBE: 'diciendo que iba a matar a David'. SV, LV, NBG: 'en dacht David te verslaan'. KJ, Buber, BJ and KBS have approximately the same rendering.

Chapter 22, the great hymn of David. It cannot be the task of 20th century philology, on the ground of arguments from reason and one's own good taste, to create a mixture of parallel texts such as II Sam.22 and Psalm 18, and to proclaim this third text, of one's own compilation, as the best text. Nevertheless a comparison of II 22 with Psalm 18 is permitted, fascinating and on several points highly relevant. My interpretation aspires to view II Sam.22 as far as possible as a self-contained text which can be understood in terms of itself and presupposes as few alterations as possible in the text. In this appendix I mention and vouch for the minimum of operations, but also at those places where I do not change anything I discuss a number of points of contact with the psalm. That which follows on ch.22 does not aim at completeness on the points of difference with the psalm. There are all sorts of minor orthographical and morphological differences which, within the framework of my research, need not be mentioned. For information on this see the discussion which Cross and Freedman offered at the time in JBL of 1953.

- 22:2-3 The first strophe differs from the parallel text to the extent of a whole colon. The psalm places a line, absent in II Sam., in initial position, so that its verse 2 is a bicolon, whilst II Sam. ends on its own colon (v.3c) which the psalm does not have. This phenomenon serves as one of the examples in the theory of J.C. de Moor on the expansion and contraction of units (foot, stich, verse, strophe, etc.): see p.195 of his 'The Art of Versification in Ugarit and Israel', UF 10 (1978) pp.187-217.
- 22:3a I change a vowel and read the first word as *'ĕlōhāy*, 'my God'; compare Ps.18 which has *'elī* here.
- 22:5a Just as the analysis shows, the form *ḥbly mwt* is inferior to what II Sam. has here, *mšbry mwt*.
- 22:7b The bicolon v.7ab is more predicatively varied in the psalm by having, in v.7b, the form *'ăšawweă'* 'I call for help' (compare the noun *šaw'ātī* in v.7d – a vertical parallelism thus) instead of a repeated *'ęqrā*.
- 22:8a The retention of the K of the first word is preferable: in this way the assonance of *wattig'aš wattir'aš* is maintained and colon C exhibits a variation and climax (hithpa'el versus qal) with colon A.

– 22:8b In the psalm the 8ab cola have the word pair earth//mountains as subject, and the combination 'the foundations of the mountains' is, of course, in order. In II Sam. heaven occurs instead of the mountains, perhaps as an anticipation of v.10a and 14a; but the combination 'the foundations of heaven' is unique. In the Biblical view of the world, however, heaven is a very solid construction which has to keep the chaos power of the waters from the earth; it is 'stamped firm' as the word *rāqīă'* of Gen.1 puts it. That is why *mōsᵉdōt haššāmayim* does not seem impossible to me and I do not alter the text here.

– 22:11b The consonantal text of the first word differs by one letter from that of the psalm. The *wyd'* of Ps.18, 'he glided', is more specific and more plastic than *wyr'*, 'he was seen', in II Sam.22.

– 22:12 'Sieve' proposed by McCarter and HAL for the word **ḥašrā*, quoting a contribution to JNES 9 by Feigin, and in the footsteps of various Ugarit experts (in the Ba'al cyclus there is a reference with *ḫṯr* which the majority, like Aistleitner WUB no.1109, Gordon, UT § 19.1027, translate by 'sieve'; Del Olmo Lete however (in his Mitos y Leyendas de Canaán, glossary s.v. *ḫṯr*) prefers 'pitchfork', see on the choice De Moor, 'Seasonal Pattern' p.210) is doubtful whilst Ps.18 has another word, *ḥęškat* (which is put forward in Ges.-B and KBL2 as an improvement for our reference). BDB supposes (without further data) 'collection, mass'. I myself opt for a cognate of the arabic *ḫṯr*, 'thick, become stiff, solidify' [of fluids], (an alternative, mentioned by McCarter) and guess at a meaning such as 'thick mass' or 'layer of condensation', also in view of the *'ābē šᵉḥāqīm* (gloss or no gloss) which follow. The predicatively-used *sukkōt* can be translated in exactly the same way as the *sukkātō* of Ps.18 without changing the text: interpret the number as a poetic plural and treat the suffix as being understood. For the rest we might have to construe the text of v.12 in the Psalm in a different way, e.g. as a tricolon, in the nominal colon B of which *sukkātō* is then predicate or subject. For Sam. my translation does not differ much from the JPS which offers the following: 'He made pavilions of darkness about Him,/ Dripping clouds, huge thunderheads;'

– 22:16a This time II Sam. is more specific than the psalm, by having 'sea' instead of 'water'. The *mayim* of Ps.18 is perhaps subject to the influence of the waters in v.17b from which the poet is saved.

– 22:16cd The Psalm has the second person suffix with 'roaring' and 'nostrils'. I wonder if this has to do with the desire to mark the end of the section on the theophany formally somewhat stronger.

– 22:23b The verb, in the qal here, is a hiph'il in the psalm so that 'his laws' has become the object there. The fact that in II Sam. a *sing.* suffix refers back to this plural occurs now and then in poetry and cannot be called erroneous or incongruous.

– 22:27 I view *tittābar* as a divergent form which has arisen under the influence of the *tittammām* at the end of 26b and is a variant of the *titbārar* of the psalm. Things get more difficult with *tittappāl*. The hermetic structure of the strophe, which is based on maximum synonymous parallelism, requires a meaning such as 'being wily' and not a form of **tfl*. I allow myself to be supported by the *ttptl* of the psalm and assume that here in 27b a taw has disappeared due to haplography.

– 22:28a The *kī 'attā* as the beginning of colon A has good credentials in view of the continual working with anaphoras in this section of the song. Moreover the nota objecti is dubious. It appears, strikingly, in initial position without the functionality of this being clear, is too much of a *rara avis* in this ancient poetry (in spite of 20a) and introduces an indefinite nominal phrase here. This accumulation of improbabilities leads me to reading *w't* as a case of *scriptio defectiva* for *w*^{e}*'attā*. As it also does Cross and Freedman, note 62, McCarter (who mentions five other references), and Goslinga. The psalm marks the start of the three successive lines of poetry with the attractive series *kī 'attā* (bis) plus *kī b*^{e}*kā* of v.30a.

– 22:28b A slight difference in endings leads to an entirely different meaning of the predicate *tašpīl* in the parallel texts! The psalm has: 'but haughty eyes You humble', and II Sam.22 has, literally: 'and lower Your eyes on the haughty' (i.e. You look with scorn on them). Making a choice between these variants, which both function well in the context, is not necessary. Moreover they are poetically of approximately the same standing.

– 22:29a Instead of *yhwh* the psalm has the word *tā'īr*, so that colon A becomes a verbal clause. The combination with lamp also occurs in Num.8:2. Correspondences arise with the *yaggī^{a}h* of colon B in the psalm: assonance, morphological and semantic parallelism; moreover four cola in a row have a hiph'il, and this is stylistically the strong point of the reading in the psalm. The nominal clause of II Sam.22:29a is linguistically sound, however, and is, besides, a pure metaphor: God himself is the lamp here. I retain this version.

– 22:32 just as v.7 doubles its *'eqrā*, this verse doubles the word *mibbal'ădē*, whilst Ps.18 in the second instance varies with *zūlat*.

– 22:33a If need be one can defend *ma'uzzī ḥayil*, lit. 'my stronghold in strength' (whereby *ḥayil* is an adjunct which functions as *b^{e}ḥayil*). I am, however, inclined to favour the variant *ham-m^e'azz^{e}renī* of the psalm, which is now also attested by 4QSam^a. We then get the following picture, after the nominal verse 32 with its anaphoral interrogative forms: the verbal clauses are resumed in 33a and carry on uninterrupted throughout this entire section (thus up to and including v.46) – the pi'el participles of vv.34-35 are, as a part of this long series, to be interpreted as predicates – and the (restored) pi'el participle of 33a gets a telling continuation in the strophe vv.34-35. Also of importance is a link with a similar passage, the strophe of vv.40-41, which also works with the combination *'zr* (pi) + *ḥayil*.

– 22:33b The form *wayyatter* is in difficulties due to competition with the simple and attractive *wayyitten* of Ps.18. The problematics of the word lie purely in the relative unfamiliarity of the root(s). The trouble with this is tellingly reflected by the lexicons: Ges.-B recognises one root *ntr*, BDB two and HAL three! For our verse the latter gives the qal of *ntr* II, *wayyittar*, 'davonspringen' (intransitive therefore; but what/who is the subject?). (This *ntr* II is approximately the *ntr* I of BDB.) Perhaps the handed-down hiph'il (of 'set free' or the like, i.e. II *ntr* of BDB, *ca.* = *ntr* in Ges.-B) functions with a wider or watered-down meaning, so that it becomes practically the same as *wytn*. Compare the difference between 'give' and 'make' which nevertheless both lie within the broad semantic field of the root *ntn*. Something else is the solution of CT, pp.306-307, which envisages a metaphorical use of 'set free':

'et il a dégagé parfaitement ma carrière'. I myself take the word *tāmīm* to be predicative rather than adverbial.

– 22:36b The psalm begins with a sizeable plus here, two words which form an entire clause and for this reason more or less force us into making a tricolon of v.36, which is problematic in this poem that plies its tricola thriftily and functionally. Neither do I have much confidence, at the same time, in the word *'*ănāwā* of the psalm. II Sam. has '*ănōt*^{e}*kā*, which I interpret as the infin. of '*nh* III, 'concern oneself with', as in Eccl.1:13 and 3:10 (where his '*inyān* comes from also, so familiar to us from post-Biblical Hebrew), and translate: 'your concern [*or*: care] has made me great'. The JPS rendering 'your providence' is probably based on the same choice.

– 22:39a The MT begins here with an extra verb, *wā'ăkallem*. I delete it because it weighs down the colon semantically (with three predicates!) and metrically and because the root *klh* has already just been used at the end of 38b; the finite verb directly afterwards is an ugly repetition, whilst its informative contribution has already been guaranteed by *wā'ęmḥāṣem*. The same decision has been made by Cross and Freedman, note 88, Geller p.187, BJ, KBS, McCarter.

– 22:41a I see the form *tattā* as either an old (dialectal?) variant of, or an erratum for, the fuller *nātattā*. The latter is rhythmically more pleasant to realise, the former alliterates more effectively with the three words which begin with t- in the strophe.

– 22:42a The form of the root *š'h* is acceptable and not inferior to the variant *y*^{e}*šaww*^{e}*'ū* of Ps.18 as concerns the play on sounds with the word *mošīă'*. But the presence of (the hoped-for but not received) '*ānām* is an argument that the auditive term is more fitting than the visual one; compare also the noun *šaw'ā* in the proximity of so many forms of **yš'* in vv.3-7.

– 22:43 Both the third word of colon A and the third word of colon B are preferable to the variants in Ps.18. I view the text at the end of 43b, however, as a conflate reading which gives us the choice between *'ădiqqem* and *'ęrqā'em*. Viewed purely semantically the forms do not differ much. Cross and Freedman wrote in JBL 72, p.32 note 95: 'In the two texts, there are three variant readings, all apparently derived from the same original. From the textual point of view, any one of the three may be regarded as the original reading, and the others ex-

garde'. In v.13a CT follows the Qere's *šelōšā* and reads *me-haššālīšīm* straight after (not 'thirty' thus) on the ground of the Targum, Peshitta, Radaq, and Isaiah of Trani. The translation of v.13a runs: ' ... trois, l'élite d'entre les gardes'. In v.18c 'in the three' is retained but in v.19a *min haššelōšīm* is read, in view of S *min taltīn* and T *min gibbārayyā* (the MT has 'the three' here). In vv.22-24 the numbers given by the MT are retained.

– 23:8c the words *'dynw h'ṣnw/y* are obscure and can no longer be used. Perhaps they reflect a name plus *gentilicium*. But in any case what their text misses is a predicate after the fashion of 'he brandished his spear' – as in v. 18b, a line of similar structure and position. According to KBL, BJ, HAL p.330a, NBE, KBS, GNB the weapon is 'his battle-axe', originating from **ḥaṣīn* which is well-known in Akkadian and Ugaritic.

– 23:9abc In my line-up the links of these three lines are wooden and so is their syntax. A much more pleasant series arises if we fit 'of the three heroes' into 9a, interpolate the words *hū hāyā* from Chron. (as do NEB, Goslinga, BHK for example), and position them initially in 9b, then borrowing the place name from Chron. for the end of 9b, so that the designation 'there' in 9c gets a neat antecedent. We then obtain: 'Next to him was Eleazar ..., one of the heroic three. He was with David at Pas-dammim. Whilst/because they laughed at the Philistines the latter gathered for battle'. Compare my colometry with the JPS rendering. In my arrangement 9b is a predicative nominal clause and we can think of *wayhī* in front of 9c.

– 23:9c the verb *ḥrf* exhibits prepositional rection here and the qāmeṣ is a qāmeṣ ḥāṭūf (not in the Ms. L, but in the Cairo and Aleppo Mss. however) so that I take the infin. to be in the qal: 'when they poked fun at the Philistines'. See also CT which also mentions the choice of the qal by Abulwalid and Radaq.

– 23:9d The going up of the Israelites is in this situation a withdrawal as e.g. Smith, Hertzberg, BJ, Goslinga, KBS, JPS and McCarter have seen. To this end we might have to repunctuate *wy'lw* as a niph'al, compare 2:27 for the meaning. We ought to view the movement in connection with the counterpart in v.10e, where 'the soldiery returned behind him', westward thus and descending in order to pillage.

– 23:11b together with, amongst others, Wellhausen, Driver, NBG,

KBS, Buber, Goslinga, NEB, NBE, McCarter and CT I
maintain, it is true, *lḥyh* of the MT, but with another vocalisation, *lęḥyā*, i.e. the locative of the place name Lechi. This
name is the antecedent of 'there' in the following line. The
word *ḥayyā*, 'gang', is hardly relevant in v.11b, whilst it is
authentic in v.13c.

– 23:13a   The position and meaning of the word *rōš* is difficult here.
Does it mean that 'three of the chiefs' take the lead whilst a
way is fought down to Adullam? Some translations link the
word with the harvest and then translate with 'at the beginning of harvest time'; as do BJ, NEB, NBE, GNB. This
yields good sense, it is true, but entails a minor relocation. CT
reads *mēhaššālīšīm rōš* and, without discussing word order,
renders it 'l'élite de la garde'.

– 23:13b   *'ęl qāṣīr*. The parallel text writes 'on the rock', *'al haṣṣūr*, at
this point. I do not adopt this, because there are already three,
four explicit designations of place in the text (requiring seven
words which form a clear series at the end of 13bc + 14b),
besides it is not aesthetically pleasing for a spatial term to
occur both prior to and after *'ęl dāwīd* in one clause. Neither
am I attracted to the view that *'ęl qāṣīr* is a temporal term, 'at
the time of harvest'. It is, on the other hand, possible to
interpret *'ęl* as a pregnant *'al* used *in bonam partem*: 'they
came to David for the harvest', i.e. to protect the harvest.

– 23:20a   add the lamed, with the Qere, and read *bęn ḥayil*.

– 23:21a   I read the word *'yš* with the Qere and translate, in line with a
long tradition, 'a man of striking appearance' (I read these
words in the NEB).

– 23:24-39   I print the names without alterations with respect to the MT
and refer to CT and McCarter for further philological and
historical-critical study of the list.

– 24:5b   I follow here, amongst others, Wellhausen, Driver, Skehan
(CBQ 1969), Schenker (note 42), CT, and McCarter who
translates: 'After crossing the Jordan, they began from Aroer
and the city in the wadi of the Gadites near Jazer.' On the
ground of the LXX (Mss. boe₂ of the Antiochian recension)
and the passages Josh.13:9, 16 and Deut.2:36 the following
Hebrew has been construed: *wayyaḥellū mē'ărō'er umin
hā'īr 'ăšęr b'tōk hannaḥal haggādī 'ęl ya'zer*.

– 24:6a   Since Thenius, Wellhausen and Driver the majority change the impossible *tḥtm ḥdšy* of the MT into *haḥittīm qādešā*; e.g. LV, NEB, NBE, CT, Schenker (note 43). I agree with Skehan (CBQ 1969) and McCarter that the Hittite Kadesh and the Orontes are much too far north, *pace* CT, and I concur with their emendation, which, apart from this, is already older (Graetz, followed by Schulz and Goslinga): *taḥat ḥęrmōn*. This word combination is attested by Josh.11:13. What Buber did, with a minimum of encroachment upon the text, is interesting: apparently he read *tḥt ym qdš*, translated 'bis zum Land unter dem Kadeschsee' and was thinking of Lake Huleh I imagine; in which case it concerns the Kadesh of Naphtali, a realistic possibility. An explanation of the corrupt *tḥtym ḥdsḥy* is, perhaps, that the gaze of the tired copyist slid to 8b, where *tš'h ḥdšym* occurs; the mistake could have been fostered by the fact that 8b begins with the form *wayyābō'ū* just like v.6a (and 6b and 7a).

– 24:6b Also corrupt is *y'n*. I read the place name Iyyon (*'yn* in *scriptio defectiva*) as do Klostermann, Schulz and Goslinga, who refer to I Ki.15:20, and with KBL2 and HAL *s.v. y'n*. The adverb *sābīb* which follows need not necessarily be changed into a verbal *wysbw*. What is more an emendation like this would disturb the threefold anaphora *wayyābō'ū* and is, therefore, to be discouraged on the ground of style. The translation of the whole of v.6 now runs: 'They came to Gilead and to the region at the foot of the Hermon; and they came to Dan and Iyyon, and around to Sidon.'

– 24:10a The combination *'aḥărē ken* is demonstrative and therefore impossible at this point – right in the middle of a compound sentence in which a conjunction is required. We are compelled to read a single *'aḥărē* or the combination *'aḥărē 'ăšęr*: after this conjunction an infin. is more usual than a form in the perfect. Perhaps the given text, line 10a as a whole thus, is a conflate reading of these two alternatives: a) *wayyak leb dāwīd 'ōtō 'aḥărē ('ăšęr) sāfar 'ęt hā'ām*, b) a shorter text which does not mention the counting: *wayyak leb dāwīd 'ōtō 'aḥărē ken*. (Also compare for this final position of 'after that' what I noted at 21:14c.) Those who grant themselves much more freedom than I do myself in rectifying the text, might consider a third alternative, in view of the fact that II 24:10 has apparently been inspired by I 24:6; in which case we would get: *wayhī 'aḥărē ken wayyak leb dāwīd 'ōtō kī* (or: *'al 'ăšęr*) *sāfar 'ęt hā'ām*.

Appendix II
Colometry

In the preceding volumes I discussed a number of rules and considerations in effect for arriving at the proper colometry. Now I am able to restrict myself to pointing out a few particulars.

– 2:23ef one line has 10 words, the other only one. Nevertheless *wayyamot*, as part of the relative clause and as the continuation of *npl*, goes with line e (the relative clause mirrors 23d incidentally); *wymt* is not an independent link in the narrative chain, *wy'mdw* is. Here we have an example of wyqtl not always requiring its own colon. The same situation occurs in 8:10b with *wayyakkehū*.

The same argument is in force syntactically for 2:5e, *wat-tiqb*^{e}*rū 'ōtō*, also part of a relative clause and a continuation of the perfect *'ăśītęm*. In this case, however, I have given the clause its own colon because of the importance of its content.

– 2:26a I do not award an isolated *wayyōmęr* after 'he called' its own colon; see also II 15:2c and I 29:6a. Compare the situation *wayyiqrā ... lēmōr* of I 24:9c, 14a, or *wayyiš'al ... lēmōr* of I 30:8a, II 2:1d, 20a and 5:19a, or the points at which 'he answered and he said' are joined. The element 'he said' is new in 3:24b, 28b and merits, as a new act, a line of its own, as do 3:8b and 5:1b, 20c.

– 3:7a The decision to include the short nominal clause with the mention of the name in 7a also, is partly a question of taste;

compare I 25:2a and II 13:1b.

– 3:9bc and 10ab: After the exordium of the oath, v.9a, comes the oath's content in 9bc + 10ab, which is introduced by 'truly'. The main clause 9c repeats this *kī* quasi-redundantly (compare I 14:39 and Gen.22:16sq.) so that, as an anaphora, it marks the lines 9bc as a pair and underlines the scheme 'just as ... so ...'. Subsequently the doubling of *l*[e] with a hiph'il infin. ensures that the infinitival clauses of 10ab each merit their own colon. The parallelism of their content reinforces this decision.

– 3:25cd These two lines are a similar kind of case: two infinitive clauses which, moreover, place the same verb in front as anaphora.

– 3:29c still belongs to 29b syntactically, but has been set apart both for practical reasons (length) and stylistic ones (three construct chains).

– 3:33b-34c are a poem. That is why 34ab has been printed the way it is: a bicolon.

– 3:37 The position of the time adjunct 'on that day' fosters an independent position (37b) for the object clause. Note, in contradistinction to this, how an object clause after 'know' does *not* need its own colon in 2:26c, 3:38b or 5:12a.

– 5:8b The right colometry is dependent on interpretation here.

– 5:11b Just as in 3:29c I place the three construct chains apart. Note that the address 'to David' has immediately been placed after 'messengers', so that a hardly perceptible break is necessary.

– 5:14-16 The Masoretes too found it necessary to distribute the long enumerative concatenations over 'verses'.

– 5:23b This 'he said' should have been attached to 23a – see *ad* 2:26a.

– 5:25a/b The importance of the 'so ... as' is the reason for my giving a line to each clause.

– 6:5 is one sentence which I spread out over 5a and 5b for practical reasons. It is noticeable that the five specific kinds of musical instruments form a series, whilst 5a has an encompassing *kol* both at the beginning and at the end.

– 6:19 Verse 19ab offers a similar situation. In 19a the encompassing phrases (with *kol* twice and the man/woman merismus) occur, after which 19b demonstrates the distribution through three specific kinds of food (each of which is accompanied by the numeral one).

– 7:6b-7a If the context had been lost I would have given this compound sentence as a colon. Now the concentric structure of vv.5c-7c leads to its being spread out over two cola.

– 7:12a Because *wškbt* is governed by *kī*, I accord its clause a place in 12a and not later.

– 7:23bcd The distribution of the increasingly longer infinitive clauses is chiefly a matter of taste. Notice, however, that the words 'gods, redeem, people' of 23b return chiastically in 23d.

– 8:11-12 Even though 'with the silver' is a formal complement of the clause 11a, two observations lead me to separating 11a and 11b: the doubling of *hiqdīš* and the temporal aspect of 11b + 12ab, which are largely a flashback. The enumeration 12a with its five names is the added specification of 'all the people' in 11b; whilst 12b brings an enemy (now a king, not a nation) especially to the fore, thus referring back to, and forming an inclusion with, vv.7-9.

– 21:1b For stylistic reasons I accord this striking temporal apposition a line of its own.

– 21:7 The length of the sentence and the repetition of the phrase 'Jonathan, the son of Saul' lead me to distributing the whole over 7a and 7b.

– 21:8 A well-nigh identical situation.

– 21:12c After the main clause 12b a flashback appears which goes increasingly further back, reversing the chronological order *hakkōt – tālā – gānab*.

– 23:24-38 The division into two columns mirrors the masoretic arrangement of verses and the repeated placing of the *zāqef*.

Index of biblical verses treated

This index is limited to the texts from I-II Sam. and I Kings 1-2. It disregards the Contents, Appendix II, the lists on pp. 20-22, the headings of my chapters and §§, and some enumerative notes (like p.154 notes 2-4, p.169 notes 38-39, p.253 note 91, p.300 and 336).
There are three parts:
A) Sections and Acts
B) Larger units, i.e., bible chapters and scenes (for the division into units and their verse-numbers see pp. 20-22).
C) Smaller units and bible verses.

A. *Sections and Acts*

B. *Larger units (chapters and scenes)*

C. *Smaller units and verses*

ACT IX

II Sam. 2:1-11

2:1 ויהי אחרי כן
b ויׁשאל דוד ביהוה לאמר
האעלה באחת ערי יהודה
d ויאמר יהוה אליו
עלה
f ויאמר דוד
אנה אעלה
h ויאמר
חברנה
2 ויעל שם דוד וגם שתי נשיו
אחינעם היזרעלית ואביגיל אשת נבל הכרמלי
3 ואנשיו אשר עמו העלה דוד איש וביתו
וישבו בערי חברון
4 ויבאו אנשי יהודה
b וימשחו שם את דוד למלך על בית יהודה

c ויגדו לדוד לאמר
אנשי יביש גלעד אשר קברו את שאול
5 וישלח דוד מלאכים אל אנשי יביש גלעד
b ויאמר אליהם
ברכים אתם ליהוה
d אשר עשיתם החסד הזה עם אדניכם עם שאול
ותקברו אתו
6 ועתה יעש יהוה עמכם חסד ואמת
וגם אנכי אעשה אתכם הטובה הזאת
אשר עשיתם הדבר הזה
7 ועתה תחזקנה ידיכם
b והיו לבני חיל
כי מת אדניכם שאול
d וגם אתי משחו בית יהודה למלך עליהם

8 ואבנר בן נר שר צבא אשר לשאול לקח את איש בשת בן שאול
ויעברהו מחנים
9 וימלכהו אל הגלעד ואל האשרי ואל יזרעאל ועל אפרים ועל בנימן ועל
10 בן ארבעים שנה איש בשת בן שאול במלכו על ישראל ישראל כלה
ושתים שנים מלך
אך בית יהודה היו אחרי דוד
11 ויהי מספר הימים אשר היה דוד מלך בחברון על בית יהודה שבע שנים
וששה חדשים ||

2:12-23d

12 ויצא אבנר בן נר ועבדי איש בשת בן שאול ממחנים גבעונה
13 ויואב בן צרויה ועבדי דוד יצאו
ויפגשום על ברכת גבעון יחדו
וישבו אלה על הברכה מזה ואלה על הברכה מזה
14 ויאמר אבנר אל יואב
b יקומו נא הנערים
וישחקו לפנינו
d ויאמר יואב
יקמו
15 ויקמו ויעברו במספר
שנים עשר לבנימן ולאיש בשת בן שאול
ושנים עשר מעבדי דוד
16 ויחזקו איש בראש רעהו
b וחרבו בצד רעהו
ויפלו יחדו
d ויקרא למקום ההוא חלקת הצרים אשר בגבעון
17 ותהי המלחמה קשה עד מאד ביום ההוא
וינגף אבנר ואנשי ישראל לפני עבדי דוד

18 ויהיו שם שלשה בני צרויה יואב ואבישי ועשהאל
ועשהאל קל ברגליו כאחד הצבים אשר בשדה
19 וירדף עשהאל אחרי אבנר
ולא נטה ללכת על הימין ועל השמאול מאחרי אבנר
20 ויפן אבנר אחריו ויאמר
b האתה זה עשהאל
ויאמר
d אנכי
21 ויאמר לו אבנר
b נטה לך על ימינך או על שמאלך
ואחז לך אחד מהנערים
d וקח לך את חלצתו
ולא אבה עשהאל לסור מאחריו
22 ויסף עוד אבנר לאמר אל עשהאל
b סור לך מאחרי
למה אככה ארצה
d ואיך אשא פני אל יואב אחיך
23 וימאן לסור
b ויכהו אבנר באחרי החנית אל החמש
ותצא החנית מאחריו
d ויפל שם וימת תחתו

←

23e ויהי כל הבא אל המקום אשר נפל שם עשהאל וימת
f ויעמדו
24 וירדפו יואב ואבישי אחרי אבנר
והשמש באה
והמה באו עד גבעת אמה אשר על פני גיח דרך מדבר גבעון
25 ויתקבצו בני בנימן אחרי אבנר
ויהיו לאגדה אחת
ויעמדו על ראש גבעה אחת
26 ויקרא אבנר אל יואב ויאמר
b הלנצח תאכל חרב
הלוא ידעתה כי מרה תהיה באחרונה
d ועד מתי לא תאמר לעם לשוב מאחרי אחיהם
27 ויאמר יואב
b חי האלהים
כי לולא דברת
d כי אז מהבקר נעלה העם איש מאחרי אחיו
28 ויתקע יואב בשופר
b ויעמדו כל העם
ולא ירדפו עוד אחרי ישראל
d ולא יספו עוד להלחם
29 ואבנר ואנשיו הלכו בערבה כל הלילה ההוא
b ויעברו את הירדן
וילכו כל הבתרון
d ויבאו מחנים
30 ויואב שב מאחרי אבנר
ויקבץ את כל העם
ויפקדו מעבדי דוד תשעה עשר איש ועשהאל
31 ועבדי דוד הכו מבנימן ובאנשי אבנר
שלש מאות וששים איש מתו
32 וישאו את עשהאל
b ויקברהו בקבר אביו אשר בית לחם
וילכו כל הלילה יואב ואנשיו
d ויאר להם בחברון
3:1 ותהי המלחמה ארכה בין בית שאול ובין בית דוד
ודוד הלך וחזק
ובית שאול הלכים ודלים

←

3:2-14

3:2 ויולדו לדוד בנים בחברון
ויהי בכורו אמנון לאחינעם היזרעאלת
3 ומשנהו כלאב לאביגיל אשת נבל הכרמלי
והשלשי אבשלום בן מעכה בת תלמי מלך גשור
4 והרביעי אדניה בן חגית
והחמישי שפטיה בן אביטל
5 והששי יתרעם לעגלה אשת דוד
אלה ילדו לדוד בחברון ||

6 ויהי בהיות המלחמה בין בית שאול ובין בית דוד
ואבנר היה מתחזק בבית שאול
7 ולשאול פלגש ושמה רצפה בת איה
ויאמר איש בשת אל אבנר
מדוע באתה אל פילגש אבי
8 ויחר לאבנר מאד על דברי איש בשת
b ויאמר
הראש כלב אנכי אשר ליהודה
d היום אעשה חסד עם בית שאול אביך אל אחיו ואל מרעהו
ולא המציתך ביד דוד
f ותפקד עלי עון האשה היום
9 כה יעשה אלהים לאבנר וכה יסיף לו
כי כאשר נשבע יהוה לדוד
כי כן אעשה לו
10 להעביר הממלכה מבית שאול
ולהקים את כסא דוד על ישראל ועל יהודה מדן ועד באר שבע
11 ולא יכל עוד להשיב את אבנר דבר מיראתו אתו
12 וישלח אבנר מלאכים אל דוד תחתו לאמר
b למי ארץ – לאמר
כרתה בריתך אתי
d והנה ידי עמך להסב אליך את כל ישראל
13 ויאמר
b טוב
אני אכרת אתך ברית
d אך דבר אחד אנכי שאל מאתך לאמר
לא תראה את פני
f כי אם לפני הביאך את מיכל בת שאול
בבאך לראות את פני
14 וישלח דוד מלאכים אל איש בשת בן שאול לאמר
תנה את אשתי את מיכל אשר ארשתי לי במאה ערלות פלשתים ←

15 וישלח איש בשת
ויקחה מעם איש מעם פלטיאל בן ליש
16 וילך אתה אישה הלוך ובכה אחריה עד בחרים
b ויאמר אליו אבנר
לך שוב
d וישב
17 ודבר אבנר היה עם זקני ישראל לאמר
גם תמול גם שלשם הייתם מבקשים את דוד למלך אליכם
18 ועתה עשו
כי יהוה אמר אל דוד לאמר
ביד דוד עבדי אושיע את עמי ישראל מיד פלשתים ומיד כל איביהם
19 וידבר גם אבנר באזני בנימין
וילך גם אבנר לדבר באזני דוד בחברון את כל אשר טוב בעיני ישראל ובעיני
20 ויבא אבנר אל דוד חברון ואתו עשרים אנשים   כל בית בנימן
ויעש דוד לאבנר ולאנשים אשר אתו משתה
21 ויאמר אבנר אל דוד
b אקומה ואלכה ואקבצה אל אדני המלך את כל ישראל
ויכרתו אתך ברית
d ומלכת בכל אשר תאוה נפשך
וישלח דוד את אבנר
f וילך בשלום ||

22 והנה עבדי דוד ויואב באו מהגדוד
b ושלל רב עמם הביאו
ואבנר איננו עם דוד בחברון
d כי שלחו וילך בשלום
23 ויואב וכל הצבא אשר אתו באו
b ויגדו ליואב לאמר
בא אבנר בן נר אל המלך
d וישלחהו וילך בשלום
24 ויבא יואב אל המלך
b ויאמר
מה עשיתה
d הנה בא אבנר אליך
למה זה שלחתו וילך הלוך
25 ידעת את אבנר בן נר
b כי לפתתך בא
ולדעת את מוצאך ואת מבואך
d ולדעת את כל אשר אתה עשה ←

3:26-39

26 ויצא יואב מעם דוד
b וישלח מלאכים אחרי אבנר
וישבו אתו מבור הסרה
d ודוד לא ידע
27 וישב אבנר חברון
b ויטהו יואב אל תוך השער לדבר אתו בשלי
ויכהו שם החמש
d וימת בדם עשה אל אחיו
28 וישמע דוד מאחרי כן
ויאמר
נקי אנכי וממלכתי מעם יהוה עד עולם מדמי אבנר בן נר
29 יחלו על ראש יואב ואל כל בית אביו
ואל יכרת מבית יואב זב ומצרע
ומחזיק בפלך ונפל בחרב וחסר לחם
30 ויואב ואבישי אחיו הרגו לאבנר
על אשר המית את עשהאל אחיהם בגבעון במלחמה
31 ויאמר דוד אל יואב ואל כל העם אשר אתו
b קרעו בגדיכם וחגרו שקים
וספדו לפני אבנר
d והמלך דוד הלך אחרי המטה
32 ויקברו את אבנר בחברון
b וישא המלך את קולו
ויבך אל קבר אבנר
d ויבכו כל העם
33 ויקנן המלך אל אבנר ויאמר
הכמות נבל ימות אבנר
34ab ידך לא אסרות ורגליך לא לנחשתים הגשו
c כנפול לפני בני עולה נפלת
d ויספו כל העם לבכות עליו
35 ויבא כל העם להברות את דוד לחם בעוד היום
b וישבע דוד לאמר
כה יעשה לי אלהים וכה יסיף
d כי אם לפני בוא השמש אטעם לחם או כל מאומה
36 וכל העם הכירו
וייטב בעיניהם
ככל אשר עשה המלך בעיני כל העם טוב
37 וידעו כל העם וכל ישראל ביום ההוא
כי לא היתה מהמלך להמית את אבנר בן נר
38 ויאמר המלך אל עבדיו
הלוא תדעו כי שר וגדול נפל היום הזה בישראל
39 ואנכי היום רך ומשוח מלך
והאנשים האלה בני צרויה קשים ממני
|| ישלם יהוה לעשה הרעה כרעתו

4:1-7

4:1 וישמע בן שאול כי מת אבנר בחברון
וירפו ידיו
וכל ישראל נבהלו
2 ושני אנשים שרי גדודים היו (עם) בן שאול
שם האחד בענה ושם השני רכב
בני רמון הבארתי מבני בנימן
3 כי גם בארות תחשב על בנימן
ויברחו הבארתים גתימה
ויהיו שם גרים עד היום הזה
4 וליהונתן בן שאול בן נכה רגלים
b בן חמש שנים היה בבא שמעת שאול ויהונתן מיזרעאל
ותשאהו אמנתו ותנס
d ויהי בחפזה לנוס
ויפל ויפסח
f ושמו מפיבשת
5 וילכו בני רמון הבארתי רכב ובענה
ויבאו כחם היום אל בית איש בשת
והוא שכב את משכב הצהרים
6 והנה שערת הבית לקטה חטים
6abc: LXX!
ותנם ותישן
6c/7a ויבאו רכב ובענה אחיו הבית
7b והוא שכב על מטתו בחדר משכבו
ויכהו וימתהו
d ויסירו את ראשו
ויקחו את ראשו
f וילכו דרך הערבה כל הלילה ←

vv.6a-7a according to the MT:

6 והנה באו עד תוך הבית לחקי חטים
ויכהו אל החמש
ורכב ובענה אחיו נמלטו
7 ויבאו הבית

4:8-5:5

4:8 ויבאו את ראש איש בשת בן שאול אל דוד חברון
b ויאמרו אל המלך
הנה ראש איש בשת בן שאול איבך אשר בקש את נפשך
d ויתן יהוה לאדני המלך נקמות היום הזה משאול ומזרעו
9 ויען דוד את רכב ואת בענה אחיו בני רמון הבארתי
ויאמר להם
חי יהוה אשר פדה את נפשי מכל צרה
10 כי המגיד לי לאמר
b הנה מת שאול
והוא היה כמבשר בעיניו
d ואחזה בו ואהרגהו בצקלג
אשר לתתי לו בשרה
11 אף כי אנשים רשעים הרגו את איש צדיק בביתו על משכבו
ועתה הלוא אבקש את דמו מידכם
ובערתי אתכם מן הארץ
12 ויצו דוד את הנערים ויהרגום
b ויקצצו את ידיהם ואת רגליהם
ויתלו על הברכה בחברון
d ואת ראש איש בשת לקחו
ויקברו בקבר אבנר בחברון

||

5:1 ויבאו כל שבטי ישראל אל דוד חברונה
ויאמרו לאמר
הננו עצמך ובשרך אנחנו
2 גם אתמול גם שלשום בהיות שאול מלך עלינו
b אתה היית המוציא והמביא את ישראל
ויאמר יהוה לך
d אתה תרעה את עמי את ישראל
ואתה תהיה לנגיד על ישראל
3 ויבאו כל זקני ישראל אל המלך חברונה
ויכרת להם המלך דוד ברית בחברון לפני יהוה
וימשחו את דוד למלך על ישראל
4 בן שלשים שנה דוד במלכו
ארבעים שנה מלך
5 בחברון מלך על יהודה שבע שנים וששה חדשים
ובירושלם מלך שלשים ושלש שנה על כל ישראל ויהודה

||

– – –
– –
–

ACT X
5:6-16

5:6 וילך המלך ואנשיו ירושלם אל היבסי יושב הארץ
b ויאמר לדוד לאמר
לא תבוא הנה
d כי אם הסירך העורים והפסחים – לאמר
לא יבוא דוד הנה
7 וילכד דוד את מצדת ציון
היא עיר דוד
8 ויאמר דוד ביום ההוא
b כל מכה יבסי ויגע בצנור
ואת הפסחים ואת העורים שנאי נפש דוד
d על כן יאמרו
עור ופסח לא יבוא אל הבית
9 וישב דוד במצדה
ויקרא לה עיר דוד
ויבן דוד סביב מן המלוא וביתה
10 וילך דוד הלוך וגדול
ויהוה אלהי צבאות עמו
11 וישלח חירם מלך צר מלאכים אל דוד
ועצי ארזים וחרשי עץ וחרשי אבן קיר
ויבנו בית לדוד
12 וידע דוד כי הכינו יהוה למלך על ישראל
וכי נשא ממלכתו בעבור עמו ישראל

13 ויקח דוד עוד פלגשים ונשים מירושלם אחרי באו מחברון
ויולדו עוד לדוד בנים ובנות
14 ואלה שמות הילדים לו בירושלם
שמוע ושובב ונתן ושלמה
15 ויבחר ואלישוע ונפג ויפיע
|| 16 ואלישמע ואלידע ואליפלט

5:17-25

17 וישמעו פלשתים כי משחו את דוד למלך על ישראל
b ויעלו כל פלשתים לבקש את דוד
וישמע דוד
d וירד אל המצודה
18 ופלשתים באו
וינטשו בעמק רפאים
19 וישאל דוד ביהוה לאמר
b האעלה אל פלשתים
התתנם בידי
d ויאמר יהוה אל דוד
עלה
f כי נתן אתן את הפלשתים בידך
20 ויבא דוד בבעל פרצים
b ויכם שם דוד
ויאמר
d פרץ יהוה את איבי לפני כפרץ מים
על כן קרא שם המקום ההוא בעל פרצים
21 ויעזבו שם את עצביהם
וישאם דוד ואנשיו

22 ויספו עוד פלשתים לעלות
וינטשו בעמק רפאים
23 וישאל דוד ביהוה
b ויאמר
לא תעלה
d הסב אל אחריהם
ובאת להם ממול בכאים
24 ויהי כשמעך את קול צעדה בראשי הבכאים
אז תחרץ
כי אז יצא יהוה לפניך להכות במחנה פלשתים
25 ויעש דוד כן
כאשר צוהו יהוה
ויך את פלשתים מגבע עד באך גזר

||

6:1-16

6:1 ויסף עוד דוד את כל בחור בישראל שלשים אלף
2 ויקם וילך דוד וכל העם אשר אתו מבעלי יהודה
להעלות משם את ארון האלהים
אשר נקרא [שם] שם יהוה צבאות ישב הכרבים עליו
3 וירכבו את ארון האלהים אל עגלה חדשה
וישאהו מבית אבינדב אשר בגבעה
ועזא ואחיו בני אבינדב נהגים את העגלה [חדשה
4 וישאהו מבית אבינדב אשר בגבעה] עם ארון האלהים
ואחיו הלך לפני הארון
5 ודוד וכל בית ישראל משחקים לפני יהוה בכל עצי ברושים
ובכנרות ובנבלים ובתפים ובמנענעים ובצלצלים
6 ויבאו עד גרן נכון
b וישלח עזא אל ארון האלהים
ויאחז בו
d כי שמטו הבקר
7 ויחר אף יהוה בעזה
ויכהו שם האלהים על השל
וימת שם עם ארון האלהים
8 ויחר לדוד על אשר פרץ יהוה פרץ בעזה
ויקרא למקום ההוא פרץ עזה עד היום הזה
9 וירא דוד את יהוה ביום ההוא
ויאמר
איך יבוא אלי ארון יהוה
10 ולא אבה דוד להסיר אליו את ארון יהוה על עיר דוד
ויטהו דוד בית עבד אדום הגתי
11 וישב ארון יהוה בית עבד אדם הגתי שלשה חדשים
ויברך יהוה את עבד אדם ואת כל ביתו
12 ויגד למלך דוד לאמר
ברך יהוה את בית עבד אדם ואת כל אשר לו בעבור ארון האלהים
וילך דוד ויעל את ארון האלהים מבית עבד אדם עיר דוד בשמחה
13 ויהי כי צעדו נשאי ארון יהוה ששה צעדים
ויזבח שור ומריא
14 ודוד מכרכר בכל עז לפני יהוה
ודוד חגור אפוד בד
15 ודוד וכל בית ישראל מעלים את ארון יהוה בתרועה ובקול שופר
16 והיה ארון יהוה בא עיר דוד
b ומיכל בת שאול נשקפה בעד החלון
ותרא את המלך דוד מפזז ומכרכר לפני יהוה
d ותבז לו בלבה

←

17 ויבאו את ארון יהוה
ויצגו אתו במקומו בתוך האהל אשר נטה לו דוד
ויעל דוד עלות לפני יהוה ושלמים
18 ויכל דוד מהעלות העולה והשלמים
ויברך את העם בשם יהוה צבאות
19 ויחלק לכל העם לכל המון ישראל למאיש ועד אשה
לאיש חלת לחם אחת ואשפר אחד ואשישה אחת
וילך כל העם איש לביתו
20 וישב דוד לברך את ביתו
b ותצא מיכל בת שאול לקראת דוד
ותאמר
d מה נכבד היום מלך ישראל
אשר נגלה היום לעיני אמהות עבדיו
f כהגלות נגלות כאחד הרקים
21 ויאמר דוד אל מיכל
b לפני יהוה אשר בחר בי מאביך ומכל ביתו
לצות אתי נגיד על עם יהוה על ישראל
d ושחקתי לפני יהוה
22 ונקלתי עוד מזאת
והייתי שפל בעיני
ועם האמהות אשר אמרת עמם אכבדה
23 ולמיכל בת שאול לא היה לה ילד עד יום מותה ||

7:1 ויהי כי ישב המלך בביתו
ויהוה הניח לו מסביב מכל איביו
2 ויאמר המלך אל נתן הנביא
b ראה נא
אנכי יושב בבית ארזים
d וארון האלהים ישב בתוך היריעה
3 ויאמר נתן אל המלך
כל אשר בלבבך לך עשה
כי יהוה עמך ←

7:4-17

4 ויהי בלילה ההוא
ויהי דבר יהוה אל נתן לאמר
5 לך ואמרת אל עבדי אל דוד
כה אמר יהוה
האתה תבנה לי בית לשבתי
6 כי לא ישבתי בבית למיום העלתי את בני ישראל ממצרים ועד היום הזה
ואהיה מתהלך באהל ובמשכן
7 בכל אשר התהלכתי בכל בני ישראל
הדבר דברתי את אחד שבטי ישראל אשר צויתי לרעות את עמי את ישראל לאמר
למה לא בניתם לי בית ארזים
8 ועתה כה תאמר לעבדי לדוד
כה אמר יהוה צבאות
אני לקחתיך מן הנוה מאחר הצאן להיות נגיד על עמי על ישראל
9 ואהיה עמך בכל אשר הלכת
ואכרתה את כל איביך מפניך
ועשתי לך שם גדול כשם הגדלים אשר בארץ
10 ושמתי מקום לעמי לישראל
b ונטעתיו ושכן תחתיו
ולא ירגז עוד
d ולא יסיפו בני עולה לענותו כאשר בראשונה
11 ולמן היום אשר צויתי שפטים על עמי ישראל
והניחתי לך מכל איביך
והגיד לך יהוה כי בית יעשה לך
12 והיה כי ימלאו ימיך ושכבת את אבתיך
והקימתי את זרעך אחריך אשר יצא ממעיך
והכינתי את ממלכתו
13 הוא יבנה בית לשמי
וכננתי את כסא ממלכתו עד עולם
14 אני אהיה לו לאב
והוא יהיה לי לבן
אשר בהעותו והכחתיו בשבט אנשים ובנגעי בני אדם
15 וחסדי לא יסור ממנו
כאשר הסרתי מעם שאול אשר הסרתי מלפניך
16 ונאמן ביתך וממלכתך עד עולם לפניך
כסאך יהיה נכון עד עולם
17 ככל הדברים האלה וככל החזיון הזה
כן דבר נתן אל דוד ←

7:18-29

18 ויבא המלך דוד
b וישב לפני יהוה
ויאמר
d מי אנכי אדני יהוה
ומי ביתי כי הביאתני עד הלם
19 ותקטן עוד זאת בעיניך אדני יהוה
ותדבר גם אל בית עבדך למרחוק
וזאת תורת האדם אדני יהוה
20 ומה יוסיף דוד עוד לדבר אליך
ואתה ידעת את עבדך אדני יהוה
21 בעבור דברך וכלבך עשית את כל הגדולה הזאת להודיע את עבדך
22 על כן גדלת אדני יהוה
כי אין כמוך
ואין אלהים זולתך ככל אשר שמענו באזנינו
23 ומי כעמך כישראל גוי אחד בארץ
b אשר הלכו אלהים לפדות לו לעם
ולשום לו שם ולעשות להם הגדולה ונראות
d לארצך מפני עמך אשר פדית לך ממצרים גוים ואלהיו
24 ותכונן לך את עמך ישראל לך לעם עד עולם
ואתה יהוה היית להם לאלהים
25 ועתה יהוה אלהים
הדבר אשר דברת על עבדך ועל ביתו הקם עד עולם
ועשה כאשר דברת
26 ויגדל שמך עד עולם לאמר
יהוה צבאות אלהים על ישראל
ובית עבדך דוד יהיה נכון לפניך
27 כי אתה יהוה צבאות אלהי ישראל גליתה את אזן עבדך לאמר
בית אבנה לך
על כן מצא עבדך את לבו להתפלל אליך את התפלה הזאת
28 ועתה אדני יהוה אתה הוא האלהים
ודבריך יהיו אמת
ותדבר אל עבדך את הטובה הזאת
29 ועתה הואל וברך את בית עבדך להיות לעולם לפניך
כי אתה אדני יהוה דברת
ומברכתך יברך בית עבדך לעולם ||

8:1-18

8:1 ויהי אחרי כן
ויך דוד את פלשתים ויכניעם
ויקח דוד את מתג האמה מיד פלשתים
2 ויך את מואב
b וימדדם בחבל השכב אותם ארצה
וימדד שני חבלים להמית ומלא החבל להחיות
d ותהי מואב לדוד לעבדים נשאי מנחה
3 ויך דוד את הדדעזר בן רחב מלך צובה
בלכתו להשיב ידו בנהר פרת
4 וילכד דוד ממנו אלף ושבע מאות פרשים ועשרים אלף איש רגלי
ויעקר דוד את כל הרכב
ויותר ממנו מאה רכב
5 ותבא ארם דמשק לעזר להדדעזר מלך צובה
ויך דוד בארם עשרים ושנים אלף איש
6 וישם דוד נצבים בארם דמשק
ותהי ארם לדוד לעבדים נושאי מנחה
וישע יהוה את דוד בכל אשר הלך
7 ויקח דוד את שלטי הזהב אשר היו אל עבדי הדדעזר
ויביאם ירושלם
8 ומבטח ומברתי ערי הדדעזר לקח המלך דוד נחשת הרבה מאד
9 וישמע תעי מלך חמת כי הכה דוד את כל חיל הדדעזר
10 וישלח תעי את יורם בנו אל המלך דוד לשאל לו לשלום ולברכו
b על אשר נלחם בהדדעזר ויכהו
כי איש מלחמות תעי היה הדדעזר
d ובידו היו כלי כסף וכלי זהב וכלי נחשת
11 גם אתם הקדיש המלך דוד ליהוה
עם הכסף והזהב אשר הקדיש מכל הגוים אשר כבש
12 מארם וממואב ומבני עמון ומפלשתים ומעמלק
ומשלל הדדעזר בן רחב מלך צובה
13 ויעש דוד שם בשבו מהכותו את ארם
(ויך את אדום) בגיא מלח שמונה עשר אלף
14 וישם באדום נצבים
b בכל אדום שם נצבים
ויהי כל אדום עבדים לדוד
d ויושע יהוה את דוד בכל אשר הלך
15 וימלך דוד על כל ישראל
ויהי דוד עשה משפט וצדקה לכל עמו
16 ויואב בן צרויה על הצבא
ויהושפט בן אחילוד מזכיר
17 וצדוק בן אחיטוב ואחימלך בן אביתר כהנים
ושריה סופר
18 ובניהו בן יהוידע והכרתי והפלתי
ובני דוד כהנים היו

\- - -
\- -
\-

||

ACT XIV
21:1-10

21:1 ויהי רעב בימי דוד
b שלש שנים שנה אחרי שנה
ויבקש דוד את פני יהוה
d ויאמר יהוה
אל שאול אל ביתה דמים
f על אשר המית את הגבענים
2 ויקרא המלך לגבענים ויאמר אליהם
b – והגבענים לא מבני ישראל המה כי אם מיתר האמרי
ובני ישראל נשבעו להם
d ויבקש שאול להכתם בקנאתו לבני ישראל ויהודה
3 ויאמר דוד אל הגבענים
b מה אעשה לכם
ובמה אכפר
d וברכו את נחלת יהוה
4 ויאמרו לו הגבענים
b אין לנו כסף וזהב עם שאול ועם ביתו
ואין לנו איש להמית בישראל
d ויאמר
מה אתם אמרים אעשה לכם
5 ויאמרו אל המלך
האיש אשר כלנו ואשר דמה לנו
נשמדנו מהתיצב בכל גבל ישראל
6 יתן לנו שבעה אנשים מבניו
b והוקענום ליהוה בגבעת שאול בחיר יהוה
ויאמר המלך
d אני אתן
7 ויחמל המלך על מפיבשת בן יהונתן בן שאול
על שבעת יהוה אשר בינתם בין דוד ובין יהונתן בן שאול
8 ויקח המלך את שני בני רצפה בת איה אשר ילדה לשאול את ארמני ואת מפבשת
ואת חמשת בני מרב בת שאול אשר ילדה לעדריאל בן ברזלי המחלתי
9 ויתנם ביד הגבענים
b ויקיעם בהר לפני יהוה
ויפלו שבעתם יחד
d והמה המתו בימי קציר בראשנים בתחלת קציר שערים
10 ותקח רצפה בת איה את השק
ותטהו לה אל הצור מתחלת קציר עד נתך מים עליהם מן השמים
ולא נתנה עוף השמים לנוח עליהם יומם ואת חית השדה לילה ←

11 ויגד לדוד את אשר עשתה רצפה בת איה פלגש שאול
12 וילך דוד
b ויקח את עצמות שאול ואת עצמות יהונתן בנו מאת בעלי יביש גלעד
אשר גנבו אתם מרחב בית שן
d אשר תלאום שמה פלשתים ביום הכות פלשתים את שאול בגלבע
13 ויעל משם את עצמות שאול ואת עצמות יהונתן בנו
ויאספו את עצמות המוקעים
14 ויקברו את עצמות שאול ויהונתן בנו בארץ בנימן בצלע בקבר קיש אביו
ויעשו כל אשר צוה המלך
ויעתר אלהים לארץ אחרי כן ||

15 ותהי עוד מלחמה לפלשתים את ישראל
b וירד דוד ועבדיו עמו
וילחמו את פלשתים
d ויעף דוד
16 וישבי בנב אשר בילידי הרפה
b ומשקל קינו שלש מאות משקל נחשת
והוא חגור חדשה
d ויאמר להכות את דוד
17 ויעזר לו אבישי בן צרויה
b ויך הפלשתי וימיתהו
אז נשבעו אנשי דוד לו לאמר
d לא תצא עוד אתנו למלחמה
ולא תכבה את נר ישראל
18 ויהי אחרי כן
ותהי עוד המלחמה בגוב עם פלשתים
אז הכה סבכי החשתי את סף אשר בילידי הרפה
19 ותהי עוד המלחמה בגוב עם פלשתים
ויך אלחנן בן יערי בית הלחמי את גלית הגתי
ועץ חניתו כמנור ארגים
20 ותהי עוד מלחמה בגת
b ויהי איש מדון
ואצבעת ידיו ואצבעות רגליו שש ושש
d עשרים וארבע מספר
וגם הוא ילד להרפה
21 ויחרף את ישראל
ויכהו יהונתן בן שמעה אחי דוד
22 את ארבעת אלה ילדו להרפה בגת
ויפלו ביד דוד וביד עבדיו ||

22:1-31

22:1 וידבר דוד ליהוה את דברי השירה הזאת
ביום הציל יהוה אתו מכף כל איביו ומכף שאול
2 ויאמר

יהוה סלעי ומצדתי ומפלטי לי   [3]אלהי צורי אחסה בו
3bc מגני וקרן ישעי משגבי   ומנסי משעי מחמס תשעני
4 מלל אקרא יהוה   ומאיבי אושע

5 כי אפפני משברי מות   נחלי בליעל יבעתני
6 חבלי שאול סבני   קדמני מקשי מות

7 בצר לי אקרא יהוה   ואל אלהי אקרא
cd וישמע מהיכלו קולי   ושועתי באזניו

8 ותגעש ותרעש הארץ   מוסדות השמים ירגזו   ויתגעשו כי חרה לו
9 עלה עשן באפו   ואש מפיו תאכל   גחלים בערו ממנו

10 ויט שמים וירד   וערפל תחת רגליו
11 וירכב על כרוב ויעף   וירא על כנפי רוח

12 וישת חשך סביבתיו סכות   חשרת מים עבי שחקים
13 מנגה נגדו   בערו גחלי אש

14 ירעם מן שמים יהוה   ועליון יתן קולו
15 וישלח חצים ויפיצם   ברק ויהמם

16 ויראו אפקי ים   יגלו מסדות תבל
cd בגערת יהוה   מנשמת רוח אפו

17 ישלח ממרום יקחני   ימשני ממים רבים
18 יצילני מאיבי עז   משנאי כי אמצו ממני

19 יקדמני ביום אידי   ויהי יהוה משען לי
20 ויצא למרחב אתי   יחלצני כי חפץ בי

21 יגמלני יהוה כצדקתי   כבר ידי ישיב לי
22 כי שמרתי דרכי יהוה   ולא רשעתי מאלהי
23 כי כל משפטיו לנגדי   וחקתיו לא אסור ממנה

24 ואהיה תמים לו   ואשתמרה מעוני
25 וישב יהוה לי כצדקתי   כברי לנגד עיניו

26 עם חסיד תתחסד   עם גבור תמים תתמם
27 עם נבר תתבר   ועם עקש תתפל

28 ואת עם עני תושיע   ועיניך על רמים תשפיל
29 כי אתה נירי יהוה   ויהוה יגיה חשכי
30 כי בכה ארוץ גדוד   באלהי אדלג שור

31 האל תמים דרכו   אמרת יהוה צרופה
c מגן הוא לכל החסים בי

←

22:32-51

32	כי מי אל מבלעדי יהוה	ומי צור מבלעדי אלהינו	
33	האל מעוזי חיל	ויתר תמים דרכי	
34	משוה רגלי כאילות	ועל במותי יעמדני	
35	מלמד ידי למלחמה	ונחת קשת נחושה זרעתי	
36	ותתן לי מגן ישעך	וענתך תרבני	
37	תרחיב צעדי תחתני	ולא מעדו קרסלי	
38	ארדפה איבי ואשמידם	ולא אשוב עד כלותם	
39	אמחצם ולא יקומון	ויפלו תחת רגלי	
40	ותזרני חיל למלחמה	תכריע קמי תחתני	
41	ואיבי תתה לי ערף	משנאי ואצמיתם	
42	ישעו ואין משיע	אל יהוה ולא ענם	
43	ואשחקם כעפר ארץ	כטיט חוצות אדקם ארקעם	
44ab	ותפלטני מריבי עמי	תשמרני לראש גוים	
44c-45ab	עם לא ידעתי יעבדני	בני נכר יתכחשו לי	לשמוע אזן ישמעו לי
46	בני נכר יבלו	ויחגרו ממסגרותם	
47	חי יהוה וברוך צורי	וירם אלהי צור ישעי	
48ab-49a	האל הנתן נקמת לי	ומוריד עמים תחתני	ומוציאי מאיבי
49bc	ומקמי תרוממני	מאיש חמסים תצילני	
50	על כן אודך יהוה בגוים	ולשמך אזמר	
51	מגדול ישועות מלכו	ועשה חסד למשיחו	לדוד ולזרעו עד עולם

23:1-7

23:1	ואלה דברי דוד האחרנים		
bc	נאם דוד בן ישי	ונאם הגבר הקם על	
de	משיח אלהי יעקב	ונעים זמרות ישראל	
2	רוח יהוה דבר בי	ומלתו על לשוני	
3	אמר אלהי ישראל	לי דבר צור ישראל	
cd	מושל באדם צדיק	מושל יראת אלהים	
4	וכאור בקר יזרח שמש	בקר לא עבות	
4c/5a	מנגה ממטר דשא מארץ	כי לא כן ביתי עם אל	
5bc	כי ברית עולם שם לי	ערוכה בכל ושמרה	
de	כי כל ישעי וכל חפץ	כי לא יצמיח	
6	ובליעל כקוץ מנד כלהם	כי לא ביד יקחו	
7	ואיש יגע בהם	ימלא ברזל ועץ חנית	ובאש שרוף ישרפו בשבת

8 אלה שמות הגברים אשר לדוד
ישבשת החכמני ראש השלשים
הוא עדינו העצנו על שמנה מאות חלל בפעם אחת
9 ואחריו אלעזר בן דדו בן אחחי
b בשלשה הגברים עם דוד
בחרפם בפלשתים נאספו שם למלחמה
d ויעלו איש ישראל
10 הוא קם
b ויך בפלשתים עד כי יגעה ידו
ותדבק ידו אל החרב
d ויעש יהוה תשועה גדולה ביום ההוא
והעם ישבו אחריו אך לפשט
11 ואחריו שמא בן אגא הררי
b ויאספו פלשתים לחיה
ותהי שם חלקת השדה מלאה עדשים
d והעם נס מפני פלשתים
12 ויתיצב בתוך החלקה ויצילה
ויך את פלשתים
ויעש יהוה תשועה גדולה
13 וירדו שלשה מהשלשים ראש
ויבאו אל קציר אל דוד אל מערת עדלם
וחית פלשתים חנה בעמק רפאים
14 ודוד אז במצודה
ומצב פלשתים אז בית לחם
15 ויתאוה דוד ויאמר
מי ישקני מים מבאר בית לחם אשר בשער
16 ויבקעו שלשת הגברים במחנה פלשתים
b וישאבו מים מבאר בית לחם אשר בשער
וישאו ויבאו אל דוד
d ולא אבה לשתותם
ויסך אתם ליהוה
17 ויאמר
b חלילה לי מיהוה מעשתי זאת
הדם האנשים ההלכים בנפשותם
d ולא אבה לשתותם
אלה עשו שלשת הגברים ←

18 ואבישי אחי יואב בן צרויה הוא ראש השלשים
והוא עורר את חניתו על שלש מאות חלל
ולא שם בשלשה
19 מן השלשים הכי נבבד
ויהי להם לשר
ועד השלשה לא בא
20 ובניהו בן יהוידע בן איש חיל רב פעלים מקבצאל
הוא הכה את שני אראל מואב
והוא ירד והכה את הארי בתוך הבור ביום השלג
21 והוא הכה את איש מצרי איש מראה
b וביד המצרי חנית
וירד אליו בשבט
d ויגזל את החנית מיד המצרי
ויהרגהו בחניתו
22 אלה עשה בניהו בן יהוידע
ולו שם בשלשה הגברים
23 מן השלשים נכבד
ואל השלשה לא בא
וישמהו דוד אל משמעתו

24 עשה אל אחי יואב בשלשים   אלחנן בן דדו בית לחם
25 שמה החרדי   אליקא החרדי
26 חלץ הפלטי   עירא בן עקש התקועי
27 אביעזר הענתתי   מבני החשתי
28 צלמון האחחי   מהרי הנטפתי
חלב בן בענה הנטפתי   אתי בן ריבי מגבעת בני בנימן
30 בניהו פרעתני   הדי מנחלי געש
אבי עלבון הערבתי   עזמות הברחמי
32 אליחבא השעלבני   בני ישן יהונתן
שמה ההררי   אחיאם בן שרר האררי
34 אליפלט בן אחסבי בן המערכתי   אליעם בן אחיתפל הגלני
חצרי הכרמלי   פערי הארבי
36 יגאל בן נתן מצבה   בני הגדי
צלק העמני   נחרי הבארתי נשא כלי יואב בן צריה
38 עירא היתרי   גרב היתרי
39 אוריה החתי
כל שלשים ושבעה ||

24:1-9

24:1 ויסף אף יהוה לחרות בישראל
ויסת את דוד בהם לאמר
לך מנה את ישראל ואת יהודה
2 ויאמר המלך אל יואב שר החיל אשר אתו
b שוט נא בכל שבטי ישראל מדן ועד באר שבע
ופקדו את העם
d וידעתי את מספר העם
3 ויאמר יואב אל המלך
b ויוסף יהוה אלהיך אל העם כהם וכהם מאה פעמים
ועיני אדני המלך ראות
d ואדני המלך למה חפץ בדבר הזה
4 ויחזק דבר המלך אל יואב ועל שרי החיל
ויצא יואב ושרי החיל לפני המלך לפקד את העם את ישראל
5 ויעברו את הירדן
ויחנו בערוער ימין העיר אשר בתוך הנחל הגד ואל יעזר
6 ויבאו הגלעדה ואל ארץ תחתים חדשי
ויבאו דנה יען וסביב אל צידון
7 ויבאו מבצר צר וכל ערי החוי והכנעני
ויצאו אל נגב יהודה באר שבע
8 וישטו בכל הארץ
ויבאו מקצה תשעה חדשים ועשרים יום ירושלם
9 ויתן יואב את מספר מפקד העם אל המלך
b ותהי ישראל שמנה מאות אלף איש חיל שלף חרב
ואיש יהודה חמש מאות אלף איש ←

24:10-19

10 ויך לב דוד אתו אחרי כן ספר את העם
b ויאמר דוד
חטאתי מאד אשר עשיתי
d ועתה יהוה העבר נא את עון עבדך
כי נסכלתי מאד
11 ויקם דוד בבקר
ודבר יהוה היה אל גד הנביא חזה דוד לאמר
12 הלוך ודברת אל דוד
b כה אמר יהוה
שלש אנכי נטל עליך
d בחר לך אחת מהם
ואעשה לך
13 ויבא גד אל דוד
b ויגד לו ויאמר לו
התבוא לך שבע שנים רעב בארצך
d אם שלשה חדשים נסך לפני צריך והוא רדפך
ואם היות שלשת ימים דבר בארצך
f עתה דע וראה מה אשיב שלחי דבר
14 ויאמר דוד אל גד
b צר לי מאד
נפלה נא ביד יהוה
d כי רבים רחמיו
וביד אדם אל אפלה
15 ויתן יהוה דבר בישראל מהבקר ועד עת מועד
וימת מן העם מדן ועד באר שבע שבעים אלף איש
16 וישלח ידו המלאך ירושלם לשחתה
b וינחם יהוה אל הרעה
ויאמר למלאך המשחית בעם
d רב
עתה הרף ידך
ומלאך יהוה היה עם גרן הארונה היבסי
17 ויאמר דוד אל יהוה בראתו את המלאך המכה בעם
b ויאמר
הנה אנכי חטאתי
d ואנכי העויתי
ואלה הצאן מה עשו
f תהי נא ידך בי ובבית אבי
18 ויבא גד אל דוד ביום ההוא
ויאמר לו
עלה הקם ליהוה מזבח בגרן ארונה היבסי
19 ויעל דוד כדבר גד
כאשר צוה יהוה

←

24:20-25

20 וישקף ארונה
וירא את המלך ואת עבדיו עברים עליו
ויצא ארונה וישתחו למלך אפיו ארצה
21 ויאמר ארונה
b מדוע בא אדני המלך אל עבדו
ויאמר דוד
d לקנות מעמך את הגרן
לבנות מזבח ליהוה
f ותעצר המגפה מעל העם
22 ויאמר ארונה אל דוד
b יקח ויעל אדני המלך הטוב בעיניו
ראה הבקר לעלה
d והמרגים וכלי הבקר לעצים
23 והכל נתן ארונה המלך למלך
ויאמר ארונה אל המלך
יהוה אלהיך ירצך
24 ויאמר המלך אל ארונה
b לא כי קנו אקנה מאותך במחיר
ולא אעלה ליהוה אלהי עלות חנם
d ויקן דוד את הגרן ואת הבקר בכסף שקלים חמשים
25 ויבן שם דוד מזבח ליהוה
b ויעל עלות ושלמים
ויעתר יהוה לארץ
|| d ותעצר המגפה מעל ישראל

– – –
– –
–

Published in the series STUDIA SEMITICA NEERLANDICA:

1. *Dr. C. van Leeuwen*, Le développement du sens social en Israel avant l'ère chrétienne.*
2. *Dr. M. Reisel*, The mysterious Name of Y.H.W.H.*
3. *Dr. A.S. van der Woude*, Die messianischen Vorstellungen der Gemeinde von Qumrân.*
4. *Dr. B. Jongeling*, Le rouleau de la guerre des manuscrits de Qumrân.
5. *Dr. N.A. van Uchelen*, Abraham de hebreeër.*
6. *Dr. H.J.W. Drijvers*, Bardaiṣan of Edessa.*
7. *Dr. J.H. Meesters*, Op zoek naar de oorsprong van de Sabbat.*
8. *Dr. A.G. van Daalen*, Simson.*
9. *Dr. Leon A. Feldman*, R. Abraham b. Isaac ha-Levi TaMaKh. Commentary on the Song of Songs.*
10. *Dr. W.A.M. Beuken*, Haggai-Sacharja 2-8.
11. *Dr. Curt Leviant*, King Artus, a Hebrew Arthurian Romance of 1279.*
12. *Dr. Gabriel H. Cohn*, Das Buch Jona.*
13. *Dr. G. van Driel*, The Cult of Aššur.*
14. *Dr. H. Jagersma*, Leviticus 19. Identiteit, bevrijding, gemeenschap.*
15. *Dr. Wilhelm Th. In der Smitten*, Esra. Quellen, Ueberlieferung und Geschichte.*
16. Travels in the world of the Old Testament. Studies presented to prof. M.A. Beek, on the occasion of his 65th birthday.*
17. *Dr. J.P. Fokkelman*, Narrative Art in Genesis. Specimens of stylistic and structural analysis.*
18. *Dr. C.H.J. de Geus*, The Tribes of Israel.
19. *Dr. M.D. Koster*, The Peshitta of Exodus. The Development of its Text in the Course of Fifteen Centuries.
20. *Dr. J.P. Fokkelman*, Narrative Art and Poetry in the Books of Samuel. A full interpretation based on stylistic and structural analyses. Volume I: King David (II Sam. 9-20 & I Kings 1-2).
21. *Prof.dr. J. Hoftijzer*, The Function and Use of the Imperfect Forms with Nun-Paragogicum in Classical hebrew.
22. *Dr. K. van den Toorn*, Sin and Sanction in Israel and Mesopotamia.
23. *Dr. J.P. Fokkelman*, Narrative Art and Poetry in the Books of Samuel. A full interpretation based on stylistic and structural analyses. Volume II: The Crossing Fates (I Sam. 13-31 & II Sam. 1).
24. *Dr. L.J. de Regt*, A Parametric Model for Syntactic Studies of a Textual Corpus, Demonstrated on the Hebrew of Deuteronomy 1-30.
25. *Dr. E.J. van Wolde*, A Semiotic Analysis of Genesis 2-3. A Semiotic Theory and Method of Analysis Applied to the Story of the Garden of Eden.
26. *Dr. T.A.M. Fontaine*, In Defence of Judaism: Abraham Ibn Daud. Sources and Structures of ha-Emunah ha-Ramah.
27. *Dr. J.P. Fokkelman*, Narrative Art and Poetry in the Books of Samuel. A full interpretation based on stylistic and structural analyses. Volume III: Throne and City (II Sam. 2-8 & 21-24).

200-201 [illegible]